LEBANON

T0333437

ANDREW ARSAN

Lebanon

A Country in Fragments

HURST & COMPANY, LONDON

First published in the United Kingdom in 2018 by
C. Hurst & Co. (Publishers) Ltd.,
41 Great Russell Street, London, WC1B 3PL
© Andrew Arsan, 2018
This paperback edition, 2020
All rights reserved.
Printed in the United Kingdom

ISBN: 9781787383654

This book is printed using paper from registered sustainable and managed sources.

www.hurstpublishers.com

For Sophie

CONTENTS

CONTENTS

ACKNOWLEDGMENTS

I have been told that I thank too many people, so I will try to keep these acknowledgments short. I am grateful, first of all, to everyone at Hurst for making sure that this book exists at all—and particularly to Michael Dwyer for his faith in me, and for his good humour and bonhomie in the face of endless delays, excuses and apologies; to Jon de Peyer for his wry efforts to track this manuscript down; and, most importantly of all, to Farhaana Arefin, for patiently shepherding it to completion and for her careful, incisive edits and comments. An author is nothing without a good publisher and good editors, and I count myself very lucky to have now worked with everyone at Hurst on two projects.

This book could not have been written without very many people in Lebanon who spoke to me on or off the record, introduced me to others, pointed out particular features of its contemporary life, or simply shared their frustrations and hopes with me. I thank all those who spoke with me, and especially Abir Saksouk-Sasso, who laughed at my Arabic, explained to me what was wrong with my first book, and took the time to share with me the work that she and her colleagues at Dictaphone and the Public Works Studio—in particular Nadine Bekdache—have been doing, carefully and lovingly recording the lives and memories of Beirut's working people and fighting for their continuing right to the city. This is essential work.

Anyone who glances at my footnotes will realise that I also owe a deep debt to the many scholars, Lebanese and non-Lebanese, who have sharpened our understanding of the country in recent years. The last two decades have witnessed an efflorescence of exhilarating work on

ACKNOWLEDGMENTS

Lebanon, and a book like this one would have been impossible without the path-breaking research of scholars such as Ziad Abu-Rish, Hicham El-Achkar, Hannes Baumann, Lara Deeb, Mona Fawaz, Laleh Khalili, Marieke Krijnen, Mona Harb, Hadi Makarem, Franck Mermier, Sabrina Mervin, Maya Mikdashi, Jamil Mouawad, and many others. Some of these scholars I know—some only digitally—others I have not met, but I am thankful to all of them. It is a pleasure to stand on their shoulders, as it were.

This book would also have been an impossible feat were it not for the continuing work of Lebanon's journalists and activists. Readers will see that a pessimistic streak runs through it, but if there is one bright star in the sky, it is the continuing dedication of print and television journalists and activists to record the rights and wrongs of Lebanese democracy, to take its politicians to account, and to inform its public. These men and women work in increasingly trying financial and political circumstances, but they are the very lifeblood of the Lebanese body politic. Their work must be praised, but it must also be protected if Lebanon's democracy, such as it is, is to survive and thrive. As Joni said, you don't know what you got till it's gone.

I also owe a special debt to those who have hosted me in Lebanon: my aunt and cousin, Mona and Marc Tarazi; the staff at the Mayflower Hotel, my other home away from home in Beirut; and Samir Khalaf, Waleed Hazbun, and Samer Frangieh, who all served as my academic hosts on various stints at the American University in Beirut. I am particularly grateful to two formidable scholars and organisers, Guita Hourani and Nadya Sbaiti. Guita and Nadya have been both wonderful hosts and true friends, always ready to make time in their busy lives to have a conversation. They are, in short, models of scholarly generosity, and I am immeasurably grateful to them both for their warmth, their sense of humour, and the vast reserves of knowledge that they are willing to share so readily.

In Britain and the United States, I am grateful to Nadim Shehadi, Gilbert Achcar, and Akram Khater for all their encouragement over the years. I began working on what would become this book a long time ago, when I was still a post-doc at Princeton. I owe a debt to the Department of Near Eastern Studies—and, in particular, to my mentor, Michael Cook—for creating the ideal conditions for a young

ACKNOWLEDGMENTS

researcher to get on with his work. For the last five years, I have been back at Cambridge. The terms may be brutal but at least, to paraphrase Hobbes, they are short, and it remains a joy to work here. I am thankful to my colleagues in the Faculty of History and at St John's College for the friendship and moral and intellectual support they have provided over the last few years. I am particularly grateful to all those who have listened to me witter on more than most over lunch, wine, or coffee: Renaud Morieux, Sarah Pearsall, Helen Pfeifer, Sylvana Tomaselli, Andrew Preston, Sujit Sivasundaram, Shruti Kapila, and Arthur Asseraf. I have also learned a great deal about what it means to be a scholar from my doctoral 'students'—not quite the right term—and am particularly grateful to Chris Wilson, Hana Sleiman, Ayşe Polat, and Chloé Kattar. Long may you thrive and create a better university.

In London, thanks to mandem in the Lycée crew for keeping me sane—you all know who you are—and to Will and Em for wine talk and baby photos. Tic, thanks for being the most constant of friends—and for putting us up in Coleridge Road. Stef, thanks for doing the same in Queen's Park. Will, one day I might eventually write a book that is not about Lebanon... In Glasgow, Ben White kept me fed and watered and well-oiled for a few days while I cranked out a chapter. We don't see each other often enough, but he is a sound comrade and a good friend. Thanks, too, to 'Sophie's friends'—Coleraine High and Prairie Dogs. I won't name you all—Sophie already thinks these acknowledgments are too long—but you make life much boozier and much funnier than it might otherwise be. Special props, though, to Willoughby—shine on you bright star.

I must also thank those who have made this research financially possible: the Master and Fellows of St John's, the Faculty of History, the Cambridge Humanities Research Grant, the British Academy, and the Council for British Research in the Levant. I am particularly grateful to Claire Aspinall and Ed Mayes, the administrators who have processed so many of my forms, with never so much as a word of complaint. More than just money, my Faculty and my College granted me a term of leave, during which the bulk of this book was written. I am grateful to them—and in particular to Larry Klein, Tim Harper, Chris Dobson, and Frank Salmon—for freeing me from teaching and administrative responsibilities.

ACKNOWLEDGMENTS

Last but not least, I owe thanks to my two families: the Arsans and the Eastwoods. My parents, Jane and Adel, share my love for, and my ambivalence about, this place we all still sometimes call home. They have listened to me rant on, corrected my Arabic, and shared their own memories, while putting me up—and putting up with me—during unhappy adventures in the London housing market. In Coleraine, Chris and Dave Eastwood have also fed and sheltered me, and have dealt with my repeated invasions of their space with all the patience and quiet humour you would expect. One person, though, has kept me going over the last five years. Only Sophie knows how difficult it has been—and how difficult I have been—but she has kept me going at every point of the way, even when this manuscript has taken me away from her. This book is for her.

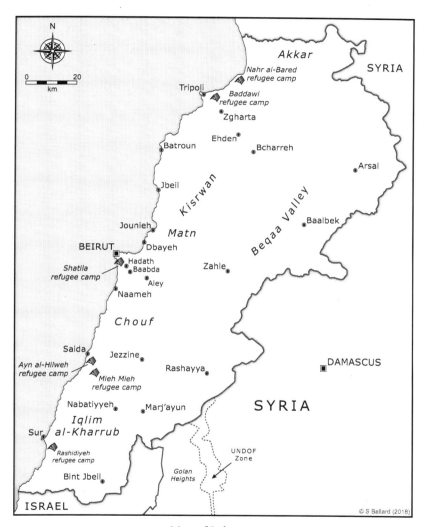

N

0   20
    km

Akkar

SYRIA

Nahr al-Bared
refugee camp

Tripoli

Baddawi
refugee camp

Zgharta

Ehden

Bcharreh

Arsal

Batroun

Jbeil

Kisrwan

Beqaa Valley

Baalbek

Jounieh

Matn

BEIRUT

Dbayeh

Shatila
refugee camp

Hadath
Baabda

Zahle

Aley

Naameh

Chouf

Saida

Jezzine

Ayn al-Hilweh
refugee camp

Mieh Mieh
refugee camp

Rashayya

DAMASCUS

Nabatiyyeh

Marj'ayun

SYRIA

Iqlim
al-Kharrub

Sur

Rashidiyeh
refugee camp

UNDOF
Zone

Golan
Heights

Bint Jbeil

ISRAEL

© S Ballard (2018)

Map of Lebanon

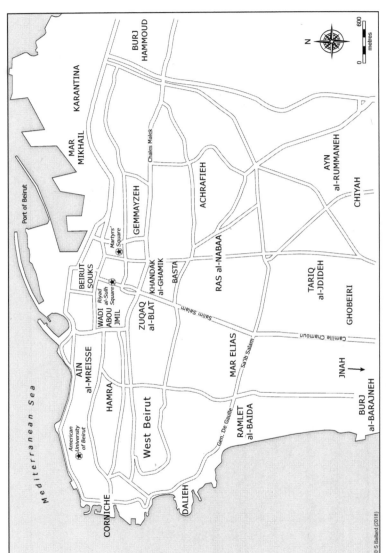

Map of Beirut

INTRODUCTION

LEBANON AND THE TWENTY-FIRST CENTURY

Thirteen years. Three presidents. Thirty-four months without a president. Five prime ministers. More than twenty months of interim government while various parties wrangled over ministerial portfolios. A ruinous war between Hizballah and Israel, which caused the deaths of anywhere between 1,035 and 1,191 Lebanese civilians, the flight of a million internally displaced people, and the destruction of much of Lebanon's infrastructure.[1] Forty-eight bombings—devices left in industrial lots and car parks, outside churches, shopping centres and banks in the middle of the night, or detonated by suicide bombers in crowded cafés and at busy intersections, army checkpoints or mosque entrances. Twenty-one assassinations or assassination attempts on politicians, party cadres, journalists, and army and intelligence officers, killed or maimed by explosives planted under car seats and roadside booby traps or shot down while sat in traffic. One flirtation with civil war: the 'events' of May 2008, when Hizballah and its allies took over large swathes of Beirut and Mount Lebanon in a lightning operation. Ongoing civil strife in the northern city of Tripoli, where fighting has broken out at regular intervals between the neighbouring quarters of Bab al-Tebbaneh and Jabal Muhsin—one Sunni, the other Alawi. Repeated confrontations between the Lebanese armed forces and Islamist groups, the most recent of which—the large-scale campaign that the army and Hizballah waged in tandem in August and September 2017 against Daesh and Jabhat al-Nusra men encamped in eastern

1

Lebanon—was celebrated as a new dawn, freeing the country from the pernicious presence of these subversive elements, even as many saw it as a sign that Lebanon was being drawn ever further into the bewildering, wrenching chaos of the Syrian civil wars. A seemingly unending garbage crisis, which has left the streets of Beirut strewn with rubbish bags and thick with the smell of rotting matter on repeated occasions. And, of course, the arrival of over a million Syrian refugees—men, women, and children torn from their hometowns and villages by conflict, in the greatest humanitarian crisis this century has seen.[2] This is the bleak tally of Lebanese life since the Cedar Revolution in 2005.

This book is about these thirteen eventful years in the life of Lebanon. They have been, it is clear, a time of recurring crisis for the country—political and economic, but also social, demographic and environmental. Others have sought to explain the origins of crisis through the conventional tools of political science and international relations, painting a picture of internal disarray, growing sectarian tension and deteriorating regional conditions to account for the blockages and false starts that have been the hallmark of Lebanese political life since 2005. My ambitions are rather different. Where most have concentrated on the sleights of hand of high politics and the zero-sum games of geopolitics, I attempt to map out the landscapes of everyday life. I want in this book to understand how the existences of Lebanon's inhabitants have been shaped—or bent out of shape—by the succession of disruptive episodes that have punctuated the years since 2005, moments of strife that puncture and rip the fragile weave of normal life.

What does it mean, and how does it feel, to attempt to live an ordinary life in extraordinary times? What are the joys and expectations, the fears and anxieties, the aspirations, hopes, disappointments and sorrows that have marked the lives of the men and women who have lived through these unusual times? And how have they striven to maintain a hold over their own lives, in an effort to keep the years from drifting away on the currents of contingency? What strategies for everyday living and political action have they devised to fight the pull of events, to stay afloat and keep their heads above water? What are the discourses and rhetorical devices—from jokes to slogans, and sectarian polemics to political programmes—to which they have resorted to make sense of the unfamiliar, uncanny landscape of the present? And what are the structural and political conditions in which they live? It has often seemed over the last thirteen years as though the ordinary order of things had been suspended, giving way to the exceptional and the makeshift, the unexpected, the contingent and the provisional. Uncertainty and precarity have come to leave their indelible imprint on the lives of many, often taking as profound an emotional and psychic toll as they exact an economic cost. If Lebanon's politicians have sometimes appeared to be indulging in what—to borrow a term from the political scientist Lisa Wedeen—could be called the politics of 'as if', then its inhabitants have simply been engaged in the politics of getting by. Every act, every choice is political in contemporary Lebanon. Whether it signals a tacit acceptance of prevailing social norms, an attempt to deflect the weight of structural forces, or an outright rejection of the status quo, it is also always a reminder of the sheer effort required just to muddle through and get on with the day-to-day in times of crisis. This book argues that, if we are to understand Lebanon in the twenty-first century, we cannot ignore the fraught politics of the everyday in times like these, times out of joint when all seems awry.

But why should any of this matter? To most outside the small circle of academic specialists and foreign policy analysts who work on Lebanon, the country seems of limited significance. It is not India, China or the United States, Russia, South Africa or Brazil, countries whose importance seems self-evident, a function as much of their immense territorial extent as of their demographic, economic and geopolitical heft. Lebanon, by contrast, is a small state. With a population roughly equivalent to that of New Zealand—at least before its ranks were swollen by the coming of Syrian refugees—it is just a little bigger than the Bahamas, and smaller even than other Middle Eastern states hardly reputed for their size, such as Kuwait and Qatar. But that is perhaps why Lebanon does matter. For it can seem at times a microcosm of the contemporary world, a petri dish in which we can observe the microbial strains of late modernity. This was certainly the response of my partner on her first visit to Lebanon in 2013. After a few days in the country, she turned to me as we were walking through the barren web of streets that is Beirut's central business district and said: 'so this is what neoliberalism looks like'. The point, of course, is not that the effects of neoliberal logic might not be apparent in Britain or the United States—far from it—but that the workings of the contemporary world can perhaps best be glimpsed in miniature, and from elsewhere. As Jean and John Comaroff have noted, it might make sense to begin from the post-colonies of the Middle East, Africa or Asia if we are to understand our own times, for 'many of the great historical tsunamis of the twenty-first century appear to be breaking first on their shores'.[3]

From the glinting lures of populism, with its dual illusion of government for the people, by a man of the people, to populism's obverse, technocracy and its fantasies of an antiseptic world of expertise, cleansed of inconvenient political realities; from the strains put on the social body by mass displacement, to policies that foster inequality and precarity in the name of perpetual growth and the exhausting sense of living in a time of permanent crisis—so much of what seems to characterise our contemporary condition can be found in Lebanon. By concentrating, if even for a while, on this small country, we can better understand the workings of those techniques of government, those dispositions and ideologies, those bundles of words and practices and sentiments that frame the way we live now. And perhaps nothing defines our contemporary predicament more than the sense of living in a permanent present. Whether we are held in the sway of contingency, uncertain of what this day or the next might bring, or caught up in a tangle of constant consumption and compulsive, episodic living, forever checking what might have happened in the machine worlds we are tethered to, we seem to live an existence characterised by the 'dissolution of past and future alike'.[4] On the one hand, the 'horizon' of the future 'is apparently closed': there is no way for people to know where they are heading, no pensions or political programmes to cling on to.[5] The future is simply 'unthinkable … unimaginable'.[6] On the other, 'the past has apparently receded'.[7] Once the live matter from which the present was shaped, the past is now reduced to bitter memories or 'dusty images', grounds only for resentment and nostalgia.[8] This seems particularly clear in the case of Lebanon, where so many live day-by-day, where politics is devoid of ideology—devoid, in other words, of any consideration of the future—and where the past is commemorated or destroyed, but never fully remembered, never fully reckoned with.[9] But we can also glimpse, in looking at Lebanon, the outlines of alternative strategies for living—efforts to devise different ways of being in the world, less complicit in the compromises, the illusions and disillusions of late modernity, and founded in the making of community. Looking at Lebanon, in other words, can help us to understand the world in which we live now.

A short history of the Lebanese twenty-first century

But to plot out the terrains of the everyday in contemporary Lebanon, we also have to understand what has come to pass there, and across the Middle East, since 2005. On Valentine's Day of that year, the Sunni business magnate and politician Rafiq Hariri was assassinated, the victim of a powerful truck bomb detonated as his motorcade passed along the Beirut seafront. Prime minister for ten of the fifteen years since the end of Lebanon's civil war in 1990, Hariri had established himself in that time as the dominant figure of Lebanese politics. Now his death seemed to signal the unravelling of the system in which he had thrived—one premised on a clear division of the spoils of post-war Lebanon between Lebanese politicians and Syria, whose troops had been present in Lebanon since 1976, and which emerged as the country's de facto ruler after 1990. Hariri—a charismatic, wily, wilful figure, who had made his wealth as a building contractor in Saudi Arabia and continued to benefit from the support of that country's royal family—enjoyed a relatively free hand in matters of economic policy. Stamping his imprint on Lebanon through an ambitious—and controversial—programme of liberalisation, he sought to transform the country into a regional hub for transport, tourism, and banking, a place where wealthy Gulf Arabs could feel comfortable spending their holidays and squirrelling away their dollars. In politics, however, Hariri had to contend with the powerful presence of the Syrian security apparatus that effectively governed Lebanon after 1990. Carefully managing the country's politics, Ghazi Kanaan, the head of Syrian military intelligence in Lebanon until 2002, and his successor, Rustum Ghazali, vetted electoral candidates, approved appointments, and kept a tight watch on dissidence, using their Lebanese underlings as enforcers. The restrictions imposed by this system of indirect rule had long rankled with Hariri, who increasingly failed to disguise his displeasure at moves such as the decision to extend by two years the term of the Lebanese president, Emile Lahoud—a placeman for Damascus, and one of his most bitter rivals.

For many at the time, the explosion that killed Hariri could only have been the work of the Syrian security services. Within days, bitter crowds began to gather in Martyrs' Square, in central Beirut, chanting slogans laying the blame for his death squarely on the Syrian Baathist regime and its Lebanese allies. But anger at Hariri's assassination was not simply the preserve of his supporters. Rather, it helped to crystallise growing resentment of Syria's hegemony over Lebanon, drawing hitherto disparate currents of discontent into a single upswell of protest. Week by week, the demonstrations in Martyrs' Square grew larger, culminating in a massive gathering on 14 March—a month to the day after Hariri's death. As a sea of people filled Martyrs' Square, holding aloft Lebanese flags, politician after politician took to the stage to reiterate the same demands: truth and justice for Hariri, the immediate withdrawal of Syrian troops from Lebanon, free parliamentary elections, and 'freedom, sovereignty, and independence' for the country after fifteen years of foreign domination. All the while, diplomatic pressure on Damascus to withdraw intensified—from the United Nations Security Council, which had passed Resolution 1559 in September 2004 calling for the holding of free and fair elections and the withdrawal of all 'foreign forces' from Lebanese territory; the United States, eager to portray Lebanon as an example of Middle Eastern democracy in action; Saudi Arabia, which had seen Hariri as one of its own; and France, whose president, Jacques Chirac, and Hariri had been friends. By late April, Bashar al-Assad was ready to cede to diplomatic pressure and to put an end to almost three decades of military involvement in Lebanon. On 26 April, the last Syrian troops left Lebanon, their tanks snaking over the mountain passes and across the border. The era of Syrian hegemony had seemingly come to an end.

Not all in Lebanon, though, were happy with these developments. On 8 March, hundreds of thousands gathered in central Beirut at the behest of Sayyid Hassan Nasrallah, Hizballah's charismatic secretary-general. Though relations had not always been easy between Hizballah and Damascus, by 2005 a modus vivendi had been established, and Nasrallah took on the responsibility of reminding the Lebanese of everything they owed Syria and its ruling party. In an impassioned speech, interrupted by the cries of a crowd bearing Lebanese flags and images of Hafiz and Bashar al-Assad, Nasrallah extended his thanks to Damascus for its role as the protector of Lebanon, and condemned in stinging terms the international community's attempts to break up the relationship between Lebanon and Syria. The two states, he insisted, were bound together by fraternal ties, and nobody but their own governments could pronounce on the terms of their future relations. As for Resolution 1559, which had called for the 'disarmament of all Lebanese and non-Lebanese militias'—a phrase widely interpreted as targeting Hizballah's armed wing, which had held on to its weapons after the end of the civil war: two years after the occupation of Iraq, this was but another instance of American intervention in the Middle East, and had no other purpose but to weaken armed resistance to Western imperialism and Israel. This message is what Damascus would have wanted to hear. But it was also one that resonated with many Lebanese.

The dividing lines were drawn in these March days between the two alliances that would come to define political life after 2005. On the one hand is the 14 March alliance. Centred round the Future Movement, established by Hariri as a vehicle for his own political ambitions within the Sunni community, it brought together for a time an unlikely coalition of longstanding opponents of Syrian interference and erstwhile allies of Damascus, secular leftists and Islamists. Loudly proclaiming its opposition to Syria's presence in Lebanon, 14 March has presented itself as the guarantor not just of the country's independence and sovereignty, but also of its stability, adopting a discourse of state-building which emphasises the need to bring all armed groups under the umbrella of the Lebanese government. Confident of the support of the United States, the European Union, Saudi Arabia and other Gulf states, 14 March spoke—and continues to speak, if with diminishing returns—a language foreign diplomats could understand: one that stresses disarming the national 'resistance' headed up by Hizballah, national partnership in the task of technocratic government, continued foreign direct investment in the Lebanese economy and, since 2011, support for the Syrian opposition in its struggle against Bashar al-Assad—though this has grown increasingly muted as the Syrian regime and its Russian, Iranian, and Lebanese backers have gained ground. On the other hand are ranged the forces of 8 March—Hizballah, its Shia rival and partner Amal and, since February 2006, the Free Patriotic Movement of the popular Christian leader General Michel Aoun. Staunchly attached to the resistance's weapons, 8 March has portrayed itself as part of a regional 'axis' ranged against the forces of Western neo-imperialism, Zionism, and Sunni jihadi obscurantism. In this view, it stands firm alongside Iran and the Syrian regime in its opposition to nefarious plans for the division and destruction of the Middle East—of which the Syrian conflict is but the latest manifestation. It is along these lines that the parliamentary elections of 2005 and 2009—both won by 14 March with relatively comfortable, if contested, majorities—were fought, as much as around matters of domestic policy. But if 8 March and 14 March have defined themselves largely in external terms, the divisions between them have had profound consequences for Lebanon's democracy and the lives of its people.

For in the thirteen years since Hariri's death and the demonstrations of March 2005, Lebanon's inhabitants have grown all too accustomed to the sight of political polarisation and inaction. They have become used to the making and unmaking of electoral alliances, the embrace and disavowal of political principles, the insults and accusations, counter-accusations and reconciliations. They have watched with increasing weariness the tempestuous talk show appearances, fiery press conferences, and stage-managed summits that are the mainstays of Lebanese political life—so much empty bluster and chatter relayed in minute, mind-numbing detail by the country's newspapers and TV channels. Impotent witnesses to the cabinet sessions that come and go in a flurry of pronouncements and proposals, delayed budgets and deferred laws, they have looked on as the arteries of representative government have grown sclerotic, obstructed by endless, tedious disputes over ministerial appointments and constitutional protocols and slowed down by walk-outs, boycotts, abstentions and resignations. Since 2008, they have seen countless 'national dialogue' sessions pass them by, without the shadow of an agreement. (Eighteen were held, by my count, under President Michel Sleiman alone. He left office in May 2014, leaving behind a vacancy that remained unfilled for twenty-nine months.) After the end of Sleiman's term, they had to watch as parliament held forty-six sessions before finally electing Michel Aoun as president in October 2016. This has only compounded the sense that the chamber of deputies is a mere talking shop filled with self-serving and vain incompetents. For, having argued for two years over a new electoral law, putting together ever more byzantine and outlandish proposals in their efforts to preserve their own interests, Lebanon's deputies voted in May 2013 to postpone the parliamentary elections scheduled for the following month, extending instead their terms in office for seventeen months. In November 2014, they met again to extend parliament's life for another thirty-one months, putting back the elections until June 2017. In 2017, they were again postponed for another year. At the time of writing, they are scheduled for May 2018. It can all too easily seem as though the only thing Lebanon's politicians can agree on is their own importance.

These are scenes as unedifying as they are absurd. Sweeping up to parliament in convoys of armoured cars ahead of each session, taking their seats in cabinet, issuing statements, Lebanon's politicians seem engaged in a simulacrum of representative government, mummers playing out a script that everyone—actors and audience alike—knows is a fiction. For all are too aware that this is simply the pretence of normality, and that things are anything but as they should be. Since 2005, the exceptional—in the form of interim cabinets, executive vacancies, parliamentary extensions, and administrative decrees—has become the norm in Lebanon. It would be easy to ignore this game of make believe, leaving it to fade into the background like a television set left on mute, were it not to have such dire consequences. This is not simply a bad script played out by mediocre actors. Lebanon's parliamentary democracy, held in abeyance by the civil war and much traduced under Syrian hegemony, now lies suspended in a state of half-life, like a patient left on a ventilator.

And alongside this stasis have come death and disorder. Many can reel off with tired familiarity the roll call of 'martyrs' of all sides, from the anti-Damascus editorialists Samir Kassir and Gebran Tueni, blown up by car bombs within six months of each other in 2005, to the Hizballah commanders Imad Mughniyyeh and Mustafa Badreddine, killed in Syria in 2008 and 2016. And, as the Syrian civil war has intensified and Hizballah's role in the conflict grown ever more significant, so too have 'security incidents' on Lebanese territory become more frequent—and murderous. The Lebanese have become used to bad news stories, from the fighting that pitted the Lebanese army against followers of the charismatic Salafi shaykh Ahmad al-Asir in the southern city of Saida in 2013 to suicide attacks like the twin explosions that killed forty-three in the Beirut suburb of Burj al-Barajneh in November 2015 and five in the Beqaa village of Qaa, hit by eight explosions in a single day in June 2016.

Unsurprisingly, political uncertainty and rising insecurity have taken their economic toll. Reliable figures are hard to come by for the Lebanese economy, but those that exist make for unsettling reading. Though GDP growth rose from 1.6% in 2006 to a high of 10% in 2009, bolstered by the combined effects of a brief period of political optimism and the paradoxical effects of the global financial crisis, which led many in the diaspora to move their money into Lebanese banks, it has since wavered again, falling to a low of 1.3% in 2015. (It has since stabilised a little.)[10] By the end of 2014, Lebanon's net public debt stood at US$57.3 billion, an annual increase of 7.69%.[11] Unemployment, meanwhile, remains well above the 6% mark.[12] But even these indicators do not tell the full story of an economy stunned by systemic shock and sent reeling by repeated crisis. The tally is a long and familiar one, from the series of assassinations that followed Hariri's death in 2005 to the July war of 2006, the fighting in 2007 between the army and the Islamist group Fatah al-Islam in the northern Palestinian refugee camp of Nahr al-Bared, and the 'events' of May 2008. For a time each new spring seemed to beckon a fresh outbreak of violence, throwing into jeopardy the summer tourist season that Lebanon, like a faded seaside resort, has come to rely on as a source of revenue and an indicator of economic health.

Little, though, could have prepared Lebanon for the effects of events in Syria since 2011. These have cast a dark cloak over the Lebanese economy, like a dust cloud rising from a destruction site. For as its neighbour has been dragged from peaceful protest into a brutal zero-sum war of barrel bombs, sieges, suicide attacks, foreign interventions and splintered factions, Lebanon, too, has had to live with the consequences of violence. The Syrian war has sent the tourism sector—so dependent on the perception of safety and stability—into a prolonged crisis. Wary of 'spill-over', the wealthy Gulf Arabs who long flocked to Beirut every summer, filling its five-star hotels and chic restaurants, have largely stayed away since 2011. Those not put off by fears of disorder have been dissuaded by official warnings. The sharpest of these came in February 2016, when Saudi Arabia, the United Arab Emirates and Bahrain, angered by Hizballah's vociferous response to the killing of the Saudi Shia cleric Nimr al-Nimr and by its continuing military involvement in Syria, urged their citizens to avoid all travel to Lebanon. (A further call for all Saudi citizens to leave Lebanon came in November 2017, coinciding with Saad Hariri's mysterious resignation in Riyadh.) Not for the first time, Lebanon has been caught up in a regional conflagration. The effects are palpable. The cafés and bars of downtown Beirut, once largely frequented by visiting Arab tourists, now lie empty. Those summers when the streets around Martyrs' Square resounded with the guttural roars of red Maseratis and canary-yellow Porsches shipped from Abu Dhabi or Qatar for a few weeks of play seem a lifetime ago. Hariri's Beirut is now a ghost quarter. But the effects are felt much further afield. When I was last in Lebanon in late 2017, the only other guests in my hotel in a down-at-heel part of the capital were Syrians in flight—whole families of them, the parents anxiously fretting with cigarette packs and mobile phones while their children indulged in the unlimited pleasures of the breakfast bar—and aid workers, serious men and women in light summer clothes earnestly poring over tables of figures or chatting about their days in the camps.

This is just one small reminder of the profound demographic trans-formation Lebanon has undergone in the last few years. It has, of course, long been a country of migrants—a place formed, defined and redefined by movement. The Lebanese themselves, like the Irish or the Italians, are an unusually diasporic people, migrating in their hundreds of thousands in a series of waves that began in the late nineteenth century. This propensity for movement has made their homeland heavily dependent on the financial investments and emotional attachments of its prodigal ones. But Lebanon has also taken in—often not without a certain marked reluctance—successive generations of refugees. First came Armenians, Kurds and Assyrians fleeing southern Anatolia, northern Syria and Iraq in the decades after the First World War. Then, after 1948, followed the Palestinians. In December 2017, the Lebanese government announced that there were 174,422 Palestinian refugees dwelling in the country; there were once more than 400,000.[13] Many of these families have now been in Lebanon for seventy years; several generations have known nothing but life in the country's twelve refugee camps and 156 informal Palestinian settlements. Alongside these refugees—some, like the Armenians, a distinctive thread in the weave of Lebanese society, others like the Palestinians carefully kept apart and cantoned in their camps—must be counted the migrant workers on whom Lebanon has developed such a heavy dependence. The Syrian agricultural labourers and construction workers who began to cross the border in the 1950s and 1960s have been joined since the 1980s by Egyptians and Sri Lankans, Filipinos, Nepalese, Indians, Ethiopians, Sudanese and Madagascans. It is these men and women who build the homes of the Lebanese and pick the rubbish off their streets, who fill their cars at petrol stations and nurse their children. But these long-standing trends have only been amplified in the last decade. Many Lebanese have once again taken the well-trodden paths of migration, seeking relief in the Gulf, Western Europe, North America, and Africa from under-employment, depressed wages and depressing uncertainty. And as they have left, Lebanon has become a landing point for so many of those fleeing the Syrian war.

On 3 April 2014, the UNHCR announced that the number of registered Syrian refugees in Lebanon had reached a million.[14] Since then, numbers have stood more or less constant around the million mark, rising or falling slightly with each new regime offensive on opposition strongholds. Only Turkey, where some 2.6 million have found a haven of sorts, has taken in more Syrian refugees than Lebanon. Though head-counts are made more difficult by the Lebanese government's insistence in 2015 that UNHCR stop registering new arrivals from Syria, there are now, in early 2018, almost 230,000 Syrian households in Lebanon, scattered across the length and breadth of the country.[15] To compound matters, 80 per cent of those who have fled to Lebanon are women and children, many of whom live in desperately precarious circumstances.[16] (In late 2015, the UNHCR reported that around 89 per cent of Syrian households in Lebanon had run into debt to purchase food, pay for rent, heating, schooling and legal fees; the figure rose to almost 100 per cent if those who had borrowed money more than three months before the survey were included.)[17] This influx has profoundly reshaped Lebanon's demography. This is true at the local level: a notable example is the eastern border town of Arsal, whose population grew threefold to over 100,000 in late 2013, as Syrians flooded across the border to flee brutal fighting in Qalamun and Qusair between Hizballah and opposition groups. But it is also true at the national level. A quarter of Lebanon's inhabitants are now refugees. This has strained the binds of conviviality, sometimes revealing nasty blotches of nativism beneath, and has placed a heavy weight on the shoulders of an arthritic Lebanese state.

Living in times of crisis—or the politics of getting by

Whether written by political scientists or journalists and commentators, most accounts of contemporary Lebanon tend to move along two well-set grooves. While some focus on the inner workings of the Lebanese political system, others concentrate on its external regional circumstances. For those who look within, seeking to discern the origins of crisis in the country's political anatomy, there are few aspects more significant than the byzantine political arrangements devised to deal with the country's exceptional degree of religious pluralism. Thus, many regard sectarianism as 'a crucial, if not defining, feature of Lebanese politics and society'.[18] They are perhaps not wrong to do so. After all, the Lebanese state affords official recognition to eighteen religious communities: four Muslim sects and twelve Christian churches or groups of churches, along with the Druze and Jews (the latter still counted despite the miniscule number who still remain in Lebanon). Parliamentary seats, ministerial appointments, and positions in the army and the civil service are all distributed on the basis of confession. Thus, while by convention the president of the republic is a Maronite Christian, the prime minister a Sunni, and the speaker of parliament a Shia, the 128 seats in the chamber of deputies have, since the 1989 Ta'if accord, been divided up equally between Muslims and Christians. And sectarianism seems to determine the complexion of party politics, too. It is common for commentators to speak of Hizballah, say, as a Shia political force, or the Phalange and Lebanese Forces as Christian—if not specifically Maronite—parties. What's more, few are the political leaders who attempt to address voters outside of their own communities, becoming adept instead at tugging at the strings of communitarian affirmation and confessional resentment.

Of course, things are more complicated than this. At an elite level, the Lebanese political system is not just built on inter-sectarian jostling and jockeying for position. Intra-communal rivalries like the long-standing rift between General Michel Aoun and the leader of the Lebanese Forces, Samir Geagea—recently patched up in dramatic fashion in a telegenic reconciliation ceremony—play their part. And so do cross-sectarian pacts such as the unlikely alliance between Aoun and Hizballah, or the rickety deal that bound together for a time the Progressive Socialist Party of the Druze leader Walid Jumblatt and the Future Movement, a political formation built around the spectral presence of Rafiq Hariri. What's more, it is by no means exceptional under Lebanon's existing electoral arrangements, in which voters in each district choose candidates from lists representing different factions and blocs, for members of one religious community to vote for candidates of another confession. This is commonly the case, for instance, in the eastern constituency of Rashaya and the West Bekaa, where in the 2009 elections a majority plumped for a 14 March list made up of six candidates—one Maronite, one Shia, one Greek Orthodox, one Druze and two Sunni.

But perhaps because they are so complicated, the workings of the sectarian system exert an enduring fascination on scholars of Lebanon, for whom the country's politics represent an irresistible bundle of paradoxes. On the one hand, Lebanon seems a paradigm of 'corporate consociational government'—to use the ungainly term coined by the Dutch political scientist Arend Lipjhart to describe what he called 'government by elite cartel designed to turn a democracy with a fragmented political culture into a stable democracy'.[19] Founded on a power-sharing compact dividing up political office amongst the country's several sects, Lebanese consociationalism is in this reading the product of a series of experiments in communitarian government. Beginning under Ottoman rule in the mid-nineteenth century, these have continued unabated until the present day, bequeathing to contemporary Lebanon a tradition of 'consensus and compromise'.[20] In this reading, this is a system capable of transmuting an apparent weakness—religious and social diversity—into a potential strength. For a 'strong confessional division of power' provides a basis for 'democratic governance', ensuring not just equitable representation—at least in theory—but also 'built-in checks-and-balances' against the monopoli-sation of power by any one group or figure.[21] Inherently pluralistic, this is a model of government that provides 'freedoms' for all, not by expunging signs of religious difference from the public sphere, but by making religious belonging the basis of political representation.[22]

On the other hand, contemporary Lebanon remains a 'deeply divided society'.[23] Twenty-eight years after the end of its civil war, and thirteen years after the withdrawal of Syrian forces, it is still riddled with 'sectarian tensions' and beset by the urge of competing communi-ties to 'monopolise state and territory' by converting 'communal claims' into 'national ones'.[24] Where once Maronite Christians saw Lebanon as their own, it is now the Sunni and the Shia who vie for dominance. The players may have changed, but the game remains the same. These endless rounds of rivalries have left the Lebanese state weak and exhausted, a hollow shell incapable of governing, let alone resolving the country's deep structural problems. All these resentments and grievances have left the country vulnerable to renewed bouts of strife, as the relentless competition for resources among politicians and sectarian groups forever threatens to devolve into the futile bloodlet-ting of civil war. Unable to learn from its past mistakes, Lebanon can seem at times like a repeat offender fated to fall back into bad old habits. Mired in 'endless cycles of internal conflict', the country repre-sents 'an example ... of the tragic pitfalls of violent communalism'.[25] Rather than a symbol of the potential of corporate consociationalism, Lebanon is a reminder of its flaws.

If some focus on the workings of a political system built around sectarianism, others seek an explanation for the country's on-going woes in geopolitics and the fluctuating course of international rela-tions. Amongst the explanations they have furnished for the seemingly chronic vulnerability of Lebanese institutions can be counted the unfortunate position of this small sliver of land: hemmed in between Israel, Syria, and the deep blue sea, Lebanon has been a hostage to broader Middle Eastern conflicts, serving as a chessboard on which regional and global powers can make their moves. The country's small size, too, has contributed to this trend. In this reading, Lebanon is something like a puny child mercilessly teased and bullied by its bigger classmates, who steal its pocket money and use it as a go-between carrying back and forth threatening messages. But if all this smacks of geographical determinism, others have taken a more historicist tack to explain Lebanon's lack of stability. A hodge-podge of communities, each with a differing understanding of its place in the world, the country has suffered in this reading from a century-long 'national identity crisis' which has made it exceptionally susceptible to the shifting ideological winds blowing through the region, from pan-Arabism to Islamism. Established to satisfy the Maronites' craving for a state of their own, Lebanon was long caught, in this account, in a tug of war between its Christian and Muslim citizens. While the former broadly sought to isolate themselves from the Arab Middle East, adhering instead to a particularistic vision of the Lebanese nation, the latter generally regarded themselves as Arabs and wished for stronger ties, if not outright political union, with neighbouring countries. This contest between 'Lebanonism' and Arabism could ultimately be resolved only through the cataclysm of the civil war that began in 1975.

In recent years, these accounts have been dusted down and updated to allow for new developments. The tensions of old may have waned in the wake of the war—a period that, ironically, saw the birth of a new-found attachment to Lebanon amongst its Muslim communities. However, they have only been supplanted by growing animosity between the Sunnis and Shia. This relatively novel phenomenon has been stoked, to be sure, by domestic factors. On the one hand, many Shia resent the Ta'if accord, in their eyes an unfair settlement that does not provide them with the share of power their demographic preponderance should command. On the other hand, Sunnis feel they are held at ransom by Hizballah's arms and its dominance—alongside Amal—of particular neighbourhoods they once regarded as 'theirs'. This sense of living in a stranglehold has only been heightened by the 'events' of May 2008 and the Special Tribunal for Lebanon's indictment, in 2011, of five Hizballah operatives for the assassination of Rafiq Hariri. But the tensions between Sunnis and Shia have hardly been eased by regional events. Lebanon's Muslims only had to cast a glance at Iraq in the years after 2003 to see Sunni suicide bombers and Shia killing squads doing the dirty work of confessional 'cleansing'—a sight replaced in recent years by the ghoulish apparition of Daesh and its opponents in the largely Shia militias of the 'popular mobilisation forces'. Looking across

16

the border at Syria, Lebanon's Shia see Daesh, Jabhat al-Nusra—or Jabhat Fatah al-Sham, as it is now known—and other Sunni jihadi groups as a threat to their very existence as a community. The country's Sunnis, for their part, see Hizballah as deeply complicit in Assad's relentless counter-revolution, and as guilty of brutal acts of repression against their coreligionists in Qalamun and Qusair, Homs and Aleppo. And, across the Middle East, they have seen the bitter geopolitical and ideological contest between Saudi Arabia and Iran—one the self-appointed patron of Lebanon's Sunnis, the other Hizballah's longstanding sponsor—spread and metastasize into proxy war in Yemen. All of this, then, means that Lebanon is—to use the phrase of the political scientist Tom Najem—a 'penetrated society', its political system riddled with the effects of foreign influence like a patient worn out by illness.[26]

But while some attribute this vulnerability to Lebanon's weak immune system, as it were—its inefficient state and sectarian divides— or lay the blame on cynical regional and global powers all too ready to exploit the country's position and resources, others argue that this is to neglect its politicians' propensity to enlist foreign support. This is a deeply ingrained habit, for if today's political leaders and blocs look to Saudi Arabia and Syria, Qatar, Iran or the United States to throw their weight behind them and unlock impasses, their predecessors once appealed to Nasser's Egypt and Eisenhower's United States or, in Ottoman times, to the protection of Britain and France. As Marie-Joëlle Zahar has argued, 'foreign intervention in Lebanese politics is, in great part, a function of Lebanese factions seeking to gain advantage over each other'. It is in this pattern of seeking assistance outside of Lebanon's borders that accounts for the country's 'permeability and vulnerability', not geographical factors or sectarianism *per se*. Be that as it may, the consequences are still ruinous: 'international interventions … have created a vicious cycle', worsening 'communal fears' and transforming the Lebanese state from a sovereign body into an instrument of international politics.[27] The internal and the external are thus not separate processes, but are intimately bound up by Lebanon's self-destructive dependency on foreign forces.

Despite their superficial differences, these various explanations for Lebanon's predicament have a great deal in common. They share a propensity for grand narratives, for regarding big men and large-scale forces as the only meaningful agents of change, and therefore as the only worthwhile subjects of inquiry. Some linger on the political intrigues and machinations of Lebanon's politicians, these flawed 'leaders of men' whom they treat as the 'modellers ... and creators, of whatsoever the general mass of men contrived to do or attain'.[28] Others are like weathermen, tracking the gales of regional conflict and sectarian tension as they sweep over the country. But all see everything—or everything worthy of note—as 'the outer material result' of the larger-than-life personalities and sweeping structural forces that take up centre stage in their accounts.[29] In their focus on high politics, on intra-elite rivalries and inter-state animosities, they tend to take certain forms of power as given. This is particularly true of sectarianism, which analysts view as the master key capable of unlocking the mysteries of domestic and regional politics alike. In treating it thus, as an essence that permeates all aspects of Lebanese life, like an oil slick that leaves its dark stain on everything it touches, such readings tend to freeze the status quo in place. Obviating any interpretation of confessionalism as a product of historical contingency, a changeful cluster of practices and ways of speaking about and understanding the world that rise in intensity at certain moments but wane at others, they regard the current prescription as the product of unwavering, constant forces. And, in doing so, they also negate the possibility of future change. It was ever thus, they seem to suggest, and forever will be.

What's more, in keeping their eyes trained on the crowded field of high politics, these accounts tend to overlook the ordinary. They have little to say about ordinary people, except as pieces of straw blown this way and that by the winds of change or as stock figures thrown in to the mix to add a little bite of the exotic to the narrative. And nor do they have much to say about ordinary moments, those mundane, banal moments that still occur in the midst of crisis—and that are often the effects of crisis. For time is not singular, a river whose strong currents carry us along a straight course from the past into the future. It is rather, as Achille Mbembe has written, an 'entanglement' of temporalities, of distinct but 'interlocking' presents, of different pasts and varying futures. Interwoven with the prolonged interruptions and jolting lurches of political time is another time, the 'time of existence and experience'.[30]

INTRODUCTION

If the first part of this book gives more attention to the time of politics, the second focuses on this time of experience—the time of everyday life, with its daily rituals and routine occurrences, its repetitions, its disruptions and 'disturbances' and particular ebbs and flows—and on the people who inhabit it.[31] The focus of these chapters is that realm of the ordinary that Kathleen Stewart has described as the 'shifting assemblage of practices and practical knowledges, … of liveness and exhaustion', filled with 'dream[s] of escape or of the simple life'—the world of work and city streets, of nights out and weddings that we all inhabit.[32] These pages linger on the everyday practices and sentiments of ordinary people, on the 'life worlds' they construct for themselves out of the 'material practices, signs, figures, superstitions, images and fictions' they have inherited and refurbished or picked up along the way, cutting and splicing and customising these ways of speaking and doing and living until they just about fit.[33] Its focus, then, is on 'those things which have not yet been talked about, those things that … give some … indices of the fragility' of life in the present, with its precarity and its stabs of passing beauty.[34]

And yet, I do not want to slip into facile celebration of the agency of the weak, attempting to 'right the balance' of scholarly neglect by showing that housewives and domestic workers, labourers and taxi drivers also possess the will and wherewithal to shape their own lives.[35] It is not enough to establish that 'the dominated … have a rich and complex consciousness [and] … are capable of challenging their oppression'.[36] There is a danger, at times, of celebrating a little too eagerly each act of cannibalisation, each small piece of handiwork as a victory in itself, and of losing sight of the ways in which customisations and canny subterfuges might signal instead a tacit acceptance of the norms that govern Lebanese society. This was brought home to me when I spoke on my work at the School of Oriental and African Studies in London, going on at some length about the reliance of the Lebanese on the road on shortcuts and swerves, and presenting these as acts of creative appropriation. After I was done, a student in the audience raised her hand. Were these tactics, she asked, really signs of cunning and creativity, of refusal of the stagnant realities of everyday life? Were they not, instead, further evidence of the individualism and misrule that reigned in contemporary Lebanon? Getting ahead meant keeping others back. It signalled self-interest and atomisation, not resistance. It meant refusing not the status quo, but the very possibility of community. We must consider not just attempts to resist or subvert dominant modes of thinking about the political and the social, from partisan alignment to confessional loyalty or commodity fetishism, but also the ways in which Lebanon's inhabitants fall into line with these hegemonic discourses, which infuse their lives with meaning and shape their view of the world.

We cannot, then, neglect the political. Quite the contrary—it would be impossible to write about contemporary Lebanon without considering the workings of politics, the main focus of this book's first part. I do, though, want to make the case for an expanded definition of the political, reaching beyond conventional topics of inquiry. To confine oneself simply to the realms of party alignments, parliamentary debates, of legal texts, cabinet minutes, international diplomacy and regional conflict, is to attempt to grasp a 'world of shadows'. This is not just because so much of high political life is carried on behind the scenes, in an endless synchronised dance of secretive phone calls and closed-doors meetings, whose contents, if they ever do filter out to the public, do so in the form of off-the-record briefings and scraps of rumour, allusion, and allegation. More than this, it is because to comprehend politics in contemporary Lebanon, we must understand how its inhabitants 'experience and live politics in their daily existence'.[37]

This is as true of the members of the country's *tabaqa siyasiyya* or 'political class' as it is of those with no stake in politics as they are conventionally understood. For all are connected. And all are, in a sense, ordinary. Counter-intuitive as it may seem, the *zu'ama* and *aqtab*, the 'leaders' and 'poles' of Lebanese political life, inhabit the realm of the everyday. Try as they might to insulate themselves from its more niggling aspects in their air-conditioned apartments and villas, with their swimming pools, security fences and gilded furniture, theirs is a world constantly invaded by the quotidian concerns and demands of their followers, for whom they must arrange jobs and loans, secure introductions and patch up differences. The lives of these men—for all are men—are measured out in the daily exchange of gripes and favours, in shared coffee cups and mezze lunches and telephone calls. This is an intensely personal, banal mode of politics. And their public pronouncements are as much rooted in the everyday as their private dealings, for the tropes that punctuate their speeches and press conferences—of resistance to foreign invasion or fear of demographic displacement, of state-building, resilience and fair representation—are products of the preoccupations, anxieties and desires that they share with their listeners. For both speaker and listener, these are not mere catchphrases or abstractions, but dense clusters of meaning. Each one is a cue, prompting recognition of the ways these notions evoke, and shape, personal experience—conjuring up memories of the civil war or the 'July war' of 2006, of neighbourhood disputes and disagreements over real estate, of jokes and dinner-table gossip and conversations with classmates or colleagues. Just as the everyday is steeped in the political, so too is politics steeped in the mundane.

And just as we must understand even high politics as a fundamentally quotidian operation, so too do we have to account for the ways in which certain political discourses act as force fields shaping social relations. As Michel Foucault long ago pointed out, power, in the form of particular conceptions of the world, courses through the capillaries of society. Reaching each of its members, these discursive constructions and disciplinary mechanisms inform individual ways of being and relating to others. This is evident in Lebanon in the immanence of sectarianism in daily life. It is felt by the Lebanese as a haunting, a presence that is rarely spoken aloud but that is always there, lurking within conversations and beneath seemingly innocent questions, arranging space and settling like a thin layer of dust on social intercourse. And, though opinions differ as to whether it is a natural feature of Lebanese society, an organic growth as ineradicable as the nose on one's own face or an unnatural imposition, a tool of division wielded by cynical rulers, many ordinary Lebanese regard it as a defining characteristic of their country.

The same is now true of crisis. It is understood through the familiar explanatory frameworks furnished by television talk shows and politicians' interviews—political blockage, Shia-Sunni conflict, US interventionism, Israeli aggression—figures of speech that saturate the public sphere and are endlessly parsed in everyday conversation. But it is also experienced as a series of symptoms and signs both large and small. Thus, crisis is manifest not just in electricity cuts, in uncollected rubbish and traffic jams, but also in that fraction of a second when one wonders whether the blurt of a text message signals a missive from the Israeli Defence Forces or just another promotion for two-for-one loo paper from the local supermarket, or when one unthinkingly checks under one's car for a booby-trap at the end of a night out. Is it any surprise, then, that many should think of insecurity and instability, too, as features of life in contemporary Lebanon? A source alternatively of weariness, of wry amusement, disgust and abject anger, crisis frames the way in which the Lebanese relate to their own country. What Naveeda Khan has written of Pakistan is also true of Lebanon: its inhabitants come 'to attach' themselves to the country and 'claim it as [their] own', not just through embracing its pleasures, but also 'through disclaiming' its dysfunctions.[38] To live in contemporary Lebanon is to live in crisis, always aware of its troubling presence, even as life ticks along according to its own particular rhythms.

This book is a critical history of the Lebanese present. Each of its eight chapters takes as its starting point a particular conception of contemporary Lebanon: as a place of political unrest and upheaval; as a stage for conflict; as a site of foreign intervention, a state whose sovereignty is uncertain and perforated; as a society held captive by sectarian sentiment and patrimonial politics; as a testing-ground for neoliberal economics; as a country of refuge; as a hedonistic land; and, finally, as a failed state, a place of collapsing infrastructure and malfunctioning institutions. Working through these, I want to examine them critically, to unpick and complicate the way that we think about this place. Instead of getting caught up in these tropes, in other words, I want to take the present as it is, as it comes—that great chaotic current of feelings and thoughts and information and images that surges over us daily, without fail, till we are no longer here—till the things we lived through have passed and till we, too, are a thing of the past.

This book does not seek to understand how we arrived here—or at least not in conventional terms. It is not the sort of book a historian is supposed to write about the present. It does not go in search of origins or antecedents, attempting to single out in the past a few features that might define and make the present, giving it its particular cast. Nor does it work backwards from the present, seeking to identify the point when this or that particular characteristic of our own times first emerged. Instead, it asks: 'What is happening today? What is happening now? What is this "now" in which we all are? What is the frame of our current experiences and of our potential futures?' It seeks its answers in the fragments of daily life—in conversations, interviews and scenes recorded over thirteen years of visits; in newspaper articles, caricatures, talk shows, blogs, comment boards and memes, Facebook posts, tweets and YouTube clips; in political posters, graffiti and the walls on which they are plastered and painted, the ever-shifting urban fabric of Lebanon. For thirteen years, I have kept notebooks in which I have scrawled small moments and scraps of conversation and folders stuffed with the ephemera and digital junk of modern life. These are the archives for this book. It is an 'ontology of the present', an effort to understand what it means, and how it feels, to live in Lebanon, and the world, in the early years of the twenty-first century.[39]

PART I

THE TIME OF POLITICS

1

INTIFADAT AL-ISTIQLAL, OR THE
INDEPENDENCE UPRISING

THE MOMENT THAT PASSED

The assassination

It was an unseasonably warm morning that Valentine's Day in 2005. Rafiq Hariri's day had followed the patterns of his routine. After eating his usual breakfast—a few spoonfuls of *labneh* doused in olive oil and garnished with mint, tomatoes and olives—alone, he had met with his advisers for about an hour and a half to discuss the day's developments, as was his habit. Around 10.35, Hariri and his security convoy left his ten-story villa in Koraitem, in western Beirut, for the Lebanese parliament, where he was due to meet the Druze MP Marwan Hamadeh, a member of the opposition Bristol Gathering, who had recently survived a bomb attack. At about 12.25, Hariri left parliament and crossed Nijmeh Square towards the Café de l'Etoile where Nejib Friji, the Tunisian head of the UN Information Office in Beirut, was briefing a number of prominent journalists. After chatting a little with the group about recent political events, Hariri briefly spoke alone with Friji. The two men each sought advice from the other—Hariri asking about Rustom Ghazaleh, the all-powerful head of Syrian military intelligence in Lebanon, and Friji about how best to handle Hizballah. Shortly

27

before one, Hariri called for his convoy to pick him up. He was ready to return home to Koreitem for lunch. At five to one, Hariri's armoured S-600 Mercedes was nearing the St George Hotel,[1] on the Beirut seafront, when a suicide bomber parked in a Mitsubishi Canter van detonated a charge of around 2,500 kilograms of explosives.[2] The suicide bomber, Hariri, eight of his companions and security detail, and thirteen bystanders were killed; 231 were injured in the blast, which left behind a crater more than 30 feet wide.[3]

The reaction to Hariri's death was one of disbelief and apprehension. Hariri was not the first Lebanese politician to be targeted by a bomb attack in recent months. In October 2004, Hamadeh, a member of the Druze leader Walid Jumblatt's parliamentary bloc, had been left badly hurt by a car bomb explosion that killed his bodyguard and injured his driver. But an attack of this magnitude, and on a figure of Hariri's significance, had not been seen since the dark days of the 1980s. The dominant political figure of post-war Lebanon, Hariri had long seemed untouchable. He was, it is true, unpopular amongst some, particularly Christians opposed to Syria's presence in Lebanon, who were resentful of his hold on power and his accommodating, pragmatic stance towards powerful figures such as Ghazi Kanaan—until 2003 Damascus' proconsul in Beirut and a symbol of Syrian 'hegemony'. There were those, too, who were critical of his reconstruction projects, which they saw as a means of transforming central Beirut into his personal fiefdom, and stripping it of its old identity in the process. And yet, few Lebanese could accept the idea that he could be dispensed with in so crude and spectacular a fashion. For many, there could only be one culprit capable of carrying out such an act.

For Hariri's relations with Syria had been put under intolerable strain in recent years. The election of Emile Lahoud as Lebanon's president in 1998—in reality an appointment by executive fiat—had first tugged at the seams of Hariri's relationship with Damascus. It was hard not to see the dour, obdurate former military commander as anything but a counterweight to Hariri, whose largesse and bonhomie were central features of his political persona. Lahoud was determined to establish himself as a strong Christian leader, and there could be no more flagrant way of doing so than by putting Hariri in his place, checking the Sunni community's pretensions with one swipe of the paw at its leader. Hariri, meanwhile, viewed Lahoud as little more than a grey placeman, parachuted into the presidential palace by Damascus. But only after Hafiz al-Assad's death from cancer in 2000 did the cracks really begin to show. The priority for the callow and craven Bashar and his advisers, eager to profit from the power now at their fingertips, was to keep the extractive mechanisms that siphoned revenue away from Lebanon and towards Damascus in good order. In their eyes, the growing antipathy between Lahoud and Hariri was only so much detritus clogging up the pipes. And it was clear that the younger Assad and his courtiers saw Lahoud as their man. He had the advantage, after all, of being entirely in Damascus' debt; by contrast, Hariri's wealth, political experience and close relationship with Saudi Arabia suggested a worrying capacity for independent action.

An early portent of this came in the 2000 parliamentary elections, in which Hariri's bloc routed many of Lahoud's candidates. In Beirut, Hariri's list swept the board, taking all nineteen parliamentary seats. Even Selim el-Hoss, the beleaguered incumbent prime minister, lost his seat. Ironically, Hariri's success was in part a product of Syrian policy, for his candidates benefited from the new 2000 electoral law, the confection of Ghazi Kanaan. No friend of Lahoud, Syria's man in Lebanon was determined to prop up his old ally Hariri. This was further evidence to the younger Assad that things needed to change if they were to remain the same. To maintain his grip on Lebanon, he would have to weaken Hariri's own hold on power. This strategy became apparent in 2002, when Damascus and Lahoud offered their surreptitious backing to the premiership bid of the wealthy Saudi-Lebanese prince and businessman Walid bin Talal. At the opening of his new Mövenpick hotel on Beirut's beachfront, Talal laid out an economic recovery plan for Lebanon that it was hard not to read as a statement of political intent. Many of Hariri's supporters attempted to laugh off this challenge. (The information minister, Ghazi Aridi, commented waggishly that if each new hotel launched in Beirut augured a new premier, then Lebanon would go through fifteen or twenty cabinets a year.)[4] But Bashar's intent was clear. It became clearer still the following year, when it was announced that Ghazi Kanaan was to be retired and replaced with Rustom Ghazaleh. Kanaan was a fearsome figure, to be sure, but also a familiar one, with whom many Lebanese politicians—or, at least, those who had accepted the post-war status quo, coming to play the game according to rules laid down in Damascus—felt they could do business. Ghazaleh, meanwhile, was as opaque and shallow as a faded mirror. Dull and thuggish, he proved 'easily buyable with financial privileges', but subservient to Damascus in a way that his more biddable predecessor, with his long experience of Lebanese politics, had not been.[5]

Hariri, it was becoming increasingly clear, could not hope for any improvement in his relations with Damascus as long as Lahoud remained in office. In April 2003, he had to accept a new cabinet made up of staunch 'loyalists' such as Qassem Qanso, the head of the Lebanese branch of the Syrian Baath, and Assad Hardan, the head of the Syrian Social Nationalist Party.[6] It was hard not to read this not just as a reassertion of Damascus' control, but also a belated reprimand for the cheek Hariri had shown during the 2000 elections. Though Hariri stayed on as premier, seeing this as the only means of keeping Lahoud in check, he found his position increasingly untenable. In a rare unguarded moment after one particularly laborious cabinet session, he told the Lebanese newspaper *al-Safir* that Lahoud 'does not want to reconcile with me. I do not want to have a problem with him but he insists on provoking me'.[7] And there was little sign that Lahoud was going anywhere. As 2003 wore on, rumours began to swirl about suggesting that Damascus was eager to extend Lahoud's presidential term—a decision the man himself was hardly likely to oppose.

The international situation hardly helped Hariri's relations with Damascus. In March 2003, American and British troops had poured into Iraq, toppling Saddam Hussein. Many presumed that Syria was next. Late in 2003, the US Congress passed the Syria Accountability and Lebanese Sovereignty Act, imposing political and economic sanctions on the country. Describing Syria as a 'state sponsor of terrorism', the act charged that Damascus harboured organisations such as Hamas and Hizballah, supported forces hostile to the Coalition in Iraq, and flouted international law and treaties through its continued 'encroachment upon Lebanon's political independence' and sovereignty, its blockage of the Arab-Israeli peace process, and its ballistic and chemical weapons programmes.[8] Washington was clear: through its actions over the decades, Syria had wilfully put itself beyond the pale. But far from reining in Syrian policy in Lebanon, foreign pressure only increased Assad's determination to hold on to the country. Like a scolded child, reprimands merely seemed to spur Bashar on. By mid-2004, his mind was made up. Lahoud would get his second term, even if it meant pressuring the Lebanese parliament into voting through the necessary constitutional amendment. Jacques Chirac—an old friend of Hariri's increasingly worried by the new turn in Syrian policy—and George W. Bush would see just how little their criticism counted.

In late August, Hariri was called to Damascus, where Bashar told him of his decision. Hariri would later tell friends and colleagues that he had tried to discuss the matter with the Syrian president. Assad's response was as clear as it was final: 'There is nothing to discuss. I am Lahoud and Lahoud is me. If your friend Chirac wants me out of Lebanon, I would sooner break Lebanon on your head and the head of Chirac than break my word.'[9] The meeting lasted barely a quarter of an hour.

This was not the first time that Hariri had been forced to endure Assad's vitriol. In late 2003, a few days after Lebanon's Independence Day celebrations, which Hariri had chosen to boycott—underlining his increasingly public feud with Lahoud—he had been summoned to Syria for a dressing down. For three quarters of an hour, Assad, surrounded by Kanaan, Ghazaleh, and Kanaan's aide, Muhammad Khallouf, berated Hariri, accusing him of abetting France and the United States in their plots against Syria. So shaken was Hariri that he had to be led out of the meeting by Kanaan, his nose bleeding from the nerves.[10] But this new announcement signalled a decisive shift. There could be no going back. On 28 August, the Lebanese cabinet met. There was just one item on its agenda: the bill proroguing Lahoud's term in office.

International condemnation and Syrian obduracy followed each other in a cycle becoming increasingly familiar to the Lebanese. On 2 September 2004, the UN Security Council voted in favour of Resolution 1559. The product of a joint diplomatic initiative by the United States and France, it called for a 'free and fair presidential election in Lebanon conducted according to Lebanese constitutional rules devised without foreign interference or influence', 'the withdrawal of all non-Lebanese forces' from Lebanon, and 'the disbanding and disarmament of all Lebanese and non-Lebanese militias'.[11] The latter clause, which clearly targeted Hizballah, was deemed a disaster by many Lebanese observers, who feared it would split the country down the middle, pitting the party against those opposed to Syria's presence in Lebanon and putting Hariri and his allies in an impossible position. The following day, the Lebanese parliament met to vote on the constitutional amendment that would secure Lahoud's second term: ninety-six voted in favour, including Hariri himself, who declared himself duty-bound to go along with a motion his own cabinet had approved. But for all his weary compliance, Hariri's time was up. He was too powerful, too hostile to Lahoud, too close to Chirac, for Bashar's comfort. On 20 October, Nabih Berri, the speaker of parliament, delivered Hariri an ultimatum on behalf of Damascus. He had two hours to resign, or he would face a mass walkout from his cabinet, pulling the ground from under his feet. He was replaced by Omar Karami, the ageing head of a Tripolitan political dynasty.

Even this ousting, however, could not resolve Hariri to break entirely with old habits and join the anti-Syrian opposition. Lahoud's extension had emboldened longstanding critics of Syria's interference in Lebanese affairs, and had turned politicians once well disposed towards Damascus against Bashar and his coterie. Particularly prominent were the Maronite patriarch, Mar Nasrallah Boutros Sfeir, and the Druze leader Walid Jumblatt. The two made unlikely bedfellows. The wizened, diminutive Sfeir had long been an outspoken opponent of Syrian overrule in Lebanon. Like many of his predecessors, he regarded the Maronite Church not just as the guarantor of the Christians' rights, but also as the guardian of Lebanese sovereignty. With his resolve, Sfeir had helped to compensate for the diminished power of Christian political leadership, decimated by the flight into exile of figures like Michel Aoun, Amin Gemayel and Dory Chamoun and the arrest and solitary confinement of Samir Geagea. Under his stewardship, these parties' remaining representatives had gradually grown more vocal in the wake of Bashar's accession to power. Meeting in the Matn town of Qornet Shehwan in 2001, they had called for the redeployment of Syrian forces to the border region of the Beqaa, in anticipation of a full withdrawal. This gathering would provide the core of the anti-Syrian front that coalesced in the autumn of 2004.

Jumblatt, meanwhile, provided a convenient—if unlikely—figure-head, a former staunch ally of Syria who had taken the road away from

Damascus. Careful to avoid the fate of his father Kamal, who had been assassinated in 1977, he had sought for much of the 1990s to protect both his own interests and those of the Druze community by tacking close to the wind. But, like Hariri, Jumblatt had not found a friend in Lahoud, who was eager to curb his power in his efforts to assert himself. When his opposition to the extension of Lahoud's term in office was met with barely veiled threats from the petulant Bashar, Jumblatt aligned himself with the Christian opposition. In December 2004, he chaired the 'Bristol Gathering'. Held at the Bristol hotel in Beirut, the meeting brought together members of Jumblatt's Progressive Socialist Party, the Democratic Left and the Lebanese Communist Party with all the components of the Christian opposition: the Qornet Shehwan group, the main coalition of Christian opposition parties, but also Geagea's Lebanese Forces and Aoun's Free Patriotic Movement, both outlawed by Damascus. The Gathering's message was clear. Echoing UNSC Resolution 1559, it asserted Lebanon's 'right to self-determination' and called for 'free and fair' elections. Hariri flirted gingerly with the Bristol Gathering, asking a Christian member of his parliamentary bloc—the Maronite doctor Ghattas Khoury—to attend in a personal capacity. But he could not yet bring himself to do more. Hariri's party, the Future Movement, was not among the signatories to the Bristol accord.

Over the next few months, however, Hariri, faced with yet more attempts to humiliate and reduce him, travelled the long road from ally to opponent. As the attentions of Lebanon's political class began to focus on the parliamentary elections scheduled for May 2005, he opened up channels of communication with Sfeir and the leaders of the Qornet Shehwan gathering. In a show of his desire to build a common front, he signalled his willingness to assent to the use of *qada*—or districts—as the basis for electoral constituencies, an option favoured by the Christian parties that regarded these smaller districts as preferable. That he had few options left but opposition to Damascus was increasingly clear to all. He spent what would turn out to be his last weekend attempting to clear up the mess caused by the arrest, on trumped-up charges of electoral corruption, of four employees of one of his charities, the Beirut Society for Social Development. Valentine's Day fell on the following Monday.

The independence intifada

As news of Hariri's death spread, confusion, shock and apprehension began to turn into anger. Barely an hour and a half after the blast on the seafront had shaken central Beirut, someone had called Al-Jazeera's local offices, claiming that the attack was the work of a previously unknown jihadi group known as al-Nasr wa al-Jihad fi Bilad al-Sham. A few hours later, a videotape was left in a tree a few hundred metres away. Broadcast at around 5:00 p.m., it showed a turbaned figure gravely explaining that Hariri had been killed for being Saudi Arabia's 'agent' in Syria.[12] Few gave these claims much credence. Stunned, the members of the opposition met that evening in Hariri's palatial compound in Koreitem, in west Beirut. Outside, a crowd had gathered. Somewhere in the throng of grievers, one young man yelled out: 'if we want to know the truth, it is Syria that killed Hariri.'[13] Even a few hours earlier, to utter such an accusation in public would have been unthinkable, particularly for a Sunni. But the anger was too much to keep in. Inside, the politicians mulled what to do next. A statement was drafted, then another. The final draft placed the blame squarely on the shoulders of 'the Lebanese and Syrian authorities, given that the latter are the de facto authorities in Lebanon, responsible for this and other crimes in Lebanon'. Though the text stopped short of accusing Damascus directly of ordering the attack, it made it clear that it could not have been carried out without its tacit assent. The statement went on to call for the immediate resignation of Prime Minister Omar Karami's cabinet and the formation of a national unity government, the withdrawal of all Syrian troops from Lebanese territory before the coming parliamentary elections, three days of national mourning, and an international investigation into the killing. These would remain the core demands of the demonstrators who would descend into the streets in the coming days. Already, the crowds gathered around Hariri's home could be heard chanting *suriya la-barra*—'Syria out'.[14]

Over the next few days, popular anger found an outlet in a series of public gatherings. First came Hariri's burial, on Wednesday 16 February. Rejecting the offer of a state funeral, his family insisted that this would be an affair of the people, uniting Hariri one last time with his followers. Hariri, they announced, would be buried on a small plot of land next to the unfinished Muhammad al-Amin mosque, the grandiose neo-Ottoman edifice he had financed in Martyrs' Square, and whose construction had been plagued by controversy over what some perceived as his ongoing appropriation of central Beirut. In death as in life, Hariri's own fate, then, would remain symbolically and materially bound up with that of Beirut. Images of the day show angry, confused, scenes. Some are startlingly personal: Hariri's sister, Bahiyya, swallowed up in the mass, led through the fray by a bodyguard, his hand placed on her shoulder to guide her; a stolen glance of the camera at his son, Saad, his eyes faraway, tired, before he closes them, turning his face away; Hariri's widow, Nazek, standing in tears besides a mournful Jacques Chirac, before collapsing onto her knees before her husband's grave.

Others convey something of the scale of the event and the anger and grief that convulsed the crowds that day: Hariri's sons straining to keep the coffin aloft on their shoulders as the mourners gathered outside the entrance to his home surge and jostle; young men leading the crowd in chants or attempting to touch the coffin; Muslim clerics in their immaculate white turbans, leading the funeral procession from Koreitem to Martyrs' Square, and behind them crowds of people surrounding on all sides the ambulances that carried Hariri and his companions, some holding up images of a smiling Hariri and signs calling for Syria's departure, others—Druze men bussed in from the mountains for the occasion, carrying the distinctive red flag of Jumblatt's Progressive Socialist Party.[15] Jumblatt's followers were joined by members of General Aoun's Free Patriotic Movement, who called for the 'liberation' of Lebanon from foreign overrule. Other participants—many of them civil society activists who had long called for greater freedom—saw the funeral as an opportunity to federate opposition to Damascus' heavy-handed, brutal tactics. The events organiser Asma Andraos, a key figure in the early days of the protest movement, had put together placards with the simple message 'IT'S OBVIOUS, NO?' written across them in English. If Andraos chose allusion and humour to signal her disillusion, others, like Ziad Majed, the vice-president of the Democratic Left, were more forthright. As he would later tell the Lebanese-American journalist Michael Young:

> We chose our slogans prior to the funeral because we feared people
> would be silent ... I remember when we started ... people around us
> were shocked, scared, and many tried to change their place in the pro-

cession so as not to be associated with us. Then suddenly more and more people began joining in the slogans and the songs against Bashar, Lahoud, against the Baath and for independence ... I cannot forget the scene when we passed near Aisha Bakkar, through Munla, and onto Karakol Druze [all Sunni working-class areas of Beirut], how people started screaming from the balconies when we were chanting against the *mukhabarat* [intelligence services] and the Syrian regime and then women started throwing rice and sugar at us. We were probably a group of 150 to 200 when we gathered at Verdun [near the march's starting point]. By Karakol Druze there were thousands with us.[16]

As Majed's recollection suggests, the funeral procession was not just a moment of final communion between the Sunnis of Beirut and their leader, but also the making of a broader movement. This rapidly gathered pace over the next few days and weeks. A week after Hariri's death, on 21 February, a crowd of some 25,000 gathered at the site of his killing near the St George, before making its way to Martyrs' Square, the central gathering place that, more than just the site of Hariri's grave, had been the symbolic heart of Beirut's political and cultural life for over a century. As they wound their way through the city's streets, finally arriving in the square, the demonstrators chanted defiant slogans: *ma badna jaysh bi lubnan, illa al-jaysh al-lubnani, ma badna jumhuriyyeh, taht al-jazmah al-suriyyeh*—'we don't want any army in Lebanon, but the Lebanese army, we don't want a republic, under Syrian boots'.[17] In their early stages, these demonstrations were expressions of popular anger—a moment of almost unthinkable possibility that suddenly opened up with Hariri's wrenching death. While for some, like Hariri's supporters within the Sunni community, the demonstrating and sloganeering were a breach with past practice, an unexpected recourse to protest, for others, both on the left and among the Christian 'sovereignist' parties, his death offered an opportunity to reprise old tactics and realise longstanding wishes.

One participant in the early gatherings in Martyrs' Square recalled that they had grown, for her, out of the political contestation of the early 2000s, when a loose grouping of left-wing parties had come together around issues such as solidarity with the Palestinian struggle, opposition to Syrian security practices, and anger at neoliberal economic policies such as the raising of VAT. In this genealogy, several events, both internal and external, had served to galvanise this movement—first the second Palestinian intifada and the 2001 World Social Forum meeting in Doha, then the occupation of Iraq and, in 2004, the Lebanese transportation drivers' strike, in which four van drivers were killed. While some of those who took up prominent positions at such moments were 'old leftist intellectuals'—the same familiar faces that had rallied behind pan-Arab causes since the 1970s—many others were younger labour activists or students, weary of sectarianism and angry at their leaders. It was these young men and women who would organise a procession from the St George hotel to Martyrs' Square a week after Hariri's death to protest the descent into violence. In these first days of popular mobilisation, it was possible to see among the demonstrators a religious Druze man in his distinctive white cap and black clothes holding up a Quran with a rosary wrapped around it—an image eagerly seized upon by press photographers. But it was not long before Lebanon's political parties took over this space of unaffiliated, free protest. Walid Jumblatt's wife Nora took in hand food distribution to the camp in Martyrs' Square, handing out care parcels stamped with party names. The youth wings of the National Liberal Party and the Kata'ib, two of the main Christian opposition parties, staked out territory, marking out sections of the camp as theirs. The kind of behaviour she had witnessed a year earlier during the transportation drivers' strike, when participants had cursed Hariri and Hizballah alike, was now almost unimaginable. It was becoming increasingly difficult to be unaffiliated. One had to take up a party line—to be a supporter of the PSP, the Lebanese Forces or the Future Movement—in order to protest and occupy public space.[18] As the political space narrowed and became more segmented, certain possibilities were closed off.

In many ways, this account tallies with that of the journalist Michael Young, who was there himself in those heady, angry days in late February and early March, and of the other participants he interviewed in the years after 2005. This is the tale of an up-swell of popular feeling captured and canalised by well-practised PR executives and political machines flush with cash. One of the key moments of the early days of the demonstrations was when the event organiser Asma Andraos started a petition protesting Lahoud's continued presence in office on a white sheet. Headed by a single word—DÉMISSIONS!, or resignations—it soon grew to over 600 feet, as people added their signatures and tacked on ever more fabric. This seems a potent symbol of the growing anger and boldness of a grassroots movement without political affiliations. But the suggestion to add that one word—DÉMISSIONS!— came from the crusading human rights lawyer and political operator Chibli Mallat. The idea of adding the S to the end of the word, calling for multiple resignations and an overhaul of the political class, came from Gebran Tueni, the editor of Lebanon's most prominent newspaper, *al-Nahar*. Others provided assistance of a more practical kind. A 'prominent banker opened an account at his bank to collect donations' in support of the demonstrations. The Virgin Megastore that looms over the southern edge of Martyrs' Square, facing *al-Nahar*'s offices, supplied electricity and—patchy—internet connections to those camped outside its doors. Soon, political families and movements swept in to lend funds and logistical support. Nora Jumblatt provided not just food, but also a stage, a sound system, and portable toilets. The Future Movement, meanwhile, helped to cover the costs of rallies, paying for printing posters and the like.[19]

Particularly significant in this process was one man—the advertising and PR executive Eli Khoury, the head of Quantum Communications in Beirut. In late 2004, Khoury and his friend Samir Kassir—a fierce and eloquent essayist whose attacks on Bashar al-Assad in *al-Nahar*'s commentary pages stood out for their cogent commitment to Arab democracy—had begun to draw up plans for what they expected would be the electoral campaign of May 2005, around the slogan 'Independence '05'. Both firm supporters of a Syrian withdrawal, Khoury and Kassir regarded the upcoming elections as a potential watershed, which created the conditions for creating a democratic opposition to Syrian overrule. Now, as circumstances raced ahead of them, the two men decided to roll out the slogans and logos they had drawn up ahead of time. The demonstration that gathered strength after Hariri's killing owed the two men the bicolour red and white scarves that so many wore in Martyrs' Square, and the phrase 'Independence '05'—that easy, catchy brand so appealing to foreign observers and journalists.[20] But herein lay the problem for some. Khoury's company, Quantum, had a strong working relationship with George Bush's American administration. It had drawn up slogans—with Kassir's help—for the 2005 Iraqi elections. And more than that, it had provided all the technical and logistical support necessary for Al-Hurra, the Arabic language channel created by the Bush administration in the wake of the 2003 occupation, to produce shows in Lebanon.[21] Though Khoury loudly proclaimed himself a proud Lebanese patriot, and though few sought to question Kassir's Arabist credentials, such associations were always likely to raise the suspicion of some.

Increasingly, the course of events slipped out of the hands of the civil society activists who had led the *masirat al-istiqlal*, or 'independence march', from the St George and built the tent city in Martyrs' Square. But even as they were changing in character, the demonstrations were beginning to achieve some success. A first breakthrough came on Monday 28 February, two weeks to the day after Hariri's death. Though the army and security forces had begun to cordon off Martyrs' Square late on Sunday, some protesters had still slipped through. Pushing through the barriers or climbing over fences, they had settled down in the square overnight. Huddling under blankets in the tent city they had put up in what had been, only a few weeks before, a giant outdoor car park, they sought to reclaim and remake the square, transforming a vacant space into a place of popular participation. For want of anything else with which to fend off the light as they slept, some used the red and white cotton scarves the demonstrators had begun to wear as makeshift eye-masks.[22] Those who arrived the next morning found even less resistance. Though small scuffles broke out here and there, for the most part the soldiers who had taken up positions around the square let the crowds slip through their arms—acting, some would later say, under the orders of the army's commander-in-chief, General Michel Sleiman. For their part, some of the demonstrators gave out red roses to the soldiers, a symbolic gesture intended to show that they regarded them as brother citizens who served as the legitimate guardians of Lebanon's sovereignty.[23] If this was a sign that some within the Lebanese state were beginning to waver, the demonstrators would soon have a 'concrete result' to cheer.[24]

For as a crowd tens of thousands strong massed into Martyrs' Square, waving a sea of Lebanese flags, the prime minister, Omar Karami, announced his resignation. Reading out a statement broadcast on giant screens to the demonstrators gathered only a few hundred metres from his offices in the Grand Sérail, Karami insisted that his government would not be 'an obstacle before those who want the good of this country'. The cabinet's resignation was met with cries of joy, which would soon turn into defiant chants of 'Karami has fallen, your turn will come, Lahoud, and yours Bashar'.[25] Many of those who were there that day felt that this victory was theirs, and theirs alone, and that it owed nothing to the political leaders seeking to capitalise on this upsurge in popular feeling. As the protagonist of a short film made by Ziad Majed put it, 'we made the government fall'.[26] This sentiment was echoed by the activist Nabil Aboucharaf, who told Young that 'this was ... something we could work on. Christians and Muslims had brought down a Muslim prime minister', seemingly breaking the 'taboos' and conventions of sectarian politics to craft a new cross-confessional front.[27]

The ides of March

But further victories were still a way off. Evidence of this came on 8 March, when Hizballah organised a rally in Riyad al-Sulh Square, just a few hundred metres from Martyrs' Square, where anti-Syrian demonstrators were still camped out. In his speech to the throngs of thousands gathered beneath him, the party's charismatic secretary-general, Sayyid Hassan Nasrallah, batted away calls for Syrian withdrawal. Could the 'hundreds of thousands' who had come to listen to him, he asked, be dismissed simply as 'agents of the Syrian intelligence services'? Among the crowd, he reminded his audience, were 'the families of martyrs, were the injured, were freed prisoners [of the Israeli occupation] and the families of detainees' still held in Israeli jails, and 'the martyrs of the resistance and the army'. 'You', he told them, 'have defended Lebanon's dignity and honour, its independence and sovereignty'. Reclaiming these terms from the anti-Syrian demonstrations of the previous weeks, Nasrallah made it plain that those calling for the departure of Syria's troops did not have a monopoly over Lebanese patriotism. Hariri's assassination, he said bluntly, 'could not be used for political polemic'. And nor could anyone attack their fellow 'citizens and partners in the nation' in the way that some had attacked Hizballah and Amal. Transgressing 'the bounds of morality', the party's political opponents had also insulted Syria, using regrettable words for which Nasrallah now took it upon himself to apologise. On the contrary, he went on, the Lebanese people owed thanks to Syria. Indeed, it was for this that he and his followers had come together—to 'thank Syria, the Syria of Hafiz al-Assad and Bashar al-Assad, Syria with its steadfast people and its Arab army ... which has remained alongside us through all the years of ... resistance', and which had 'rebuilt and preserved and protected' the squares of central Beirut 'destroyed by Israeli occupation and internal wars'. 'No-one', Nasrallah exclaimed, his voice hoarse from rising above the cheers, 'could expel Syria from Lebanon, and from the minds and hearts of the Lebanese'—neither 'foreign powers', nor his fellow Lebanese who had now turned their backs on Damascus in a bewildering show of ingratitude. 'Syria was part of Lebanon's past, of its present' and, he insisted, 'of its future'.[28]

What's more, it was time for the Lebanese to look to each other and their fellow 'partners' in the state. Only the Ta'if accord—which, Nasrallah reminded his listeners, Hariri had done so much to broker—could serve as the framework for any potential Syrian withdrawal, and not UNSC Resolution 1559, which he rejected out of hand. And only a 'government of national unity and national accord' could rescue the country from this 'crisis'. It would not be the first time that Nasrallah would make such demands—rejecting the UN's role in the investigation into Hariri's death as an unwarranted intervention serving the interests of Israel and the United States, with its plans to redraw the Middle East into a set of pliant protectorates, and calling for a national dialogue and the formation of a government drawing together all of Lebanon's increasingly fractious parties and factions. These would become refrains to which he and other Hizballah cadres and MPs would return again and again over the following decade. But perhaps the most significant—and striking—aspect of the speech was its unwavering commitment to Syria's presence. Hizballah had not always been a friend to Damascus in the past, but now the Sayyid stuck his flag firmly to the mast.[29]

Those calling for Syria's departure now had to find a response. The opportunity to do so would come only six days later, on 14 March—a month after Hariri's assassination. Politicians and civil society activists had called for a massive turnout to surpass the crowds that had filled Riyad al-Sulh on 8 March, and their call was answered. From early in the morning, tens and hundreds of thousands flocked into Martyrs' Square. The news helicopters circling above head captured them coming in from every entrance, and spilling out into the adjoining streets and roads, a heaving multitude bedecked in red and white and waving Lebanese flags. But for all the rumours of a million turning out for the occasion, this was in many ways not the apotheosis of the popular movement that had taken shape since mid-February, but a reassertion of the political will. Over twenty politicians, party officials, and journalists were invited to the stage to deliver speeches to the assembled crowds. No representatives of the tent city were invited to take the nostrum. What's more, many of those who did speak covered much the same ground. Repeating that holy triptych *hurriyya, siyada, istiqlal*, they reiterated their commitment to Lebanon's 'freedom, sovereignty, and independence', and called again and again for the truth to be revealed, Hariri's killers to be brought to justice, and Syria to withdraw from Lebanon. This did not make these demands any less significant, or any less meaningful to the crowds listening. But it did contribute to a deadening of the vital discourse of those weeks, which began to stiffen into the dried-up matter of political rhetoric.

Ironically, perhaps the most memorable speech of all was that which paid greatest heed to the popular forces that had surged forth in the wake of Hariri's assassination—that of Gebran Tueni, the editor-in-chief of *al-Nahar*, whose offices sat on the square's northern edge. A red and white scarf tied around his neck, he spoke back to Nasrallah's claims, a few days earlier, that Syria had built Lebanon back up from the ground after the war, protecting it from its foreign foes and internal discords. Eulogising Hariri, he told the crowd that it was he who had 'built Beirut, not Syria'—and if he 'had built Lebanon from stone', then he had also rebuilt 'the human Lebanon', helping the wounds of war to heal. Tueni then moved on to congratulate the crowd on 'Lebanon's independence'. This, he told them, was not the achievement of any politician. It was their work—the result of their 'determination and will'. 'You', the people, 'came to ask for the truth, and for sovereignty, real sovereignty without *mukhabarat* and soldiers and despotism'—not the politicians or the parties. 'If only Bishara al-Khuri, Riyad al-Sulh, Kamil Sham'un' and the other political leaders who had secured freedom from French rule, he went on, 'could see you', reclaiming Lebanon's independence once more.[30]

Just as the political parties joined in opposition to Damascus—the Future Movement, the Progressive Socialist Party, the Christian parties of the Lebanese Forces, the Kata'ib, and the Free Patriotic Movement, and others besides—were using the occasion to cement support, Tueni was asserting the potential of popular mobilisation. But perhaps the most moving part of his speech came at its end, in a prayer-like 'oath' which he asked the crowd to repeat after him: 'we swear by God the almighty / Muslims and Christians / To remain one and united / Until eternity / In defence of Lebanon the great'. Tueni's speech, with its hopeful vision of a new independence for Lebanon, was rendered all the more poignant by his assassination in December 2005—killed, like so many others who spoke out in those months, by a car bomb placed by the side of the road.[31]

The mismatch between Tueni's rhetoric and that of his colleagues in the anti-Syrian movement now appears just one of the fault-lines within what would soon be known as the 14 March movement. As early as late February, some had quietly expressed frustration at the fact Hariri followers often favoured the Future Movement's sky blue over the red and white that had become the official colours of the demonstrators, and that their placards and banners often demanded *al-haqiqa*—the truth, if even 'for the sake of Lebanon', as it was often put in those days—rather than independence, freedom, and sovereignty. This was a reminder of the hasty, improvised nature of this coalition. For these had long been the treasured demands of the Christian activists who had chanted those three words—*hurriyya, siyada, istiqlal*—in the face of police batons and water guns throughout the late 1990s and early 2000s. The demonstrations that gathered pace through February and March were, for the parties to which these young men and women belonged—the Lebanese Forces, the Free Patriotic Movement, the Kata'ib, and the Chamoun family's National Liberal Party—an opportunity to set the agenda. As their demands also became those of the Sunnis and Druze, they saw a chance to re-enter the political mainstream—to bring an end to the hated Syrian occupation, but also to field candidates and gain parliamentary seats, and to pave the way towards a new electoral law providing what they saw as fairer representation for Lebanon's Christian communities. Perhaps most important of all for supporters of the two largest of these parties—the Lebanese Forces and the Free Patriotic Movement—was the return of their leaders. For while the head of the Lebanese Forces,

Samir Geagea, had languished in solitary confinement in a cell beneath the defence ministry at Yarze since his conviction in 1994 on charges of terrorism and murder, the leader of the FPM, Michel Aoun, had lived in France since his exile from Lebanon in 1990. What's more, the Christian parties themselves were by no means a united front, but fractured by old disputes and battles—not least the lasting rancour between supporters of Geagea and Aoun, who had fought a bitter war for control of 'Christian Lebanon' in the last months of the Lebanese civil war in 1989 and 1990. How to reconcile these varying demands and conciliate these different elements would become in time an existential matter for 14 March. But for now, there remained a more pressing and immediate question: how and when would the Syrian presence in Lebanon end?

For though many treated the immense gathering of 14 March as a victory—a triumphant statement of unity and joint purpose in the face of oppression and violent intimidation—it was clear to many that more would be needed than just speeches and slogans to make Damascus budge. This was particularly true of the more wizened politicians within 14 March, who understood that Syria's position would shift only under international pressure. This would prove to be the case. On 5 March, Bashar al-Assad had addressed the Syrian people's assembly— that simulacrum of a parliament stuffed with placemen. Bashar had spent much of his speech mocking the Lebanese opposition, suggesting at one point that the cameras broadcasting the Beirut demonstrations should pan out to reveal how thinly attended they were. (Every one of his jeers and contemptuous chortles was answered in kind by the watching protesters in Martyrs' Square.) But amidst the disdain, the speech also contained a significant concession: Syria, Bashar announced, would withdraw its troops to the Beqaa valley in the east of the country, and then to the border between the two countries. It was no coincidence that Bashar's speech should have come a day after he had met the Saudi crown prince, Abdullah. According to some, Abdullah had squarely accused Syria of killing Hariri, asking Bashar why it had done so, before sharply advising him to withdraw his soldiers and intelligence agents from Lebanon. Should he fail to do so, Saudi Arabia would leave Syria out in the cold. Though Bashar attempted to deflect the accusations, losing the support of perhaps the most powerful of Arab states was not a risk he could take. On 6 March, the UN's envoy, Terje Roed Larsen, obtained an assurance from Damascus that its troops would leave Lebanon by the end of April.[32]

Further pressure came in early April, when France and the United States presented a joint draft resolution to the UN Security Council, calling for an international investigation into Hariri's assassination. In doing so, they sought to underscore their shared commitment to Lebanese affairs. The administration of George W. Bush saw in the protests gathering in Beirut an opportunity to further its vision of a new, more 'democratic', Middle East—it was the US undersecretary for global affairs, Paula Dobriansky, who coined the phrase 'the Cedar Revolution', a media-friendly appellation that deliberately suggested a parallel with Ukraine's recent 'Orange Revolution'. For the French president, Jacques Chirac, this was as much a personal affair as a geopolitical one—his concern for shoring up French influence in the Middle East deeply entangled with his old friendship with Rafiq Hariri. Resolution 1595 was passed unanimously. It committed the UN to the establishment of an 'international independent investigation Commission … to assist the Lebanese authorities', and the latter to providing their 'full cooperation … including full access to all documentary, testimonial and physical information and evidence in their possession'.[33] A little more than a month later, on 13 May, the German prosecutor Detlev Melhis would arrive in Beirut as the head of the United Nations International Independent Investigation Commission, or UNIIIC.

France, the United States and Saudi Arabia, it was clear, were all determined to rein in Damascus' actions, bringing an end to the impunity it had enjoyed since 1990, when Hafiz al-Assad had haggled dominance over Lebanon for support of the first Gulf war. In the face of this formidable pressure, his son found himself obliged to keep to his word. On 26 April, Syria's remaining troops filed out of Lebanon, their tanks snaking over the mountain passes as a guard of honour lined the road from the military base of Rayak to the border. In the end, it was the blunt force of international diplomacy, as much as the self-affirming rhetoric of the Beirut demonstrations, that led to Assad's decision to withdraw. After twenty-nine years of Syrian military presence in Lebanon, and fifteen years of direct political dominance, this seemed a momentous day.

The general's return

Many of the country's politicians, however, had already shifted their attention to the coming parliamentary elections, scheduled for June. On the face of it, the events of recent months shaped the leitmotifs of the campaign. Now under Saad Hariri's callow leadership, the Future Movement called loudly for *al-haqiqa, li-ajl lubnan*—or 'the truth, for the sake of Lebanon'. For their part, Hizballah and Amal called for continued adherence to the values of resistance—again, in the name of a Lebanese nation to which all the country's parties now loudly proclaimed their allegiance. Christian parties such as the National Liberal Party, the Kata'ib, the Lebanese Forces and the Free Patriotic Movement, meanwhile, now redeployed as electoral slogans the protest chants of the early 2000s. The Syrian withdrawal, they insisted, did not guarantee freedom, sovereignty, and independence. More needed to be done to dismantle the security apparatus built up over a decade and a half, a boil that had bored its way deep into the skin of the Lebanese body politic. But despite their rhetorical differences, these parties lined up in sometimes surprising formations. Perhaps most bewildering was the alliance drawn up between the Future Movement, on the one hand, and Hizballah and Amal on the other in a show of stark political cynicism. Putting aside for the moment their radically divergent views of the Lebanese state and its relationship to Syria, the parties agreed to form joint lists in several districts. To many, this represented the final defeat of the *intifadat al-istiqlal*, or independence uprising, that had begun to coalesce in the public squares of Beirut in the weeks after Hariri's death. For the political scientist Karim Makdisi, the deal-making was a rank betrayal 'of all those demonstrations which represented a moment of true popular anger with the system.' Those— civil society activists, avowedly secular old leftists, or even disillusioned citizens exhausted by all the ceaseless politicking—who had hoped that Hariri's assassination might mark the beginning of a new era, free of the confessionalism and corruption of old, were to be disappointed. As Makdisi put it, 'it could have gone in a different positive direction but it was taken over by the political sharks who used that idealism for their own purposes'.[34]

But the young protesters of the tent city were not the only ones frozen out of these deals. Another conspicuous loser was the Free

Patriotic Movement of Michel Aoun. Aoun had first come to prominence in 1988, when the then-president, Amin Gemayel, had named
him interim prime minister shortly before the end of his own term in
office. The commander-in-chief of what was left of the Lebanese army,
Aoun used this position to secure his political position. From the presidential palace at Baʻbda, where he took up residence, he proclaimed
himself leader of a free Christian Lebanon. For almost two years, Aoun
held out. Rejecting as illegitimate the Taʼif accord that had brought the
Lebanese civil war to an end, he sought to assert his position on the
ground, resisting Syrian military advances and launching a brutal 'war
of elimination' against the Lebanese Forces of Samir Geagea, perhaps
the most powerful of the Christian militias that had emerged over the
course of the conflict. This bloody internecine conflict would leave
deep scars on Lebanon's Christian communities for years to come. For
Aoun's actions brought him bitter condemnation from some, but also
fanatical adoration from the throngs that camped out around the presidential residence—a place many took to calling the *qasr al-shaʻb*, or
palace of the people. As the diminutive general harangued the crowd in
his creased fatigues, they would fill the air with chants of *bi-ruh, bi-dam,
nafdik ya ʻimad*—'with our souls and our blood, we will sacrifice ourselves [for you], oh general'. Encircled by Syrian forces, Aoun had
finally fled to the French embassy—and on to exile in France—on
13 September 1990, a date long commemorated by his supporters like
the loss of a loved one.

Aoun himself returned from fifteen years' absence on 7 May 2005.
Visibly aged and dwarfed by the bodyguards ringed around him, he
addressed a sea of followers who had flooded into Martyrs' Square to
listen to him, covering its expanse in the red and white of the Lebanese
flag and the FPM's newly chosen colour—a bright, spring-like orange.
Quietening the chants of *ʻAwn w Allah*—'Aoun and God'—ringing
through the square, he began: *ya shaʻbu lubnan al-ʻazim*, 'oh great people
of Lebanon'. This phrase, so familiar to his supporters from the heady
days of 1989 and 1990, brought exultant cheers from the crowd. Little
that Aoun said that day was memorable—much of it the stock phrases
of nationalism, with its tributes to the martyrs who had given their
lives and youth to 'the Lebanese cause' over the years and its encomia
to the people, whose voices had reached the world's rulers, helping to

ensure that Lebanon was once again 'free, independent and sovereign'. But if some of Aoun's Christian rivals had hoped that his long absence might have dimmed his followers' passionate, messianic support for 'the general' then this ecstatic reception would surely have dispelled any of their illusions.

Aoun's return, regarded by his supporters as a veritable second coming, presented his opponents with an irresolvable quandary. Should they bring him into the fold, at the risk of seeing their own share of the vote diluted in favour of Aoun's candidates, or leave him out in the cold in the hope that the Future Movement's electoral machine could 'steamroller' any opposition standing in its way—to use a phrase beloved of Lebanese political commentators? In the end, they chose the latter—a decision no doubt made easier by Aoun's own obduracy and egotism. When Aoun suggested that the Syrian withdrawal was the result of his own efforts in Washington—he had appeared before a congressional committee in September 2003 to lend his support to the Syria Accountability and Lebanese Sovereignty Restoration Act— Jumblatt retorted that only 'Hariri's blood' had secured this victory for the Lebanese people.[35]

And yet many wondered, even at the time, whether Jumblatt and others were right to shut Aoun out. The results of the elections appeared to give reason to the doubters. The newly formed Future Movement, it is true, had emerged as the single largest party in the new parliament, with thirty-six MPs, while Walid Jumblatt's Progressive Socialist Party secured sixteen seats. In Beirut, the 'Rafiq Hariri Martyr List' swept the board, taking all but one of the nineteen seats up for grabs in the capital—by prior arrangement, one had been left uncontested for a Hizballah candidate. This story was repeated in the north, where the list took all twenty-eight seats. In the south, meanwhile, the 'Resistance and Development Bloc' formed by Hizballah and Amal took twenty-two of the twenty-three seats on offer, leaving one for Rafiq Hariri's sister, Bahiyya. In other parts of the country, however, the Future Movement, Hizballah and Amal could not simply divide the spoils amongst themselves, and fierce electoral contests were waged. This was particularly the case in Christian areas of the Matn and the Kisrwan. In these places, Aoun's share of the vote dwarfed that of his rivals. He and his allies—who included, incongruously, staunch allies of Damascus like Sleiman Frangieh—won fifteen constituencies. The Lebanese Forces, by contrast, won six, and the Kata'ib a mere two. This result lent credence to Aoun's claims that he was the true voice of Lebanon's Christians, and that victory against Syria would have been impossible without the intervention of his supporters. But Aoun's electoral success was also significant in other ways. For it stopped the loose coalition forming around the Future Movement from securing a truly decisive majority in parliament—and, in doing so, prevented Lahoud's opponents from calling a vote of no confidence in the hated president. In one of those ironies particular to Lebanese politics, one former army commander, who made no secret of his own presidential ambitions, helped to keep another former army commander in the presidential office.

Aoun's strong showing notwithstanding, the loose coalition of parties that had come together to push for Syria's departure now formed the single largest bloc in parliament, with sixty-nine MPs. On 30 June, Fouad Siniora—a close associate of the Hariri family who had served as Rafiq Hariri's finance minister in the 1990s—was tasked with forming a cabinet. After several weeks of negotiations and backroom deals, Siniora announced the formation of his government on 19 July—a national unity cabinet bringing together representatives of most of Lebanon's main parties and factions. Only one remained conspicuously absent—Aoun's Free Patriotic Movement. This failure to reach agreement would prove significant in time. Unsurprisingly, the new government was dominated by members of what many were already informally referring to as the 14 March movement—named after the landmark demonstrations of that day. The Future Movement itself took eight portfolios. As well as the premiership, these included the ministries of the economy and the interior. Siniora's old job as minister of finance was taken up by Jihad Azour; nominally an independent, he had served as a senior aide to the new prime minister in the 1990s. Jumblatt's Progressive Socialist Party, meanwhile, secured three ministries—including telecommunications, information, and the Ministry of the Displaced, since the early 1990s a key source of power and patronage for the Druze leader. Their Christian allies picked up the scraps. The Lebanese Forces' Joe Sarkis was appointed minister of tourism, the Kata'ib's Pierre Gemayel minister of industry, and the independent Nayla Moawad, the only woman in the cabinet, minister for social affairs. Sitting alongside them in this unity cabinet were also men loyal to President Lahoud as well as representatives of Amal and—for the first time—Hizballah. The latter's decision to send ministers to cabinet, in particular, was seen as a symbolic gesture of openness and conciliation after the fractious demonstrations and counter-demonstrations of March. There was symbolism, too, in their choice of ministries. The new health and agriculture ministers, Jawad Khalifeh and Talal Sahili, belonged to Amal, and those of energy and labour, Muhammad Fneish and Trad Hamadeh, to Hizballah. Though unaffiliated to any party, the minister of foreign affairs, Fawzi Salloukh, was also a Hizballah nominee. In taking up these unglamorous, difficult portfolios, the two parties signalled their continued commitment to the joint stewardship of the *mahrumin*, or dispossessed, of the Shia community, with its tobacco and vegetable farmers, its poor taxi drivers, hospital orderlies and nurses, and its many migrants scattered through the Gulf, West Africa, and the United States.

Despite the veneer of unity, cabinet meetings and parliamentary sessions grew increasingly fractious. The various parties sitting together in government could agree neither on domestic issues such as the programme of privatisation to which Siniora remained committed, nor on international matters such as diplomatic relations with the West. And, perhaps most significant of all, they could not agree on Syria and the international investigation into Hariri's death. Tellingly, the two blocs that were beginning to coalesce in parliament came to be defined by the stances they took towards Damascus. For it now became increasingly common to speak not just of the 14 March coalition—composed of the Future Movement, the Progressive Socialist Party, the Lebanese Forces, the Kata'ib and several smaller parties—but also of 8 March, a countervailing bloc centred on Hizballah and Amal. As the divisions rose to the surface, what had been loose enough coalitions now became organised blocs. 14 March, in particular, established a general secretariat which provided representation for all the smaller groups that did not have deputies in parliament or ministers in cabinet—in the main Christian organisations like the National Liberal Party or Raymond Edde's National Bloc, and independent Christian politicians like Nassib Lahoud. Symbolically, it was headed up by Fares Souaid, an independent Maronite politician from the Kisrwan. This was a deliberate attempt to present the bloc as a coalition of principle, whose shared commitment to justice, truth, sovereignty and freedom from foreign intervention transcended differences of confession and party.

In response, Hizballah moved to create its own cross-sectarian alliance. The Lebanese Forces and the Kata'ib were already firm allies of the Future Movement and had made clear their opposition to Hizballah's military arsenal, which they considered not a legitimate means of resistance, but an illegitimate imposition putting the Lebanese people to ransom. Only Michel Aoun remained—a considerable political presence, with his parliamentary bloc of sixteen MPs and his devoted popular following in Christian areas of the country, but also an isolated figure, unsure of his place in the new dispensation and casting about for allies. In late 2005, the two parties began negotiations, led on the side of the Free Patriotic Movement by Aoun's son-in-law Gebran Bassil and on that of Hizballah by Ghaleb Abu Zeinab. On 6 February 2006, Michel Aoun and Sayyid Hassan Nasrallah, accompanied by some of their closest advisers, met at Mar Mikhail Church, in the southern Beirut suburb of Chiyah. The choice of venue was pregnant with meaning—a Maronite church that had been destroyed during the civil war, located in what had once been a small Christian village some way from the city, but was now a bustling, densely populated, suburb largely inhabited by Shia migrants to Beirut. There could be no better symbol of coexistence.

After a three-hour-long meeting, Bassil and Abu Zeinab read out a memorandum of understanding that laid out the two parties' joint stances on issues ranging from the need for root-and-branch reform of government to security, relations with Syria, and sovereignty. In some ways, this was very much a product of compromise and mutual concessions. Hizballah acquiesced in the FPM's insistence on establishing full diplomatic relations between Lebanon and Syria, replacing the old structure of joint coordination and 'brotherly relations' with formal embassies. The FPM, meanwhile, acknowledged that Hizballah's arms were 'a noble and sacred means' of waging resistance against Israel's continuing occupation of Lebanese territory. In others, however, it also served their common interests. In some ways, the most politically significant parts of the document were its opening paragraphs. These called for national dialogue, bringing together 'all parties that have a political, popular, and national status'; a renewed emphasis on 'coexistence' and on discarding the 'majority/minority formula' in favour of 'consensual democracy'; and a new electoral law guaranteeing 'the accuracy and fairness of popular representation'.[36] These words belied not just the bitterness of the FPM's leaders, who regarded themselves as the only legitimate voice of Lebanon's Christians and were still smarting from their perceived rough treatment at the hands of the Future Movement and the PSP, but also Hizballah's frustration at what its own leaders regarded as the overweening, domineering conduct of Lebanon's Sunnis since Hariri's death. Uniting the two parties was a shared sense that they spoke for Lebanon's under-represented masses—all those Christians and Shia who, together, made up the majority of the country's population, but who received so little representation in a cabinet dominated by the Hariri family's political allies. In their joint press conference, Aoun and Nasrallah gave voice to these sentiments. While the FPM's leader proclaimed the arrival of 'a new culture' in Lebanon—'to collaborate [and] to discuss views until we find solutions'—Nasrallah lauded the coming together of 'two great Lebanese currents'. This was 'a call to all to come together in dialogue and to put an end to talk of erasing, eliminating and obliterating' political rivals.[37] If the memorandum of understanding provided a formal roadmap for the two parties' collaboration, then this shared sense of grandeur and resentment bound them together as much as, if not more than, strategic interest. Whatever the case, by early 2006 a seismic shock had reshaped Lebanese politics. On one side of the fault-line lay 14 March, on the other 8 March. The independence intifada, with its idealistic hopes of renewal and reconciliation, transcending the party politics and deal-making of old, seemed a distant memory.

The white Alfa

There were other signs, too, that the 'Beirut spring' was rapidly fading. The emancipatory zeal of the months after Hariri's assassination had always been tempered by fear of insecurity and sectarian tension and awareness that it would not be easy to rid Lebanon entirely of Syrian influence. To many, such anxieties were justified by a wave of bombings in late March and early April. On 19 March, a device had exploded in the residential suburb of Jdeideh, wounding eleven. Three days later, another device targeted a shopping centre in the seaside resort of Kaslik. The device, left in a leather bag near the entrance of the closed mall, went off at 1:30 a.m., killing three night-workers. The explosion caused the mall's roof to collapse and blew out shop windows, leaving the streets strewn with sharp splinters. On 26 March, a bomb went off in the night in an industrial zone in Sad al-Bouchrieh. Late in the night of 1 April, a fourth bomb went off in the Rizk Plaza shopping centre in the pretty mountain town of Broummana, another popular tourist resort, with its hotels, pine trees, and outdoor restaurants. The bomb injured twelve and, once again, caused severe material damage.[38]

A pattern was now becoming clear: all of the devices had been left in Christian areas of the country, and two had targeted commercial premises in places popular with Arab tourists, returning Lebanese migrants, and Beirutis looking to get away from the city. No-one claimed these night-time bombings. But, for many, the identity of the perpetrators was beyond doubt. The timing and location of the bombings suggested that they were the work of the Syrian security services and their Lebanese underlings—a transparent attempt to scare off foreign travellers, crippling the country's tourist economy, and to play on the fears of persecution of Lebanon's Christians. That this was the case seemed to be confirmed by the location of another bomb that exploded in the Christian town of Jounieh on 7 May. The device had been left in an alleyway between Mar Yuhanna Church and the offices of Sawt al-Mahhaba, the Maronite Church's radio station. But if this was indeed a campaign of intimidation aimed at keeping Lebanon's Christians quiet, then it was not one that succeeded.

Soon, though, the violence took a different turn. Shortly before 11:00 a.m. on the morning of 2 June, inhabitants of the quarter of Zahret al-Ihsan, in a Christian part of east Beirut, heard a dull detonation. This was the bomb that killed Samir Kassir, as he started his beloved white Alfa Romeo to head to the downtown offices of *al-Nahar*. Passers-by reported seeing a white flash, and then a cloud of pale grey dust billowing up from the car—the same dust that covered Kassir's body, which a journalist reported seeing slumped still at the wheel, as though asleep, as security agents frantically milled about.

Whoever had set the device knew what they were doing. The paint-work of the 4x4 parked behind Kassir's Alfa had barely a scratch on it, though its window had been shattered by the sheer force of the blast. So too were the windows of Supermarket Achrafieh, which occupied the ground floor of Kassir's apartment bloc. Though she was sitting at her till only a few metres from the explosion, the shop's cashier was unhurt—if so traumatised that she was unable to speak. It was not long before anger began to seep through the crowd gathered at the scene. When the interim prime minister, Najib Mikati, attempted to address the onlookers shortly after his arrival at the scene, he was cut short by a well-to-do woman who shouted out, her arms crossed in defiance: 'What use are your condemnations? They have never saved innocent people from dying. You are a shame. What are you doing here? Go hang yourselves, you bunch of incompetents, [you're all] incapable of stopping innocent people from being assassinated'.[39] It was not long before this anger found other targets. Interviewed while he was standing at the scene, Gebran Tueni—Kassir's editor at *al-Nahar*—squarely accused 'the Lebanese-Syrian security regime' of having killed his colleague and sometime sparring partner. 'The Syrian regime in Ba'bda'—a none-too-subtle reference to Emile Lahoud's proximity to Bashar al-Assad—'the head of the Republican Guard, Mustafa Hamdan, and the former director of the General Security, Jamil Sayyed' were responsible, he declared.[40] Standing by Tueni's side, his uncle, the MP Marwan Hamadeh—who had himself survived a car bomb less than a year earlier—repeated his nephew's charge, calling for the full withdrawal of the 'Syrian security services from Lebanon'.[41] Soon, others joined this chorus of accusation. The expert nature of the operation was cited as evidence, but so too was the fact that Kassir had grown ever bolder and angrier in his editorials in recent months and weeks, anathematising the Baathist regime in a series of coruscating articles depicting the independence intifada as the first stage in the liberation of the Arabs from the tyrannical regimes that had ruled over them for decades.

Kassir's assassination led to an outpouring of grief and anger. For he had been in life a figure capable of straddling and joining together different worlds. Born in Lebanon to a Palestinian father and a Syrian mother, he moved easily between the biting, lacerating Arabic of his editorials and the elegant, flowing French in which he wrote the history of his beloved Beirut. Indeed, he had lived for several years in Paris, first as a doctoral student—he had written his thesis on the Lebanese civil war—and then, in the 1990s, as a cultural correspondent. And yet he remained deeply rooted in the Levant, identifying passionately with broader Arab causes for which other Lebanese, caught up in their parochial struggles, often had little time. Handsome and charismatic, his charm spiked by a sharp temper, he was as beloved of the students and young activists who had set up the tent city in Martyrs' Square as he was admired, and feared, by journalists and politicians. The day after Kassir's killing, a cortege of ministers, MPs, dignitaries, and ambassadors filed through the offices of *al-Nahar* to offer their condolences. Behind a closed door could be glimpsed Kassir's desk, still strewn with days-old newspapers and filled ashtrays. On his chair, someone had placed a white rose, a Lebanese flag, and one of the red and white scarves that Kassir had helped design—and which he rarely took off in the weeks before his death.[42] In Kassir, civil society organisers like Ziad Majed had seen the embodiment of a new idea of Lebanon as a tolerant, cultured place, free of sectarianism, authoritarianism and corruption, comfortable with its Arab identity and capable of sweeping others along on a wave of popular fervour for democracy and freedom. With Kassir's death, these hopes seemed to fade. As the French-language newspaper *L'Orient-Le Jour* noted in its editorial the next morning, his assassination was also, in a sense, a way of 'killing the Beirut spring and the independence intifada'.[43]

Sadly, Kassir's death would not be the last. On 21 June, the former head of the Lebanese Communist Party, George Hawi, was killed by a bomb as he drove through the Beirut neighbourhood of Musaitbeh. Like Kassir, Hawi was a founding member of the Democratic Left, a grouping of anti-authoritarian secular leftists established in 2004, and an outspoken critic of the Baathist regime. On 12 July, a bomb targeted the motorcade of the defence minister, Elias al-Murr. Murr survived, suffering bad injuries to his legs, but two by-standers were killed. The son-in-law of Emile Lahoud, Murr was considered a pro-Damascus figure. This, however, did not prevent some from pointing the finger at the Syrian intelligence services, which they accused of a cack-handed attempt at throwing investigators off the scent. More explosions followed over the summer: on 22 July, a bomb left in Rue Monot in Achrafieh, known for its bars and clubs; on 22 August, another device in Zalka; and then a third on 17 September, killing one person. This time the attack was in Geitawi, like Zalka a largely Christian working-class neighbourhood. As in the spring and early summer, the pendulum soon swung back from relatively small devices planted in public places to sow fear and disorder to targeted attacks on particular individuals. On 25 September, the TV journalist May Chidiac—well-known for her unsparing criticism of Damascus—was severely injured by a car bomb that exploded as she started her car. And then, on 12 December, came Gebran Tueni's assassination.

Since Kassir's death, Tueni had stayed, for the most part, in Paris—keeping out of the way of those who, he had been told, wanted to kill him. He was under no illusions that others were also under threat. As Saad Hariri told the journalist Nick Blanford, Tueni had been clear with him when the two had talked about going back to Lebanon. 'Don't even think about it', Tueni had said. But Tueni could not resist the pull of Beirut and his newspaper, returning on 10 December to a Lebanon readying itself for the Christmas holidays. As Blanford and others noted, Tueni's assassins must have trailed him carefully from the moment he left the airport to head to his home in Beit Meri, up in the mountains above Beirut, for they had a clear sense of his movements. Two days later, Tueni was taking the back road around Mkalles to Beirut—perhaps to escape the seasonal traffic—when his car was hit by a car bomb placed at a bend in the road. The sheer force of the blast sent his armoured Range Rover 4x4 cartwheeling a hundred metres down the steep mountainside. By the time the security services arrived at the scene, it lay in the valley, a burnt-out wreck. Around it lay fragments of glass, twisted and mangled bits of iron—all that was left of the crash barrier the explosion had scythed through—and human remains. This was a meticulously planned operation. Shortly before 9:00 a.m., one of the CCTV cameras installed on the industrial estate that ran along the road—a bleak set of low warehouses, mostly occupied by garages and car shops—caught two men parking a Renault Rapide weighed down with around 40 kilograms of explosives. A few minutes earlier—at about quarter to ten—Tueni had left his home. At five to ten, someone set off the device, as Tueni's driver, Nicolas Flouty, took the bend. The two men were killed instantaneously. Dozens of others were injured.[44]

Tueni's funeral was held on 14 December. His coffin, draped in the Lebanese flag, was carried through the thick crowds that thronged the route—first parliament, whose members had assembled to pay their final respects to their colleague as the bells of Beirut's churches rang in unison, then the Greek Orthodox cathedral of St George, a few short metres from parliament, and then finally the Orthodox ceme-tery of Mar Mitr in Achrafieh, where Tueni's body was laid to rest in the family vault. Among the pall-bearers were a Sunni shaykh and the Druze journalist Ali Hamadeh—not just Marwan Hamadeh's younger brother, and therefore a relative of the dead man, but also one of *al-Nahar*'s editorialists. This symbolic show of cross-confessional comity was underscored when the Muslim cleric led the crowds in Tueni's famous oath, with its call for Muslims and Christians to remain united for eternity. Along the way, mourners waving Lebanese flags called out *Allah ma'k Jibran*—'God be with you, Gebran'—and clapped, their applause ringing out like church peals against the winter sky. Some carried images of Tueni adorned with the slogan *al-farq bayn al-zulm wa al-hurriyya, kalima...*—'the difference between tyranny and freedom is a single word'. Watching these images again, more than a decade later, it feels as though these men and women had lost a friend, a relative—one of their own, rather than a distant political figure removed from their lives.

Perhaps most moving of all are the scenes of the funeral itself—of Tueni's wife, Siham, her tear-swollen eyes hidden behind dark glasses, her hair unkempt, draining a glass of water; of his daughter Nayla weeping over the coffin; and of his father, Ghassan, sitting amidst the throng, weary with grief, his shoulders hunched over, his eyes search-ing for something in the distance. In her speech, Nayla sounded a note of defiance. 'In the name of all the free people of Lebanon and the Arab region', she insisted, fighting back the tears, 'our objective has not been broken, our aim [remains] freedom. My father did not die—he was not put out like a light'. Her grandfather, however, called only for 'all this hatred, all these contrary words, to be buried along with Gebran'—his voice cracking only for an instant as he spoke his son's name. Tired of so much loss, so much death and waste, he did not want 'revenge or hate', but only an end to the killing. These were the words of an old man. Seventy-nine in 2005, Ghassan Tueni had lived through the civil war—serving during its early stages as Lebanon's ambassador to the UN—watching as friends and colleagues were killed, and as his city, Beirut, was decimated. But he had also known uncommon grief, outliving his wife, the poet Nadia Tueni, who died of cancer in 1983, and his two other children—a girl, Nayla, who also died of cancer at the age of seven, and another son, Makram, who died in a car crash when he was twenty-one. Now he buried the last of his children.

Conclusion

With Tueni's death ended a long year. 2005 had begun, in a way, with the assassination of Rafiq Hariri—an event that remained shocking, despite growing political opposition to Syria's occupation of Lebanon. The months since had witnessed the popular protests of the tent city and the political deals of the electoral campaign, the withdrawal of Syria's forces from the country and the killing of some of its boldest critics. Taken together, these events were almost beyond comprehension. How could Syria's hegemony have unravelled so quickly, and how could so many have come together in opposition to its rule? How could the demonstrations of February and March have brought out not just the activists and students who had protested state practices since the early 2000s, but also middle-class, middle-aged doctors and accountants in neatly ironed polo shirts and well-to-do housewives in pearls and shades, Christian supporters of Aoun and Geagea, Sunni followers of Hariri, and Druze loyal to Walid Jumblatt?

But the verve and optimism of these months was also melded with fear and disappointment. Syria's soldiers were gone, but the killings and night-time explosions had come back, calling to mind the days of the war. The elections had been held, bringing a swathe of new deputies to parliament—not least the Christian representatives of the Lebanese Forces and the Free Patriotic Movement, whose parties had been outlawed under Syrian overrule, and whose members had largely refused to stand as independents, boycotting elections that they complained were marred by gerrymandering, corruption, and outright repression. A government had been formed, bringing together ministers from—almost—all sides. But this restoration of politics as normal was accompanied by new disputes, new alignments and divisions. Hizballah's ministers joined the cabinet for the first time, and men still loyal to Lahoud sat alongside members of the Future Movement. But the differences in outlook on key issues both international and domestic remained unbridgeable. By early 2006, these differences had congealed and hardened into two distinct blocs—14 March and 8 March, two rival camps defined by their divergent stances towards Syria, as much as by their contrasting understandings of Rafiq Hariri's legacy and the place of Hizballah's weapons in the state. These divisions would define Lebanese politics in years to come. The moment of the independence intifada—those few, short, weeks when some had glimpsed the possibility of a new Lebanon growing out of grief and anger—had passed. Rancour, recrimination, and fear had now replaced the fervour and fragile, daring hope of the Beirut spring.

2

AL-HAWADITH, OR THE EVENTS

LEBANON'S TUMULTUOUS YEARS

The death of Gebran Tueni in December 2005 marked the waning of the hope and optimism that had sprung from the demonstrations of February and March 2005, those displays of unshackled, mordant protest which seemed, if only for a brief moment, to reclaim politics for the people. But it did not signal the end of the assassinations. For Tueni would not be the last outspoken opponent of Syria's actions in Lebanon to die. With weary regularity, the deaths continued to come, like the change of the seasons: in November 2006, that of the Kata'ib MP Pierre Gemayel; in June 2007, that of the Future Movement MP Walid Eido; in September 2007, that of another member of the Kata'ib, Antoine Ghanem. It was hard to avoid the sense that this was a concerted campaign to punish Syria's critics, chipping brutally away at 14 March's already slim parliamentary majority, which Ghanem's death reduced to a mere three MPs. The conviction that all these deaths were somehow linked to the assassination of Rafiq Hariri—or were, at the very least, the product of the same baleful forces—would be bolstered by the assassination of Brigadier General François el Hajj in December 2007, and that of Captain Wissam Eid in January 2008. Both men were rumoured to be working on the investigation into Hariri's death at the time of their deaths.

These killings did little to ease the political deadlock into which Lebanon had descended soon after the parliamentary elections of May and June 2005. The events of that year had undoubtedly consolidated the position of the Hariri family and its closest advisers, who were now able to proclaim themselves not just the uncontested representatives of Lebanon's Sunni community, but also the central part of the anti-Syrian coalition that had emerged that year. But the leaders of the Future Movement were not the only ones to regard the demonstrations and elections of 2005 as having strengthened their claims to representativeness. Both Hizballah and General Michel Aoun's Free Patriotic Movement could insist—not without reason—that they spoke on behalf of Lebanon's Shia and Christians. Significantly, however, both parties felt that their own concerns had been overlooked in the post-election settlement of 2005. Though two Hizballah ministers now sat in cabinet for the first time, the party remained uneasy about several of 14 March's demands—not least its attachment to the disarmament of the resistance and its calls for an international investigation into Hariri's death, which the party's leaders decried as evidence of an unwarranted willingness to suspend Lebanon's sovereignty. Like a spouse warily agreeing to give a dysfunctional marriage another try, the party seemed forever on the verge of a walkout. As for the Free Patriotic Movement, its exclusion from the deal-making of 2005 did little to alleviate its leaders' longstanding tendency to regard themselves as courageous opponents of the post-war status quo, scorned for their attachment to Lebanon's independence and persecuted for their attempts to protect the rights of its Christians. While the Kata'ib and the Lebanese Forces—parties with far fewer seats in parliament—were invited into cabinet, the FPM sat on the margins, joining the ranks of the opposition.

These unresolved tensions would play themselves out over the following years. Stubbornly clinging to their stances, Lebanon's politicians continued to regard politics as a zero-sum game, shunning compromises that they feared would inevitably weaken their own positions and increase their opponents' strength. These were years of near-permanent uncertainty, of nerve-jangling anxiety and frustrating atrophy, as walk-outs, boycotts and ultimatums succeeded each other with exhausting frequency. Alongside such tactics came a marked increase in sectarian tension, for figures such as Saad Hariri, Sayyid Hassan Nasrallah and Michel Aoun did not shy away from insisting on their capacity to speak for their own, playing on their followers' sense of communal pride and resentment by representing themselves as confessional leaders. Perhaps inevitably, such tactics led to repeated outbreaks of violence, as Lebanon's parties and blocs engaged in shows of force and confrontations with enemies both internal and external. The first of these would come early in July 2006.

Summer 2006—the war

At around 9:00 a.m. on the morning of Wednesday 12 July, Katyusha rockets launched from southern Lebanon landed on the Israeli settlement of Shlomi. Located in northern Galilee, only a few kilometres from the Lebanese border, the settlement had been hit before by Hizballah rockets. This time, however, things were different. For at about the same time, a small group of Hizballah guerrillas stole across the border. Surprising an Israeli military Humvee on patrol, they killed three of its passengers, wounded two, and took captive two more: first sergeants Ehud Goldwasser and Eldav Regev, whom they carried back across the border to Lebanon. Shortly after, Hizballah announced that Regev and Goldwasser would only be freed in exchange for the release of 'Arab detainees'. Israel's response was swift. Even as Prime Minister Ehud Olmert condemned the abduction as an 'act of war' for which the Lebanese government would pay a 'heavy price', Israeli warplanes bombed Hizballah positions in southern Lebanon and ground troops entered Lebanon for the first time since Israel's withdrawal from the country in 2000.

These events would mark the beginning of Israel's offensive on Lebanon. Known to Israelis as the 'second Lebanon war' and in Arabic as *harb tammuz* or 'the July war', this was an odd and asymmetrical conflict. It was fought in Lebanon, and yet it was not one in which the Lebanese state was an active combatant. And though it began in July, it eventually only stumbled to a halt on 14 August, when both sides, worn down to a stalemate, agreed to abide by UN Security Council Resolution 1701, which called for an immediate cessation of hostilities. For more than a month, Israel and the 'Lebanese Resistance' waged fierce war against each other. On one side was the IDF, with its tanks, its armoured vehicles and warplanes, and its massed ranks of ground troops. Perhaps sensing the scale of operations to come, the Israeli army command called up reservists on the very first day of fighting. By 10 August, some 10,000 troops were active in Lebanon. This number had tripled to 30,000 by the time the bombs eventually fell silent a few days later.[1] On the other were the men of the *muqawama*, or resistance—combatants drawn in the main from the ranks of Hizballah and its awkward ally Amal, but also from the Lebanese Communist Party and Ahmad Jibril's Popular Front for the Liberation of Palestine– General Command, a Palestinian faction loyal to the Baathist regime across the border in Syria. Numbering at most a few thousand, the forces of the 'resistance' mustered rocket launchers, light artillery, and machine guns against the might of the IDF. The conflict would play itself out not just in the low-lying hills and valleys of southern Lebanon, where the 'resistance' used its superior knowledge of the terrain to wage an effective guerrilla campaign against the ground troops and tanks of the Israeli army, but also in the skies above Lebanon and Israel.

For neither side showed much regard for the distinction between civilian populations and military targets. While Hizballah sent down daily showers of rockets on Israeli settlements and towns in the northern Galilee, hitting Haifa on thirteen occasions, Israeli warplanes bombed targets across Lebanon. As early as 13 July, fighter jets hit the Beirut–Damascus highway, the military airbases of Rayak and Qulayy'at, and Rafic Hariri International Airport, damaging two runways, as Israel set about imposing an air and sea blockade on Lebanon. Not content with besieging Lebanon, the Israeli army also strove to leave the country in the dark. On 14 and 15 July, Israeli planes hit the power station of Jiyyeh, south of Beirut. The damage caused some 30,000 tonnes of fuel to spill into the Mediterranean, creating an oil slick that would eventually affect some 120 kilometres of coastline, putting a stop to fishing and endangering species such as the green turtle. Photographs taken in late July in the port of Jbeil, 60 kilometres north of Jiyyeh, show a harbour covered in a dense film of oil, like black ice glistening in the sun.[2] In early August, Israeli bombs hit pumping stations, channels and pipes which supplied water drawn from the Litani river to more than twenty-three villages in southern

Lebanon and the Bekaa, leaving 10,000 acres of farmland without irrigation.[3] For thirty-three days, then, Lebanon found itself caught up in a war not of its own making. As in the 'first Lebanon war' of 1982, the country as a whole suffered the ruinous consequences of a war fought on its land.

Justifying such attacks, Israeli officials made it clear they saw no distinction between Hizballah and the Lebanese government. As Danny Ayalon, the Israeli ambassador to the United States, put it in an interview with PBS' Jim Lehrer on the day the hostilities began: 'we have been attacked by Lebanon, from Lebanese soil, by terror organizations'. One could simply not differentiate between Hizballah and the Lebanese state. 'Hezbollah is a part and parcel of the Lebanese government. They have ministers who sit in the [cabinet].' Moreover, it was incumbent upon the 'Lebanese government, in order to be viable' to 'exercise their sovereignty ... and also perform their duty and obligation according to international law'. 'If they cannot control Hezbollah', Ayalon continued, 'maybe they are not a viable government'. The implication was clear: the Lebanese government's inability to keep Hizballah in check had shown that it did not possess a monopoly over force within its own territories. This was, in other words, no sovereign entity, but a failed state which showed neither the capacity nor the desire to police its own unruly people. Intervention, then, was fully justified. For 'if they do not control the Hezbollah, we will have to do the work.' And nor could Lebanon expect to go scot free for its dereliction of its own sovereign duties. On this Ayalon was clear: 'if they do not keep peace and quiet along our northern border, they cannot have impunity'.[4]

Throughout the conflict, Israel would abide by this logic. Holding the Lebanese state to account for the errant actions of one part of Lebanese society, it sought, as in the West Bank and Gaza, to mete out collective punishment against the Lebanese people as a whole. As the IDF's Chief of Staff, Dan Halutz, put it at the outset of its offensive, Israel would 'turn back the clock in Lebanon by twenty years' if Hizballah did not release the abducted soldiers immediately.[5] But the Israeli state made it clear that its objectives extended far beyond the release of Goldwasser and Regev. More than this, it intended 'to remodel the security situation along the [Israeli–Lebanese] border and to prevent Hizballah from reaching Israeli territory', 'to weaken the

Hizballah organization', and to compel the 'Lebanese government to exercise its sovereignty over its own [territory] and activities that emanate from its territory'.[6] The hope was that brute and indiscriminate force would achieve the last two of these objectives, turning Lebanon's inhabitants and government against Hizballah and pushing them to bring the party into check.

Only this can account for the sheer volume of strikes on Lebanon between 12 July and 14 August. According to figures compiled by Human Rights Watch (HRW), Israeli warplanes launched no fewer than '7,000 bomb and missile strikes' on Lebanon in little over a month— and this is without counting the 'numerous artillery attacks and naval bombardment[s]' that accompanied these aerial attacks. These, HRW concluded, resulted in a high civilian death toll for one very simple reason: a disregard for the essential distinction between 'military targets' and 'civilians'. To be sure, the blame could not lie entirely with the IDF. In its investigations, HRW did find evidence that Hizballah had, on occasion, used unoccupied houses to store weapons. This was the case, for instance, in the village of Ba'arshit where, on 13 July, an Israeli airstrike hit the homes of Najib Husayn Farhat and his brother, who had moved to Beirut in 1996. The strike killed Farhat and his 16-year-old daughter, Zaynab, and injured his wife, son, and daughter. Unbeknownst to the Farhat family and other villagers, Hizballah had rented out his brother's house, turning its basement into a weapons cache. Only when rumours of this deception spread through the village did the party acknowledge its actions, offering the Farhat family compensation for their loss.[7] It also appears that Hizballah did at times fire rockets from civilian areas. On the night of 18 July, an Israeli airstrike hit the southern village of 'Aitarun, killing nine members of the 'Awada family who were sheltering in their home in the centre of the village. In the wake of the attack, several surviving members of the family testified that Hizballah fighters had been firing rockets 'from 100 or 150 meters away from our house, from inside the village'.[8] On the whole, however, Hizballah did not locate its military facilities in built-up areas, preferring to build its bunkers and weapons storage facilities in fields and valleys on the outskirts of southern villages and establishing 'security cordons' around these areas to keep out non-members. The inhabitants of Ayn Ibl, for instance, told HRW investigators that

Hizballah had placed a number of fields 'off limits' to local people in the wake of the Israeli withdrawal in 2000, before beginning work on military installations.[9]

Rather, HRW concluded, the high number of civilian casualties on the Lebanese side could be accounted for by Israel's presumption that its calls for evacuation had been heeded. Choosing to believe 'all Lebanese civilians had observed its warnings to evacuate villages south of the Litani river', the Israeli army operated on the basis that all who remained could be treated as combatants, and that the region as a whole could be considered a military zone. There was, therefore, no need to 'discriminate between military objectives and civilians'.[10] This, of course, was wishful thinking at best. At times, indeed, Israeli officials appeared to acknowledge that their claims were without foundation. On 24 July, for instance, the IDF's Chief of Staff, Dan Halutz, noted on the record that 500 inhabitants of the southern town of Bint Jbeil had stayed behind despite repeated warnings to leave.[11] The effects of this policy rapidly became apparent, as the IDF targeted civilian cars and trucks which it assumed to be military vehicles simply because of their presence in the conflict zone. On 15 July, an airstrike killed twenty-three civilians, including fourteen children and seven women, fleeing the village of Marwahin; on 19 July, six were killed and eight more injured as they attempted to leave 'Aitarun; on 23 July, six ambulance drivers and three passengers were wounded in Qana. All movements were apparently deemed suspicious: on 25 July, a drone targeted Sa'da Nur al-Din as she was driving back to the village shelter in Ghassaniyeh from her home, where she had gone to collect some food.[12] After the war, Israel's deputy ambassador to the UN, Daniel Carmon, attempted to justify the country's military actions in southern Lebanon by claiming that 'there is hardly any distinction between Hezbollah and the civilian population [in southern Lebanon]. This whole region was a region in which you could not make a distinction between the one and the other'.[13]

And nor did Israel see much difference between Hizballah's military wing and its political and charitable arms. Determined to extirpate what one Israeli parliamentarian described as the 'cancer' of Hizballah from the Lebanese body politic, the Israeli army took aim not just at the locales of its charitable foundations, research centres and schools, but also at the homes and offices of its MPs and officials. On 16 July, an Israeli airstrike targeted what the IDF mistakenly believed were the 'Hizballah headquarters' in the southern Lebanese city of Sur, killing fourteen civilians; it later emerged that these were the headquarters of the Lebanese Civil Defence. On 13 August, meanwhile, Israeli warplanes launched an attack on the Imam Hassan Building Complex in the Beirut suburb of Ruways, razing ten eight-story buildings and killing at least thirty-six civilians and four low-level Hizballah operatives.[14] It is clear from this example that Israel's determination to demolish the party's political and charitable institutions and to treat all its members as legitimate targets, regardless of their functions, could not but have dire consequences.

These policies' effects were only exacerbated by Israel's widespread use of cluster bombs during the July War. In a report published in February 2008, HRW estimated that the IDF fired as many as 4.6 million submunitions on southern Lebanon in 962 separate strikes, peppering an area of around 1,400 square kilometres—roughly the size of Rhode Island—with cluster bombs. This was the most extensive use of these devices anywhere in the world since the 1991 Gulf War, and both HRW and the UN 'judged the level and density of post-conflict contamination in South Lebanon to be far worse than that found in Iraq, Afghanistan, or Kosovo following the use of cluster munitions in those countries'.[15] Many of these devices fell on villages and towns such as Tibnin, Nabatiyyeh, Bint Jbeil, Zawtar al-Gharbiyyeh and Zawtar al-Sharqiyyeh, Ayn Ata, Dayr Qanun, Hasbayya and Rashayya.[16] The effects of such tactics can be seen from just one incident. At 3:00 p.m. on the afternoon of 19 July, a cluster bomb landed on the home of Maryam Ibrahim, in the southern Lebanese town of Blida. The explosion killed Ibrahim. At least two submunitions fell into her basement, where the Ali family was seeking shelter. Ahmad Ali, the father of the family, lost both his legs in the explosion. His wife and mother-in-law also suffered injuries, as did five of his children—the youngest of whom was just one at the time of the attack.[17] On returning home after the conflict, many villagers found their homes and fields strewn with unexploded submunitions. 'Unexploded cluster duds' were found 'inside houses, in the streets, in gardens, on roofs, on patios, and hanging from trees and fences'.[18] On 13 August 2006, just fifteen hours before the ceasefire came into effect, a hospital in Tibnin was hit, leaving around 375 trapped inside the hospital building, their way out obstructed by unexploded cluster bombs.[19]

Indeed, what made Israel's policy all the more perverse was that '90% of ... cluster munition strikes took place' in the last seventy-two hours of its offensive on Lebanon, after the UN Security Council had passed Resolution 1701 calling for an immediate cessation of hostilities. As one officer told the Israeli newspaper *Haaretz*: 'What we did was insane and monstrous; we covered entire towns in cluster bombs' in the last days of fighting. The effects of this tactic were felt long after the end of the conflict. In the sixteen or so months between August 2006 and January 2008, 172 Lebanese civilians were injured and twenty lost their lives as a result of unexploded cluster munitions, as they tried to clear stray devices or simply attempted to return to work in the tobacco fields and orange and olive orchards that surrounded their homes. Children, who stumbled across devices as they were out playing, were particularly affected: a third of the casualties were under the age of eighteen.[20]

These casualties can be added to those incurred during the war itself. In those thirty-three days, 1,109 Lebanese—the vast majority of them civilians—were killed and 4,399 injured. Around a million people—a quarter of Lebanon's population—were internally displaced, and tens of thousands of homes damaged. In Bint Jbeil alone, more than 800 houses were completely destroyed; in 'Aita al-Sha'ab, the toll was 750. It is no surprise, then, that the most lasting and affecting images of the conflict are of utter devastation: of streets of apartment blocs in the southern suburbs of Beirut reduced to rubble, concrete slabs fallen at awkward angles strewn with household stuff, of distraught aid workers holding in their arms the lifeless remains of children, of weeping women standing amidst the destruction and young tear-stained thirsty faces peering at the camera lens.[21]

But perhaps the most famous image of all—and the most deceptive—is that which captures best the confusing realities of the war, and of Lebanese society. On 15 August, a day after the ceasefire had finally brought an end to the violence, the American photographer Spencer Platt was in the *dahiyeh*, the southern 'suburbs' of Beirut, when he saw a young group driving through the rubble in their red Mini Cooper.

Platt rapidly captured the scene: a twenty-something man, his long hair pushed back by a band, his aviator glasses screwed on, and around him four women, also in their twenties, in halter neck tops and tight white t-shirts. The one in the front seems almost out of her seat, her body pushed forward, her neck craned as she drinks in the devastation. One of those behind is capturing the scene on her mobile phone, while another holds a tissue to her nose. Three of the women also have sunglasses on; they glint in the sun, reflecting the destruction they shut out, reflections that can also be seen in the car's immaculately polished body. Platt's photo seemed a perfect representation of the divisions within Lebanese society, between those who had been affected by the war and those who had escaped its effects, between the haves, with their expensive foreign cars, and the have-nots, some of whom can be seen in the background, going about their business or speaking on their phones, and between Hizballah's pious followers in the southern suburbs, people like the woman visible behind the car—her back turned to the camera, so that one sees only her headscarf and long navy coat—and these outsiders, with their brazen glamour. Picked up by Getty Images, the photo was used across the world with the caption 'Affluent Lebanese drive down the street to look at a destroyed neighbourhood 15 August 2006 in southern Beirut, Lebanon'. Making explicit the contrasts the image appeared to capture, one Dutch magazine published it under the headline: 'The Cool People vs. Hezbollah'.[22]

And yet these captions hid a much more complex truth. Four of the car's passengers, it soon turned out, were inhabitants of Beirut's southern suburbs: the driver, Jad Maroun, and his sisters Bissan and Tamara had all grown up there, as had Nour Nasser, who had moved there as a teenager. They were not members of a gilded elite, disaster tourists come to inspect the miseries of their compatriots, but merely returning home to survey the damage. And, in their own way, all four were embodiments of *dahiyeh*'s social complexities.[23] The Maroun siblings were Christian, their family leftovers from the days when neighbourhoods like Haret Hreik and Burj al-Barajneh were largely Maronite villages far outside the confines of Beirut proper.[24] As Jad Maroun told the BBC: 'My problem with the … picture is that [it] emphasises some of the misconceptions people have—that it would be unusual for people like us to be in the area, they expect the area to be full of veiled women, to be dirty and impoverished'. Nasser, too, complained that the image did not accurately portray the realities of life in *dahiyeh*: 'We are part of the working middle class and we can afford some things, like nice clothes and sunglasses, but not everybody here can'. But Nasser's own life was complicated in other ways too. Though a Shia, she told the BBC, she was 'not a Hezbollah supporter'; 'I'm a liberal, but I'm not bothered by them. I don't like my neighbourhood though. I don't have any friends there, people look at you, they gossip'.[25] The lives of the Maroun siblings and Nasser were reminders that the southern suburbs were by no means as monochrome or monolithic as some will make them out to be, but were marked by both socio-economic differentiation and a measure of confessional diversity. At the same time, however, Nasser's words also spoke not just of the ways in which some of *dahiyeh*'s inhabitants refused to acquiesce in Hizballah's hegemony, but also of the costs such a refusal might entail. As ever in Lebanon, things here are not quite as simple as they might appear at first. But Platt's image also caught the odd disjuncture of devastation and banality that characterised those thirty-three days of war and their immediate aftermath. It is this disconcerting jumble of life and death, of normality and utter abnormality, that artists such as Mazen Kerbaj and Ali Cherri strove to capture.

In his work *Starry Night*, Kerbaj set out to record one night of bombardment over Beirut, early in the war. On the night of 15 to 16 July, he went out onto his balcony to pick up what he could hear—and to answer back to the bombs. The first sound you hear is the intent chirping of crickets in the darkness, like on any summer night. But then something else comes into earshot, something that sounds at first like mosquitoes buzzing about in the air, until you realise it is the faint hum of warplanes up above. And after the faint hum come in quick succession the high-pitched whistle of the bomb falling, the thud of an explosion somewhere in the city, the cacophony of car alarms that go off in the empty streets, warning nobody in particular of something everybody knows about. Against the noise of war, Kerbaj musters the distorted, looped sounds of his trumpet, sheets of grey noise raging against the dying in the night. Standing alone on his balcony, he offers what he can against the explosions as they grow closer and louder, against the barking of frightened dogs, against the war that has come to Lebanon.[26]

At the same time, Kerbaj kept a diary of a kind of the war: more than 250 drawings, most of them in hasty, intricate black pen or ink, their stark unrelenting monochrome a reflection on the times, uploaded to his blog. Some capture despair and bewilderment. 'Beirut 16 July 06 2.10 am', box-like apartment buildings, their windows rendered as little slots and grids and crosses, overwhelmed by a dense swell of black smoke. And somewhere in Beirut, Kerbaj himself, represented only by a speech bubble: 'how can i show sound in a drawing?' 'Television Blues', 9 August, five TV screens, and on each a few words in Arabic: 'day after day', 'we stay in front of the TV', 'and we watch our children and our people in the south and the suburbs of Beirut', 'die', 'die', 'and we watch'. 'Since the first day', 7 August 2006, intestines winding their way in white through a black torso and above them the words, *'andi 'uqda*—'I have a knot'. 'Question', 6 August 2006, a face marked out in shadows, its features replaced by the words 'Where are we, WHO are we?' Another from the same day, '130': again a face, within its eyes the words 'We are', on its nose 'dying', and its mouth replaced by the crossed-out words 'IN SILENCE'. Others speak of the odd banality of events and the disquiet that haunts the body and upsets its workings. An image of the artist musing, cigarette in one hand, whisky glass in the other, in his favourite Gemmayzeh bar. The speech bubble reads 'I AM IN TORINO (AGAIN & AGAIN). IT IS 12.05AM. THE COUNTRY IS BURNING. MY COUNTRY. I AM DRINKING WHISKEY . . .'. Then an image of the artist squatting over the toilet, spewing up his guts: 'in the toilets of Torino I am vomiting . . . I never—even when I was 15—vomited after only 2 whiskeys HRRRGGLL'.

The best known of Kerbaj's drawings, however, sum up with mordant humour the sorrow, the anger and frustration felt by so many, caught up in a war not of their own making. An image of the southern city of Sur, besieged and bombarded by Israeli troops, cast off the shore and cut off from Lebanon, its centre turned into a fireball rising up above the apartment towers. Above, the words: 'Sur, from a city became an island.' Beneath, simply one word: 'she burns'. Or 'Let's play', with its three games for the Lebanese to play with 'our friends from the Israeli air force': 'the maze', with its attempt to reconnect a body to its detached parts, 'match the numbers', with its bodies and coffins, and 'spot the differences', with its two images of Beirut, one a colourful array of higgledy-piggledy buildings, the other a grey wreck.[27]

Some of these images call to mind the iconography of solidarity, conjuring echoes of the posters produced from the late 1960s to the 1980s by OSPAAL, the PLO and other leftist groups—images of lone women and distraught men, of bombs and fallow fields which drew attention to the suffering of the Palestinian and Lebanese people and called on the world to stand by them. But Kerbaj's drawings are only elliptically political. Eluding any overt alignments, they are intensely personal in their unremitting focus on the bellyaches and sleepless nights of war, and on the ways in which even small moments of joy can be polluted by thoughts of a conflict that breaks the routines of men and animals alike. One drawing, for instance, shows Kerbaj sitting in a friend's garden, sipping a coffee; seeing a small kitten in the foliage, he thinks, 'how lucky you are not to know you were born in Lebanon', the thought not so much a disavowal of his homeland as a sorrowful recognition of its predicament. Another shows Israeli warplanes circling, birds on a wire chirping, and Kerbaj's own tired face, his eyes sleep-deprived sinkholes circled with deep black lines and, between, the words: 'Night of 10 to 11 August, 6 am. The planes have not slept. The birds wake. I don't know what I'm supposed to do.'

Insomnia, fraught nightmare-ridden sleep, digestive trouble, drinking and drunkenness, endless TV watching and talking and fretting, and in between visits to the mountain to see his partner and their son, or to his parents to eat *mujaddara* and cabbage salad: Kerbaj's drawings capture not just the disruption of war, but also its odd banality.[28] They conjure how close, and yet also how distant, the war could feel to those who did not live in neighbourhoods and towns directly hit by the Israeli air force. This was a war that was lived on two planes at once—in real time, as one listened for the flight patterns of the aircraft up above and watched the bombs fall over the city, and in the hyper-reality of television and radio. And, like the Lebanese civil war, this was a conflict whose effects were felt unevenly. I know of some who spent most of those thirty-three days of war up in the clouds, fortunate enough to be able to afford a bolthole in the ski resort of Faqra. High in the mountains and faraway from Beirut, these wealthy boys and girls experienced the war not just as a flight from reality, but also as an intensification of normality, in which all the usual features of the Lebanese summer season were accentuated: seemingly endless leisure, entire days whiled away lolling by the pool, long lunches and late nights. Others, meanwhile, lived down in the inferno, reality suspended, life kept in abeyance while they stayed awake waiting for the bombs to fall.

This sense of life in wartime as uncanny, like a nightmare in which one visits a familiar place but finds it changed in some imperceptible and troubling way, is also captured in the work of artist Ali Cherri. In his *Untitled (To The Lebanese Citizens)*, completed in 2006, Cherri superposes the message the Israeli military broadcast to the Lebanese people on 21 July, capturing the frequency used by Voice of Lebanon, over images of the warships Western states sent to Beirut to evacuate their citizens. A plangent Arabic love song is interrupted by a stern male voice, reading out a warning:

> To Lebanon's citizens: Hizballah's military operations directed at Israel's territories have led you to the situation in which you currently find yourselves. You should know that Israel will continue its operations with force to put an end to the terrorist attacks against it…

And then the voice fades away again, drowned out by static, and the love song returns like a head bobbing up to the surface in the sea waves. Beneath this soundtrack, a series of slides show a city scene—flat rooftops, radio aerials, a minaret—and, beyond, the sea and the sky, both as effortlessly and endlessly blue as they can be on a Lebanese summer day. Moving across the screen, disappearing and reappearing, one sees one warship, then two, then three.[29]

In Cherri's piece, two forms of intervention are juxtaposed, the entry into Lebanese territorial waters of the warships despatched by Canada, the US, Australia, France and the UK to save their citizens from harm set alongside the Israeli infiltration of the airwaves—one more invasion of the everyday lives of the Lebanese, robbing them even of the comfort of music. One gets a sense, in watching this piece, of the claustrophobia of the Lebanese, forever watched over by foreign forces, there to save them, to warn them, to fight against them and bombard them. But one is also reminded of the way war punctures normality: a love song broken up by a military press release, a summer sea dotted with warships. The homespun nature of the piece—Cherri made the recording on his mobile phone while listening to Voice of Lebanon on 21 July, and took the photos he used from his bedroom window—with its deliberate use of an artless default font, Calibri, to convey information, only adds to the sense that the war injected new and alien elements into an otherwise familiar reality. As one Lebanese blogger noted, Cherri's piece 'brings back the mix of monotony and fear we felt during those days' of boredom and dread.[30] Time, for many, was torn to pieces by the war. For others, however, it merely stood still, the conflict a surreal, nightmarish interlude.

That is the way it must have seemed to those nominally in power in Lebanon in those summer days. For even as Hizballah and Israel both spoke repeatedly of the conflict as one that involved all the Lebanese and their state, they took little heed of the government and its entreaties to rein in the violence. Isolated and powerless, Lebanon's prime minister, Fouad Siniora, was reduced to making impotent pleas for assistance from the United States, the United Nations and the Arab League. In one meeting, Siniora broke down in tears before his fellow Arab leaders, perhaps all too aware of just how futile and empty the platitudes of Arab solidarity and the duties of brotherhood really were. Those sympathetic to Siniora saw his tears as a sign of his sincere dedication to the welfare of his country. To his opponents, however, they were mere crocodile tears, a mark of the hypocrisy of a government that indulged in empty speechifying and lachrymose sentiment while its citizens were dying under Israeli bombs. To make matters worse, they were unmanly, an unseemly image of impotence broadcast to the world. Many Hizballah supporters drew an explicit contrast between the unedifying sight of Siniora exposing his weakness on the international stage, a crestfallen and powerless figure, and the composure and confidence of their own leader. In his very first intervention of the war on 13 July, Sayyid Hassan Nasrallah gave a message of steadfast resistance. Dismissing the posturing and empty rhetoric of Lebanon's Arab neighbours, he mocked Israel's government. The Israeli people, he insisted, would soon realise just how unready their rulers and military commanders really were for the challenge of taking on Hizballah, whose *mujahidin* had imposed on Israel its first defeat in 2000. Nasrallah's defiant speech culminated in a stunning act of theatre: even as he spoke, he explained, an Israeli warship was in flames off the coast of Beirut, hit by a Hizballah rocket. There would be, he promised, many more such shocks in store.[31]

Indeed, while 14 March and the Israeli government both collapsed into fits of soul-searching in the wake of the July War, Hizballah's stock was as high as it ever had been. Turning a military stalemate into a triumph of resistance, it proclaimed its defeat of Israel a 'victory from God'—*nasr min Allah*, a neat pun on Nasrallah's own name. Posters celebrating the party's 'divine victory' and images of the martyrs who died in its pursuit were plastered up and down Lebanon's highways, far beyond nominally Shia areas. And this, Nasrallah proclaimed to the crowds that gathered on 22 September 2006, forty days after the end of the fighting, was not just a victory over Israel, its armies and its ambitions, but also a blow to America's project for a 'new Middle East'. This, he went on, citing the words of Hugo Chávez before the United Nations, was a victory 'for all the resistances of the world', and 'for all those who resist submission' to the great powers. Writing now in the shadow of the Syrian war, it seems hard to believe that this, the high tide of Hizballah's popularity amongst anti-imperialists across the Arab world and beyond, was little more than ten years ago.

December 2006—the walk-out

By late 2006, Hizballah found itself in an ambiguous position. On the face of it, the party was stronger than ever. Its reputation as a fierce fighting unit bolstered by its performance in the 33-day war, it was able to claim that it had achieved what Arab states had never succeeded in doing—standing up to, and even defeating, the mighty juggernaut of the Israeli military. Moreover, the party was able to draw upon a carefully crafted set of political alliances, which ensured it the support not just of Nabih Berri and his Amal movement, whose ministers sat alongside the party's own representatives in cabinet, but also of Michel Aoun's Free Patriotic Movement, whose fifteen MPs made up the largest single Christian grouping in parliament. More than just political leverage, these alliances allowed Hizballah to claim for itself popular legitimacy, arguing that it represented a majority of Shia and Christians—and, thus, the majority of Lebanon's inhabitants.

And yet, Hizballah's most prominent members remained frustrated with a status quo they condemned as unjust; according too much untrammelled executive power to a single party—the Future Movement—the current dispensation allowed the latter to pursue its foreign dalliances, compromising Lebanon's sovereignty and security in the process. The only means of pulling Lebanon out of the political crisis in which it remained mired, Hizballah's clerics and MPs argued, was the formation of a national unity government in which the opposition would hold a blocking third, allowing it to veto any cabinet decisions. This was not simply a means of checking the tyranny of the majority and ensuring a fairer form of government by consensus. More than this, it would pave the way for a new dispensation, in which each of Lebanon's major religious communities—the Sunnis, the Shia, and the Christians—would be accorded a third of parliamentary seats and ministerial portfolios. It was time, in other words, to do away with the makeshift arrangements reached at Ta'if, replacing them with a fairer system according the Shia their due share of political representation. This was, to be sure, a long-term aspiration. There is no denying, however, that it also served as a useful political instrument in the short-term, allowing Hizballah to prevaricate, stall, block and bluster, by accusing its opponents of abusing executive power whenever they sought to introduce a measure the party disliked, and threatening to walk out of cabinet if their demands were not met.

Indeed, the arrival on 21 October of a draft UN plan for the creation of a special tribunal to try those accused of Rafiq Hariri's assassination led to a noticeable intensification of the party's rhetoric.[32] The very next day, Shaykh Muhammad Yazbek, one of the members of the party's legislative council, insisted in a speech that only a 'national unity government' built upon cooperation between Hizballah and the Free Patriotic Movement could lay the foundation for a 'strong, dignified, and capable state'. The same day, Muhammad Fneish—then the minister of water and energy, and one of the party's most prominent MPs—made it clear that Hizballah would use any 'legitimate means' at its disposal to secure its aims.[33] A few days later, Hassan Nasrallah himself threw his weight behind these demands. In an interview with Hizballah's TV channel, Al-Manar, he accused the 'party in power'—in other words, the Future Movement—of seeking to transform the United Nations Interim Force in Lebanon (UNIFIL) into 'a multinational force operating under Chapter 7 of the UN Charter to occupy Lebanon ... and disarm the Resistance'. There was nothing new, he continued, about this idea. Long before the 'Israeli aggression' of July 2006, the 'majority' had already buckled to 'American-Israeli demand[s]', attempting to implement a 'project' that would transform Lebanon into 'another Afghanistan or Iraq'—a violent and unstable place overrun by foreign forces. Unable to put into effect this 'dangerous' scheme, this clique had fallen back on crude exploitation of its majority in cabinet, reducing Hizballah's ministers to mere 'scenery'. It was no surprise, then, that it should have 'lost all credibility'. '[T]he majority of the Lebanese'—around 70 per cent, Nasrallah asserted—'want a unity government, capable of facing up to the dangerous challenges facing the country'. Confident of popular assent in its actions, Hizballah would resort to 'all peaceful and democratic means' to ensure that the desires of the people were honoured and the country spared another 'civil war'—the natural result, in its own particular logic, of the abuses that had become customary under Fouad Siniora. If the national dialogue called for by Nabih Berri did not lead to the creation of a more consensual, representative cabinet and early elections, then the party would call on its supporters to descend into the streets to exert pressure on its opponents. For what use was a government 'that had only a slim majority in parliament … and no popular majority'?[34] Ever the rhetorician, Nasrallah made canny use of the language of popular sovereignty, presenting his followers and allies as an oppressed majority, whose rights had long been traduced by a faction beholden to foreign interests. Right, he insisted, was on the side of the many, who represented Lebanon's true face. His opponents, meanwhile, were nothing but illegitimate stooges, determined to bring the country to its knees.

Despite such fiery talk, the party went along with Nabih Berri's national dialogue. For the first ten days of November, the Lebanese newspapers were full of reports of fall-outs and deals, of boycott threats and potential solutions to the deadlock. But, despite the occasional thin chink of light breaking through the glum mood, it was apparent to all that neither side was ready for compromise. On the eve of the first round of meetings, Saad Hariri made his own position clear in an interview with the journalist May Chidiac. There could no 'blocking third', he insisted, when Lebanon already had a 'blocking president'—his father's old foe, Emile Lahoud, whose opposition to the tribunal was either an 'attempt to protect himself, or to protect the Syrian regime'. Rejecting out of hand Hizballah's claims, Hariri argued that '99 per cent of the government's decisions were taken in a consensual fashion'. Hizballah, he reminded Chidiac, had approved the creation of a tribunal in the wake of the assassination of Gebran Tueni, in December 2005, and 'there was not a single word of Resolution 1701' that the party had not signed off on. There was now no going back, and there would be 'no concessions' to the 'Syrian–Iranian axis', either on 'sovereignty, or the tribunal, or Paris III'—the upcoming round of talks on international financial assistance to Lebanon.[35]

Given such intransigence, few could have expected the national dialogue to last long. And yet, as always in Lebanese high politics, the participants could not resist a little dramatic flourish at the end. As the session of Saturday 11 November collapsed into acrimonious wrangling, Nabih Berri suddenly interrupted proceedings after receiving a handwritten note, announcing that the meeting was suspended. Shortly after came the news that the cabinet's five Shia members had resigned with immediate effect. If their intention was to force Siniora into dissolving cabinet and announcing his own resignation, then the gambit failed. Responding to the news, the prime minister declared that he refused their resignation, and that the cabinet meeting called for Monday 13 November to discuss the workings of the international tribunal would still go ahead. Then came Lahoud's turn to enter the fray, the president announcing that he deemed the cabinet unconstitutional in the absence of Shia ministers, and would not attend any of its meetings. But this grandstanding was not enough to dissuade Siniora and his allies in 14 March. Meeting at Koreitem, they issued a defiant statement, which Saad Hariri read out in his hesitant Arabic. Lebanon's enemies in Damascus 'had tried to oppose the international tribunal and to plant traps on the path of independence', killing opponents of the Syrian regime, 'multiplying explosions in the Kisrwan, the Matn, and Beirut, [and] creating problems with the army. They tried everything, and when they failed, the Syrian regime tried to undermine the independence intifada, dynamiting decisions taken in the national dialogue, [and] accusing [14 March] of treason'. Little else could be expected from Damascus, but it was 'unthinkable that Lebanese currents should seek to undermine the international tribunal' on behalf of the 'Syrian regime'.[36] On Monday, the cabinet met as planned, signing off on the UN's draft plan—a symbolic show of resolute defiance.

Lebanon now found itself waiting for the next move in this tense and laborious game. When it came, it was shocking in its brutality. On 21 November, Pierre Gemayel—the minister of industry in the Siniora cabinet and Amin Gemayel's son and heir apparent as head of the Kata'ib party—was gunned down as he drove through the Christian neighbourhood of Jdeideh. As his rented Kia stopped in traffic, unknown assailants opened fire, riddling the car with thirteen rounds of gunfire.[37] Gemayel died at the scene of gunshot wounds to the head. He was thirty-four years old.[38] With the grief came renewed recriminations. The day of Gemayel's funeral in the grand Maronite cathedral of St George in downtown Beirut, at which the Maronite patriarch Mar Nasrallah Boutros Sfeir officiated, hundreds of thousands of partisans descended into the streets of Beirut to manifest their anger at the perpetrators. Choking up the streets around Martyrs' Square, they held aloft party banners, Lebanese flags, and signs that insisted, reprising a slogan much heard in March 2005, that 'Lebanon is the country of life' or protested 'No to the culture of death' which 14 March supporters associated with Hizballah, with its putative idealisation of suicidal sacrifice. In this view, if 14 March's martyrs had been taken from the arms of their supporters, snatched away too early, those of Hizballah had given themselves willingly to death. When Walid Jumblatt addressed the demonstrators, telling them that Gemayel had joined the ranks of the 'other martyrs who refused' Syrian 'trusteeship', with its 'killings and assassinations', the crowd's anger reached a paroxysm. 'Down with Syria, down with Lahoud', they chanted and screamed, 'we want to go to Baabda'. For few 14 March supporters held any doubts about Gemayel's killing.[39] Coming a day before the UN Security Council voted on the special tribunal for Lebanon, the assassination had reduced the cabinet to eight members, lending further weight to the claims of those who insisted it was no longer constitutional and pushing it closer to collapse. This, in their eyes, was no coincidence. It couldn't be. So crass, so cynical and calculated was this act of violence committed in the mid-morning sun, so confident were its perpetrators that they would remain unpunished, that it was hard to avoid the conclusion that Damascus and its Lebanese allies were behind Gemayel's killing.

Those who had hoped that the death of the young minister might bring the Lebanese political class back round the negotiating table, though, were to be disappointed. After a brief truce during which MPs and ministers of all sides rushed to extend their condolences to the Gemayel family and to condemn this brazen act of violence, 14 March and 8 March fell back on their old positions. Barely a few days after Gemayel's burial, Hizballah and its allies in 8 March called on their supporters to come out into the street to call for the dismissal of a government they condemned as illegitimate. On 1 December, hundreds of thousands heeded their call, swarming into Martyrs' Square and Riyad al-Sulh Square. *Ya Siniora, fil, fil*—'leave, Siniora, leave'— they chanted, or 'Yellow, green and orange, we all want the fall of the government', in allusion to the colours of the three largest parties in attendance, Hizballah, Amal and Aoun's FPM. Some hurled ad hominem attacks at the despised Siniora, calling out 'leave Siniora, we need a man to take your place' or 'Siniora, dry your tears and look at the people who are hurting'. Indeed, the personal contempt in which he and his allies in 14 March were held was apparent from the words of those questioned by reporters. As 'Isam Ali Hasan, a carpenter from the village of Abla in the Beqaa, explained, he had come to Beirut aboard one of the coaches that Hizballah and Amal had laid on for the occasion to demand the 'departure of this government. Not only does it not offer us any social services, it also had the cheek to ally itself with the West during the summer war. Prime Minister Siniora met with Condoleezza Rice when Israel was pouring down American bombs' on Lebanon. Others shared this sense of personal betrayal. Fadi Tanios, a 25-year-old architecture student and FPM member, explained that he was 'one of the guys who were beaten and sprayed with water cannons at each and every anti-Syrian demonstration' in the 'leaden days' of the 1990s. 'At the time', Tanios went on, 'Rafiq Hariri was prime minister and Walid Jumblatt a super-minister, combining several cabinet positions'. He couldn't 'help but laugh hearing the PSP or the Future Movement accuse the FPM, now of being pro-Syrian, now of being pro-Iranian'. Where men like Jumblatt were craven hypocrites, weathervanes tacking to the changing winds, Aoun and Nasrallah had remained steadfast in their commitments. Others went further still. Walking through the crowd, the journalist Jad Semaan saw one small group of teenage Amal supporters reeling round and chanting *Pipo met met w Ja'ja' waynu waynu*—'Pipo [Pierre] died, died, and Geagea where is he, where is he?' Before being able to speak to them, Semaan was ushered away by a member of Hizballah's *indibat*, or crowd control team, who apologised profusely for their behaviour, while insisting firmly Semaan could not want to speak to a few 'uncouth' bad seeds.[40]

Before long, the caustic brutality of these words turned into physical violence. On 3 December, 21-year-old Amal supporter Ahmad Mansur was gunned down as he returned home from central Beirut. While no-one knew who had killed Mansur, journalists wrote of growing tension and rancour among the Sunni and Shia inhabitants of Beirut's densely populated working-class neighbourhoods. Each night, local residents reported, bands of young men would gather on either side of intersections like that at Bechara al-Khoury. Armed with slings, stones, and sticks, they shouted slogans in support of the Future Movement, Hizballah or Amal and their leaders: the shaykh, Saad Hariri, the sayyid, Hassan Nasrallah, and the *ustadh*, or master, Nabih Berri, a term the speaker of parliament had earned thanks to his legal training. Mixed into these chants of praise were sectarian taunts, Shia 'insulting the *sahaba* [companions] of the Prophet—Uthman, Omar, and Abu Bakr—as well as Hariri and Siniora', while Sunnis mocked 'Imam Ali and Nasrallah'. But this, as the journalist Jad Semaan noted, 'was not a new chapter in a thousand-year war', as some in the West were wont to see the renewed sectarian tension between Shia and Sunnis across the Middle East, but a neighbourhood matter, born of deprivation and a fierce loyalty to one's own quarter and patrons. Indeed, some could remember easier times. 'For decades', one local pharmacist told Semaan, 'we lived together, without asking ourselves who is Sunni and who Shia'. There is a hint here of retrospective revision, but there is no doubt that this fierce confessionalism was a new phenomenon, and not a secular matter. As one old man put it, 'everything started with the assassination of Rafiq Hariri' and the ideological stand-off that followed.[41]

But this did not make the violence any less frightening or destabilising. After a period of relative calm over Christmas and Eid al-Adha, 8 March called for a general strike for 23 January, to coincide with Paris III, the international donor conference held in the French capital to discuss financial assistance to the Lebanese state. Once again, the opposition showed its capacity for an unsubtle kind of political theatre. As Fouad Siniora sat down with representatives of the United States,

Saudi Arabia, France and the European Union in a Parisian conference room, his political opponents descended into the streets. The intended contrast was clear. While Siniora was away cosying up to the foreign powers that propped up his illegitimate government at the expense of Lebanon's sovereignty and financial autonomy, the opposition stood for the people—they were, in fact, the people. However, the tension and resentment of the previous months soon burst into violence, as the protesters blocked off roads with burning tires and some pelted the police with rocks and stones. The demonstrations brought economic life to a standstill, closing Beirut's airport for the day, but they also left a toll of four dead, 133 injured, and 132 arrested.[42] There would be more deaths two days later, when a dispute between Sunni and Shia students at the Beirut Arab University turned violent, before spreading into the surrounding streets. Soon these resembled a war zone of burned-out cars and turned-over bins, and the fighting had spread to the neighbourhoods of Tariq al-Jdideh, Mar Elias, Bechara al-Khoury and Zuqaq al-Blat. The army, which deployed heavily to dampen down the fighting, was not spared, and the sight of a patrol coming under fire from unknown gunmen was captured by Al-Jazeera cameramen. For a few awful hours, the prospect of a wider conflict between Sunnis and Shia seemed a very real possibility, and the dark spectre of civil war hung over Lebanon.[43] Only the imposition of a curfew by the army, and the intervention of Hizballah and Future Movement leaders, brought the fighting to an end.

And still, both sides dug in. Within a week of the demonstrations of early December, the protests had turned into a carefully organised sit-in, as partisans of Hizballah, the FPM and Amal set about building a tent city. Rigorously sticking to the party line, with its stress on cross-sectarian comity, those interviewed by reporters in its early days insisted that this canvas town was inhabited day and night by 5,000 activists—half Christian and half Muslim, they represented all of Lebanon's many confessions, joined together in opposition to a government that had impoverished the country's people and done nothing to protect them from harm and foreign aggression during the summer war.[44] Few of those camping out would have disagreed with the Maronite opposition leader Sleiman Frangieh when he told the crowd in early December that they would 'spend Christmas, [Eid] al-Adha, the

New Year and Easter' in their makeshift homes, staying out in the street as long as it would take to meet their demands.[45] Though effectively locked into the prime minister's offices, encircled by the warren of tents outside, Siniora proved no less intransigent. 'The solution', he declared from his gilded cage, 'will not come from the street'. While everyone was allowed their freedom of expression, such demonstrations were comparable to the coups that had shaken Lebanon's Arab neighbours over the decades. So long as he enjoyed the confidence of parliament, Siniora told the reporters allowed into the Serail to listen to him, he would not bow to the threat of force. 'I am going nowhere', he insisted, a seemingly meek man demonstrating unexpected reserves of stubborn defiance.[46]

True to his word, Siniora would remain in office for another eighteen months. Staying all the while in the Serail, a virtual prisoner, he presided symbolically over a government whose ministers were themselves under effective house arrest. For in the wake of Gemayel's assassination, many 14 March MPs and dignitaries were effectively forbidden from moving about on security grounds; leaving their homes, they were put up in luxurious confinement in temporary accommodation dotted about Beirut's more affluent neighbourhoods, under the close watch of a coterie of bodyguards and security agents. One member of Lebanon First, Hariri's newly formed parliamentary bloc, recalled holding his daughter's engagement party in his small furnished apartment, the joy of the occasion tinged with the sadness and uncertainty of internal exile. Outside Siniora's office the tent city, too, stayed in place. Though only a skeleton crew of party cadres and devoted followers were left—one would see them sometimes sitting out amidst the tents smoking *arghileh* and playing backgammon under glum winter skies—their presence was enough to keep up pressure on the government. The tent city's inhabitants brought the cafes and luxury stores of the downtown area to a standstill, transforming the pleasure ground that Hariri's Solidere company had designed for summering Gulf Arabs and well-off Lebanese migrants into what local entrepreneurs described in panicked terms as a 'ghost town'.[47] More than just a pacific siege of the Grand Serail, this was also a symbolic occupation of a part of Beirut long considered off-limits to many of Lebanon's citizens. For a time, the people of the periphery—of the capital's southern suburbs, of the villages of the Beqaa or the northern reaches of Mount Lebanon—took possession of the symbolic centre of Hariri's reborn, reconstructed capital, turning his vision on its head.

Indeed, the standoff between the prime minister in his office and the demonstrators in the square below was also one between two visions of Lebanon—as a state of resistance which empowered the marginal and lifted up the deprived, and as a neoliberal dreamscape open to foreign investment and founded on a faith in the capacity of wealth to trickle down through society. Neither side would cede ground until May 2008, when the Doha Agreement—reached in the wake of brutal fighting between Hizballah and Amal fighters, on the one hand, and Future Movement and PSP men on the other—installed a new president and a national unity government presided over by Saad Hariri. Lebanon's governing institutions were effectively paralysed. But soon another, more violent, crisis would come to distract the country's inhabitants from these dire straits.

May–August 2007—the camp

Late on Saturday 20 May 2007, or in the early hours of Sunday 21 May—the accounts differ—gunmen robbed a branch of BankMed in Amioun, a town in the northern region of the Kura. Making away with $125,000 in cash, they fled by car towards Tripoli, some 26 kilometres to the north.[48] In pursuit was a squad of the Internal Security Forces, which followed the gunmen's trail to an apartment building in the well-off neighbourhood of Mitayn. Little, though, could have prepared this patrol for the response that met them as they attempted to enter the building. For the men they had followed, it would eventually transpire, belonged to a cell of the armed Islamist group Fatah al-Islam, which had taken over four of the bloc's flats. A relative upstart which had first appeared in the Palestinian refugee camps in late 2006, the group had risen to prominence in the wake of the Bikfayya bombings of 13 February 2007, in which three were killed and twenty-one injured in twin attacks on mini-buses travelling through a Christian region of the mountain. Though its leader, Shaker al-'Absi insisted the group had played no part in these, the Lebanese authorities were quick to point the finger at the group, arresting four of its members the day after the bombings.[49]

Facing heavy machine-gun and mortar fire from within, the ISF patrol called for army reinforcements. Before long, armoured vehicles and tanks surrounded the building. Attempting to break the deadlock, the besieged gunmen in turn called for assistance from their companions in Tripoli and its surroundings. In the Palestinian refugee camp of Nahr al-Bared, some 16 kilometres from the city, Fatah al-Islam members attacked the army post on the camp's outskirts, killing four soldiers in their sleep. In the town of Qalamun, on Tripoli's outskirts, the group's gunmen ambushed an army patrol, killing seven of its members. In the Tripoli neighbourhoods of Tell and Zahiriyya, meanwhile, members of the group engaged patrolling soldiers in open gun battles in the streets before retreating, outnumbered, into residential buildings where they barricaded themselves with hostages—including, in one case, two young children. What had initially seemed a straightforward enough bank robbery was rapidly turning into the worst clashes between the Lebanese army and Islamists since 2000, when violent confrontations had broken out in the northern town of Diniyyeh. Late on Sunday evening, the ISF finally declared Tripoli 'clean' of Fatah al-Islam gunmen. This achievement, though, had come at a cost. In more than twelve hours of ambuscades, sieges and street fighting, twenty-three soldiers had lost their lives and more than thirty were injured; fourteen Fatah al-Islam gunmen had been killed, while local residents were left surveying the pockmarked walls and burned-out cars around them.[50]

What's more, this was not the end of the battle, but the beginning of a long and costly confrontation between the Lebanese army and Fatah al-Islam. Determined to destroy the group and avenge the loss of its soldiers, the army moved on Nahr al-Bared, where 'Absi and most of the group's members had hidden. By Sunday evening, hundreds of soldiers had taken up positions around the camp, closing off all its entrances. Over the next few days, the camp's 31,000 or so inhabitants found themselves caught between the gunmen of Fatah al-Islam and the Lebanese army's shelling as the PLO attempted to broker a settlement. For a time, it looked as though they might be successful, as a series of temporary truces allowed many of the camp's Palestinian inhabitants to flee. On 31 May, however, Fatah al-Islam rejected the ceasefire plan put together by the PLO. The following day, commando troops launched an assault on the camp, in which 3,000 to 8,000 refugees were still trapped.[51] But if the generals and the politicians had hoped for a swift and painless resolution, they were to be disappointed. Bolstered by shipments of equipment from the United States, France, and Arab states, the army threw all its might at Fatah al-Islam. Up to 5,000 army personnel—infantry, but also members of the special forces and armour, air force and naval divisions—participated in the assault on Nahr al-Bared.[52] Throughout, the army kept up a barrage of bombardment: while tanks and artillery shelled the camp from their positions on the high ground, helicopters flew above the camp, strafing militant positions. At the height of the offensive, up to ten shells were being fired every minute towards Nahr al-Bared.[53]

Time and again, the army high command announced that victory was imminent. On 3 June, the National News Agency reported that the army had 'full control over all the axes' within the camp.[54] On 13 June, the army announced that it was 'cleansing' areas of the camp newly under its control and advancing steadily on 'positions where Fatah al-Islam extremists are holed up'.[55] On 29 July, the army's commander, General Michel Sleiman, assured reporters the 'final assault against Fatah al-Islam is imminent', with other sources reporting that the fighting might be over in time for Army Day, on 1 August.[56] And yet it was not until 2 September that the army finally took control of Nahr al-Bared, its soldiers firing celebratory salvos into the bomb-stained air above the camp.[57]

In the end, Fatah al-Islam proved an obdurate and resilient opponent. Though it could never count on more than 500 to 700 fighters, it derived tactical advantage from its members' knowledge of Nahr al-Bared's alleyways, dead-ends, and bomb shelters, drawing the Lebanese army into booby-trapped houses and ambushes. Moving laboriously through the debris and shelled out buildings, always wary of sudden fire or explosive devices, soldiers could fight for sixteen hours at a time and come away with little more than 20 metres of captured ground. Though strength in numbers and sheer firepower eventually told, the Lebanese army's victory came at a dire cost: some 446 lost their lives in the fighting, including 168 soldiers. To add embarrassment to injury, the army could not even claim the capture of Fatah al-Islam's leader. Though Shaker al-'Absi's second-in-command, Abu Hureira, was killed in the final phases of the fighting, 'Absi himself fled in a well-coordinated breakout on 2 September. Vanishing into the wilderness, he would later reappear in Syria, where he apparently died in 2008, the victim of an ambush by the Baathist state's security forces.[58]

But if the resounding achievement proclaimed by the army high command seemed to many Lebanese a pyrrhic victory at best, then to Nahr al-Bared's Palestinian residents it signified nothing more than abject humiliation and defeat. The camp lay in ruins, and most of its 31,000 inhabitants crowded into the northern camp of Baddawi, to which they had fled in late May and June. Though UNRWA sought to hasten the reinstallation of displaced residents, announcing in October 2007 that some 800 families had returned, it struggled to make the camp fit for habitation. Those who made it into the camp in the aftermath of the fighting found scenes of utter devastation. As the Lebanese journalist Wafic Nawari reported: 'it looks like Hiroshima, the infrastructure is all ruined with no running water, no electricity or even toilets' and 'many houses ... looted, stripped of everything'. 'The refugees who returned', Nawari continued, 'couldn't sleep ... because of the rats, the insects and the dust'. UN posters glued to the walls of burned-out houses warned of unexploded mines and munitions. The conclusion was as simple as it was unavoidable: 'the camp is not liveable'.[59] In the lead-up to an international donor conference held in June 2008, UNRWA estimated that it would cost more than $450 million to rebuild Nahr al-Bared. In the meantime, the 1,900 families that had returned lived in temporary accommodation like 'the barracks'— 'long lines of prefabricated steel units, stacked two high', crammed on the edge of the ruined camp.[60] The bulk of its inhabitants—some 2,400 families—still had not returned.[61]

The fighting shone an unwelcome spotlight on the Lebanese state. Not only did it take fifteen weeks for its army to overcome a small and obscure Islamist group. What's more, the manner in which it did so raised questions about both its fighting effectiveness and tactics. While the army was celebrated in Lebanon and its fallen 'martyrs' commemorated as heroic defenders of the nation, its heavy bombardment of Nahr al-Bared throughout the 106 days of the conflict drew condemnation from critics at home and abroad. Though the army insisted the shelling had targeted its opponents' positions, for many such heavy and persistent bombing of civilian areas could not be anything but indiscriminate.

What's more, this was an unpleasant reminder for the Lebanese state that it did not remain immune from the threat of *takfiri* ideology, with its brutal insistence that all who do not adhere to its radical interpretation of the creed are apostates to Islam. Many—Muslim and Christian alike—must have felt a shudder of fear at the sight of videos like that sent out to Lebanese television channels, in which a man claiming to be an Al-Qaeda representative condemned the military offensive on Nahr al-Bared as a 'brutal crusade'. His head wrapped about with a keffiyeh, his chest heavy with bullet pouches, he addressed Lebanon's Christians, threatening to 'rip out your hearts with bombs', covering Lebanon in 'seas of blood', if the Maronite patriarch Mar Nasrallah Sfeir did not 'hold his dogs away from our coreligionists'. 'Do not', he warned, 'be fooled by the support of the Arab apostates'. The implication was clear: Lebanon's Christians were, ultimately, on their own, and particularly vulnerable, like those of Iraq or Egypt, to jihadi ire.[62]

But those who felt that this reel, with its near-perfect depiction of an ogre-like Islamist villain, had something of the pastiche about it may not have been entirely wrong. It is not that Islamist movements were absent from Lebanon. Far from it: while groups such as Jund al-Sham were solidly implanted in the Palestinian refugee camps in the south, Salafi preachers and movements like the heterodox al-Ahbash had found receptive audiences among the young men of Beirut, Tripoli and Saida in the 1990s and early 2000s.[63] And nor is it that groups that purport to practise violence in the name of Islam do not resort to such flagrant imagery. The videos of ISIS, for instance, with their hyper-real depictions of death peopled by murderous ghouls, deploy the visual rhetoric of horror to nightmarish effect.[64] Nevertheless, many within 14 March could not quieten their suspicions about the sudden emergence of Fatah al-Islam, regarding it as the creation of the Syrian security services which, still smarting from their ejection from Lebanon, were determined to destabilise the country and reassert their presence. This was plainly the view of the head of the Internal Security Forces, the powerful Sunni general Ashraf Rifi, who claimed that Fatah al-Islam was nothing more than another name for Fatah al-Intifada, a Palestinian faction 'which works closely with the Syrian intelligence services'. Walid Jumblatt's Progressive Socialist Party followed suit. Condemning the Bikfayya attacks in a press release as the work of the 'Syrian regime', he insisted that the latter was more intent than ever upon throwing 'obstacles in the way of the international tribunal which will show the role it has played in [past] attacks'.[65] Such allegations surfaced again once the fighting in Nahr al-Bared had begun. Could it really only be a coincidence, some asked, that Fatah al-Islam should have ambushed the Lebanese army, drawing it into open confrontation, just as the UN Security Council was readying itself to vote on Resolution 1757, which provided for the establishment of an international tribunal for Lebanon?

'Absi's own uncertain past did little to assuage such doubts. Born in the West Bank, he had trained as one of the PLO's few fighter pilots in the 1970s, before joining Fatah al-Intifada, then based in Libya, in 1983. In the late 1980s, 'Absi moved to Damascus, where he became a close confidant of Fatah al-Intifada's second-in-command, Abu Khalid al-'Amleh. While 'Absi remained active within the movement, he had become, by the late 1990s, increasingly drawn to Salafi Islam. In 2000, the Syrian authorities arrested 'Absi on charges of weapons smuggling, sentencing him to three years in prison. Upon his release, he headed for Iraq, where he joined the growing Sunni insurgency against the United States occupation forces and became—so it was said—an associate of Abu Mus'ab al-Zarqawi, Al-Qaeda in Iraq's feared commander. In 2004, a Jordanian military court sentenced the two men to death in absentia for their role in the assassination of an American diplomat. The following year, 'Absi was again back in Syria. From there, he made his way across the border to Lebanon. He would remain there until he fled the country on the last day of the fighting in Nahr al-Bared.[66] For many in 14 March, there were too many unanswered questions about 'Absi's close association with Fatah al-Intifada, his time in Syria and his possible links to the Syrian intelligence services. Had they freed him to go fight in Iraq? Had they allowed him back into the country after his death sentence? And, crucially, had they aided and abetted his installation in Lebanon, providing funding and support for Fatah al-Islam? To their opponents in 8 March, however, such questions were absurd. 'Absi himself denied any link to the Syrian state. What's more, this was, in any case, a staunchly secular entity, which saw the *takfiri* movements that proliferated in the wake of the invasion of Iraq as a threat to its own existence and sense of self.

As this suggests, the elaborate displays of national unity politicians and army commanders put on throughout the conflict could do little to disguise the continuing discord between different factions. I was in Senegal that June, conducting research for my doctoral dissertation on the Lebanese of West Africa, and I attended a mass at Dakar's Maronite church, Notre-Dame du Liban, in honour of the soldiers who had died in the fighting. Surrounded by parishioners in their very finest Sunday best, all lace dresses and shiny ties, I remember being struck by the ostentatious welcome which the priest extended not just to the ambassador and consul, but also to the Shia and Sunni clerics who took their seats in the front pews. But this mass—and other ceremonies of togetherness—was but one side of the coin. On 25 May, Sayyid Hassan Nasrallah insisted Hizballah would not offer its 'cover' to a new 'war of the camps' punishing the Palestinians. 'The army was a red line', he made clear, but so was Nahr al-Bared. Should the army enter its precinct, breaking a long-held convention keeping the Lebanese state out of the camps, a general 'conflagration' could well be the result, whose victims would be 'the army, the Palestinian people and Lebanon'.[67] This stance brought rapid condemnation from all sides. While Fouad Siniora insisted that Nasrallah's failure to condemn Fatah al-Islam unequivocally was tantamount to a show of tacit support, his Future Movement colleague Ahmad Fatfat accused him of 'sowing discord' with his comments.[68] Even the Aounist deputy Ibrahim Kanaan acknowledged that the conflict had strained Aoun's alliance with Hizballah, insisting that the priority was to 'eradicate this group from the camp and the entirety of Lebanon'.[69] These differences would break out into open conflict in early May 2008, almost a year to the day after the Lebanese army took on Fatah al-Islam.

8 May 2008—the takeover

On Friday 2 May 2008, the quarrelsome and quixotic Druze leader Walid Jumblatt made a shocking allegation. Somebody had lined Beirut International Airport's Runway 17, which runs along the seashore towards the poor neighbourhood of Ouzaï, with a wall of containers. And within one of those containers, they had hidden a remote-controlled camera, recording the comings and goings along the tarmac. One of the airport's oldest, Runway 17 was used nowadays only by small private planes—many of them the jets that ferried 14 March politicians back and forth to their assignments in the Gulf and Europe. Whoever was capable of placing a surveillance camera in a spot like this, Jumblatt continued, was more than capable of 'launching a Sam-7 missile capable of destroying a civilian plane in flight'. Though he did not name the culprit, Jumblatt left it in no doubt that he thought Hizballah had installed this device to plot its next attack on 14 March. But this was not all. For Jumblatt went on to claim the party had established a private telecommunications network, connecting the southern suburbs of Beirut to the main cities and towns of southern and eastern Lebanon, Sur, Nabatiyyeh, Mashghara, Kfar Huna, Baalbek and Hermel. And this network was not completed: a new extension was now being laid down in the valley between Jbeil and the Kisrwan. This was a charge intended to trouble not just Jumblatt's Christian allies within 14 March, but also Hizballah's partners in the FPM, who all regarded this region as one of the heartlands of Christian Lebanon. Despite Hizballah's hurried dismissal of these allegations as the products of Jumblatt's 'nocturnal nightmares and inner perturbations', the fuse had been lit.[70]

Four days after Jumblatt's speech, the cabinet met to discuss his allegations, placed on the agenda by the minister of telecommunications, Marwan Hamadeh, a longstanding friend and ally of the Progressive Socialist Party's leader.[71] After a long, tense session that lasted through the night, the cabinet issued a press release in the early hours of 5 May outlining its decisions. Under no circumstances could Hizballah's actions be justified. The creation of an illicit telecommunications network and the installation of unauthorised surveillance devices at Beirut International Airport were no acts of resistance, but grave breaches of the law, which undermined the sovereignty of the Lebanese state and the security of its citizens. As such, they would be referred not just to the Lebanese courts, but also to the Arab League and the United Nations, before which the government promised to lodge a complaint about Iranian involvement. The cabinet announced the immediate removal of the head of airport security, Wafic Choucair—an officer widely considered to be sympathetic to Hizballah, which had opposed his reassignment—and the uprooting of the party's telecommunications network from all areas the party did not control militarily.[72]

By sheer coincidence, Lebanese trade unions had called a general strike for the following day, Wednesday 7 May, to protest stagnating wages and rising costs. Through Tuesday, as angry recriminations and vehement denials and counter-attacks saturated the airwaves, fears rose that demonstrations might spill over into violent confrontation with security forces. As morning broke on Wednesday and shops across Beirut kept their shutters down, tense negotiations continued between the authorities and the Lebanese confederation of trade unions. At 10:30 a.m., just half an hour before its march was due to set off, the confederation's president, Ghassan Ghosn, announced its postponement. What came to pass that day, however, was much worse. In the place of trade union demonstrators, with their banners and chants and demands, young supporters of the Future Movement, Amal and Hizballah descended into the streets. Early that morning, some of the latter had already set about dragging tyres and sprung mattresses into the entrance of the Selim Salam tunnel in central Beirut, before setting them alight, closing one of the capital's main traffic arteries. By lunchtime, several roads and intersections had been blocked off with makeshift barricades of burning tyres and bin bags, upturned skips and bits of concrete. The Damascus road, which cuts between Achrafieh— largely Christian and self-consciously bourgeois, despite its great socioeconomic diversity—and the working-class neighbourhood of Ras al-Nabaa, with its population of poor Sunnis and Shia, was closed in this fashion. So too was the road to the airport, as the Tayyuneh roundabout was filled with din and dust and smoke: trucks dumping sand brought in to build barricades; empty burned-out cars strewn across the road; hectoring, excited shouts as young men covering their mouths with keffiyehs rushed about, heady with disruption.

By mid-afternoon, the arguments and jostling and stone-throwing of the morning had turned into armed altercations between supporters of Amal and Hizballah, on the one hand, and those of the Future Movement on the other. Fighting broke out across the densely populated quarters of west Beirut, whose Sunni and Shia inhabitants were bound together in space but divided by political allegiance. In Mazra'a and Barbir, sporadic rounds of gunfire could be heard. In Nuayri, the Future Movement's office was hit by rocket fire. In Musaytbeh, clashes broke out between the men of Amal and the PSP. Reports circulated of

Amal gunmen marching through the streets of Beirut, weapons in hand. As night fell and the fires of the day petered out, a tense curfew was imposed on the Lebanese capital. Bursts of gunfire rang out here and there. The road to the airport remained closed.[73]

The next morning, Lebanon woke with a sense of foreboding. Then, shortly before 10:00 a.m., Hizballah's secretary-general, Sayyid Hassan Nasrallah took to the airwaves to address the situation. The cabinet's demands were, he made clear, 'despotic decisions' which, like the assassination of Rafiq Hariri, had inaugurated a 'new phase' in the history of Lebanon. And, just as in 2005, the country had been irrevocably changed overnight. The telecommunications network that Hizballah had established, he made clear, was not simply a phone network which it operated for its own profits, setting up a 'ministry' to collect taxes and bills from its users. These, he insisted using a Qur'anic citation, were nothing but the distortions of his opponents, 'who knew the truth but denied it'. Rather, this was an 'integral and fundamental' part of Hizballah's military apparatus. The party's opponents, he claimed, knew this all too well. What's more, this network was not new, and many of those who now made up 14 March had been happy enough to acquiesce in its existence when they had worked alongside Hizballah in the early 2000s. What, then, could have changed? The cabinet's sudden resolve to address the issue seemed to Nasrallah the product of a wider plan to diminish the forces of resistance in the region. If the 2006 war was not evidence enough, then one needed only to look at Iraq or Palestine—or indeed at Iran and Syria, treated as pariahs by the international community. This, then, was war by other means.[74]

In agreeing to pursue others' grudges and prosecute others' conflicts, 14 March had revealed not just its true 'allegiances' but also the utter moral bankruptcy of its 'methods'. Fouad Siniora was no head of state, but a 'cheap, miserable employee'. In reality, none other than Walid Jumblatt ran the government. And he, in turn, was nothing but 'Condoleezza Rice's employee'. The dismantling of Hizballah's telecommunications network had nothing to do with Lebanon's much vaunted 'sovereignty and independence', Nasrallah went on, mocking his opponents' slogans, and everything to do with a desire to strip the resistance of its weapons, drawing its leaders out into the open so that their external enemies could kill them. 'All the red lines had been crossed' on that 'dark night' when the government had taken its fateful decisions. 14 March was 'complicit in murder', and its actions tanta-mount to a declaration of war. And 'no matter who declared war' on the resistance, 'be they a father or a brother, let alone a political oppo-nent', it was 'our right to defend ourselves, our weapons, our resis-tance and our existence'. 'The hand that attempts to touch our resis-tance, to whomsoever may it belong, we will cut.' That it should belong to a mere 'gang'— *'isaba*—headed up by a man, Jumblatt, who was nothing more than 'a liar, a thief, and a murderer' who openly bragged of the crimes he had committed during the civil war and since, only made Hizballah's decision easier. [75]

Within minutes of the end of Nasrallah's speech, fighting broke out again in the streets of west Beirut. In mixed neighbourhoods like Barbur, Mar Elias, or Tariq al-Jdideh, in which one side of a thorough-fare could 'belong' to the Future Movement and the other to Amal, the staccato jackhammer sound of automatic gunfire rang out, punctuated by the dull whistle and thud of RPGs. But for all the attempts of Future Movement supporters to defend their positions, it rapidly became clear that they were outnumbered and outdone by their opponents. In a few hours, all the rumours that had been doing the rounds for months on social media of Sunni militias preparing for confrontation with Hizballah in Saudi-funded training camps unravelled. This was no even match. On the one side were ragtag groups of young men, many of them barely out of their teens, their bravado and desperation no com-pensation for their lack of preparation. On the other were ranged not just Hizballah's well-equipped and well-drilled fighters, but also men loyal to Amal and the Syrian Social Nationalist Party, unruly but expe-rienced combatants who took evident glee in the routing of their Sunni opponents. Photographs of the day's events show burly men, some well into middle age, crouching at intersections and firing RPGs and machine guns round street corners. While some are dressed in civilian gear—heavy anoraks, incongruous in the springtime, or tight black t-shirts displaying their gym-worked muscles—others wear battle fatigues or, even, in one image, uniforms of the Internal Security Forces, their chests draped in bandoliers and bullet pouches. A few have tried to hide their faces behind balaclavas or keffiyehs, but many have not bothered. They want their opponents to know who they are, and they do not fear the state's sanction. As one young man supposedly told a reporter on 7 May: 'these soldiers look like cartoon characters. We scare the Israelis. We're not going to be put off by a few Lebanese soldiers.'[76] And as Hizballah and its allies gained the upper hand, the purpose of their offensive became clear: not just to seize control of Beirut, but also to humiliate the Future Movement, punishing it for its insolent attempt to check the autonomy of the resistance. The offices of Future TV were set alight. Those of *al-Mustaqbal*, the Hariri family's newspaper, were briefly overrun by gunmen before the army regained control, while the family's palatial compound at Koreitem was hit by mortar fire.

It did not take long for Saad Hariri to take to the air. Shocked, stumbling over words, he described Beirut as a 'besieged city'. The events of that morning, he insisted, demonstrated the 'bankruptcy of the resistance'. No longer did it fight on the border with Israel, in Ayn Ata or Bint Jbeil. Instead the battalions of the resistance had morphed into 'armed groups', whose acts, 'the invasion of Beirut's streets, the destruction of houses, the arrest of citizens on the basis of their identity', recalled the dark days of the civil war. Indeed, what had befallen Beirut was *fitna*, discord within the ranks of the community. Did the Sayyid, Hariri asked, not understand that 'jettisoning the unity of Muslims is abandoning the existence of Lebanon'? He called on Nasrallah to stop short of throwing himself, and the country, into free-fall, hurtling towards civil war.[77] But these belated words of conciliation could do little to change the mood of Hariri's opponents. They were not ready to surrender their advantage for a political compromise. So Hariri did the only thing he could do, sending out word to his supporters to draw back from the streets.

By the following morning, west Beirut was firmly under the control of Hizballah, Amal and their SSNP allies. The city, usually so frantic on a Friday morning with the rush of the oncoming weekend, was eerily quiet. Here and there people could be seen hurrying to the supermarkets to buy up what they could readying themselves for the uncertain days ahead, or quitting their homes to leave the capital for a time. The streets, though, now belonged to the gunmen. This was a city under occupation, living in suspended time. Outside their offices in Hamra, heavily armed SSNP supporters took up watch, ogling and heckling and jostling anybody who happened to pass by. Amal fighters walked the streets firing off celebratory salvos in the air and pausing for press photographers. In one photo, five middle-aged men, machine guns in hand, can be seen dancing a celebratory *dabke* dance before an image of the Amal leader Nabih Berri, their faces cracked into exultant grins.

Their Sunni opponents put back in their place in humiliating fashion and reminded of the resistance's brutal efficacy, the leaders of Hizballah and Amal declared themselves ready for negotiations. On 15 May, the two parties signed up to the agreement drawn up by the Arab Ministerial Committee, which had rapidly intervened to prevent the fighting from spiralling into all-out civil war. Declaring an immediate end to hostilities, they agreed to send emissaries to Doha, where the Amir of Qatar had offered to bring together Lebanon's warring parties to broker a political solution to the crisis. Over six days, Hizballah, Amal, the Future Movement and their peers would hash out what became known upon its publication on 21 May as the Doha Agreement. All parties reiterated their renunciation of violence, their readiness to uphold 'the sovereignty of the state', and their willingness to participate in a 'national dialogue' on Lebanon's future. And, perhaps most importantly, they agreed to the election of the former army commander, Michel Sleiman, as a 'consensus president', tasked with overseeing the creation of a thirty-strong 'national unity' cabinet and the implementation of legislative elections the following year on the basis of the 1960 electoral law.[78] And, for once, the country's politicians were true to their word: with surreal and almost indecent haste, they despatched the members of their parliamentary blocs to the hemicycle, where they elected Sleiman president on 25 May. Three days later, Fouad Siniora was reappointed prime minister, eventually forming a cabinet that would include representatives of Hizballah, Amal, the SSNP and the Free Patriotic Movement, as well as the Future Movement, the Progressive Socialist Party, the Lebanese Forces and the Kata'ib. The wheel, it seemed, had come full circle, the violence of early May apparently forgotten.

But the conciliatory poses of politicians could not disguise their supporters' feelings. Indeed, many in the Future Movement found it hard to forgive their leaders' pusillanimous stance during the fighting. 'They put us on the front line of the confrontation and then abandoned us', one young fighter still smarting from the humiliation of surrender told a reporter. Another chimed in, insisting that 'Saad Hariri let us down'; 'we don't want the Future Movement any more, or the whole Hariri family', he continued.[79] For all the politicians' insistence that the crisis of May 2008 had ended well and the cataclysm of civil war averted, the Future Movement's supporters had no doubt of the outcome. Dismissing talk of *la ghalib wa la maghlub*—'no victor and no vanquished', an old phrase regularly trotted out by Lebanese politicians to describe the results of reconciliation—as so much mealy-mouthed rubbish, they knew that they had been roundly defeated, their shame matched only by the glee their opponents took in victory. This outcome would open up lasting sores. It led many to question, at least for a time, the Future Movement's leadership—and, in particular, that of Hariri, whom some came to see as a callow upstart, better suited to the playboy life to which he had been accustomed than to the brutal realities of Lebanese politics. And, of course, it only increased Sunni resentment of Hizballah, which some of its more virulent opponents took to calling *hizb al-shaytan*—'the party of Satan'—on bulletin boards and comments sections. As an acquaintance—a well-to-do member of the Sunni bourgeoisie, whose family had flourished thanks to its dealings with the Hariri family—told me once over lunch, throwing a spot of darkness into a sun-filled day: 'we'll never forgive them for what they did in 2008. Never.'

3

AL-FARAGH, OR THE VACUUM

LEBANON BETWEEN TWO PRESIDENTS

Never had the capacity of Lebanon's political life for paradox seemed more apparent than in May 2008. Barely two weeks after the country's political leaders had sent their followers into the streets to fight, pushing them into the fray with communitarian battle cries that brought Lebanon to the edge of civil war, they assembled in Doha in their best suits, heeding the invitation of the Emir of Qatar to sit down for reconciliation talks like obedient schoolboys. Political opponents arrived arm-in-arm, Syria's old friend Michel el-Murr—no young man himself—propping up an ailing Ghassan Tueni, while bitter rivals spoke to the press together, the Hizballah MP Hussein Hajj Hassan smiling benignly as Amin Gemayel addressed reporters.[1] The gathering did, it is true, lead to the election of Michel Sleiman as president of the republic. This was a success on two fronts: ending the presidential vacuum that had begun with the expiration of Emile Lahoud's term on 24 November 2007, it also consigned Lahoud to history, putting in his place a man who strove to present himself as an unaligned moderate open to all.

But any hopes that Sleiman would help to heal a bruised nation, bringing together the political factions packed into the opposing scrums of 8 March and 14 March, would prove short-lived. For despite the small measure of stability that his election brought, his years in office

99

would be defined by continued wrangling and obstructions. The issues that had paralysed Lebanese politics since 2005—the international investigation into Hariri's death and the question of Hizballah's weapons and their use, but also the thorny topics of power-sharing and electoral and constitutional reform, and of Lebanon's foreign relations and ties to Syria, Saudi Arabia, Iran and the United States—became, if anything, more divisive in these years. And the most divisive issue of all—that which had helped to define and crystallise the differences between 8 March and 14 March—became all the more complex and enswathed with accusations and counter-accusations after the outbreak of the Syrian revolution in 2011. As the fearless peaceful demonstrations of Daraa, Homs, and Hama were swallowed up in brutal repression, and as countless parties—from the Free Syrian Army to myriad local defence groups and Islamist militias—piled into the fray, Lebanese politicians found themselves having to adjust to a remarkable turnaround. Where once they had defined themselves by the stances they took on Syrian involvement in Lebanese affairs, they now found themselves defined by their views on Syria's own predicament and their own involvement, alleged or real, in the events unfolding across the border. Though all announced themselves determined to prevent the conflagration from spreading across the flimsy firewall between the two countries, the conflict could not but cast a dark shadow over Lebanese politics. But for all the fear of 'contamination' and civil war, Lebanon's political class showed little willingness or ability to modulate its repertoire. Still engaged, as they had been since 2005, in a relentless war of attrition, its members used the self-same tactics that they had long relied on, resorting to ultimatums and threats, resignations and walkouts, rhetorical one-upmanship and stalling as they attempted to harry and weary their opponents into concessions. For almost a decade, the defining phrase of Lebanese politics became *al-faragh*—the vacuum—as the country had to make do with interim prime ministers and lame duck cabinets, extended parliaments and presidential vacancies.

25 May 2008—the inauguration

The eleventh president of the Lebanese republic, Sleiman could not have done more to differentiate himself from his predecessor. He was, it is true, a military man with reported links to the obscure world of Syrian high politics. After joining the army in 1967, Sleiman had risen through the ranks to become commander of the armed forces in 1998—thanks in large part, according to the whispers that circulated at the time, to the fact his Syrian brother-in-law was Hafiz al-Assad's official spokesman.[2] Though Sleiman had taken a carefully neutral stance during the demonstrations of February and March 2005, following the command from on high to the letter by deploying troops around central Beirut's squares and avenues, but ordering his men to allow the streaming thousands through, such associations inevitably aroused the suspicion of some. Others, meanwhile, were concerned about the growing influence of the army on Lebanese political life—which, unlike that of Syria or Egypt, had remained relatively free of military men. Despite the army's questionable performance during its confrontation with Islamist fighters at Nahr al-Bared in the summer of 2007, many—particularly amongst Lebanon's Christians, always fearful of the ghoul of Islamic extremism—celebrated Sleiman. The appearance, shortly after the end of the fighting, of roadside billboards carrying his image and the simple slogan *taht amrak*—'at your command'—did little to assuage such fears, hinting at a growing idealisation of military force, at least amongst Lebanon's Christians.[3]

But in his first few weeks in office, Sleiman did his utmost to dispel these fears. His efforts to present himself as a conciliatory figure eager to bring together the nation were apparent from his opening address in parliament. Fighting back the emotion, he delivered a message of reconciliation. 'I call on you all, people and politicians, for a new beginning', he said as white doves were launched into the sky above the parliament building. 'The people have given us their confidence to fulfil their aspirations, not to afflict them with our petty political disputes.'[4] These were plain words, but soothing ones. For after three years of exhausting invective, many Lebanese found themselves feeling like sick children craving only the most bland and comforting food. The contrast with his predecessor could not have been clearer. Many had come to see Lahoud as the symbol of Syria's perversion of Lebanese politics, its way of using a band of clients to twist the letter of the law into ever more baroque and distorted forms—a thin-skinned, sneering placeman whose high-handedness and propensity for self-indulgence had become notorious. Sleiman, meanwhile, strove to appear free of personal vanity and political allegiances, a man driven by duty and whose only ambition—to serve his nation—had been fulfilled twice over. To complement this, he fostered the image of an uncomplicated, undemanding everyman, whose simple, petty bourgeois habits distinguished him from the profligate Lebanese politicians of the post-war years. In this, he was helped by the frequent presence by his side of his wife, Wafaa, an unglamorous but thoroughly respectable—and unusually active—first lady. Trained as a teacher, she dedicated much of her time in the presidential palace to education and women's issues.

There were other ways, too, in which Sleiman sought to portray his election as a new beginning for Lebanon. A week after his election, he took the highly unusual step of calling for the removal of all posters and banners depicting him or bearing his name. While grateful for the 'outpouring of support and affection' that had come his way since his election, he announced in a press release, he saw it as unnecessary. This, though, wasn't simply an attempt to signal to his detractors that he had no desire to capitalise on the broad support he enjoyed since the Doha Agreement to transform himself into a *za'im*, or political leader, building a following of his own. More than this, Sleiman sought to set a new precedent for political conduct, calling on 'Lebanese leaders to take all possible steps in a similar direction and remove pictures, banners and slogans' in order to cleanse Lebanese politics of its more noxious aspects.[5] This was in itself, of course, a move calculated to increase his popularity—though Sleiman appeared, for the moment at least, genuinely uninterested in building up a sizeable electoral following.

But if Sleiman truly did hope that such measures would help to transcend the relentless polarisation that had found its inevitable release in the street clashes of May 2008, then he was also all too aware of the magnitude of the task at hand. In his inaugural speech to parliament, he had described the resistance led by Hizballah as a 'strategic need to liberate the land that is still under occupation'—a reference to fragments of land like the Shebaa farms, which Israeli forces still occupied and which Hizballah claimed belonged to Lebanon. 'This makes it important', he had continued, 'to find a defence strategy and to benefit from the power of the resistance'.[6] This was an attempt to strike a delicate rhetorical balance. But what supporters of Hizballah might read as an attempt to curb the effectiveness of the resistance by bringing it under the supervision of a Lebanese state susceptible to outside pressure, others in the Future Movement or the Lebanese Forces might interpret as a dangerous recognition of the resistance's importance. As awkward as these stilted phrases were the interactions among foreign observers at Sleiman's inauguration. Seated close to each other, the Syrian and Saudi foreign ministers, Walid Muallem and Saoud al-Faysal, studiously ignored each other for the duration of the proceedings. The situation was made only more delicate by the late arrival of the Iranian foreign minister, who found his seat between them.[7] Throughout his presidency, Sleiman would butt up against these obstacles, both internal and external, as he attempted to devise a new 'national defence strategy' capable of satisfying both Hizballah and its opponents.

The first year of Sleiman's presidency would pass peaceably enough. In July 2008, a new national unity government was formed, with Fouad Siniora returning to the position of prime minister. In his cabinet sat many of those who had supported the sit-in that had left him trapped in the Grand Sérail for a year and a half—Hizballah and Amal members like Jawad Khalifeh and Muhammad Fneish, whose resignations in November 2006 had prepared the way for the demonstrations of the following month—but also, for the first time, members of the Change and Reform parliamentary bloc centred on the Free Patriotic Movement. After much wrangling, Aoun secured for his party and its allies five seats in the cabinet. Not least among these was the Ministry of Telecommunications, which Aoun gave to his son-in-law and heir-apparent, Gebran Bassil. Despite its apparent lack of glamour, this was considered vital not just for the lucrative contracts that might be secured in the event of privatisation, but also for its clear strategic importance in a country where a dispute over phone lines had almost led to a civil war. Their colleagues, meanwhile, included stalwarts of the 14 March movement—men like Rafiq Hariri's former financial adviser, Muhammad Chattah, or Walid Jumblatt's loyal lieutenants Ghazi Aridi and Wael Abou Faour. If any of these men found this déjà vu disconcerting, they did not say so in public. There was, though, one welcome development about the new cabinet: the inclusion of the president's ministers, politically unaffiliated men chosen by Sleiman for key portfolios. These included the aging lawyer Ibrahim Najjar, an advocate for the abolition of the death penalty and the recognition of marital rape as a criminal offence, and his younger colleague Ziad Baroud, a dynamic and well-liked civil society activist installed at the Ministry of the Interior. Despite the unseemly haste with which former enemies rushed to sit at the cabinet table, these appointments were enough cause for cheer for those Lebanese who had become desperate for good news.

I was in Lebanon for much of the summer of 2008, and I remember well the optimism of those months. For the first time since 2006, Lebanese migrants and Arab tourists had returned to Beirut, spilling out of the downtown cafés and restaurants that had lain empty for much of the period since 2005. In the night-time neighbourhoods of Hamra, Gemmayzeh, and Monot, crowds of moneyed young Lebanese jostled elbow against elbow in crowded bars. For some, at least, the Lebanon of the pre-2005 years—a place where profit and hedonism were put ahead of political concerns, and where unanswered existential questions could be put in abeyance—appeared to have returned. But looming on the horizon were the parliamentary elections of 2009. Rather than signalling the coming of a new age, these would furnish further proof of the difficulty of overcoming the polarisation that had set in after 2005, congealing Lebanese politics into set patterns.

June 2009—the election

There was much to be celebrated in these elections. For the first time, they were held on a single day, 7 June, rather than in a series of regional rounds spread out over several weeks. And for the first time, too, an independent electoral commission watched over proceedings, accompanied by a bevy of international observers from the European Union, the United States and Canada. These reforms were in line with the findings of the Boutros Commission on electoral reform, which had issued its report in 2006. In other respects, though, the elections signalled the resumption of politics as usual. Few of the Boutros Commission's other recommendations were implemented. There was no overseas voting for Lebanon's migrants, no standardised ballot paper, and no reform to the country's majoritarian voting system. Parties and blocs remained free to hand voters customised ballots, printed with their own candidates' names. And, more important still, seats in each constituency continued to be allocated on the basis of confession, with voters of all communities choosing their favoured candidates from lists of those standing. This, in effect, was a version of the first-past-the-post system designed to accommodate both constituencies with multiple seats and the constitutional requirements that voters can elect candidates of any confession, but that deputies must represent their own confessional communities. In practice, this meant that in the West Beqaa and Rashayya, for instance, with its six seats—two reserved for Sunnis, and one apiece for Shia, Greek Orthodox, Druze and Maronite deputies—the two Sunnis with the highest share of the overall vote would take the two Sunni seats, while the Druze candidate with the largest number of votes would take the seat reserved for his community, and so forth.

The bargaining in Doha did result in the adoption of a slightly modified version of the 1960 electoral law, which used the *qada* or administrative district as the basis for twenty-six relatively small constituencies across most of Lebanon.[8] The exceptions to this were in Beirut, whose nineteen quarters were drawn together into three electoral districts, and in the south and east of the country. In the south, the *qada* of Saida was divided into two districts, Saida and Zahrany. In the east, the six *qada*-s of Marj'ayun and Hasbaya, Baalbek and the Hermel, and the West Beqaa and Rashayya were amalgamated into three electoral districts.[9] On the face of it, the adoption of smaller districts followed the Boutros Commission's recommendations. This, however, was no benevolent attempt at reforming a broken system. Underlying both the norm and the—numerous—exceptions was a crude confessional calculus. Smaller districts in the north and Mount Lebanon satisfied Christian political leaders who complained—sometimes in cipher, at other moments quite openly—of their being forced to rely in larger multi-confessional electoral districts on Muslim voters whose interests, they feared, might be inimical to their own. This ensured the existence of mono-confessional districts like Bcharreh—the smallest of all in demographic terms, whose 45,000 registered voters elected two Maronite deputies—the Koura, with its three Greek Orthodox deputies, or the Kisrwan, with its five Maronite deputies. A similar logic underwrote the separation of Saida and Zahrany, a split that protected the interests of Sunni and Shia powerbrokers in the region. In other districts, like Marj'ayun-Hasbaya and the West Beqaa–Rashayya, this logic was turned on its head. Here, the imperative was to dilute the Shia vote to bolster 14 March's candidates against their Hizballah and Amal opponents.

Despite such concerted gerrymandering, many refused to see the result as a foregone conclusion. Speculation focused in particular on how the two largest parties in parliament, the Future Movement and the Free Patriotic Movement, would fare. Saad Hariri and Michel Aoun, analysts argued, had frittered away their popularity, the one by gravely mishandling his confrontation with Hizballah, the other by siding with the party despite growing misgivings among Christians about its weapons and strategy. Indeed, some went so far as to predict a slim 8 March victory, overturning the parliamentary order that had prevailed in 2005. Whatever the case, the campaign was fiercely fought. In the general absence of programmes and policies—for few were the parties that bothered with publishing manifestos ahead of the election—the election was fought on the terrain of lofty principles and foreign alliances and misalliances. Thus, Hizballah urged supporters to 'resist with your vote', showing their support for its values at the ballot box. The Future Movement, meanwhile, called on its own followers to put 'Lebanon first'—ironically, the old slogan of the 'sovereignist' Christian parties, which Saad Hariri had recently adopted for his parliamentary bloc. Competition was particularly bitter in Christian areas of the country like Jbeil and Batroun, or mixed districts like Baabda, where candidates traded in highly charged sectarian accusations and counter-accusations. While FPM supporters portrayed the Lebanese Forces and the Kata'ib as lackeys of the Hariri family and its Saudi patrons, on whose largesse they had been rendered utterly dependent, their opponents accused Aoun's supporters of propping up Hizballah's armed hegemony—and, through it, Iranian and Syrian encroachments on Lebanon's sovereignty. Whether they portrayed the other as servants of Wahhabism on Saudi retainer or agents of *vilayet-i faqih* and Iranian theocracy, each side painted their opponents as a traitor to the Christian community and the Lebanese nation. Far more than an electoral contest, this was presented as an existential struggle.[10]

In the event, though, the elections held fewer surprises than some might have expected. 14 March maintained its parliamentary majority, winning 71 of the 128 seats up for grabs—only one less than in 2005. Though big beasts like the Future Movement or Jumblatt's Progressive Socialist Party had, on the face of it, lost seats, they had in many cases given these up to their smaller allies within 14 March, in their efforts to shore up this broad alliance. In Jumblatt's electoral stronghold in the Chouf mountains, for instance, one of the three Maronite seats on offer was taken—as it had been in 2005—by the Lebanese Forces' Georges Adwan while the National Liberal Party leader Dory Chamoun took the second; only one was kept for Jumblatt's affiliate, Elie Aoun. But if Christian parties like the Lebanese Forces and the Kata'ib had cause to celebrate—each gained two seats, bringing their respective totals to eight and five—so too did the Free Patriotic Movement, which increased its share of deputies from fifteen to nineteen.[11]

Indeed, the election's results served only to confirm the deep polarisation of Lebanese politics. The final count was more or less evenly split between the two main blocs: 14 March won 50.4 per cent of the vote, and 8 March 49.6 per cent, and each secured a majority of seats in thirteen of the country's twenty-six electoral districts. In most districts, one or another alliance took a clean sweep of seats—in Baabda, Jbeil, the Kisrwan, or the Beqaa and Hermel, 8 March; in the Shuf, Tripoli, Bcharreh or two of Beirut's three districts, 14 March. Only the unequal distribution of seats among the country's various districts accounted for 14 March's relatively sizeable majority.

What's more, the direction of the vote was largely predictable, reproducing patterns established in 2005—if not earlier. Only in two or three constituencies were there upsets—in Batroun, where Gebran Bassil failed to win a seat in a fierce contest against the Lebanese Forces and the independent Maronite deputy Boutros Harb, and in Zahle and the West Beqaa–Rashayya, where bitter campaigns resulted in 14 March victories.[12] But even in such places, the results may not have been quite as unexpected as they appeared on the night, as the final counts filtered in to TV stations and news websites, for the first time giving Lebanese viewers and readers a comprehensive sense of the new lay of the land.

For it was not long before allegations surfaced of systematic vote-buying on all sides. In keeping with the tenor of their electoral campaigns, 14 March and 8 March each accused the other of using foreign money to influence the elections' outcome. Allegations swirled about of vast shipments of Saudi dollars funnelled into Lebanon by Hariri and other Future Movement leaders, or of Qatari, Iranian and Syrian funds piling into the campaign chests of Hizballah, Amal and the FPM. Some of the evidence appeared to bear this out. An unnamed Saudi source confirmed to a *New York Times* reporter that 'We're putting a lot into this ... we're supporting candidates running against Hezbollah, and we're going to make Iran feel the pressure'. When asked to quantify Saudi Arabia's contribution, he put it in the hundreds of millions of dollars. One candidate was brave, or foolish, enough to go on the record about these backroom deals—Ahmad al-Assaad, the 46-year-old heir to an old Shia political dynasty fighting an ultimately doomed campaign to regain some of the dominance his family had lost with the rise of first Amal, then Hizballah. Saudi Arabia, he was happy enough to confirm, was a 'significant source of support' for his electoral efforts. 'I need tools to fight back' against Hizballah and Amal with their funds and security services, he told the *New York Times*, 'and if the Saudis have an interest in building a state here, why shouldn't I take advantage of that?'[13] Others in 14 March seem to have benefited from similar largesse. One candidate I spoke to in the wake of the election estimated he had been given $100,000 for his electoral costs. As is often the way in Lebanon, one euphemism masked another. For we might surmise that, besides the usual roadside posters, placards and banners, these 'costs' largely consisted of *khidmat shakhsiyya*, or 'personal services'—the catch-all term the Lebanese use for the material assistance voters receive in exchange for their support. This can range from bunches of rumpled dollars or cheques to booklets of fuel coupons, mobile phone top-up cards, to more extensive support such as jobs or assistance with medical bills or school and university fees—the exceptional patterns of electioneering shading into the regular, sustained routines of clientelism.[14]

In 2009, these services also extended to free flights from Dubai, West Africa, or the United States for those willing to barter their votes for a holiday back home. For Lebanese migrants, unable to vote abroad, represented a significant means of tipping the balance one way or another—if enough of them could be enlisted to do so. Some panicked observers asserted that as many as 120,000 Lebanese had been flown in to cast their vote in key districts up and down the country. Other estimates, while more conservative, were still significant. The market research company Information International calculated on the basis of arrival data at Beirut International Airport that some 48,000 migrants had returned for the holiday season, while the actuarial firm Muhanna & Co. put the number at 25,000. But though the actual numbers would remain a 'mystery even to the most sophisticated actuarial modelling tool', it was clear that many had been offered incentives of the kind one 'Lebanese professional' living in Dubai described.[15] While sitting in a restaurant one day, he remembered, he was approached by a group of fellow migrants who knew that he hailed from the Christian town of Zahle in the Beqaa, a key electoral battleground. Asking him whom his family voted for, 'they told me that I know people who would vote' for their candidate, they would 'provide them with everything'. It wasn't long before he 'got a call from the other camp and the woman also gave me a sales pitch—offered to fly me to Beirut, take care of expenses and transport on voting day'.[16] This was yet another way in which—perhaps deliberate—foot-dragging on reform had created gaps and loopholes in the electoral system: the failure to provide overseas voting encouraged candidates and movements to view migrants as a crucial asset up for grabs, reserves to be deployed in an electoral battle.

But, as the political scientist Daniel Corstange has demonstrated, these practices were not the monopoly of any one faction or sect. On the basis of data gathered from 2,500 interviewees across Lebanon, Corstange estimated that around 26 per cent of Lebanon's resident voters freely confessed to having sold their votes when asked directly. When asked indirectly, the percentage rose to 55 per cent. Just as significantly, Corstange found that the proportion did not vary much between major confessional groups, despite the impression that electoral corruption was most widespread amongst the Sunnis, flush with the Hariris' money. While 54 per cent of Sunnis appeared to have sold their votes in 2009, 56 per cent of Christians and 64 per cent of Shia had seemingly done the same. What varied was merely the willingness of respondents to admit to these transactions when asked directly. Furthermore, this suggested that vote-buying was just as widespread in predominantly Shia regions of the south, where the victory of Hizballah and Amal candidates was a foregone conclusion, as in sharply contested districts like Zahle or Batroun—a reminder that more was at stake than electoral seats. In safe districts like Nabatiyyeh and Sur, it was getting the voters out that mattered. For as Corstange astutely pointed out, a low turnout could all too easily signal a worrying lack of engagement and dwindling support for the resistance.[17] That the turnout rate mattered just as much, at times, as the final result shows just what was at stake here: the ability to claim that one's own party represented and spoke for the majority of the Lebanese. The problem, of course, was that the results—despite the substantial majority 14 March enjoyed thanks to Lebanon's particular variation on the first-past-the-post system—were so evenly poised that both 14 March and 8 March could, and did, claim to be the true representatives of the Lebanese people.

March 2009—the tribunal

The suspicion that the elections had failed to resolve Lebanon's enduring political deadlock was confirmed by the difficulties Saad Hariri faced in his efforts to form a government. Though tasked with doing so on 27 June, barely three weeks after he had been confirmed as the leader of the parliamentary majority, his cabinet was not announced until 9 November—almost five months later. The delay was in part the product of the usual traffic of influence that follows each Lebanese election, with various factions angling for ministries they regard as particularly useful to their clientelist ends or as vested with particular symbolic weight. In this particular instance, it was the FPM that held firm to its positions, insisting both that Aoun's designated successor at the head of the movement, Gebran Bassil, remain in the cabinet, and that the party should control the ministries of telecommunications and energy.

These two ministries mattered to Aoun and his followers for a complex stew of reasons. Poor telephone lines and interrupted electricity stood, for many, for the ineptitude of the Lebanese state and the political class that controlled it, turning its ministries into engine-rooms of clientelism. For the FPM, they offered the opportunity to live up to their reformist creed, showing their efficiency and competence in government by addressing swiftly issues no previous government had resolved successfully. But there was another dimension, one linked to the confessional and partisan realignments of the 1990s. For Lebanon's blackouts and crackling phone lines underscored, in the eyes of many FPM members—both high up and rank-and-file—the extent to which the years of Hariri's dominance had been a dark episode in Lebanon's history, his talk of reconstruction an empty promise which disguised his corruption and confessional favouritism. Many staunch supporters of the general remembered the 1990s as a bleak time. Persecuted for their political views and forced to live without their exiled leader, they were also—so they insisted—consistently passed over for contracts in favour of their Sunni competitors; undercut and over-taxed, they had borne the brunt of the changes that had come in with Hariri's rise to power. Now, at long last, the time had come for them to claim back a share of political and economic power from what they described as *jama'at Hariri*, 'Hariri's gang'. And, as this suggests, the FPM's refusal to budge on these two ministries was also born of self-interested con-siderations, for any restructuring of electricity supply or telephone and internet networks presented potential opportunities. In the end, the obdurate general got what he wanted, showing again that his favoured tactic—stubbornly repeating the same demand until his flagging oppo-nents simply gave way out of sheer exhaustion and frustration—could reap reward. Though unpopular both with many Lebanese and—one suspects—with his fellow politicians, Bassil became energy minister. Charbel Nahas—an engineer known both for his fondness for reform-ist pronouncements and for his uncommon ideological journey, from communism, through a brief flirtation with Rafiq Hariri in the 1980s and 1990s, and now to partnership with the FPM—took on Bassil's old job at the Ministry of Telecommunications.

But another matter, too, held up negotiations—that of the composi-tion of the government. 8 March insisted on a 'blocking third'—in other words, on having the capacity to veto any cabinet decision it opposed. 14 March, for its part, would not countenance such obstruc-tion, which got in the way of the business of government. At stake here were not simply competing definitions of the Lebanese political sys-tem, one based on consensus rule, the other on a more majoritarian understanding of executive power. For who held the final say in cabinet would determine not just the course of domestic policy—such as it was—but also the government's stance on the international tribunal charged with prosecuting those accused of assassinating Rafiq Hariri.

This, of course, had already pushed one government into a prolonged coma, when the resignation of Shia ministers from Fouad Siniora's cabinet in November 2006, in protest at Siniora's insistence on endorsing the UN's proposal for the tribunal, had plunged Lebanon into an eighteen-month-long constitutional crisis. Now the exact same issue threatened to make another government stillborn. For, after much delay and uncertainty, the Special Tribunal for Lebanon (STL), as it came to be known, had finally opened its doors in The Hague on 1 March 2009.

The tribunal sat uneasily at the heart of political debate, a constant source of friction and misunderstanding. While 14 March insisted that only pursuing those guilty of Hariri's assassination could end the era of impunity and bring closure to a country desperate for truth and justice, 8 March clung doggedly to its view that the tribunal would only pit the Lebanese against each other, sowing pandemonium and serving the interests of inimical foreign states—not least Israel, still smarting from the 2006 war. In the event, the deadlock was eventually broken through a fudge of sorts: a national unity government of thirty ministers—fifteen for the majority, ten for the opposition, and five for the president, including the neutral Shia minister Adnan Hussein. While President Sleiman emerged strengthened from the process, with his image as a conciliatory figure burnished and with what appeared a solid block of moderate, unaligned ministers to his name, 14 March could believe it held the majority, while 8 March remained confident that it could secure what the Lebanese press christened a 'third + one' veto by drawing one of Sleiman's ministers to its side. In other words, the problem was simply pushed downstream, and the solution deferred to another day.

For the investigation into Hariri's assassination continued to hover over Lebanese politics like a dark cloud pregnant with rain, much as it had done since 2005. This had always been an international affair—to the delight of those who regarded the Lebanese state as a corroded entity, eaten from within by years of Syrian influence and corruption, but to the dismay of those, like Hizballah, who regarded this as tantamount to intervention. Soon after Hariri's death, the Lebanese authorities had called in foreign investigators to assist with their inquiries. In late February 2005, Kofi Annan despatched a team led by the deputy commissioner of the Irish police, Peter FitzGerald, to help with the investigation. In March, a Swiss forensic team had arrived in Beirut to conduct an examination of the crime scene at the St George, amidst fears that the initial investigation had—perhaps intentionally—missed crucial clues and destroyed vital evidence. In April, UNSC Resolution 1595 was passed, establishing a UN International Independent Investigation Commission, which would join forces with the Lebanese authorities as they continued with their inquiries. Searching around for an investigator with experience of complex cases of this kind, Annan appointed the German prosecutor Detlev Melhis, who had spent a decade investigating the 1983 bombing that had torn through the French consulate in west Berlin, killing one person.[18] Melhis, who arrived in Beirut in early May, energetically set about making up for lost time. Between mid-June and early October, thirty investigators of seventeen different nationalities gathered up 16,711 pages of documents. These included 244 witness statements, 22 suspect statements, and 293 investigation notes. The investigators also seized 453 crime scene exhibits.[19] But the Lebanese and international press was less interested in the minutiae of the investigation than in the case it was building.

In October 2005, Melhis published his first report. A clear indication of what its contents would be had come on 30 August, when the Lebanese authorities had arrested four generals: the head of Lahoud's presidential guard, Mustafa Hamdan; the head of the General Security Directorate, Jamil al-Sayyed; Ali al-Hajj, the head of Interior Security; and the head of Military Intelligence, Raymond Azar. But the report's findings were still shocking in their concision and clarity. 'There is probable cause to believe that the decision to assassinate former Prime Minister Rafik Hariri', Mehlis and his team wrote, 'could not have been taken without the approval of top-ranked Syrian security officials and could not have been further organised without the collusion of their counterparts in the Lebanese security services'. This single sentence sent shockwaves through the Lebanese political scene, comforting those who had believed since February 2005 that the Baathist regime in Damascus had ordered Hariri's death. To add fuel to the flames, the report was first released to journalists as a Word document, still showing track changes. Where the final, redacted version, spoke only of unnamed 'top-ranked Syrian security officials' and their Lebanese counterparts—itself a strong enough claim—the unbowdlerised version explicitly named Bashar al-Assad's brother Maher, their brother-in-law Assef Shawkat, the former head of Syrian military intelligence Hassan Khalil, the head of the Syrian General Intelligence Directorate, Bahjat Suleiman, and the head of the Lebanese General Security Directorate, Jamil al-Sayyed. Whether it was a dire mistake born of ineptitude or Melhis' attempt to increase pressure on the Syrian regime by leaking names he had been encouraged to keep out of the public eye for the moment, this 'gaffe' only further divided opinion on the Melhis investigation. To some it was leading a canny judicial campaign against a criminal regime. To others, Melhis was at best a gullible fool who had let himself become the instrument of those intent on undermining Lebanese and Syrian sovereignty, and at worst a Trojan horse for these nefarious foreign interests.

It did not help that much of Melhis' case appeared to rest on the testimony of two witnesses. The first of these was a man of 'Syrian origin but resident in Lebanon, who claims to have worked for the Syrian intelligence services in Lebanon'. It was this source who confirmed what others' evidence only suggested: that 'approximately two weeks after Security Council Resolution 1559 ... senior Lebanese and Syrian officials decided to assassinate Rafik Hariri'. The cabal had worked out their plan of action in a series of meetings held either side of the border in late 2004 and early 2005. These secretive conversations had taken place in hotel boardrooms, security offices and on several occasions, the witness claimed, at the Syrian presidential palace itself. But this source's allegations did not stop there. In the days running up to Hariri's assassination, he had visited several Syrian bases in Lebanon. At one such base, in the mountain town of Hammana, he had seen a white Mitsubishi Canter van—the same model and colour as that used in the assassination. A white tarpaulin had been stretched across its flatbed. This van, which had been driven from Syria to Hammana in late January, left the base on the morning of 14 February, just hours before Hariri's killing. On 13 February, the same witness had driven another senior Syrian officer to the St George on what he 'subsequently understood' to have been a 'reconnaissance exercise'. On the day of the killing, the witness was 'in the vicinity of the St George' when he received a phone call from a senior Syrian intelligence official, who asked him where he was. On hearing the witness' answer, the official advised him 'to leave the area immediately'. What's more, the witness told Melhis' team that Jamil al-Sayyed and two other high-ranking Lebanese security officials with close ties to Damascus, General Raymond Azar and General Mustafa Hamdan, had 'cooperated closely' in the assassination. Keeping in communication with Rustum Ghazali and the head of the Popular Front for the Liberation of Palestine–General Command, Ahmad Jibril, Hamdan and Azar 'had provided logistical support, including money, telephones, cars, walkie-talkies, pagers, weapons, identification cards, etc.'.[20]

The second of the witnesses rolled out in Mehlis' report was a low-ranking Syrian officer, Muhammad Zuhair Saddik, who had agreed to give evidence to the commission. Saddik claimed in his testimony that killing Hariri had first been suggested by the Lebanese Baath party and its leader, Nasser Kandil, who had grown increasingly frustrated at Lahoud's inability to freeze his powerful opponent out of the 'political scene'. Over the course of several months, 'seven senior Syrian officials and four senior Lebanese officials' had met in Lebanon to plot the attack, first in Saddik's apartment in Khaldeh, and then in another flat in the southern suburbs of Beirut. Several of the plotters had visited the area around the St George to stake out their ground. Saddik also testified that he had seen the Mitsubishi Canter van in a camp at the Syrian town of Zabadani, just across the border from Lebanon, where he had watched mechanics emptying out its doors and the sides of its flatbed to fill them with explosives. These, he had been told, were of a special kind only used by jihadis in Iraq, in order to deflect attention onto Islamic extremists. If to some, all of this seemed incontrovertible evidence of the carelessness and callousness of Syria and its Lebanese underlings, to others the testimony of these all-knowing, ever-present super-witnesses seemed so convenient as to stretch the bounds of credibility.

Equally unhelpful was the perception that the international support for the investigation was—at least in part—the product of personal vendettas waged by leaders in Paris and Riyadh. Hariri had not just been a trusted confidant of the Saudi king, who had helped to make him 'one of the major Sunni leaders of the Middle East', as one Western diplomat described him in 2008. More than this, he had been a close personal friend to Jacques Chirac, lending him his splendid *hôtel par-*

ticulier in Paris and, some said, offering him the use of his private jet to take Chirac's daughter, gravely ill with anorexia, for treatment. When the Lebanese political commentator Paul Salem told the American journalist Joshua Hammer in 2008 that Hariri's assassination had 'stirred up personal animosity' between Riyadh and Damascus and that 'Abdullah still holds Assad responsible for it', he was doing no more than restating conventional wisdom.[21] How could the investigation's findings be trusted, its detractors asked, when it was so patently the product not just of Chirac and Abdullah's grief and anger, but also of the vainglorious and grand delusions of American strategists?

But if 8 March's spokesmen relentlessly denigrated the commission as an instrument of great power strategy, others maintained that the diplomatic pressures that had initially allowed the UN investigation free rein had, in time, come to hold back its work. His reputation damaged by the botched release of his initial findings and his life facing a number of credible threats, Melhis was to publish just one more report, in December 2005, before stepping down. In a sign of his growing frustration, much of this second report was taken up with an account of his efforts to secure Syrian cooperation. In January 2006, the Belgian prosecutor Serge Brammertz replaced Melhis. Where the latter had been an ostentatiously public figure, a 'sensationalist' in a hurry who had gone out of his way to court the press, Brammertz was a reticent, cautious figure, happy to recede into the shadows, working quietly away at his highly protected base at the Monteverde Hotel, up in the mountains above Beirut. As one Western diplomat unkindly observed, 'Brammertz was so absent from the public eye that he projected the sense that nothing was happening'. What evidence he did release did little to dispel this impression. His reports were highly technical affairs, which shrank away from Melhis' bolder claims, presenting individuals the latter had named as suspects as mere 'persons of interest'. Political support for Brammertz in Lebanon soon ebbed away, as 14 March figures began to mutter about his uncooperative attitude and lack of initiative. While Brammertz himself was the target of much of this criticism, it was made all the sharper by fears that the international tide had turned and that American officials, in particular, had lost much of their initial enthusiasm for the commission.[22]

The blithe optimism of Beltway neoconservatives who had hoped that the fall of Saddam Hussein would soon be followed by that of Bashar al-Assad had begun to fade, by 2006, into a sour fear of sectarian conflict and growing Iranian influence in the region. In February of that year, the Shia 'Askari mosque in Samarra, Iraq, with its distinctive golden dome, was destroyed in a massive explosion. For weeks afterwards, Iraq's cities witnessed murderous reprisals, as Shia militias slaughtered Sunnis and thousands fled their homes. And while Shia 'death squads' dragged Sunnis out of cars and hospital beds to kidnap and kill them, more and more Sunni jihadis detonated their suicide bombs in markets and job queues, wreaking destruction. As they saw their delusions collapse before their eyes, American officials contracted what one member of the UN's investigation commission called 'Iraq syndrome'. 'When you talk to American diplomats about Syria being involved at the top', this figure explained to Joshua Hammer, 'the reaction is hedging'. This equivocation was born of the fear 'Syria could become another Iraq'. Swayed by theories that saw Assad's regime as one part of the 'Shia crescent' drawn across the Middle East, from Iran through Iraq to Lebanon and the Mediterranean coast, they continued to regard it with suspicion. But at the same time, they feared that bringing a case against Assad's closest associates—or even the Syrian president himself—might sow confessional disorder, further destabilising the region. As one diplomat told Hammer, 'Imagine if the Syrian regime is proved to have planned and executed this assassination. What will the Sunni majority in Syria think about a leadership that took out one of the major Sunni leaders of the Middle East?'²³ And another vicious confessional civil war that many would blame on their meddling was something the Americans could do without for the time being.

By the time a 'tired' Brammertz stepped down after two years in January 2008, to be replaced by the Quebecois prosecutor Daniel Bellemare, the geostrategic considerations had changed yet again. In 2007, Assad had sent discreet feelers out to Ehud Olmert about the possibility of resuming indirect negotiations between Syria and Israel. The Israeli prime minister, still bruised by the discomfiture of the 2006 war and determined to curb Hizballah's power, proved receptive. Backchannel talks started up again, focusing on a simple but elusive proposition: Israel would abandon the Golan Heights; in return, Syria would recognise Israel's existence, move away from Iran, and curb its support for Hizballah and Hamas. Assad had begun to come back in from the cold. Flaunting his capacity to control Hizballah and Hamas—the one reliant on arms supplies funnelled across the Syrian border to Lebanon, the other headquartered in Damascus and dependent on the goodwill of the Baathist state—he began once again to present himself as 'a peacemaker'. As a Syrian exile told Hammer, 'he believes that if he takes care of politics, the tribunal will be finished'. In other words, Assad would become a model neighbour. Mending his errant ways, he would keep his guard dogs on the leash and stop throwing his trash over the fence into Lebanon, but help instead to patch up the rows next door, using his enduring influence to shore up the country's fragile stability. This was a shtick of which many in Lebanon were deeply wary, but it appeared to work on at least some foreign leaders. In July 2008, the French president, Nicolas Sarkozy, invited Assad to Paris to attend the EuroMediterranean summit. The implications for the work of the UN commission were clear. As one UN official put it, many of its members feared that 'the investigation will be sold down the river, or it will lead to a minor official being indicted'.[24]

All the while, however, the work of the UNIIIC continued, while the Security Council laid the foundations of an international tribunal, after the possibility of a court operating in Lebanon had been abandoned because of security risks. In March 2006, UNSCR 1664 was passed, calling on Kofi Annan to consult the Lebanese government on the establishment of an international tribunal. In October 2006, the Security Council sent the Lebanese government a draft plan. On 23 January 2007, Fouad Siniora's hamstrung government agreed to the formation of this tribunal. In May, however, Siniora wrote to the secretary-general to explain that Nabih Berri had refused to convene parliament to put this agreement to a vote—the opposition once again using every resource it had to stonewall a measure it deemed unacceptable. On 30 May, the Security Council took the highly unusual step of creating the Special Tribunal for Lebanon under Chapter VII of the UN Charter, which authorised it to take appropriate measures to 'restore international peace and security'. UNSCR 1757 and its annexes set out the modalities and statutes of the Special Tribunal for Lebanon. An odd hybrid entity under the joint aegis of the Lebanese state and the UN, this would be located on foreign soil but apply Lebanese law. The Lebanese government undertook to pay 49 per cent of its operating costs, and the UN 51 per cent. Four of its eleven judges would be Lebanese, but its prosecutor would be a foreigner, who would pick up the work of the UN investigation. Indeed, the court's first prosecutor was also the last head of the UNIIIC—Daniel Bellemare.

As all knew too well, however, setting up the tribunal was only half the work. The Syrian exile who spoke to Joshua Hammer in 2009 predicted that 'it will have financial problems, it will have trouble bringing people to the court. You will hear, "This one vanished, this one was killed, this one is a liar." At the end, the tribunal will achieve nothing.'[25] His prediction would prove at least partially accurate. In April 2009, Bellemare asked for the release of the 'four generals'—Mustafa Hamdan, Ali al-Hajj, Raymond Azar, and Jamil al-Sayyed—detained by the Lebanese authorities in August 2005, and held without charge since then in the military prison at Roumieh. After four years, the investigation had no suspects in custody. Their release was greeted with jubilation, as fireworks were let off, shots fired into the sky, sheep slaughtered, and sweets handed out on the streets of their hometowns and villages. Saad Hariri was quick to insist that their release was of no consequence. Sounding as eager to reassure himself as his supporters, he insisted he did not 'feel one iota of disappointment or fear over the fate of the international tribunal'. The release of the generals was not a sign of failure, but an 'indication that the international tribunal has started work and it will reveal the truth'. 'This court is here to stay', Hariri emphasised, 'and is not up for bargaining'.[26]

It was not long, however, before Jamil al-Sayyed—whom Melhis had named in his initial, unedited report as one of the planners of Hariri's killing—went on the attack. In an interview with Al-Jazeera on 18 May 2010, he accused Mehlis' investigators of attempting to blackmail him. Almost five years earlier, on 31 May 2005, he alleged, the head of the investigating team, Gerhard Lehmann, had visited him at home to ask him to pass on a message to Bashar al-Assad: 'Syria will set up a local inquest, which will choose a significant victim. This person will confess to having committed Rafiq al-Hariri's assassination for personal or material reasons that have nothing to do with the regime. Then, this person will be found dead, having committed suicide'. What's more, Sayyed told Al-Jazeera that he had been promised several 'presents' to sweeten the deal—not least a 'ministerial portfolio'.[27] As with so many conspiracies, this took fact as its dough and fiction as its yeast. After all, was it not true that Ghazi Kanaan—Syria's old proconsul in Lebanon, replaced by Rustom Ghazali in 2002—had been found dead, from an apparently self-inflicted gunshot wound, weeks after Mehlis' team had interviewed him? The day after his interview, Sayyed filed a suit in the French courts for defamation and obstruction of justice against Detlev Mehlis and the former Lebanese ambassador to Paris, Johnny Abdo.[28] Though many dismissed Sayyed as an embittered crank intent on throwing a spanner in the works, this was another unwanted bad news story for the beleaguered investigation.

As some had predicted, the tribunal's case against Damascus and its Lebanese henchmen appeared to be unravelling. Few, though, could have foreseen the next twist in this long and sorry tale. In May 2009, an article appeared in the German magazine *Der Spiegel*, which claimed 'that the Hariri case is about to take a sensational turn'. After more than four years, 'the investigation has yielded new and explosive results ... that it was not the Syrians, but instead special forces' of Hizballah 'that planned and executed the sensational attack'. Beneath the crude tabloid prose there lay a grave charge indeed: Lebanese security officers under the command of Captain Wissam Eid had painstakingly worked through data from mobile phone masts, isolating eight phones that had been used again and again in the area of the St George in the days leading up to Valentine's Day 2005 and on the day of Hariri's death. Activated six weeks before the attack, they were used only to communicate with each other—and none were used again after 14 February. This was what the investigators—or sensationalist German journalists—called the 'first circle of hell': the phones of the team that had carried out the attack on Hariri. Around them could be traced a 'second circle of hell'—twenty phones used in close proximity to those of the hit team, and often in the area around the St George. These had been identified as belonging to the 'operational' arm of Hizballah—in part because one man, 'Abd al-Majid Ghamlush, had slipped his guard and called his girlfriend from one of the 'hot phones'. Besides its schlocky prose, the piece was not without its inaccuracies— Jamil al-Sayyed, for instance, was named as Jamal, while the Beirut suburb of Hazmiyyeh, where Wissam Eid had been killed in a car bomb in January 2008, was rendered as Hasmiya.[29] But for all its small errors of fact and lack of subtlety, the piece caused an uproar in Lebanon.

It was not long before fears about what the tribunal might turn up and how those accused might react began to reshape Lebanon's already dynamite-scarred political terrain. In August 2009, Walid Jumblatt announced his departure from 14 March. One of the stalwarts of this coalition since its creation, he now sought to distance himself from its work. 'Our alliance with [14 March] forces was driven by necessity', he declared. It was now time to return to the leftist, pan-Arab policies of old, abandoning the 'sectarian, tribal' politics that had come to characterise the alliance, and to atone for his decision to draw close to the American neoconservatives who had advocated the creation of a new Middle East. His meetings with the Bush administration, he now said, were a 'black point in the [PSP's] white history'. It was not the party's 'policy to meet with those who have spread chaos in the Middle East'. Circumstances only had dictated this rapprochement—not least Jumblatt's desire to see the truth out in Hariri's assassination. But the circumstances had now changed, and Jumblatt was no longer quite so certain of Syria's guilt, nor as willing to think of the special tribunal as a boon to a bereaved country. In fact, the STL was a 'synonym for nightmare'. 'Looking back', he wrote in his weekly column in the party newspaper, *al-Anba*', 'I think I committed the sin of voicing too many anti-Syrian slogans'.[30]

Jumblatt's defection was a blow for 14 March. He had worked closely alongside Saad Hariri to provide a countervailing force to Syria's allies in Lebanon, just as he had worked alongside his father to prop up Syrian rule in the 1990s. But for many, it did not come as a surprise. Always a savvy strategist careful to tack to the prevailing winds, Jumblatt knew that Syria was no longer the pariah that it had been in 2004–5. The neoconservatives' dreams had resulted only in Iraq's destruction, and Bush was now gone, replaced in office by a younger, more cautious president, less eager to launch himself heedlessly into foreign adventures. Speaking from Al-Azhar in Cairo, Obama had called in June 2009 for 'a new beginning between the United States and Muslims around the world; one based upon mutual interest and mutual respect', rather than force, the imposition of freedom and the waging of a war without end.[31] These emollient words would be drowned out, in time, by the quiet hum of drones above Yemeni, Pakistani and Somali encampments, Obama's preferred mode of engagement with the Islamic world. But it was clear that the more blatant tactics of the early 2000s were out of favour: no longer would dictators' statues be brought low triumphantly in the public squares of foreign capitals, and all talk of toppling Assad faded away. If Obama was keen to engage the Syrian regime, and even the Saudi king was rumoured to be willing to resume relations, what political capital could be gained from anathematising it?

Mingled with these geostrategic considerations were more immediate domestic ones. Jumblatt's men had shown resolve in May 2008, pushing back their more numerous Hizballah and Amal opponents. But he had been concerned at the way in which the fighting had opened up divisions in the Druze community, threatening to pit his own followers against those of his rival, Talal Arslan, a member of 8 March. And what's more, he had resented being left alone to face down Hizballah and Amal, as the Future Movement's feeble efforts had rapidly petered out. He and his community had been caught in the middle of a fight they had not picked. Now, as the revelations leaking out of The Hague threatened to throw Lebanon's delicate equilibrium into jeopardy and political commentators began to talk seriously of another conflict between Sunnis and Shia, Jumblatt feared that the Druze would again find themselves in the midst of a conflict not of their own making. It was time to sever his ties to 14 March, before it was too late.

Jumblatt's decision, though, could hardly have come as a surprise. Back in April 2009, someone had leaked grainy mobile phone footage of Jumblatt speaking to a group of Druze men of religion. Surrounded by these old men with their luxuriant white beards, Jumblatt opened 'the subject of the Shia' as he sipped from a cup of Turkish coffee. Britain, he told his listeners, 'is opening up to Hizballah. America is talking to Iran'. But if these global realignments mattered, then so did local power relations. 'We were besieged in Beirut', 'when you saw that guy, what's his name, Samir Geagea', Jumblatt went on—groping dismissively for the name of his nominal ally, once a bitter foe in the mountain war of the 1980s—it was impossible not to realise that 'the Christians' were 'hoping we'd engage with the Shia', letting the Druze take on Hizballah while 'they watched on'. If this was unsurprising coming from 'the Christians', who hoped that such a conflict would rid them of two sectarian rivals, more disappointing was the fact that 'even some of the Sunnis' were also 'hoping' for a confrontation between the Druze and the Shia. After all, they had 'brought a thousand men from Akkar within a quarter of an hour' to help Future Movement fighters, but not a single one had lent a hand to the Druze in their own battles with Hizballah and Amal. Though the Druze had emerged from the battles of May 2008 with 'our heads held high', there was no getting away from the fact that it was 'impossible to engage in open battle on existential, political, and confessional fronts with the Shia'. It was quite simple: 'there was no need to make an enemy of the Shia'; the Druze only stood to lose from an ongoing confrontation with Hizballah.[32] It was time for Jumblatt and the Druze to move on.

January 2011—the collapse

Jumblatt's withdrawal into safe centrism only further complicated Hariri's efforts to create a government, already hampered by the ongoing distraction of the tribunal. For after several months of silence, Sayyed sprung back to life, like a devilish jack-in-the-box. On 31 August 2009, he gave an inflammatory press conference, in which he accused Lebanon's judges and politicians of being complicit in his persecution. Lebanon's chief prosecutor, Saïd Mirza, was a 'criminal'. The judge Ralph Riachi lacked any integrity, having accepted bribes from the security services when he was one of those who presided in the highly politicised case against Samir Geagea, in the early 1990s. Walid Jumblatt had called for 'hanging the generals and wrenching tears of blood from their families'. Saad Hariri had no right to invoke the tribunal, 'having accepted lies, fraud, and injustice for four years'. Mirza, Riachi, and their fellow judge Sakr Sakr, the security officials Wissam Hassan and Samir Chehade, and the political figures Marwan Hamadeh, Fouad Siniora, and Johnny Abdo were all 'symbols of corruption' who had led the campaign against him. It was time for Michel Sleiman to 'become again the general ... I knew' and to 'clean up' the filth cluttering Lebanon's halls of power.[33]

Prominent 14 March politicians were quick to dismiss Sayyed's unpleasantness as the empty strutting of a vainglorious and insignificant figure whose marginal status still rankled, with the Future Movement MP Nohad Machnouk calling him a 'hate-filled peacock ... spitting out spite' in all directions. Sayyed, Machnouk continued, 'had brought back a new account of the facts' from his recent visit to Damascus.[34] But Sayyed's ravings had a way of distracting from more pressing matters, not least the formation of the government. So too did the interventions of the Syrian regime, always eager to shore up the stability of its neighbour. In September 2009, the Syrian foreign minister, Walid Muallem, wrote to the UN Security Council requesting a new inquiry into Hariri's killings. Sayyed's allegations the previous May, Muallem insisted, had shown that the current investigation lacked even the slightest semblance of impartiality. The aim of the UNIIIC had been, from its very inception, to 'implicate Syria at any cost'. 'When Sayyed refused' to do its bidding, 'he had been imprisoned for four years'. This was a grave 'abuse of power', and one that the UN secretary-general owed it to the world to investigate.[35] But while for some the tribunal was a means of holding up the business of government and throwing Lebanon into turmoil, for others it was a useful bargaining chip in the ongoing haggling over cabinet positions. After all, an undertaking to endorse funding for the tribunal might be usefully exchanged for the promise of this or that ministry—telecommunications, say, or labour. Hariri's frustration at such manoeuvres was becoming clear. During one *iftar* meal in late August, he had told those looking for concessions to go knock on the door of the tribunal in The Hague.[36]

Against all expectations, however, the government finally came together in November 2009. It still carried around the tribunal, though, like a bad cold it could not shake off, going from one embarrassing scandal to another. In April 2010, the star witness of Mehlis' first report, Zuhair Siddik, reappeared to insist that Hizballah had helped Damascus to carry out Hariri's assassination. Siddik's inopportune intervention did little to restore confidence in the STL. Shortly after his interview with Mehlis, Siddik had taken refuge in one of the palatial residences that Rifaat al-Assad, Bashar's exiled uncle, owned in Puerto Banos on the Costa del Sol. Notorious for his presumed role in the massacre of Muslim Brotherhood supporters in Hama in 1982, Rifaat had attempted to seize power in late 1983, taking advantage of his brother's illness. When Hafez's heart problems proved to be less serious than first presumed and he returned to power, his brother found himself disgraced and rusticated. Since 1984, he had lived out his days in gilded exile, nursing his resentment for the brother who had wronged him and the nephew who had succeeded him. That Siddik had taken up with such a compromised figure, so overtly hostile to the Syrian regime, cast doubt, in the eyes of many, on his testimony. Taken in hand by the French security services, Siddik was soon revealed to have lied about his position within the Syrian intelligence apparatus. As some accused Saad Hariri and Walid Jumblatt of paying Siddik to give his false testimony, the Lebanese government issued charges against him for perjury. Though arrested by the French authorities, he was soon let go after France refused to extradite him to Lebanon. On his release, he took up residence in the suburbs of Paris, where the DGSE, France's external intelligence agency, was supposed to keep a watchful eye on their wayward charge. But in March 2008, Siddik suddenly vanished, only to emerge several months later in the United Arab Emirates, in possession of a fake Czech passport. Arrested by the Emirati authorities, he was sentenced to six months in prison for possession and use of a false identity document, before being released. Once safely back in Europe, he accused Nicolas Sarkozy's office of supplying him with his Czech passport, insisting all the while he had no idea it was a forgery. Not for the first time, this odd, shifty figure's declarations served to weaken the prosecution's case, suggesting it was built on the fantabulous lies of a delusional witness—shoddy foundations indeed.

Over the next year, the question of the false witnesses—for Siddik was not the only one accused of telling tales, and the reliability of several other witnesses was called into doubt—would come to take up more and more of the government's time, as the opposition latched on to it as a means of undermining the STL's legitimacy. This time, figures with rather more clout than Jamil al-Sayyed waded into the debate. First Hassan Nasrallah weighed in, dismissing the inquiry as a scheme cooked up by the great powers to worm their way into Lebanese affairs and undermine the resistance. 'How can we have faith', he asked, 'in the workings of an investigative commission whose members were nominated by the British and American governments and are close to their intelligence services, which are themselves linked to Mossad'? 'Justice' was essential, but 'not at the expense of the resistance'.[37] Aoun soon followed Nasrallah's lead, declaring in July 2010 that the 'tribunal has fallen because it relied on false witnesses to accuse Syria' and had dismissed too hastily the 'Israeli hypothesis'—the notion, which Hizballah's media arm had clung to since the beginning, that the attack had been committed by Israeli intelligence in an effort to sow discord. Sleiman Frangieh, too, stressed the importance of maintaining Lebanon's stability. Any indictment, he insisted in an interview to Hizballah's TV station, Al-Manar, would only 'provoke disorder on the domestic front, rather than unmasking Hariri's assassins'.[38] In early August, Nasrallah again went on the offensive, explicitly accusing Israel, in two grand multimedia press conferences, of having killed Rafiq Hariri.[39]

By mid-August, Saad Hariri had been forced by his cabinet colleagues' campaign to agree to an inquiry, led by the minister of justice, Ibrahim Najjar—not quite the commission that Nasrallah had called for in July, but a significant concession nonetheless.[40] Eager to shore up his premiership, Hariri was prepared to go even further. In an interview published in early September in the pan-Arab daily *Al-Sharq al-Awsat*, Hariri acknowledged that false witnesses had misled the inquiry into his father's death, damaging ties between Lebanon and Syria and 'politicising the assassination'. What's more, Hariri confessed to having been at fault. 'We have evaluated the mistakes that happened on our side with Syria', mistakes that 'harmed the Syrian people and the relationship between the two countries'. 'At a certain stage', he went on, we accused Syria of assassinating ... Rafiq Hariri, and this was a political assassination'.[41] This was as close to an apology to Damascus as Hariri could come without entirely giving up his dignity.

But this was still not enough for Hariri's opponents. Throughout the autumn, leading figures in 8 March kept up their calls for the case to be referred to the Lebanese courts, demanding a ministerial vote on the matter. As the question of the tribunal once again got in the way of ordinary government business, the cabinet found itself sharply divided. This time, though, it broke down into three camps: 8 March, eager to bring the matter to a vote; 14 March, who refused to countenance such a move; and, stuck in the middle, ministers who owed their seats to Walid Jumblatt and Michel Sleiman, who attempted to interpose themselves as moderating influences holding the government together. For all knew full well that any vote would split the cabinet, effectively precipitating its collapse.[42] 8 March deputies and ministers continued to portray the tribunal as a 'great plot, which sought'—in the febrile words of the Druze deputy Talal Arslan—'to use creative destruction to eliminate Lebanon, as part of a joint American-Israeli strategy to conquer Lebanon and the entire region'.[43] For their part, 14 March MPs condemned their antagonists' actions as tantamount to a 'coup d'état' whose intention, they alleged, was not just to undermine the STL, but to sap the very foundations of the Lebanese state which the parliamentary majority was committed to building up.[44]

By the end of 2010, the seemingly irresolvable question of the tribunal had once again pushed Lebanese politics into an impasse—and this in spite of the theatrical intervention of Lebanon's regional neighbours. In July, Michel Sleiman—ever the conciliatory force, eager to please all sides—had invited Saudi Arabia's King Abdullah and Bashar al-Assad to Beirut for a summit intended to defuse the growing tension among his cabinet colleagues. On 30 July, both men arrived amid much pomp, ceremony and security. After passing through streets garlanded with Saudi, Syrian, and Lebanese flags, and banners thanking these two foreign potentates for their benevolent intervention, they sat down for a brief meeting with Lebanese politicians of all sides. That Bashar al-Assad had deigned to attend—and that 14 March politicians were willing to countenance his presence, let alone seek his help—was a sign of the thaw in relations between the Lebanese parliamentary majority and the Syrian regime. Lebanon and Syria had, it is true, exchanged ambassadors in 2009—the opening of embassies in Beirut and Damascus marking a formal diplomatic recognition that successive generations of Syrian politicians, always reluctant to recognise Lebanon's independence, had refused to grant. But this was still a symbolic occasion—Bashar's first visit to Lebanon since 2005, to meet the Lebanese president as a nominal equal, rather than as a dependent who ruled at his sufferance. As Bashar left, he raised his thumbs to the waiting reporters, exclaiming: 'it was an excellent summit'. The Saudi king proved even less loquacious, but the Lebanese presidency released a statement following the meeting, during which the leaders of all three countries had 'stressed the importance of stability ... the commitment [of the Lebanese] not to resort to violence and the need to place the country's interests above all sectarian interests'.[45] This was no more than a bland restatement of the principles of the Doha Agreement—and one that might have seemed to cynics rather minimal in its ambitions. Nevertheless, it did provide some relief for those willing to put their faith in the *mubadara al-sin-sin*—or 'S-S initiative', as this joint undertaking between Syria and Saudi Arabia became known.

This time, though, even the help of their external protectors could not extract Lebanon's politicians from the morass into which they had led each other. On 11 January 2011, the ten 8 March ministers in the cabinet announced their resignation at a joint press conference chaired by Gebran Bassil. Soon after, the minister of state, Adnan Hussain—nominally a neutral figure close to the president, but vulnerable, as a Shia, to the pressures of Hizballah and Amal—announced that he, too, would be leaving the cabinet. Deprived of just over a third of its ministers, Hariri's cabinet collapsed. This was a move timed to perfection: Bassil and his co-conspirators took to the rostrum while Hariri was more than 9,000 kilometres away, in Washington, DC. As the Lebanese premier sat down in the Oval Office with Barack Obama, his rebellious ministers announced that they could no longer share government with a 'party incapable of eluding American pressure' and resolving the 'crisis that had resulted from the international tribunal'. Seemingly lacking the slightest semblance of self-awareness, the resigning ministers blamed Hariri and his allies for the 'blockage' that had held up Lebanese politics since the formation of the government.[46] But perhaps they did not need self-awareness—always a hindrance for politicians eager to achieve their aims, after all. For they had achieved exactly what they wanted to achieve: to bring down the government, while underscoring what they regarded as Hariri's unseemly proximity to the United States. And yet, for all the theatrical panache, the end of Hariri's term in office could not have come as a surprise to anyone. For, like a middle-aged man collapsing with a heart attack, this was a government that had long suffered from sclerosis, its arteries obstructed and its organs overloaded with the stress of the tribunal. And it was the STL that finally led it to keel over. For as Bassil and his 8 March colleagues knew all too well, Daniel Bellemare was due to submit his sealed indictment to the tribunal's pre-trial judge, Daniel Fransen, on 17 January—a deadline which lent their manoeuvres real urgency. The indictment would remain confidential, for now, but many suspected—and feared—that it would inculpate

Hizballah, either alone or in collaboration with Syria and Iran.[47] The storms over Lebanon were not close to letting up.

June 2011: the indictment

And so, barely fourteen months after the formation of its last government, Lebanon found itself waiting again for a new prime minister. This time, the man charged with the task of forming the cabinet was the Tripoli-born billionaire Najib Mikati, who had made his fortune in telecommunications, but whose business interests extended by this point to a range of holdings—including, as Lebanese friends never tired of pointing out, the French clothing brand Façonnable. Mikati had already been prime minister once before, serving as the interim premier between April and July 2005, after Omar Karami resigned in the face of mounting popular protest. Perhaps more importantly, he was regarded as an amiable and moderate political operator on good terms with most of Lebanon's competing factions, and a strong and wealthy Sunni politician, respected by others within his community but free of binding attachments to the Hariri family and its money.

But Mikati's task remained a difficult one. He benefited, it is true, from the goodwill of an international community eager to shore up Lebanon's stability at all costs, with Turkey and Qatar, who sought to use the Arab spring—then in its early, heady stages—to establish themselves as regional powerbrokers lending their support to a series of moderate Sunni governments, playing a particularly prominent role.[48] But for all this foreign encouragement, Mikati could still not be sure of internal support. Lebanon's MPs remained split between those who simply could not bring themselves to endorse Mikati, because they regarded his predecessor's ouster as nothing short of an unseemly coup, and those who were only too eager to draw a line under the previous government. Mikati, then, faced a tricky balancing act: he had to placate Hizballah and meet Aoun's always onerous demands to ensure the participation of 8 March in his government, but find a way of doing so without giving the impression of weakness or appearing a traitor to those Sunnis still reeling from the fighting of May 2008 and the humiliating manner of Hariri's dismissal.

In the end, Mikati was able—just about—to reconcile these seemingly opposing pressures. After barely six months of the usual horse-trading—accompanied, as always, by frantic announcements in the media of breakthroughs, hold-ups, reconsiderations and reconciliations—Mikati announced the formation of his government on 13 June. Thanks to the intercession of Nabih Berri, who gave up one of the six Shia seats in cabinet to his Sunni counterpart, Mikati was able to claim a numerical victory of sorts for his premiership and his community. For he had done what Saad Hariri had not succeeded in doing, breaking the informal power-sharing formula and ensuring that seven Sunnis, and only five Shia, would sit in cabinet. Despite such cosmetic touches, however, there was no disguising the cabinet's distinctly pro-8 March complexion. Indeed, in many ways, its make-up emphasised 14 March's growing disarray. While Walid Jumblatt shored up his self-acclaimed status as a moderating centrist force in Lebanese politics by securing three ministries in return for lending Mikati his support, the formation of the cabinet precipitated further splits in the ranks of 14 March, with the Tripoli MP Mohammad Safadi—elected in 2009 on the coalition's list—joining his fellow northerner Mikati in cabinet. The clear winner in numerical terms, though, was Michel Aoun, whose maximalist tactics resulted in an impressive yield. The ageing general secured eleven seats for members of his Change and Reform Bloc—just over a third of the portfolios up for grabs. For the first time, these included not just telecommunications, labour, and energy—now firmly in the hands of Aoun and his acolytes—but also key 'sovereign' ministries such as justice and defence. While the former was given to the lawyer Shakib Qortbawi, a member in the early 2000s of the Christian opposition group known as the Qornet Shehwan gathering, the latter was handed to Fayez Ghosn, a client of Aoun's ally, Sleiman Frangieh. Though perhaps still not enough to sate Aoun's appetite, this represented a blow not just to his Christian opponents in 14 March—the Lebanese Forces, the Kata'ib, and smaller outfits like the National Liberal Party and the National Bloc—but also to Michel Sleiman. The president—whom many had seen as a potential challenger to Aoun for Christian hearts and votes in the wake of his election in 2008—now seemed a diminished force, with just three ministers: the deputy prime minister, Samir Moqbel, the minister of the interior, Marwan Charbel—who, for all his good intentions, lacked the charisma and reforming verve of his predecessor, Ziad Baroud—and the minister of the environment,

Nazim Khoury. But for all the totting up of seats won and lost—that breathless tallying of ministerial musical chairs—few had any illusions about where the cabinet's centre of gravity sat. Though Hizballah, as was its habit, claimed only two ministries, it was clear to informed observers that neither Aoun nor, for that, Mikati could have secured anything without the party's support. This was very much its cabinet.

Despite its newfound dominance, 8 March still could not rid itself entirely of the troublesome matter of the tribunal. On 30 June—a week to the day after Mikati had announced the formation of his cabinet—the STL passed on its indictment to the Lebanese government. Four men—all Lebanese nationals—were named in the indictment: Mustafa Badreddin, Salim Ayyash, Hussein Oneissi, and Assad Sabra. They were charged variously with a series of offences under Lebanese law, ranging from 'Conspiracy aimed at committing a Terrorist Act' to 'Committing' or 'Being an Accomplice to' a 'Terrorist Act by means of an explosive device', 'Intentional Homicide (of 21 persons in addition to the Intentional Homicide of Rafik HARIRI) with premeditation by using explosive materials', and 'Attempted Intentional Homicide (of 231 persons ...) with premeditation by using explosive materials'.[49] Though the indictment took care not to identify the confession or political allegiances of the four accused, the Lebanese media proved rather less scrupulous, naming all four as Hizballah operatives. Indeed, in one case, this was hardly worth doing. For one of the four, Mustafa Badreddin, was as notorious as he was elusive. Known as *dhu al-fiqar* after the Imam Ali's sword—given to him, in legend, by the prophet Muhammad himself—Badreddin was one of Hizballah's best-known military commanders. Like his cousin and brother-in-law Imad Mughniyyeh, whom he replaced as the head of foreign operations after the latter was killed in Damascus in 2008, Badreddin had joined the fledgling organisation during Israel's occupation of Lebanon in 1982, rapidly rising through the ranks thanks to his mastery of explosives. Over the years, he had been identified—together with Mughniyyeh— as one of the planners of the bomb attack that tore through US and French barracks in Beirut in 1983, killing 305 people, convicted of the bombing of the US and French embassies in Kuwait—he was sprung from prison in 1990, during the Iraqi invasion of the country—and accused of cross-border attacks against Israeli military targets and of assisting Iraqi insurgents in their campaign against American and British troops.[50] Now Badreddin was charged with being the 'overall controller of the operation' that killed Rafiq Hariri and twenty-one other people, on Valentine's Day 2005. Lebanon had thirty days to respond to the indictments.

Politicians of all sides scrambled to react. While Mikati's press office released a cautious statement emphasising the need for 'truth in the crime against Rafik al-Hariri', 14 March saw an opportunity to regain some much-needed political capital. The coalition's secretary-general, Fares Souaid, made clear that it would hold Mikati to account. While lauding the premier's commitment to truth and justice, Souaid emphasised that 'Mikati must realise that we will face any shortfall ... with all our strength in a peaceful and democratic way'. From his Parisian haven, meanwhile, Saad Hariri called for an 'end to the episodes of killing'. In ominous tones, he went on: 'the era of the murderers is over and the time for justice is close'. Piling pressure on Mikati—whose barely-formed government was already beleaguered—Hariri insisted that there was no reason for the government to 'run away from [its] responsibility'—though he knew full well, of course, that at least one of the parties in the cabinet might well take a rather different view.[51] For how could Hizballah support a tribunal that had charged four of its own members with the murder of a former Lebanese prime minister—and twenty-one others?

On 3 July, Nasrallah gave another of his long, overflowing multimedia press conferences. Its aim was clear: to demolish the STL's credibility. Since Hizballah's victory against Israel in the 2006 war, he insisted, some had been bent on curbing the organisation's growing power by framing it for Hariri's assassination. This campaign had begun with an article planted in *Le Figaro* in August 2006, and had continued with *Der Spiegel*'s infamous accusations in May 2009, before culminating in the announcement of the indictment and its publication. At each stage, the timing was suspect. The *Spiegel* article had been published just weeks before the parliamentary elections of June 2009, the indictment handed to the pre-trial judge during the parliamentary consultations on Hariri's successor, the revised indictment issued on 13 March—the day before the annual rally held in downtown Beirut—and its contents published days before a parliamentary vote of confidence in Mikati's new government. More than this, there was plentiful evidence of collusion between the inquiry, Israel and the United States at each stage. Several members of the UNIIIC and the prosecutor's team had shown 'partiality' and 'a declared hostility to Hizballah'. These included the Australian Nick Caldas, a former intelligence officer who had worked in Iraq during the American occupation, the Briton Michael Taylor, a former counter-terrorism expert at Scotland Yard, the American Darrel Mendez, an ex-marine with known ties to the CIA and the FBI, and Robert Baer, a former CIA field officer in Beirut whom some accused of having helped to plan the bomb attack against the Shia cleric Sayyid Muhammad Husain Fadlallah that killed eighty-five civilians in 1985. Worse still, Nasrallah showed his viewers a short extract from the Herzliya conference, in which one of the speakers acclaimed the STL's instructing judge, Antonio Cassese, as 'a great friend to Israel'. And if this was still not enough to persuade some of the STL's untrustworthiness, then what were naysayers to make of evidence of its corruption? For among the other videos Nasrallah showed was a clip showing the German investigator Gerhard Lehmann—whom Jamil al-Sayyed had accused of attempting to bribe him into serving as a go-between to Bashar al-Assad—handling wads of cash, clear evidence, for Nasrallah, that wrongdoing had undermined the investigation at every stage. If this corruptible, flawed man was capable of 'selling witness statements for a handful of dollars', Nasrallah commented acidly, 'what would he do in return for millions'? Nasrallah made his stance clear: the four men charged with Hariri's murder would never be given up— 'not in thirty days, not in thirty years, and not in three hundred years'. The resistance could not be broken by crude political manoeuvres.[52]

Speeches alone, however, were not enough to stall the tribunal's cogs, for its hybrid nature—half-Lebanese and half-international— ensured that it remained insulated from the effects of polemic, its employees working relentlessly away in their offices in Leidschendam, in the suburbs of The Hague. There was one way, though, in which 8 March could impede its work—by refusing to countenance Lebanon's payment of its share of the STL's annual operating budget, due in late November. As the deadline for transfer of the funds approached, 8 March ministers and MPs, well-versed in the arts of obstruction, embarked on their campaign of invective and condemnation. When Mikati placed the STL's finances on the agenda for a cabinet meeting scheduled for 30 November—the very last day on which Lebanon could make payment without finding itself in breach of its international obligations—the ministers of Michel Aoun's Change and Reform Bloc flatly refused to attend, prompting the meeting to be adjourned. Many expected 8 March to rack up another victory, bringing another prime minister to his knees and precipitating yet another new political crisis. And the coalition might well have won, were it not for an unexpected masterstroke on the prime minister's part. For in place of the scheduled cabinet session, Mikati held a press conference, in which he announced that he had paid Lebanon's share of the STL budget that very morning out of discretionary funds attached to the prime minister's office. This was, he made clear, a 'national decision protecting Lebanon from regional repercussions', born of three considerations: his desire to 'preserve Lebanon', saving it from internal discord and external interference; his 'unshakeable attachment to seeing justice done'—for it was 'impossible', he explained, 'to ignore' a case like this one; and his refusal to give up on Lebanon's commitments, 'withdrawing [the country] from the international community'. With this announcement, Mikati did not just ensure that the country's obligations were honoured; he also saved his premiership, bolstering his position among Sunnis and calling the bluff of those ministers who had insisted they would resign should he act peremptorily.[53] For now, at least, the prime minister stayed in place, and the tribunal's work continued. Somehow, the Lebanese political class had stumbled through this most uncertain of years—even if it resembled at times nothing so much as a drunk man clattering through a dark room, uncertain, ungainly, and full of bad excuses.

However, there is no getting away from the fact that all this artificial chaos, all this froth and tumult generated by Lebanon's politicians like so many wave machines churning away in a cheap water park, had a deadening effect on the work of government. As MPs and ministers of all sides remained caught up in an alternate universe of cabinet formulas, ministerial vetoes and prerogatives, casting about in desultory fashion big words like justice, truth, dignity, sovereignty, and resistance, they neglected the quotidian matters that concerned their constituents: inflation, falling real wages, under-employment, failing infrastructure and an absent state.

The years since 2005 had already witnessed attempts at large-scale labour mobilisation. In January 2007, the CGTL—the general confederation of trade unions—had called a strike to protest the international donor conference known as Paris III, with its agenda for further privatisation of Lebanese public assets. In May 2008, taxi drivers, teachers and farmers called another strike, asking for a higher minimum wage, an end to the freeze on public sector pay in place since 1996, and anti-inflationary measures. Both of these had been overshadowed, however, by the actions of 8 March: first the demonstrations of 23 January 2007, when Hizballah, Amal and the FPM had gone to the streets in protest at the formation of the STL, then the fighting of May 2008. But as ministers prevaricated in the face of a deteriorating economic situation, Lebanon's trade unionists returned to the streets in growing numbers. In 2012 alone, the Union Coordination Committee—a new body federating over forty trade unions, many of them representing state employees like public schoolteachers—organised fourteen strikes, sixty sit-ins, and four large-scale demonstrations.[54] Hamstrung by its desire not to alienate private sector employers, the government's only response to this resurgence of labour discontent was to engage in an endless process of consultation and wage negotiation.

March 2011—the revolution

2011, however, was not just the year of the indictment. It also marked the beginning of the Syrian revolution—that impossible feat of protest, which soon unravelled into brutal domestic violence. As demonstrations began to spread from the south-eastern city of Daraa, where the protests had first begun in mid-March in response to the arrest and torture of a group of young boys who had dared to write anti-regime slogans on the walls—one of them, Hamza Khatib, was elevated into the revolution's first martyr after he died as a result of his injuries—they gained both in amplitude and in boldness. Thousands, and then tens of thousands, began to stream everyday through the streets of Homs, Hama, Dayr al-Zur and other Syrian cities. And as these protests became a daily communion, the participants' chants began to change. At first, many had called only for dignity and reform, insisting that they sought not to destroy the Assads' state, but to work with it to create a better Syria. Soon enough, though, they began to call—like others in Tunisia, Egypt, Bahrain, and Yemen—for the downfall of the regime and the creation of a new political community.

But these experiments in participatory politics, whose songs and placards sketched out a vision of radical democracy born of the streets and public squares of Syria, were faced with the full repressive powers of the state. Crack army troops—some of them under the command of Bashar's younger brother, Maher—moved from city to city in a blitzkrieg operation, firing at 'rebellious' neighbourhoods and districts from their tanks. (Barrel bombs, packed full of explosives before being dumped from helicopters, would come later.) Trustworthy intelligence units, like those belonging to the air force—long a bastion of support for the Assad family—were deployed. Their modus operandi was all too familiar to those who had dared to oppose Baathist rule: demonstrators, or those suspected of sympathising with them, were arrested in the street or grabbed from their homes and taken to the regime's jails, where they were beaten and tortured—their nails pulled out, their testicles electrocuted, their anuses penetrated, the soles of their feet beaten, their shins broken. Many of those who died in detention were simply dumped at their families' doors, their faces unrecognisable under the bruises, their bodies mutilated. No less familiar than the *mukhabarat*—or intelligence men—were the shadowy figures known as *shabbiha*—'ghosts', a term used in colloquial Syrian to denote the loyalist thugs who did an increasing share of the regime's dirty work. Some of these men had worked, it would appear, as the retainers and bodyguards of the new Alawi elite that had come to the fore with Bashar's consolidation of power—men like the president's cousin, Rami Makhlouf, who had accumulated a fortune built on his dominance of Syrian telecoms. Now, the state relied upon them to do the work of repression. These men became notorious for their brutality and the vicious relish they took in inflicting suffering. Some took to the roofs and balconies of abandoned buildings to snipe at the civilians in the streets below, jeering and joshing as they took pot-shots at women scurrying to get some water or men attempting to extract relatives from the rubble of a fallen building. Others, however, adopted blunter means. Social media was rife, in the summer and autumn of 2011, with blurry clips of *shabbiha*, their tattoo-spattered muscles swollen into nightmarish, grotesque shapes by a diet of steroids, beating and abusing harried demonstrators or army deserters. Their ghoulish laughter still rings in the ears.

As the localised protests of the early spring spread to towns and cities across Syria, and as the regime's repression grew ever more brutal and relentless, Lebanon's politicians quickly took sides. Their stances were, to a large extent, in keeping with their pre-revolutionary views of the regime in Damascus. What changed, however, was their sense of what was at stake. Before March 2011, the Baathist regime had been for some an obstacle, and for others an enabler. But whether they deemed it a nuisance or a useful ally, Lebanese politicians recognised the new constraints on Syria's reach. To be sure, Damascus could still yield influence in Lebanon—not least through the threat of instability—but it was no longer the hegemonic force it had been until 2005. This was evident enough from the reduced status of pro-Syrian figures like Elie Ferzli, Karim Pakradouni, Ali Qanso, Wiam Wahhab, Sleiman Frangieh, or Talal Arslan. Looking for all the world like yesterday's men, these figures still lingered on the margins of Lebanese politics— some, like Ferzli, forlornly attempting to claw back their positions and their seats in parliament, others like Wahhab or Arslan stubbornly barking their provocations at talk show hosts and journalists like defanged guard dogs.

Now, with the prospect of the Assad regime collapsing seeming to many a real possibility, the Syrian revolution became a zero-sum game for Lebanese politicians. To the Future Movement and its Christian allies, the revolutionary enthusiasm unleashed in Syria promised to yield a moderate Sunni government approximating to democracy—not unlike that, in fact, that Hariri father and son, and their partners, had envisioned for Lebanon since the 1990s. And as this suggested, the revolution presented an opportunity to reset the relationship between Lebanon and Syria, so poisoned by the events of the 1990s and early 2000s. Indeed, the leaders of the Syrian National Council, hastily formed in Istanbul to federate the fissiparous forces of Syrian opposition, made all the right noises. As Burhan Ghalioun, the greying political exile and sociology professor who briefly headed up the SNC, put it in late 2011: 'Democracy for Syria is the best support for the independence of Lebanon'.[55] And more than this, it would asphyxiate

Hizballah, cutting off its supplies of support from Iran, and helping to free Lebanon of the stifling weight of weapons. Conversely, a quick victory for Assad would spell disaster: marking a significant blow to the Arab spring that, they insisted, Lebanon's independence intifada had prefigured, it would also signal the rise of a new Shia ascendancy across the region, from Iran through Syria and into Lebanon, a 'Shia crescent' of authoritarian obscurantism that would blot out any possibility of democratic renewal or Sunni renaissance.

Hizballah and the FPM, however, looked rather differently on the events unfolding in Syria. The fall of Assad would result only in the creation of a deliberately weak state, a ward propped up by foreign backers and in thrall to the United States, Turkey, Saudi Arabia or Qatar. Entirely dependent on their goodwill, the new state would come under intense pressure to sever ties with Iran, Hizballah and Hamas, breaking what so many in Lebanon called the *mahwar al-muqawama*, or 'resistance axis'. Normalisation with Israel would soon follow. Unthinkable as this was, a worse alternative existed. The Syrian state might dissolve under the weight of protest, creating a vacuum that could be filled only by a proliferation of jihadi groups bent upon exterminating minorities—chief among them Shia and Christians. The new Syria, in other words, would not be another shiny Sunni variant on neoliberalism, like Lebanon, Qatar or Turkey, but another Iraq—a nightmarish vision of Western-induced state failure, sectarian warfare, and genocidal violence. A victory for Assad, however, would only strengthen the resistance, helping it to cement the position it had been building up since its victory in the summer war of 2006—if not since the liberation of southern Lebanon from Israeli occupation in 2000. For, as the Amal MP Ali Hassan Khalil told a conference organised in Beirut in April 2011 'in support of Syria against the conspiracy': 'if it wasn't for Bashar Assad's Syria and Hafez Assad's Syria, Lebanon would not be a country of resistance'.[56]

In other words, this was as much an existential matter as an ideological one. Many in 14 March were sympathetic to the cause of Syrian demonstrators, activists, exiled dissidents, and deserting army officers, but they also understood that on their success hung the chances of a major regional realignment, which would only favour them. For the most part, one would have thought that 8 March had even less ideological sympathy for Assad's regime, despite the ties of personal alliance and material interest binding many of its constituents to the Syrian president and his coterie. But they too knew that victory for their side could lead to a significant shift in the regional order, bolstering their own position. And both 14 March and 8 March politicians were aware that their own constituents had quite different reactions to the events unfolding across the border. Many of the Future Movement's Sunni rank-and-file, even as they insisted on the national and cross-confessional character of the demonstrations in Syria, saw the repression that followed each protest as the workings of a sectarian clique bent on keeping power from the majority. But ordinary members of Hezbollah, the FPM, and Amal, like their leaders, saw the protests as the reassertion of a rampant Sunnism, which would result only in the curtailing of freedoms for minorities like the Shia or the Christians—if not worse, were *takfiri*-jihadi groups to gain a foothold amidst the chaos, as they had in Iraq. It was this clear-sighted appreciation of the Syrian revolution's potential consequences for the Middle East, and for Lebanon, that shaped the discourses of both sides in its first year or two.

Spinning the tale they had told since the mid-2000s into new shapes, 8 March politicians spoke of the events in Syria as the product of the same Western machinations that had torn apart Iraq. In many ways, indeed, Syria was the culmination of these plotters' attempts to create a new, and more pliable, regional order. As the former deputy parliamentary speaker Elie Ferzli, a stalwart of the Syrian order in Lebanon, told the audience gathered at the Bristol Hotel in April 2011 to show its 'support for Syria against the conspiracy', the confrontation in Syria was a 'central battle' for the future of the region. Assad's triumph over the provocateurs and foreign agents undermining Syria's hard-won stability 'would continue the resistance's July war victory'.[57] Dismissing the optimistic prognostications of their 14 March opponents as the wild-eyed delusions of possessed men, Lebanon's pro-Syrian politicians insisted on Assad's imminent victory. And, as the northern Maronite politician Sleiman Frangieh, an old friend of Bashar—the two men had gone hunting together as teenagers—insisted in October 2011, Syria would emerge 'stronger than before from this trial'. Held together by its people's love for their president, its army's resilience, and its leader's 'alertness', the country would remain free of the 'sectarian unrest' that had torn apart Lebanon and Iraq.[58] This was a clear echo of official Syrian rhetoric, which had long stressed the country's exceptional ability to maintain harmony and stability in the face of hostile regional forces, and which now presented the protests unfolding across the country as the product of foreign intelligence services planning to bring low the last bastion of pan-Arab resistance to Israel. It was time, therefore, for the Syrian people to 'give up the bullets and return to the ballot box', as Michel Aoun put it, in his characteristic homespun fashion, in August 2011. Once one of Damascus' most dogged critics, Aoun now closely toed the Assad regime's official line. It was important, he stressed, not to overstate the significance of the protests. For 'anyone who went to Syria could see that it was quiet'. After all, where were the demonstrators in Syria's largest city, Aleppo, or, for that matter, in the capital? Those who inveighed against the Syrian state's actions should be clearer about their objectives. They did not want the 'implementation of reform, but compliance with international demands', not least 'cutting ties with Iran, Hamas, and Hizballah, and beginning negotiations with Israel'. And there was no doubt who was behind this—the United States, which 'created wars in the same way it created debt crises'. But the wanton irresponsibility of successive American administrations could still 'not lead to the creation of regimes given over to the United States' in the region, because of the strong 'popular contempt for such regimes, and for the United States' itself. Resistance would triumph in the end, once the Syrian people had come to their senses. This was quite a turnaround for a man who had once testified in the House of Representatives against Syria's involvement in Lebanon. In the end, though, the same interests and concerns drove Aoun and his colleagues on. As the former high-ranking Kata'ib cadre Karim Pakradouni, who had gone over to Damascus' side in the 1990s, told the audience gathered at the Bristol Hotel in April 2011: 'we support Assad because we love Lebanon'—or, at least, a certain vision of the country and their own place within its politics.[59]

From the beginning, meanwhile, 14 March saw solidarity with the demonstrators of Syria as a means of burnishing its ideological credentials, multiplying its calls for protection for the refugees streaming— first in their hundreds, then their thousands and tens of thousands— from Syria into Lebanese border towns and regions like Arsal and Wadi

Khalid, for recognition of the Syrian National Council and stronger international sanctions against the Assad regime. But as the leaders of 14 March explicitly recognised, their vocal support could never be disentangled from domestic considerations. At its loftiest and most elaborate, this argument presented the Syrian revolution as the inevitable outcome of a decades-long confrontation between the forces of freedom and the oppression and brutality of the Assad regime, one that had begun during the Lebanese civil war and continued through the fifteen years of Syrian 'hegemony' in Lebanon and the demonstrations of the independence intifada, and was now coming to a climax in Syria itself. As Samir Geagea put it in his speech to the dignitaries assembled in Beirut on 14 February 2012 to mark the seventh anniversary of Rafiq Hariri's death, there was a straight line to be drawn 'from Achrafieh and Basta al-Fawqa ... and Ayn al-Rummaneh and 'Aley and Zahle and Bab al-Tebbaneh'—Lebanese sites of Syrian sieges and killings during the 1980s—to 'Homs, Hama, Idlib, Ladhqiyya, Dayr al-Zur and Daraa', the battlegrounds of the Syrian revolution. Where the Lebanese people had once borne the brunt of the Assad regime's violence, it was now the turn of Syrians to stand up to tyranny, paying the cost of their courage. For the heroes of Lebanese independence, 'Kamal Jumblatt and Bashir al-Jumayyil, Rafiq Hariri, Samir Qassir, and George al-Hawi', and the martyrs of popular uprisings in Tunisia, Egypt, and now Syria, 'Muhammad Bu 'Azizi, Khaled [Sa'id], the child Hamza Khatib, and Ibrahim Qashush' were all 'one man' and represented 'one cause': that of 'freedom, dignity, and justice'.[60] Geagea's argument required some intellectual gymnastics—not least in its rather flexible view of the past—but it amounted to a single point: a victory for the Syrian revolution would also be a victory for those who had fought for Lebanon's independence, sovereignty, and freedom from extra-legal arms.

Perhaps the fullest summation of this stance came in Saad Hariri's speech at the same rally in February 2012. In his intervention, which he gave via video link from his Parisian exile, Hariri did not equivocate. 'I bear the responsibility', he told his audience, 'for my solidarity with the Syrian people, and [my] support for their right to establish a democratic regime, just as I bear the responsibility for preventing discord amongst the Lebanese, and in particular between the Shia and the Sunnis'. Taking on the twin mantles of statesman and revolutionary, Hariri announced himself and his cohort ready for duty. It was incumbent upon 14 March, he continued, to pursue the path of 'freedom and dignity', for his was the party of 'freedom of opinion and religious practice, freedom of thought and speech and behaviour, of individual and collective liberties'. But Hariri was not just preaching to the converted. In the second part of his speech, he opened up to the doubters. Whatever would come to pass in Syria, he insisted, 14 March would live up to its slogan, 'putting Lebanon first'. It always had been, and remained, the party of 'independence, sovereignty, and democracy'. To the Christians who feared that the revolution in Syria would lead to the rise of Islamic 'extremism' in Lebanon, Hariri spoke reassuring words: 'we are the party of moderation, of coexistence, and pluralism'. And to the Shia who believed that 'the victory of the revolution in Syria would lead to a Sunni offensive against them to avenge the blood' of his father, Hariri offered a remarkable concession: 'we do not hold our Shia brothers in Lebanon responsible for the blood of Rafiq Hariri, for we consider that blood to be their blood just as it is our blood and the blood of all the Lebanese'. But alongside such overtures also came a challenge. For, Hariri reminded his Shia listeners, 'we do not regard [keeping] weapons' as an indispensable marker of 'confessional or sectarian identity'. 'These are political weapons that define a political identity', and their 'spread' posed a veritable 'threat' to the shared political life of the Lebanese.[61] He presented his compatriots, then, with a stark choice: chaos or joint participation in the construction of a unitary state capable of reconciling Lebanon's various communities. As the slogan that had adorned the backdrop of a Future Movement rally held in Tripoli in November 2011 had it: *kharif al-silah, rabi' al-istiqlal*—'the autumn of weapons is the spring of independence'. With these simple words, their white letters standing out against the red bands of the Lebanese flag, the Future Movement and 14 March announced their ambition to present Hizballah's weapons as a repressive mechanism comparable to the authoritarian states then collapsing across the Middle East, and their own demands as an extension of the struggle for freedom spreading across the region's borders.[62]

But this was no longer just a war of words. In November 2011, an ugly spat broke out on the air between Fayez Chokr, the secretary of the Lebanese branch of the Baath party, and the Future Movement member Mustafa Alloush, who confronted each other as guests on the popular political talk show 'Bimawdouiye'. When Alloush dared to say that he did not believe Bashar al-Assad's latest pronouncements on the state of Syria, Chokr erupted angrily: 'who are you not to believe him?' Goading his opponent on, Alloush responded: 'I don't believe him because he's a liar.' As the show's presenter, Fadi Abboud, attempted to calm them down, the two men traded insults like schoolchildren in the playground. There was nothing particularly unusual about this—for it is not uncommon for Lebanon's political shows to descend into slanging matches, the presenters mere referees attempting to make themselves heard above the shouts and accusations—until Alloush called his opponent a *sabe al-mukhabarat*—'boy of the spies', suggesting both that he owed his all to the Syrian intelligence services, and that he was no more than a child, an unmanned weakling with no independent capacity. At this, Chokr erupted. 'I have more honour than you', he shouted. But Alloush, with all the calm containment of the judo black belt that he is, simply sat back in his chair and told his antagonist to 'eat shit and shut your trap'. Finally snapping into movement, Chokr flung his glass of water across the studio, missing Alloush by some way.[63]

This was unseemly enough. More serious, though, were the reports that multiplied over the latter half of 2011 and the first half of 2012 of arms caches, weapons smuggling, and fighters passing across the porous border between Lebanon and Syria. In August 2011, two men were arrested as they were preparing to load a shipment of weapons onto a boat waiting in Beirut marina. According to Lebanese media, they had already carried out more than thirty such trips, ferrying large quantities of arms to the Syrian port of Banias. What made the matter particularly sensitive was the fact that the marina belonged to Solidere, which was forced to issue a statement denying all knowledge of the men's activities.[64] In February 2012, two more men were arrested carrying weapons across the border, in the hills above the Sunni town of Arsal, on the Lebanese side of the border.[65] Only two months earlier, the Lebanese defence minister, Fayez Ghosn, had announced that 'extremists' belonging to Al-Qaeda 'are sneaking into Lebanon' and hiding in and about Arsal, fast becoming a gathering point for refugees fleeing across the border—a claim that led to loud protests not just from the town's inhabitants, but also from 14 March.[66] A few days after the arrest of these smugglers, Mustafa Alloush was forced to deny the charge—made by the Lebanese Alawi leader Rif'at Eid—that a warehouse filled with weapons that had gone up in flames in the Abi Samra neighbourhood of Tripoli had belonged to the Future Movement, who had allowed 'gangs of Lebanese and Syrian opponents' to use these arms 'to sow disorder in Lebanon and Syria'.[67] Allegations were mounting, then, of collusion between Lebanon's Sunnis and their Syrian coreligionists—a collaboration that could only result, for many in 8 March, in the implantation of extremist elements on Lebanese soil.

For 14 March, the threat of 'spill-over'—or, as it was often put in Arabic, in'ikasat salbiyya, or negative repercussions—was just as real, but the guilty parties were the Assad regime and its Lebanese allies. The kidnapping of Syrians on Lebanese soil, the assaults on Lebanese demonstrators protesting outside the Syrian embassy in Beirut, and the wounding and killing of Lebanese and Syrian nationals crossing the border—all of these were intolerable violations of Lebanese sovereignty and of the rights enshrined in the Lebanese constitution.[68] What's more, evidence was beginning to mount of Hizballah throwing its military weight behind the Syrian state. In February 2012, the Hariri family's al-Mustaqbal newspaper reported on the strange disappearance of two bodies from the Italian-Lebanese Hospital, in the southern Lebanese city of Sur. The two bodies, both of which bore the traces of violence, had been taken away from the hospital before investigators could examine them. Though Hizballah was quick to deny its involvement in the matter, Future TV drew rather different conclusions. The whole affair was a clear indication that the party's men were fighting—and dying—in Syria, and that those who lost their lives propping up Assad's rule were being buried in secret in Lebanon.[69]

For all that their readings of the situation diverged radically, both 8 March and 14 March feared that Lebanon would be pulled into the Syrian maelstrom. Their fears would be realised soon enough. In February 2011, violence broke out between the adjacent Tripoli neighbourhoods of Bab al-Tebbaneh, whose Sunni inhabitants were fiercely sympathetic to the Syrian revolution, and Jabal Mohsen, whose Alawi residents saw events across the border as a threat to their own existence. Separated only by one of the city's main thoroughfares, Syria Street—the mordant irony was not lost on anyone—the two quarters had engaged in intermittent clashes since 2008. But now the worsening fighting in Syria reignited the slow-burning animosity between their residents, who found themselves on opposing sides of what many regarded as a confessional war of all against all. As men armed with RPGs and Kalashnikovs moved through the city's emptied streets, Lebanese army patrols deployed in a vain attempt to restore order. Once again, Lebanon's cities were living through violence.[70]

Caught between these irreconcilable stances, Mikati and Sleiman struggled to find a policy capable of holding together the government—and the country. They had to do so in the face of continuing internal discord and growing social unrest. In early 2012, the FPM began a campaign to secure the appointment of its own candidates for a series of administrative posts—the party's brazen clientelism dressed up, as always, as an honourable defence of Christian rights and constitutional prerogatives.[71] Only a few months earlier, Aoun's ministers had boycotted cabinet meetings and threatened to bring down the government over Lebanon's share of the STL's budget. Now they did the same in the name of what they presented as the 'principle' of equal representation. For many, there was some bleak amusement to be found in the yawning disjuncture between the FPM's talk and its actions—its insistence on presenting itself as a party devoted to the battle against corruption, efficiency and sound governance belied by its dogged pursuit of its own interests, its attempts to parachute its own men into positions of power and profit, and its choice of obstructionism as its favoured tactic.

The party's cause was little helped by growing criticism of the conduct of two of its ministers, Gebran Bassil and the minister of culture, Gaby Layoun. In the summer of 2010, Bassil—elevated to ever more senior positions by his ageing father-in-law, but derided by his many critics, who, punning on his name, called him Gebran Imbecile—had launched a new energy plan which, he promised, would bring uninterrupted electricity to all of Lebanon. Predictably enough, every detail of his plan—from his proposals to buy supplies from Turkey to his suggestion that Lebanon lease boats loaded with generators that, moored off the coast, would make up for the country's electricity shortfall—was debated, dissected, and dismissed by his opponents, whom FPM supporters accused of standing in the way of Lebanon's progress. But by the summer of 2012, it was Bassil himself who stood accused of affecting the country's electricity supplies by his intransigence in dealing with striking day-workers who sought the same rights and protections as the permanent employees of Electricité du Liban (EDL), Lebanon's state-owned electricity provider. As the strikers staged a sit-in at EDL's headquarters in Beirut and the country experienced ongoing black-outs, the FPM's commitment to change and reform came under increased scrutiny. Layoun's behaviour that hot, heavy summer did not help. In June, the minister of culture became mired in controversy when construction work began on a new luxury development in Mina el-Hosn on archaeological site BEY194, which Layoun's predecessor, Salim Wardeh, had designated a place of preserved 'cultural heritage' on the basis of a report naming it as the location of a Phoenician harbour. Layoun's decision to give the go-ahead to the developers, Venus Towers Real Estate Development Company, was cause enough for protest. But more disquieting still was the fact that work had already begun two days before the publication of his ministerial decree in the official gazette.[72] If the FPM was committed to fighting governmental malfeasance and incompetence, it seemed to have an odd way of showing it.

And yet, for Mikati, there was little consolation to be found in his opponents' disarray. For he knew full well that Bassil and Layoun were ministers in his own government, and that their actions could not but reflect poorly on the cabinet as a whole. While politicians of all sides took each other to task, for many ordinary Lebanese it hardly mattered who was to blame. All they knew was that the situation was getting worse. This general air of anxiety and deflation was only exacerbated by the descent of Syria into civil war over the spring and summer of 2012. On 25 May, over a hundred civilians were slaughtered by *shabbiha* in what came to be known as the 'massacre of Houla'. As the inhabitants of the village of Taldou, on the outskirts of the town of Houla, gathered for Friday prayers, readying their placards for the weekly demonstration that had become a ritual across parts of Syria that had joined the opposition to Bashar al-Assad, a round of shelling began. This marked the beginning of a brutal, relentless attack on the village. It is estimated that

108 died that day, including thirty-four women and forty-nine children.[73] As images of the killing circulated on social media, the fragile ceasefire between loyalist and opposition forces that UN negotiators had brokered fell apart for good. In the wake of Houla, the Free Syrian Army and a range of smaller militias and Islamist factions—perhaps the most prominent of them the jihadi group Jabhat al-Nusra—launched a series of attacks against regime-held positions across Syria, from Qusayr, on the Lebanese border, to Saraqeb in the north-west, Ayn al-Arab in the north-east and Raqqa in the east. And for the first time, they launched major offensives against Damascus and Aleppo. Pushed out of the capital by mid-July, opposition forces turned their attention to Aleppo, taking a series of outlying neighbourhoods, military bases, and checkpoints. The battle for Aleppo, which would continue until early 2017, when regime forces finally regained control of the entire city, would soon become known as *umm al-ma'arik*, or the mother of battles, for its intensity. As the fighting spread across Syria like a remorseless forest fire, the country's inhabitants fled in their hundreds of thousands. In April 2012, the UNHCR estimated that there were 18,000 Syrian refugees in Lebanon. By April 2013, that figure had risen to 356,000.[74] Their arrival and installation in hastily assembled camps did not just impose new strains and pressures on Lebanon's already arthritic public infrastructure; it also created intense controversy. While some in the FPM and other political parties—haunted by fears of these new arrivals and their effect on Lebanon's confessional make-up—suggested repatriating them to 'safe zones' inside Syria or setting up a harsh regulatory regime, others deplored the racism and inhumanity of these proposals.

Harried by all sides, an embattled Mikati adopted what he came to call as *na'i bil-nafs*—literally, 'keeping oneself out of the way'. Perhaps wishing that he, too, could abstract himself from the situation, Mikati insisted that this was the only sensible option available to a government facing such a complex and irresolvable situation. Effective neutrality, he argued, was the only means for Lebanon to 'keep discord in check', remaining 'steadfast in the face of the storms surrounding' the country and protecting it from the 'repercussions' of the Syrian conflict.[75] But Mikati knew that this stance was sustainable only if all in the government adhered to the same line, staying out of the wars raging across the border and refusing to take sides. And he knew, too, that this was asking for the impossible. For one party in particular was playing an increasingly prominent role in the fighting—Hizballah. In October 2012, Sayyid Hassan Nasrallah had been forced to admit that party members had been fighting in Syria, but that they were doing so in a personal capacity, defending the shrine of Sayyida Zaynab in Damascus and a number of Shia villages. But this claim became ever harder to sustain as the Assad regime mounted a counter-offensive against opposition forces in early 2013, attempting to regain ground lost the previous summer. In February, Syrian revolutionaries reported a Hizballah offensive in the region around the Syrian town of al-Qusayr, just a stone's throw from the Lebanese border. The party, already in control of eight villages along the border, had now moved to take three more from the Free Syrian Army, which responded with tank artillery. Two Hizballah fighters were killed, and fourteen more injured.[76] But still the party refused to acknowledge its participation in the Syrian war. Only on 25 May, amidst reports of heavy Hizballah participation in a much wider offensive on al-Qusayr, did Nasrallah finally admit to the party's presence across the border. 'Syria', he told his followers in the speech he gave each year to mark the Israeli withdrawal of 2000, was 'the back of the resistance, and the resistance cannot stand, arms folded while its back is broken'. For should Syria fall into the hands 'of America, Israel, and the *takfiris*, the resistance ... will be besieged and Israel will enter Lebanon and impose its will'.[77] This was, as Hizballah had maintained since 2011, an existential struggle—and one that it could not afford to stay out of. But by the time Nasrallah made his admission, the Mikati government was already a thing of the past. For the prime minister had resigned on 22 March, frustrated by his inability to reconcile pro- and anti-Assad forces and by his failed attempts to oversee the creation of a new electoral law in time for the parliamentary election scheduled for that spring. In the statement he had issued on Twitter announcing his decision, Mikati had called for the formation of a 'government of salvation'.[78] For many, it would take more than another cabinet to save Lebanon from itself.

24 May 2014—the vacuum

With Mikati's resignation, Lebanon entered another period of drift and stasis—its politics characterised not so much by the rule of exception as by government through prevarication. A new prime minister was designated soon enough—Tammam Salam, the scion of one of Beirut's most distinguished Sunni dynasties and a longstanding fixture of the capital's political scene. But, like his predecessors, Salam struggled to create a cabinet. Charged with this task on 6 April 2013, he only announced the formation of his government on 15 February 2014. In the end, this was another 'national unity' government—an awkward assemblage of twenty-four ministers, in which Sleiman and Salam, 8 March, and 14 March received eight portfolios apiece. An arrangement intended to guarantee a measure of equilibrium between Lebanon's dissonant political forces, it brought only discord and atrophy. A bad situation was only made worse by the end, on 24 May 2014, of Michel Sleiman's term in office. After struggling to secure his appointment as prime minister, Salam now found himself also taking on the mantle of caretaker president, as Lebanon's deputies demonstrated their singular ability to prevaricate by meeting forty-five times before they were able to agree on a new president in October 2016, when they finally elected Michel Aoun. The parliamentary elections, put off in May 2013 until November 2014, were again postponed—this time for three years, until May 2017, MPs citing Lebanon's worsening security situation to justify this *tamdid*, or extension. An electoral law could still not be agreed upon. Nor could a comprehensive budget, addressing the demands of striking public sector workers. In April 2014, UNHCR announced that the number of Syrian refugees had passed the one million mark; their numbers had almost tripled in the space of a year.[79] All the while, Hizballah became ever more deeply involved in Syria, engaging in fierce offensives on the opposition strongholds of Zabadani in western Syria in July 2015. By that point, the trash crisis had already broken out. With no-one to pick up the rubbish, mounds of refuse piled up along streets and highways. Riverbeds, mountainsides, forests—all were used for fly-tipping as the inhabitants of Beirut and Mount Lebanon ran out of space for the waste they continued to produce with depressing, inevitable regularity. The crisis did not just bring unwelcome attention to a country that prided itself—even at the risk of self-delusion—on its natural beauty and hospitality; it also precipitated a wave of civil unrest, as ordinary Lebanese began to call for the end of an unsustainable political system built on *muhasasa*—or division of the spoils. By the time Tammam Salam stepped down in November 2016, giving way to Saad Hariri— the prodigal son returned from exile—he might well have been relieved to go.

4

AL-ZA'AMA

ON POLITICAL LEADERSHIP AND PARTISANSHIP
IN LEBANON

It was the summer of 2007. A by-election had been called in the Matn district in the wake of the assassination of Pierre Gemayel, gunned down the previous November. This was viewed as a major test for 14 March and its fragile majority—reduced, since Gemayel's death, to a single seat in parliament—and the Free Patriotic Movement and its allies were widely expected to win the contest. The day was hot and filled with tension, as the representatives of rival Christian parties took up their positions outside polling stations to hand out their prepared lists of candidates, as is the way in Lebanon, which lacks official ballots. Violence hung heavy in the humid July air. Around lunchtime, a roadside scuffle broke out between the son of a *za'im*, or political leader, known for his longstanding opposition to Syrian interference and members of the Tashnag, one of Lebanon's two Armenian parties, which had joined the ranks of 8 March alongside the FPM. The row was nothing, just a few shouts and insults and fisticuffs, and the son was known, in any case, for his hot temper and high-handed ways. His father was elderly, but still vigorous, and the party over which he presided was a diminished force, weakened by the inter-Christian fighting of the 1980s and the oppression of the 1990s. The son, now well into middle-age, threw his weight around as only a thwarted heir could.

But as radio stations reported an altercation and mentioned his name, one of the za'im's retainers—once one of the fighters in his militia, who now made his meagre living as a janitor in a state hospital near his hometown—took to the roof of the apartment building in which the za'im and his family lived, in the outer suburbs of Beirut. A bandolier wrapped around his body, laden with carriages like ripe grape bunches, he lay down on the roof edge like a sniper, his Kalashnikov ready. Lustrous with sweat, his lips frayed with white from the thirst, he kept muttering 'they're coming, they're coming'. For hours, he could not be brought down, for all the efforts of the za'im's drivers and the small cohort of gendarmes the Ministry of the Interior had tasked with his safety. I would hear the story twice in the following weeks. Once, it was the za'im's own wife who told it. In her telling, pity was the dominant strain—'the poor man', she kept saying, her face showing bewildered concern for this errant soul, 'the poor man'. When the drivers told me the story, however, they did not find it moving, so much as funny. Playing their friend's behaviour for laughs, they described the sight of him, stalking the roof for hours, talking to himself, his gun pointed into the empty distance in expectation of an attack never to come. But for them, too, incomprehension was mixed in with ridicule—*kan majnun*, they would say, 'he was possessed', 'insane'. There was no way of accounting for this behaviour in rational terms, of placing it within the settled regimes of everyday life. It was entirely aberrant, a brief and disturbing breach of the normal order.

To be sure, their friend's behaviour spoke of a deeper disquiet within him, a psyche possessed by past trauma. And yet these men remained reluctant to consider the ways in which his acts did fit within the troubling patterns of the everyday in contemporary Lebanon. For, as the anthropologist Sami Hermez has argued, this is a country whose people are caught between the recollection of violence past and the anticipation of violence future, the memory of the civil war that was and the fear of what might still come to pass. Disintegrating, destructive violence of the kind that tore the country apart from 1975 to 1990 is always felt as an immanent presence, a haunting of the present, like a chronic ache carried around in the body that flares up at moments of tension and stress. And, of course, violence—both political and banal—is more than just an imagined possibility. It is a constant feature of life, from the young men killed by other drivers in fits of murderous road rage and the bullets fired into the air by men celebrating an election or an exam result, cheering a wedding, or grieving a relative, to the car bombs that have killed a string of politicians and army and intelligence officers since 2005, the street fighting of Tripoli, Beirut, and Saida, and the confrontations against jihadi groups at Nahr al-Bared in 2007, and, ten years later, in the heights above 'Arsal. To deny that violence is there all around them, to pretend that it is a faraway thing or a remote possibility—these are strategies that many rely on in Lebanon to deflect its presence and to lessen their quotidian anxieties. But this in itself is just another way in which violence weaves its way into the everyday lives of the Lebanese and structures their comportment.[1]

There are other ways, too, in which this retainer's behaviour was in keeping with the norms of the political in contemporary Lebanon: the intense personal loyalty and devotion towards the *za'im* and his family, intermingled with fear of his whims and fits of temper and obligation towards this man who provides wages and favours and keeps others afloat; the intimate comingling of leader and followers, that feeling of being so very close and yet also, at the same time, so utterly distant, of sharing space and yet inhabiting different worlds; the coarse, dismissive masculinity of the *za'im*'s retainers, playing backgammon and smoking as they swap stories, and the importance of particular discourses of the political, particular ways of representing the world and making sense of actions—all of these, I want to suggest, are characteristic of the worlds of the *zu'ama*, or political leaders, the everyday world they inhabit and the way in which they project their power into the everyday worlds of others.

The makings of leadership

It is upon the characteristic features and workings of *za'ama*, or political leadership, in contemporary Lebanon that this chapter concentrates. This is a mode of accumulating and projecting power that is at once intensely 'personal' and structural.[2] For the way in which the *za'im* conducts himself in everyday life, constructing his charisma out of small acts and throwaway words, matters as much as the grand gestures and pronouncements that he will make in public appearances on the national stage. Moreover, the *za'im*'s political power is built, in large part, out of his ability to act—for good or bad—in the everyday lives of his followers, to intercede on their behalf, to procure work and provide food or medication, as well as to punish, to take away and exclude. This may take the form, increasingly, of institutional support through charitable foundations, schools, clinics, cooperatives and microcredit initiatives. But it is understood by all as a personal connection, holding leader and follower together in a reciprocal bind of mutual obligation. The terms of the arrangement are unequivocal: the *za'im*'s generosity must be repaid in kind, through political support at the ballot box and in the street.

Given such material underpinnings, it is not surprising that scholars long understood the relationship between *za'im* and partisan in economistic terms. This was no more than a mutually beneficial material arrangement, if one underwritten by primordial ties of region and religion. As the political sociologist Arnold Hottinger put it in the mid-1960s, 'a *za'im* in the specifically Lebanese and contemporary sense is a political leader who possesses the support of a locally circumscribed community and who retains this support by fostering or appearing to foster the interests of as many as possible from amongst his clientele'. A political operator and fixer who leverages his personal wealth for political gain, and uses political office for personal enrichment, he 'exchanges the betterment of his client group in all ways, economic, social, and political, for their political support'. However, while some modern men—'lawyers, businessmen, ... professional politicians' and the like—exhibited many of the traits of the *za'im*, this role was in many ways a holdover of tradition—or rather a peculiarly Lebanese retrofitting of tradition to modernity. Though most *zu'ama* did not possess the feudal prerogatives that had once defined the position, all had to belong to the same confession and region or locality as their followers; they were not national leaders, who presided over parties with a reach that transcended the narrow, parochial bounds of community and place. This was an arrangement that could survive only so long as Lebanese democracy retained its particular characteristics, and remained defined by religious belonging.[3]

Hottinger's definition has been echoed by generations of scholars. In the midst of Lebanon's uncivil wars, Michael Johnson described the politics of pre-1975 'Sunni Beirut' as bearing all the trappings of a 'clientelist system', 'in the sense that individualised contacts or agreements were made between the patron and client, whereby welfare services of various kinds were exchanged for political, and particularly electoral, support'. To ensure both that these services were provided and that clients complied with the *za'im*'s expectations, the latter's retainers developed 'sophisticated machines' to govern the 'dyadic' relationship between leader and follower—'an articulated set of structures which functioned to maintain social and political control', channelling political energies into confessional sentiment and personal loyalties, and preventing the development of class consciousness among the country's poor.[4] In her study of Lebanon's post-war political elites, meanwhile, Rola el-Husseini defined the *zu'ama* who still loomed large in the 1990s as 'community leaders who are perceived as intercessors for their clients or followers'. The latter, she argued, 'vote for their leader's person, not for a political program. In many cases, the leader may not even *have* a political platform, beyond an established ability to further the interests of clients'.[5] This material definition, then, has remained remarkably stable through the turmoil of war, reconstruction, and political crisis.

Indeed, it may well be that this typology is not without its uses. After all, it is clear that political leadership and charisma are still bound up, in complex and intimate ways, with confessional belonging. Rafiq Hariri may have prided himself on providing welfare assistance and scholarships to all Lebanese regardless of their religion. When it came to building a sustainable electoral following, however, he found that his most viable and expedient option was to tack to established rules and expectations, ramping up his offerings to Sunni localities and neighbourhoods, and winning over or displacing Sunni notables in Saida, Beirut, and Tripoli.[6] Sayyid Hassan Nasrallah may enjoy the admiration of Christians, who—sometimes begrudgingly—acknowledge the force and emotional charge of his oratory; still, it is hard to conceive of non-Shia identifying so closely with his words, with their evocation of a particular experience of deprivation, occupation, and resistance and their way of weaving this into a longer, sacred history of martyrdom and injustice.[7]

And yet, as this suggests, the relationship between the *za'im* and his followers—what the French scholars Franck Mermier and Sabrina

Mervin have called the 'partisan societies' that remain invested in Lebanon's politics—is not just an economic arrangement, an exchange of favours lubricated by self-interest.[8] Affect and emotion matter here—aspirations, enmities, and beliefs in common, shared grief and joy, but also intense, fervent personal admiration and love, apprehension and awe and, at times, quietly voiced anger, bemusement and resentment. What's more, the *za'im*'s power is built as much out of words as out of things and acts. It is not made simply of material offerings, but also of discursive gifts, particular tropes that are blandishments in their own right. By turns comforting, cajoling, and anger-making, these speech acts serve to hold leader and follower in a close rhetorical clench and to spur the *za'im*'s supporters into political action and personal commitment. In the absence of programmatic politics, these stock phrases and refrains, these patterns of argumentation and ways of envisioning the community, the nation, and the world stand in place of manifestoes and policy pledges. Ceaselessly repeated by the *za'im* and other ranking members of his party, movement, or parliamentary bloc, they are taken up in turn by followers—and mocked or contradicted by opponents. For as much as the *za'im* places himself above questioning—avoiding, for instance, the rough and tumble of the talk show—his power and prose are never uncontested. On the contrary, his words—these pronouncements that take the place of deeds—are constantly questioned, disputed, debated and derided.

These are conversations that involve not just the *za'im*'s opponents, but also his supporters. All are drawn into endless discussion of the motives and reasons of this or that announcement or decision by the *za'im*'s deliberate refusal to provide whys and wherefores for his actions. In doing so, Lebanon's political leaders contribute to the construction of a form of power that is deliberately unaccountable—both in the sense that they see no need to account for their actions to anyone, convinced as they are that they retain an 'absolute ... freedom of action, unconstrained' by the forces of convention, law, and due process, and in the sense that their acts are therefore difficult to reckon with, lacking as they do clear causal explanations or a relation to a particular manifesto or programme.[9] One or another *za'im* will break this pattern at times, either to contest his rivals' actions by appealing to the constitution, say, or the rules of parliamentary procedure, or to draw his partisans more closely into the intimate discursive relationship he has constructed—a device that Nasrallah, alone amongst Lebanese political leaders, uses regularly. But on the whole, what is not self-evident—and self-evidently in the interests of the community or the nation—remains inscrutable. In such circumstances, in which the facts of political negotiations and private dealings are so carefully hidden from the eyes of the public, analysis and inquiry are replaced by rumour, supposition and speculation. Journalists and *muhallalun*, or political analysts and commentators, but also partisans and opponents whiling away the hours in cafés, on bulletin boards and comments sections, endlessly guess at reasons and quarrel over causes. The *za'im*, then, is like a figure standing behind a wall of opaque glass; the details of his life, of his way of being in the world and doing things are as imperceptible as its outlines are clear.

The changing face of *za'ama*

To speak of the *za'im* in the singular is, perhaps, somewhat of a misnomer. For there is no one type of political leader in contemporary Lebanon. There are the scions of the old houses that held office and prestige before the war—urban notables like the Sunni Hoss and Salam families of Beirut or the Karami, Jisr and Ahdab of Tripoli, and rural grandees like the Druze Arslan and Jumblatt. There are the families—mostly Christian—that owe their position to the prominence of a forebear in the politics of the early Lebanese republic. This is the case, for instance, of the Chamoun, Edde, and Gemayel families—all dynasties with some local standing, but which projected their power onto the national stage only from the 1940s and 1950s onwards. There are those—of whom perhaps the best known are Samir Geagea and Michel Aoun—who derive their standing from the power and renown they accumulated during the civil war and their refusal of the post-war order. There are the entrepreneurs who made their fortunes in the Gulf and elsewhere, and who leveraged their wealth into political careers. The most famous of these, of course, is Rafiq Hariri, but Najib Mikati may also be counted in this category.[10] And last, but not least, there are Nabih Berri and Hassan Nasrallah, the leaders of Amal and Hizballah. The two owe their positions to quite different social and institutional bases—Berri to the access to state resources he enjoys as speaker of parliament and his canny transformation of bodies such as the Council of the South into levers of political power, and Nasrallah to his position as the secretary-general of Hizballah, his religious charisma and powerful oratory, by turns affable and shuddering. And yet for all the ostensible differences between Berri, the upwardly mobile lawyer with his expensive suits and reputation for lavish ostentation, and the cleric Nasrallah, with his black *sayyid*'s turban, his dark robes and his ascetic lifestyle, the two men do share, in some ways, a common trajectory. Both entered politics through the 'movement of the dispossessed', or *harakat al-mahrumin*, founded in 1974 by the Iranian cleric and social reformer Musa al-Sadr, who had settled in Lebanon in 1957; Berri became its president in 1980, following Sadr's disappearance in Libya in 1978, while Nasrallah broke away with a host of others in the 1980s to form the movement that became Hizballah.[11] Both acquired their current positions in 1992, when Berri was elected speaker of the Lebanese parliament and Nasrallah secretary-general of the 'party of God'. And, significantly, both have presided over the marked ascendancy of the Shia community, navigating the turbulent waters of post-war Lebanon with skill to establish themselves as dominant figures in national politics.

But, as this suggests, distinctions among *zu'ama* are not always as clear cut as their public images might suggest. What's more, though scholarly representations of the ideal-type of the *za'im* have stayed static over the last fifty years or so, the fortunes of various leaders have waxed and waned, moving with the shifting currents of war, reconstruction, and regional growth.[12] The 1990s was, in this regard, a time of flux and restructuring. Figures like Walid Jumblatt and the Maronite *za'im* Sleiman Frangieh adroitly adjusted, it is true, to the new dispensation created by Syrian overrule. The end of the war had curtailed the opportunities for economic profit it had thrown up, compelling them to diversify their activities once again—in the case of Jumblatt, by gaining access to state resources in the form of the Fund of the Displaced, and in that of Frangieh by capitalising on his close relations with members of the Syrian elite to secure lucrative private contracts. Though these men still carefully cultivated the regional roots of their status, their economic standing was largely divorced by the 1990s from their families' histories of landowning and local authority. This trend was already apparent in the 1960s and 1970s, when many of the *bekawat*, or notables, had moved to Beirut, the locus of political and economic power in Lebanon, with its opportunities, its international schools in which to educate the children, its clothes stores, restaurants and nightclubs. But the civil war, and the establishment of what some have called—perhaps rather too euphemistically—the Pax Syriana, only accelerated this transformation of the old rural *zu'ama* into canny political entrepreneurs whose prosperity depended upon packed and diverse portfolios of commercial undertakings.[13]

Other members of the old, pre-war political elite, however, did not fare so well. This was the case of members of the old Sunni notability, like Tammam Salam and Selim el-Hoss. Though they had clung on through the civil war years, adapting awkwardly to this time of militia capitalism, they were eclipsed in the 1990s by the new 'contractor bourgeoisie'—as Hannes Baumann has called this group—preeminent among them Rafiq Hariri, who set about creating a reliable electoral base in Beirut and other Sunni regions in the mid-1990s.[14] Ironically, Hariri did so by emulating the tactics that had underpinned the political success and standing of these families for generations. For not only did he turn the Hariri Foundation, which he had established during the civil war to provide university scholarships and healthcare, into an instrument of patronage within the Sunni community; he also lent his support to the new Mufti of the Republic, Lebanon's chief Sunni cleric, and made his own the Maqasid Foundation—the Sunni charitable organisation that had long been the domain of Beiruti families like the Salams and the Daouks—ensuring that Saudi Arabia, which had suspended its funding, turn the taps on again and parachuting his aides onto its board.

For their part, the ranks of the Christian *zu'ama* were decapitated by exile, assassination, and repression. Amin Gemayel left in 1988, before the war was even out. Michel Aoun, who had built up a messianic following in 1989 and 1990, fled to France in 1991. Dany Chamoun was assassinated with his family in 1990; his brother and successor Dory left for France soon after. Samir Geagea was arrested and tried in 1994, indicted on four charges of murder—including those of Rashid Karami, the former prime minister assassinated in 1987, and of Dany

Chamoun and his family—and on a charge of planting a bomb in a church in Zouk Mosbeh in 1994. Though he was cleared of the latter offence, he was convicted on all counts of murder and given four life sentences. He would spend the next eleven years in solitary confinement, locked up in his cell beneath the Ministry of Defence in Yarze. These men were replaced by more pliant figures like Elie Hobeika, Michel el-Murr, Elie Ferzli, and Karim Pakradouni, who seized the opportunities that Syrian hegemony presented. Their followers, meanwhile, either gave up, migrated away from Lebanon themselves—the crosses and cedars on the walls of the restaurants and hair salons they have opened in Paris, Brussels, Montreal or London discreet signs of their enduring allegiances—or moved into a clandestine world of sombre rallies and student protests.

By contrast, the years after 2005 can be seen as a time of unprecedented consolidation within the political class. For the bipolar nature of Lebanese politics in this period has necessitated the crafting of sprawling, sometimes unwieldy, coalitions and unlikely alliances to provide the central parties of 14 March and 8 March—the Future Movement on the one hand, and Hizballah on the other—with a panoply of partners from across Lebanon's regions, electoral districts and communities. Both these blocs, after all, make much of their respective claim to be the legitimate representatives of the Lebanese people as a whole. This claim, if it is to hold water, must be buttressed by recruiting a large cast of parties and independent players—Sunni and Shia, Maronite, Greek Catholic and Greek Orthodox, Druze and Armenian. These coalitions serve, in effect, as vast canopies under which leaders both large and small can shelter, and as means of gaining access to patronage, privileges, and political leverage. Like an executive scheme for the political class, they provide everything from funds for electoral campaigns, to support for demands for ministerial positions or administrative appointments and armoured SUVs and enhanced security details. Paradoxically, even the problems that beset 14 March after 2011 afforded others opportunities for office, with both Najib Mikati and Tammam Salam finding something to gain from the Future Movement's discomfiture. The post-2005 period, then, has been a time of *zu'ama*.

Welfare parties

These are the men—and they are, almost without exception, men—who make up Lebanon's political class, a class that is as diverse in its composition as it is dependent on the same mechanisms and levers to exert and preserve its power. Prime amongst these is welfare. For all either provide—if they have the means—their supporters with alternatives to deficient state services, or act as funders and brokers, ensuring supporters' access to healthcare and education and helping to subsidise private school or hospital fees. This partisan welfare provision is often spoken of as a particularly Lebanese practice, the *wasta* or mediation that is required to get anything done—from getting a parking ticket cleared to securing a civil service job—another feature of that exceptionalism that the country's people at once bemoan and pride themselves on. Others present it as characteristic—alongside individualism, honour, and shame—of that Mediterranean culture that prefers personal intermediation and negotiation to the anonymous workings of bureaucracy, and regards the state with suspicion as a hostile and interfering presence that meddles with private matters, rather than a force for good.[15]

However, there is no escaping the fact that this reliance on private means and networks to provide welfare is a structural feature of late capitalism, with its ideological distaste for state intervention. One need only think, for instance, of the local authorities in Britain that place housing benefit recipients in private flats and houses, lining the pockets of landlords rather than investing in new public accommodation, or the American municipalities that think it more economical to rely on 'car transportation' companies than to keep funding their bus networks. In this logic, it makes more sense to subtract responsibility from a state supposedly ill-fitted to provide services than to add to its capacity to assist its citizens. If there is anything that distinguishes Lebanon, though, it is the deep history of practices that can be traced back into the late Ottoman period and the years of the French Mandate, and the complex arithmetic of confessional and partisan considerations that determines who receives welfare, how much they will receive, and through what channels.

Perhaps the best known of Lebanon's overlapping networks of welfare provision is that of Hizballah. Foreign journalists and commentators will often note the existence of its social services as a means of making sense of its popular appeal—an instrumental reading of partisan loyalty that is often used to explain the pull of other Islamist parties across the Middle East, such as Hamas and the Muslim Brotherhood. However, these explanations, with their stress on the self-interest of claimant and supplier alike, do not do enough to help us understand both the close and intimate relation that ties Hizballah to its supporters and its motivation for building such an extensive set of social welfare institutions. To be sure, these calculations do matter: supporters have needs that they know the party and its pendants will supply, and the party knows, too, that its munificence will be rewarded with loyalty and votes. But Hizballah is, like Amal, the heir to Musa al-Sadr. This is a contested legacy, complicated by the fighting between these parties during the civil war and the underlying current of tension and conflict that runs beneath the official rhetoric of partnership and collaboration. What's more, Hizballah now tends to speak of its constituency as the *mustad'afin*—those who have been weakened—rather than the deprived or *mahrumin*—a rhetorical shift that allows it at once to mark itself out from Amal, and to suggest that its followers' condition is not a permanent one and that, though brought low for a time, they retain the potential to raise themselves up again.[16] Nevertheless, it is clear that Hizballah has inherited Sadr's concern for uplifting Lebanon's Shia. Its central concern remains ensuring the socio-economic elevation of its constituents while crafting a society respectful of the ethical precepts of Islam and dedicated to the task of resistance.

These are the considerations—as much as the simple arithmetic of the ballot box—that have informed the party's action, as it has spun a dense web of social welfare organisations around itself since the 1980s. Designated in the party's promotional literature as *mu'assasat al-khidma*, or service foundations, these include the Mu'assasat al-Shahid, or Foundation of the Martyr, which provides assistance to the families of dead fighters and civilians, and the Mu'assasat al-Jarih, or Foundation of the Injured, which provides medical care and financial aid to those hurt in fighting or bombing raids. Both established in 1982 as subsidiaries of Iranian parent organisations, they remained for a time under the Islamic Republic's auspices. Since Hizballah's appearance in 1985, however, they have come under the party's aegis, taking on a central role in its welfare provision. Several other institutions have followed a similar pattern. The Mu'assasat al-Qard al-Hasan was established in 1982 as an 'Iranian initiative', and provides—as its name suggests—interest-free loans to those in need in the southern suburbs of Beirut, Sur, Nabatiyyeh and the Beqaa. The Mu'assasat Jihad al-Bina al-Inma'iyya—roughly 'the foundation for development and construction', better known as Jihad al-Bina, or the 'construction effort'—was set up in 1985 as the subsidiary of the Iranian Jehad-e Sazandegi. Al-Imdad, also known as the 'Islamic philanthropic committee', was established in 1987 by Hizballah with the financial assistance of the Islamic Republic to provide donations and loans to families whose heads cannot meet their needs, and which are not eligible for assistance from other institutions. Finally, the Rasul al-A'zam Hospital opened its doors in 1988, and was financed first by the Iranian Foundation for the Martyr, and then by its Lebanese counterpart. Perhaps alone in not having been established on an Iranian blueprint or initially funded by Iranian money is the Ha'ya al-Suhhiyya al-Islamiyya, or Islamic Health Committee. Established in 1988, this oversees Hizballah's health policies, running dispensaries, preventive healthcare centres, and a hospital in southern Lebanon.[17]

That many of these organisations owe their origins to Iranian investment and initiative in Lebanon in the 1980s is hard to contest. Nevertheless, it would be wrong to regard them merely as vehicles for the continuing projection of Iranian power or as symbols of Hizballah's enduring submission to foreign forces. There is no denying that the party maintains a close, if complex, relationship with the Islamic Republic. Indeed, it has recognised Ayatollah Ali Khamenei as its *marja'*, or 'source' of spiritual authority and guidance since the mid-1990s, when the Supreme Leader named two of the parties' leaders—Nasrallah and Muhammad Yazbak—as his *wakil*-s, or agents, in Lebanon.[18] Iran's influence is visible not just in Hizballah's theology, with its clear commitment to *vilayet-i faqih*—the ideological keystone of the Islamic Republic—but also in the party's foreign policy. The clearest sign of this is perhaps its involvement in Syria, where Hizballah has fought alongside Iranian forces on key fronts since 2013—if not earlier. On the other hand, it would be reductive in the extreme to regard a party with motivations, interests, and agendas of its own as a mere puppet answering to the bidding of its Iranian masters. The party's combat operations in Syria—and now, since July 2017, in Lebanon—are also born, for instance, of its disquiet at the proliferation of Sunni jihadi movements and factions, which it regards as existential threats not just to the Shia community, but also to the fragile weave of Lebanese comity. And what is true of its foreign adventures also holds for its domestic commitments. The extensive network of welfare organisations that have developed in Shia parts of Lebanon—the southern suburbs of Beirut, the south, and the Beqaa and Hermel in the east—since the early 1980s have long since fallen firmly within Hizballah's ambit, playing a central role in its efforts to construct a *mujtama' al-muqawama*, or 'resistance society' in Lebanon.

What's more, each of these organisations performs a subtly different part. The Foundation of the Martyr and the Foundation of the Injured, for instance, prop up Hizballah's image as a militant force, doing battle with the forces of neo-colonial oppression and providing succour to the meek and the weak. Jihad al-Bina, meanwhile, has helped to shape the spatial and economic fabric of Shia villages, towns, and neighbourhoods since the 1980s. It has done so in a variety of ways. Perhaps the most conspicuous of these has been its role in rebuilding private dwellings and public buildings damaged in Israeli raids, and making up for the infrastructural shortcomings and absences of the Lebanese state. Between 1988 and 1997, the organisation was responsible for the construction or reconstruction of forty mosques, thirty-two schools, seventeen cultural centres, three hospitals, and eleven dispensaries, as well as 15,000 private homes. As Mona Harb has pointed out, this building work underwrites the efforts of the resistance, ensuring that Shia displaced by conflict return quickly to their homes and villages and preserving the social weave of 'its' communities.[19] (Much the same logic underwrote the efforts of al-Wa'd, or 'the promise', the organisation established in 2006 to reconstruct the southern Beirut neighbourhoods that bore the brunt of Israeli air raids.)[20] But Jihad al-Bina has also helped Hizballah-run municipalities to embellish their localities by designing 'fountains, public gardens, and roundabouts'. And it has built social centres for the Foundation of the Martyr and the Foundation of the Injured, medical centres for the Islamic Health Committee and schools for the Islamic Foundation for Education and Learning, many of which share the distinctive cube-like design and bright colours of the Foundation's flagship school in Burj al-Barajneh—a reminder of the tight integration and interpenetration between Hizballah's different 'satellite organisations', as Harb has called them.[21]

But many of Jihad al-Bina's activities go beyond simple building. In the rural areas of southern Lebanon that Hizballah deems in need of uplift, Jihad al-Bina has not just laid down new roads and dug irrigation canals, but has also opened nurseries, veterinary clinics and agricultural training schools and introduced environmental awareness and microcredit schemes. In Beirut, meanwhile, it has helped since the 1980s to collect waste and to provide water and electricity. Though it has increasingly left the latter to the private syndicates that hire out their generators to apartment buildings and communities across Lebanon, there is no denying the importance of such infrastructural support.[22] All in all, then, Jihad al-Bina resembles in significant ways its Iranian forebear, Jehad-e Sazandegi (construction effort in Farsi) which did not just build roads, bridges, clinics, and libraries across rural Iran, connecting villages to the electricity and water networks and digging trenches during the Iran–Iraq war of 1980–88, but also played a key part in the Islamic Republic's intelligence and propaganda efforts, gathering information on smugglers and dissidents, distributing Qur'ans and prayer sheets and working to maintain the morale of the revolution's footmen in the villages and on the front.[23] For Jihad al-Bina's operations undergird Hizballah's efforts to create in Shia parts of Lebanon a *hala islamiyya*—an 'Islamic condition' or 'sphere'—or what its adherents sometimes also call, in more informal terms, a *jaw islami*—an 'Islamic mood' or 'atmosphere'.[24]

A similar function is performed by Hizballah's schools and scout troops, known respectively as *madaris al-mahdi*, the 'schools of the Mahdi', and *kashshaf al-mahdi*, or Mahdi scouts. There are now sixteen Mahdi schools across predominantly Shia regions of Lebanon, from Ayn Mizrab and Bint Jbeil, only a few kilometres from the border with Israel, to Baalbek and Nabi Sheet in the Beqaa, Hadath in the suburbs of Beirut, and the organisation's flagship establishment, the Shahed school in Burj al-Barajneh, whose building overlooks the airport highway that scythes through the *dahiyeh*.[25] Overseen by the Islamic Foundation for Education and Teaching, one of Hizballah's many 'satellite organisations', these establishments welcomed 17,415 pupils in 2011–12.[26] As Catherine Le Thomas has shown, they prize not just educational attainment, but also *iltizam*, or commitment, seeking to foster in their students observance of the faith and attachment to the party.[27] The Foundation thus seeks, in its own words, to 'provide an example of pioneering Islamic education, bringing together pure and authentic Islamic education with exceptional modern learning', in order to create a 'learned and conscious missionary generation [*jil risali*], committed to the values of Islam'.[28]

This twin commitment is evident as much from the schools' ceremonies as from their social media pages. The 'celebration of achievement' held at the Mahdi secondary school in Sur, for instance, began with the audience—pupils wearing yellow Hizballah sashes and their parents—and assembled dignitaries reciting verses of the Qur'an and singing the two anthems of Lebanon and Hizballah, before an audiovisual presentation of the pupils' achievements over the course of the academic year. This was followed by the speech of Hizballah's regional cadre, Ahmad Safi al-Din. Flanked by the flags of Lebanon, the party, and the Foundation, he enjoined his audience to appreciate that 'in truth, it is a stronger and more capable resistance that ensures our unity ... and not weakness and submission to this or that regime, or to the international community that danced in our blood in every massacre committed during the wars waged against us'.[29] A similar admixture of objectives and messages can be found on the alumni association's Facebook page, whose profile picture is an image of Sayyid Nasrallah: posts congratulating one former pupil on receiving her nursing diploma from the American University Hospital in Beirut, and mourning the death of another as a martyr in Syria, as well as images of religious devotion. One photograph shows primary school pupils dressed all in black and holding black balloons in commemoration of the death of the Imam Husain; its caption reads, simply, 'a picture that speaks, a picture of school life'. Another post is a devotional image of the Imam Ali and the Prophet Muhammad together, arms aloft and hands interlaced, beneath the saying 'were it not for you, Ali, the believers would not know any after me'—a powerful reminder of the legitimacy of Shia Islam.[30]

These schools' efforts to socialise young Shia into what is commonly known as *thaqafat al-muqawama*, or the culture of resistance, are buttressed by Hizballah's scout troops, the *kashshaf al-mahdi*. Despite competition from Amal's *kashshaf al-risala* and Sayyid Fadlallah's *kashshaf al-mabarrat*—Lebanese scouting is a crowded field, with eighteen different federations representing different confessions and school networks—the organisation counted 24,452 boys and 21,289 girls amongst its members in 2005. By the end of the 2000s, there were perhaps as many as 60,000 children enrolled in the Mahdi scouts.[31] Many of these also attend the schools run by the Islamic Foundation for Education and Learning or Hizballah's charitable organisation al-Imdad, participate in youth clubs run by party associations, and pray in mosques identified with the party. The 'paths' or curriculum set out for the organisation's scouts seek to foster in them piety, moral comportment, and loyalty to party and nation. Thus, the scout must believe in God and obey his leader in the same way as pious Shia must observe 'the rule of the jurisconsult'—*vilayet-i faqih* or, as it is known in Arabic, *wilayat al-faqih*; he or she will be a 'trusted and polite friend, who will work with his peers and refuse to deal with the enemies of God and the nation'. Endurance, thrift, duty, love of learning and effort, and environmental concern are all encouraged, as are knowledge of the Qur'an and the tenets of Shia Islam.[32] These political and religious aspects are particularly evident in the Mahdi scouts' activities. Physical strength and stamina and service to the community are significant here, of course: scouts gather in 'scout cities' like the vast Imam Khomeini recreational complex, established by al-Imdad in 1991 in the Beqaa village of al-Taybe or the Mahdi scouts' own centre near Nabatiyyeh, embark on hikes, and go white-water rafting on the Litani river, which wends through southern Lebanon, and they help to clean mosques and, on occasion, churches. But the Mahdi scouts' marching bands specialise in patriotic anthems of a particularly martial bent, and its troops organise visits to Shia shrines like that of Sayyida Zaynab in Damascus and events to commemorate important religious occasions. In 2005, 47,268 people attended the events held to mark 'Ashura, and another 37,645 those put on for Ramadan.[33]

For their part, the hospitals and dispensaries that fall under the aegis of the Islamic Health Committee perform a dual function, serving both the party's humanitarian rhetoric and its electoral calculations. To be sure, these facilities are largely situated in predominantly Shia parts of the country—a concentration that party officials justify by pointing to their history of relative deprivation and state neglect, and their more recent experience of Israeli occupation and bombing. But they pride themselves on working with a range of partners—from the Lebanese state to international organisations—to provide care and health education to all, regardless of faith or need. The Committee's slogan—*al-sahha lil-kull, wa ma' al-kull*, or 'health for all and with all'—is a telling sign of these ambitions to transcend confessional difference. In similar fashion, the Rasul al-A'zam Hospital—still by far the largest medical facility in the southern suburbs of Beirut, which, despite their demographic weight, remain a healthcare desert devoid of a single public hospital—also declares itself open to all. This is apparent from its take-over of the Saint-Georges Hospital in the Beirut suburb of Hadath—still one of the few localities scattered around the southern rim of the Lebanese capital in which sizeable numbers of Christians and Shia comingle—as well as from the tone and content of its digital presence.

On the day that I visited the hospital's website, it carried news items on a conference organised by the hospital's maternity and feminine health section to mark the International Day of the Midwife, and on the visit of the Lebanese TV presenter George Kordahi—best known for hosting the Arabic version of 'Who Wants to Be a Millionaire', as well as for his staunch support of the Assad regime—to fighters injured in the combats between Hizballah and Sunni jihadi forces in eastern Lebanon. The intent of the latter was clear enough: to provide evidence of the cross-confessional understanding and consensus around the role of the 'Islamic resistance' in Lebanon's defence from foreign threats that Hizballah's media channels regularly insist upon.[34] The former, meanwhile, served to showcase Rasul al-A'zam's close working relations with national partners—from the Lebanese University professor who lectured on 'the role of midwives in social health centres' to the national syndicate of midwives, with whom the hospital worked to organise the conference. The photograph accompanying this short news item is the very picture of confessional comity and female empowerment: a group of women, some wearing the headscarf, others not, all smiling warmly at the camera, and wearing much the same outfits—jeans, trainers, and heels, chunky watches and handbags. Some may be observant Muslims, it appears to suggest, others not, and others still

Christian or Druze—but that is of little import. What matters more are the essential issues of female health—cervical and uterine cancer, breastfeeding, post-natal care and the like.[35]

To be sure, the principal purpose of these institutions is still to provide care for the Shia community, while remaining open to working with other sectors of Lebanese society. This ambiguous order of priorities is apparent from the Committee's mission statement, in which it declares its purpose as providing 'the best medical services and care to the weakened, resistant Lebanese society'—*al-mujtama' al-lubnani al-muqawim al-mustad'af*—in order to enable it to 'reach up to a better life'.[36] This is language that does not differentiate explicitly between different confessions, but which instead organises Lebanon's inhabitants according to their varying levels of socio-economic need and ideological proximity to the principles of resistance. It goes without saying that those most in need of this assistance, and most closely aligned with these values, will be—in Hizballah's view—the country's Shia. And yet, at the same time, the party's medical organisations do provide care to others. The political scientist Melani Cammett was told by one Sunni inhabitant of Beirut's southern neighbourhoods that 'there are Sunni families living in the southern suburbs and Hezbollah generally does not approach them. But these families do use Hezbollah's health centres and always receive good care there. My mother recently had the flu and went to a Hezbollah clinic'. The same appears to be true in the central Beirut district of Basta, where Sunnis and Shia live in often tense proximity—and yet where the Committee's clinic offers assistance to all regardless of confession.[37] This appears born of a genuine concern to care beyond the confines of sectarian community.

In this respect, however, medical provision appears to be the exception that confirms the rule. For other Hizballah institutions do follow more closely the calculated logic of sectarian, partisan and electoral provision. Thus, one Shia inhabitant of the southern Lebanese town of Nabatiyyeh reported that he had been turned away by the party's social services because of his past association with Amal, which had once had a strong presence in the locality. The same was true of a Maronite woman living in a Christian area of Mount Lebanon who travelled to the southern suburbs of Beirut to seek out help, and who was told that she was not eligible for assistance because she came from a region in which the party 'does not organise'. By contrast, welfare appears to have been opened up to Michel Aoun's supporters, after his Free Patriotic Movement and Hizballah signed a memorandum of understanding in February 2006. The same logic appears to dictate the party's provision of social welfare to Christian inhabitants of districts such as Jezzine, in southern Lebanon, or the Western Beqaa, marginal electoral constituencies in which Maronite, Greek Catholic, and Greek Orthodox seats have been fiercely contested in recent years. These calculations also appear to serve as the motivation for its recent efforts to reach out to the small Shia communities of the largely Christian regions of Kisrwan. In the years since 2005, the party has stepped up its assistance to Shia inhabitants of the small coastal town of 'Amshit and the villages around Jbeil, opening health clinics and paving roads with what the locals have taken to calling 'Iranian asphalt'. These efforts appear to have paid off: in 2009, 68 per cent of Shia voters in the *qada* of Jbeil went to the polls—the highest turn-out since 1990—and 89 per cent of those who did cast their ballots for the FPM.[38] Welfare, then, serves several purposes for Hizballah: it fulfils its commitments to a more 'human' approach to politics, founded on the principles of Islamic ethics; it burnishes its credentials as a national party, as committed to the Lebanese nation-state as it is to religion and resistance; and it allows it to secure both the long-term allegiance of supporters and the fleeting, but essential, endorsement of non-committed voters open to enticement.

Much the same admixture of motives is at play in the welfare policies of the Hariri family's Future Movement. Rafiq Hariri made his first forays into philanthropy in the early years of the Lebanese civil war, establishing a fledgling scholarship programme based in his hometown of Saida in 1979, before beginning work on the Kfar Falous Cultural and Medical Complex in 1980. Built in partnership with the Jesuit Université Saint-Joseph, the American University of Beirut and the private, English-language International College, this included a university and a vocational training school, a teaching hospital and a medical centre, a sports complex and a power station. The location of this project, in the village of Kfar Fallus, situated between 'Sunni' Saida, 'Shia' southern Lebanon, and 'Christian' Jezzine, was deliberately chosen to make it 'a meeting point for all the Lebanese family'. The complex was damaged during the Israeli invasion of 1982, before being destroyed in 1985 by the Lebanese Forces and Antoine Lahd's Free Lebanese Army, a Christian proxy for the Israeli occupation forces. Nevertheless, Kfar Fallus already bore all the characteristics of Hariri's distinctive approach to philanthropy: it focused on education and uplift, it worked closely with international partners, projecting an image of Lebanon as Western-oriented and open to progress, and it broadcast loudly its cross-sectarian, national credentials as a Lebanese institution open to all.[39]

Hariri's next—and rather more enduring—initiative, set up in the aftermath of the Israeli invasion, was the establishment of the Hariri Foundation, to provide loans to Lebanese students entering higher education. Between 1983—when the foundation was established—and 1996, the organisation provided assistance to around 32,000 young Lebanese. Like Kfar Fallus, the organisation worked closely with the American University of Beirut, which set the examinations through which applicants were assessed and provided language training and career guidance to beneficiaries. This Western orientation was also apparent in other ways. Though financial considerations compelled the organisation to jettison its initial aim of despatching two-thirds of its students to 'Western Europe [...] America and Canada', which the Foundation's director, Fadl Shalaq, regarded as the 'truthful source' of culture, the American University of Beirut and Beirut University College—later the Lebanese American University—remained destinations of choice for those it funded. As their names suggest, both were English-language, American-funded institutions with a proud tradition of training in subjects such as engineering and medicine.[40]

However, the Foundation's stated desire to cater to all Lebanese was hampered both by its lack of personnel on the ground and by the spatial segregation created by the civil war. It thus relied heavily—particularly in its early stages—on Sunni religious dignitaries and charities to publicise its activities and attract potential recruits. In Akkar, Sunni shaykhs were asked to mention its loan programme in their Friday sermons. In Tripoli, meanwhile, the Foundation collaborated with the Association of Islamic Youths. Unsurprisingly, a survey of loan recipients studying at the American University of Beirut carried out between late 1990 and early 1991 found that 62 per cent of recipients were Sunni, 18 per cent Shia, 11 per cent Druze and 10 per cent Greek

Orthodox. None were Maronite Christians, perhaps a product of their tendency to gravitate towards Francophone schools and universities, as well as of the dangers of crossing into west Beirut in the final stages of the civil war. What's more, while 55 per cent of Sunni respondents had not relied on contacts to secure financial assistance, almost 90 per cent of non-Sunni respondents had done so. For the testimony of those working at the Foundation in those early days suggests that it came to be seen by some outsiders as a vehicle for their own clientelist ambitions. As one employee put it in 1991, 'community leaders, influential businessmen, friends and acquaintances also press top Hariri officials to consider their requests'. While this suggests that some simply sought favours for their own children or those of their relatives and friends, it also shows the way in which this technocratic institution could be captured by political patrons like the 'community leader' who once 'imposed upon the Foundation a list of 400 applicants after the application deadline'. Despite Hariri's ambitions to provide 'non-political' assistance to Lebanese of all religious backgrounds without any strings attached, he found himself pulled back into the quicksands of confessionalism, intercession, and war capitalism.[41]

And, as Hariri himself sought to build a political following, he found himself increasingly adopting the same tactics—using education, healthcare, food packages, and the like to secure the lasting loyalties of some, and the temporary allegiances of others. By the late 1990s, Hariri had realised that the modes of technocratic governance he had favoured in the first part of the decade were not enough to ensure the successful implementation of his policies; he also needed a solid and reliable bloc of deputies willing to vote for his measures—and, to do this, he needed to mobilise a political following in Beirut and other heavily Sunni parts of Lebanon, such as Saida, Tripoli, Akkar, and the Iqlim al-Kharrub. This change in tactics, which had begun with the parliamentary elections of 1996, accelerated in 1998 with the election to the Lebanese presidency of Emile Lahoud and the demotion of Hariri's Syrian allies, 'Abd al-Halim Khaddam and Hikmat Shihabi, before culminating in the lead-up to the parliamentary elections of 2000. Aware that he needed to secure an overwhelming victory against opponents such as Selim el-Hoss and Tammam Salam, Hariri outspent his rivals lavishly—with one media source estimating he had disbursed

$50 million, much of which had gone towards incentives for voters, such as university or technical college fees or $200 in food vouchers. By contrast, Hoss put his own electoral expenditure at $273,940.[42]

Alongside these election-time outlays, Hariri also invested heavily in what Melani Cammett and Sukriti Issar have called 'bricks and mortar clientelism'.[43] This was not the first time Hariri had put his money into schools, clinics, dispensaries and the like. After the destruction of the complex at Kfar Fallus, the Hariri Foundation had reached an agreement in 1985 with the Mission Laïque Française to administer Beirut's French *lycée* jointly, before acquiring in 1986 the old Lebanese Evangelical School for Boys and Girls.[44] But the late 1990s witnessed a radical change of pace—and, some might argue, of intentions. In 1998, Hariri added to his portfolio of schools, opening a large new establishment in the working-class Sunni Beirut neighbourhood of Tarik el-Jdideh.[45] In 2000, the Hariri Foundation established six health centres across Beirut.[46] Five—the Foundation's flagship clinic in Tarik el-Jdideh, as well as those in Ras al-Nabaa, Zarif, Unesco, and Karm al-Zeytun, were opened between January and July; a sixth, in Ras Beirut, opened its doors in October.[47] The timing was no coincidence—the parliamentary elections of that year were held in late August and early September. What's more, it is telling that all but one of these centres—that in the working-class and lower-middle-class Christian neighbourhood of Karm al-Zeytun—are in neighbourhoods in which Sunnis form a significant component of the population.

Indeed, even the seemingly inexplicable decision to open a centre in Karm al-Zeytun—whose inhabitants, many of them displaced during the war, display their fierce allegiances to the Lebanese Forces, the Kata'ib and the FPM on their walls—obeyed electoral demands. For this quarter is situated in the electoral constituency known as Beirut I—a large district that englobes the largely Christian neighbourhoods of Achrafieh and Saifi and the Muslim neighbourhoods of Mazraa and Ras al-Nabaa. Try as they might to claim that they are driven entirely by humanitarian concerns for the needs of their recipients, the Hariri Foundation's officials cannot entirely shirk off the charge that such moves are politically motivated. This is certainly the perception of some within Karm al-Zeytun itself, such as the director of a Christian medical charity, who remarked that 'it's all for political reasons ...

When elections come, the rates at the clinics go down and food aid increases. Then, little by little, these services disappear until the next electoral period'.[48]

Others, however, contradict this account of contingent and calculated outlays. A Shia woman who lived in Chiyah, for example, stressed to Melani Cammett that she and her family had been well treated in its clinics, and when, in the late 1990s, her husband had needed a major operation, the Foundation had offered generous financial assistance. In similar fashion, several inhabitants of Achrafieh told Melani Cammett that they visited the health centre in Karm el-Zaytun because it offered cheaper and more reliable care than other clinics. Indeed, the Hariri Foundation's arrival in neighbourhoods like Karm al-Zeytun or Zuqaq al-Blat, a working-class neighbourhood in which both Sunnis and Shia live, and where Hizballah and Amal are also active, inadvertently creates a market for welfare, in which ordinary claimants of various confessions can shop around for the best deal.[49]

Nevertheless, it is clear that the Foundation's clinics are strategically located. Thus, the Sunni inhabitants of Ouzaï—a poor and predominantly Shia neighbourhood in the southern reaches of Beirut—have long complained of continuing neglect in the face of their 'misery'. As one woman put it in 2007, 'in the summer you find fire, in the winter you find flooding. When it rains, water', both from the sky above and the swollen sea, 'enters the homes of the people'. To be sure, 'the parliamentarians come to see the … situation. They come, make video clips and they leave'. But 'did Shaykh Rafiq … do anything for Dahiyeh? From the Summerland [resort on the seashore] to Ouzai'—that is to say, along the whole length of Tarik el-Jdideh itself, the road that splits the Sunni neighbourhood to its north from Shia Ghobeiri to the south—'we put up pictures and banners for the ministers and the MPs'. And yet, 'when it comes to us, they know us only during elections'. For Cammett, this neglect is quite simple. It would not be politically profitable to invest in welfare infrastructure in Ouzaï, a neighbourhood that falls within the electoral district of Baabda, in which the Future Movement cannot hope to compete with Hizballah and its Christian allies.[50]

Since the early 2000s, then, the Hariri family seems to have deployed its resources in an increasingly strategic and calculated fashion—the logic of spatial concentration trumping, at times, the rhetoric of universal provision. Between 2000 and 2013, the Hariri Foundation's Directorate of Health and Social Services opened thirty-five new health centres, which offer medical and dental consultations, medication, X-rays, and tests, all at a heavily subsidised rate, and which help to coordinate preventative medicine programmes.[51] Many are either in Sunni localities such as Saida, Tripoli, its northern neighbour of Minieh, Arsal in the Beqaa or Fneydak in Akkar, or in mixed towns and villages that play an important part in the Future Movement's electoral sums. This is the case, for instance, of Taanayel, in the western Beqaa, and of Rashayya, both located in a 'hot district' that was the scene of keen contests in the elections of 2009.[52]

The activities of the Maktab al-Ra'is al-Shahid Rafiq al-Hariri li-l-Musa'adat, or The Martyred President Rafiq Hariri's Office for Assistance, follow a similar spatial logic. Based in the Beirut neighbourhood of 'Aysha Bakkar, a Future Movement stronghold, the organisation has branches in Tripoli, Saida, Akkar, and Baalbek, as well as in largely Christian areas such as Batroun and Jbeil, though not in Shia parts of southern Lebanon, where it is conspicuous by its absence.[53] Established in 1982 as the Hariri Aid and Relief Bureau—it was renamed after Rafiq Hariri's assassination—the organisation offers temporary 'medical and social assistance' to those in need.[54] In practice, this most often means covering the costs of medical treatment for the uninsured, but its other activities include a food aid programme. The latter is well-known for distributing vouchers and boxes, particularly on religious occasions such as Ramadan—and Christmas. In recent years, the Office has significantly increased its presence in Christian and mixed parts of Lebanon, such as the northern regions of Bcharreh and the Koura and the Beqaa in the east.

This expansion has led to charges from its detractors that it is no more than an adjunct to the Future Movement, buying up votes for the party with enticements that range from hampers containing simple and durable items such as 'lentils, fava beans, sugar, milk, cans of tuna fish and mortadella meat, pasta, cheese, cooking oil, margarine, biscuits, and chocolate spread' to kerosene for cooking—what some call *mazut siyasi*, or political fuel.[55] But though the Office stresses its charitable status, insisting that it has no connection to the Hariri family's political work, these allegations are made harder to fend off by the fact its food programme is administered by the Jam'iyyat Bayrut li-l-Tanmiyya al-Ijtima'iyya, or Beirut Association for Social Development, whose director, Saleh Farroukh, describes it as the 'social arm' of the Future Movement.[56] What's more, it is often difficult to disentangle personal loyalty and admiration for Rafiq Hariri from participation in the welfare programmes he left behind after his death. As Melani Cammett observes, the Beirut Association for Social Development's headquarters are plastered with images of the dead leader and messages of remembrance.

In reality, then, it is hard to regard the Hariri family's welfare work—initiated by Rafiq before his death, and now taken up by his widow, Nazek, his sister, Bahiyya, and his son and political heir Saad—as either fully self-interested, the product of cynical electoral calculation, or as an entirely altruistic effort born of generosity and patriotism. There is no doubt that, since the 1990s, welfare has increasingly served a useful political function, underwriting the Hariris' attempts to present themselves as both Sunni leaders and Lebanese statesmen, lifting up at once community and nation. This is a process that, if anything, has gained speed since Rafiq Hariri's assassination in 2005—and, particularly, since the street clashes of May 2008, which have left behind rancorous memories among the Sunnis of Beirut. What's more, the family's personal wealth, access to Saudi finances, and famed largesse towards both supporters and less well-funded political allies have led to a view, in certain quarters of Lebanon, of the Future Movement as exceptionally corrupt.

But this is no doubt a reductive view, which does not account for the range of motivations that underpin the work of the Hariri family—and, crucially, that of the employees who manage scholarship schemes, distribute food aid, or work as teachers and lecturers in its schools and universities, or as nurses and doctors in its health centres. To take but one example, the Hariri Canadian University—established in 1999, and renamed the Rafik Hariri University in 2011—is many things at once.[57] It is a commercial undertaking, one of the many universities that have crowded the Lebanese marketplace in recent years, if one that does live up, to an extent, to its commitment to providing an 'affordable, accessible education'.[58] Fees for the 2016–17 academic year range from 300,000 Lebanese lira—or $200—per credit for courses in the

College of Arts, to 430,000LL—just under $287—per credit for those in the College of Engineering.[59] By contrast, the American University of Beirut charges up to 1,009,000LL—or $669—for courses in the humanities and social sciences, and 1,206,000LL—$800—for engineering courses.[60] As this suggests, it is not just a business, but also a philanthropic venture. Its website thus lists its various scholarships and support schemes, from competitions to introduce high school students to various subjects to 'merit scholarships' awarded to incoming students, a 'work study program' which provides students with both valuable professional 'experience' and 'skills' and a 'modest income', and a financial aid program, which underwrites the fees of students deemed worthy on the basis of the 'severity of [their] financial difficulties and the level of [their] scholastic achievement'.[61]

What's more, the university serves to embody Rafiq Hariri's conception of Lebanon as an inclusive, tolerant, and entrepreneurial place open to the global forces that will help it to realise its full potential for growth. Thus, its website makes much both of the university's international partnerships and global outlook, and of its attempts to foster inter-confessional understanding and comity. As it puts it, Hariri's 'dream of establishing a ... university' could not be realised without 'the help of experts from a country that had made great strides in the field of education'.[62] With their help, he was able to create 'a community that advocates and promotes diversity and tolerance as a priority of academic and civic life'.[63] Indeed, in an echo of the Kfar Fallus project, the university's main campus is in the village of Mechref, near Damour in the Chouf—a confessionally diverse region to the south of Beirut. The university's alumni page on Facebook, meanwhile, trumpets one entrepreneurial success after another, from an artisan chocolate company and the food franchise Shawarma w Saj, to marketing companies and one start-up that 'develops and produces devices' linked to the 'internet of things'.[64] But, at the same time, it is a means of showing the family's commitment to its own community. Many of the university's senior administrators are Sunnis, as is its president, Ahmad Smaili, a professor of mechanical engineering who has held positions in Oman, the United Arab Emirates, and Saudi Arabia, as well as in Lebanon and the United States.[65]

Much like Hizballah, then, the Hariri family has built up a dense lattice of overlapping welfare institutions since the early 1980s. Driven by a host of different considerations, their role is perceived in radically different ways by the dynasty's supporters and detractors. For what some may see as the cynical buying of souls by an organisation that exploits philanthropy for political gain, others will regard as the legacy of a life defined by generosity and service, and what some criticise as a deeply sectarian organisation, others praise as the embodiment of a vision of national unity. In the end, though, these binary distinctions are of little analytical use. Rather than viewing the choice between community and nation as a categorical one between sectional interest, on the one hand, and public-mindedness, on the other, we would do better to trace the overlap between two equally powerful conceptions of the common good. For, much like those who run Shia educational and charitable establishments like Ayatollah Muhammad Hussein Fadlallah's al-Mabarrat, employees of the Hariris' philanthropic organisations regard service to the community *as* service to the nation.[66] As they see it, these are but 'two faces' of the same coin. Furthermore, we may well have to accept that the Hariris' motivations may be more complex than simple dichotomies allow: vanity and generosity, patriotism, local pride, communitarian attachments, and political convenience—all play a part to varying degrees. As one of Rafiq Hariri's close associates, Fadl Shalaq, put it, 'he felt he had an obligation. Of course this satisfied his political ambition. So if you are a sceptic you say he did it for political reasons. If you are a believer in Hariri, you say it was because he was a good person'.[67] There is no means here of uncoupling the personal from the institutional: just as the Hariri Foundation and its satellites have been the projections of the particular worldview of Rafiq Hariri, his relatives and advisers, so too are their perceptions shaped by the way in which others look on his person and the party he has left behind.

For the remainder of Lebanon's political parties, the personal and the institutional are interlaced in a rather different way. Though many have attempted to build up their own welfare services, none possesses an infrastructure comparable to those of Hizballah and the Hariri family. They are forced, instead, to act as brokers and funders, facilitating the access of their supporters to state resources and helping to finance their treatment and education. Perhaps the clearest illustration of this is Amal. The movement may have thirteen health clinics and two hospitals, administered by the Jam'iyya Lubnaniyya li-l-Ri'ayya al-Suhiyya wa al-Ijtima'iyya, or Lebanese Association for Health and Social Protection, and an educational network of eight schools and six higher education institutes, all overseen by the Mu'assasat Amal al-Tarbawiyya, or Amal Educational Foundation.[68] But much of its welfare work takes place elsewhere, in what are widely known by the generic term of *makatib al-khadamat*, or service offices. There are three of these. One deals with education, distributing bursaries and using its employees' personal contacts in the Ministry of Education and the hundreds of informal agreements it has reached with schools to secure places for applicants; another deals with healthcare, again relying on its main administrator's personal relations in the Ministry of Education to secure medicine and hospital places; and a third provides assistance with matters of infrastructure and daily life, such as rubbish collection, potholes, and electricity supplies. Already smudged by the back-and-forth between Amal functionaries and their counterparts in the civil service, the lines between state, political movement, and society are rendered almost invisible by the reliance of many of its cadres on bureaucratic positions for their livelihoods. As Mona Harb has put it, the party has effectively 'grafted itself on to the state', using its 'direct and indirect access to a range of public services and resources' to 'maintain and renew its capacity for mobilisation'.[69]

Much the same is true of Lebanon's Christian parties. The Kata'ib operate a small network of clinics in neighbourhoods such as Mar Mikhail, in eastern Beirut. The Lebanese Forces, meanwhile, have their own food aid programme and health insurance scheme. The first of these, administered by the NGO Auxilia, distributes monthly vouchers that poor families can use in its *ta'awuniyya*, or cooperative, supermarkets in Baabda, Antelias, Jounieh, Jbeil and Bijdarfe. Open only to party members, the latter partially covers the cost of such basic procedures as X-rays, urine and blood tests, and MRIs. In 2008, the party began to open dispensaries in strongholds like Ayn al-Rummaneh, which offer basic care in return for an annual subscription of $20.[70]

In more innovative fashion, several businessmen close to the Free Patriotic Movement set up in 2005 a company which they named 8 Oranges—both because of the party's colour, a garish orange, and because there are eight letters in Michel Aoun's name when spelled in

Arabic, and eight beats to the strident refrain that supporters hammer out on their car horns.[71] In return for an annual subscription of $11, the scheme offered personal insurance, underwritten by Cumberland Insurance and Reinsurance. Members could also enjoy discounts at a range of 'gas stations, supermarkets, [and] pharmacies' owned by FPM supporters, and order fuel and cooking gas—'Orange fuel'—to their own homes, and purchase Orange Cascade mineral water from Orange Kiosks. Though the company—which now seems to have gone under—was eager to stress that it was a private, commercial undertaking and that membership in its loyalty schemes was open to all, its communications director also took pains to make clear that 'more than 25 per cent' of its proceeds would go to the FPM, and that it would 'recruit FPM members and followers, because they suffered for 15 years [of Syrian occupation], when they were sacked from their jobs just because they were FPM supporters'.[72]

But a scheme like this remains very much the exception, rather than the rule, and most Christian partisans continue to rely on the kind of informal procedure that one informant described in an interview with Melani Cammett. When this interviewee, a Kata'ib supporter who lives in the Christian neighbourhood of Sin el-Fil, in the Beirut suburbs, required medical treatment, they sought out the head of its municipality, Nabil Kahale, also a Kata'ib member with whom they already had 'good relations'. Kahale helped to arrange discounted treatment in Sin el-Fil's municipal clinic, and for the party to pay what fees were not covered by Lebanon's meagre social security. In such instances, welfare provision is undergirded by essentially personal relations of trust and shared partisan allegiance.

Indeed, the deeply personal task of allotting welfare can draw even the *za'im* himself into the world of his followers, and his followers into his own world. In the exchanges that bring them together, both play a role in an elaborate performance of political obligation and authority, which suggests at once 'intimacy' and 'distance'. At the centre of this performance—in part reliant on stock phrases and shared expectations, in part improvised with each new visitor—is the *za'im* himself. Each Saturday morning, for instance, the Druze leader Walid Jumblatt holds open sessions in the *diwan*, or meeting room, of his ancestral palace in Mukhtara, in the Chouf mountains to the south of Beirut.

Dressed in his uniform—stonewashed jeans, a white shirt, and a dark leather jacket—his tousled hair falling each side of his bald pate, the *bek*, or notable, sits in a white chair facing away from the balcony and into the room. His visitors, as they file in, find their places on the low sofas that line the walls of the *diwan*. As he deals with each new case, Jumblatt's entire mien changes—he will whisper confidentially with one visitor, before loudly chiding another that he is 'wasting my time and my coffee with your story', or take out his wallet and hand some-one a few notes, before absent-mindedly accepting their invitation card, his eyes already fixed on the next interlocutor. One minute, he will slump into his chair, his long legs curled beneath him, lost in thoughts, before jumping up again to receive the greetings of an old Druze lady; his shoulders bent low to allow her to kiss his forehead, he will gladly accept her good wishes. The next, he will respond to the very same wishes with an angry exclamation: *hillu 'anni w ma tatawalu w ma takasru 'amri*—'leave me alone and don't make my life any shorter or longer'. In constant motion, he will 'get up, sit, go out onto the balcony', take one of his 'administrators'—each of whom deals with a different kind of request, from procuring jobs in the army or the gen-darmerie to taking care of medical cases—aside for a word, or 'disap-pear into another room ... leaving a visiting delegation waiting'. As the anthropologist Isabelle Rivoal has argued, the *diwan* is 'more here than simply a place for words, and for the affirmation of status hierarchies' that other scholars have described; it is also a stage on which are played out the tensions between the *bek* and his visitors. Ever motile, ever shifting, the leader cannot let his followers know how he will react or what he will do; he must remain responsive, without becoming pre-dictable. He is forced, therefore, to play out this elaborate masque, performing the role of the whimsical, quixotic, irritable leader to keep his followers on their toes, forever second-guessing his moods.[73]

But not all the *za'im*'s work must take place in such formal sur-roundings. One long, sticky summer afternoon, I sat by a country club swimming pool and watched an ailing *za'im*—a figure who had enjoyed much influence under the Syrian occupation, but who had lost his posi-tion with the departure of Damascus' troops in 2005—do his work. For hours, he sat on the edge of his white plastic deck chair, hunched over small pieces of scrap paper that he shuffled between his fingers.

Only occasionally would he reach to his side to grab another cigarette, or to take a short sip from the beer that sat on a little table. There was something incongruous about the way he looked. His fashionable sunglasses, driving shoes and expensive French swimming trunks and, most of all, the baseball cap he wore turned backwards gave him the air of a younger man. But everything else about him spoke of weariness, of a life saturated with experience—the grey hair he had pulled up under his hat, the slight paunch of his belly, the muscles giving up and losing their tautness with age, the scarred, time-worn face and pocketed eyes and, most of all, the gravelly voice with which he made phone call after phone call. For on each of those scraps of paper, in hurried Arabic script, was marked a different favour to be fulfilled, or a reminder to make a condolence call to a recently bereaved wife, to arrange a mass or a visit, to send apologies for a wedding or a christening. After each call, he would add another little note or scratch out whatever was written with the biro that sat on his beach towel, and put another scrap on the pile building up by his ashtray.

One felt there was something practised, almost ritualistic, about this work. This was something the man had done many times before, and expected to do again. It was part of the pattern of his weeks and months, and the words came easily to him—the little nudges to someone he knew could secure a job or a contract for one of his clients, the stock phrases of congratulation or commiseration that were reserved for particular occasions. With his concentrated, serious air and his ability to modulate his tone to each new conversation, he resembled a parish priest going about his pastoral duties, or perhaps an accountant calling after his clients. For, as Michael Gilsenan observed some years ago, there is nothing gratuitous about the generosity of the za'im; it always presupposes reciprocity.[74] The favour must be returned someday, one way or another.

Herein lay something of the pathetic aspect of this scene. Though the man still possessed his way of working with words, he had been pushed aside from power. His chances of returning to elected office hinged, therefore, on his capacity to render service to those who had once voted for him—but his ability to do so was now hampered by his lack of position, as his interlocutors knew all too well. To make a promise that could not be kept, to ask for a favour that would increase his own debt to others—these were dangerous things for the *za'im*. His is a form of power that hinges not just on verbal dexterity, on the ability to say the right things and to extract concessions, but also on the ability to negotiate this economy of favours—one in which success depends on an intimate knowledge of the person one is speaking to, whether it be a retainer or a fellow politician, a priest or an army officer—of their circumstances and inclinations, who they are related to and where they come from, their financial situation, their susceptibility to particular pressures and their openness to particular compromises and, finally, their knowledge of one's own circumstances. It is out of this stuff, the empirical details of a lived life, the ability to place an individual within a network of kin and place and political position, that the authority of the *za'im*—his capacity to act, to do things—is made. Just as a follower might have to guess what the *za'im*'s mood might be before making a request, so too must the leader be adept at these mental calculations. Economistic and institutional analyses, with their impoverished sense of the transactions and agreements that structure the *za'im*'s life and reach, are not enough to explain this particular kind of intimate power.

Of parties and partisans

This interlacing of the personal and the institutional is apparent, too, in the way in which the very understanding of political leadership has itself been transformed over the last three decades or so, with the growth of party structures—some relatively amorphous, like that of Amal, others, like Hizballah, tightly organised in a descending cascade of responsibility. This shift has been particularly visible since 2005, with the emergence from clandestine half-life of the FPM and the Lebanese Forces and the reorganisation of the Future Movement. It is common now for parties—and coalitions like 14 March—to hold yearly conferences and commemorations, to organise electoral rallies, and to possess various means of mobilisation, from a student section—not infrequently managed by balding, paunchy eternal students of indeterminate age and occupation—to a more or less cohesive social media presence. The more organised of Lebanon's political movements have long had their media outlets—the newspapers *al-Anba'* and *al-'Amal* in the case of the Progressive Socialist Party and the Kata'ib or *al-Mustaqbal*, which

Rafiq Hariri founded as he moved into electoral politics in 1999, or TV stations like LBC, established by the Lebanese Forces in 1985 and bought out by a private consortium in 1992, or Al-Manar, which Hizballah opened in 1991.[75] But this is now complemented by an endless drip feed of news, rumour, and commentary on Facebook pages and bulletin boards—some official, others not.

But this transformation of the political landscape, which marked a break—if not a complete one—with the traditional practice of cobbling together lists of allies at election time and assembling rickety coalitions in parliament, can be traced back to the late 1990s and early 2000s. This period of uncertainty witnessed not just the creation of the Future Movement, but also the emergence of smaller political organisations like the Lebanese Democratic Party of the Druze leader Talal Arslan. The descendant of a family of *muqata'ji*-s, or tax-farmers, whose extensive domains stretched through the southern reaches of Ottoman Mount Lebanon, Talal is the son of Majid Arslan, who took up a prominent position in Lebanese politics thanks to the alliances he forged with the country's first two presidents, Bechara al-Khoury and Camille Chamoun. After seizing the leadership of his family from his elder brother Faysal in 1991, and contesting two elections—in keeping with traditional practice—under the banner of the *tayyar al-arslani*, or 'Arslan current', he established the LDP in 2001. This ostensibly bears all the hallmarks of what some would call a 'modern' political organisation: it has published a programmatic statement enunciating its guiding principles; it holds regular—though not annual—conferences; and it has a political bureau and an executive committee whose members handle different portfolios, from information to sport and foreign affairs. Significantly, the members of this political bureau are drawn from across Lebanon's confessions, in a transparent effort to break the party's association with the Druze community and to present it as a truly national enterprise.[76]

But for all such window-dressing, the LDP remains little more than a vehicle for Arslan's political ambitions. The party's general congress might elect twelve members of the political bureau, but its president— Arslan himself—chooses six others, and it is he who names the executive committee's members. The LDP's vice-president, Ziyad Choueiri, was clear in his interview with the Lebanese political analyst Chawkat

Ichti: it was Arslan, and no-one else, who took the bulk of the decisions. If he had chosen such an elaborate structure over the rather simpler vessel of the current, it was to project his ambitions onto the national stage and, paradoxically, to shore up his local electoral fortunes by presenting himself as a national leader with a reach extending beyond his strongholds. This paradox is apparent to all those who have driven past the party's offices in Choueifat. Alongside the LDP's banner—a deliberate attempt to present an inclusive vision of the Lebanese nation, with its invocation of the national flag's red and white and its use of a cartographic representation of Lebanon in place of the cedar that so many associate with Christian exclusivism—flies the five-coloured flag associated with the Druze community.

In similar fashion, the Maronite leader Sleiman Frangieh has attempted to create a party mechanism around himself in the form of the *tayyar al-marada*—the Marada current or movement. Named after the mythical warriors from whom some of Lebanon's Maronites insist on tracing their descent, the party has its origins in the Frangieh family's Marada militia—hence its martial name. Its creation, however, was only formally announced in 2006, at a ceremony held in the Frangieh family's northern homestead of Zgharta, and attended by representatives of Frangieh's allies in 8 March, Hizballah, Amal, and the Free Patriotic Movement. Like other Lebanese parties, the Marada have their own 'hymn, party, and colours' designed to provide the party with a distinctive image.[77] Its new emblem—a white Pi sign set against a green background and framed within a compass—is a clear attempt to break with the Maradas' earlier history, when its badge was suitably militaristic and nationalistic: a green cedar whose yellow edges marked out lightning strikes, and whose trunk doubled as a cross-like sword.

And yet this new image—like the party's name itself—still hints at the Frangieh family's northern origins and associations with Christian Lebanese nationalism. While the Pi sign that stands in its centre seems an allusion to the belief that the Phoenicians gifted mathematics to the ancient world, transmitting an understanding of arithmetic and geometry to the Greeks through figures like Pythagoras, the compass that rings it shows only one coordinate—N for North. The movement's official website, meanwhile, does not even use this new symbol, but reverts instead to the old crest of the Marada militia, an insignia supposedly supplanted by the party's more modern trappings. Indeed, the site makes little effort to disguise a history known, in any case, to all. Tellingly, its brief history of the Marada gives the date of the movement's foundation not as 2006, when it was incorporated as a political party, but as 1968, when Tony Frangieh, Sleiman's father, formed the Marada militia. As the site recounts, this faction—otherwise known as the *jaysh al-tahrir al-zghartawi*, or Zgharta liberation army—fought 'several battles against the Lebanese National Movement and the Palestinians in the north and Beirut in the early stages of the civil war', defending 'the region of Zgharta-Zawiyya', the family's 'traditional stronghold' from leftist incursions.[78]

A similar awkwardness pervades the party's organisational reforms. Like Arslan, his 8 March ally, Frangieh has sought to appoint figures who do not hail from Zgharta and its region to the Marada's political bureau, in an effort to undermine perceptions of the movement as a distinctly parochial instrument of dynastic ambition.[79] One of its ministers in the 2011 cabinet was the Greek Orthodox Fayez Ghosn, who served as the minister of defence. But it is telling that the Maradas' other minister should have been Salim Bey Karam, like Frangieh the scion of a family of *bekawat* who have long dominated the village of Ehden, which neighbours Zgharta. Indeed, the party's two other MPs, Istfan Douaihy and Emile Rahme, hail, like Karam and Frangieh himself, from villages that cling to the steep escarpments of northern Lebanon. The Douaihy are also from Ehden, while the Rahme hail from nearby Bcharreh. This all gives the party's representation a distinctly local feel. Even Ghosn hails from the Kura—a region with a clear sense of itself, but one that is in the foothills of the steep mountains the Frangieh family hails from, and in which Sleiman Frangieh has business interests, not least in the vast cement factories of Chekka, which leave a white dust hanging over the highway at all hours of the day.

There are other ways, too, in which Frangieh finds it difficult to sever his ties to the past. His family's *za'ama* does not have the deep roots on which the Arslan or the Jumblatt can pride themselves. Unlike these Druze families, which owe their positions to their role as brokers for the early modern Ottoman state, its political status was only achieved in the early twentieth century, when one of its members seized upon the coming of the French Mandate to translate into political office his position as a *shaykh al-sulh*—in which he was charged with acting as an arbiter within the village community and reconciling those who had fallen out.[80] But the family had assiduously and rapidly built up its position. By the 1970s, Sleiman Frangieh the elder—after whom his grandson, the family's current leader, is named—had reached the highest office in the land, presiding over the country's disintegration into civil war. Over the course of the decades, the family has assiduously cultivated a reputation for violence, both given and received. One forebear, Kabalan, was known to go down into Tripoli at election time to coax reluctant voters to the ballot box, shotgun in hand. In 1957, Sleiman Frangieh was accused of prosecuting a brutal blood feud against the Douaihy family. Accused of murdering twenty members of the family, gunned down during a church service in the northern town of Miziara, he fled across the border into Syria—where he met Hafiz and Rifaat al-Assad, laying the seeds of a fruitful political friendship—before returning to Lebanon, thanks to the amnesty declared in the wake of the civil strife of 1958. The massacre did not prevent his election as president thirteen years later. Sleiman's son, Tony, was himself murdered in 1978, in an incident known as the 'Ehden massacre'. As conflict between rival Christian factions intensified, an armed squad—largely believed to have been led by Samir Geagea, then a young militia leader—broke into the Frangieh redoubt, gunning down forty people, including Tony, his wife, and his daughter. Sleiman Frangieh the younger escaped the slaughter only because he was in Beirut at the time. Martyrdom forms a rather more important part of the family's efforts to present itself to the world than murder, with solemn occasions like the memorial mass held each year for Tony, his family, and those who died alongside them opportunities to reassert its power over the region, a bond forged in blood.

Frangieh, however, is not shy of reminding his followers of the violent streak that runs through the family. In 2009, a video circulated on social media of the *bek* berating a crowd in Zgharta. 'Whoever wants to act like an *'abaday* [a tough guy], can go do that with the *'uwwet*, [Lebanese Forces],' Frangieh screams, his hoarse voice cracking, his movements sharp and charged with aggression. When one of his followers, a small man dressed in a grubby white vest, attempts to embrace him, he pushes him away. When another lets a word slip to his neighbour, Frangieh yells *sid buzak inti*—'shut your trap, you'—slapping down the man's hand as he puts it to his chest to proffer his apology. 'There are 3,000 asses in this village,' he continues, 'go back home, you dogs.'[81] There is something deeply revealing about the proprietorial way in which Frangieh addressed his followers, reducing them to unthinking, imbecilic animals, and about the way in which he handled his own body and those of others. It is clear who possesses power—the power to touch, the power to speak, to order and compel others—and who must simply obey, like children or chattel. This is not just an empty analogy. For though this is a discourse of brute sovereignty, buttressed by the very real potential for physical violence, it is also one that is strikingly familiar. Frangieh speaks in the same way as his followers. He has the same, thick, mountain accent and adopts the same crude register that they use among themselves.

This distinctive admixture of familiarity and distinction, of proprietorial nonchalance and power dressed up in affability is apparent in the different ways that *za'ama* will act around their confidants, their visitors, and retainers—the bodyguards and enforcers who, in the old days, would have been called their *'abadayat*, or strongmen.[82] During my time with one *za'im*, I noticed the frank, masculine nature of his exchanges with the drivers, guards, and gendarmes who ferried him about and kept his person safe. Everything about their comportment conveyed the impression that these were men at ease with each other, acting out together a performance of strength and bluntness: the harsh, loud tone of their voices; the language they used, all curses and coarse jokes and put-downs, anecdotes and hard laughter; the way they held their bodies and occupied space, but also the way they handled the things about them—their weapons and cars, the men resting their machineguns on their knees or slipping them under the seat, keeping a foot on them, and wrapping their seatbelts around their seats with a frustrated sigh so that the 4x4's safety system would not beep.

But there is no doubt that this was, for the *za'im*'s retainers at least, a show of nonchalance. I would watch them sitting about beneath the building or lying across their small metal-frame bunk beds—enveloped in the off-white smoke of their cigarettes and water pipes, they would eat with haste and greed, one eye on the television that was blaring loudly away somewhere inside, the news broadcast distorted by static, their shoulders slumped or sagging with weariness, their legs spread-eagled wide or stretched out beneath them. When the maid would ring down to announce the *za'im*'s descent, they would quickly pull themselves together like a unit of new recruits surprised by its drill sergeant, hastily buttoning shirts over their sweat-stained vests, pulling their backs up, sweeping down their car seats and stubbing out their cigarettes. At such moments, only the *za'im* himself was at ease. For their part, his men had to watch out—like visitors to Jumblatt's *diwan*—for his moods. Who was he seeing today? Did he like them? And if he did not, would they bear the brunt of his annoyance? Would he want to drive himself? Would he mind today if they smoked in the car? These were not idle questions, for they knew full well that a wrong move would be rewarded with a sharp reprimand, if not a hard slap to the back of the head, forms of violence that could not be answered because they came from on high, invested with authority and privilege.

Each knew his place, then, both literally and figuratively. Only some could enter the apartment in which the *za'im* and his family lived, and even then they were only allowed to enter certain rooms: the kitchen, that space of service and work, in which they picked up their food or dropped off their empty plates or, if invited to do so, the balcony where the *za'im* would sometimes sit to eat. This was where his advisers and certain trusted followers, whose families had long and certain ties to the *za'im*'s own forebears, would meet him too. Sat beside the *za'im*, they would make calls for him and listen in on his conversations, advising occasionally with a whispered word or a nod of the head, spread papers out before him, and talk in that easy, confidential manner that characterises the interactions between close partners, equally invested in the operations of the political enterprise. Others who came to see the leader at home—delegations from a village known for supporting his party, old fighters in his militia, claimants seeking his *wasta* or intermediation—had their own place, a front salon or reception room reserved for such visits. It is telling that not once did I see the *za'im* and his family sit in this part of the house when alone; it was used only for social occasions. Whenever the doorbell would ring, the *za'im* would emerge from the private parts of the flat to take his place among his visitors in this space, which was at once part of the home and outside it. This division of the home into several distinct spaces, some more intimate and private than others, is by no means, of course, the sole preserve of politicians. In Lebanon, as elsewhere across the Middle East, those who can afford it will keep two salons, a formal, slightly stuffy one for visitors bearing all the necessary and conventional markers of affluence and hospitality, and another for the family arranged in a more comfortable fashion better suited to the household's tastes and needs. But this bifurcation of domestic space is particularly stark in the case of those politicians who work from home, bringing together, and yet always keeping separate, the personal and the political.

For this was, in effect, a public place nestling within a private sphere, a meeting room contained within the home. Carefully set out to accommodate the occasions that brought leader and follower together, it bore the subtle trappings of power. The sofas were arranged in a horseshoe to fit a group or delegation. Two armchairs—just ever so slightly higher than the sofas, so that the *za'im* would always be looking down on his visitors, in a subtle reminder of rank—were placed side-by-side to seat the *za'im*, and perhaps a particularly important visitor it was necessary to place in equivalence. A low table sat in the middle, with ample room for the fresh pot of Arabic coffee served to each new set of visitors, for all the cups and glasses of ice cold water. Amidst the chintz were placed bowls of plastic-wrapped nougat, nut confectionaries, and chocolates, which a maid might offer to visitors if they were important enough. And, taking pride of place within this setting were photographs of the *za'im*'s dead relatives, in their heavy silver-gilt frames—his brother, who had died during the civil war, and his father, who had founded this political line, in the company of important dignitaries, both Lebanese and foreign. These spectral presences—these dead men who sat among the living, listening in on their conversations—served as reminders that the *za'im*'s position was not simply the product of his individual authority and competence, but was embedded in his family's genealogy, with its capacity to conjure up sharp affective responses from those who felt they shared its history and values.

This attempt to underscore the authority of the living by surrounding them with the dead is also apparent in Lebanon's public spaces—its highways and alleyways, its streets and roundabouts and squares. In neighbourhoods of the *dahiyeh* such as Burj al-Barajneh, Mreijeh,

Ghobeiri, and Haret Hreik, which are under Hizballah's control, representations of the Ayatollah Khomeini, of the party's former secretary-general, 'Abbas Musawi, assassinated in 1992 by the Israeli Defence Forces, or of dead commanders like Imad Mughniyeh, killed by a car bomb in Damascus in 2008, or Mustafa Badreddine, who died in Syria in 2016, crowd around those of Hassan Nasrallah or the Ayatollah Khamenei. In Amal neighbourhoods like Hursh al-Qatil, Cocodi, Jnah, or Chiyah, images of the movement's founder, Musa al-Sadr, are placed alongside those of its current leader, Nabih Berri.[83] Often, the two men are placed together within the same visual frame, just as Nasrallah is shown alongside Musawi or Khomeini and Khamenei, the living and the dead intermingling in a display of charisma and authority, grief and pride. The same is true of Saad Hariri, shown alongside his father Rafiq in posters and banners that line the streets of Beirut neighbourhoods such as Ras al-Nabaa or Tarik el-Jdideh. Along the streets of Christian quarters such as Furn al-Hayek or Yasu'iyya, meanwhile, it is perhaps more common to encounter images of the dead—figures like Bashir Gemayel, assassinated in a bomb blast in 1982, only a few weeks after he was elected the president of Lebanon, or his nephew Pierre, gunned down in 2006, or Camille Chamoun, who died in 1987, and his son, Dany, assassinated with his family in 1990—than the living, their contemporaries and successors. At times, the walls of these neighbourhoods become a palimpsest, the dead still visible within the faces of the living. I still recall the graffiti I saw on the walls of Furn al-Hayek in the wake of the 2009 parliamentary elections. Stencilled in black spray paint every few yards were cameo portraits of the Kata'ib parliamentary candidate Nadim Gemayel, designed to bring out his eerie resemblance to his father, Bashir. So close, in fact, was the resemblance that it required a double-take to distinguish these images from the many posters and billboards of Bashir that saturate the visual sphere in Achrafieh. Beneath this image was inscribed a single word—*thabitun*, 'we remain', 'we persist', a message of defiance like those so often encountered in these Christian parts of Beirut.

But alongside these images of the illustrious and the powerful, there also exist numerous representations of the common foot-soldiers who have died in the cause of one party or another. The streets of the *dahi-*

yeh, like those of the Beqaa or of southern towns like Nabatiyyeh and Bint Jbeil, are thus lined with posters of those who have died for Amal or Hizballah. Pinned to electricity pylons, they gaze down sternly on the drivers filing past all day, their young features softened and smoothed out to give them the glow of martyrdom. And what is true of the physical spaces of the city is also true of virtual arenas like YouTube or the unofficial Lebanese Forces discussion board Sawte. com. On its threads can be found lists of the 'Lebanese Forces martyrs and Christian resistance, which also includes Kataeb, Ahrar, Tonzim, and the guardians of the Cedars martyrs [sic]', which commemorate fighters like 'Martyr Elias Mansour Taouk, died in Qlaiaat during battles against the Aouni cult and their gangs', or 'martyr Tony Werdan from the northern town of Hadchit. He died in the battle of Bhamdoun, he spilled his blood defending Lebanon from the barbaric Syrian regime … A great hero from Lebanon'.[84]

Death and its remembrance, then, provide a means for partisans to come together. The ceremonial calendars of Lebanon's parties are punctuated by masses, services, and commemorations. Some, like the events that Hizballah holds to mark 'Ashura and Jerusalem Day, signal at broader concerns born of the party's distinctive political theology. But many mark the relatively recent passing of political figures, both obscure and well-known. At times, these are small, mournful occasions, like the masses held each year to mark the death of Dany Chamoun or Tony Frangieh, solemn services held in their hometown's main churches, in which their families are joined by a congregation of locals and partisans, followed perhaps by the laying of wreaths or a short speech. At others, they are rather larger in scale. This is the case, for instance, of the ceremony held each year on 14 September in Sassine Square, in Achrafieh, to mark Bashir Gemayel's death—crowds gather in the street, closing off this busiest of thoroughfares, torches are lit, speeches are made—or of the annual *mahrajan*, or festival, that Amal organises in Ras al-'Ayn, on the outskirts of Baalbek, to commemorate the disappearance of Musa al-Sadr. I can still remember driving up the road that leads from Beirut to the Beqaa with my brother one August morning in 2005, when we were overtaken by mini-bus after mini-bus loaded with Amal supporters, singing, waving to others, and letting their green party flags sway in the wind as they rushed up towards their destination. Like the pilgrimages to Hariri's *darih*, or mausoleum, in central Beirut—that *mazar al-watan*, or 'national shrine'—which became customary for Future Movement supporters in the years after 2005, these occasions serve multiple purposes. At one level, of course, they serve the *zu'ama's* own needs, allowing them to reinforce their ties to particular communities or places—Deir al-Qamar in the case of the Chamoun family, or Achrafieh and Bikfayya in that of the Gemayels—and to restate their commitment to particular causes. These complex politics of grief are apparent in the transformation of Hariri's *darih*. As Ward Vloeberghs has shown, this was in its first few months an improvised and ecumenical space—in which candles of the Christian saint Mar Charbel could be found alongside copies of the *fatiha*, the opening passage of the Qur'an. But it increasingly became a space of 'Islamic piety', with the installation of a 'large stone Qur'an, standing on a book holder … dedicated "to the soul of the martyr Rafiq al-Hariri"' and the *sotto voce* sounds of the *tartil*, or recitations of the Qur'an, played on loop over the shrine's PA system.[85] And yet, the site lost nothing of its national character, remaining enshrouded in Lebanese flags and garlands and wreaths in its colours. As Roschanack Shaery-Eisenlohr has argued, it is wrong to regard confessionalism and nationalism as mutually exclusive options; on the contrary, the two often overlap, with many of all backgrounds seeing service to the community as service to the nation, and service to the nation as service to the community.[86]

But these sites and moments of commemoration are not simply opportunities for leaders to harvest and reinvest political capital. They are also partisan occasions, moments for those who share in a tradition of faithful support and fervent belief to gather together, to commemorate the sacrifices of their own forebears—as exceptional as they are ordinary—and to lay the foundations of the political future. This is apparent, for instance, in the Lebanese Forces' annual 'martyrs' mass', held each year in the Christian town of Jounieh 'in remembrance of the martyrs of the Lebanese resistance'—the term that the Forces' members have used to designate their movement, but one that has taken on added resonance in the years since 2005, when it serves as a rhetorical counterpoint to Hizballah's Islamic resistance, with its own claim to work in the name of the nation.

It is important not to lose sight of the meanings that occasions like these possess for simple partisans. For, as Philippe Abirached has argued, za'ama is not simply a set of remarkable attributes that cling to the person of the leader, like an ostentatious garment marking him out from his followers. Rather, it is a relationship between leader and supporters—one that is constructed by both. For as much as the za'im claims to represent his followers, so too do they claim to represent him—seeing themselves in him, they defend him and speak up for him, presenting him as particularly deserving of their allegiance. Abirached, then, is right to argue that the political, in Lebanon, is not simply the preserve of those who lead, but is also the domain of those who follow. However, it is not entirely the case that 'it is impossible to bypass the leader, it is necessary to go through him (whether through identifying with him or, on the contrary, by distinguishing oneself from him), to gain access to the political'.[87]

The personal characteristics of the za'im matter a great deal—even, or especially, when they seem so very different to those that have gone into making the archetype of the Lebanese leader. This is particularly the case of three central figures of contemporary Lebanese politics: Sayyid Hassan Nasrallah, Samir Geagea, and Michel Aoun. Regarded by their supporters as contemplative, ascetic figures uninterested in personal gain and gifted with unusual insight and dedication to their respective causes, they are seen as the very antithesis of the corrupt, ostentatious and flighty zu'ama of caricature, men who care only about the next election and the next contract. For his supporters, Nasrallah is the very embodiment of the iltizam, or commitment, that they strive for. Often depicted in the many representations that circulate on posters, banners, car stickers, cigarette lighters and keyrings as a benign, smiling figure, he is possessed both of the inherited religious charisma of the sayyid, or descendent of the Prophet Muhammad—signalled by his black turban, but also by his rhotacism, which some attribute to his revered descent—and of an inherent holiness. Despite the embonpoint noticeable beneath his robes and his known fondness for sweets and ripe, succulent fruit, he is seen as a figure whose piety and detachment from earthly pleasure had marked him out from childhood, a deeply dedicated and determined figure ready to give his life—and indeed, that of his son, Hadi, killed in clashes with Israel in southern Lebanon—to the resistance. This is particularly so since 2006. For Nasrallah now lives a clandestine existence; constantly moving from one safe house to another, he makes only the rarest of public appearances, addressing his followers instead through live video-links. This image of piety and commitment is one that Nasrallah's hagiographers have constructed with care, and that he has himself contributed to building up in his rare personal interviews, in which he speaks of growing up an unusually religious child in the poor Beirut neighbourhood of Karantina, then under the sway of the secular revolutionary ideas of the time. But equally important to his followers are his empiricism and rhetorical gifts, his ability to speak truth and to reveal hidden realities in his televised speeches—often presented as didactic displays in which Nasrallah seeks to correct the dangerous misapprehensions of others, and to call out their lies and distortions. This gift for expression and worldly insight is at the heart of the image that Nasrallah and his followers have constructed, together, in a joint act of political participation.

For all the homespun effectiveness of their pronouncements in press conferences and interviews, Aoun and Geagea lack Nasrallah's rhetorical gifts—his rare ability to compel the listener and move a crowd and his capacity for changing registers, shifting from the lofty language of the cleric to the simple, familiar cadences of the colloquial like a singer gliding up and down scales. Nevertheless, their followers attribute to them many of the same qualities that make Nasrallah so distinctive in his own supporters' eyes. It is common for Aoun's supporters to contrast his public persona as a recalcitrant and valiant military leader, a crusading defender of Christian rights, and his gentle private demeanour, his 'proximity' and warmth with supporters, with whom he speaks 'in a simple language', 'like a grandfather' with whom one is having a 'family conversation'. At the same time, however, they also see him as a figure capable of reading the runes of Lebanese politics like few others. As one FPM member insisted to the French anthropologist Bruno Lefort, Aoun, alone among Lebanon's politicians, saw the danger of Islamist violence breaking out in the years after 2005.[88]

Supporters of the Lebanese Forces have gone further still. Where Hizballah partisans customarily refer to Nasrallah simply as *al-sayyid*, and those of the FPM to Aoun as *al-'imad* or *al-jiniral*—the general, in Arabic or Arabicised French—or even simply as GMA—General

Michel Aoun—in their online discussions, those of Geagea call him *al-hakim*. This means at once, in colloquial Lebanese, 'the doctor' and 'the wise one', and refers both to his short time as a medical student, and to his liking for authors such as the Jesuit philosopher Teilhard de Chardin and to his reputed sagaciousness and insight. From the 1980s onwards, Geagea and his followers began to construct an image of the man as a peasant intellectual, whose famed—or infamous—brutality was inflected with an unexpected philosophical bent. One old fighting companion thus remembered his surprise when Geagea handed out mimeographed extracts of Hobbes' *Leviathan* and Sun Tzu's *The Art of War* during a meeting in a cold monastery chapel high up in the Lebanese mountains. This reputation only grew during and after Geagea's long imprisonment. For it was said that he devoted himself to religious and philosophical reading on Christianity, but also on Islam and Hinduism, during his eleven years in solitary confinement. Geagea's time in prison, which many of his partisans came to see as a kind of death—martyrdom, even—also added to their sense that he was an unusually devout and saintly figure, who carried the sins and hopes of others on his shoulders. As one Lebanese Forces sympathiser told the French anthropologist Emma Aubin-Boltanski, Geagea 'is not a politician like others. He is straight, he doesn't change his ideas, but always keep the same vision. Like the Christ he carries the Cross, our Cross, that of Lebanon's Christians'.[89]

But ascetism, self-restraint, a bent for learned rumination are not the only characteristics these men appear to share. For all are seen as leaders whose seeming lack of interest in self-enrichment distinguishes them sharply from their predecessors and peers. This categorisation depends on a mix of sociological observation and rhetorical embellishment. For their partisans have seized, since the late 1980s, on the lower-middle-class or working-class origins of these men and their fierce animosity for the established order, to make of them revolutionaries and rebels, committed to overturning the status quo and creating a fairer Lebanon. As one of Aoun's old companions put it, he 'is not a *za'im*, but a rebel'.[90] Like Nasrallah, Aoun is not averse to contributing to this fashioning of his persona and ideology. In his interviews with the French journalist Frédéric Dumont, he thus opined that 'three forces oppose the project of reform in Lebanon: political feudalism, repre-

sented by the traditional notability, the communitarian warlords recon-
verted into politicians, and the business-political class'.[91] Aoun, of
course, presents himself as the sole alternative to men like Walid
Jumblatt and Saad Hariri—a man of humble origins, from the poor
Beirut suburb of Haret Hreik, who rose through the ranks of the army
to become its commander, before turning his wrath against the warlords who wanted to parcel out Lebanon's resources or sell the country
down the river.

Geagea's supporters have followed a similar line. Thus, one hagiog-
rapher has written that he had to confront 'in his birthplace, Bisharri,
a terrible feudalism, the conservatism of the [established] families, the
tribal narrowmindedness'. The simple son of 'an army corporal and a
working woman' who grew up in the shadow of great families like the
Frangiehs, he developed a deep animus for 'the system of "the nation
in the service of the region, the region in the service of the tribe, and
the tribe in the service of the *za'im*"'. This representation of Geagea as
a Maronite 'Robin Hood' has endured in the years since 2005, and—
like those of Aoun—his supporters will often remark that he and his
wife, Sethrida, the MP for Bcharreh, do things differently to other
politicians. They have not 'opened their house' to supporters, and they
do not engage in the customary *wajbat*, or obligations, that other
zu'ama spend much of their time on, attending weddings and visiting
the bereaved. There are other ways, too, in which they differ from
their peers. Though a 'political couple', they are 'without children'.
While rivals like Sleiman Frangieh and Walid Jumblatt groom their
sons for succession, the way in which Geagea and his wife shirk
dynasty-building, like much of their conduct, marks them out from
their peers.[92] For, like Aoun, who has only daughters, and Nasrallah,
who lost his son, Geagea and his wife do not have a boy to take up
their political mantle.

But if the personal conduct of the *za'im* matters to supporters who
assemble from the fragments of biography and the remembered elements of history a strikingly intimate image of their leader that
bypasses the formal structures of party, so too do ideas. Though
Lebanese politicians have little by way of detailed policy offerings for
their publics, leaders and partisans partake together in the shared construction of an internally coherent vision of Lebanon's past, present,

and future. As one FPM militant told Philippe Abirached, 'we follow Michel Aoun not as a person but as an idea, as a way of thinking'.[93] These ideological discourses range from that of the Future Movement, with its stress on *bina' al-dawla*, or 'the construction of the state', a deliberate evocation of Rafiq Hariri's infrastructural legacy, to Hizballah's insistence on Islamic morality and Islamic resistance, and Christian parties' deep-seated concern for their political rights, often presented in the language of *al-tamthil al-sahih*, or fair representation. In this regard, the views of an FPM activist who told Bruno Lefort that the Ta'if accord is 'an accord against the Christians', a Saudi-brokered compact that reduced the president from a strong figure of executive authority to a 'mere secretary', are shared by partisans of the Kata'ib and the Lebanese Forces as well as Aoun's own sympathisers. There the similarity ends. For if FPM supporters see the general as 'the last hope of the Christians', members of the Lebanese Forces are driven by a fierce allegiance to their own party and its leader. This is captured in the slogan one so often hears at their rallies: *al-'uwwet w bas, al-hakim w bas*—'the Forces, the doctor, and nothing else'.[94]

For partisanship consists, of course, not just of the vertical bonds between leader and follower, but also of the horizontal connections that tie supporters together. This partisan sociability is constituted out of shared experience, out of a shared sense of place, and out of shared ideas. For followers of the Future Movement, these experiences include the death of Rafiq Hariri, a moment of profound, wrenching bereavement, as the man who spoke and worked for them was taken away, and the clashes of May 2008, which left lasting rancour at what many called—in a tellingly territorial gloss—Hizballah's 'invasion' of Beirut, as though the 'party of God' were a foreign force occupying their own sovereign land. For Hizballah or Amal supporters from the villages and towns of southern Lebanon and the *dahiyeh*, the war of 2006 figures among these recent memories of collective experience— a moment of loss and suffering, but also a time of togetherness and *sumud*, or steadfastness, which culminated in the *nasr min Allah*, or the 'victory from God'. For members of Christian parties, meanwhile, it is not just older memories of the civil war—now experienced by many only as a set of well-rehearsed stories recounted by parents and older partisan companions—or of momentous days like 14 March 1989, when Aoun declared his 'war of liberation' against Syria's forces in Lebanon on 13 September 1990, when he fled the presidential palace at Baabda, but also of more recent events like those of August 2001, when the arrest of several FPM activists prompted demonstrations, brutally broken up by the security forces and their hired hands, or 10 March 2004, when a rally held by student activists in the Kata'ib, the FPM, the Lebanese Forces and the National Liberal Party in the precinct of the Université Saint-Joseph was met with repression.

These are homespun histories, then, of popular partisan 'resistance' and 'steadfastness'—for Lebanon's Christian parties, with their view of themselves as righteous combatants for 'freedom, sovereignty, and independence' from oppression and foreign occupation, rely on many of the same affective tropes as Hizballah. Tellingly, they are preserved and archived, not in official repositories, but in countless online posts and homemade YouTube clips. Some of these, to be sure, focus upon the actions of this leader or that. Thus, one *tayyari* or FPM clip commemorating the events of 7 August 2001 begins and ends with lengthy montages of Michel Aoun, dignified stills of the leaders in military uniform, his arms aloft and his hands in a victory sign, or melancholy portraits of the general lost in thought on his Parisian balcony, a disconsolate figure in exile. Many are accompanied by a brief slogan: *lubnan al-qawi*, 'strong Lebanon', say, or *al-rabi' al-ati*, 'the coming spring', as though Aoun himself were the personification of his nation and his people's hopes and beliefs.[95] Another clip, of the student demonstrations of November 2004, focuses on the actions that day of the young Sami Gemayel—the son of the former president and head of the Kata'ib party Amin, but then leading his own 'sovereignist' movement—showing 'Samy ... al Moukawem', the resistant Sami, leading the demonstrators in chants of *ma badna jaysh bi-lubnan, illa al-jaysh al-lubnani*—'we want no army in Lebanon, but the Lebanese army'—and urging those marching behind him to keep their flags high.[96] Others, however, see these occasions as moments of partisan communion. As the FPM activist Elsy Moufarrej puts it in her account of August 2001, the protests 'embodied the movement's history of struggle' in the face of liberation, its resolute refusal to surrender. While it uses many of the same few scraps of archive footage as others, hers is a clip that focuses not on the absent presence of Aoun, the longed-for liberator, but on the 'activists' who organised and led the demonstrations, who were beaten, dragged across the ground, shoved into waiting army trucks and led to police stations. As important as Aoun, the ageing general faraway in Paris, in this account are young partisans like Ramzi Kanj or Ziad Abs, named as key figures within the party on the ground, or the dozens of others who remained unnamed, but whose bravery and determination the camera lingers on.[97] Commemorative documents like these seem to envision ways of participating in the political, of joining in partisan society, which rely less on vertical ties of allegiance to the leader, and more on a fierce adherence to common values and shared recollection of particular events and moments of communion and sacrifice.

Despite these complex entanglements of experience, sentiment, ideas and affect, it remains common for the Lebanese to think of the political allegiances of others in a reductive way as simple matters of confession and place. As one inhabitant of the Christian village of Dayr al-Ahmar in the Beqaa put it: 'if I meet someone for the first time in Beirut and I tell them [where] I come from … this person will automatically think: "Oh, so he's from Dayr al-Ahmar, he must be Lebanese Forces".'[98] In this logic, those from the Gemayels' hometown of Bikfayya are seen as either 'with the' Kata'ib, or 'against' them—in which case they must belong to the Syrian Social Nationalist Party. There is, of course, a sociological truth here. The inhabitants of Jnah or Cocodi in the *dahiyeh* are likely to be Amal supporters, those of Burj al-Barajneh, Ghobeiri or Haret Hreik almost certainly Hizballah supporters.[99] One part of Ras al-Nabaa will be beholden to the Future Movement, another to Amal—the fringes of their respective territory marked out by flags and images of martyrs.

But these are not the primordial, inescapable, loyalties the Lebanese—and others—sometimes think they are. Place does not predetermine political allegiance. As another inhabitant of Dayr al-Ahmar quietly confessed, many of his fellow villagers were more sympathetic to Aoun, though they rarely showed such allegiances in public. Rather, it is again the sense of belonging to a community of experience that helps to shape these loyalties. Christian inhabitants of the poor Beirut suburb of Ayn al-Rummaneh, which borders the Shia neighbourhood of Chiyah, will stencil the distinctive sword-shaped cross that once stood for the Lebanese Forces onto the walls on the fringes of their own territory, 'to show them that we're not a Muslim neighbourhood'.[100] This is a practice that is shaped by sharp memories of the fighting of the 1980s, when Ayn al-Rummaneh came to be known among some Christians as the *'asimat al-sumud*, or capital of resilience. I saw much the same pattern in Sur's small Christian quarter, hemmed in on all sides by Shia neighbourhoods. Here, too, the walls were marked with spray-painted images of the cross hanging from a rosary bead and stencilled symbols of the Kata'ib and the Lebanese Forces. All too aware of the demographic realities of the places in which they live, the inhabitants of this place see membership of the Lebanese Forces, and the defiant acts that must accompany it in their view, as a means of holding on and holding out, of protecting their neighbourhood from the suffocating advances of others. Here partisanship and confession work together to define each other: these men and women are Lebanese Forces supporters because they are Christian, but they also understand what it means to be Christian in contemporary Lebanon through the lens of partisan allegiance.

Indeed, party members define themselves not just through their engagement in a wider community of sentiment, but also by distinguishing themselves from others. This can follow, it is clear, a confessional logic. But it also works to lay down demarcations within a single religious 'sect'. Amal supporters, for instance, will mock those of Hizballah for being excessively devout and beholden to Iran, while those of Hizballah will decry the lack of manners and morals that characterise those of Amal, whom they see as *bala marba* and *bala ikhla'*—without education and morals. In a coarser vein, I remember once stumbling across a Facebook group named *pedeyyet al-tayyar*—or 'Tayyar fags'—which derided, in a crude homophobic fashion, FPM members as emasculated, weak idiots. (Others will speak of the Kata'ib as *hizb tantet al-ashrafieh*, or the Achrafieh aunties' party, deriding it for its perceived fustiness and supposed origins as a party of the petty bourgeoisie.) On another occasion, I was sitting at a lunch table with a group of young men, all, as I was then, in their mid- to late-twenties. I knew one of them well, but the others—all old school friends of his, with whom he had grown up—I was meeting for the first time. The conversation, which till then had focused on the happenings of the night before in some club or another, soon turned to politics, and my friend began recounting a scene he had taken part in at an expensive Beirut restaurant. Slightly the worse for wear, the diners had started parsing their political differences. *Inta ma' min*, 'who are you with', they started asking the waiters: *ana ma'Awn*, one would say, 'I'm with Aoun', or *ana ma' al-'uwwet*, 'I'm with the Forces'. Then, finally, they asked one waitress who till then had not spoken. *W inti, inti ma' min?* 'And you, who are you with?' *Ana ma' al-marada*, she replied—'I'm with the Marada', Sleiman Frangieh's militia-cum-party. *Kis ikht al-marada, min henne*, one of the young men replied—'fuck their sisters' cunts, who are the Marada anyway'—before the group collapsed into laughter.

Partisanship is made of these rough forms of male sociability, with their assertions of superiority and their verbal and physical force. On another occasion, I was told a story of two groups facing off in a nightclub with the distinctive hand signals of the FPM—a thumb and index finger held up in a tick sign, mimicking the movement's symbol—and the Lebanese Forces—the fingers of two hands held together to form a triangle, standing for the cedar on the party's flag. But partisan bonds are forged not just through vain, suggestive peacocking or appeals to histories of shared struggle, but also through the endorsement of certain shared ideals that shape one's understanding of the present and sense of the future. The *za'im*, of course, is not by convention to be crossed or contradicted directly—an act that would run counter to the hierarchical arrangement of the political. It is telling, in this respect, that he will not appear on the many talk shows that populate Lebanon's television stations, sending in his stead fierce proponents of his stance. As subordinates, rather than leaders in their own right, men like Ibrahim Kanaan, in the case of Aoun, or Okab Sakr, in that of Saad Hariri, can engage in the unrelenting scrimmage of these exchanges, which so frequently disintegrate into flare-ups and slagging matches, without any loss of face or standing. What's more, their verbal dexterity may well exceed that of their rather more ponderous leaders, whose favoured mode of encounter is the press conference or the 'special' two-hour interview with a prominent TV journalist like Marcel Ghanem or Walid Abboud—monologues dressed up as dialogues, in which the *za'im* will never be pressed too hard, but allowed the opportunity to roam and ramble, to digress and ruminate, dredging up old stories and settling old scores. But that does not prevent partisans from engaging in intense, feverish discussion of the official line, or from expressing dissent and discontent when the leader appears to depart from the principles to which all should be beholden.

This is apparent, for instance, from the internal politics of the FPM. Many of its followers share with Aoun the belief that this movement serves not just the *tahrir* or liberation of Lebanon from foreign overrule, but also its *taharrur* or emancipation from corruption, confessionalism, and clientelism. What is needed, then, is the creation of a new Lebanon founded on the values enshrined in the constitution—fair representation, respect for the rights of all, *ta'ayush* or coexistence and, in due course, an end to the corrosive practices of *al-ta'ifiyya al-siyasiyya*, or 'political sectarianism'. This legalism is acted out by figures like Kanaan in their talk show appearances, in which they play out their commitment to the law by bringing heavily highlighted and annotated legal texts into the studio, reading out passages in their loud, declamatory fashion, waving the pages about and pointing to one fluorescent section or another to drive a point home. But it is also held dear by FPM supporters who believe that theirs is a popular movement built on ideals, rather than a vehicle for the personal interests and ambitions of its leaders.

Aoun's decision in 2015 to push his son-in-law Gebran Bassil's candidacy for the FPM's presidency—effectively making him the heir to the sonless and ageing general—thus caused deep rifts within the movement. In June 2017, Ziad Abs, Ramzi Kanj, and a number of other founding FPM members who had broken rank after Bassil's installation, two years earlier, announced that they would stand as independents on the 'civil society lists' created for Lebanon's next parliamentary elections, scheduled for 2018. As Abs explained in a televised interview, they were not the *mu'arada 'awniyyeh*, or Aounist opposition, that some spoke of, but men who had 'given [to the party], who founded the Free Patriotic Movement, and who still share in the principles and ideas that are in its charter'. This unbending commitment to the party's founding principles and ideals, rather than loyalty to any particular figure, would guide their participation; they were not after making back-alley deals—*tahalufat bi-l-zawarib*—but would 'go down', or form alliances, with those 'with whom we share values and ideas'.

For *al-shabab*—the lads, as Abs called his colleagues—'are far more FPM than some of the faces you see on your television', a sharp criticism of erstwhile colleagues like Bassil and Kanaan.[101] Some of the Orange Room's users dismissed this news—it was, as one put it, '3al fade', empty or useless—while others discussed the dissidents' chances of causing an electoral upset. But others dissected the personal characteristics of the two sides—Abs, Kanj and their colleagues, on the one hand, and Bassil on the other. For some, Abs was a traitor to the party and its leader. For all that he may have been—as one commentator noted—'with PMA', or President Michel Aoun, 'since 84', he was 'now working against' him and undermining his project of reform. To others, however, Bassil was a 'phoney' who did not represent the movement and its values. As one member—his avatar a recent photograph of Aoun as president striding down a corridor surrounded by the army high command—opined, 'What has Lord Gebran done for FPM compared to these heroes? Nothing. Just lucky that he is PMA son in law [sic]'. How, some asked, could the members of a movement opposed to feudalism and dynastic succession accept the manner in which *usuliyyin*, or original members, had been side-lined to facilitate Bassil's accession, or the purges that Bassil had embarked upon to transform the party into his personal instrument? And who would act out of 'socio-political concern and interest', rather than to serve 'their own selfish interests'? As one commentator put it: 'We care about programs that will benefit us and our country (and, as Christians, our future survival, and the survival of our political power, in Lebanon)'. In this view, personal allegiances could not override ideological principles, and it remained to party members to prove 'to GMA', in a show of popular sovereignty, 'that it is us the free willed who decide about our leaders and MPs. We cannot bow down to his personal wishes while we paid with human lives dreaming of a better political practice and democratic environment'. Though the political tittle-tattle and ad hominem attacks strewn through the eighteen pages of this ill-tempered thread suggest that not all FPM members may have shared this idealism, it is clear that this was, for some, above all else a question of ideological commitment. Conduct and character mattered, to be sure, but only as the outward manifestations of deeply held principles. The only question to be asked was who best represented, as one commentator put it, 'the true spirit of the FPM', embodying the movement's values. And this, ultimately, was a matter for its members to decide.[102]

Conclusion

It is not enough, when all is said and done, to reduce Lebanese partisanship simply to primordial, instinctive, unshakeable allegiances to community and region, to material self-interest or blind obeisance to the *za'im*. There is no denying, to be sure, the significance of sect and locality and the ways in which these can be used to articulate political belonging, anchoring individual subjects within wider communities of meaning. And nor can we overlook the trappings of the *za'im*'s power, the ways in which he embodies authority, carrying about his person the sovereign capacity to remake lives—for good or ill—or the material structures of partisan allegiance, these webs of intercession and welfare provision into which supporters are drawn. The belief that one leader will provide better, more effective protection to the community and more generous individual assistance than another, or that he possesses greater moral integrity than his competitors, and even the conviction that one is bound to support one *za'im* over another because of one's origins, carrying allegiance around like a family heirloom, are all powerful considerations. Yet we should not lose sight of the importance of shared sentiments, shared experiences, and shared ideas in shaping partisanship. For all the poverty of partisan political thought in contemporary Lebanon, with its reliance on the trite tropes of nation and sovereignty, service, duties, and rights, loyalty and resistance, these are words that carry an affective charge and that help to make up the minds of partisans. In the end, then, partisan allegiance is always an active process, a wilful, thoughtful product of individual choices rather than a matter of passive acquiescence to the ineluctable sociological facts of confession and place.

PART II

THE TIME OF THE EVERYDAY

5

AL-MISHWAR, OR THE WALK

ON SPACE AND CAPITAL IN CONTEMPORARY LEBANON

It isn't easy to walk in Beirut. One stifling morning in mid-September 2015, when the city still lay beneath the oppressive heat that had come with the red sandstorms moving in from the Syrian desert, I decided to walk from my hotel in Hamra, in west Beirut, to Gemmayzeh, in the east of the city, where I was due to meet an interviewee. This was a walk I had taken many times before, and I set out with my backpack slung across one shoulder and a large bottle of water in hand, leaving a little early to give myself time to go at an easier pace. I walked down towards Bliss Street, and then eastwards past the American University Hospital and the Gefinor Tower, that twenty-story monument to Lebanon's pre-war ambitions, and on through Clémenceau and Jumblatt, down a gentle slope strewn with discarded mattresses and bags of stale bread and past the Maronite al-Hikma school, and towards Kantari. I soon reached Avenue Fakhreddine, as the map calls the wide thoroughfare that leads from the Murr Tower and the grand old ruined villas of Zokak el-Blat to the seafront. After hesitating a little, I crossed, cutting through the unceasing traffic, now rushing for a step and now slowing down almost to a standstill. Safely on the other side of the road, I wended my way down past Mar Elias Maronite Church and the Ecole des Soeurs de Besançon towards Bab Idriss and its banks, intending to cross through Beirut's central business district, carved out of its old markets and alleyways in the 1990s and 2000s.

Just as I reached the Beirut Souks, the new luxury mall opened in 2009 and named after the markets that once stood in its place, I came up against an unexpected obstacle—metal railings pulled across the width of the street. Before them were members of the General Security, with their distinctive desert camouflage uniforms. A step behind them were a clutch of men in plain clothes. The protests that had begun that summer with the outbreak of Lebanon's trash crisis were still going on but, naively, I had not thought that so much of central Beirut would be closed off in an attempt to prevent demonstrators from gathering in its squares and parking lots. I walked up to the men, still hoping to find a way through with a reasonable explanation as I rubbed my sunglasses on my t-shirt, nervously trying to clean away the sweat that had built up on my walk. But before I spoke, one of the General Security men—immaculate in his mottled grey uniform and aviator sunglasses—asked me 'where are you going? The centre of town is closed'. I told him that I was heading to a meeting in Mar Mikhail, out on the other side of Martyrs' Square. 'Is there no way I can get through this way? I'm running late', I asked. Shaking his head patiently and taking off his sunglasses to speak to me, he explained courteously that he just could not let me through. No-one was allowed to pass. It was at this point that one of the men standing behind the barrier took an interest in me. A wiry thing in his early forties, a short-sleeved yellow shirt slung over his slight frame, his eyes were lined with small pouches ridged with thin lines, from years of smoking. *Shu baddak?* 'What do you want?' *W leh 'am btimshi?* 'And why are you walking?' he asked, in a brusque, dry bark. I tried to explain, but even as I spoke he had already lost interest. He couldn't understand why I would walk, and he didn't care why I did. His eyes turning away from me, he waved his cigarette absently. His voice thin and violent, like the hit of a cane, he said simply *khud tani tari'*, 'take another route'.

And so I did. Walking back upon myself and turning up a side-street, I found myself up at Mar Elias Church. I kept walking past it, up towards the ring, the 1960s flyover that transects the heart of Beirut, a tarmac river separating the working-class neighbourhoods of Zokak el-Blat, Bashoura, Serail, Basta, Khandak al-Ghamik and Bechara al-

Khoury, that dense clot of housing on the hills above the manicured streets that house parliament, the prime minister's office and the municipality of Beirut. I walked as far as I could, or dared, up the fly-over, until the thin pavement ran out. Up ahead of me, two Syrian men kept on, one behind the other, their bodies leant against the crash barrier and away from the traffic like trees bent by the wind. Too afraid to do the same, I looked for another way. As I stood there, I saw a bright flash of colour moving almost beneath my feet; looking down, I glimpsed the turquoise smock of a young woman as she reached the bottom of a set of stairs that led down from the ring. To one side sat the regional headquarters of ESCWA, the United Nations Economic and Social Commission for Western Asia, safely barricaded behind breeze-blocks and barbed wire. To the other lay a road that seemed to make its way beneath the ring and up into the neighbourhoods to its north. I followed the woman down. Soon enough I found myself in a world quite different to the wide avenues of downtown Beirut, with their lay-away luxury apartments, their constant flutter of development, their fancy shops and overpriced cafés—a world of noise and life, of car horns and shouts and loud chatter, of taxis and scooters and pedestrians weaving around each other, of greengrocers and butchers displaying the day's wares, the stripped carcasses hanging in their shopfronts dripping blood into the gutter. I began to walk, but, unsure of my bearings and without a phone to guide me, I looked around for help. Seeing a gendarme sitting on a plastic chair sipping his coffee, I asked for the way towards Bechara al-Khoury. From there, I knew my way through Sodeco and Monot and down towards Gemmayzeh. Slightly bemused by the appearance of this pale man in a sweaty green t-shirt, he gave me a few directions—up around Bashoura's Muslim cemetery, and back down Khandak al-Ghamik until I reached Bechara al-Khoury, the wide avenue named after independent Lebanon's first president, whose statue sits stranded alone in a dusty traffic island, a forlorn monument to the faded hopes of the past. Before long, I found myself on familiar ground. Within the half-hour, I had reached Gemmayzeh—late, my bottle empty, and my shirt drenched.

As futile as all these detours were, this is a walk that reveals much about contemporary Lebanon's political economy, its infrastructure and state. For the sheer difficulty of walking through the city is one of the most mundane, and most immediate, symptoms of a system designed for accumulation and founded on an understanding of the citizenry as an aggregate of atomised consumers. This is an economic model in which the parts—these individual economic agents, with their cars and credit cards—will always count for more than the whole—the thick, complicated weave of the social fabric. Even as politicians harp upon 'the construction of the state'—*bina' al-dawla*—they can envisage no other way to shore up Lebanon's sovereignty than through corporate initiative. For these actors, private actions will always trump public works.

A Singapore on the Mediterranean

To retrace the lineaments of Lebanon's economy in the years after 2005, it is necessary to look back across the twentieth century: to the policies first sketched out in the immediate wake of the First World War by the propagandists of the Revue Phénicienne, who sought to make of Lebanon a new Switzerland, its prosperity founded on tourism, commerce and finance; to the independent nation-state's first presidents, Bechara al-Khoury and Camille Chamoun, who capitalised on the profound political upheavals that affected the Middle East in the 1940s and 1950s—the creation of the state of Israel, the succession of coups that upset Syria's precarious order, and the revolutions that toppled the Egyptian and Iraqi monarchies—to make of their small state a hub for finance and air and sea transport at the disposal of local and global banks and corporations; but also to the splintering of Lebanon's state and territory during the civil wars of 1975–90 into a series of cantons, administered by militias dependent on external trade and crude forms of fiscal extraction.

From Lebanon's very inception in the wake of the First World War, its economy has been built on circulation, on transit, on movements of capital, commodities and people. In their attempts to channel and dam these evanescent, flighty flows, its politicians and entrepreneurs have variously thought of the country as an entrepôt and a conduit, an entry-point into the Levant for Western manufactured wares, and a terminus for the oil and gas pipelines coming from the East; a key node in the networks of land, sea, and air transport that criss-cross the

Middle East; a centre of learning, whose relative cosmopolitanism makes it a port of call for intellectuals and scholars eager to find a bridgehead in the region; and a financial safe haven that might serve as a receptacle for the investments of enriched Lebanese migrants and wealthy Gulf speculators. For all the ruptures that have marked and punctuated Lebanon's history over the course of the short twentieth century, there is no doubt that its distinct phases, when considered all together, add up to a long and continuous history of extraversion—of an economy turned outwards, like a sun-seeker eagerly squinting into the midday orb.

There is no doubt, however, that this history entered a different phase in the 1990s, with the growing ascendancy of a new economic and political caste. For the end of the civil war brought into prominent positions two groups of actors that, together, have reshaped Lebanon's economy and society. The first of these were members of what Hannes Baumann has called the 'contractor bourgeoisie'—men like Najib Mikati, Mohammad Safadi, Issam Fares and, most famous and powerful of all, Rafiq Hariri, who had made their fortunes building palaces, malls, skyscrapers and highways in the Gulf.[1] The second set of actors—not always as noticeable as the first, but just as significant—were the technocrats who oversaw Lebanon's macroeconomic policies from the early 1990s onwards. With their degrees from Western universities and business schools like Harvard, Wharton, and the INSEAD and their stints working for investment banks or management consultancies like Merrill Lynch and Booz Allen Hamilton, or international bodies like the IMF and the UNDP, this group—which included Fouad Siniora, Jihad Azour, Raya Hassan, and the late Bassel Fuleihan and Mohammad Chattah—provided the expertise and professional experience that lent legitimacy to Hariri's visions of neoliberal rebirth. Since the early 1990s, figures such as these—comfortable in their own cosmopolitanism and persuaded of the power of regulatory reform and transnational capital to transform Lebanon for the better—have worked hand in glove to effect profound changes in Lebanon's political economy.

As scholars like Baumann and Hadi Makarem have argued, the politicians and technocrats who have dominated the higher echelons of government and state hoped to transform Lebanon into a kind of Singapore on the Mediterranean—a futuristic scape of sky-scraping banks and real estate developments, whose luxury hotels and favourable tax rates would draw in crowds of leisure-makers and investors, creating wealth that would, in time, trickle down through society.[2] This is a vision that has, of course, much in common with previous economic dispensations that relied on tourism, financial services, and transport to prop up the Lebanese economy and to provide the country's inhabitants with regular rents. But if there is anything distinctive about the policies these actors have implemented over the last twenty-five years, it is their aggressive attempts to reshape the country's urban fabric and regulatory framework to bring about structural transformation. For, as Baumann and Makarem have shown, 'actually existing neoliberalism' in Lebanon, as elsewhere, has depended both on the state's extensive intervention in particular sectors of the economy through manipulation of interest rates and monetary tinkering and on its abnegation of responsibility for other aspects of governance such as the administration of urban space or the provision of welfare and utilities, which it has increasingly surrendered into private hands.

This Janus-faced approach to government can be traced back to the early 1990s, when Hariri and his advisers first began to acquire power over the Lebanese economy. In December 1991, the Lebanese parliament voted in Law 117. This allowed the Council for Development and Reconstruction—the powerful quasi-autonomous body tasked with overseeing Lebanon's infrastructural redevelopment—to entrust real estate holding companies with the task of rebuilding war-damaged areas. Much discussed at the time, this act effectively set in place the legislative framework for the outsourcing of public works to private corporations. With Hariri's accession to the premiership in 1992, the work of reconstruction gathered speed. In 1993, the CDR—headed up since 1991 by Hariri's trusted adviser Fadl Shallaq—published its Horizon 2000 masterplan, a bold statement of its intention to catapult Lebanon back to its rightful 'position among the world's upper-income nations in the first years of the twenty-first century'.[3]

Central to this vision was the reconstruction of central Beirut into a lush scape of luxury housing and expensive office space, a display cabinet for the country's ambitions and a magnet for foreign tourists, real estate investors and corporations seeking a regional base.[4] In 1994, the Société Libanaise pour le Développement et la Reconstruction du

Centre-ville de Beyrouth—better known simply as Solidere—was incorporated to realise this utopian scheme. Reporting directly to the CDR, the company did not have to answer to the municipality or governor of Beirut, putting it out of the reach of local government. As this administrative exemption suggests, this new corporate entity enjoyed from the off extensive powers of exception which underwrote its claims to economic sovereignty over the centre of Beirut. Perhaps the most important of these were the compulsory purchase powers which allowed it to acquire the property rights of around 100,000 to 150,000 residential and commercial landlords and tenants, ranging from notable families like the Salam, Beyhum and Daouk to charitable organisations like the Maqasid and small shopkeepers and artisans who had held stalls in the souks for generations. Around 90 per cent of those involved acquiesced, accepting shares in Solidere in return for giving up their claims to properties in downtown Beirut. Only a small number resisted, challenging the company's authority in the courts. This mass transfer of property rights effectively established Solidere's hold over this area. It soon turned this into a tabula rasa, demolishing around 80 per cent of the buildings left standing in the area that fell under its remit. Having razed so much to the ground, the company was now free to begin afresh, doubling building density and floor space in order to maximise its gains from rent. Solidere's pursuit of profit was only made easier by the substantial fiscal benefits it enjoyed. The company's income, the dividends it released to shareholders, and the capital gains on sale of its shares, were all 'exempt from tax for ten years'. The state's justification for entrusting a private corporation with the task of reconstruction, and for granting it such extensive exceptions and exemptions, was simple. Worn down by fifteen years of war, it could simply not afford to undertake the work itself. And it was only logical—and fair—that incentives should be offered to the private entrepreneurs willing to accept this heavy burden and the investors propping them up. Such soothing talk, however, did little to alleviate the suspicions of some that Beirut's central district had been transformed, in the space of only a few years, into the private monopoly of a single corporation—and the man widely regarded as its progenitor and master, 'Mr. Lebanon' himself, Rafiq Hariri.[5]

These efforts to reshape the heart of Lebanon's capital were accompanied by a concerted attempt to remould the country's economy. At the centre of this macroeconomic policy was a single principle: the need to ensure, at all costs, the stability of the Lebanese currency in order to foster investor confidence. For what good would it serve to build a shiny new central business district as a showcase for Lebanon's ambitions, if no-one—whether Lebanese or foreign—had any faith in the country's economy? And, as Hariri and close advisors like Fouad Siniora and the new governor of the central bank, Riad Salame, knew all too well, the lira had been blighted during the civil war by damaging speculation and bank runs. When Hariri began his first term as prime minister in September 1992, the currency had gone down from a pre-war exchange rate of 3 lira to the dollar to stand at 2,420LL to the dollar—the result of a painful bout of hyperinflation.

The remedy to these ills, Hariri and his advisors came to believe, was bolstering the currency's value and, in due course, pegging it to the dollar. Together, Hariri, Siniora, and Salame mapped out the path by which they would achieve these aims. The first step was releasing treasury bills denominated in Lebanese lira, at artificially high interest rates designed to draw in investors. The Lebanese economist Toufic Gaspard has estimated that these stood at around 18%, when a more realistic interest rate, reflecting the credit-worthiness of the state and the potential volatility of the currency, would have been around half that. It was not long before the effects of this deliberate attempt to stir investor attention were felt. Between 1993 and 1998, government debt as a proportion of GDP more than doubled, from 50.7% to 109.1%. In the same period, the assets of Lebanon's banks—the main purchasers of these bills—grew by an astounding 387%. Around a third of this, economists have estimated, was down to treasury bills. Between 1994 and 1998, Lebanese banks earned some $6.3 billion in interest on state debt. A significant proportion of these earnings—some 53.3% of all interest on Lebanese treasury bills—went to only six banks. By the late 1990s, these institutions—which included the Banque Libano-Française, Bank Audi, and Hariri's own Banque Méditerranée—had established themselves as the dominant players in Lebanon's financial sector. But the banks were not the only beneficiaries of the Hariri government's macroeconomic policies. Their clients, too, drew handsome profits from interest rates on Lebanese-lira-denominated accounts, which fluctuated between 11.1% and 19.1% over the course of Hariri's first term in office. This, Baumann has argued, only served to increase the financial power of a small number of private and institutional clients. In 2002, the UNDP estimated that 0.6% of account-holders controlled 40% of deposits in Lebanon's banks.[6]

By 1997, some of the desired effects had been achieved. The share of foreign-currency deposits in Lebanese banks had fallen from 86.8% in September 1992 to 54.7% in March 1997. Though it would rise again to 63.7% in November 1998, this was enough to achieve the government's objectives. By 1997, the lira's stock had risen to 1,507LL to the dollar. It has stayed pegged at this level ever since, the putative anchor holding the Lebanese economy in place. All Lebanese have grown used to keeping two ledgers in mind, dividing or multiplying salaries, shop and restaurant receipts, bank balances and utility bills by 1500—the unofficial conversion rate. But this had come at great cost to the state, which now faced an 'extraordinary debt burden,' and depended heavily on Lebanese banks' continued willingness to finance this debt. In short, the stability of the Lebanese economy hung on a remarkable balancing act: the currency anchor depended on the government's ability to keep servicing its debts, but this depended in turn on the easy convertibility of the lira into dollars—a convertibility, ensured, of course, by the currency peg. For some, this was the key to what they regarded as Lebanon's economic miracle, a resurrection inconceivable to most observers at the start of the 1990s.

But for critics of these policies—and there were many—they had served only to increase sectoral imbalance and socio-economic inequality, by establishing the financial sector as the key to Lebanon's continued stability and favouring the concentration of assets in the hands of a few institutions and individuals. For who had benefited from all this macroeconomic manipulation? Certainly not, they charged, the 28 per cent of Lebanese that a 1996 UN report found to be living below the poverty line, subsisting on less than $618 a month. But if resilient deprivation and rising inequality were causes for concern, so too were the long-term prospects of the Lebanese economy. For what some regarded as a miracle, others dismissed as a mere prestidigitation trick. In their eyes, the anchor was no more than a magic wand. What would happen, they asked, when this astounding sleight of hand was finally discovered?[7]

Almost twenty years later, little has changed. Lebanon's sovereign debt remains as unwieldy as ever. In 2016, the IMF estimated that it represented 144% of the country's GDP, and forecast that this would rise to 160% by 2021.[8] Debt repayments currently eat up around a third of the country's annual revenues. To meet its obligations, the Lebanese state continues to issue Eurobonds denominated in US dollars, as it has done at regular intervals since 2001, when Rafiq Hariri first resorted to this strategy. In March 2017, the Ministry of Finance issued another $3 billion of Eurobonds. In a development that may surprise those unfamiliar with the circular workings of the Lebanese economy, these were oversubscribed. For though Eurobonds, denominated as they are in a foreign currency, are considered by most observers as external debt, the principal client for these bills remains the Lebanese banking sector. Together, Lebanon's central bank, the Banque du Liban, and its commercial banks own more than 85% of the country's sovereign debt. These holdings, in turn, represent some 60.7% of their assets. The trade-off is clear. As one expatriate Lebanese banker put it: 'Lebanese banks are the only reason why the state still holds'. They are rewarded handsomely for this loyalty, which allows the state to keep servicing its ever-growing debt. Treasury bonds in Lebanese lira pay more than 7.5% in annual returns—an extravagant rate that ensures that banks have effectively come to 'live off the debt'. The profits of the Lebanese banking sector—which now counts some fifty commercial banks—grew by more than 12% in 2016, and Lebanon's top fourteen commercial banks control more than $200 billion in deposits.

But this remains a difficult and dangerous balancing act, built as much on interdependency as on a shared belief in Lebanon's exceptional resilience. Should the state default, systemic shocks would tear through the banking sector—a catastrophe for ordinary Lebanese who have come to rely on the handsome interest rates that banks flush with government debt are able to offer on their savings accounts to top up their slim earnings. As one 'senior banking executive' explained to the economic consultant Rosalie Berthier, 'average Lebanese clients are so squeezed by a failing economy that they desperately need the additional income they make' thanks to interest rates of 6 per cent on their savings accounts. In other words, neither the banking sector nor its clients can afford to lose confidence in the state.

It is perhaps this which accounts for the narratives of extraordinary economic resilience that have taken hold in recent years—with the Central Bank's longstanding governor, Riad Salame, fêted as a sage whose percipient measures have helped to ward off the consequences of the 2008 financial crisis and to protect the country, since 2011, from the dire effects of regional instability. There are unmistakable echoes here of the personality cults that have surrounded other central bankers like Alan Greenspan or Mervyn King, figures whose lauded gift for pulling the strings of monetary policy supposedly helped to insulate their countries' economies from crisis. Continuity at the central bank may well be a 'very good thing', as the Lebanese economist Nassib Ghobril told me in an interview in August 2012, helping to preserve 'confidence' in its ability to weather the storms of global economic crisis and regional political turmoil.[9] But surely more important than any one individual to Lebanon's remarkable economic conjuring trick is the currency peg. This is attractive for Lebanese banks, which know that they 'can exchange dollars to buy [lira-denominated] sovereign bonds' and, if need be, convert their investments 'back into dollars at any given time, at an unchanged rate'.[10] In the eyes of these institutional actors, Lebanese sovereign debt is 'both profitable and, so long as the state is solvent, risk-free'. For much the same reasons, it is attractive to Lebanese migrants—particularly, but not exclusively, those who work in the Gulf or West Africa, and for whom their home country's banks offer a profitable safe haven, where their initial capital will not be lost, and where it can always be easily withdrawn. And it is utterly indispensable to Lebanese consumers. In a country in which 80 per cent of goods—from the wheat used to make *khobz* or Arabic bread and the Turkish Ülker biscuits that have flooded local *dukkan*-s, or corner shops, to the white goods in people's kitchens and the electricity that powers them, and the Chloé bags and Tiffany necklaces on sale in the shops of downtown Beirut—are imported, 'everybody lives off the peg'; by keeping their currency at a fixed rate, it gives the Lebanese 'an artificially strong purchasing power'. No wonder that Prime Minister Saad Hariri, whose cabinet was plunged into crisis in September 2017 by the Constitutional Council's declaration of its new tax law as unconstitutional, should have declared, in an effort to soothe tensions, that his government remained committed 'to the interests of every Lebanese, and most important of all the financial and currency stability that guarantees the value of their incomes and expenses'.[11]

Here, then, is another weak point in Lebanon's supposedly crisis-proof economic system. For if the state depends on the banks, and the banks on the state, then both depend on collective faith in the currency peg. Without it, Lebanese banks would suddenly begin to look far less attractive to expatriates, Lebanese firms would find it much more difficult to purchase imports, and confidence would crumble in the state's ability to meet its debt obligations. Preserving the currency's stability, then, is 'one of the most important things the central bank is doing; it is essential for preserving confidence in the system'.[12] Ghobril expressed much the same sentiment to me in 2012, insisting that the currency peg—and the role that the Banque du Liban maintained in keeping it afloat—represented the 'anchor' of Lebanon's macroeconomic 'stability'.[13] This stability does not just depend, however, on wishful thinking, but also on the ability of the state and the commercial banks to maintain sufficient reserves of US dollars. Until recently, both benefited from the remarkable effects of the 2008 financial crisis, which brought an increase of 23 per cent in foreign currency deposits, as Lebanese migrants wary of banks and economic circumstances in the Gulf, North America, or Europe transferred funds to Lebanon.

There are signs, though, that the tide is beginning to turn against the Lebanese economy. In 2015–16, the country's currency reserves dropped for the first time since 2005. To provide the treasury with the US dollars it requires in ever-increasing quantities to service its debt—$6–7 billion at the current rate—the Ministry of Finance and the Central Bank resorted to an 'elaborate exercise in financial engineering' known simply as 'the swap'. In May 2016, Banque du Liban exchanged treasury bills denominated in Lebanese lira against $2 billion of Eurobonds. Between June and October, the central bank sold these on—along with other debt products coming to a total value of $11 billion—to several Lebanese commercial banks, which resorted to their US dollar reserves, dollar deposits held in their foreign branches, and contributions from some of their more important private clients to purchase these bonds. Though Banque du Liban took care not to publicise the interest rates on these debt products, we can safely assume that they were generous enough to entice the commercial banks. But the central bank also offered a further incentive: should they purchase the Eurobonds it was putting up for sale, it would in return buy 'back from the banks lira-denominated bonds, paying on top of their actual price a bonus corresponding to half the total interest these bonds would have yielded had they been held until maturity'. According to the IMF's estimates, the banks made an unexpected profit of $5 billion, while the Banque du Liban was able to claw back a much needed $13 billion. But, as Berthier has pointed out, this transaction was built on a paradox: to save the peg, Lebanon's central bank 'implicitly [devalued] the national currency' by selling lira at a cut-price rate.[14] This is a risky move in a system in which everything hinges on continued inflows of dollars from expatriates willing to trust in the resilience of the home country's banks, and a sign of the desperation of the Ministry of Finance and the Banque du Liban. So far, their luck has held, and faith in Lebanon's famed ability to escape crisis like Houdini slipping out of his chains has not yet evaporated. But this is the crucial point. This is a system built not on structural strength and resilience, but on mutual trust and shared faith in the banking sector's capacity to keep thriving. And should this faith be shaken and one link in the chain break—should Lebanese migrants lose trust in the Lebanese banking system, say, or the Lebanese state default on its debts—then the whole house of cards will come tumbling down. For, as Ghobril told me, the banking system is, 'contrary to cliché', not 'immune' to crisis.[15]

And what is true of the banking sector holds for the Lebanese economy as a whole. This is a system highly reliant on 'consumer confidence and investor sentiment'—and on the willingness, in particular, of migrants and Gulf Arabs to deposit their capital in Lebanese banks, but also to spend currency in its hotels, restaurants, beach resorts, and nightclubs, to buy apartments and villas, and to invest in local businesses. And where, in other places, fluctuating markets, taxes or unemployment might all affect consumer and investor confidence, in Lebanon these are 'almost exclusively affected by ... politics'.[16] Paradoxically, it may be that both these sets of contributing factors helped Lebanon to attract deposits in the years after 2008, when banks across North America and Europe fell apart, the economies of the Gulf contracted sharply, and Lebanon experienced renewed optimism with the election of Michel Sleiman as president of the republic and the holding of legislative elections in 2009. As I noted earlier, deposits made by Lebanese abroad increased by 23 per cent during the financial crisis. One influential school of thought has argued—yet again—that this surge was the product of Riad Salame's wise leadership at the Banque du Liban. Salame, so this narrative goes, saw early on the systemic dangers that sub-prime debt posed, and imposed strict prohibitions on Lebanese banks investing in instruments such as CDOs. Only his prescient actions inoculated the sector against infection, and helped to make of it a welcome haven of migrants seeking a safe berth for their fugitive capital.[17] But perhaps just as significant as Salame's stewardship was the palpable sense of hope that came with the apparent return of political stability to Lebanon.

This would appear to be borne out by the indicators relating to tourism and real estate—both key sectors of the Lebanese economy and both, like banking, particularly susceptible to the dispositions of visiting Arabs or migrants flitting back for the summer. In 2007, 1,017,032 tourists visited Lebanon, and hotel occupancy rates stood at 38%. By 2009, their numbers had jumped to 1,850,000, and hotel occupancy rates had almost doubled, at 73%. Though a desire to put capital no longer deemed safe in banks into bricks and mortar may have played a part in the growth of real estate transactions in these years, it is clear that the same picture of renewed consumer confidence also holds for this sector. In 2007, construction permits were granted for properties totalling 9,038 million square metres; in 2008, for 16,067 million square metres, and in 2009, for 14,343 million square metres. Over the same period, the number of property sales jumped from 67,041 to 83,622. Indeed, the years between 2008 and 2010 now appear boom years, with GDP growth averaging 9.1% according to the Lebanese state's own reckoning, and 8.3% even by the World Bank's rather more chary estimates. Before long, however, the growing turmoil across the border in Syria brought endless talk of in 'ikasat salbiyya, or negative repercussions. As fears of geopolitical uncertainty and domestic political instability spread, growth for 2011 contracted to 2.0%, and visitor numbers fell back yet again to 1,655,051.[18] As Nassib Ghobril put it sharply the following year, the 'political class' had been 'too busy arguing with each other' to 'isolate Lebanon' from the 'Syrian crisis'. 2012, he estimated, had brought another decline in tourist numbers, which had fallen 25% in two years as Gulf Arabs fearful of kidnap and security incidents stayed away in droves, warned off Lebanon by their governments.[19]

This, however, serves not only to bear out Ghobril's insistence on the importance of political stability to consumer confidence, but also to underline the importance of the diaspora to the Lebanese economy. It is no coincidence that the corridors leading passengers arriving at Beirut International Airport towards the immigration desks should so often be lined with posters for projects such as Tilal Bhersaf. Set in the 'lush landscapes' of the Matn mountains above Beirut, with their 'mild and healthy climate', this is billed by its developers as the 'perfect gated community', with its private gardens, pools, walkways, and children's playgrounds.[20] A 'unique blend of nature and luxury'—this last word is repeated four times in the pitch's twelve short sentences—it provides what Lebanese entrepreneurs imagine migrants want: 'panoramic views' over the sea and the forest green mountains, 'relaxation … comfort', 'security and privacy'—an ersatz Lebanon, in other words, made all of nostalgia, and insulated and abstracted from its surroundings.[21] It is not, of course, that those who live in Lebanon do not find these things attractive. Not so long ago, an acquaintance living in Lebanon who had bought an apartment off-plan in a similar development, Beit Misk, told me that he was drawn to it because, as he put it, moving between Arabic, French, and English, *ma fiha pollution*—'there is no pollution there'—and *bhibb al-security*—'I like the security'.[22] But advertisements such as these do provide evidence of real estate developers' famed dependence on expatriates' desire and funds.

It is not just Lebanon's property firms, though, that look to migrants for support. Remittances from relatives living abroad have increased year-on-year over the course of the 2000s, offering much needed assistance to Lebanon's inhabitants confronting rising prices and stagnating wages. In 2003, remittances stood at $4,343 million. By 2007, they had increased to $5,769 million, before jumping to $8,177 million in 2010. The financial crisis may have contributed to this leap, encouraging migrants to put their capital into family ventures—refurbishing the old house in their home village, say, or helping their relatives to set up a business in return for a share of the profits. But, whatever the case, there is no disputing the fact that by 2009, remittances represented a full 21.7% of Lebanon's GDP. The average across the Middle East and North Africa was 3.5%.[23] This is no blip, no one-off occurrence born of an exceptional global conjuncture. On the contrary, it should be seen as the continuation of a longstanding pattern of dependence. In the early 1990s, for instance, it was found that the 2,500 remaining inhabitants of the village of Lala, in the western Beqaa, relied on its 7,500 or so migrants to supply 70% of their income.[24] In similar fashion, the Lebanese sociologist Mounzer Jaber concluded in 1995 that around 64% of the inhabitants of Beirut's southern suburbs received regular assistance from relatives living abroad, in West Africa, the Gulf and elsewhere. Certain villages, like Miziara in northern Lebanon, with its *qusur* or 'palaces' built with wealth brought back from Africa, have acquired a reputation as particularly dependent on remittances, but this is a pattern repeated in uneven and complex ways across many parts of the country.

What's more, the period since 2005 has been one both of steady migration and continuing dependence on those who have left. In 2014, it was estimated that the total stock of first-generation migrants stands at around 885,000. In other words, perhaps a quarter of the country's citizens have chosen to live outside its confines, searching for better opportunities elsewhere.[25] There is every indication, furthermore, that a significant proportion of these men and women have left in the last twenty years. The economist Marwan Abi Samra estimates that 350,000 migrants departed between 1997 and 2007, with 214,000 doing so after 2002.[26] This would seem to be borne out by a survey of 13,500 Lebanese households carried out in 2009 by the Central Administration of Statistics. Some 6.3% of these had seen at least one of their members depart between 2004 and 2009. Most of those, it would seem, were young men and women who saw migration as a surer path towards professional success and social mobility than staying put. 77.4% of those who left were under the age of 35, and 68.8% were the daughter or, for the most part, the son of the head of the household. Indeed, most—some 76.3%—were young men, and many were educated; some 44.4% had a university degree. A significant majority—65.9%—were leaving in search of work.[27] Is this really so surprising, in a country where average starting salaries for a junior accountant stood in 2013 at $600–900 a month, a web developer at

$700–900 a month, and an advertising account executive $800–950, but where a basic mobile phone contract can cost $60 a month?[28] Most of those who left during this period—39.2%—headed towards Arab countries, 19.5% towards Europe, 19.7% towards North America, and 12.1% towards Africa.[29] This certainly tallies with the tales of those I know, or know of: countless graphic designers and management consultants working in Dubai and Sharjah, engineers and hotel managers in Doha and Riyadh, and bankers and shawarma chefs in London and Paris, but also a hospitality graduate who moved to Cape Verde to work in a beach resort owned by the Chagoury family, or a group of young men who left together to set up a telecoms company in Kinshasa. Meanwhile, remittances only continue to rise. In 2014, the World Bank estimated that Lebanon received $7.5 billion from migrants.[30] As such, it has the dubious honour of being among the top twenty remittance-receiving countries in the world. A rough calculation based on the (admittedly flimsy) assumption that there are around 4 million Lebanese citizens resident in the country would give us a figure of $1,875 per capita. This is hardly a statistically accurate way of measuring the distribution of this inflow, but still it represents an approximate per capita sum far higher than those for Vietnam, Nigeria, and other remittance-receiving nations.

But if for many Lebanese families the opportunities presented by departure must be balanced against the pains of distance, of absence, then the Lebanese state takes a rather more hard-headed approach to its diaspora. For all their sentimental talk of Lebanon as a bird of two wings—*al-janah al-muqim*, 'the resident wing', and *al-janah al-mughtarib*, or the 'migrant' wing—and their insistence that those who have left remain 'an inseparable part of Lebanese society', most ministers and bureaucrats tend to view migrants as a vital economic resource to be exploited for all it is worth.[31] This is apparent from Gebran Bassil's recent attempts to enlist the diaspora's considerable 'human capital', putting it in the service of the Lebanese state and economy. At the first Conference on the Migrant Economy, held in late 2016, he boasted that Lebanon's migrants represented its 'greatest wealth'. Why, then, not make full use of this formidable resource, both by creating new initiatives such as Buy Lebanese, a promotional drive for home-grown products, or the real estate investment drive Invest to Stay, and by employing them as unofficial emissaries, representatives of Lebanon in the world spreading the good word about its great potential?[32] Bassil spent much of his trip to North America in September 2017—officially to accompany his father-in-law, Michel Aoun, to the United Nations General Assembly—glad-handing at a string of gala dinners like the one held in Las Vegas to open the 2017 Conference on Migrant Energy. In its discussions, Bassil—the minister of energy before he moved to the Ministry of Foreign Affairs in 2014—outlined his vision of greater migrant investment in the energy sector, in the provision of utilities such as water and electricity, and in the emergent sectors of gas and oil, on which Lebanese politicians have staked so much in these years.[33]

But Bassil is not alone in speculating on the future. In an economy largely built on the fluctuating currents of confidence, any sign of stability or any hint of an economic boon is enough to lift the spirits, if only for a short while. This was the case in 2008–9, when the election of Michel Sleiman as president and the holding of parliamentary elections brought a wave of optimism washing over the country, and again in late 2016, when Michel Aoun's election to the presidency precipitated a flurry of real estate purchases, with one developer reporting that he 'suddenly started receiving 30 phone calls a day, instead of 30 a week'.[34] For several years now, Lebanon's politicians have pinned their hopes on gas and oil reserves hidden under the Mediterranean, bickering over how best to exploit this boon and divide up the spoils. But, like children on a sugar rush, they are already turning their attention elsewhere, to the rich pickings they hope will be up for grabs once the war in Syria is over. Rather than confront the realities of their present, they seem always to be keeping one eye on the future, in the hope that they can glimpse the next miracle to lift Lebanon out of the morass.

The private city

It is perhaps for this reason that the building that makes of Beirut one giant construction site has still not ceased, in spite of everything. In recent years, two developments in particular have attracted the attention of journalists and scholars—both, of course, the work of Solidere. The first of these are the Beirut Souks, which opened their doors in 2009 after almost two decades of planning, construction, delays and speculation. The second, meanwhile, is the Beirut Waterfront Development (BWD), a 50–50 joint venture between Solidere and the London-based Stow Capital Partners. Covering what Solidere's own website describes as '20000 m2 of prime waterfront land', this project consists of two parts—Zaitunay Bay, with its restaurants and shops, and the Yacht Club, with its marina, clubhouse and luxury apartments.[35] To the west, jostling against the St George Hotel—whose owner, Fadi el-Khoury, remains one of Solidere's most longstanding and vociferous opponents—sits Zaitunay Bay, which occupies around 6,000 square metres of the shoreline.[36] Despite its developers' ambitions to make of it a 'hub destination' whose 'specialty stores', 'outdoor spaces and public areas for displaying artwork' would draw visitors from across the city and beyond, this is now a glorified food court.[37] Among the tenants of what Solidere has christened the 'Quayside Restaurant Strip' can be counted international chains such as Starbucks, Paul and those stalwarts of the American mall, Pinkberry and P.F. Chang's, alongside the Lebanese-owned Kikomo, Roadster Diner, Classic Burger Joint, and Al Forno.[38] Indeed, it seems somehow fitting that one of the tenants should be named the Babel Bay.[39] For this list of offerings, from spaghetti alfredo, cheeseburgers, orange chicken, frappuccinos and frozen yoghurts to the sushi burrito—itself a monstrous by-product of culinary globalisation—is so deliberately difficult to place, so entirely detached from its context, that one could be anywhere in the world. And that, one suspects, is the point.

Just as noticeable as this cosmopolitan consumerism is the growing dominance of chain restaurants. Since Zaitunay Bay's opening in 2011, these have gradually replaced the initial tenants. Many of these were high-end restaurants like Zabad, owned by the Lebanese-French chef Karim Haidar, where a nine-course tasting menu could set diners back 86,000LL—or $57—per person, or the Cro Magnon Steakhouse and Bar, with its 'cigar cabinet, leather banquettes and ... vaulted brass ceiling', where a 'bone-in filet mignon'—'dry-aged U.S.D.A.', it goes without saying—cost $48.[40] These places fit squarely with the ambition of the strip's developers to make of it a 'world-class ... landmark and destination'.[41] But in a country where the minimum salary remains $500 a month, they could be a destination but for the very few—a fact that perhaps accounted for the 'almost eerily quiet' atmosphere noted by one *New York Times* journalist sent to investigate in January 2012.[42] Though still out of the reach of many, chains like Zaatar w Zeit and Leila, which have replaced these early occupants, are perhaps more readily accessible to Beirutis looking for something to eat after a stroll on this private 'urban beach'. In a 2014 interview with a Lebanese business magazine, BWD's chairman and general manager, Farouk Kamal, admitted as much, stressing that 'we know that for a project to be successful in Lebanon … you need to depend on the local people, the middle class professional people. This is because if you are not successful with them, tourists will come to that place. But if it's only tourists that come here, the locals will probably not come'.[43] In adjusting to the harsh realities of the post-2011 Middle East, when the Gulf tourists who had once flocked to central Beirut now stayed away, Solidere and its partners had no choice but to move away from their ambitions to make Zaitunay Bay into a preserve of luxury.

These ambitions, though, are still fully in evidence in the Yacht Club, with its 'clubhouse … nine club suites, swimming pool … bar, club restaurant, lounge bar, library, game room, and fitness and wellness centre'.[44] Covering 14,000 square metres—an area more than twice as large as Zaitunay Bay—this is trumpeted on its website as 'the premier seaside destination for luxury living and recreation in Lebanon, catering exclusively to the region's cultural and social elite'.[45] In a few bland words of marketing talk, this description aptly captures BWD's ambition to appeal to only the wealthiest. Membership does not come cheap, carrying a fee of $15,000 for an individual and $20,000 for a couple. This, of course, is precisely the point. As Kamal explained, the club's members—their numbers strictly limited to 500—would 'want to enjoy a certain kind of exclusivity and at the same time rub shoulders with the right people'. Not for nothing was the club contemplating offering embassies complimentary memberships, to ensure the frisson of diplomatic company for the financiers, corporate executives and wealthy heirs who would join its ranks.[46] These are men and women accustomed to thinking of themselves as part of a global elite, a detached caste whose members, if they do not themselves possess political power, know that it is always within reach. Wearing their cosmopolitan affluence like a badge of identity, they expect nothing less than the most luxurious, refined, and reassuringly expensive of surroundings. In the club's restaurant, 'members' special requests are always welcomed, as a highly trained service staff will provide an unparalleled level of service at every turn'.[47] In its 'exquisitely designed' suites, they will enjoy a 'restful, memorable and comfortable stay', sleeping on king-size beds, lounging on landscaped outdoor terraces—each one, of course, private, for the rich expect to be spared at all costs the inconvenient presence of others, even those as well-off as they are—and reclining on furniture picked out especially by interior architects.[48]

Atop the yacht club sit forty-four 'executive' residences. At around $20,000 per square metre, these 150-square-metre apartments averaged out at $3 million when they were first put up for sale in 2014—in addition to which any prospective buyer had to stump up club membership fees, presumably a relatively small premium for those willing to invest such sums.[49] In return, interested parties could choose between apartments in one of two styles: 'timeless', a mix of sleek, polished wood floors, cream and beige furniture, and silica white walls enlivened with 'white marble touches throughout'; and 'avant-garde', with its black basalt floors, copper fittings and black PVC furniture. All enjoy views of the sea or the private landscaped parks that the developers have built around this island of affluence.[50] And all are equally characterless and impersonal. Designed to cater to the needs of those who want only clean lines, immaculate whites, and spotless floors, they resemble nothing so much as high-end hotel rooms or airport executive lounges.[51] This, again, is perhaps the point, for this aesthetic seems a particularly expensive rendition of what has sometimes been called 'AirSpace'—a 'generic' blend of 'minimalist furniture' and 'symbolic blankness' intended for those who take relish in 'frictionless, 'ceaseless movement', flitting easily between places every few weeks or months, knowing that wherever they end up, they will lay their head on the same taupe cushions and memory foam pillows and look up at the same insulated off-white ceiling.[52]

Few of those who have purchased properties here, or who moor their super-yachts in the club's waters, can dwell much on the site's odd and disquieting history. For this is a place quite literally built out of trash, an exclusive preserve reclaimed from waste. Where the Yacht Club now stands once was the Normandy landfill. The product of more than fifteen years of fly-tipping into the sea, this was a vast amalgam of plastic bottles, toilet paper, sanitary towels, and decomposing food, 'old household appliances, wrecked cars and car parts, old tires, medical wastes, and industrial wastes including lubricants and cleaning agents'. In time, even the municipality of Beirut came to use this spot as a dumping ground, emptying its rubbish trucks into the Mediterranean. To these mounds of miscellaneous refuse were added the iron and concrete carcasses of destroyed buildings, a practice that began during the war and continued after its end, when Solidere set about flattening much of central Beirut. Upon the landfill's eventual closure in 1994, it stretched over some 360,000 square metres, jutting out 600 metres into the Mediterranean. Twenty metres deep, it resembled nothing so much as an iceberg of trash, its peaks stretching up into the sky to beckon to the seagulls circling up above. Around its manmade shores lapped filthy water, the outflow of Beirut's broken-down sewage system.[53] Between 2001 and 2005, marine engineers set about dredging and reinforcing this vast artificial promontory, clearing out the bay and reshaping the rubble and detritus into new shapes, bolstered against the waves by Accropodes—immense structures of reinforced concrete built to protect against the untiring churn of the waves, rushing forth day after day against this new and unexpected opponent. Piles of these remain stacked along the seafront—parts of a jigsaw few passers-by know anything about.[54]

But perhaps just as discomfiting as this tale of salvaged luxury is that of the property speculations and regulatory agreements that led to the construction of the Beirut Waterfront Development.[55] In September 2000, the government of Selim el-Hoss passed Decree 3808, ruling that 'additional areas obtained through reclaiming the sea resulting from marine protection works are to be considered public property, and Solidere shall have no right thereof'. On Rafiq Hariri's return to the premiership the following month, however, this decree was swiftly dismissed as one of the 'retaliatory reforms' that Hoss' government had taken to punish Hariri, and overturned. Soon after, Solidere acquired the rights to exploit the land for a fifty-year period. In return, the company undertook to cover the costs of reclamation—dredging, consolidation and the like—and to pay the state the modest sum of 2,500LL per square metre in annual rent—$1.66 at the official exchange rate, not enough to buy an espresso in many of Beirut's more exclusive cafés.[56] In February 2004, just as the reclamation work was nearing completion, Solidere announced that it would be entering into an agreement with Stow Capital Partners. Under its terms, Solidere would contribute 'in kind 22,351 squ m of land', and Stow would inject 'US$31.6 million' in cash. The new joint venture would be known as Beirut Waterfront Development, or BWD.[57] Though Stow is registered in the Cayman Islands, its head offices are in London. Indeed, this is where the bulk of its portfolio is concentrated, in the golden rectangle around its base in Brook Street, in Mayfair. (At the time of writing, its holdings included 425 Oxford Street, occupied by Adidas' flagship UK store, the Argentine embassy at 65 Brook Street, and 33 Davies Street, a set of offices and ground-floor retail spaces primed to take advantage of the 'dynamic change that Crossrail will bring to Mayfair in 2018'.)[58]

This joint venture presented, it would seem, two key advantages for Solidere. Firstly, it allowed the project to receive the support of the Investment Development Authority of Lebanon, or IDAL, the country's 'national investment promotion agency'. Now that the development of the waterfront was ostensibly backed by 'British' investors, IDAL was free to contribute $80.9 million to the project. But public financing—the main source of IDAL's funds—was not the only benefit that the investment authority's backing brought with it. For upon his return to the premiership in 2000, Hariri set about significantly bolstering IDAL's powers. Under the terms of Law 360 of 2001, 'the Authority shall exclusively supersede all public administrations, authorities and municipalities in issuing required administrative permits and licenses, except those granted by the Council of Ministers'.[59] In other words, this autonomous body, which reported directly to the president of the Council of Ministers—none other than Hariri himself—was handed immense regulatory power, side-lining large swathes of the Lebanese state.[60] With IDAL's backing, BWD no longer had to worry about applying for building permits to the municipality of Beirut or the city's *muhafiz*, or governor; most—though, as we shall see, not all—of its wishes would be granted by this body. What's more, the company would enjoy exemption from income tax for two years, in recognition of its willingness to contribute to the economic development of Lebanon's littoral, known as Zone A. All it had to do in return, under the terms of the 'package deal contract' it entered into, was complete its project and ensure that 'the local labor force is preserved through employing at least two Lebanese nationals against one foreigner, and registering them in the National Fund for Social Security'.[61] This might seem, on the face of it, an inconvenience, given the dominance of Syrian labour within the construction industry. But it would not be impossible to envisage a scheme under which the requisite number of Lebanese citizens might be recruited to serve as ghost employees in return for registering for social security—hardly an onerous commitment, one would have thought—while continuing to employ cheaper Syrian workers. Whatever the case, it is clear that Solidere benefited from the investment and regulatory support of a body whose explicit purpose was to encourage foreign direct investment in the Lebanese economy.

There remained, however, one apparent sticking point. Plots 1455 and 1456, on which much of the landside parts of the project would be built, still fell under the strict planning regulations that ostensibly governed building height and land use across Beirut's central business district. As the product of a ministerial decree, these could not simply be waved aside with IDAL's assistance. Here again, Stow's involvement came in handy. For, though it might seem—at least in a fiscally fluid sense—a British entity, one of its main shareholders is the Tripoli-born businessman and politician Mohammad Safadi. Like Hariri and his fellow Tripolitan, and close ally, Najib Mikati, Safadi had made much of his initial fortune as a contractor in Saudi Arabia, before moving to London and becoming the business manager for Prince Turki bin Nasser, then the head of the Saudi air force.[62] Though Safadi's name does not appear on Stow's shareholders register, which lists for the most part offshore entities in Gibraltar and Jersey, Lebanese journalists have suggested that he owns a stake of 25 per cent in the company.[63] Farouk Kamal, BWD's chairman and general manager—and also, coincidentally, the executive chairman of Stow Capital Partners, in which he also retains shares—is happy enough to confirm Safadi's interest.[64]

An MP for Tripoli since 2000, Safadi was named in July 2005 minister of public works and transport in Fouad Siniora's cabinet. It was in this capacity that Safadi apparently began to push for what would become, in due course, Presidential Decree 15456. Signed by President

Lahoud, Prime Minister Siniora, and Safadi himself, as the minister responsible for planning law, this 'exempt[ed] the port buildings located on cadastral plots Minat al-Husn 1455 and 1456 from … [both] general regulations and those specifically intended for Beirut's central business district'. The maximum height for the building on lot 1456— the future Yacht Club—was raised to 13 metres, and all buildings on both plots were exempted from regulations dictating the surface area of balconies and surrounding 'green areas'. In addition, the electricity station to be installed by EDL to power the marina, as well as requisite 'technical installations', would not be counted as part of the overall built-up surface area, allowing greater room for manoeuvre. Finally, the decree changed zoning regulations for all land within development Zone A. Henceforth, 'cafes, restaurants, and touristic' installations would be allowed along the coastline, in addition to 'sports and leisure activities, commercial premises and homes', in order to stimulate the 'development' of this zone.[65] With one strike of the president's pen, BWD was now free to realise its projected vision for the waterfront. That those involved were willing to alter the regulatory framework governing much of Lebanon's coastline in order to achieve their aims is telling.

But it is not just such deft manoeuvring—always tiptoeing like a tightrope walker along the edge of the law—that has provoked the ire of activists and fellow politicians like Ghazi Aridi, Safadi's successor as minister of public works, who accused his predecessor of corruption in a very public spat.[66] Equally troubling, in the eyes of many, is the way in which a swathe of Beirut's shoreline has been brought under private control. It is galling enough that the Yacht Club, which takes up the lion's share of the BWD, should be accessible only to members and their guests—presumably drawn, like them, from the gilded but exiguous elite that holds much of Lebanon's wealth. But this is not all. For though Zaitunay Bay loudly trumpets its public areas, with their 'spaces for events, cultural festivals, concerts, [and] exhibitions', it remains very much a private domain, which imposes its own regulations and polices the public's use of its domain. Signs discreetly placed on planters on the upper walkway—a stretch of pavement that might easily be confused for public land—remind passers-by, in emphatic capital letters, that they are on 'PRIVATE PROPERTY', and ban music, loud talking, food, shisha smoking, hawking, picking the flowers, littering, cycling, rollerblading, and allowing dogs to foul the pavement. To ensure that the rules are upheld, the company employs private security guards—though these men, far from preserving the peace, are capable on occasion of attracting unwanted attention for their employers. In September 2015, a man whom Lebanese media identified as a private security guard in Solidere's pay was caught on camera as he attempted to wrestle free of police officers to confront demonstrators who had gathered to stage a protest at Zaitunay Bay, which they saw as a symbol of the growing privatisation of the commonweal that had resulted in the complete breakdown of rubbish collection in the capital. As one agent tried to drag him away by the arm, and another to reason with him, the man screamed *ana 'am bihki ma'u, ru' shway, triki, triki*—'I'm trying to speak to him [one of the demonstrators], calm down, leave me alone, leave me alone'. As the investigative journalist Habib Battah noted laconically, 'this would probably be considered assault of a police officer in many countries', but in Lebanon 'he was just left alone when police left'.[67] There is no doubt that there is something unusual about such brazen impunity. But perhaps we should not be too eager to consider Lebanon as entirely exceptional. For with its mix of public and private financing, its exploitation—and creation—of a highly favourable regulatory environment, and its power to govern and police the spaces it owns, imposing and enforcing its own regulations as it sees fit, Zaitunay Bay is not unlike regeneration projects in the United Kingdom, the United States and elsewhere, which have carved out similar sovereign spaces of capital.[68]

It is entirely understandable that so much attention has been lavished on Solidere, its partners, and their visions for Beirut's central districts. With their sheer ambition and their brazen embrace of luxury, their associations with the Hariri family—for so long a source of fascination for Lebanese and foreign observers alike—and their enlistment of famous architects like Zaha Hadid and Renzo Piano, grand schemes like the Souks, the Beirut Waterfront Development, and the projected Pinwheel skyscrapers, just a few hundred metres to its east along the shoreline, seem emblematic of the transformation of Lebanon's cityscapes. But they are, in a sense, no more than the most conspicuous products of the neoliberal approach to urban planning that has gripped the country since the 1990s—a set of policies that have placed public means at the disposal of private ends and transformed hitherto public places into private enclosures. Everywhere one goes in Beirut, one finds streets, and skylines, in transformation. Everywhere, old houses and apartment blocks, built in late Ottoman times or under the French Mandate, or even in the 1950s and 1960s, disappear in a matter of hours and days, leaving behind them only a few distressed piles of rubble. Sometimes, buildings will vanish overnight in the roar of diggers, as developers ignore ministerial decrees ordering a stay of execution. One turns a corner expecting to find a familiar building, only to be greeted by a gaping space, like a missing tooth in a boxer's grin. A parking lot might open for a while, charging drivers three or four thousand lira to leave their cars off Beirut's choked, narrow streets. Often, though, this little enterprise does not last, giving way soon enough to more ambitious exercises in spatial speculation. All over Beirut, vast craters pockmark the city and building sites spit acrid, chalky dust out onto the roads, covering cars and trees and jasmine vines. Diggers jut out, their fat backsides blocking the onward progress of impatient cars sounding their horns like an angry herd. Concrete mixers vomit out the products of their innards. Labourers—small, lean men from the east of Syria—rush busily about. Cranes reach up into the heights, hovering above the scene with imperious detachment.

Soon, another sky-scraping luxury apartment block is born. The names of these developments range from bland placeholders—many are simply christened after the cadastral plots on which they sit—to more poetic handles like that of the much discussed Achrafieh sky-scraper Sama Beirut. At 193 metres, this is the tallest building in the Lebanese capital. Looming like an emaciated giant over its neighbourhood, it sits amidst its own private park—4,000 square metres of 'landscaped areas equipped with enjoyable lighting and fountains'. Its lower floors are given over to offices, while the upper stories are taken up by palatial flats that range 'from 253m2 to 526m2', equipped with 'state-of-the-art smart home technologies for increased comfort and reduced energy consumption'. Superseding even these 'is a sumptuous 1,414m2 penthouse, a villa in the sky, … with its own amenities: a private internal elevator, a 35m2 internal garden, a 30m2 pond in the main living area, a solarium of 147m2 together with a 30m2 pool in the upper floor, together with an internal mezzanine for the staff'.[69]

One would have thought such ostentation more than enough. But I recall once being told that the owner of this penthouse—for somebody did buy it, a Lebanese entrepreneur who made his fortune in the beauty industry—called for more and more embellishments: first a wood oven, flown in from Italy so that he could make his own pizzas, then a DJ booth so that he could entertain his guests with his own mixes, and finally a helipad so that he could return home in the most convenient of ways, passing over the traffic down below. His fellow residents, understandably reluctant to have their expensive tranquillity broken by the throb of helicopter blades, refused this last demand. But it is telling that they should only have balked at this point. It matters little, I think, whether this particular anecdote is true. That some should recount it, and others listen so eagerly, is in itself revealing of the tales of luxury that middle-class Lebanese tell each other as they watch the transformations about them, attempting to find a way not to be left behind.

Sama may be exceptional in its absurd grandiosity, but there are many other buildings that share not just its infatuation with the ostentatious, the new-fangled and the expensive, but also its aesthetic of isolation. Typically, the new high-rises stand some way back from the street. Set at a safe distance from the public thoroughfare, they are protected from its occupants by a wall or metal fence. This barrier is broken by just one or two openings: a small pedestrian door, of expensive, elegant, solid pine or oak, for those coming on foot—a domestic servant returning from the corner-shop, perhaps—and a larger opening for cars, leading down to the underground parking that sits in the building's foundations. Both are electronically activated and equipped, often enough, with cameras. Beside one of these doors might sit a plastic garden chair, flanked perhaps by a pot of Turkish coffee and a half-drunk bottle of water—the essential accoutrements of the sleep-deprived security guards who serve, at all hours of the day and night, as uniformed gatekeepers between the private spaces within and the public space all about. Between this fence and the building's main entrance stands another protective membrane—small patches of lawn and pebbles, and olive or palm or cypress trees, lit at night from beneath with floor-spots buried amidst their gnarly roots. The walk through this little garden—on basalt paving stones, perhaps—leads up into a spacious, iridescent lobby—all marble or immaculate white surfaces. The swift trip in the elevator—whose barely perceptible hum contrasts with the wheezing and groaning of the lifts in older apartment buildings—takes one up onto the landing and into large, enviably spacious flats, all high ceilings and unbroken stretches of floor. These expansive surface areas are only swollen further by balconies that effectively serve, in many cases, as extensions of the living room. This spatial inflation was made possible by the 2004 Building Law, which ruled that balconies could be covered with glass all year round. As one of the parliamentarians who examined the law at the committee stage put it: 'I, as a citizen, want to take advantage of my balcony. So you allow me to use it in summer but not in winter?' This logic appears to have won over his colleagues, for only one objected, arguing that glass covers would only 'be favouring rich people'.[70] This is but one of the ways in which systematic regulatory engineering has helped to engender this building boom.

This runs counter to one of the narratives the Lebanese like to tell themselves about life in the post-war years. For the rapid spread of these luxury developments is often put down, like so many other aspects of Lebanon's recent economic history, to the incapacities of a 'weak' and 'absent' state fatally wounded by fifteen years of civil strife and content to remain a tired and old night watchman.[71] But, as Marieke Krijnen and Leila Fawaz have argued, their construction has on the contrary been made possible by a number of quite deliberate 'public interventions'. Taken together, the 2004 reform of building regulations (Law 646/2004), which considerably loosened the restrictions on high-rise residential buildings, and laws passed in 2001 and 2006 which eased the restrictions on non-nationals acquiring real estate and creating companies have created a highly favourable regulatory framework for property developers. These measures, however, are not just the work of public servants, of disinterested politicians and neutral bureaucrats in their drab ministry offices. On the contrary, the 2004 law was in large part the product of concerted lobbying and detailed proposals 'by a handful of developers who have since … flaunted their role'.[72] It is no surprise that the head of the Building Promoters Federation of Lebanon, Elie Sawma, should have expressed his satisfaction with a 'modern law [that] responds to the expectations of investors, engineers, and developers'.[73] Such talk does not just reveal the discursive frames in which developers place their actions, thinking of themselves as beneficent agents of modernisation and economic growth. It also reminds us that perhaps the most significant aspect of this recent history of real estate has been the growing entanglement of state and private interests. This has gone hand-in-hand with what Krijnen and Fawaz call the growing 'informalisation' of decision-making. For since the turn of the century, the state has increasingly abdicated its responsibilities, turning over the work of regulating and ruling on new projects to autonomous bodies like IDAL and the Higher Council of the Directorate General of Urbanism.[74]

The Higher Council, in particular, has acquired extensive powers over the future shape of the city, as decisions on new projects have increasingly been routed towards it, bypassing the municipality of Beirut. This hybrid public–private body is made up not just of representatives of the internal security services and the ministries or departments of housing, archaeology and justice, but also of the heads of the Orders of Engineers and Architects of Beirut and Tripoli, as well as two representatives of the 'profession' chosen for their 'excellence' as developers. It operates in a strictly ad hoc fashion, often taking decisions on shifting, highly subjective aesthetic grounds. For, as several developers have attested, its members assess each case individually on the basis of '*taste*. They have no regulations, no book they follow. It's not a technical study like at the municipality'. As another developer put it, 'it's a question of personal judgment ... there are no requirements on a list which you can look at'. The matter is quite simple: 'if they don't like it for some reason ... it won't pass'. But if the members of the Higher Council do like a project—or if they happen to be willing to do a favour to a developer they know—then they are ready to make extensive use of the exemptions allowed under the 2004 Building Law for developments that present '*special architectural and urban characteristics that may benefit the neighbourhood where it is located*'. On this point, Krijnen and Fawaz's sources were clear. In recent years, 'almost every high-end development ... has benefited from one exemption or another'. This is nothing less than the mark of a new 'mode of government'. Founded on a neoliberal willingness to use the law to protect the needs of capital—that putative engine of wealth creation and urban improvement—it has increasingly entrusted private actors with seemingly public decisions. In the process, it has transformed regulatory work into a personal matter of friendly favours and subjective judgments, creating a process that is as opaque as it is inconsistent. As one 'frustrated public sector employee' complained to Krijnen and Fawaz, 'the exception is the … rule here'.[75]

One particular aspect of this growth of high-end high-rise housing has been its spatial dispersion through Beirut and beyond. Unlike in many other places, luxury apartments and property developments are not necessarily concentrated in particular neighbourhoods, havens of affluence deliberately cut off from the surrounding quarters. (Think, for instance, of San Isidro in Lima, or L'Oeuf in Dakar, neighbourhoods that with their cube-like white villas, their quiet tree-lined streets and private security forces, are designed to be the obverse of the cities around them.) This is apparent from the compilation of average property prices per neighbourhood published each year by *Le Commerce du Levant*. Its figures for 2017 indicate that a first-floor flat—by no means the most desirable of acquisitions when so many buildings stretch at least eight or nine stories up nowadays—still costs upwards of $3,000 per square metre everywhere in central Beirut but Hayy Surian and the area around the French *lycée*. In the former, the square metre will now set you back $2,450. This is still an almost unthinkable sum for what was once, not so long ago, a firmly proletarian neighbourhood of Assyrian Christians, after whom it is named, and Syrian and South Asian migrant labourers, the kind of place in which those capable of paying more than $300,000 for an apartment would not have dreamed of living. Prices in most other quarters are significantly higher. In east Beirut, the average going price per square metre in Mar Mikhail is $3,967, in Furn al-Hayek $4,675, and in Sursock $5,000. In the central district and west Beirut, prices are comparable, if not higher still—$7,100 per square metre in the old Jewish quarter of Wadi Abou Jmil, now a succession of chic apartment blocks that promise, as the hoarding on one development has it, 'a luxury haven in the heart of downtown Beirut'; $4,487 in Hamra; $5,367 in Ain al-Mreisse; and $8,500 in Manara, whose sea frontage promises un-endangered Mediterranean vistas. In only twelve of the twenty-nine districts examined do average prices come in at less than $4,000.[76]

In a recent article, Nadia Alaily-Mattar has argued that this remarkable inflation in real estate prices is in part a product of demographic changes provoked by the civil war, which pushed people about Lebanon, leading to the collapse of older patterns of coexistence and creating increasingly homogeneous confessional enclaves.[77] In short, those who can afford it are willing to pay a premium for the security of living among others of the same community. One is tempted to agree when one hears conversations between well-to-do Christian women about what the *musiciens*—as they call Muslims in barely concealed code—are really like, or when an estate agent in a Christian part of east Beirut tells a prospective client the building they are in 'only rents to Christians, so don't worry about the area. It is clean'.[78] Indeed, the last few years have been marked by a series of controversies surrounding property ownership and development in particular areas, many of them fomented by Christian parties concerned to protect their communities from the depredations of Muslim others. Perhaps the most infamous of these has centred on the small mixed village of Lasa, in the mountains high above Jbeil, whose Shia inhabitants have long disputed the Maronite Church's claim to own two-thirds of the 3 million square metres of cadastral land attached to the village. This dispute was reignited when the Miqdad family began building on some of this land. While the Church condemned what it regarded as illegal appropriation, politicians and reporters aligned with 14 March claimed that this was no private action, but the doing of Hizballah. Pointing to repeated instances of intimidation against reporters filming at the scene and resistance against the Internal Security Forces' attempts to stop construction, the MTV reporter Joyce Akiki argued that this was no less than the establishment of 'the republic of the *dahiyeh* in Lasa'. Hizballah's oppressive rule, which already stifled the southern suburbs of Beirut, was now spreading deep into Christian country, as the party waged a 'continuing offensive on the church's lands' and 'the rights of the people'. The question had to be asked: 'what does Hizballah want in Lasa?'[79] The logical outcome of these polemics, with their conception of particular regions and localities as the irredeemable property of one community or another, was the draft law put forward in 2011 by the veteran Maronite politician Boutros Harb, implementing a fifteen-year ban on property transactions between Lebanese of different sects.

In response to his many critics, Harb brazenly insisted that he was only 'saying aloud what everyone is thinking'.[80]

But we should perhaps not overstate the power of sectarian considerations to shape Beirut's real estate market, with its fantastical distortions of value. For, as Marieke Krijnen and Hicham El-Achkar have both argued in persuasive fashion, this is very much a boom driven by supply-side factors.[81] Paradoxically, the very same law that protects longstanding tenants from rent hikes and provides them with security of tenancy is also cited by landowners as a justification for entering into partnerships with property developers or selling on the land. If they cannot secure a new rent law which affords them fairer—that is to say, higher—returns, then, landowners plead, they are left with no course of action but the most radical: knocking down the buildings their fathers or grandfathers had put up, in order to release the capital locked up in their land.[82] Krijnen and el-Achkar both draw on Neil Smith's influential 'rent-gap' theory of gentrification, which posits that buildings depreciate as they get older, while land only increases in value, to argue that landowners and developers have striven in recent years to close this gap, realising the value of the land that lies beneath—and then some—and maximising their earnings by building high-value, high-rise housing.[83] Even the most cursory of glances at the official statistics will confirm this. In 2006, sixty construction permits for 'luxurious' developments in Beirut were granted, seventy-eight for what authorities qualify as 'good' housing, three for 'medium' standard, and none for 'popular' housing. Indeed, between 2006 and 2008, no permits at all were granted for 'popular' projects. Over the same three-year period, however, 210 permits—or just shy of 40 per cent of the total—were granted to 'luxurious' projects.[84] This cannot but have effects on neighbourhoods and the communities that live in them.

Developers like HAR Properties—one of whose main shareholders is Fahed Hariri, son of Rafiq and brother of Saad—make much of the special appeal and quirky charm of quarters like Mar Mikhail, where HAR began work on a new $30 million project, the AYA-tower, in 2011. Once a working- and lower-middle-class neighbourhood whose largely Armenian inhabitants worked as mechanics and furniture-makers, this has experienced rapid social transformation in recent years, as young foreigners and Lebanese—many of them members of that free-floating, footloose caste of NGO workers, artists, designers, and freelance journalists who need only a laptop and a flat white to get to work—have flocked to it. And, as is so often the case, the property developers soon followed in their wake, seeking to capitalise on this ideal conjunction of cheap land with new-found cool and cachet. In its promotional material, HAR promises that buyers would soon befriend 'the Man'kouche salesman from the Nile' who will 'introduce you to his own fellows', become 'the next door grocer's best confident [sic]', listening to tales of his 'sciatica', play backgammon with the neighbourhood hairdresser's friends, learn a few words of Armenian, and 'watch the boiling underground arts scene' unfold at a local bar. There is little evidence, though, that prospective buyers are interested in the life of 'surprises and oddness' promised in such excruciating terms.[85]

For the suspicion lingers that many of those who have purchased real estate in central Beirut in recent years have been motivated, in part, by financial considerations. This is particularly so when one remembers that many analysts insist that Lebanese migrants and Gulf Arabs make up a significant proportion—if not the bulk—of these buyers. According to one well-informed source, Lebanese 'expatriates began to buy in bulk' in the wake of the independence intifada of 2005, which seemed to augur a new period of political stability and economic prosperity. While some may have wanted to spend more time in a Lebanon free of Syrian overrule, others were in all likelihood hoping that these favourable conditions would help their investments to appreciate rapidly. The global financial crisis of 2008 brought, in turn, another wave of capital, as many migrants came to see 'land value' as 'the safest' form of investment in highly volatile times.[86] It is inevitable that this preponderance of overseas investment will lead to low rates of occupancy, as many of these newly built apartments are used as holiday homes for only a few weeks or months a year, or simply left alone to grow in value, like a stock certificate stashed away for a rainy day in a drawer. This has the effect of transforming parts of Beirut into a ghost city, inhabited only by the spectres of speculation. As I walked back home one recent evening, I counted no more than three or four apartments with the lights on in all of the new developments that line the hill of Wadi Abou Jmil.

But even those who live year-round in their new apartments seem to have little desire to venture out into the neighbourhoods that sur-round them. If they have a dog, it will likely be the maid who will walk it once or twice a day, and who will be charged with picking up after it. And it is she, too, who will watch the kids if there is room for them to play outside the building—and if they are allowed to play downstairs. And should *monsieur* and *madame* need something from the shops that they forgot to pick up on their weekly car trip to the supermarket, it will fall to the housekeeper or the driver to pick it up.[87] This social isolation complicates the argument that Lebanon's rich choose to live within the comforting cocoon of sectarian community. For the wealthy of all confessions tend to cluster and mingle in their own spaces—restaurants, cafés, exhibition spaces, malls, and shops, beach clubs, beauty salons, and health clubs that, like their own homes, are scattered across the city. These are easy enough to recognise by their prices and their menus, on which Lebanese mezze are rechristened and given a fusion twist—*baba ghanuj*, for example, becomes a *caviar d'aubergine*—and new fashions like quinoa salad and avocado toast jostle with reliable old favourites like *filet mignon*. The same small rotating cast moves between these places, a clientele of young women in expensive sports clothes, their hair tied in a pony-tail as if ready for their Pilates class, older women in maxi dresses and stack heels, tables of corpulent middle-aged men, joshing as they smoke their cigars and sip their Pepsi and their Perrier, who go to this or that place—whose owner they will often know, inquiring of the waiter whether *sittna*, 'our lady', is about today—knowing that they will encounter friends, acquaintances and business partners. The rich thus live in a strangely segmented city of disconnected dots on the map. Their points of reference are not proximate ones, the familiar markings of neighbourhood. Insulated in their air-conditioned SUVs, high above the traffic that surrounds them, they spend their days in transit, moving slowly through a series of 'tunnels' and 'corridors' that cut across the city. Only rarely, while waiting outside a restaurant for the valet to return their car, or calling their driver to come pick them up, do they tread on public ground. You will see them walking gingerly over uneven pavements, uncertain of their surroundings, or staring intensely at their mobile phones like shy teenagers, desperate to maintain the pretence of disengagement.[88] These men and women are never fully in—and never fully of—the city, and yet they claim to own its rights.

243

LEBANON

The presence of these atomised figures in their midst cannot but have an effect on longstanding inhabitants of neighbourhoods like Yasu'iyya and Furn al-Hayek, in east Beirut, or Ain al-Mreisse, in the west. The results of a survey of Achrafieh residents carried out by Hicham El-Achkar in October 2011 are deeply suggestive in this respect. 68% of those he spoke to were tenants, and the vast majority—74%—lived in buildings of between three and nine floors. When asked how often they interacted with fellow residents who did not live in high-rises, 65% responded that they did so 'often' and another 35% 'socially'. But when asked if they interacted with high-rise residents, 77% told el-Achkar that they 'never' did so, and only 23% that they did so 'socially'—exchanging greetings on the street, or crossing each other in a shop—with no-one responding that they did so 'often'. When asked for their opinions of high-rise buildings, 62% had a negative opinion; only 14% responded positively.[89] Such findings add up to a sense that many are beginning to feel like strangers in their own neighbourhoods, displaced—whether literally or figuratively—by the new developments crowding them out. Indeed, el-Achkar found that 350 families had been evicted from their homes between 2000 and 2010, as fifty old apartment buildings were knocked down to make room for high-rises.[90] Many have been forced to relocate to the outer peripheries of Beirut, where they have attempted to make new homes in unfamiliar surrounds. This process has not only added to the pressure on housing in densely built-up areas like Dora and Jal al-Dib to the north, or Hadath, Chiyah and Ayn al-Rummaneh to the south; it has also fuelled a burst of new developments on the hills of Hazmieh, Fiyadiyyeh and other outlying suburbs. These have been captured in Manuel Alvarez Diestro's recent photographs of concrete frames sprouting up, alien structures amidst the pine trees, of patches of apartment blocks surrounded by raw earth and rock, like moon colonies, and of immense chunks of earth bitten out of the mountainside.[91] These eerie images remind us that among the consequences of Beirut's gentrification must be counted not just social dislocation, but also environmental degradation. For the dismantling of longstanding communities has only accelerated the city's sprawl ever deeper into the mountain, taking a heavy toll on Lebanon's already compromised ecosystems.

But even those ordinary tenants who have stayed put in their neighbourhoods are living in increasingly precarious circumstances. In January 2012, twenty-seven inhabitants—sixteen of them Sudanese, Egyptian, Filipino and Jordanian migrant workers—died when a six-storey apartment building in the Fassouh quarter of Achrafieh collapsed.[92] A Syrian labourer working on a nearby construction site told Al-Jazeera that he had seen 'small pieces of stone falling down but no-one paid any attention at the start. Then large chunks of stone started falling and people began screaming for everyone to get out. Within minutes, the building was on the floor.'[93] The tragedy suddenly brought into the media spotlight the effects of rampant property speculation. The building's collapse, investigators concluded, had been provoked by a combination of factors: the demolition of a weight-bearing wall on the ground or first floor, which exacerbated existing structural flaws; the material out of which these two floors had been built in 1940, before another five stories were added in stages between 1940 and 1967; and the recent construction of a building on the adjoining plot, which had damaged one of the apartment block's supporting pillars and reached into the water table, causing subsidence. But most important of all was the building's age and state of disrepair.[94] As one of the residents told an Al-Jazeera reporter, 'the building was extremely run-down and the owner had warned tenants not to remain there shortly before it disintegrated'.[95] In 2015, its owners—two brothers, Michel and Toufic Saade—were sentenced to two years in prison and ordered to pay almost 2 billion LL in compensation to the building's surviving residents. Here, then, were the two sides of Beirut's building boom: a new building had been put up too quickly, causing structural damage and dangerous levels of subsidence, an old building had been deliberately left to fall into decay, its tenants' safety neglected, and all in the name of profit.

The stories of those who survived, meanwhile, reveal the growing precarity of Lebanon's working classes. Among them were two Sudanese men, al-Tayyeb Daoud Ismail and Ismail Abou Bakr, who were rescued from the rubble by Red Cross volunteers only to be arrested and taken from their hospital beds by officers of the Internal Security Forces, who detained them for illegally entering the country; they were deported to Sudan two weeks later.[96] Jeanne d'Arc Naïm and her daughter, Gladys, managed to escape from their first-floor apartment as the building started coming down around them. Her sons, Jihad, Charbel, and Farhat stayed behind to help their father, Tanious, who was disabled and in a wheelchair. None of the four survived. As she explained to a journalist from *L'Orient-Le Jour*, she and her family had moved into the building five years earlier, when they were evicted from their apartment in the sector of the Lycée, in Achrafieh. She was now staying with one of her other daughters near the Hôtel Alexandre, in another run-down part of Achrafieh.[97] Albert Yazbeck had lived in the building for forty-five years. He had worked until his retirement at Sleep Comfort, a bed store. When he became too old for this work, he took up a seat in a neighbourhood parking lot, living off the tips that drivers handed him and the small sum that one of the local shopkeepers gave him each month. His partner, Thérèse, died in the disaster. She had been watching television when the building started caving in. Albert had been downstairs, lighting votive candles in the small shrine in the entrance hall. As he explained, 'me and Thérèse, we never got married ... She was my cousin, we were young... Then she got married, and her husband died, I got married too on my end and then divorced. We don't have any children, either one of us. Twelve years ago, Thérèse came to live with me. She's my wife, my companion, my friend... We were together all the time.' Without anyone to go to, Albert was placed in a care home, paid for by the Bachir Gemayel Foundation—which raised more than $300,000 for the victims of the disaster. But, without Thérèse, his health quickly deteriorated. He died on Monday 30 April 2012.[98]

Albert, Jeanne d'Arc, al-Tayyeb and Ismail lost everything. Theirs are stories of quiet grief, but also of deportation, of eviction and displacement, of hand-to-mouth existences and dependence on private goodwill and the flickering, inconstant kindness of strangers, of attempting to maintain dignity and decency in the face of neglect, absent public services and ever-present uncertainty. But, in a bitter irony, the association of landlords presented themselves as victims of the Fassouh disaster. 'The State, and not the building's owners, are solely responsible' for this catastrophe, they declared in a press release in December 2012, for it was 'the State that has still not taken the initiative of putting to the vote a new tenancy law that would give landlords the means to restore buildings'. In other words, in their eyes, the Saade brothers were not guilty of negligence, but were in fact the victims of an iniquitous attempt to maintain rents at artificially low and 'mediocre' rates, depriving them of the revenue that was theirs 'by right'. Could 'any human conscience', they cried out, 'accept that an apartment of more than 150m2 be rented out for 30,000 Lebanese lira'—or 200 dollars—'per month'? Landlords were being forced into penury and neglect, while among their tenants were 'well-off people who could easily adapt to a rise in rents'. If the Lebanese did not wish to see another disaster like Fassouh, what was needed was a new and 'just' tenancy law.[99]

This might well seem a perverse attempt to make good on catastrophe, a petty declension of disaster capitalism, twisting the discourse on rights and equity into aberrant and repulsive forms. In June 2014, however, parliament appeared to side with the landlords, introducing a new rent law removing many of the controls that had previously governed tenancies. Under this act, the landlords of the 140,000 or so tenants who still had 'old rent' contracts would be free to increase rents in increments over a period of six years, in order to bring them into line with current rates. The law forecast that rents would rise by 15 per cent in each of the first four years, before rising in increments of 20 per cent in the fifth and sixth years of the tenancy. After this period, tenants would be offered a new contract for only three years, in line with inflation. After this, 'rents' would be 'free'—that is to say unregulated.[100] In short, this amounted to a comprehensive liberalisation of Lebanon's rent laws, stripping low-income tenants, many of them well into old age, of the safeguards they had hitherto enjoyed, and plunging them into uncertainty.[101] Only those whose income was no more than three times the minimum salary, and who did not own a second property anywhere in Lebanon—an important concession to landlords who complained that many tenants retained a house in their home villages, a sign in their eyes not of the lingering attachments of relatively recent migrants, but of their tenants' deceptive affluence—would be entitled to any assistance from the state.[102] On the one hand, the minimum monthly salary was $500. On the other, average yearly rents could range anywhere between $7,000 and $10,000 in much of Beirut.[103] It was hard to see, as *L'Orient-Le Jour* noted sharply, how a social crisis could be avoided.[104] It is no surprise that a coalition of architects, lawyers, economists and activists should have sharply condemned the new law, which they accused of stripping 'city dwellers of their housing guarantees without providing them with any alternatives'. A 'flagrant violation of the right to the city', the new legislative framework would lead to 'mass eviction', and 'automatically transform lands with rent-controlled buildings into targets for real-estate developments'.[105] As the graphic designer and urban activist Nadine Bekdache has written, 'old tenants' remain 'an obstruction to landlords' opportunities to profit from their skyrocketing land price', their 'mere continuous presence ... the only substantial challenge to the real estate growth machine' that has ploughed through Beirut in recent years.[106] Once again, the authors of this open letter argued, the state had chosen to uphold the interests of private enterprise and capital. And, once again, the most vulnerable were to pay the price. This message was more pithily conveyed in the handwritten placard held up by one of the protesters who rallied against the new law in December 2014, a dignified old lady wearing her best hat for the occasion. It read, simply: *la li-bi' bayrut li-sharikat 'iqariyya*—'no to the sale of Beirut to real estate companies'.[107]

Lebanon's working classes, however, are not just confronting growing residential insecurity. They must also make do with both uncertain and declining living standards and what might be called infrastructural deprivation. A map of central Achrafieh that Hicham El-Achkar drew up neatly brings this home, presenting a bleak picture of neglected public space and unplanned development. On his walks through the area delimited by Avenue Charles Malek to the south and Avenue de l'Indépendance to the north, Mar Mitr to the east and Rue de Damas on the west, el-Achkar counted eleven phone-boxes, all situated on these busy main roads, four benches, one recycling bin, and one public space—the small park that faces the Greek Orthodox church of Mar Niqula, to the south. In the same small quadrant of the city, he found twelve stretches of broken street lights—many spread over several streets; eight stretches of metal bollards and barriers obstructing the path of pedestrians; and twenty-one green bins blocking the road or the pavement. And, scattered through this map are nineteen high-rise luxury developments. Informality, both high and low, has taken over this neighbourhood, as a host of actors—from shopkeepers who sit out, taking up the thin sliver of pavement with their plastic chairs, to property developers whose projects envelop their surroundings in noise and dust—occupy public space, making it their own. No wonder, then, that 70% of residents should judge their quarter to be ill-fitted for pedestrians. Moreover, the vast majority crave more public facilities: 96% would like more green spaces; 94% more litter bins; 90% more benches and street lighting; 80% more children's playgrounds and phone boxes; 68% more post boxes; 54% more public art.[108] All of these amenities—the universal markers of public space—are absent in their neighbourhood. It is the same story in much of Beirut. From Verdun or Ain al-Tine in the west to Jeitawi and Qubayyat in the east, night-time streets are unlit by streetlamps. If some are illuminated by the fluorescent glare of the shops, fast food joints and bars that line them, others are forests of shadows, in which small clearings are opened up by the light cast off an apartment block, until one is sunk back into the darkness, stepping awkwardly along broken, dipping pavements.

What's more, this lack of public amenities has inevitable effects on private incomes. For all, rich and poor alike, are forced to pay—sometimes twice, once to the state and again to private providers—for essential services, run by private operators. This is true not just of schools and hospitals—around 62 per cent of Lebanese pupils, for instance, attend private schools—but also of smaller everyday expenses.[109] Those who do not have off-street parking at their home or workplace must pay, as I already mentioned, 3,000 or 4,000 lira a day or take out a monthly *ishtirak*, or subscription, to leave their cars in a private parking lot—often an informal installation turning vacant space to profit, as landowners or even, in some cases, churches, seek to extract whatever value they can from land. Those who do not have cars of their own—the young and the old, migrant labourers or soldiers on service—must rely either on *service*-s, or shared taxis, or on the many private mini-bus companies that run through Beirut, and far into its hinterland. Those who wish to spend a day sunbathing or swimming must all too often pay a steep entrance fee to gain access to a rooftop pool or beach club—often, as investigative journalists and activists have found, built illegally on seafront land that belongs to the state. And those who do not wish to drink the tap-water must either find ways of purifying their supply, or—as around half of all households do—buy bottled water.[110] In every supermarket and corner-store you will find six-packs of Tannourine or Soha mineral water, stacked high to the ceiling next to the tills. All of these expenses, large and small, quickly add up, only increasing the wearying, pressing weight of the everyday. But perhaps the most infamous and egregious of these additional charges are those levied on electricity.

Energy slumps

Since the civil war, Lebanon's inhabitants have effectively had to rely on two parallel electricity systems. One, official but intermittent, is overseen by the state utility company, Electricité du Liban. Another, run by a number of private operators, supplies the generators that maintain power for homes and commercial premises when the electricity cuts out—as it does, every day, with numbing regularity. So frequent are these outages, so part of the familiar weave of everyday life, that people barely mark the shift from light into darkness. In a university library, the chatter and tip-tapping of fingers on laptop keys will continue, the students' faces lit up by their screens. In a café, the conversation will stop for a breath, registering the change, before picking up again, as though nothing had changed. People will shower in the dark, lit by a small torch, or come to meetings late with shampoo still in their hair, if their electric shower has given up for the day. And yet people have come to treat these disruptions, these sudden bursts of darkness, as nothing out of the ordinary, just another tedious quotidian inconvenience amongst many. The frequency of the cuts varies across the country. Beirut usually tends to suffer only from outages of between three and four and a half hours each day. Elsewhere in Lebanon, however, average daily supply is only sixteen to eighteen hours, and consumers must find other means to light their homes and power their appliances for six to eight hours a day.[111] This is borne out by the Ministry of Energy's own figures, which put the number of lost hours of power per month at 245 for March 2017, and 191 for April.[112] In certain regions, or when high oil prices or hot weather affect supply and demand, EDL can barely supply electricity for twelve hours a day.[113]

Into this gap have crowded a number of generator operators. Since the 1980s, these informal enterprises—many, it is alleged, with firm ties to assorted political parties and their leaders—have established a firm hold on the market. Indeed, so tight is their stranglehold on the sector—and so close, some say, their ties to powerful political patrons—that the Lebanese state shrinks away from curbing what remain illegal operations, preferring instead timid and intermittent attempts to regulate their activities, formalising the informal through restrictions on tariffs and the like. In May 2017, the energy and economy ministers, César Abi Khalil and Raed Khoury, held a joint press conference in which they announced their plans to install electricity counters in private residences and commercial premises across Lebanon. These devices—whose cost, they stressed, would be borne by generator operators rather than consumers—would keep track of both the number of hours without official current and the number of kWh of energy homes and businesses were drawing from generators. This would enable the state to act against those operators who were charging more than the official tariffs set by the Ministry of Energy— sometimes, Abi Khalil alleged, under the noses of municipalities willing to turn a blind eye to such flagrant abuses. Prices, he reported, ranged from 7,000LL—or $4.50—for five amps in certain regions to 40,000LL—$26.50—in others, a discrepancy so wide that it could only be explained by sharp practices.[114]

This announcement brought immediate condemnation from the generator operators themselves. Though they carefully maintained, as always, their anonymity, they rejected the tariffs imposed by the Ministry of Energy, inveighing against what they viewed as unreasonable attempts to restrict their activities. As one anonymous source put it to *L'Orient-Le Jour*, the ministry's tariffs 'obliges me to charge $6.60 per month for a subscription of 5 amps. But I would have to charge at least $20 to even cover my costs'.[115] Another generator owner who supplied power in the Kisrwan echoed this claim: 'We can't do decent work with these prices, which don't take into account the cost of our equipment. We should be able to charge at least 35,000 lira [or $23] per month in order to get by'. 'If the ministry digs its heels in', he threatened, 'we will have to mobilise'.[116]

Though the idea of these faceless cabals organising a public demonstration appears as absurd as that of private landlords holding a sit-in outside the Ministry of Justice to protest the supposed iniquities of rent control—a nonsensical perversion of the idea of commonweal and public interest—it is clear that these men appear willing to defend their right to profit by any means available. But these are the slippages that neoliberalism makes possible, with its conflation—and confusion—of private interest and public good and its utilisation of the language of rights and liberties to protect free enterprise, and that the executive encourages by treating these illegal operators as legitimate entrepreneurs whose only offence is an occasional propensity to overcharge the customer. If the state cannot do anything more, it is for a complex concatenation of reasons. The networks of interest in which these operators are firmly ensconced are one cause for its relative inertia, but so too is its own commitment to the language—and practice—of free and untrammelled private enterprise, even when this appears to operate on the margins of the law. But another reason is perhaps as self-evident as it is painful: Lebanese politicians know that, so long as EDL cannot supply twenty-four hours of power a day, the country's inhabitants must face the choice between languishing in the dark or turning to alternative supplies of energy.

Since 2010, successive energy ministers have remained committed to an ambitious $4.87 billion plan to reform Lebanon's electricity sector. Trumpeted by Gebran Bassil and his successor, César Abi Khalil, as the solution to Lebanon's longstanding energy woes, this is built upon an admixture of infrastructural modernisation and corporate restructuring. New state-operated power stations would be built, the most important of them at Deir Ammar, in the northern Beqaa, existing installations at Jiyyeh and Zouk Mosbeh extensively refurbished to boost production, and the private sector enlisted to build power stations of its own. Renewable energy would play a greater part. The state would refurbish hydraulic power stations, like the one in the northern valley of Qadisha, one of the oldest sources of electricity in the country, and develop the capacity to transform waste into energy. Here too, the private sector would play a part, building wind farms that could supply somewhere between 60 and 100 MW each year. Improvements would be made to the national grid, finally finishing a section held up by the protests of local residents in Mansourieh and completing work on a substation at Ksara, in the Beqaa, which connected Lebanon's electricity network to that of Syria. These works would enable the state to cut down on technical inefficiencies, which made up around 15% of the total power supply lost each year, Bassil estimated in 2010. 'Theft', or diversion of power cables for private supply, made up 20%, and non-payment of bills another 5%.[117]

All of this would be financed through five years of state funding, through international loans, and through private–public finance initiatives. Indeed, one of the ways in which Bassil hoped to cut down on costs was to entrust private companies with distribution. Henceforth, the latter would be tasked with rehabilitating the supply network, installing smart meters, and collecting bills, in return for which they would be granted 'distribution licences'. Freed of the demanding task of ensuring supply to Lebanon's businesses and households, EDL would henceforth be allowed to concentrate on production. But these were not the only cost-saving measures Bassil hoped to enforce, in order to bring into line the company's $1.5 billion running deficit. In an interview with *Le Commerce du Levant*, he outlined three other initiatives. He aimed, in the first instance, to foster a culture of responsible consumption—both by clamping down on bill evasion, associated in the popular consciousness with some of his political allies and their partisans, and by educating consumers in energy efficiency. He forecast a revision to consumer energy prices, slashing the subsidies that meant that it cost EDL 255LL to produce a kWh that it sold on for 127LL. And he predicted, in due course, the privatisation of EDL after a period of corporate restructuring which would cost the state some $165 million—much of it in subsidies to laid-off employees.[118] All in all, this amounts to a familiar neoliberal dispensation: a growing reliance on the private sector, culminating in privatisation proper and accompanied by cost-cutting job losses; a willingness to borrow from international creditors who expect such structural reforms; and, finally, the tendency for the state to subsidise private initiative, transferring public wealth into corporate—and individual—hands, while at the same time passing on many of the associated costs and responsibilities to the citizen, re-imagined as a free-standing and self-reliant consumer and 'educated' in the need for efficient consumption even as she is told to accept the logic of the market and pay more to finance the costs of modernisation.[119] According to Bassil, only such radical reform would boost Lebanon's flagging energies. Boosting supply from 11,522 GWh in 2010 to 15,000 GWh in

2015, it would make good a shortfall of 23 per cent in energy supplies over five years, while putting an end to the financial troubles at EDL, long an immense drain on state finances.[120]

The trouble is that this magic bullet has not worked. They rarely do. In March 2017, Abi Khalil announced a five-point 'rescue plan' for Lebanon's electricity supply. Its main, and perhaps most controversial, proposal was to extend for another five years Lebanon's reliance on the 'Turkish boats'—floating power stations operated by the Turkish company Karadeniz Powership Orhan, first enlisted in 2013 to supply 370 MW per year. In addition, two more barges would be leased, to provide another 890 MW per year. Estimates put the total cost of this undertaking at $340 million a year—a significant share of the $4 billion or so that Abi Khalil proposed to spend over the same period.[121] It was hoped that this measure, and the installation of new motors in the power stations at Jiyyeh and Zouk, would enable more power over the summer—always the most difficult period for households because of the constant need for air conditioning and, it is said, the influx of returning migrants and tourists who put a strain on an overworked and sclerotic grid. In mid-July, official sources announced with quiet confidence that they could guarantee 'twenty-one hours of electricity per day in Beirut, and between fifteen and eighteen hours in the rest of the country for the whole of the summer'—not the 24-hour power supply Bassil had promised so confidently only a few years ago, but an improvement, they stressed, on the previous year.[122]

Despite Abi Khalil's insistence that leasing two more barges was the most economical option on the table, this was clearly not a plan that would come cheap. To complicate matters further, allegations soon surfaced of malpractice. There were irregularities, it was said, in the tender process, and a consultancy had been recruited to assess the bids without prior approval from Lebanon's auditing authorities. In late July, the Direction des Adjudications, the body that oversees all state tenders, ruled the entire process invalid, sending the file back to the Lebanese cabinet.[123] In early August, it was announced that a solution had been found: EDL and the Ministry of Energy had reached an agreement with the Syrian state to increase power imports from Syria, from around 90 MW to 300 MW.[124] This would provide EDL and its customers with two more hours of electricity per day—making up, conveniently enough, for the drain on its resources by Syrian refugees who 'are consuming', as Abi Khalil had complained in March, '490 mega-watts, thus depriving the Lebanese from a five-hour feed, which is costing the state treasury $330 million'.[125]

That Lebanon's ministers should consider it reasonable to look to the country's war-torn neighbour for supplies while blaming its dis-placed inhabitants for aggravating its own insufficiencies gives a sense both of the sheer scale of its energy problems, and its politicians' crass-ness and lack of imagination. For it would seem that successive energy ministers and their colleagues can think of nothing other than leasing power from foreign suppliers and contractors—including, in a per-verse twist, a state whose infrastructure has been decimated by more than seven years of brutal conflict—and formalising the informal by attempting to regulate generator operators, while all the time continu-ing to uphold privatisation as the only possible solution to Lebanon's chronic shortages of energy. Meanwhile, it is Lebanese consumers who pay—quite literally—the price for both the incapacities of the formal sector and the unruliness of its informal partner. In 2015, the World Bank estimated that average household expenditure on electricity came to $1,300 each year—and this in a country where the gross national income per capita is $9,800.[126] Like Lebanon's fiscal system, with its reliance on highly regressive indirect taxation, these are charges that disproportionately affect those on lower incomes.

It is no small wonder that analysts should despair that ordinary Lebanese citizens 'care only for their daily bread and their electricity', nor that so many should turn to partisan institutions like those created by Hizballah, the Lebanese Forces, the Future Movement or Amal.[127] For if in other parts of the Middle East, informal welfare networks of this kind provide much needed 'autonomy from the state and serve as the foundations for collective action', offering a sustaining alternative to the dominant logic of the market, in Lebanon these networks are profoundly entangled in the workings of neoliberalism.[128] For the sup-port they provide allows politicians of all sides to continue to use the rhetoric of private enterprise and personal responsibility of which they are so fond. Lebanon's politicians are thus capable of envisioning the country's citizens at once as members of partisan—and confessional—communities, whose selves meld into collective units that envelop and protect them, and as atomised individual consumers bidden to the market. And this is not always as paradoxical as it might seem. For at times, the two logics—that of community, on the one hand, and that of the market, on the other—can go hand-in-hand. This is apparent, for instance, in the work of Wa'd, the private development company established at Hizballah's initiative to reconstruct the southern Beirut neighbourhood of Haret Hreik in the wake of the 2006 war. As Mona Fawaz has argued, far from an alternative to the dull visions of Solidere and other real estate developers, Wa'd followed the nostrums of neoliberal planning. For not only did it privilege private initiative; it also sought to bolster private home-ownership, elevating property-holding into one of the defining characteristics of the modern pious subject that Hizballah sought to cultivate. To be sure, the party strove to maintain Haret Hreik's distinctive demography and political leanings. But, as Fawaz has argued, it chose to do so in a manner entirely keeping with the post-civil war consensus, putting corporate initiative in the service of communitarian interest.[129]

Conclusion

On the face of it, Lebanon's contemporary political economy has inherited a great deal from earlier incarnations of the 'merchant republic'—as local and foreign observers are fond of describing this small entrepôt of a place. Thus the country remains reliant on banking and financial services, on tourism, and on the remittances of migrants, much as it did in the supposed 'golden age' in the 1950s and 1960s. Unlike, say, Egypt, Lebanon seems to have been purpose-made for the neoliberal formulas that began to gain prominence among policymakers in the 1970s. But the story is more complicated than that, as family resemblances and apparent continuities disguise significant distinctions, ruptures, and paradoxes.

One is that Lebanon's elites have freely adopted the tools and techniques of neoliberalism—the use of monetary and fiscal mechanisms to engineer growth, say, or the transfer into private hands of state funds and public prerogatives, from the provision of essential utilities to the management of urban space. It will not do, then, to see Lebanon in simple, stark terms as a client of American capitalism, a captive state, silently acquiescent in its sequester's orders. The United States has certainly contributed to the securitisation of the Lebanese state. (Some $1.5 billion of the $3.5 billion Washington has pledged to Lebanon 'in assistance for relief, recovery, rebuilding, and security' in the years since 2006 has come in the form of military hardware, with the latest evidence of this largesse coming in November 2017, when the Lebanese Armed Forces received $120 million in cash and kind 'to boost border security and counter-terrorism work'.)[130] There is much that could be said about these hegemonic practices and the ways in which they perforate and bend out of shape Lebanon's sovereignty.

But, at the same time, international financial organisations like the IMF and the World Bank have been conspicuously absent from Lebanon and have neither compelled nor enticed its elites into reforming state and economy. Thus, while the Lebanese state has been propped up with successive rounds of French and Saudi Arabian finance, it is not a direct beneficiary of the circuits of debt finance centred on Washington. If successive premiers and finance ministers have seemed such willing adherents to the Washington Consensus, it is not—or not just—because they detect opportunities for enrichment, but because they have been conditioned by their education in European and American business schools and economics departments to believe in the need to put the state in the service of private initiative, that great generator of economic growth.[131]

This, though, is not the only paradoxical effect of Lebanon's post-war reconstruction. On the one hand, Lebanon's foreign debt stands at over $30,431 million.[132] On the other hand, much of this 'foreign' debt is, as we have seen, held by Lebanese banks. Far from stretching the country into new patterns of external dependency, then, successive debt issues have created the conditions for an odd kind of involution. This feature of Lebanon's economy has only been accentuated by the departure, after 2011, of the Gulf Arabs who had previously invested their dollars in the country's real estate developments, hotels, beach resorts and malls. We should not discount the importance of foreign assistance. In important respects, however, Lebanon's economy is no longer characterised by extraversion, but by an autarky of sorts, with the country ever more reliant on two main sources of macroeconomic stability: the banks of Beirut, and the migrants who have, so far, not abandoned their homeland.

But perhaps the most significant of the differences between 'actually existing neoliberalism' in Lebanon and its declensions and variants elsewhere centres on the role of the state. As Hannes Baumann and others have pointed out, Lebanon's elites share the propensity, apparent in many other twenty-first-century contexts, to use the state's powers to create conditions propitious to private initiative and investment.[133] But where scholars such as Salwa Ismail have argued that efforts to dismantle the architecture of formal welfare allocation in countries such as Egypt have unintentionally bolstered oppositional forces by allowing them to become informal service providers, filling the spaces the state has deliberately vacated, the story is rather different in Lebanon.[134] For here, of course, the state, the private corporations that control so much of the economy, and the partisan organisations and communitarian support networks that provide welfare to the country's inhabitants are controlled to a large extent by the same actors. It is this unusually strong suture of public and private power and interest that defines Lebanon's political economy, that sustains its political system, and that bolsters the position of its political elites.

6

AL-AKHARIN, OR THE OTHERS

ON LEBANON'S REFUGEES AND MIGRANT WORKERS

There was a time when I used to take the road to Damascus every day. Every morning, I would call a taxi—I couldn't drive then; still can't— and head up from my flat in Beirut to Ba'bda, a little way up *tariq al-sham*—the Damascus road. Traced by a French concessionary company in 1858, this remains one of Lebanon's two main highways, snaking its way through the mountains, up to Dahr al-Baydar, and then back down into the Beqaa and towards the border with Syria. As with so many things in Lebanon these days, this daily route was an odd compound of the tedious and the absurd. The intermittent conversation, the heat and traffic, the crackle of the radio, which might, depending on the day, the tastes of any given driver, and his rapid assessment of my own cultural dispositions, blurt out staccato news announcements, Arabic *tarab*, Eurodance, or maudlin French *chanson*—all of these were familiar enough. But then there were days like that when the driver, his nerves drawn by the rain and creeping traffic, swept round the inside and, keeping close to the verge, knocked over someone who had stopped to change a tyre. As he sped away, he glared at his damaged rear-view mirror, muttering bitterly about the 70 dollars it would cost him to find a replacement.

Familiar, too, were the sights and sensations of the road. I came to recognise, and dread, every pothole and bump, to know the road works and roadblocks, those checkpoints manned by barely post-pubescent soldiers who sleepily cradle their machine guns against their hips, like young mothers hold their firstborns. I came to expect the sight of the young Syrian children—most five or six years old—who snaked their way through the oncoming traffic to hawk mosquito-killing contraptions that resembled electrified badminton rackets, their heads barely reaching above the window, children whose only reminders of childhood were the Disney characters clumsily printed on their blue or yellow t-shirts. I came to know when to avert my eyes, when we passed another road accident, mangled metal and strewn bodies, or when we got stuck behind one of those antique, garish lorries that crawl up the mountain, carrying not piles of furniture or white goods, but sheep or cattle, piled atop one another, bleating with pain as their limbs buckled under them. And I grew to recognise, without thinking about them too much, the hierarchies that governed these stretches: the off-white minibuses, with their load of grim soldiers on leave and Filipino and Nepalese domestic workers in their infantilising pastel uniforms and flip-flops; the weather-beaten Mazda and Mercedes, hiccoughing their way along; the Fiats and Suzukis; and, at the apex, the 4x4s and SUVs, whose drivers sat sullenly shut up behind their Ray Bans and tinted windows, tyrants of the road who ruthlessly cut in, weave through and shunt others to the side, seemingly insulated behind the darkness of their sunglasses and blacked-out windows, finding false comfort in their technological superiority.

It is not easy to go anywhere in Lebanon without seeing a car—or, for that matter, without driving, or being driven. Cars, cars everywhere—cars driving on the outside of a lane, transforming what is hardly a dual-carriageway into a racecourse, keeping on the shoulder, urgently beeping till they accelerate away with a sudden burst of energy, leaving behind a streak of fumes; cars overtaking others on the sudden, sharp bends in mountain roads, as in a deathly fit of pique; cars coming at you against the traffic; cars double-parked, triple-parked on street-corners and junctions. The Lebanese do not like to walk. It is true that some trudge along mountain roads on still hot summer evenings, utterly drenched in sweat, in a desultory concession to healthy living, or stroll along the seaside at sunset. But most regard it as the sign of a lack, an activity best left to those who cannot drive or afford a car, for serving soldiers, migrant labourers and domestic workers, and the odd quixotic Westerner. Even children whose parents are at work or otherwise engaged will be ferried to and from school in the back of a *service*—a common taxi. Why walk to get somewhere, when one could drive? Out and about, in the streets and on the roads, the Lebanese are not so much bipeds as hybrid beings, centaur-like cyborgs so closely imbricated with their vehicles that they are meaningless, and helpless, without them.

Accordingly, driving has come to stand as a symbol, and a symptom, of the predicament of contemporary Lebanon. Trite as it sounds, the sight of a nation at the wheel serves as a particularly stark, and immediate, reminder of the sharp inequalities of wealth and status that run through Lebanese society, in a country where around 8,000 individuals, or 0.3 per cent of the population, controls 48 per cent of the wealth. For on the road, it is hard to ignore the disparity between the many who soak up the thick exhaust fumes—their broken windows permanently down, their ventilation units wheezing relics—and the few who sit high up in their pristine vehicles, insulated in their crisply air-conditioned cocoons. It is no surprise that Crédit Suisse ranked Lebanon sixth in its global wealth inequality index, behind only Ukraine, Denmark, Kazakhstan, the Seychelles, and Russia.[1] If the car still stands for some for the treasured bourgeois values of 'freedom, self-possession, self-discipline, and ease', others have long since had to let go of these twentieth-century dreams of individualism.[2] For many, the car stands not for moneyed self-affirmation, the confirmation of a comfortable present and the promise of a better future, but merely for a lack of better alternatives, a beat-up reminder of the past and its travails and disappointments. No longer does the car carry the promise of 'dignity as free subjects', capable of 'governing [themselves]', as Charles Taylor put it.[3] Far from an engine of democracy, the car is in contemporary Lebanon a signifier of inequity.

And at the bottom of this hierarchy are those who go by foot. There are the migrant workers: the Filipino, Sri Lankan, Nepalese or Eritrean women who take their *madames'* little pooches down for a walk twice a day and sit by the pool as middle-class children splash about; the Sudanese, Egyptian or Nigerian men and women who fill up the cars of the Lebanese at petrol stations, and wipe away their piss and their shit in the toilets of restaurant and malls; the Indian and Pakistani bin-men who jump down from their rubbish trucks to pick up the trash left out on the streets, or who stalk the roadsides, diligently sweeping up the empty soft drink cans, torn food wrappers and plastic bottles thoughtlessly tossed from car windows; the Ukrainian or Romanian women who walk about towns like Maameltein, allowed out from their work (as 'hosts' in the country's 'super nightclubs'—or brothels) to run their errands in shops adorned in Baltika beer hoardings and adverts for phone cards and wire transfers.

Even lower still, however, are Lebanon's refugees: the 170,000 or so Palestinians whose grandparents and great-grandparents arrived here in 1948, fleeing war and expulsion, and the million men, women, and children from Syria who now make up more than a quarter of Lebanon's population. For if Nepalese and Filipino domestic workers and Indian bin-men are excluded from the networks of partisan and confessional support and kin solidarity that provide some sustenance to Lebanese citizens in these persistently hard times, then Palestinians and Syrians find themselves locked out of all but the most precarious and low-waged of informal work. More than just non-citizens, they are perceived by many Lebanese as threats to their own citizenly status, to their fragile, stubbornly protected entitlements. Lebanon's Syrian and Palestinian inhabitants are subjects who live in a state of constant impermanence, who are refused the status of permanent residents because their instal-lation and naturalisation would throw off-kilter Lebanon's unsteady confessional equilibrium. And yet they are not, of course, simply refu-gees, inactive recipients of aid awaiting their eventual return to their homelands. They work, just as they have always done, performing the most arduous tasks, those that the Lebanese themselves have long since abandoned and do not want to go back to. They are the fruit and vege-table pickers who work in the orange and banana orchards of the south or in the vineyards and potato fields of the Beqaa; the construction workers that you see waiting by the roadside for a foreman to pick out his crew, or busily moving about building sites, short wiry men from the Syrian north and east, who sleep in half-finished buildings, their lives hidden away behind improvised curtains hanging from the breezeblocks; they are the scrap metal collectors and rag-and-bone men who wade waist-deep in Beirut's waste bins, sorting through the detritus to find something of value; the building superintendants who unblock drains and keep an eye out for intruders; the 10- and 12-year-old boys who put shoppers' goods away in plastic bags for a coin or two of change, if they are lucky; and the shoe-shines and beggars who sit on flattened cardboard boxes in the street. For begging, too, is work. It requires extraordinary resilience to walk the streets all day long, to sleep rough, to be hungry and dirty and exhausted and scared and indebted and lonely, to withstand the cold and the heat and hold out against the abuse and contempt of passers-by who pretend not to hear you or push past, swatting you away as they would a fly. But it also calls upon other resources: on courage and resourcefulness and creativity, to be able to speak to others, to confront them with one's own abject condition, to face their disgust without forgetting your own humanity and sense of self, and to shape one's experiences into narratives that capture their compassion, when one has no other means of getting by than pleading for others' charity. It is work to be at the end of your tether and still to go on and get by—just about.

In the world of the camp: Lebanon's Palestinians

On Boxing Day 2017, Saad Hariri, still reeling from his mysterious resignation in Riyadh, took to the nostrum at the Grand Sérail, the prime minister's offices in central Beirut. Before an audience of dignitaries—American, European, and Arab diplomats, fellow members of parliament, and representatives of the PLO—he announced the long-awaited results of the census of Lebanon's Palestinian refugees. Born of the joint efforts of Lebanon's Central Administration of Statistics and the Palestinian Authority—just one of the signs of a rapprochement between the Lebanese and Palestinian states that would have been unthinkable even a few years ago—this made for surprising reading. In late 2017, there were 174,422 registered Palestinian refugees living in Lebanon. While 45 per cent live in Lebanon's twelve officially recognised refugee camps—Baddawi and Nahr al-Bared in the north; Burj al-Barajneh, Shatila, Mar Elias, and Dbayeh in greater Beirut; Ayn al-Hilweh and Mieh Mieh, near Saida; Burj al-Shemali, El-Buss, and Rashidiyeh, near Sur; and Wavel, in the Beqaa—the majority of the refugees, 55 per cent, live in 156 informal encampments and shantytowns. (The census did not enumerate those Palestinians who have not acquired—and indeed cannot acquire—Lebanese citizenship, but who live not in these separate settlements, but in Lebanon's towns and cities.)[4] This figure was a far cry from the 449,957 refugees recorded in the registers of the United Nations Relief and Works Agency, or UNRWA, the organisation established in 1949 to provide assistance to the Palestinians displaced in 1948 by the establishment of the state of Israel and the outbreak of the first Arab–Israeli war.[5]

Though sociologists and political economists had insisted for years that the number of Palestinian refugees in Lebanon had fallen sharply with out-migration, Hariri's announcement still came as a surprise to many observers.[6] If some were relieved at this revelation, happy to learn that years of flight from discrimination and poverty had reduced a presence they saw as a cankerous imposition on Lebanese society, others remained wary of these figures, which they feared were no more than a prelude to the permanent installation of the Palestinians in Lebanon. For that is what is at stake here—not just Lebanon's oft-repeated commitment to Palestinians' right to return to their historic homeland, but the deep-seated fear that these refugees will set the confessional order off balance, undermining Lebanon's sovereignty or strengthening one community at the expense of others. Well aware that some might construe his comments as paving the way towards *tawtin*— the 'naturalisation' or 'resettlement' of the Palestinians—Hariri was at pains to stress that this was no statistical Trojan horse, repeating several times that 'this census does not open the door for the Palestinians' implantation'.[7] For Hariri knew all too well that the preamble to the revised Lebanese constitution of 1990 explicitly states that 'there shall be ... no settlement of non-Lebanese in Lebanon'—a phrase that all understand to refer to Lebanon's Palestinians.[8] And he knew, too, that both Christian and Shia political parties were at once wary of any measure they feared might increase the relative demographic weight of the Sunni community, and eager to seize upon any opportunity to discredit him. Since the end of the civil war—a conflict that many in Lebanon have come to regard as *harb al-akharin* or *la guerre des autres*, a 'war of others', provoked in large part by the international community's attempts to force Lebanon into accepting the burden of the Palestinian presence—all the country's political parties have stated and restated their opposition to *tawtin*. Hariri, his position still insecure, was not about to break with precedent.

These fears of implantation have a deep history, which can be traced back to the 1950s and 1960s, when the government of President Fouad Chehab sent the agents of the Second Bureau—Lebanon's military intelligence—into the refugee camps to surveil their inhabitants, whose commitments to pan-Arab causes it deemed suspect. Relations between the Lebanese state and Palestinian political organisations only took a turn for the worse after the Six-Day War of 1967, when the PLO and its dominant factions, Fatah, the Popular Front for the Liberation of Palestine, or PFLP, and the Democratic Front for the Liberation of Palestine, or DFLP, began to conceive of Lebanon's refugee camps as rear-bases for their armed struggle against the Israeli state. In 1969, the Lebanese Armed Forces and the PLO signed the Cairo Agreement, which gave 'Palestinians resident in Lebanon' the right to 'participate in the Palestinian revolution through the Armed Struggle'. Henceforth, the PLO's commandos would be allowed to move through Lebanon and its commanders to attend meetings in the Ministry of Defence. In 1970, the PLO moved its operations to Beirut, after the clashes of Black September against the Jordanian army forced it to leave Amman.

Over the course of the early 1970s, the PLO's armed presence in Lebanon would become a sore point of controversy in Lebanese politics. Though the Cairo Agreement had stated explicitly that Palestinian actions should not breach 'the principles of the sovereignty and security of Lebanon', many—particularly on the 'Christian right'—viewed this as an empty pledge. For politicians like Camille Chamoun, the head of the National Liberal Party, or Pierre Gemayel, the leader of the Kata'ib, the PLO was a 'state within the state', a foreign entity with dangerous pretensions to sovereignty, whose presence in Lebanon eroded the state's authority and posed a threat to the country's stability.[9] Clamouring ever more loudly for a way to keep in check the PLO's growing power and audacity, they were dismissed by their opponents on the Lebanese left—the Progressive Socialist Party, the Communist Party, the Baathists and others—as 'isolationists', whose refusal to put Lebanon in the service of the Palestinian *qadiyya*, or cause, showed that they were no more than stingy, small-minded petty bourgeois reactionaries, whose errors would soon be lain bare by the forces of history. In the initial stages of the Lebanese civil war, from 1975 until the early 1980s, Palestinian factions fought alongside the men of the Lebanese National Movement against the militias of the rightist Lebanese Front. While the former regarded themselves as a revolutionary vanguard, fighting for a fairer dispensation at home and the end of neo-colonialism across the region, the latter saw themselves as a resistance force, defending the rights of Lebanon's Christians and holding out against their nation's absorption into an overwhelming territorial entity, like Jonah being swallowed by the whale.

By the mid-1980s, however, the tide had begun to turn against the PLO—and Lebanon's Palestinians. First the Israeli occupation of 1982 forced the organisation to go into exile once again, as they hastily abandoned Beirut for Tunis, and Palestinian society was shattered by the Sabra and Shatila massacres, in September of that year, when Lebanese militias allied to Israel killed as many as 3,500 Palestinian refugees living in these two camps on the outskirts of Beirut. Then Baathist Syria—an active participant in the Lebanese civil war since 1976, when it first sent reinforcements to prop up the Lebanese Front—turned its wrath against what remained of the PLO in Lebanon. The 'war of the camps' lasted from 1985 to 1988, a brutal offensive led on the ground by Damascus' Lebanese and Palestinian proxies—Amal, Al-Sa'iqa and the Popular Front for the Liberation of Palestine–General Command. For three years, camps like Ayn al-Hilweh, near Saida, and Rashidiyeh, outside of Sur, were besieged and subjected to bombardment from the ground and the air. They still bear the scars of these assaults. In 1987, the Lebanese government—or what stood then for a government—repudiated the Cairo Agreement.

By 1990, when most of Lebanon's warring factions and parties finally sat down for peace talks in the Saudi city of Taif, many had found new enemies to resent and new causes to prosecute. Still, all could agree, as they went about drawing up a new political dispensation, that the Palestinians—diminished and decimated—could serve as a useful scapegoat. Over the following decade and a half, Lebanon's Palestinians would face growing securitisation and discrimination. Lebanese and Syrian security services transformed many of the country's refugee camps into what the anthropologist Julie Peteet has called 'spaces of containment', encircling their perimeters with a constant military presence. At Ayn al-Hilweh, in the south, soldiers stationed at a checkpoint at the camp's entrance would stop all cars entering or leaving its precinct between 9:00 p.m. and 6:00 a.m., taking down registration numbers and the names and identity card numbers of all drivers and passengers. Often, the *shabab*, or young men, of the camp would be subjected to rough treatment, the soldiers screaming at them to 'get down' and 'give me your identity card!' As one of Peteet's interlocutors put it, the point of such measures was 'humiliation'; after all, the Palestinians had long since ceased to be a 'political threat'.[10] At Rashidiyeh, one of the few camps in the country where Fatah still maintained a significant popular following, the army would go so far as to stop anyone attempting to bring building materials to repair the homes damaged in the violence of the 1980s, in an effort 'to punish' its inhabitants for their 'pro-Arafat orientation'.[11] In the north of the country, where Syria's security services exercised a more direct and forceful influence, they lent their support to the PFLP–GC, Al-Sa'iqa and Hamas, which came to exert their dominance over the camps of Nahr al-Bared and Baddawi. Over time, these parties would become known as *al-tahaluf* or 'the alliance', a sign that they were thought of as a loose coalition beholden to Damascus.[12]

If these measures appear contradictory—on the one hand subjecting some camps to ever greater constraints and surveillance, while on the other hand passing internal matters into the hands of Syria's Palestinian proxies—they obeyed the same logic: to create a perception of the camps as wormholes in Lebanese sovereignty, spaces of exception or, as they are often called, *juzur amniyya*, 'security islands', guarded from without because they are lawless from within. The Lebanese army may have changed tack in recent years, entrusting greater authority to the local representatives of the PLO and Fatah, whom they have tasked with ensuring security in the camps. But this policy is plagued by inconsistencies and practical constraints. At one level, the tendency of the Lebanese Internal Security Forces and military intelligence to treat members of the camps' security committees as mere 'informants' and subalterns carrying out their orders has the unintended effect of delegitimising and disempowering these men. For who among the camp's inhabitants would be willing to trust these agents of the Lebanese state in their midst?[13] But more than this, the tendency to trust the PLO and Fatah ignores entirely the changing political landscape of the camps and relies on a twin set of flawed assumptions—that Fatah continues to ensure a wide measure of popular legitimacy and that, as a consequence, it is in some way an impartial arbiter capable of presiding over Palestinian society in the camps and adjudicating in its internal disputes.

But, as scholars such as Sari Hanafi and Bernard Rougier have argued, Fatah's legitimacy—much like that of the popular committees—has been eroded in recent years, as other modes of informal governance more reliant on the ethical guidance and counsel of Islamic associations and factions have gained in popularity. Increasingly disillusioned with the insecurity of their surrounds, the inhabitants of camps such as Nahr al-Bared, Baddawi, and Ayn al-Hilweh have gravitated over the course of the early twenty-first century towards those groups that appear capable of providing both physical safety and moral stability. Thus many in Nahr al-Bared, left in ruins by the brutal fighting between the Lebanese army and the Islamist group Fatah al-Islam in 2007, initially welcomed the latter's presence in the camp. As one shaykh recalled after the camp's destruction: 'I am one of those who approved of some of the accomplishments of Fatah al-Islam, when you consider dealing with the drunkards and the fact that our girls could come and go without anyone misbehaving with them'.[14] He was not alone in feeling that Fatah, preoccupied with the tasks of security, had forsaken the more important work of moral oversight. And, as Islamic groups of varying ideological inclinations have increasingly captured the ground once held by Fatah and other 'secular' factions, the organisation has increasingly been drawn into confrontation with these new rivals. At times, this can lead the entire 'security system' to break down, as it has done on several occasions in recent years in Ayn al-Hilweh, which has witnessed repeated bouts of armed fighting. (In one of the most recent bouts of fighting, in August 2017, Fatah found itself taking on a coalition of Islamist groups led by Jabhat al-Nusra, or Fatah al-Sham, as it is now known.)[15] As Hanafi has argued, the securitisation of the camps—the reduction of rule to the mere maintenance of order—seems to show a strikingly impoverished and dysfunctional sense of what government might entail, endlessly reproducing the problems it is supposed to resolve.[16]

This, though, is perhaps the point. For only the utter collapse of the 'security system'—such as some would argue happened in Nahr al-Bared in 2007—can allow for a new kind of control over Palestinian lives to be established, one in which their camps would be 'open to the Lebanese army and the police and would be under the sovereignty of the Lebanese state'.[17] Moreover, the enduring power of these discourses of lawlessness is not without its uses. In recent years, partisan mouthpieces like the FPM's website, *tayyar.org*, have increasingly depicted Ayn al-Hilweh as a Hobbesian site of war of all against all, a place of unrest and misrule, or as an open-air holding pen for all the criminals of the land. This is a place, journalists and commentators will claim, whose alleyways teem with fugitives eluding the grasp of the Lebanese state and, increasingly, with malevolent jihadi fighters, stolen across the Syrian border to lay down their bombs in Christian churches, Shia mosques, and army checkpoints. But these nightmarish visions only help to bolster the growing militarism of certain sections of Lebanese society, with their enthusiastic endorsement of the army's growing reach and power. And at the same time, they lend powerful justification to the arguments of those who maintain that the 'social integration' of the Palestinians into Lebanese society will never be possible, that they will always remain a boil on the body politic, but that it is possible to send some to the West Bank and Gaza and transfer others to sympathetic Western states like Canada, while leaving a smaller and more manageable population of 50–60,000.[18]

At the same time as they became caught up in revised security arrangements, Lebanon's Palestinian refugees were increasingly ensnared in a web of legal discrimination. The Palestinians, of course, have long been considered an exceptional set of subjects under Lebanese law, a special category unto themselves. In 1962, the Lebanese state defined Palestinian refugees as 'foreign nationals who do not possess identity papers from their country of origin'.[19] At once neither entirely foreigners, nationals of another state who might enjoy all the benefits of reciprocity, nor refugees in the full sense of the term, possessing the particular entitlements that came with this status, the Palestinians were an anomalous and undefined presence. The consequences of this paradoxical position would become apparent over the next few years. In 1963, Palestinians were deemed ineligible for social security: as stateless people, they could not benefit from the principle of reciprocity.[20] But by legislation introduced in 1964, they were assimilated to other foreigners and required to obtain an employment permit before seeking work in Lebanon.[21] In other words, their status came with all the duties of foreignness, but none of the rights of statehood. In treating Palestinians in this fashion, Lebanon was itself exceptional. It ratified the Casablanca Protocols of 1965, which gave Palestinians living in Arab states the 'right to employment on a par with their citizens' and the right to receive 'upon request, valid travel documents', only with reservations, insisting that Palestinians could only work in Lebanon 'in accordance with the prevailing social and economic conditions' in the country and that it could make the entry of Palestinians into Lebanon 'whenever their interests demand it' 'conditional upon their obtaining an entry visa issued by the concerned Lebanese authorities'.[22]

This legal architecture of exemptions and conditions—what we might call the law of ifs and buts—afforded the Lebanese state a great deal of latitude, on which successive governments would capitalise during the 1980s and 1990s. In 1982, at the height of the civil war, Ministerial Decree 1/289 prohibited Palestinians from working in 'over 70 commercial and administrative professions'. (They had already been excluded from syndicated sectors, like medicine, law and engineering, which were regulated by bilateral and reciprocal agreements; now, they were banned from being tailors, mechanics, company directors and secretaries.)[23] These prohibitions were reinforced in 1983, and again in 1993 and 1995, as the post-war political elite turned the nativist language of 'Lebanon for the Lebanese' to its own ends.[24] Indeed, the governments of the 1990s and early 2000s sought increasingly to restrict not just the participation of Palestinians in the labour market, but also their capacity to travel freely in and out of the country—another entitlement that might have come with the full recognition of their status as refugees—and to acquire real estate. In 1995, the minister of the interior, Michel el-Murr, made it compulsory for Palestinians wishing to enter Lebanon to obtain a visa from Lebanese diplomatic missions abroad, and for those wishing to leave the country to obtain an exit permit. He justified his actions by explaining that he did not want Lebanon to become a 'dump' for 'human waste' expelled from other Arab states.[25] In 2001, a longstanding convention allowing Palestinians, as fellow Arab citizens, to acquire real estate in Lebanon was overturned, when the country's property law was reformed to ensure that 'all forms of real estate are forbidden to any person who [does not hold] a nationality of a recognised state'. In other words, Palestinians were disbarred from owning property, for fear that their acquisition of a plot of land or an apartment might facilitate their 'permanent settlement'.[26] It is no wonder, then, that Palestinians in the 1990s often spoke of the Lebanese state's hopes of 'eliminating the Palestinians from Lebanon', not through the violent tactics of the war years, but through 'strangling' them with law, leaving them no recourse but emigration.[27]

This situation only really began to change in the mid-2000s, when Prime Minister Fouad Siniora established the Lebanese–Palestinian Dialogue Committee to re-establish channels of communication with the PLO. As one Lebanese official with knowledge of the 'refugee file' in these years put it, Siniora approached this question with 'an open mind'. While rejecting *tawtin*, he came to see that 'the Palestinian is not an enemy' and began negotiations both with the Palestinian organisations within Lebanon, and with the PLO in Ramallah. These ultimately paved the way not just for the creation of the LPDC, but also for the reopening of the PLO's legation in Beirut in 2006, twenty-four years after the organisation's offices in the city had closed after its departure for Tunis.[28] Indeed, these years witnessed a rapprochement of sorts between the Future Movement and the PLO, which came to see each other as fellow travellers of sorts. Like the Future Movement, the PLO—or at least Fatah—was a 'moderate', secular movement, not unsympathetic to the United States, and caught in a bitter rivalry with a pious party wedded to the ideal of violent struggle. While the Future Movement had to live with Hizballah, the PLO had to deal with Hamas. If these two parties could be staunch allies within the 'axis of resistance', then why could the Future Movement and the PLO not work together? As Are Knudsen has argued, these feelings were reciprocated by the PLO. In 2007, Abbas Zaki, the head of the organisation's legation in Lebanon, issued the 'Beirut Declaration' in which he apologised to 'our dear Lebanon' for all the harm that the Palestinians had done to the country.[29]

This intensification of relations soon began to result in modest reform. As the official that I spoke to in 2012 put it, Siniora developed a commitment of sorts to Palestinian 'dignity under [Lebanese] sovereignty'.[30] In 2005, Ministerial Memorandum 1/67 overturned the draconian restrictions introduced in the 1980s. Henceforth, 'Palestinian refugees who are born in Lebanon and who are registered with the Lebanese Ministry of Labour' would be able to work legally as cooks, barbers, or electricians.[31] However, there are still at least nineteen groups of syndicated professions that Palestinian refugees in Lebanon are barred from practising today. These do not just include occupations such as medicine, dentistry, law, engineering and accountancy; Palestinians are also prohibited from working as nurses and physiotherapists, money changers and tourist guides.[32] Further reform followed in 2010, when the Lebanese parliament ratified an amendment to article 9 of the Social Security Law, making registered Palestinian refugees eligible for pensions and redundancy benefits. And yet, despite all the effort that civil society activists, advocacy groups, and NGOs put into this initiative, and all the fanfare and controversy that surrounded its passing, this remains in practice a modest legislative change, and Palestinians are still not eligible for statutory protection in case of sickness or pregnancy.[33] Many, even among those who regarded themselves as sympathetically disposed towards Palestinian refugees, took no issue with these limitations. As my interviewee put it in 2012, why should the Palestinians have the *daman*, or national insurance, when two-thirds of Lebanese workers did not benefit from this measure?[34]

What's more, it is telling that a mere 1.6% of Palestinian refugees across Lebanon benefit from pensions.[35] For despite limited reform to the legal status quo in the years since 2005, these men and women continue to confront de facto discrimination in the labour market—just one of the factors that contribute to the precarity and deprivation of their lives. In December 2017, Saad Hariri announced that the unemployment rate among registered Palestinian refugees stood at 18.4%, almost three times as high as that among Lebanese of working age.[36] Youth unemployment was higher still: almost 24% for 20- to 29-year-olds and almost 26% for 15- to 20-year-olds. In all, only 51,939 Palestinian refugees were in work, less than a third of those who lived in the camps and settlements.[37] But alongside unemployment, we must also reckon with under-employment, and the deep effects on lives and livelihoods of casual, insecure labour. If those in the camp of Mar Elias, in the sprawling southern suburbs of Beirut, have been able to capitalise on its position at the intersection of several densely populated neighbourhoods to open grocery stores, restaurants and workshops catering to a Palestinian and Lebanese clientele, others do not benefit from the same advantages of location.[38] In Sur, for instance, 31.1% of Palestinian workers subsisted on day work. In Saida, this percentage rose to 35.5%. In Tripoli, it stood at 73.9%.[39] Paradoxically, however, Sur has by far the highest proportion of Palestinians in low-paid seasonal and occasional work—on construction sites, say, or as agricultural labourers in the orange, lime, and banana orchards of the region. In Rashidiyeh, some 46% of those in work are occupied in these sectors. In the northern camp of Baddawi, however, only 11% work in what UNRWA has called 'elementary occupations'; 46% are 'craft and related trade workers' and 'machine operators'—in other words, hairdressers, mechanics, *kandarji*-s or shoe-menders, and the like.[40] Though this skilled work might sound preferable to the wearying labours of the fields, these remain modest, low-paid occupations in which casual, informal contracts appear to still be the norm. Under such conditions, it is hardly surprising that only 1.5% of all Palestinians in work had a fully notarised employment contract, and that 82.6% made do with mere oral agreements with their employers and overseers. Nor is it surprising that more than half of Palestinian workers earn less than 500,000LL, or $333, per month—almost $150 less than the legal minimum wage for Lebanese workers.[41]

These working conditions have ripple effects through the lives of Lebanon's Palestinian refugees, affecting their diet and physical and mental health. In 2010, some 58% of those questioned reported that they were vulnerable to food insecurity—often finding fresh fruit, meat, and dairy products out of their financial reach. Fifteen per cent reported severe food insecurity—struggling, in other words, to provide adequate food for the household on a regular basis. A third of Palestinians reported chronic illness, with many suffering from hypertension in particular, and just over a fifth reported experiencing depression or anxiety—an entirely unsurprising statistic given the financial and physical pressures that so many face. But it is not just work and the absence of work that leaves its bruising imprint on the lives of Palestinian refugees.

Equally wearying are the material circumstances in which they live—the state of their streets and homes, of their camps and settlements. One need only take the briefest of looks at UNRWA's descriptions of Lebanon's twelve officially recognised refugee camps to gain a sense of the tiring effect of these spatial surrounds. At Wavel Camp, in the Beqaa, 'housing is unhealthy as many refugees still live in original Mandate-era army barracks, which lack daylight and ventilation'.[42] At Ayn al-Hilweh, on the outskirts of Saida, 'shelters in the camp are small and very close to each other. Some still have sheet metal roofing'.[43] At Shatila, in Beirut's growing spread, 'environmental health conditions … are extremely bad. Shelters are damp and overcrowded, and many have open drains. The sewerage system needs considerable expansion'.[44] Even Mar Elias, whose inhabitants often stress the 'relative quality' of their water and electricity supplies, insisting that it is 'one of the best camps in Beirut', is marred by 'bad' housing conditions and failing infrastructure. It is, as Mohamed Doraï has written, a 'pocket of poverty' enfolded within the fabric of the city. Indeed, it is this relative deprivation that lends its inhabitants an advantage in certain matters, for they can capitalise on the lack of regulation that prevails in the camp to make marginal gains. While shopkeepers and restaurant owners can keep operation costs low, bringing in customers drawn in by the cheaper fare, others can turn themselves into irregular landlords, leasing out informal housing to Syrian, Egyptian, Sudanese or South Asian migrant labourers who cannot afford rents in other parts of the city. This is the case, for instance, of one man who decided in the mid-1990s to 'build a supplementary floor on the top of my house', which he divided into 'a two-room apartment' and 'one single room separated by a small terrace'. 'The room is rented by two Sri-Lankan domestic workers and the apartment by a Sudanese family with two children', providing him with a supplementary income of $200 per month.[45]

For others, however, poor housing and failing infrastructure are not so much opportunities for small gains as sapping, tiresome facts of the everyday. There are exceptions, of course, and, despite its ongoing financial problems, UNRWA has made great efforts to improve the infrastructure and housing stock of certain camps, such as Burj al-

Shemali, with its electricity network, potable water, and sewerage and storm water drainage systems.[46] But it remains the case that many live in desperately inadequate conditions. In 2010, 40 per cent of respondents to a survey of Palestinian households reported 'water leaking through their roofs or walls', and another 8 per cent told of living in shelters made of 'corrugated iron, wood and asbestos'. A similar proportion reported living in overcrowded conditions, with more than three people living in one room.[47] Children and adults, the young and the elderly, all piled together with nowhere to go, no place to escape from the noise and the smells—of food, of sweat and sour breath, of farts and shit—and the constant presence of each other. Such things take a toll, and conditions are worse still in Lebanon's informal settlements, like Jal al-Bahr on the outskirts of Sur.

The everyday strains on refugees are only exacerbated by the dependence of so many on UNRWA. In a country in which healthcare is largely a private commodity, a third of Palestinian refugees requiring treatment fall back on the agency's clinics and dispensaries, while another 10 per cent rely on the Palestinian Red Crescent.[48] Even as the organisation provides essential relief, there is no escaping the fact that some are saddened by what they see as debasements that come with dependency. Already, in the 1990s, Julie Peteet chronicled the growing sense of frustration at the failings of the popular committees that govern camps like Shatila, and of the embarrassment engendered by undignified reliance on international organisations. In one story, Peteet's interlocutor Umm Khalid recounted her efforts to secure the committee's assistance for a disabled man, wounded in the fighting of the 1980s, and who now fed his family on the rations that UNRWA provided. 'I marched in' to the popular committee's offices, Umm Khalid told Peteet, 'and I said to all of those men sitting there, "You are sitting here, your presence or nonpresence is the same thing!" ... We just ignore the poor and don't care for them? When he is strong he is ours and when is weakened we throw him away?' In this tale, a woman's frustration with the ineptitude and self-interest of the camp's self-appointed male leaders intermingles with political disillusion and cynicism, the revolutionary ideals of the 1980s faded into washed-out, hollow phrases, but also with shame that the Palestinians are no longer a people seeking self-determination, but merely refugees reduced to reliance on external bodies. A similar sense of hopelessness pervaded the words of another of Peteet's acquaintances, Suha, who had been dropped by her graduate supervisor. When Peteet asked her what she was going to do, she responded: 'What can I do? We are Palestinians and refugees. We have no rights. There is no one to appeal to.'[49] As Hannah Arendt once argued, rights belong to those who belong to nations. 'The calamity of the rightless' is that they 'no longer belong to any community whatsoever'.[50] As Lebanon's Palestinians have lost a sense of themselves as a people and their identity has become little more than a legal category, so too have they given up on the rights they once thought were theirs for the taking.

And yet, as the anthropologist Sylvain Perdigon has argued, Palestinians can find ways of eluding and rejecting these ways of apprehending their own lives and place in the world. In his work on the camps of Sur, places like Rashidiyeh, al-Buss, and Mieh Mieh that are among the most socio-economically deprived of Palestinian settlements in Lebanon, Perdigon notes a persistent 'reticence' to speak of oneself as poor. It is not that his interlocutors do not know what poverty might entail. On the contrary, it is an ever-present part of the assemblages of their everyday, of that world of 'ordinary calamity' in which they live, plagued by the sensory awareness of 'a leaking roof, a lingering untreated pain' or a sputtering electricity generator, the troubling knowledge that 'a damp sleeping room … will give [the] children asthma', and the nagging fear that one does not have 'food for tonight's family dinner', a fear felt as a physical ache, a disquieting tightness in the throat. These are men and women who live, it is clear, 'at the mercy of what each day brings'. Still, though, they resist the language of poverty. Even as they grasp and acknowledge that their condition is born of 'something political'—*shi siyasi*—that it is a structural effect, in other words, of particular governing practices, they continue to insist that their predicament is distinct to that of the global poor of South Asia or Latin America—*nahna ghayr*, 'we are different'. For Perdigon, this signals the adherence of these men and women to alternate modes of envisioning sovereignty, as a political condition founded in *sabr*, or patience, in endurance, in the capacity to put up and carry on, moving wearily but steadily from the present into the future.[51] But there is something else here, that Perdigon only hints at: a refusal to acquiesce in the sovereign schemes of the Lebanese state, with its pursuit of pre-carisation: its attempts to foster 'uncertainty', 'insecurity', and 'vulnerability' as instruments of 'social regulation and control'.[52] In short, this reluctance to lapse into the language of poverty, to recognise oneself as poor, is a way of preserving a measure of dignity, of worth, of mastery over oneself and one's place in the world. As Perdigon has argued, the 'moral codes' and languages of 'self-making' that these men and women rely upon provide the makings of a particularly resilient kind of subjectivity. Far from stranded figures, stripped of all but the most 'basic' of 'biological dependencies' and standing naked before the state like a tree caught in the gales, Palestinian subjects find meaning and succour in the ethical and affective language of kin and community.[53]

The labours of abjectness: Syrian refugees in contemporary Lebanon

The Palestinians of Lebanon, however, are not the only figures to be framed by Lebanese officials and foreign donors and scholars as exemplars of 'bare life' or mere recipients of aid. Strikingly similar discourses have swirled about the Syrian refugees who have arrived in Lebanon since 2011. Like the Palestinians before them, they are imagined as abject beings, shorn of all the trappings of political subjectivity. And like the Palestinians, they are feared as security threats, dangerous pathogens infecting the Lebanese political system. If the latter view appears a disturbing product of the growing nativism and militarism of Lebanese society, then the former can seem a simple reflection of statistical fact.

As of January 2018, the UNHCR estimates that there are 995,512 Syrian refugees in Lebanon—though, as it freely acknowledges, the fact that it has not registered new arrivals since May 2015, at the request of the Lebanese government, may well mean that this is an undercount. Most remain clustered in the eastern valley of the Beqaa, which provides a refuge of sorts to 357,395 Syrians. There, as many as half still live, in some cases almost seven years after their arrival, in makeshift tent cities exposed to the elements—blustery winds and snow in winter, burning heat in summer. Another 266,058 have headed for the ever-proliferating sprawl of Beirut and its conurbation, and 253,173 for the city of Tripoli and the northern reaches of Akkar. Like the Beqaa, Akkar borders Syria, and some of its inhabitants have long maintained ties of kin, intermarriage, migration and trade across the border. It is no coincidence that the north-eastern district of Wadi Khaled, whose inhabitants share close relations with the region of Homs, should have been one of the first places in Lebanon to welcome refugees from Syria, as hundreds, then thousands attempted to escape the regime's brutal siege of Homs, which began in May 2011. Another 118,886 Syrians now live in the south of the country. Like the more than 30,000 Palestinian refugees from Syria—many of them fugitives from the camp of Yarmouk, in Damascus, the scene of bitter fighting in 2012 and again in 2015—who have headed for Lebanon, some of these men and women have streamed into camps like Rashidiyeh and Mieh Mieh, putting further stress on their already overstretched infrastructure.[54]

What's more, all the socio-economic indices that we have indicate that Syrian refugees in Lebanon confront severe deprivation and debt. The average monthly working income for Syrian men was $206, and $159 for women. These wages are lower still than those that Palestinians receive, and though levels of female income are roughly comparable—as we shall see—to those of migrant domestic workers, the latter often, though not always, do receive the meagre compensation of food and board. Moreover, only 53% of Syrian households had a member in employment in 2017. (A third of men found work in construction, and just over a fifth in agriculture, while 55% of women worked as farm labourers and fruit-pickers, and 24% worked in services.) More than a third of those surveyed reported that not a single member of the household had worked in the last month. It is unsurprising, under these circumstances, that 77% of households reported shortages of food or money to buy daily necessities, and 87% had borrowed money to make ends meet and put food on the table. Most families, then, relied on a variety of coping strategies, from informal loans contracted on onerous terms with Lebanese or Syrian money-lenders, to selling off household items or land and property in Syria—often, one would imagine, at severely discounted rates—or withdrawing their children from school to provide a supplementary income. While two-thirds of households had resorted to such temporary tactics to alleviate their financial strains, 96% admitted that they had been forced to reduce their food consumption in order to pull through. Indeed, it was common for most Syrian adults to consume only two meals a day, and a fifth of households reported 'low dietary diversity'.[55]

But if food is difficult to come by, so is adequate housing. Almost three-quarters of the displaced Syrians in Lebanon now live in residential buildings, a proportion that rises to 96% in Beirut and 94% in Mount Lebanon, where so many have flocked in search of transient work. Only in the northern and eastern rural marches of Akkar, Hermel, and the Beqaa, whose economies remain largely agrarian, does a significant proportion—from 22% in Akkar to 50% in Baalbek and the Hermel—still live in informal settlements. (Tellingly, female-headed households are almost twice as likely to live in these tent cities.) But this regional variation belies broad similarities. For 53% of Syrian refugees in Lebanon live 'in dwellings that were overcrowded, had dangerous structural conditions, and/or urgently needed repairs'. These are cramped outhouses in which watchmen and labourers are put to sleep; half-finished apartment blocks in which labourers live and work, the kerosene stoves on which they cook their meals sending flashes of blue light into the night air; poky extensions on informal housing in working-class quarters and suburbs like Mar Elias, Kola, and Dora. Leaking roofs and walls, damp, unsealed windows, with just an old bedsheet or some greaseproof paper closing off the room, failing sanitation, or no sanitation at all, and overcrowding—with many households, composed, on average, of four persons, living in less than 35 square metres: these are the daily lot of many Syrians, regardless of where and how they live. And yet none of this comes cheap. Nominal rents ranged in 2017 from $35 per month for a plot of land on which to pitch a tent in the Beqaa, to $328 for a room in Beirut. Less than a third of households did not have to pay additional fees for water and electricity. Though a small proportion offset these costs by working for their landlords, there is no avoiding the fact that rent often far outstrips the monthly income of most Syrian refugees, contributing not just to growing rates of debt, but also to the ceaseless, tiring transience and insecurity that plague the lives of so many. Twelve per cent of Syrian households had moved within the past six months; 38% of those had been evicted, and 20% could simply not afford the rent. Housing, food, heating, lighting, safe drinking water—all of this adds up, and the statistics tell an abject story: 76%

of Syrian households lived in poverty, and 58% were living in 'extreme poverty, unable to meet survival needs'.[56]

This has contributed to forming a particular image of the Syrian refugee as a vulnerable subject, a recipient of assistance whose life can be summed up in statistical assessments of need. But if international donors and non-governmental organisations see Syrians through the lens of philanthropic governmentality, defining them primarily as objects of humanitarian relief, Lebanon's politicians and people have increasingly come to regard them as a threat to the body politic. Earlier chapters have outlined the rancorous polemics that broke out in the early stages of the Syrian conflict over the supposed presence of Al-Qaeda and other radical groups in Lebanon's border marches. These fears of Syrian refugees as dangerous free radicals, germs of terror circulating through the bloodstream of Lebanese society, have only grown more pronounced in recent years. As President Michel Aoun put it in his address to the United Nations General Assembly in September 2017: 'Terrorists have taken shelter in refugee gathering areas and camps, transforming them into a fertile terrain aiming to carry out terrorist activities.'[57]

In these narratives, the eastern town of Arsal and its hinterland have come to play a discursive role similar to that of Ayn al-Hilweh. After 2011, Arsal rapidly became a reception point for refugees fleeing the fighting in the regions to the west of Damascus, and its population tripled, swelling to 80,000 in 2014. With this influx, it came to be seen as a nest of subversives, an unpoliced outpost through which extremists could enter Lebanon, before fanning out to plot their operations across the country. In the summer of 2014, the worst fears of the country's doomsayers were realised, when Daesh and Jabhat al-Nusra launched a joint offensive on the town after the Lebanese army arrested one of their commanders. First, they attacked the army checkpoints on the fringes of Arsal, then they seized the police station, before establishing guards throughout the town. It took the army a week to regain control. Twenty Lebanese soldiers were killed in the fighting, and another eighty-five wounded. Twenty-nine were taken captive.

The fighting in Arsal seemed confirmation of the ways in which the Syrian conflict could perforate and pockmark Lebanese sovereignty, giving rise to formidable new enemies. Lebanon's Christian and Shia communities, long petrified by the ghoulish rise of *takfiri* Islam, saw the presence of IS and Jabhat al-Nusra on the Lebanese borders as a threat to their very existence. But this brief confrontation also created a sad and cruel legacy. Though four of the soldiers were killed by their captors and sixteen, taken by Jabhat al-Nusra, were released in a prisoner exchange in December 2015, nine men remained in the hands of IS.[58] For almost two years, their relatives—the *ahali al-makhtufin*, or families of the kidnapped—kept up a protest at their disappearance. At times angry, at others dignified, they maintained their resolve, calling on the Lebanese state to do more to secure the release of their sons and brothers. They held press conferences and sit-ins. They met with officials, ministers and army officers. They gave interviews. Every few weeks and months, the Lebanese media would speak of a breakthrough, announcing the imminent release of the kidnapped soldiers. Nothing, though, came to pass until the summer of 2017, when Hizballah and the Lebanese army strove to take decisive action against IS and Jabhat Fatah al-Sham—the organisation once known as Jabhat al-Nusra.

On 20 July 2017, Hizballah laid down the markers, launching an offensive against the positions of Jabhat Fatah al-Sham along the Lebanese–Syrian border. After a week of intense fighting, during which every advance and captured position was celebrated in jubilant news broadcasts and tweets by Hizballah's media arm, the party announced its victory on 27 July. In a gesture intended to show its humane observance of Islamic norms of just war, its military command organised safe passage for the remaining *takfiri* fighters and their families, putting them on coaches to carry them to the rebel-held province of Idlib, in northern Syria. Though many rejoiced in what they regarded as the resistance's victory over the forces of obscurantism, seeing it as another decisive step in the party's attempts to create a safe zone either side of the Lebanese–Syrian border, free of radical Sunni fighters and inhabited by loyal, pliant populations, others expressed deep misgivings about the wisdom of its acts. Did such an offensive not threaten to pull Hizballah ever deeper into Syria's conflicts? Might the party drag Lebanon into the morass, as in 2006, exposing the country to 'negative repercussions' rather than making it safer? What did Hizballah's autonomy say about its attitude to the Lebanese state, not to speak of the latter's ability to assert its sovereignty, establishing a legitimate monopoly over arms within Lebanon? And could one even think of the party as a Lebanese entity any more, a legitimate instrument of resistance, when it appeared more interested in shoring up its own position and that of the Assad regime than in protecting Lebanon's territory and population from harm?

Caught in a bind, the high command of Lebanon's army decided that they, too, had to take action if they were not to be outdone and humiliated. Operations began in the heights of Ras Baalbek on 14 August, and on 19 August 2017, the army's commander-in-chief, General Joseph Aoun, announced the beginning of the operation known as *fajr al-jurud*, or the dawn of the heights. Fought 'in the name of Lebanon, in the name of the kidnapped Lebanese soldiers, [and] in the name of the martyrs of the army', this offensive would liberate Lebanon from the scourge of radical Sunni Islam, flushing out the small units of IS fighters still hiding out in the high ground along the Lebanese–Syrian border. The Lebanese army, however, did not work alone, but continued to operate in conjunction with Hizballah's military wing. In a telling indication of just how deeply the 'party of God' had been drawn into Syria's conflicts, Hizballah fighters and soldiers of the Lebanese army positioned themselves on either side of the border, launching a pincer offensive on the pockets of armed men hiding out in the heights of Qalamoun, and Ras Baalbek.[59] On 27 August, the army announced its victory. Like Hizballah, it allowed the men of IS safe passage into rebel-held Syria. But victory was tinged with sorrow and anger. Only hours after the ceasefire, Major-General Abbas Ibrahim, the head of the Amn al-'Amm, or General Security, who had spearheaded efforts to negotiate with Jabhat Fatah al-Sham for the release of the kidnapped, announced that the remains of eight men had been discovered in the seized encampments. The soldiers had been killed by their captors.[60]

These episodes speak, I think, not just of the growing tendency to think of refugees as a security threat, but also of the growing idealisation of the army. In a country in which aborted protests, surprising reconciliations, delayed elections, and incessant blockages have eroded faith in political leadership, the army is increasingly seen as an impartial and honourable arbiter, the sole custodian of Lebanon's fragile sovereignty. It has become common to see posters across Lebanon with the army's distinctive crest and motto—*sharaf*, *tadhiyya*, *wafa'*, or 'honour, sacrifice, and respect'—values whose absence from civic life many in Lebanon feel so keenly. These are sometimes, to be sure, keenly partisan tropes. Supporters of the FPM, in particular, hold up as paragons of martial virtue men like the commander-in-chief of the Lebanese armed forces, Joseph Aoun, and Brigadier-General Chamel Roukoz, who commanded elite troops in 2007 against Fatah al-Islam, in 2013 against the fighters of the Lebanese Salafi shaykh Ahmad al-Asir, and in 2017 against IS. (Not coincidentally, Roukoz is Michel Aoun's son-in-law.)

That Roukoz will be standing as a candidate in the 2018 parliamentary elections is a further sign of the erosion of the lines between security and politics in contemporary Lebanon. Another is the growing tendency of some to call for the registration and return of Syrian refugees to safe zones inside their own country. These are not new demands, but they gained greater currency with the announcement of supposed de-escalation areas inside Syria in the summer of 2017. In his address to the UN General Assembly in September 2017, Aoun made his feelings on the matter clear. 'There is no doubt', he announced, 'that it would be better for the United Nations to assist [the refugees] in returning to their homeland rather than helping them remain in camps lacking the minimum standard of a decent living.' 'As for the claim', Aoun continued, 'that these people will not be safe if they return to their country, we are all aware that this is a pretext, and it is unacceptable.'[61] And, as with the Palestinians, the Lebanese state appears to be making it as difficult as it can for Syrians to gain the security of legal standing. In 2017, over 74 per cent of surveyed Syrian refugees did not have legal residency in Lebanon, and 55 per cent of all Syrian households did not have a single registered member. In large part, this is because of the onerous fees that Lebanon's General Security charges to renew residency permits—$200, a sum easily equivalent to an entire month's income—but also because of growing fears of the state, its security agencies, and their intentions.[62] If they are registered, some will ask, will it not make it easier for the Lebanese state to turn them back towards Syria? And, as the refugees themselves knew all too well, their own country was still 'not safe', despite what Aoun and his acolytes might say. They faced no guarantee that they would not be conscripted or face retribution and punishment for their actions before leaving, or even for their decision to leave.

At the same time, however, Lebanon's Syrian refugees increasingly find themselves unwelcome. As one woman put it, 'the people here treat us badly. There's no work. We can't live a normal life'. By this point, she had lived for more than six years in one of the makeshift tent settlements of the Beqaa, caught in this world of protracted impermanence by the Lebanese government's refusal to allow international organisations to construct sturdier shelters. For such housing, better able to withstand the snow and the wind, might only encourage these men and women to stay on, becoming, like the Palestinians, another imposition on a small country. This nativism and xenophobia, of course, has long antecedents. There is a deep streak of civilizational contempt among some Lebanese for Syrians, whom they deem a backward and uncouth people. For some, particularly among Christians, this is admixed with resentment at the presence of Syrian soldiers and migrant workers in their midst, whom they have come to see as the representatives of an occupying power. After the events of the Cedar Revolution in 2005, many finally gave full vent to their frustrations in mockery and deprecation. I was once told a joke about two Syrian beggars, who would get together every evening after a day spent begging on the streets of Beirut. One night, one of the two arrived with a grin on his face, flashing a wad of $500 at his astonished friend. 'How did you get that?' the other asked, bemused. 'Oh, I just went down to Sassine Square', in the heart of Achrafieh. The next day, the two men met again. This time, the second one showed up with his face bruised and his clothes tattered. 'What happened to you?' his concerned friend asked. 'I did what you told me, I went down to Sassine, and this is what happened to me.' 'But what did you say on your sign?' asked his friend. The bruised beggar showed his friend his sign, which read simply, 'I am a poor Syrian, please help me'. 'No, you idiot, don't say that. I knew I should have told you what to say,' the first one answered. At this point, he took out his sign. It read: 'I am a poor Syrian, please help me. I need $500 to get back to Damascus'. Though some Lebanese have always seen these stories for the racist narratives that they are, there were no qualms in other quarters about expressing such sentiments in public. In 2008, I went to see the British band Gorillaz play at the Byblos Music Festival, in the staunchly Christian town of Jbeil. When lead singer Damon Albarn announced that he would be joined on stage by the

National Conservatoire of Damascus, many in the audience broke out in boos. Some would justify such actions as motivated by hatred and wariness of the Assad regime. It is clear, however, that there is more going on here—not least because of the fact that such animosities are shared by newly declared allies of the Baathist state, like Aoun himself.

In recent years, this xenophobia has increasingly been projected onto common Syrian refugees. After 26-year-old Raya Chidiac was found dead in the northern Christian town of Miziara in August 2017, and her family's Syrian doorman was arrested for her rape and murder, a sit-in was held in the neighbouring locality of Zgharta calling for the departure of all Syrians. 'Nowadays,' one demonstrator explained, 'the refugees outnumber the local people, and we no longer feel safe.' Chidiac's fiancé, who attended the sit-in, was even more explicit in his diagnosis of the problem: 'Syrians, who come from societies [sic] that are different to Lebanese society, have trouble adapting to a more open society and clash against this culture that is ours.'[63] This culture trouble could only be resolved by their expulsion and return to Syria. And yet it does not take that much for some in Lebanon to express their disgust and disdain for the refugees in their midst. One night in 2013, I was out in Beirut with my partner when a little Syrian girl—perhaps seven or eight years old—approached us. While I was speaking to her, the bar's manager rushed out to our table. He dragged her away by the sleeve and slapped the nape of her neck, screaming at her to get lost. When my partner told him that what he had done was completely unnecessary, he responded with the particular condescension reserved for a foreign, blonde woman: 'you don't understand,' he said, 'they're all thieves. They don't need to beg, they're just lying.' In this context, it is unsurprising that a growing number of Syrians—67 per cent in 2017—report being subjected to verbal harassment, most often at the hands of neighbours and employers.[64] Violent words and acts and growing discrimination, both legal and discursive, as well as the Lebanese state's deliberate cultivation of uncertainty and impermanence—these are the forces that Syrian refugees must reckon with, knowing that, still, they cannot go home.

And yet, there is another, more complicated story, hidden in plain sight in the mass of statistical material amassed by the UNHCR—that of Syrians as labourers, working as they have long done in precarious and volatile circumstances on orchards and in vineyards, on construction sites and in scrap metal yards. This is the truth that none care to say too loudly: for all the complaints of the Lebanese about 'the Syrians'—that they are dirty and uncouth, the unsophisticated rustic cousins of their more cosmopolitan neighbours, that they are untrustworthy and criminal-minded, and now that they are dangerous sexual predators, murderers, and terrorists—Lebanon's economy remains reliant on their work. As Elizabeth Saleh has shown in her work on the informal economy of the scrap yards of Beirut, these spaces, with their dependence on Syrian migrant labour, enable the Lebanese to gain profits from such activities, even while maintaining the hierarchical distinctions and inequalities between different categories of people and different kinds of labour. That the Syrians who worked in the yard were all too aware of these discriminatory distinctions, and were ready to work with and against them, was clear from the fact that they named their overseer *mu'allim sarsur*, or Master Cockroach. At one level, of course, this act of naming only reproduced 'the web of social inequalities' in which they operated. At another, however, it also allowed them to reclaim some agency, casting themselves as useful actors who 'altered the urban landscape' for the better, helping to keep it clean and ordered, and turning waste into marginal gains.[65]

In this heavy reliance on Syrian work, at least, there is continuity with the years before 2011. For, as John Chalcraft has shown, Lebanon's building sites and fields have long relied on the creation of a pooled labour market, in which Syrian workers are at once treated as moveable instruments of the economy and as objects of control and suspicion.[66] Though the Syrian conflict is in so many ways a deep caesura, a painful rip in the flesh of the region, we cannot lose sight of the ways in which these earlier patterns of mobility helped some to find their feet after 2011. In 2013, I spoke to one young man who worked as a gardener in northern Lebanon. Then in his late twenties, he had been moving back and forth between Lebanon and his hometown in the countryside of Hama since his teenage years. While working in Lebanon, he had married a girl back home, whom he left behind on his money-making sojourns across the border. When some took up arms against Assad's soldiers, he crossed back to fight alongside them. And when the violence quickly became too bad to endure, he moved his wife, and the children they had since had together, to Lebanon. Even as this signalled a significant shift from the sojourning existence of the unaccompanied male migrant to a more permanent, fixed—if not necessarily secure—kind of presence, this move was only made possible by the contextual knowledge, the networks and contacts the man had accumulated over almost a decade.

In the world of the home

But Syrians are not the only moving people on whom the Lebanese economy relies. Like other Middle Eastern states such as the United Arab Emirates or Saudi Arabia, Lebanon has built up a heavy dependence on migrant workers to do its most demanding, dirty and unattractive tasks: building and fruit-picking, of course, but also cooking, cleaning, clearing away waste, providing sexual services, and raising children. It is not just 'the lifestyles of the First World', then, that are 'made possible by a global transfer of the services associated with a wife's traditional role—childcare, homemaking and sex'.[67] A 'middle-income' country beset by 'third-world' problems—unfit infrastructure, gridlocked roads, failing electricity and a painfully slow internet—Lebanon has nonetheless benefited from the global redistribution of labour that has seen certain states, such as the Philippines, Sri Lanka and Pakistan, farm their men and women out to others, in North America and Europe, the Middle East, and elsewhere in Asia.

Nowhere is this more apparent than in the realm of the home. Since the end of the civil war, hundreds of thousands of female migrant labourers from South and South-East Asia and the Horn of Africa have toiled in the households of Lebanese employers, preparing their food, cleaning their waste, and tending to their children and their old. It seems that Filipino and Sri Lankan domestic workers first began to arrive in significant numbers in Lebanon in the late 1970s and early 1980s, only a few years after the first waves of labour migration from these regions towards the Gulf. From the off, these predominantly female labourers represented a cheap and desirable alternative to the Lebanese, Syrian, Palestinian and Egyptian women who had hitherto worked in middle- and upper-class Lebanese homes. While one might have thought that their lack of familiarity with the Arabic language and

Middle Eastern culture would have been seen as a disadvantage, in fact many potential employers regarded their utter strangeness as desirable. For not only were they far removed from the ideological conflicts that were then tearing asunder Lebanese society—conflicts that inevitably took a sectarian and racialised form, with Syrians and Palestinians thought of by some as intimate brothers and by others as dangerous strangers. More than this, their unsure footing on this new terrain— and the legal conditions on which they entered employment in Lebanon—made them easier to subjugate, sack and replace. Helping to keep wages low, these factors made this new source of labour accessible to many who would previously have considered domestic 'help' beyond their means.[68] As Michael Young noted in the late 1990s, the rush to employ newcomers from the Philippines, Sri Lanka or Ethiopia 'has often seemed less necessary than advantageous socially'. In other words, 'low-cost migrants are often instruments for the social enhancement' of their Lebanese employers.[69] This is perhaps even truer now than it was two decades ago.

In 2010, the Lebanese Ministry of Labour issued 37,732 new work permits and renewed another 80,209—all in all, some 117,941.[70] By 2015, this number had increased to over 209,000.[71] While once the bulk of these workers came from the Philippines and Sri Lanka—their origins giving rise to the practice, common enough among the Lebanese, of calling all domestic workers *sirlankiyyeh*—more than a quarter now come from Ethiopia. A significant proportion are also Bangladeshis and Nepalese—who received, respectively, 29.4% and 10.3% of the new work permits issued in 2010. Some 8%, meanwhile, come from Madagascar and other African countries, such as Togo, Cameroon, and Nigeria.[72] In return for a monthly salary of between $100 and $150 for a Nepalese migrant with little experience of domestic work, and $200 to $300 for Filipinos, who are particularly prized because of their perceived superior civilizational standing and knowledge of English, these women are expected to carry out many of the essential tasks of domestic life.[73]

As in other parts of the Middle East, domestic workers enter Lebanon under the *kafala* or sponsorship system. Built upon an array of regulations, laws, and assumptions, this is a powerful administrative mechanism whose entire purpose, it would seem, is to maintain the control of the state and the employer over any migrant labourer working in the country.[74] This is a system coordinated by the 500 or so *wikalat al-khadamat*, or 'service agencies', that secure these migrants' services for Lebanese employers. These agencies charge their clients the handsome sum of $2,000 for their services, helping prospective employers to select a 'girl' from their books, drawing up all the necessary paperwork, securing visas and buying air tickets. In practice, though, much of the work is carried out by local recruiters, who operate in places such as Nepal on a double commission, charging $200 to $300 to the Lebanese agencies that rely upon them for steady sources of labour, and anything between $300 and $700 to the migrants who see them as gatekeepers. Once in the country, however, domestic workers largely fall under the responsibility of their employers. It is they who must come to Beirut International Airport to pick up their new charge from the offices of the General Security, where they must await their arrival, and it is they who must apply for a residence permit, or *iqama*, for their housekeeper before the expiry of their initial three-month visa. As this suggests, the relationship between employer and employee is underwritten by profoundly paternalistic—or maternalistic, given the extensive part that women play in these circumstances—assumptions about the unquestioned right of the Lebanese to exert extensive jurisdiction over the lives of these racial others in their homes. Indeed, it is telling that employers are commonly referred to as the *rabb al-'aml*—quite literally, the lord or master of their charges' work—while domestic workers are spoken of as *banat*, or 'girls'. Often, when accused of racism or cruelty or pettiness towards their housekeepers, Lebanese women will exclaim that they 'treat her like my daughter'. This is a discourse, then, that seemingly excuses a great deal. But even when it is not used as a justification for abuse, it yields deeply asymmetrical relations between employer and employee. While employers retain the option to 'return' their new employee to the agency if they deem them unsuitable for whatever reason, employees are expected by convention to surrender their passports to their employers, who lock them up in a drawer, out of reach. Should they leave their employer's home without these identity documents, they are deemed 'runaways' in breach of their conditions of residence—and liable to summary imprisonment in the General Security's holding cells, where one migrant activist testified up to seventy women are detained while awaiting deportation. Though the relationship between these assumptions and Lebanese law remains a murky, uncertain one, they are widely believed to have force and are commonly put into effect. It is not for nothing that this Ethiopian activist should have exclaimed, during an event held in Beirut in September 2015, that 'the law has killed us'—*al-'anun 'atalna*.

Some scholars have argued that the 'transfer' of migrants from certain parts of the world to others has freed women of certain affluent, secure backgrounds to work outside the household, taking up professional roles in the knowledge that someone else is doing the housework and the childcare.[75] This phenomenon, however, has had rather different effects in Lebanon. Here, this influx of migrant labour has permitted Lebanese households, in many cases, to give life to a particular bourgeois ideal of the gendered division of labour. In this script, played out in affluent and aspirational homes across the country, the woman is largely emancipated from the demands of work, whether in or out of the home, and free to focus on caring for herself and her family—shopping, exercising, socialising, engaging in charity work, and cooking and tending to her children as and when she sees fit. But, crucially, she is not entirely idle. For if the husband remains the central economic player, the wife can also take on managerial functions, supervising her housekeeper's work, training her, teaching her recipes, and admonishing her.

Race, gender, and class interlock here to construct a powerful narrative of superiority. The Lebanese man and woman are jointly and separately in charge—the one responsible for providing for the family out in the public realm of business, the other for managing the family's private, domestic affairs; their subordinates, meanwhile, are not just women, but *foreign* women whose nationality, race, and putative lack of linguistic fluency and familiarity with their Lebanese surroundings mark them as different and inferior. They are envisioned as beneath their employers in cultural as well as in socio-economic terms, underlings who can perform only the most menial and abject of tasks. If their Lebanese employers are playing out a fantasy of middle-class comfort in which the woman never need lift a finger in the house because of the man's capacity to provide amply, then these domestic workers are the very embodiment of the proletariat, whose sole asset is their all too precarious physical labour. This is a vision of the household that not only reproduces in microcosmic form the 'global inequalities' on which it depends, but that is faithful to two key tenets of neoliberalism as it has developed since the 1970s: its faith in managerial expertise, drawn down in this case into the private sphere of the home, and its investment in a peculiarly conservative understanding of the nuclear family as a supposedly self-reliant unit of reproduction and care.[76] Contemporary Lebanese understandings of matrimony are, to be sure, deeply rooted in older notions of the middle-class woman as a domestic being, devoted to the tasks of being a wife, a mother, and a keeper of the house.[77] But this latter aspect has taken on particular importance with the growth of new discourses of self-care, consumption, motherhood and management which encourage Lebanese women to invest their own time and effort into particular pursuits, while strictly regimenting the time of others who work for them.

Much like the Filipino maids with whom the sociologist Nicole Constable worked in Hong Kong, the women employed in Lebanon's homes often follow a 'rigid' and punishing 'daily schedule', one that governs in careful and unrelenting fashion their use of both time and space—dictating what they must do, what they cannot do, where they must be and where they should not be.[78] For many, the rote tasks of the day—cleaning bathrooms and living rooms every day, polishing glass, ceramic and wood to leave them shining, making breakfast, washing up, preparing lunch and dinner, putting away leftovers, washing and ironing clothes, and other such duties—are broken only by the few minutes spent out of the house or apartment, walking the dog or running errands. Only then can they huddle together for a few minutes of rushed conversation with one or two friends who have been allowed out from neighbouring homes. On leaving to run errands, they will be given a wad of notes—carefully counted out to cover whatever groceries they have been asked to pick up. On their return, they must hand their employer the change, which is again counted up to make sure it is right. Many, too, are those who are locked in, and who are simply not permitted to leave their employers' homes. Such restrictions received some media attention during the 2006 war, when reports abounded of Sri Lankan workers locked up and left behind by their employers, who charged them with 'taking care of the house' while they fled for safer areas.[79] Many were those who were not allowed to leave and who died with their employers beneath the bombs. This was the case of Kundbsejen Runjani, who was with her employer in her apartment when the building they lived in was hit during the Israeli bombardment of Sur; of Raniya Josef, who died with her employers in the southern town of Borj al-Shemali; of Malika, killed in Sheem; and of the other Sri Lankans who died in the south, whose names, tellingly, Lebanese witnesses did not know.[80] But there is nothing new about such entrapping practices. In 1998, Siani, a Sri Lankan domestic worker, told of her friend Mala, whose employers 'used to lock the door and fridge and tie her hands' together when they would leave the house.[81]

With such restrictions on their movements come keen demands on their time. As Annette, a Cameroonian worker attending a Mayday rally held in Beirut in 2011, told an activist, 'because they put down 2,000 dollars in an office'—that is to say, with one of the agencies that provides the Lebanese with their domestic workers—'you have to work Monday to Sunday', all week long without a break. It is not, she explained, that the Lebanese don't know better, but that all too often they simply don't care. 'There are human rights [*droits de l'homme*] in Lebanon', she went on, 'but the Lebanese do not use them'. After all, her employer 'knows, he told me an employee has a right to rest, to six days off a month'. But this has done nothing to alter his expectations. 'Why make a human being work like that, from six in the morning to twelve at night, or till one or two, without even eating? It gives people insomnia, and that's why so many girls are sick.'[82]

Others, it is true, enjoy more latitude. They are free to take a Sunday afternoon off, spending time at the *suq al-ahad* or 'Sunday market' in the outskirts of Beirut, where some take up stalls, selling small pieces of jewellery and clothing or foodstuffs from the Horn of Africa and South and South-East Asia to their compatriots, or they get together with friends and boyfriends to cook, gossip, commiserate and flirt. But time to oneself remains scarce, and even workers who insist on the kind treatment they receive from their employers, like the Nepalese Menuka Baraili, only enjoy two hours of rest each day, 'after doing all housework'.[83] Countless times, I saw tired Sri Lankans and Ethiopians take off their shoes to come into a family room after dinner to ask if their employers needed anything else. Only once the 'lady of the house' had told them their work was done could they withdraw to their own small quarters, watching a TV turned down low or chatting in the 'maid's room'. At times, this is little more than a cruel euphemism for a cubby or airing cupboard into which a mattress is crammed. If they are lucky, they will get a small room off the side of the kitchen. Lit by a single lightbulb, this is sparsely furnished—a single bed, or a bunk if there are two housekeepers at home, and perhaps a small dresser—and decorated with pictures of relatives and small statues of the gods garlanded with plastic flowers and illuminated with little candles.

This strict regimentation of time is a reminder that even those Lebanese who pride themselves on regarding their domestic workers as 'part of the family' still think of them as commodities of some kind. Having invested in the labour of another, they must make sure they utilise it to its full potential. For some, this might mean callously—and foolishly—depleting their employees' energies and driving them to despair in an endless round of chores and abuse and isolation. For others, it means consideration and kindness and ensuring that their employees remain happy with their conditions—and, therefore, willing to stay on. Lebanese employers might offer their domestic workers presents—one family I knew gave a longstanding employee a laptop, and others buy phones and clothes—and give them phone cards and 'money to call home', or buy them flights home for a visit every few years, so long as they receive an assurance that this is only a holiday and that 'the girl' will come back after a couple of months. If a 'maid' or 'nanny' decides to leave, she will often be called upon to stay on for a few months longer or—as in a couple of cases I came across—for a year or two. 'It is hard to find a good one', Lebanese employers will say, justifying their attempts to prolong another's separation from the familiar, 'we have to hold on to the house-workers we have'. But if domestic workers remain intent on leaving, they might be asked to train up—or even to help source—their replacements. They will pass on to them the cleaning routine and show them Middle Eastern or European recipes, showing them how to select vegetables and cuts of meat in the shop, how to prepare and season meals, and how to make Arabic coffee; they will teach them a little Arabic or English or French, if they do not have some already; and they will tell them about their employers' particular expectations and demands—in cautious, earnest terms if they are present, and in less guarded terms in more private moments, when a rather less varnished portrait of *monsieur*, *madame*, little miss and little mister might emerge amidst stifled laughter. And even once a domestic worker has returned to Sri Lanka or Nepal, such pressures do not go away. As Baraili told her interviewer, she remains in touch with her former employers, with whom she still 'communicate[s] by Facebook and phone'. But such conversations are not entirely innocent. 'They are asking me whether I want to come back, they told me that if I decide to go they won't get another person' and offered to cover the costs of her flight and visa. These are tempting offers, and Baraili is 'thinking about going back to Lebanon'.[84]

As Baraili's testimony suggests, 'being part of the family' comes with its own demands. The affective discourse of daughterhood and fondness into which Lebanese employers can so readily lapse is one that creates expectations of reciprocity. For few are the gifts or the acts of perceived kindness that come without certain unspoken obligations. But this familial language also has other effects. Perhaps most palpably, it disrupts and dissolves the boundaries between work and life. I have seen some employers who will respect the lines they have themselves laid down, telling their children or husband to 'do it yourself' when 'she's off'. But it remains all too often true that what is a workplace for some is a living space for others, who forget—or prefer not to remember—that receiving service during their own hours of leisure must, of necessity, prolong the working hours of another. And working within the home, with all its ambiguities, creates new and sometimes troublesome configurations of affection. In particular, it can foster intimate relations between children and the domestic workers with whom they often spend the bulk of their time at home, and who cook for them, tidy after them, clean them up, and play with them. While some mothers look benignly on these relations, others—even as they remain unwilling to commit more of their own time to the tasks of mothering—become resentful of the hold of another on their child. They will complain, for instance, that their little boy or girl speaks with a Filipino lilt, or that their Tagalog is better than their Arabic, linguistic irks that hint at their fear that their children are being appropriated by another person and taken over by another culture. As the anthropologist Ann Laura Stoler has noted in another context, the relations between domestic workers and their employers are often as tense as they can be tender.[85] That is not to say that some Lebanese do not come to care genuinely for the migrant labourers who have worked for them. I know of one woman who, for her father's eightieth birthday, flew him, her husband and daughters to visit their former employee and her family in Sri Lanka, and of a family whose daughters remain in touch with their former housekeeper—a Filipino who met her American husband online through a Bon Jovi fan board, and now lives in suburban New Jersey—regularly exchanging Facebook messages and chatting on Skype. But rare are the cases where such enduring contact does not come with the hope, or expectation, that this lost figure will one day return to the fold.

It is not only where these women live and how they spend their time that Lebanese employers seek to take charge of, attempting to wrest control of the minutes and hours of their domestic workers' days and the months and years of their working lives. For many also impose restrictions on their appearance, their physical comportment, their diet and friendships and relationships, expecting some measure of control over the bodies of their employees, as well as their labour. This choreography of control begins at the airport, where migrant labourers coming to Lebanon under the *kafala* system are expected to stand in a different queue to Lebanese nationals and other foreigners. Quite literally placed on the margins, they line up along the wall—Nepalese, Sri Lankan, Togolese and Madagascan women, and Nigerian, Indian and Pakistani men carrying heavy, old suitcases. After their interrogation by the same immigration officials who nod at other—white—foreigners seeking to enter Lebanon, they are placed in a waiting room until their employer is ready to come pick them up in person, as they must. This can be a frightening experience—particularly if, as was Menuka Baraili's case, their employer is late, leaving them in this small room until the evening, not knowing whether anyone will come, or if they encounter some bureaucratic hitch or another, like the Nepalese migrant I knew who was held back because one official refused to believe that her tattered passport was real. This is an exercise designed to impress in newcomers and returning migrants alike the awful reality that they are subject to: the twin powers of a whimsical and unpredictable state and of their employers. What begins at the airport continues whenever employer and employee leave the house together and are seen in public: in the supermarket or the street, where the employee trails a couple of feet behind, perhaps carrying a bag or two or holding a child while her employer picks out groceries or walks the pram, taking charge as is her wont, and in restaurants and beach clubs, where the housekeeper will sit or stand a foot away from the table. Never can they be seen walking or sitting together, as equals. Their hierarchical relationship must take this corporeal form.

These disciplinary regimes extend to other aspects of bodily comportment—to clothes and food and sex—as employers attempt to control their domestic workers' lives as consumers, just as they exert mastery over their lives as labourers. There is no doubt that many are free to dress and do their hair more or less as they please, if only at particular times, and it is common—increasingly so, it seems—to see young Ethiopian women walking about Beirut in jeans and pretty tops and trainers, or whiling away a half hour arranging each other's weaves. (As I write these words, I am sitting on the St Nicolas steps in eastern Beirut on a balmy early September evening, watching a gaggle of five East African women in their early twenties do just that as the darkness falls around them, the lilt of their talk carried up in my direction by the warm air.) Others, however, have to make do with worn hand-me-downs—baggy tracksuit bottoms and t-shirts and ill-fitting cheap flip-flops—or are forced to wear pastel pink or sky-blue maids' uniforms. These are clothes designed for the house—slippers and loose tunics and shapeless trousers, like a toddler's pyjamas—and yet I have often seen women dressed in this manner out on the streets. Regardless of whether domestic workers wear something old, something borrowed or something blue, it is clear that these sartorial choices made on their behalf are designed to mark out their inferior status, robbing them of their sexuality and their womanhood and infantilising them. It is through such means that they are kept in place and reminded of their subordinate and dependent status.

A similar logic dictates the diet that some employers attempt to impose on those who work in their homes. Some will think that leftovers are enough for their housekeepers, or that they do not deserve anything else. Others will forbid them from preparing their own food, because of aromas they consider noxious. Only rarely will employers take pleasure in their housekeepers' food, asking them to prepare *pancit* or vegetable curries. This fear of wild odours and uncheckable urges also extends to other areas of migrant labourers' lives. I know of one case in which an Ethiopian housekeeper was dismissed for calmly explaining that she needed to have sex to maintain her physical health; 'returned' to her agency as unsuitable, she was no doubt instructed to keep her needs to herself and placed in another household. She cannot be the only one whose sexual life and desires are a source of disquiet to her employers. Indeed, this fear has given rise to legal measures, such as the decree that allows the Lebanese state to repatriate any domestic worker who marries on its territory as in breach of the terms of her *kafala*, or sponsorship agreement.[86]

Paradoxically, however, only some are willing—as Menuka Baraili's employers were—to provide a small budget for toiletries such as shampoo and creams, a necessary monetary concession when employees are paid only every four or five months, as Baraili was, before sending much of their meagre salary back in remittances. This reluctance was mocked mercilessly in a 2010 short film by the Shankaboot collective, in which the fictional Madame Najem, a young woman of dubious taste who boasts of changing her hair with the seasons, ridicules her Sri Lankan housekeeper's request for some shampoo. 'May God give them [what they want]', she exclaims, her vermillion nails standing out against her yellow curls, 'a poor, miserable people without money, who wash in the river and brush their hair to remove the sand, and they come here and want shampoo…'[87] Given such reluctance to provide for their bodily needs, it is ironic that some who have only one bathroom in their apartments should insist their housekeepers wash down their showers and scrub them with anti-bacterial products after using them.[88] Indeed, according to a survey carried out in 2016 by the Lebanese anti-violence NGO Kafa and the London-based advocacy group Anti-Slavery International, some 27 per cent of Lebanese believe their housekeepers to be dirty, carriers of germs who pose a threat to the health of those around them. To expose this belief, the two organisations organised a mock promotional campaign. Under the watchful gaze of a hidden camera, two bright, smiley young women in their early twenties offer a new soap to shoppers in a supermarket. Named 'Clensen Ozo-Trio', this is designed—or so the fake campaign claims—specifically with domestic workers in mind. As they approach shoppers, they explain that surveys have shown many Lebanese to have complained of their domestic workers' strong body odour. This new soap, with its mix of 'ozone and triclazone', will fix this pesky problem. Only one of those offered a free sample—an older white-haired man, his face pixelated out like those of the others shown—refuses, angrily telling the young woman 'there is nothing uglier than racial discrimination. We aren't better than them. We go and work in Europe and America like they do ... *haram* [it's not right]'. Others, when presented with the soap, offer up rather less savoury opinions. 'The blacks, the Ethiopians, they have this problem. They have a strong smell. In Nepal, the yellows don't have this problem. The black people, they have a strong smell,' explains one middle-aged lady. 'It depends on the continent,' another, younger, man opines, attempting to sound liberal-minded but falling instead into a pseudo-scientific discourse of biological racism, 'you can't generalise about all domestic workers. It depends on the type of skin.' One woman pauses for a moment, asking 'are you approved by the general association of domestic workers and human rights organisations?' When she is told that the soap has indeed been approved, she shrugs, and with a simple 'yeah, we'll try it' takes a sample.

It remains a discomfiting truth that many Lebanese who profess to be concerned about laws and rights and tolerance still seem to consider their domestic workers as racial others, disruptive presences whose bodies are inherently unclean.[89] Indeed, it remains hard for even those Lebanese who are otherwise relatively progressive in their social attitudes to imagine their domestic workers as cultural—let alone social—equals. I recall talking to one woman I know, who expressed disbelief that her housekeeper might once have worked as a schoolteacher. 'How could she?' she asked, bemused, 'she can't even speak English properly...' When I reminded her that her Nepalese housekeeper knew Nepali, Hindi and Sanskrit—thinking it best to leave unsaid the fact that her own English was hardly perfect—she merely shrugged and said, *eh, barke*—'yeah, maybe...'

One manifestation of this deep-seated prejudice is the *de facto* ban that many beach resorts and country clubs impose on visitors of certain races. This segregation is often presented as in keeping with the need to preserve order and decorum within their precincts, and to respect their clients' desire for quiet and security—notwithstanding the tendency of many to broadcast booming Eurodance over their loudspeakers and to allow groups of numbskulls to drain their cocktails in the pool amidst the dowagers paddling back and forth in visors and sunglasses like overdressed poodles. One country club catering to the rich and powerful made this prohibition clear in its internal regulations, posted at the entrance: bodyguards and handguns were strictly prohibited, and domestic workers were allowed only in the children's play area and had to remain fully dressed, in order to mark their distinction from those around them, in thongs and Vilebrequin Bermuda shorts. Notwithstanding such justifications, it is obvious that this prohibition stems from the rank racism that Shankaboot's fictional Madame Najem gave voice to, when she explained nonchalantly that she would never take her maid to the beach because she'd be 'disgusted to swim in the same water as her', and that she 'was very happy with the resorts that have respect for themselves, and that know that their clients couldn't stand to be in the same place as a servant'.[90]

So pernicious had this situation become by 2012 that the then minister of tourism, Fadi Abboud, declared after a wave of social media recrimination that any resort found to be discriminating in such fashion would face the full force of the state's wrath. However, when the journalist Rona Halabi carried out an investigation in the wake of Abboud's statement, she found that little had changed in Lebanon's resorts. Accompanied by a young Ethiopian domestic worker, Ababa Gebachristos, Halabi attempted to gain entry to eight of Lebanon's best-known beach clubs. Only three allowed Gebachristos to enter. Others, when challenged, presented a host of excuses. At the Riviera, in Beirut, the doorman asked to see her identification. When asked why Halabi herself did not need to show her identity card, he explained with some hesitation, 'if something happens, I need to know where she's from'. His manager adopted a similar line. When Halabi asked him whether an American would have to go through the same procedure, as a foreigner, he responded simply, 'I know what an American is like'. 'Ya madame,' he went on, growing frustrated, 'we're in Lebanon here, we're not living in France.' These words seemed to suggest a confounding set of attitudes. Gebachristos was suspicious merely by dint of her race. Unlike a white American, there was no saying how she might comport herself.

And despite Lebanon's pretensions to civilisation, one could not expect the same social standards to be applied as in Europe. There, liberal-mindedness and freedom from prejudice could be expected; in Lebanon, discrimination was simply the norm, and all had to accept it. The manager of the Malibu proved similarly unyielding. Upon being challenged, she replied simply: 'there is a regulation'—*qanun*, or law—in place 'for the swimming pool. We can discuss it from now until tomorrow, but there's no point.' When Halabi asked 'and what if it was a tourist coming with us', the response was immediate and dismissive. 'We don't usually receive tourists of this colour,' she said, with an emphatic movement of the head.[91] Here, the simple logic of skin colour, rather than doubtful morality or criminality, was the justification.

The owner of another chic resort, the former captain of the Lebanese national basketball team, resorted to a rather different kind of justification when asked why Gebachristos could enter his club, but could not swim in its pool. In a conciliatory voice, he explained that the case of a domestic worker was much like that of a child. Just like children, they were 'allowed to swim in one place, but not in another'. Finding that this analogy failed to persuade a dubious Halabi, he continued in another key. 'Honestly, when we first opened,' he recounts, 'I used to let them come in with their ow—their employers'; '*as—*' he blurts out, as if about to say *ashab*, or owners, before correcting himself and using instead another expression, *rab al-'aml*, which he seems to consider more acceptable despite its similarly derogatory connotations. But, he explains, 'we used to receive complaints by the dozen every day. I'm with the state, I respect the state and law and order, but at the end of the day I'm the one who made the investment and put money in, they can't pass a law that people can't accept.' In short, 'in public places', Lebanon's racial others can swim where they like, 'but this is private here' and the writ of the owner, the investor, must stand, and not that of the state. As the owner of another resort in Jiyyeh, to the south of Beirut, put it rather more bluntly: 'if the minister of tourism wants [domestic] labourers to swim, let him build a pool.'[92] Whether they regard domestic workers as potential criminals or sources of moral disruption, as quasi-children lacking the rights of full adults, or as intolerable merely by dint of their phenotype, all prove equally intolerant of their presence within their establishments. And all follow the same logic—private, quite simply, trumps public. Once within the private precincts of capital, the state no longer has a say. Perhaps they are not wrong. For, as the lawyer and civil rights activist Nizar Saghiyeh explained to Halabi, there is no law in Lebanon tackling racial discrimination against non-Lebanese nationals, a lacuna that leaves the Lebanese state without effective legal means to punish those found guilty of such flagrant racism.[93] Opprobrium, it seems, is the sole available course of action in the face of such behaviour.

In the face of such widespread and deep-seated racism, some have pinned their hopes on educating future generations. In 2009, two Lebanese children's authors, Laila Zahed and Maya Tawil, launched a series of books entitled *Mimi fi Sri Lanka*, *Mimi fi Jozor al-Philippine*, and *Mimi fi Ethiopia*, recounting the adventures of the eponymous Mimi, a young Lebanese girl, who travels in her dreams to these faraway countries, from which so many of the country's domestic workers hail. Their purpose, Zahed explained to journalists, was simple—to break the 'prevalent equation of Sri Lankan = maid, Phillipina [sic] = maid'. The books, which luxuriate in the beauty and exoticism of these places even as they seek to transcend cultural differences, include short factsheets about each of the countries Mimi visits, and teach children how to say 'thank you', 'goodbye' and other such basic phrases in Sinhalese, Tagalog, and Amharic. With these, the authors hope to break down the 'one-sided' 'relationship with foreign workers' that prevails in Lebanon. As they note, 'the domestic worker at home is often the one who adapts to our culture: she learns our language, learns to eat or even cook our food, knows our country but often no one asks her where she is coming from and how she expresses herself in her own language.' Perhaps, Zahed argues, children who read these books 'would understand and respect the people they are living with at home, and would grow into adults who are tolerant and respectful of other cultures and social classes'.[94]

Others have used rather more direct tactics to combat discrimination and abuse and to secure greater legal recognition for domestic workers. Some of these efforts, like the Anti-Racism Movement or ARM, dedicated to 'documenting, investigating, exposing and fighting racist practices through multiple initiatives and campaigns', have been spearheaded by Lebanese activists. Basing their efforts on the now universal template

301

of the NGO, they seek to work within the neutral, amorphous spaces of civil society, exerting pressure on the Lebanese state, raising the awareness of the Lebanese public, and empowering migrant workers seeking to improve their social, economic and legal situation. ARM's initiatives range from social media campaigns and press releases drawing attention to particular instances of abuse and discrimination—when I visited their site, they sought to assist an African couple living with their young child in the Beirut neighbourhood of Ras al-Nabaa, and whose neighbours had waged a racist campaign of insults and violence against them—to calls for participation in moments of mobilisation, like the Mayday marches held in Beirut each year.[95] But the organisation is perhaps proudest of its Migrant Community Centers, whose three locales in Beirut, Jounieh and Saida offer 'safe and free spaces' for migrants to gather, 'where they can meet, learn new skills, work together, and access information, resources and assistance'. With their 'language classes, ICT classes, health awareness sessions, rights education, [and] advocacy training',[96] the MCCs are built around a conventional paradigm of 'capacity-building'. They seek, in other words, to instruct migrant workers in how best to take charge of their own lives—a pedagogical model adopted by NGOs the world over seeking to uplift the objects of their attention.

In other instances, it is migrant workers themselves who play the leading part, creating organisations like the Alliance of Migrant Domestic Workers in Lebanon or the Migrant Domestic Workers' Union (MDWU). The latter has worked closely in recent years with FENASOL, or the National Federation of Employees' and Workers' Unions in Lebanon, to secure legal recognition of the rights of female migrant workers. Like ARM, it uses a diverse array of tactics, from social media to the more traditional resorts of activism—demonstrations, marches, and petitions. This synthesis of different modes of mobilisation is apparent in videos like that posted on the MDWU's page ahead of the 2017 Mayday demonstrations. In grainy footage seemingly filmed on a mobile phone, the MDWU's Founding Committee—thirteen women and one man—huddle in a close-knit group, holding up a banner adorned with slogans such as 'I heart MDWU' and 'Migrant Domestic Workers in Action'. In turn, several of them intone the same message, in English, French, Arabic, Nepali, Tagalog and other languages, calling for wide participation in a labour day demonstration asking the Lebanese government to ratify the International Labour Organization's Convention C189, recognising the rights of domestic workers. This is the face of migrant labour activism now: overwhelmingly female, proud of its participants' status as both migrants and as workers, and founded on transnational solidarity and coordination between women of different origins: Filipino, Sri Lankan, Nepalese, Cameroonian—and Lebanese.[97] Indeed, in recent years, Lebanon's Mayday celebrations have become sites of cosmopolitan sorority, female migrant workers marching together holding their respective countries' flags aloft, calling upon the Lebanese state to afford them greater recognition and to ameliorate their working and living conditions.[98]

In making their presence felt and their voices heard, domestic workers seek to combat endemic verbal and physical abuse and to strip away, one by one, the fundaments of the *kafala*, or sponsorship, system under which they must work. For it is a sad truth that instances of domestic workers insulted and harried in the street, locked into homes, screamed at, beaten and burnt remain all too numerous. In 2008, the Beirut office of Human Rights Watch reported that 'at least 97 migrant domestic workers' had died in Lebanon since January 2007. Forty had committed suicide. Twenty-four had fallen from balconies or rooftops, often while attempting to escape employers. Only fourteen had died because of health conditions. As one former ambassador put it when asked for his views, 'don't call this an embassy. We have become a funeral parlour. People die. Natural deaths, accidents, suicides'—it was all the same, and the death toll kept rising.[99] In November 2009, the organisation again drew attention to the troublingly high proportion of deaths among domestic workers, after eight women died in the previous month alone. Four had killed themselves, either by jumping from buildings or, in one case, by hanging herself.[100] These women had often been pushed to escape or suicide by continuous maltreatment. As Kamala Nagari, a Nepalese woman who recounted her fall from an apartment building, testified: 'I was locked in for two days, and they did not give me food or water. Then after two days, I wanted to run away. The apartment was on the fifth floor. I tried to go down using cable wires running along the wall of the building. The cable broke, and I do not remember what happened afterwards.'[101]

Many others testified to not being able to 'leave my employer's home' or 'call my family', of 'being lent out like property' to clean the homes of their employers' relatives, of being beaten for asking to 'go back to my country at the end of my contract', or of having their pay withheld.[102] In one particularly notorious—and harrowing—instance of abuse, bystanders filmed as Alem Dechasa-Desisa, an Ethiopian migrant worker, was beaten and abducted outside her consulate. Upon their arrival, police found the car into which Dechasa-Desisa had been bundled still at the scene. While her abuser—Ali Mahfouz, the brother of the owner of her employment agency—was allowed to go free, Dechasa-Desisa was taken to a detention centre. After the intervention of Caritas, which maintains a presence at the centre, she was transferred to the psychiatric hospital of Deir al-Saleeb. Dechasa-Desisa committed suicide there two days later. Her attacker remained free. During her brief detention, he had even given an interview to Lebanese television, in which he explained that he was trying to return her to Ethiopia because she suffered from mental health problems.[103]

If those who commit such horrific abuses can act with such impunity, it is because they operate within conditions of structural racism underwritten by *kafala*. It is no surprise, then, that in recent years migrant labourers and their advocates should have focused on overturning these structural circumstances. In the summer of 2014, they scored a rare victory when a Lebanese judge, Jad Maalouf, found in favour of a domestic worker who had sued her employer after he took away her passport. In his landmark ruling, Maalouf argued that this practice—as common as it may be—denied the migrant's right to free movement, as recognised in the Universal Declaration of Human Rights, which is incorporated into Lebanese law. Employers had no authority to keep passports to 'protect their investment'.[104] Such successes come at a cost, however. In December 2016, the Lebanese authorities deported Sujana Rana, a domestic worker who had campaigned for the legal rights of her fellow migrant labourers. She had been arrested at her employer's home, held without access to a lawyer, and 'questioned about her involvement in activism'.[105] Given such rough practices, it is unsurprising that some, like the Lebanese scholar Ray Jureidini, should argue that Lebanon's domestic workers are nothing short of modern-day 'contract slaves'. It might be argued that their condition is somewhat more akin to that of indentured workers: bound into precarious conditions by insecure and unequal contracts, they are caught up in a cycle of debt and obligation and held in place by profoundly restrictive legal conditions.

The question remains, however, why so many continue to want to come to Lebanon. Upon their arrival, many may know little about this 'new, unknown place', as Menuka Baraili described it, or may have been spun tales of plenty by the agents who recruit them—often, it would seem, relatives, like those who despatched Savitra Pulami Magar and Mira Ghising from Nepal, through Delhi and Dubai, and on to Beirut. The 'global ethnoscapes' of such women are not so much grand vistas of opportunity, dreamscapes of migration, as a cramped series of boarding hostels, airport departure lounges, immigration offices and maid's rooms. But wilful ignorance may also play a part. As one migrant who had returned to Sri Lanka insisted, those preparing to head out were often unwilling to heed the warnings of those who had been to Lebanon, dismissing them as the product of mere jealousy at their own impending good fortunes. Whatever the case, all must soon learn something of their new surrounds, even if their knowledge is sometimes restricted to the home and wherever else they go in the company of their employers. When asked by a Lebanese television presenter what she liked about the country, one Filipino domestic worker answered 'the weather, and the mountains'. 'Do you go to the mountains by yourself?' he continued. *'La, bidhar bas ma' al-madame'*—no, I only go out with Madame, came the answer. Others' answers were just as revealing—'Samir Geagea,' said one woman whose employers were fervent Lebanese Forces followers. 'And what do you think of Michel Aoun?' the presenter asked, mischievously. *'Ma bhibbo'*—I don't like him—came the answer, a disgusted crease in the face, prompting laughter from the audience. 'Mar Maroun and Mar Charbel,' said another, citing her Maronite employers' favoured saints. Such religious synthesis is perhaps less uncommon than it might appear, even among those domestic workers who are not Christian or Muslim. I remember one non-Christian Sri Lankan domestic worker who found space in her prayers for the Virgin Mary, St Rita and St Charbel, constructing a little ex-voto in the kitchen adorned with incense and plastic flowers and images and candles of these Catholic religious figures.

And yet there is no doubt that these are conventional answers, calculated—as the presenter suspected—to please their employers and placate their audience.

In less guarded moments, domestic workers reveal a rather more knowing and unvarnished view of Lebanon. In late 2014, the actor and director Zeina Daccache—who found fame on popular comedy shows, before establishing Catharsis, a drama therapy company that has also put on plays by the inmates of men's and women's prisons—assembled a cast of migrant labourers for an improvised performance at Masrah al-Madina, the fashionable theatre space in Hamra. The performance, which received support from the Migrant Workers Task Force and the Norwegian Ministry of Foreign Affairs, shows a riotous and amusing set of views on Lebanon.[106] At one moment, a male migrant labourer notes the difference between Lebanon and his native Cameroon. The former, he thought, was a developed place, till he witnessed its frequent power cuts—a phenomenon unheard of, he insists, in Cameroon. Others berate the slow speed of the internet, another frequent gripe of the Lebanese about their own country. As the camera filming the performance pans out across the audience, some are bent over in uproarious laughter, while others shift uneasily in their seats, unhappy to be reminded of Lebanon's structural failings by these strangers, whose social inferiority once seemed so pathetically certain.

And more than this, migrant labourers must cope with all the familiar pangs of displacement. I remember often sitting with one Nepalese domestic worker as she showed me her photo albums, pointing with pride at the pictures of her son and daughter, carefully preserved beneath their plastic covers. Her son, she explained, smiling, was training to be a policeman, her daughter qualifying as a teacher—as she had done herself, before abandoning Nepal for the lure of remittances, first in Dubai and then in Lebanon. 'How old are they?' I asked the first time she went to her 'maid's room' to pull the albums out of the drawer in which she kept them. 'In these photos, twelve and fourteen, but now, fifteen and seventeen,' she said, noting the passing of time only with a short, sad nod of the head. While some feel compelled to leave children and husbands behind for work, often spending long stints of ten, fifteen or twenty years in Lebanon and other Middle Eastern countries, others choose to delay marriage and childbearing in their efforts to accrue a little capital abroad. I knew one housekeeper who had arrived in Lebanon as a 16-year-old, but who returned to Sri Lanka only at twenty-eight, once she had patiently accumulated enough money to give herself a dowry capable of securing an attractive husband, and of setting up a business of her own. Soon after she returned, I heard that she had married a wedding singer—the Facebook photos showed a handsome figure with a raffish black moustache—and opened a bar. There is no doubt, then, that for some migration affords opportunities for social mobility. Why, after all, would so many take the well-trodden routes that lead to Lebanon, knowing of all the perils and pains that might come their way?

Conclusion

Neoliberalism is built on the unequal apportioning of resources, rights, and duties. To some are given new means for capital accumulation, through the transformation of public utilities into private assets, or through the regulatory engineering that has enabled new assemblages of state investment and corporate initiative, and that has cleared a way for particular patterns of urban restructuring. To others, however, are handed only the burdens of vulnerability and precarity. But if in other places across the twenty-first-century world, this stripping down of the person into an uncertain, shivering subject has been used to keep certain citizens in their place, in Lebanon these self-same processes have been used at once to enclose particular kinds of subjects and to push them away, encouraging their flight by making life untenable under present conditions. Syrians, like Palestinians before them, have become prey to such strategies. Already shut out of the circuits of partisan welfare that make up for what the state does not and cannot provide, these unwelcome guests also find themselves shut out by the combined forces of law and security. And yet, at the same time, while scarcely even acknowledging it, Lebanon's elites do rely upon these fearful foreigners, finding in them a useful and pliable source of cheap and casual labour. Much the same is true, too, of the many migrant labourers who work in Lebanon's shopping malls and homes—cleaners, housekeepers, and nannies who are subject not just to mechanisms of governmental control, but also to private regimes of surveillance and dependency.

For Lebanon's middle-class men and women need these migrant workers too much to let them go. Come from sub-Saharan Africa and South and South-East Asia, they are, in a fundamental sense, enablers of leisure, who make the lives of the Lebanese possible and free them to spend the time they have saved on household chores in other ways. But as much as they are service providers catering to the needs of their employers, they are also participants in an increasingly vivacious informal economy of leisure, producing and consuming their own modes of entertainment. When I was last in Beirut, the walls of Gemmayzeh were plastered with bright yellow posters. 'Charly Office Presents Fanos Entertainment and Events Ethiopian New Year Presentation at Beirut', they read, above a picture of the three smiling performers, Mesfin Bekele, Abiyot Kasanesh, and Yared Negu. The organisers were clearly hoping for a large turn-out, as they had booked out Chiyah basketball stadium, in the southern suburbs of Beirut. To make this possible, the concert would be held at 2:00 p.m. on a Sunday, when so many domestic workers would have the afternoon off. But not all forms of migrant leisure are necessarily as well-coordinated. Spend enough time watching the worthy videos put together by NGOs working with domestic labourers in Lebanon and you will find, among the suggested content, short home-made clips shot by Sri Lankan or Filipino men and women who have slipped away from their duties to spend a few hours on the country's public beaches. These are never more than a minute or two long. The lens wavers and catches the light as it moves about the circle, capturing the smiling, laughing faces; one person might be singing or playing the *tabla*; others are clapping along, their hoarse untrained voices joining the chorus; a bottle of spirits is passed around; some fish might be put to grill on a makeshift fire. It is to the various forms of leisure and pleasure jostling for space in contemporary Lebanon that the next chapter turns—to the hegemonic modes that shape how the Lebanese spend their nights, how they get married, and how they remake their bodies, but also to the spaces of evasion, of fun and evanescent pleasure, that can be glimpsed here, in these short clips of passing moments that someone has quietly archived away on the internet.

308

7

AL-SAHRA, OR THE NIGHT OUT

ON LEISURE AND PLEASURE IN CONTEMPORARY LEBANON

Late in the summer of 2011, a video went viral. It showed the CNN business correspondent Richard Quest doing the rounds of Beirut's 'rooftop bars'—'Skybar, Iris, White, Pier 7', as he reeled them off in his distinctive croaky tones—here moving through a crowd of gawping revellers, there sneaking in before the doors open to see the 'calm before the storm'. As Quest exclaimed in a voice-over, 'there may be fewer tourists because of the political instability'—his light way of referring to the six months it took Najib Mikati to form a government, or perhaps to the Assad regime's siege of Homs that summer. 'But worry not, the Beirutis party on.' Indeed, he explained as he entered one bar in what can only be described as resplendent leisure gear, his immaculate white trousers reflecting back the strobe lighting, 'the clubs thrive in the face of political instability. Millions of dollars are spent on new creations.' 'When you know the history of Beirut', Quest continued, 'then the rooftops start to make sense. The turbulent past, the hedonism of the present, and the what-will-be attitude to tomorrow', born of the uncertainties of living in a region preternaturally prone to conflict—these were what accounted for the Lebanese infatuation with nocturnal pleasures. 'In this city', he concluded, 'the people are voting with their feet late into the night'. Who these people might be, or how representative they might be of Lebanon's inhabitants, he did not care to ask.

But as Quest's less than mordant insight suggests, this was not a report to let a cliché go to waste. As he spoke, stock images rolled by—the Mohammad al-Amin mosque, its neo-Ottoman domes lit up against the night sky; women splashing about in the pool in their skimpy bikinis while their less-than-svelte male companions sat scowling by the side; café-goers chatting, *arghileh* in hand; diners sipping their San Pellegrino in Beirut's best emulation of a French brasserie. All that was missing, perhaps, was mention of Lebanon's religious diversity and its distinctive admixture of tradition and modernity—accompanied, as is usually the case, by an image of a minaret and a belfry jutting together into the heights, or of veiled and unveiled women strolling together. In Quest's defence, however, he was not the only one to resort to platitude. For a succession of club owners fed him all the clichés he needed. First Chafik El Khazen, Skybar's owner, explained 'this is what makes Lebanon very special. Because there's no planning, we try to have as much pleasure and fun as possible as if there's no tomorrow'. Then it was the turn of Jad Matta and Mazen Elzein, the owners of Pier 7. While Matta sipped on a pink, sugary thing of a cocktail, exclaiming 'Welcome to Beirut. I love this city!', Elzein adopted a more reflective stance. For Beirut's fondness for the night was not a 'trend', but a 'legacy', the 'legacy of a very cosmopolitan city', once fêted as the 'Switzerland of the Middle East'. Ventures such as theirs, then, were ways of paying homage to Beirut's sophisticated past and bringing it into the present. Finally, it was the turn of the restaurant owner Ziad Kamel, who told of how he had opened one venture in downtown Beirut in 2006, four days before the Israeli bombardment began. But perhaps that was not the point of the report. Perhaps Quest was just trying to do the Lebanese a favour by celebrating their remarkable ability to 'live for today because they don't know what tomorrow will bring'.[1]

It would have been unseemly, under the circumstances, to probe too deeply into how the owners of these clubs—all men in their late thirties and early forties—had found such early success. And nor would it have done to ask to whom these places catered, when a night of drinking in one of them might easily set you back $50 or a $100, in a country where the minimum wage sits stubbornly at $500. But for all Quest's harping on turbulent yesterdays and uncertain tomorrows, the present—the nagging aches and troubles and inconveniences and structural inequalities of the everyday in times of crisis—seemed oddly absent from his account of Beirut's hedonism. One could be forgiven, then, for wondering just what this little montage said about contemporary Lebanon. As the blogger and writer Nasri Atallah noted wryly of the clip: 'quite how cramming thousands of people into sweaty clubs ensures Lebanon's sustainability is quite beyond me'.[2] And yet Quest's report from the rooftops is neither the only example of the genre, nor the most egregious. After I watched it on YouTube, my feed filled up with suggestions of videos singing the praises of Beirut's nightlife, its beaches and restaurants.

That is not how all the Lebanese see themselves, and it is certainly not how many of them live their lives. It is, though, how some of them would like the world to look upon their country. For as Fadi Abboud, then Lebanon's tourism minister, put it—speaking amidst a mountain landscape of red-roofed houses and cedar trees in a vain attempt to persuade Quest that Lebanon was not all heaving nightspots—'joie de vivre is our brand'.[3] With these words, Abboud evoked the hegemonic view of Lebanon—as a place of heedless hedonism, a sun-blessed sliver of land squeezed between the Mediterranean and the mountains, which, despite the geopolitical turbulence that has plagued it, nonetheless maintains its capacity for parties and pleasure. This is a script that began to gain traction in the tourism brochures of the 1950s and 1960s, when this view of Lebanon as an entrepreneurial paradise, a blissful escapade of snowy ski slopes and perfect beaches, beautiful women and long summer nights was first deployed. Since then, it has served as the foundation for successive programmes of reconstruction and regeneration, built on an understanding of Lebanon as an economy reliant on supplies of foreign capital on the whims and urges of visiting Gulf Arabs and expatriates. Like all hegemonic discourses, this is a set of norms that ensnares people within its expectations, compelling them to ascribe and aspire to its images of ease and consumption, labouring and saving and borrowing to be able to spend the day on this beach and the night in that club.

And yet its empire over the senses—and purses—of the Lebanese is not uncontested. For the country's inhabitants deploy its tropes with a mixture of pride and ironic detachment. It is not that they don't believe that Lebanon's women might be the most beautiful in the world, or that this is a place where one can ski and swim all in a morning—even if they don't know of anyone who has ever done so—but that they are all too aware that these are convenient fictions. When they trot out these platitudes in conversation with foreigners, they do so with a knowing smile. And when they utter them to each other, they do so with biting sarcasm. This is apparent from the brutal memes that circulate online, parsing the different perceptions of Lebanon and the Lebanese. In one, six images are juxtaposed: one of RPG-toting turban-wearing Taliban, with the caption 'How the world sees us'; another of two bikini-wearing women on skis standing on snowy slopes—'How the Arabs see us'; a third of a herd of sheep—'How politicians see us'; a fourth of a chef stirring a giant pot of *mlukhiyeh*—'How Guinness Book sees us', an allusion to the odd Lebanese propensity for breaking food-related records; an image of Albert Einstein, overlaid with the word GENIUS—'How we see ourselves'; and, finally, an image of a group of non-descript men of indeterminate age sitting on plastic chairs smoking shisha—'What we actually do'.[4] In a similar vein, one juxtaposes images of women lounging on beach-towels in their bikinis, or how the Arabs see Lebanon; an informal encampment of tents and donkeys, before a ruined building, or how the 'USA sees it'; verdant valleys, how 'the Lebanese abroad see it'; and a gridlocked intersection, everyone driving into everyone else in the belief that others will yield—a more accurate representation of what many regard as a place of exceptional disarray and disorder.

These homemade images are not just, to my mind, forms of auto-critique, familiar indictments of the laziness and unruliness of the Lebanese, as conceited and convinced of their own greatness as they are incapable of producing anything. And nor are they rejoinders to resilient representations of Lebanon as a place of violence and civil strife—a way of talking about the country that has lingered for so long that one Lebanese researcher, Jad Aoun, set up a blog to keep track of all the times American firefighters tackling a tornado, or British politicians speaking of inner-city blight, reached for a comparison with Beirut.[5] They are also reminders that there exist other forms of being, other forms of enjoyment and relish in the everyday, spaces of leisure less bidden to this dominant discourse of untrammelled consumption. This chapter examines these various forms and norms of pleasure—its dominant strain, with its celebration of hedonism, but also more demotic and pious conceptions of leisure and more informal, fugitive forms of fun. In the end, I think, this is what so many are looking for: a short flight from the everyday and its grinding, tiresome preoccupations, a momentary escape from the way in which even ordinary days come burdened with uncertainty and malaise. They are not so much seeking to defer consideration of the future—though that, too, must play a part—as to construct another now, an alternative present in which to live for a while. In a place in which the todays of so many are as unsure as their tomorrows, finding pleasure, even for a few hours, matters. And yet there is perhaps no escaping the cloying grasp of the quotidian, for so many of the worlds of leisure created for those who live in Lebanon reflect its inequalities, its norms and expectations.

The nightclub

Perhaps when Lebanese and foreigners evoke this cliché of sybaritic abandon, they are really only thinking of one place—Skybar, the nightclub that sits atop the roof of the Beirut International Exhibition and Leisure Center (BIEL), on the artificial promontory that Solidere created out of the city's rubble and trash early this century. There is something of the hyperreal about this place. Bald men in polo shirts spilling out of orange and canary yellow sports cars. A bouncer on steroids, his biceps surging and tearing at the fabric of his too-tight white shirt. The lift, always too packed with gaggles of girls in ankle-breaking heels and boys with lined, disdainful eyes. The smell of cigars and cheap scent. This sense of a place that is little more than a simulacrum of pleasure does not dissipate on entering the dancefloor. For this is a venue that calls to mind nothing so much as the clubs we used to laugh at in mid-1990s Hollywood films—*Basic Instinct*, perhaps, or *Showgirls*, whose producer is, after all, Lebanese. It all feels too staged, too put on, as though it were the product of somebody's idea of what a nightclub might be like. Noise, opulence, decadence, drunkenness, sensuality—all the boxes must be ticked. Strobes light the sky, like flares from some stranded ship. Fireworks are lit. Sparklers go by, their heat too close to your face, as somebody's magnum of vodka is carried along to cheers of approval. But somehow it all ends up feeling ersatz, like being caught up in an elaborate performance of joy, but one in which the actors sometimes slip their guard, letting their smile drop for a second to show the deep weariness inside.

The club stands far out to sea—further out than it should, moored as it is on the very edge of this unnatural excrescence—an unearned position that allows it unbroken views out towards the bay of Jounieh, to the north of Beirut, a rare sight in these days of skyscrapers. Nobody, though, seems to pay the view any mind. They are too focused on each other—on working out who everyone is, whether they have a table, what they're drinking, and on whether they're having fun, more fun than they are. And if they are not, then they are staring intently at their phones, tutting occasionally, their fingers flying across the screen at speed. The music is loud, so loud that it is impossible to exchange more than inchoate, animalistic sounds—whoops of what sounds like plea-sure, shouts of 'yeah, man', slightly manic laughter. But nobody is danc-ing, really, save for the blonde women hoisted up onto the bar at regu-lar intervals through the evening, who gyrate joylessly in their silver hot-pants, before being helped down by the bouncers, their dutiful performance done, and led away into some hidden chamber. Arms are hoisted in the air, fingers are pointed, the feet might shuffle a little, the hips move in an awkward, arthritic way. But at no point does all this seem spontaneous, alive and lively and of the moment. Everyone is waiting for someone else to do something, for something to happen. They are caught in this state of endless expectation, incapable of letting themselves go. The music, with its melodic platitudes and trite lyrical odes to self-affirmation and nocturnal pleasure, hardly helps to ease this state of lulled tension. The breakdowns fall exactly where you expect them to fall, the synth chords as predictable as the canned laughter in a bad sitcom. Like the club itself, it seems a calculated exercise in engineering pleasure—something concocted by a program-mer working to a mathematical formula in a dark room somewhere. And yet the club is always too full. It is difficult to fray a path through this crowd of immobile revellers, who stand tangled together in knots of people who seem petrified, like schoolchildren on an outing, of being separated from their friends. I remember once, when a friend took me there, emerging with cigarette burns on my arm. As he was talking to his companion, the man next to me—a little caricature of a Scorsese extra, with his pot belly, his five o'clock shadow, his hooded eyes and slicked back thick greasy hair—kept jabbing his arm towards me, hitting me with the incandescent end of his Marlboro. When I tried to put my arm around him, to tell him what he was doing, he affected not to hear, not to know me, turning his face away. We were standing at the same table. Not all the club's customers are such embodiments of self-absorption, but the whole place is designed to create a sense of congestion. At the centre of the dancefloor stands a large bar, like a boat on this sea of people, reducing the amount of space. On either side, terraces of tables rise up towards the night sky, like temples to bad spirits.

But this overcrowding is also, no doubt, a product of the desire of all those present to see and to be seen, to peg others on their home-spun rankings of merit and respect, and to allow others to attest to their presence in this sanctum. For beneath the apparent disorder, this is a space arrayed according to a clear and brutal hierarchy. 'Up there', a friend explained once, with a small gesture, 'are the tables reserved for the Mustaqbal [Future Movement] guys, and there the Amal, and there the 'Uwwet [Lebanese Forces], and the Hizballah'. I looked up warily. Above us, from our spot among the mortals on the dancefloor, you could see tables arranged on the terraces. At a few sat two or three men—some young, others well into middle age—in driving shoes and white jeans, accompanied by women in mini-skirts and halter-neck tops, some sitting draped around them, others moving in slow motion, off the beat. Bottles of champagne, vodka and tequila, shot glasses, tumblers of orange and cranberry juice, ice buckets sat on the table, a barely touched disarray. Nobody was smiling. Like feudal lords gazing down on their peasants from the castle walls, they could see and be seen. And the privilege of being there, in their company, does not come cheap. That night that I was burned, the bill was $800—$1000 per man. The women don't pay. Outside, as you wait for the valets running about frantically to fetch your car, little girls from Syria or the Beqaa try to sell tatty dyed roses for a few thousand lira. Few buy them.

For this, of course, is as much a space of exclusion as it is one of heedless ostentation. A place in which pleasure is counted out in shot

315

glasses, it presents a crude self-portrait of the Lebanese elite and those who aspire to enter its ranks—a clumsy, self-conscious performance of fun, in which some play the part of abandon better than others. On this evidence, it appears a closed, inward-looking society, ordered according to hermetic considerations of capital, political influence, and reach. All that matters is who you are, whom you know, and what you can do for—or to—people. Those who do not fit into these schemas of power and worth are simply excised, treated as invisible, as I was that night. This is, by definition, a world made up in equal measure of consumption and closure. It is not, I think, that tomorrow does not matter in this world, that all this drinking and display is a necessary indulgence, a way of coping with the ever-present threats of war, political turbulence, and civil strife. Rather, the very purpose of all this consumption is to give the impression of insouciance and effortlessness, as though money really were no object and it meant nothing to throw away a few hundred dollars on marked-up vodka or tequila of an evening. As Thorstein Veblen wrote more than a century ago: 'in order to gain and hold the esteem of men it is not sufficient merely to possess wealth or power. The wealth or power must be put in evidence, for esteem is rewarded only on evidence'. Leisure here may be neither 'beautiful' nor 'ennobling'. But it does, still, serve its purpose as a 'means of gaining the respect of others'.[6]

The denizens of this world must adhere to what might be called the habitus of leisure. They must know how to hold and present their bodies in these settings—how to carry themselves as they enter, whom to greet and how, where to go and where to stand. This knowledge, of course, comes at a price—it helps to have been at the right schools, to have a surname that carries weight or parents whose networks one can use, but also to have the time and money for repeated visits, for indulgent generosity, offering drinks, gathering strays and captivating the crowds. And those who lack such knowledge are shunned, left figuratively—if not literally—outside the circles of power.

Skybar may well be the archetype of the Beirut nightclub. And yet the norms that it displays ripple through Lebanese society, encouraging others to confuse pleasure and leisure with the preening ostentatious presentation of the self. This is apparent from the reams of thumbnails that fill the pages of beiruting.com, a 'lifestyle extravaganza of a website' that peddles in the hackneyed and the sensational. Among head-lines heralding news of the Spanish footballer Cesc Fabregas and his Lebanese partner Daniella Semaan, or of another British royal preg-nancy or wedding, one can find pieces like these: 'Top 10 Lebanese stores to visit on Black Friday';[7] 'Lebanon [sic] among the world's sexi-est people', which revealed that Lebanese women were ranked tenth in the '"hot" charts' from a poll of 'over 110,000 Americans' carried out by 'MissTravel, a destination dating website';[8] and 'Beirut tops the best international cities for food', an old *Travel and Leisure* piece recy-cled for the occasion.[9] These are pieces that play, of course, to the desire of the Lebanese to see their country as an attractive destination, a sophisticated and luxurious place of pleasure inhabited by a desirable, carefree, hedonistic people—and this in spite, or perhaps rather because, of the tiresome realities of their everyday. But they also pan-der to their tendency for conspicuous consumption, whether by day, in shops like the white goods store Khoury Home, or by night, in the clubs, bars, restaurants, and hotels through which the website's pho-tographers prowl in search of content.

As you flick idly through the images crammed into the website's busy digital galleries, certain patterns of comportment quickly become apparent. Older couples in their late forties or fifties—him greying and carrying the embonpoint of middle age, her preserved with injec-tions and procedures and treatments and hair highlights—draped in status symbols. The car keys flung ostentatiously on the table, the cigar in the ashtray, the expensive cosmetic surgery—all of these are valu-able commodities in this economy of display, in which even the quality of a nose job is sharply assessed, and in which a little fat round the middle can be read as a sign of (male) affluence and indulgence. For as the old adage goes, *rjel bala kirsh ma byiswa 'irsh*—'a man without a belly isn't worth a penny'. Young couples—him in a navy blue or red polo shirt, her in a floaty thing in turquoise or white—snapped as they are taking selfies, or looking languorously into the camera, arms curled around each other. Birthday cakes, creamy confections topped with sparklers and embossed, in course, with the name of the special recipi-ent. Groups of friends—unmarried girls, in gauzy summer tops or downy winter jackets and cream turtlenecks, depending on the season, stubbly teenage boys showing off their muscles in tight t-shirts and thigh-hugging jeans—all striking the same eager poses, arms aloft in the air, fingers making peace signs, as they smile into the lens. To some, this is just a parade of unknown faces. To others—those who are captured in these Van Eycks for an age of digital reproduction and their friends and acquaintances—it is an occasion to gawp at oneself and one's friends, to recognise the faces of those one knows, to gossip and swap tales and speculate on relationships coming together or falling apart, and to scrutinise every minutia of the smiles, the eyes, the arms. For in the end these reiterative exercises in bourgeois self-fashioning really amount to an infinite celebration of the self, in which those pictured are weighed up for the status they hold in society, a status signalled in bodily appearance and accoutrements, in biceps and cup sizes, handbags and tailored shirts and cars.

Bodily matters

This commodity fetishism, this obsession with the body, all that it can signify, and all the ways in which it can be improved and adorned, places demands on all those who partake in this economy of display. This is true, if in different and unequal ways, for men and women alike, as is evident from the gender paradigms to which so many Lebanese men feel they have to conform. For many are all too eager to acquire all the trappings associated with two of the central stock characters of contemporary Lebanese popular culture, the *harbu'* and the *jagal*. The first of these terms conjures up a vision of cunning, unscrupulous cleverness and quick thinking, a figure defined by the ability to stay on his feet even when the ground appears to be moving beneath him. The term, after all, means chameleon, and it evokes for many an attribute they view as characteristically Lebanese—that striking ability to find a way of getting through, and even capitalising on, the direst of situations. At dinner parties, people will speak with disbelief and rueful admiration of the antics of successful acquaintances, men who somehow seem able to bend the rules to their own interests without feeling the consequences. The *jagal*, meanwhile, is the very embodiment of virile masculinity—bluff, muscular, and uncompromising, an image of forceful sexuality.

These are powerful codes of masculinity, and ones that shape not just heteronormative practices, but also, as Jared McCormick has shown, Lebanon's queer culture, with its captivation with the ambiguous figure of the 'bear'—or, as one of McCormick's Lebanese interlocutors put it, 'hairy masculine guys'. '[He] can be muscled or not. But [he] should be masculine!' The bear, for McCormick, is a figure of homoerotic desire, but also a convenient means of passing as straight, 'avoiding the full stigma that is associated with more outward pronouncements of one's sexuality'.[10] This is all the more crucial in a context in which, for all Lebanon's reputation as a gay-friendly place in which queer nightclubs thrive and NGOs like Helem and Proud can work more or less openly, homophobia remains rife; *tubjeh* and *manyuk*—'fag'—are common terms of abuse, homosexuality remains a criminal offence punishable by up to a year in prison, and gay men can be forced to undergo compulsory medical examinations. (A brutal reminder of this came in 2012, when thirty-six men were arrested in a raid on a gay cinema in Burj Hammoud before being subjected to a medical examination at the notorious Hobeiche gendarmerie station, where they had eggs forced up their anuses to establish whether they had engaged in intercourse.)[11] But if these codes of masculinity are open to subversion and self-preserving manipulation, then they are also not immune to playful parody. In 2010, the singer Michelle Keserwany released a song entitled 'Jagal El-USEK'—named after the University of the Holy Spirit in Kaslik, where she was still a student. In its gently mocking words, half-sung, half-spoken, she recounted an everyday story of an unwelcome encounter:

> I was sitting in the cafeteria / Not thinking about much / Drinking my Nescafé / When a young guy came / And sat down opposite / He was wearing *lunettes* [sunglasses] / His hair was drenched in gel / He said *bonjour ya demoiselle* / I'm a cool guy / I listen to 50 Cent / My car it shines / And I'm always at events / I have a chalet / And a villa in Farayya / That ex-Miss Lebanon / Yup, I'm her brother / ... I'm the Jagal of USEK / My eyes are coloured / I drink Vodka Sec / My shirt is Mousseline / *Al-papy* is a colonel / And I smoke cigars.[12]

There is something lost, inevitably, in the transcription and translation of these words—the way that Keserwany moves between languages, melding French and English with a warmly colloquial Lebanese Arabic to pick at her unwanted interlocutor's pretensions, or changes her voice to mimic his affectedly masculine timbre. But the gist of the piece is clear, with its dismantling of the way in which a certain kind of Lebanese man defines himself as *al-shabb al-cool*, 'the cool guy', through the superficial and utterly predictable trappings of desirable masculinity: the sunglasses, the hair gel and French designer shirt, the hip hop, the nightlife and the car, the right drink and the right smoke, the beach chalet, the house up in the high-end ski resort, and the beauty queen sister, all made possible by his well-connected and powerful 'daddy', with his career in the army. In other words, one glimpses here the Janus-faced nature of Lebanese masculinity—at once a figure of independence, a highly individuated vision of preening sexual self-confidence, and deeply relational, a self all tangled up in relations of kin that define who he is, what he can do, and that situate him in the world, give him worth that he cannot acquire alone. And that, of course, is the joke— not just that Keserwany's *jagal* baulks when she takes him on, but also that everything he is, everything he thinks he can do, hinges on others.

And for those who are not born with the right assets—whether aesthetic, social or economic—there is always cosmetic treatment to 'enhance', 'improve', and render the body more desirable. In 2007, *Le Commerce du Levant* estimated that around 1,000 operations were carried out in Lebanon every year, generating around $25–30 million in revenue for Lebanon's clinics and hospitals.[13] It is likely that this figure, which excludes less invasive, but no less transformative—and profitable—procedures such as Botox fillers, has only grown in recent years, despite the loss of valuable 'cosmetic tourism' from the Gulf countries since 2011. For, as some have argued, the pressure to conform to a certain ideal of bodily beauty has only increased in recent years, as the political and economic uncertainty of the last decade have deepened existing inequalities and created new anxieties. As the psychologist and anthropologist Liliane Ghazale put it, 'people feel great uncertainty about the future. They feel they are not in control of their own fate. There is an exaggerated appearance because this is one area in which people can assert control'.[14] In other words, social mobility may be closed off to those who lack patronage and do not want to leave the country. People may feel trapped in unhappy working lives with stagnating wages, running simply to stand still as prices rise and a home, married life, and successful career all seem to slip further out of reach. Only in caring for themselves can they find satisfaction and success.

Parts can be exchanged more easily than the whole, and larger biceps and fuller lips are easier to come by than a different career, a new life, a fuller, happier sense of oneself. It is telling that when, in 2007, First National Bank launched its 'plastic surgery loans'—$500 to $5,000, available on certain terms and conditions for procedures ranging from orthodontics to breast enhancements—it should have advertised these as the way to 'have the life you have always wanted'. As the bank's marketing manager put it, 'we' in Lebanon 'like to look our best', and these loans offered a 'life raft' to those sinking into despair at their own appearance.[15] One of his colleagues was blunter still. 'You cannot find a job in Lebanon if you are not good-looking. People will reject you socially.' In other words, ugliness was a kind of social death, and willingness to tolerate it an imprudent rejection of the aesthetic norms that govern Lebanese society.[16] In putting a price on beauty, the Lebanese have created new and even more callous forms of inequality, parsing not just between rich and poor, modern and 'backward', but also between beautiful and ugly. For the researcher Sarah Mallat, attractiveness is seen as 'as the greatest form of social capital in Lebanese society … the most important factor is image—how you present yourself to society—even if it means spending beyond your means and accumulating debt'.[17]

There are many men who are not immune to these pressures—men like Ali Zein, who had already undergone a rhinoplasty, a chin operation, and a procedure on his teeth by the age of twenty-four. It is estimated that men now make up some 20 to 30 per cent of the patients seen by Lebanon's two hundred or so cosmetic surgeons. But there is no doubt that these norms and expectations bear down most heavily on Lebanon's women.[18] In one story recounted by FNB's marketing manager, George Nasr, a woman sold her car to pay for nose surgery. When a shocked surgeon asked her why, she explained that 'a new nose was more important to her than a car, because every day she looked in the mirror and hated herself, believing her nose was the reason she was single and had no social life'.[19] There is something conveniently ready-made about this story, but there is no doubt that social convention—diffuse, impersonal, and yet no less biting—can affect the way in which women feel about their bodies. As the owner of one Beirut hair and beauty salon explained, 'nowadays people are very judgmental, especially women. There is this expectancy [sic], they want this first impression. A woman feels pressured to be pretty and it's increasingly alarming. It's affecting women's confidence'.[20] But beyond the nameless, faceless, forces of convention, those who insist on the need for bodily modification and 'improvement' are often—as Mallat put it—'mothers, lovers, and significant others'. One young woman, Alexandra Hajj, recounted the insidious ways in which her mother's renowned beauty had affected her own sense of self-worth. Since her childhood, others had drawn invidious comparisons—at times implicit, at others quite explicit—between her own appearance and that of her mother, a former model. From the age of eight, 'everyone would tell me, 'You're perfect, but when you grow up your nose will be too big'. Worried about her weight, she started dieting at the age of eleven. All of this, she explains, 'came from seeing my mom fix herself and look beautiful and always prioritising what she wears and how she looks. Although my mother is very smart, has a master's degree and is well spoken, her priorities were always her looks, and that worked in society because my mother was very well known and celebrated because of how she looked'.[21] It is perhaps unsurprising—if no less depressing—that husbands and boyfriends should want straighter noses, fuller lips, and larger breasts for women they regard as theirs, or that women should feel they must ward off the effects of age, keeping themselves attractive with liposuction and fillers and regular trips to the gym to maintain the interest of husbands and managers and stave off invisibility and insignificance.[22] What is more disconcerting is the way in which women enforce such conventions on those around them. For Hajj is far from alone in feeling pressure to conform to a certain ideal of beauty. I know of one woman, now in her mid-thirties, who underwent a rhinoplasty at the age of eighteen after being told for years that her unbecoming nose had spoilt her appearance. Just as insidious as the forthright words of mothers and sisters are the glances and muttered asides of friends and acquaintants. Sitting by the poolside on a summer's day, you will hear snide evaluations of this or that woman's appearance, with the hang of her breasts, the thickness of her lips, the cellulite on her thighs, the straightness of her nose and the angle of her nostrils anatomised with an almost pornographic obsession with single body parts.

All of this—gossip and anxiety and unhappiness and fear of losing those around one, of not being noticed and not getting on in life—has contributed to turning cosmetic 'improvement' into big business. Television shows like FutureTV's 'Beauty Clinic'—all dramatic music, lingering close-ups and impressionistic set pieces—are made about it,[23] and cosmetic surgeons like Nader Saab have become local celebrities. Saab's name was well-known long before he became embroiled in allegations of malpractice in 2017, thanks to a canny advertising campaign whose slogan, *al-jamal nadir wa sa 'b*, or 'beauty is rare and difficult', punned on his name. His billboards jostle for space on Lebanon's roadsides with those of companies like Silkor. Established in 1997, this firm offers services ranging from laser treatment—hence its name, a pun on silk and the French for body, *corps*—to 'Coolsculpting', a procedure intended to 'freeze your fat away with no downtime, no needles and no surgery', and surgical procedures carried out by American and Lebanese doctors.[24] It now has eighteen clinics in locations across Lebanon, ranging from 'Christian' areas such as Kaslik and Dbayeh, perceived by the Lebanese as places of relative licence, to the Hadi Nasrallah highway in the southern suburbs of Beirut, seen by many as a redoubt of staunch piety, as well as offshoots in the UAE, Kuwait, Qatar, Oman and Iraq.[25] Some estimate that some 1.5 million procedures—from Botox fillers, teeth whitening and skin peels to far more ambitious undertakings—are carried out each year in beauty clinics and hospitals like these.[26]

This drive for beauty, though, is not just an individual matter. Rather, it is bound up in broader calibrations of Lebanon's worth, particularly in times like these, when so many fear that the country's standing has been diminished by crisis and uncertainty. The status of women is often seen, of course, as an indication of a country's capacity for progress. But contemporary Lebanon differs, in that it evaluates its women according to aesthetic criteria as a means of assessing its place in the world. Again and again, you will hear the Lebanese harp on the exceptional beauty and desirability of the country's women, treating it as a badge of national pride and a measure of its standing. It is clear that these tropes are intended, at one level, for external consumption. Like the hackneyed, prurient mentions of skin-tight jeans and headscarves one finds in foreign press reports, they serve to underscore Lebanon's capacity for liberalism and tolerance—of religious difference, of different registers of femininity, even, for some, of different levels or stages of modernity. And this, in turn, seems proof enough, for those who see these things as important, of Lebanon's fragile and tenuous belonging to the West, a semi-detached annex of Europe. Indeed, it is clear that these ideals and expectations shape the way in which the Lebanese look on, and behave towards, the female body. It is not for nothing that so many crave the straight noses they associate with whiteness or that First National Bank chose an image of flawless European beauty—blond hair, blue eyes, pale skin, flushed, blushing cheeks, delicate nose, full pink lips—to advertise its loans on 900 billboards across the country.[27]

This all-consuming preoccupation with women's appearance, and what it signals about the state of Lebanese society, has worked its way into the country's political culture. This is evident from the slogan the Free Patriotic Movement chose to get women out to vote in the lead-up to the 2009 parliamentary elections. Alongside an image of a young woman, her brunette hair falling alluringly across her face, her lips puckered expectantly, were four simple French words in capitals: *Sois belle et vote*, 'be beautiful and vote', a phrase that echoed, as many were quick to point out, that misogynistic dismissal, *sois belle et tais-toi*, 'be pretty and shut up'. The FPM's political opponents were quick to mock its pretensions to capture the imagination of the young and beautiful, with many of their homemade images lapsing into sectarian fear-mongering. 'Your place after voteing [sic]', one read, showing a woman lost in a crowd at a Hizballah rally. Another used a crudely reworked image of the young woman used in the FPM billboard, now shown wearing a chador, and superimposed over a crowd of headscarf-wearing female Hizballah supporters waving party and Lebanese flags. 'Your face after voting', read the slogan at the bottom.[28] The point was clear: voting for the FPM was, for women, to vote their freedoms away, exercising their right only to bring about a theocracy propped up by Hizballah's complaisant and self-seeking Christian allies. In this confessional view of the world, there is only good and evil, right and wrong. On one side stand 14 March, the life-loving forces of order and progress and tolerance; on the other, 8 March, beholden to Hizballah, with its pious, censorious, authoritarian restrictions on freedom and its embrace of a bleak 'culture of death'.

FPM supporters dismissed these charges, insisting that the slogan was a deliberate subversion of the injunction to be quietly passive, and a statement of women's capacity to marry good looks with political agency. But the movement also faced criticism from those who saw its advertising material as an insensitive appeal to image, yet another patronising instance of Lebanon's patriarchal politicians dictating their desired stance to their voting public and talking down to women. The Beirut-based Feminist Collective, in particular, decried the campaign as 'offensive to women'. In a blog post, the collective's founder, Nadine Moawad, mocked the FPM's campaign. 'Are you implying', she asked, 'that women are too stupid to engage in real-life politics? That the only way you can appeal to their voting power is by reminding them to look pretty? ...What does being "pretty" have to do with the democratic process of electing a parliament that represents our voices?' Equally troubling, in Moawad's eyes, was the way in which the campaign partook of a visual culture that compelled countless 'Lebanese girls [to] put their bodies through pain and confinement and self-loathing to *try* and look like that model in that picture', while doing nothing to address the very real structural problems that affected women, from under-representation in parliament to issues 'like protection from family violence, the right to nationality, and protection from sexual harassment among hundreds of other things'. In the image that accompanied her twelve-point manifesto, Moawad—one of the most articulate and witty campaigners for women's rights in Lebanon—provided her own reworking of the FPM's by now notorious billboard. The word *belle* had been crossed out and replaced with *intelligente*, and the word *blanc* tacked on at the end of the sentence, so that it now read 'be intelligent, and cast a blank ballot'. Beneath it, in crude handwriting, was the simple message: *ma hada balu bi-hu'u'ik*—'nobody is worried about your rights'. To reaffirm the point that Lebanon's politicians do not care a jot for women's rights and freedoms, the pretty girl in the picture now had her left eye bruised and blackened.[29]

Legal troubles

Moawad's response is a telling indication that the epidemic of prettification that has struck Lebanon is but one of the ways in which social constraints and forces shape the lives of the country's women. As the Lebanese-American anthropologist Suad Joseph has suggested in a series of path-breaking works, personhood is always relational in Lebanon. In other words, individuals are never bounded entities, independent of others, but see themselves—and are seen—as bound up in a complex, tight skein of interpersonal relations, which define, sustain, and constrain them.[30] It is telling, for instance, that the identity documents of all Lebanese people—men and women alike—bear not just their own first names, but also that of their fathers. In this way, the name of the father marks the descent and place of each citizen in Lebanese society in the same way as the code printed on one's *hawiyya*, or identity card, that enables the authorities to identify a citizen as belonging to a particular confessional community. But women's lives bear a particularly strong patriarchal imprint, which marks the everyday in manifold ways. To take but one example, unmarried women must, by the letter of the law, receive written permission from their fathers if they wish to cross the border unaccompanied. (For married women, it is their husband who takes over this supposed duty of care.)

This unevenness, this inequality between men and women is even more apparent in Lebanon's nationality laws. For women do not possess the capacity to pass their nationality on to their children, even when these are born on Lebanese soil. In other words, the child of a foreign father and a Lebanese mother cannot be Lebanese, whereas the child of a Lebanese father and a foreign mother can acquire full citizenship. (As, indeed, can his mother, who can be naturalised as the spouse of a Lebanese national.) Political belonging, then, remains strictly patrilineal: children can only inherit membership of the Lebanese nation, and all the rights that come with it, from their fathers. Unsurprisingly, this has led to concerted efforts on the part of civil society organisations such as the *hamlat al-jinsiyya*, or 'nationality campaign', to push for a change in the law. The campaign has resorted to various methods, from recruiting lawyers such as Fadi Karam, the secretary-general of the National Commission for Women's Affairs, to lobby the government on its behalf, to organising peaceful demonstrations like that it held in January 2013 near the presidential palace in Baabda to coincide with a cabinet session under the slogan *jinsiyyati haqq li wa li-usrati*—'my nationality is my right, and my family's right'.

All this, though, has been to no avail. In 2009, the Lebanese judge John Azzi ruled that a Lebanese mother could pass on her nationality to her children, but his decision was overturned at appeal. In April 2012, the National Commission for Women's Affairs, under the presidency of Wafaa Sleiman, Lebanon's first lady, proposed a new nationality law that would rectify the gender imbalance between men and women. But, Karam warned, any change would take years.[31] In December 2012, the country's Constitutional Commission ruled against any modification to the nationality law, arguing that it would pose a threat to the 'national interest'.[32] In January 2013, the then-prime minister, Najib Mikati, promised to bring the issue to cabinet and, just as importantly, to ignore the ministerial committee's recommendations. But, despite such assurances, the cabinet did not discuss the matter, and the status quo remained.[33] In November 2015, the Future Movement again attempted to raise the issue, arguing that a mooted law setting out the procedures by which the descendants of Lebanese migrants could 'recover' their nationality should include a clause permitting Lebanese women to pass on their nationality to their children. However, it was again forced to abandon the matter in the face of concerted opposition from Lebanon's Christian parties and alarmist reports that the number of Lebanese women married to foreign men had risen to 'frightening'—*mukhifa*—levels since 2012, with the influx of Syrian refugees and Palestinian refugees from Syria.[34] Once again, xenophobia, populism, and electoral self-interest combined to stall legislative change.

This refusal to grant women rights is, ultimately, born of anxiety and a deep-seated fear of upsetting Lebanon's sectarian system. All the men called upon to legislate on women's rights agree that gender equality is an important principle in the abstract. For Azzi, 'men and women should be treated equally in all matters'.[35] Karam deplored the 'discrimination' that Lebanese women faced, asking why it was 'not in the Lebanese state's higher interest to forbid Lebanese men married to foreigners to pass on their nationality to their children'.[36] The Constitutional Council, too, was happy to concede this point. But its members argued that 'the principle of equality enshrined in the constitution cannot be applied in the presence of legal circumstances to which the implementation of [this principle] would be detrimental, or when it would harm the [state's] higher interest'. For any change to

Lebanon's nationality laws to ensure equality between men and women would cause 'great damage to the demographic balance between confessions', to 'representation', and, therefore, to the 'division of powers between the executive and legislative branches of government'. This was particularly so in light of the figures provided by the Ministry of the Interior, which revealed that a not insignificant portion of those who would benefit from this measure would be Palestinians.[37]

This, then, is but one example of the way in which 'political sectarianism'—al-ta'ifiyya al-siyasiyya, as the Lebanese call the web of discourses and practices that seek to enforce observance of the confessional order—works its way into the everyday, affecting in profound ways the lives of women like Ghada Kaakani. In the early 1970s, Kaakani, a Lebanese national, met and fell in love with Bassam Al Hidiq, a young Palestinian refugee whose family had taken up residence in Saida in 1948. The two married and went on to have four children—two sons and two daughters. While their daughters have now married Lebanese men, and have acquired Lebanese nationality through their husbands, the couple's sons are still Palestinian refugees; caught in this legal no-man's-land, they must rely on the travel documents issued by the Lebanese state to leave or enter the country. As Kaakani put it in stark terms: 'It's not fair. I am Lebanese'; it was 'painful' and incomprehensible to see her children deprived of the nationality she herself holds. As the scholar and activist Lina Bou Habib put it, Kaakani had been made an 'outcast', sanctioned for her failure to observe the codes of confessional comportment that undergird Lebanese law.[38]

But this is not the only way in which confessionalism and patriarchy still work together in contemporary Lebanon. For the country's bifurcated legal system places matters of criminal and civil law under the jurisdiction of the state, but leaves those relating to citizens' personal status to the religious courts administered by fifteen of the country's eighteen officially recognised confessional communities. It is in the interest of the latter to maintain this longstanding division of labour, for they derive from it not just significant financial benefits—in the form of the various administrative fees they receive for registering births, marriages and deaths and adjudicating in matters of inheritance and separation—but also considerable powers to police the comportment of those who fall under their remit. As a consequence, Lebanon's religious hierarchs exercise a vigilant watch over the work of the Council of Ministers and parliament, attempting to ensure that neither the executive nor the legislative branch of government oversteps the mark and traduces what they regard as their rights to determine what is permissible, and what is not, for those who fall under their oversight.

Under this peculiar set of provisions, the legal personality of all Lebanese citizens is effectively split down the middle. On the one hand, they are, at least in principle, equal under the law; they possess the same duties, if not the same rights, and face the same sanctions, irrespective of their religious beliefs and personal status. In this sense, the Lebanese state is, as Maya Mikdashi has argued, as much secular as it is sectarian.[39] On the other hand, however, Lebanon's citizens are drawn inexorably into an uneven force field of obligations and constraints, which differ according to their confessional status and the varying legal regimes to which they are perforce submitted. For their legal personhood is defined, in significant part, by their belonging to a familial unit headed up by a man, and this family's membership of a single confessional community.

Some have attempted to find a way out of these binds by requesting that all mention of their given confession be scratched out of their civil registers. As one Muslim woman, Zoubeida el-Hage, explained to a journalist, it was all she could do—short of converting, of course, though she did not mention this—to ensure that her daughter inherit her apartment.[40] But for all the efforts of civil society advocates and ordinary citizens to argue that this constitutes an escape from the cell of confessional belonging, freeing citizens finally rid of the shackles of religious law to breathe the clean air of the common law, the state refuses to see it as such. The Ministry of the Interior made this clear in February 2015, when it issued a statement insisting that removing a citizen's confession from the civil registers amounted to little more than 'hiding their belonging to one of the communities recognised by law' and 'in no way' constituted a 'departure from the religious community' in question.[41] It matters little, then, how particular men and women define themselves, or what they think they are achieving by undertaking this procedure; they could no more, in the eyes of the state, cease to be a Maronite, or a

Druze, or a Shia, and to be treated as such, than the earth could cease to be round or the rivers to run downstream.

In the face of this obduracy, activists like those who head up Chaml—whose acronym stands for *shabab muwatinun la-'unfiyyun la-ta'ifiyyun*, or Non-Violent Non-Sectarian Citizenly Youth, in its English rendition—have long campaigned for the introduction of a 'Lebanese' personal status law, or even the creation a 'sixteenth confession' for those who refuse sectarian identification. On a Friday morning in mid-April 2015, a small group of about fifty demonstrators gathered in Martyrs' Square. All wearing carnations on their breasts or holding them in their hands to invoke love, they had come together at Chaml's behest to call for a Lebanese personal status law, which would provide a legislative framework on questions of 'marriage, ... children, adoption, [and] inheritance' for all citizens regardless of confession. As one of the demonstrators, Sandy Mteirek, who had been disowned by her Muslim family after marrying a Christian, explained: 'I do not want to belong to a religion, but to a country'. For Mazen Abou Hamdan, the head of Chaml, the issue was simple: the right to a personal status free of religious trappings was a 'fundamental' one, which had 'existed for seventy-nine years'; in the absence of a national law for all, the 'different religious communities had appropriated' the various procedures and ceremonies that mark out the lives of ordinary subjects.[42] In this, Abou Hamdan was not wrong. For as even the Ministry of the Interior acknowledged, the Lebanese state had set out, as far back as 1936, the conditions for the creation of 'communities regulated by the common law'—or, in other words, by civil law. All these communities had to do to gain official recognition was 'to present to the government a summary of their structures and moral and religious principles', which the state had to ensure did not pose a threat to 'public security, public morals, or the Constitution'. This, the ministry's statement explained, had simply not happened yet.[43] Quite how supposedly a-confessional communities, whose members were to be subject to civil law could, or should, be regulated by 'religious' principles, was a question the press statement left unanswered. In short, it still remains the case, even now, that one cannot be a full Lebanese citizen without also being a member of a confessional community.

This is a condition that, in some ways, places constraints on men and women alike. Perhaps most obviously, it frustrates those who wish to contract a civil marriage, whether because they want to marry 'out' of their sect or, more commonly, because they reject the structures of imposed sectarian identity and wish to make a public statement of their 'secularism'. Some have attempted in recent years to demonstrate that it is possible to contract a civil marriage on Lebanese territory, drawing on a particular reading of the 1936 law to support their case. In 2012, a young couple, Khouloud Succariye and Nidal Darwiche, drew much attention when they announced that they had been married legally by a judge in Chiyah, in the southern suburbs of Beirut. All they had to do, they explained to the journalists who came clamouring to their door, was to request from their respective *mukhtar*-s—the men responsible for keeping their civil registers in order—that they erase their confessions—Sunni in his case, Shia in hers—from the records. In 2013, their marriage was officially recognised as legally binding in a decree signed by the then-minister of the interior, Marwan Charbel.[44] But, after two years of hopeful insistence that their case had set a precedent, during which dozens of other couples had followed their lead, the Ministry of the Interior ruled in 2015 that it was no more than an exception, which had done nothing to change the legal status quo. Civil marriages could not be registered in Lebanon. It was in this context that Nohad Machnouq, Charbel's successor as minister of the interior, argued that erasing one's confession from the civil registers was meaningless, for it did no more than disguise an inherent, indelible fact of one's being. It was only possible to have a civil marriage in Lebanon, Machnouq concluded, if one belonged to a community regulated by civil law—an untested innovation in Lebanese law.[45]

It is still the case, then, that the only option available for those who do not want a 'religious' marriage is to head abroad—most often flying the short distance to Cyprus to get married before the civil authorities in Nicosia, before returning to Lebanon where husband and wife can celebrate their wedding with friends and family. Indeed, so common are these marriages that a host of travel agencies now offer matrimonial package tours to Cyprus, Turkey, Greece, or even Italy. For $1,480, for instance, Kurban Travel will take in hand marriage arrangements in Cyprus, a fee that goes up to $2,160 if the couple wants to travel to Santorini for the occasion. Five Star Tours, meanwhile, charges $900 for its services, though this fee does not include travel tickets, visas, and the requisite documentation. (Quite what it does cover is not clear.)[46]

However, even those unions contracted abroad still need to be recognised by the Lebanese authorities before the couple's marriage can be declared legal. This is a long and complex procedure, which begins with a visit to the Lebanese Ministry of Foreign Affairs to legalise the marriage certificate issued by the Cypriot authorities. Once this is done, the couple must return to Cyprus to submit their legalised marriage certificate to the Lebanese embassy in Nicosia, along with notarised extracts of the passports and individual and family civil registers of both husband and wife—the documents that provide confirmation of their legal personhood and familial status. After the embassy has processed these documents—which takes about a month or so—the couple must obtain their documents, which are passed on, once again, to the Ministry of Foreign Affairs, the Ministry of the Interior, and the two *mukhtar*-s in whose office the documents of husband and wife are respectively held. Only at the end of this drawn-out bureaucratic circuit can the couple obtain a Lebanese marriage certificate, and a new *ikhraj qayd ʿaʾili*, or family extract of civil registration.[47]

This, it goes without saying, is a bewilderingly difficult trail of procedures. That is, of course, part of the point—but only part. For there is really no need to discourage those who want to marry abroad, apart from perhaps to preserve the economic benefits of these celebrations for the home country. Just as one cannot be a Lebanese citizen without also belonging to a sect, one cannot get married without the recognition of sectarian authorities. These various stages are deemed necessary because the marriage must be verified by the two arms of the state, the secular and the sectarian. This is why all these documents, after their long journey through the circuits of the everyday state, end up back on the desks of their *mukhtar*-s. Though these men are nominally agents of the state, they are tasked above all else with keeping in order all the documents that pertain to the personal status of Lebanon's citizens. Their primary role, then, is to ensure the good functioning of the bureaucratic apparatus that makes sectarianism work, and they play a central role in the procedures by which foreign marriages receive the recognition of the Lebanese state. The first documents that the bride and groom must obtain, before they even leave for Cyprus, are the extracts of their civil register, which the *mukhtar* will provide. These define them as persons by the name of their father, the place of their birth, and, crucially, by the confessional community to which they belong. Some months later, the process ends, again in the *mukhtar's* office, with the creation of an entry in the civil register for the newly married couple. This, too, is not simply confirmation that they are married, but also that they continue to take up a particular place in the sectarian order inscribed in the registers and files that the *mukhtar*-s keep in their offices. In other words, at no point on their Kafkaesque journey through the entrails of the state can the couple ever hope to escape the strictures of sect. There is no civil marriage in Lebanon, and no getting away from confession. But as much as this set of procedures may inconvenience or trouble the prospective husband, there is no avoiding the fact that it has far greater consequences for his wife.

Henceforth, she is known to the state, not only as her father's daughter, but first and foremost as her husband's wife. Her civil register is moved to the offices of her husband's *mukhtar*, and her personal status—should they be of different confessions—is now that of her husband. At no point, then, can she possess an entirely independent legal existence as a fully individuated citizen. Rather, she remains a person whose limited legal standing is tied up in her relations to the men about her. In short, this bureaucratic process is the manifestation of a patriarchal desire to police the conduct of women, to constrain them even while allowing husbands and fathers and religious authorities the freedom to watch over them and dictate their behaviour.

This became apparent during the ill-tempered exchanges that broke out in 2011 over the mooted law on domestic violence, which had passed through the committee stage that year. In June, Dar al-Fatwa, the body which oversees the internal matters of the Sunni community, ruled that the draft law posed a threat to Islamic personal status law, 'endangered the traditional family unit', and 'took powers away from the Islamic courts'. Though the Mufti of the Republic, Muhammad Rachid Kabbani, claimed that the law 'refused certain rights to the Muslim woman which were granted to her by the Islamic courts' and ran contrary to the 'values of our society' in its desire to 'conform to Western standards', his principal objection was to what he regarded as the unwarranted criminalisation of matters that had hitherto been deemed private concerns firmly beyond the remit of the secular state. The police, Dar al-Fatwa insisted, had no right to intervene in the realm of the family. Women could not and should not provide evidence against men. And, most grievously, the state had no right to 'invent new crimes' such as marital rape, which the law sought to make a prosecutable offence.[48] Mufti Kabbani was not alone in casting the proposed law as a potential cause of moral collapse, an explosive device that would splinter the Islamic family. Parliamentarians like Imad al-Hout, a deputy of the Jamaa al-Islamiyya, the Lebanese branch of the Muslim Brotherhood, shared his misgivings. In 2011, Hout, a member of the sub-committee charged with drafting the law on domestic violence, explained to a journalist that while he 'acknowledge[d] there is such a thing as marital rape', he feared that rates of divorce would increase should it be made a criminal offence, as abused women would hurry to leave their abusive husbands. Far preferable to this would be a search for alternative remedies. 'We would rather', he continued, 'the family resort to counselling and other services that we provide before leading to divorce'.[49] In this view, sex without consent was an issue like any other, one that might be talked out before the parties reconciled, rather than a grave injury to a woman's body, psyche and very sense of self. It was not, in other words, a crime for the courts to prosecute, but a matter best left to the wisdom and insight of Islamic judges and scholars.

When it eventually arrived, a few weeks later, the response of the law's backers proved sharp. In a carefully drafted press release, the president of the Council of the Lebanese Woman, Amane Kabbara Chaarani, rebutted each of Mufti Kabbani's points. 'It is no longer possible', she argued, 'to ignore violence against women within the family. … In the absence of a law protecting them from domestic violence, women will always hesitate to ask for a dignified life'. In the face of the Mufti's denial of 'economic violence', Chaarani asked 'what the imams have to say on the many husbands who take their wives' wages and belongings, and threaten to repudiate them or deprive them of their children if they do not hand them over'. Dismissing as senseless his claim that marital rape did not exist, she insisted that 'the draft law does not invent new crimes, but speaks of crimes that exist in numerous families and that have been recognised in your own sharia courts', before reeling off the details of several marital rape cases.[50] Chaarani was not alone in her efforts.

Kafa—'enough'—or Enough Violence and Exploitation, to give it its English name, the organisation that had initiated efforts to draft a new law on domestic violence in 2007, stepped up its campaign for the criminalisation of marital rape in 2010, pursuing a two-pronged approach. It continued to work closely with politicians already sympathetic to its cause—men like the lawyer Ibrahim Najjar, the new minister of justice, whose other reformist causes included the abolition of the death penalty, and Ziad Baroud, the new minister of the interior, like Najjar a lawyer, but also a well-liked and charismatic spokesman on issues dear to the hearts of civil society activists, like electoral reform. But knowing that this would not be enough, it strove to raise the political profile of its cause, hoping to persuade—or shame—parliamentarians into supporting its efforts to reform Lebanon's outdated and invidious domestic violence laws. It announced that 25 November, the International Day for the Elimination of Violence Against Women, would henceforth be marked in Lebanon, and it launched a highly provocative advertising campaign. A simple image showed two hands gripping bedsheets, knuckles white, a wedding band conspicuously in view. It was accompanied by an equally stark message. 'Oh deputies', it began, 'marital rape is also a crime. The law represents you'—literally, *al-qanun suratakum*, or the law is your image—'do not distort or mutilate the law to protect women against familial violence'.

Despite such bold initiatives, it took another three years for Law 293, for the 'protection of women and other members of the family from domestic violence', to be voted through parliament on 1 April 2014. In the event, the final draft represented a considerably weakened version of the original proposal. The section relating to victims of domestic violence spoke of 'the family' in general, rather than women and children in particular; the law did not discriminate between minors and children who had already reached adulthood; any charges or requests for protection, regardless of the urgency of the case, had to be taken to the relief judge, who could only be reached on weekday office hours, rather than the prosecuting judge, available at all hours; the law made no provision for circumstances in which a couple might be separated, divorced, or cohabiting, but dealt only with cases of violence within the family, defined as a legal unit centred upon a man and wife; and the new text envisioned punishment only for the bodily harm a husband might have caused while demanding his 'conjugal rights', rather than for forcing his wife to have intercourse without consent. By failing to mention the matter of consent, the law denied the very possibility of marital rape, effectively defining the issue as one of assault.[51] This appeared the most troublesome omission of all, a weak-spined concession to the pressures exerted by Dar al-Fatwa, with its stated desire to protect its own legal prerogatives and exert control over all domestic matters. To add insult to injury, none of the seventy-one deputies who had undertaken to air Kafa's concerns in parliament spoke during the session, acquiescing meekly when the president of the chamber, Nabih Berri, moved to vote on the draft law.[52]

In the end, civil society activists and lawyers agreed that the law—full of sloppy wording, deliberate omissions, and procedural slips—was difficult both to interpret and implement. In particular, the provisions for granting protection orders to women were simply not fit for purpose. In August 2014, Leila Awada, a lawyer working with Kafa, reeled off a number of cases that she had dealt with in the four months since the law's introduction, all of which highlighted its inconsistencies and lacunae. In one case, a Syrian man was arrested for beating his wife on a Friday. Normally, the organisation would have had to wait until the following Monday, and the return of the relief judge to work, to present its request for judicial protection, by which time the husband, having already been in custody for forty-eight hours, would have been released without charge and free to return to the family home. It was only by chance, Awada stressed, that the judge had been working that Saturday, and agreed to grant a judicial protection order out of hours. Had legislators placed protection orders in the hands of the prosecutor's office, no such confusion or delay could occur, and the victim's request could have been granted on her initial visit to the police station to report what had happened to her. In another case, when a wife obtained a judicial protection order against her husband, who had beaten her so badly she had been forced to spend a lengthy spell in hospital, he in turn succeeded in obtaining a protection order against her, alleging that her shouts and screams were a form of abuse and that she had once bitten his hand. (Whether she did so to ward off his blows he did not care to mention.) A case such as this, Awada stressed, under-lined the absurdity of a law that covered all instances of violence within the family. The principle might have seemed generous, but in practice it led only to abuse.[53]

A similar sense of incompleteness has plagued the other victories that campaign groups have secured in recent years, such as the abrogation of Article 522 of the penal code, which allowed a rapist to be spared pun-ishment if he agreed to marry his victim. (She had no say in the matter.) Once again, Kafa and other organisations like Abaad had used bold, provocative tactics to draw the attention of the media and the public to the issue and to coax and shame politicians into action. In December 2016, Abaad had staged a rally outside parliament, whose stark simplic-ity seemed drawn from the repertoire of performance art. Twelve women in wedding dresses stood silently, their hands wrapped up in binds and sullied with blood. One had her eyes bandaged—all at once a mocking invocation of justice and its absence, of the state's apparently wilful blindness, of the violence of rape and of the utter lack of agency of those forced to marry their abusers.[54] Such methods appear to have worked, for on 16 August 2017, parliament voted to strike out Article 522. Kafa was quick to point out, however, that this was only a 'partial achievement', for articles 505 and 518 remained in place. While the first of these provides the rapist of a child aged between fifteen and eighteen with a choice between prosecution and marriage, the second compels a man who has taken a minor's virginity to marry her. The abolition of Article 522 was a victory, no doubt, but one that did not eliminate entirely the possibility of compulsory marriage in cases of the statutory rape or 'deflowering'—*fadd al-bakara*—of a minor.[55] Even Jean Oghassabian, the—male—minister for women's rights, conceded that he had 'reservations' about the failure to abrogate articles 505 and 518, insisting that 'there can be no exception allowing [the perpetrator] to escape the sanctions provided by law in cases of rape'.[56] As Oghassabian tacitly acknowledged, the law as it stands still ignores the rights, needs, and wishes of the woman, while perversely presenting her abuser with the option of marrying his victim.

In such circumstances, it is unsurprising that assaults, sexual assaults, and murders of women continue to occur with grim frequency. In July 2013, Roula Yacoub, a 32-year-old woman from the town of Halba, in northern Lebanon, was beaten to death by her husband, Karam al-Bazzi. His blows were so violent, a coroner reported, that they had ruptured the cervical artery. Al-Bazzi fled with the couple's five children, all girls.[57] In February 2014, Manal Assi was beaten to death by her husband, Mohammad al-Nhaily, in their Beirut home. She had tried to divorce him after he had taken a second wife. He had responded only by telling her, 'you will only leave me [when you are] dead'. When he told her he was planning to get married a third time, a violent row broke out. Mohammad called Manal's mother, telling her to come pick up her daughter's 'body'. When her mother arrived in the company of two of her other daughters, he threw one daughter out and locked the other into his apartment with her mother, forcing them to watch as he continued to beat Manal. Only after having turned two ambulances away did he agree to take Manal to hospital. It was too late.[58] That same month, 31-year-old Christelle Abou Chacra died of poisoning after ingesting Demol, a pesticide. Her parents accused her estranged husband of poisoning her. Fourteen months earlier, she had fled their home; taking up refuge with her parents, she had begun divorce proceedings and sought legal advice from Kafa.[59] In March of the same year, 24-year-old Roukaya al-Mounzer was shot to death by her husband in the Beirut suburb of Burj al-Barajneh. She was pregnant.[60] In November, the body of Nisrine Rouhana was found on the shores of Nahr Ibrahim, the river that runs through Kisrwan. She had been shot to death. Two days after the discovery of her remains, her husband confessed to her murder. Nisrine had lived through long years of abuse.[61] Each of these deaths has been greeted the same way in the press and on social media, with appeals for the violence to end, for stern punishment, for legislative reform.

But still the violence does not end. In August 2017, the body of 26-year-old Raya Chidiac was found in the village of Miziara, in the north-east of the country. She had been beaten, raped, and strangled to death.[62] When her family's Syrian doorman was arrested and charged after confessing, local inhabitants were quick to call for the expulsion of all Syrian workers from the region. One woman told a journalist that she thought the murderer should be 'tortured the same way as he tortured the young woman' before being put to death. Her husband agreed. He thought the murderer should be executed on the steps of the village church, and all other Syrians banished. 'We can no longer trust them', he concluded.[63] But if some pine only for retribution and racist collective punishment, others have taken a more dignified stance. When four women—including the British diplomat Rebecca Dykes, raped and murdered by an Uber driver who picked her up after a night out—were killed in the space of five days between 13 and 18 December 2017, campaigners held a candle-lit vigil on the steps of the national museum on 23 December. Under the slogan 'It could have been me', with its echoes of the viral appeals of the #metoo campaign, the organisers read out a joint statement, which the journalist Kareem Chehayeb recorded on Twitter: 'you are 4 of thousands of victims of male violence … we reject claims that these incidents are … rare occurrences … it is not enough to ask for security forces to apprehend [the perpetrators] or to ask for harsher punishments'. Rather, it was time to reject 'victim-blaming' and 'narratives' that insisted 'not all men' were to blame, and to address head-on the insidious workings of 'patriarchy and sexism'.[64] Beneath images mounted on easels of the four dead women, women sat in silence holding their candles.[65] Others chanted: 'Don't tell me to be careful, tell him not to harass me'.[66] This message was reiterated in the organisers' comments to journalists. 'The crimes of the last week', they said, 'prove that there is no safe space for women. We suffer daily from various forms of discrimination, violence, and aggression', manifestations of 'systematic male violence' which 'society refused to see' until 'our blood is spilt and our bodies found on the side of the road'.[67] The very next day, Christmas Eve, the newspapers reported that another young woman had been killed by her husband. Her name was Malak M. She was twenty-three, and she had been stabbed to death. Her body bore the traces of other blows.[68] This is the bitterest, saddest manifestation of Lebanon's gender troubles and the profound fixation with femininity, its attractions, its dangers and constraints that runs through the country's laws and leisure spaces.

The beach

The nightclub offers perhaps the best means of examining the ways in which the inhabitants of Lebanon, these participants in an economy of display, abide by pervasive understandings of gender—norms that are enshrined in laws, but that also shape and restrict personal conduct and subjectivity. But it is telling that other sites of sociability have become more like the nightclub in recent years, in a creeping colonisation of the daytime by nocturnal forms of leisure. This is the case of the nation's beaches and sea resorts, these gated estates that have colonised Lebanon's littoral since the 1960s, reservations of pleasure that treat the shoreline as a private commodity to be parcelled out in contravention of laws that consider it to be public land. It is telling that so many of them should have sprouted up during the civil war, when the casual privatisation of public goods became the norm. But this take-over has continued apace in recent decades. A report drawn up in 2012 by the Ministry of Public Works identified 390 'unlicensed encroachments on the beach and sea' in the Governorate of Mount Lebanon alone. A further thirty-three 'installations'—most of them resorts—had obtained licences of doubtful legality, which they had gone on to breach by exceeding the area on which they were allowed to build. In total, 162,383 square metres of land, and another 1,651,707 square metres of reclaimed sea, had been taken into private hands and built over.[69]

Just how much is at stake here is evident from the repeated attacks on activists and journalists who have attempted to record these violations. One of the most recent of these occurred in June 2017, when a television crew from LBCI began filming an interview with the environmentalist Mona Khalil, who has established a turtle reserve in the small southern village of Mansouri, now threatened by the construction of a new beach complex. Not long after their arrival on the beach to film an interview with Khalil, an unknown man ran towards the crew, knocking over the cameraman, Samir Baitamouni, before punching him and insulting him. He then turned to Khalil, screaming at her that he would 'light tyres outside your house today on the orders of the Hizb', or Hizballah, 'and the Harke', or Amal. 'Get the fuck out of here', he shouted at the camera crew and the gathered onlookers around, 'I'll stick my dick in your sister's cunt'. The journalist Sobhiyya Najjar recorded the entire brutal attack on her mobile phone, even while imploring the assailant to stop.[70]

But the wild development of Lebanon's littoral has also brought with it other forms of violence. For in their rush to colonise the coastline, real estate developers have often thought little of destroying older, more demotic forms of leisure. This is apparent from the ongoing controversies around the construction of new complexes on Beirut's shorelines. In July 2014, the developer Wissam Achour formally launched his new foray, the Eden Rock Resort, at a grand ceremony attended by the minister of tourism, Michel Pharaon. This 'sanctuary of luxury and refinement', scheduled for completion in 2018, would group together a '22-storey' skyscraper of 'sea view residences', a 'five-star hotel' and 'chalets and cabins by the beach', stretching over 22,295 square metres of 'Beirut's coast'.[71] What the speeches and promotional press releases did not mention was that this new development would occupy a prime position on Beirut's only remaining public beach, Ramlet al-Baida. Though only a small portion of this long strip of white sand is owned by the Lebanese state and the municipality of Beirut, it has been regarded for generations as by right and custom the property of the city's people, who have long used it to 'swim and play and stay out late', in the words of one local resident. As Ali Darwish, the head of the environmental group Green Line, pointed out: 'Ask any older Beiruti [over] 50 or 60 and they won't even know that this is [privately] owned. It's enshrined, it's anchored in our brains that this is public land'.[72]

And yet, local inhabitants and activists have been able to do little about Achour's quiet accumulation of land on the seafront. Since 2011, he has acquired not just the substantial plots that have now been transformed into a vast building site, but also a further 30,265 square metres 'that stretch across much of Ramlet al-Baida'. The assurances of Manal Dana, Achour's marketing manager, that 'the land will be renovated so people can go down on clean sand without any garbage … But there will not be any towers on it, it will not be constructed, this area', can hardly have quelled the anxieties of residents and activists, particularly when she spoke of 'small fees to preserve' the beach, just 'like in Europe'.[73] Just as disquieting, for many, are signs that the project has exceeded even the remit of the building permit granted by the governor of Beirut, Ziad Chbib. In late June 2017, the president of the Order of Engineers and Architects, the well-respected architect Jad Tabet, compiled a report detailing eight breaches of building regulations, from the damage to maritime public property caused by building work and sewage outflow to zoning irregularities and attempts to increase the total area under construction by describing, in a piece of creative labelling on the masterplan, the complex's ground floor as part of the basement.[74] Since the work began in early 2015, those opposed to the transformation of Ramlet al-Baida into a private enclave have deployed all their considerable acumen as activists. Their campaign has combined bold action on the ground to document violations, demonstrations to manifest their discontent, and recourse to assistance from on high. For like other civil society movements, the campaign has seen no choice but to enlist the support of concerned ministers and sympathetic institutional actors. Tabet's report, for instance, was prepared using army topographic maps and aerial photographs supplied by the Ministry of Defence—and resort to the country's courts, using the skills of practised lawyers such as Nizar Saghieh, the executive director of the campaign group Legal Agenda. Though they have not succeeded in stopping the work, they have prevented developers from enclosing the beach, shutting it off to public access.[75]

In another recent victory, campaigners have also secured from the municipality of Beirut a commitment to undertake a review of land-use in the area running from Ramlet al-Baida to the Mövenpick Hotel, owned by the disgraced Saudi prince Walid Bin Talal. This is the area known locally as the Dalieh, where for decades working-class Beirutis have gathered to enjoy a few hours of leisure. Owned for much of this period by a number of local Sunni families, such as the Daouk and the Itani, this land was acquired in the mid-1990s by the Hariri family. But this change of ownership meant little to those who lived and fished on this rocky promontory, for whom it remained a shared property, enjoyed in common by the people of the city. All this changed in mid-2014, when a fence was put up around the site—first the posts, then a few days later netting and barbed wire, and then finally another layer of barbed wire atop the fence. As the journalist and activist Habib Battah noted wryly, all this made the area 'look more like Guantanamo Bay than a place for a sunset stroll'.[76] Once again, campaigners and local residents were quick to spring into action. When it was announced that the Dutch architectural superstar Rem Koolhaas had been commissioned to design a plan for the development of this site, the Civil Coalition for the Protection of the Dalieh of Beirut, established in 2013 to protect the rights of fishermen threatened with eviction, wrote an open letter detailing all the ways in which this project ran against the public good. Built on land acquired illegally, the project would destroy a 'unique ecosystem' and archaeological site. But just as importantly, it would serve only the 'narrow interests of an elite group of politicians and real-estate developers', depriving 'Beirut dwellers' and 'Lebanese citizens' of 'an important social space and a national landmark'.[77]

With the site's enclosure and development, it would no longer be open to the Beirutis who had come down for generations to enjoy the sea breeze and cook barbecues on the shore, or to the swimmers who gathered every morning to make their way through its caves and inlets; the divers whose swallow leaps into the deep blue have been captured in generations of photographs; the foreign tourists who came here from the expensive hotels around to take boat rides around the Pigeon Rock, that iconic representation of Beirut and Lebanon reproduced on postcards and banknotes; the yoga group who came together every morning at 6:00 a.m. to practise by the sea; or, Beirut's Kurdish community, whose members had used the Dalieh to celebrate Nowroz, or new year, since the 1980s.[78] All these forms of enjoyment would disappear. But so too would the way of life of the fishermen who had lived and worked on this promontory for generations, creating a cooperative to maintain their small vessels and the wooden sheds they had built to store their nets. For men like Abu 'Abd al-'Itani and Abu Husain, whose stories of Dalieh were recorded by the architects, artists and activists, Abir Saksouk-Sasso, Tania el-Khoury, Petra Serhal, and Nadine Bekdache, this was all they had. As Abu 'Abd explained:

> We were known for fishing here in this area and going about the street selling fresh fish all across Lebanon ... I've lived here forty-five years and I've brought nine children into the world and I still have chicken and pigeons and dogs. ... One time, I was offered an apartment in exchange for my hut. Of course I refused. What am I, an idiot? What would I do in a flat? My whole life is here.[79]

Along with the quantitative explosion in the number of seafront projects has come a qualitative change in their nature. For these complexes, whose cascading 'chalets' and warrens of walkways and sudden openings are oddly reminiscent of the modernist ziggurats of social housing dotted through north London, have undergone a remarkable transformation in recent years. I remember running about one of them for hours as a young child, chasing my cousins across lawns and around swimming pools, and nibbling on chips and fried cauliflower florets doused in lemon juice and salt. When I returned to the place as an adult, it was no longer the quiet playground that I had known. The children were still about, of course, their irrepressible kinetic force multiplied by generous helpings of ice cream and candyfloss. But now their laughter and shrill cries of delight were half-submerged by the constant din of dance music. The men still sat about, chipping away distractedly at sunflower seeds with their front teeth as they sipped Lebanese pilsner and played backgammon, their faces still with studied concentration, the tension signalled by the rapid rattle of rosary beads through nervy fingers. The women still talked away, some shielding their faces under vast sunhats and splodges of sun-cream like cricketers on tour, while others boldly exposed their features to the sun. Teenagers still dive-bombed into the pool, treating the staccato trill of the lifeguard's whistle as invitation rather than reproach.

And yet, superimposed on this ordinary scene like some alien soundtrack was the dull, unchanging thud of Eurodance, ploddingly uninterested in deviating from its four-to-the-floor rhythm, but churning endlessly away like a steam train driving to its destination. And this is, in a sense, what this scene feels like—like people living in the noise cloud of a railway line, but who have grown so used to its industrial cacophony that they go about their daily intercourse as though it were not there, seeping through into their every moment. So incongruous is this contrast between the humdrum, unchanging pleasures of summer days and the weary, expectant hedonism of this music, so uncanny is the effect of this disjuncture, that it can feel like watching a home movie with the wrong soundtrack tacked onto it.

Why, then, play this music at all when so few seem to pay it any mind? One answer lies in a generalised obsession with youth, an inclination on the part of Lebanon's leisure entrepreneurs to cater to those who seem the very embodiment of vitality. Another can be found in the tendency of Lebanon's leisure industry to eschew simplicity, the ordinary and the tried-and-tested in favour of the expensive and the exceptional, believing they have glimpsed the future when they are only adopting features that already feel outmoded and shop-worn. For the owners of these resorts can seem at times like so many upwardly mobile curtain-twitchers, jealously keeping an eye on the neighbours, always trying to keep up with, and outdo, their competitors. If one successful or fashionable resort owner has chosen to stage a hostile takeover of the diurnal with the sounds and rhythms of night, then others must follow, emulating beaches and bathing complexes like Lazy B, known for their sophistication and sybaritic draw. In spatial terms, many of these newer resorts are strange assemblages that splice together features borrowed from the nightclub and the cruise ship. Firmly conceived of as adult spaces, they have their chill-out zones crowded with fake mahogany four-poster beds draped in white linen and their pool areas that serve as main rooms, the shallow water becoming a dancefloor in which to preen and gyrate, drink in hand, sunglasses on, their seafood restaurants, children's areas, and entertainment spaces. Each of these resorts must strive to have its own distinguishing features—in one, for instance, roman mosaics found on the site during digging were incorporated into a submerged cocktail bar set in the middle of the pool, history turned to kitsch for those who regard George Michael's performance in Club Tropicana as the very apex of refinement. But this too is a manifestation of the same logic that compels all to search for something that will make their place stand out from the crowd even while keeping to all its shared conventions.

The wedding

But nowhere is this universal striving for uniqueness—which succeeds only in creating more repetition and reiteration—and the striking desire to recreate the sensory experience of the nightclub more apparent than in the excessive, lavish wedding parties that have become the aspiration of so many Lebanese. Of course, weddings—both Christian and Muslim—have long been as much opportunities for ostentation as occasions for communion, for joy and relish in conjugal love, parental affection and filial piety. And they serve other purposes, too—a means of signalling the crafting of a new commercial or political alliance between families, or an attempt to replace the wiring of kith and kin, connecting two bits of one family. In such performances, the material—the dress and suit of bride and groom, the flowers in her hair and about the venue, the confetti and rice and petals, the quality of the spread laid out for the dozens and hundreds of guests—matters. It is

345

cause for pride and embarrassment, for performances of impression and harsh whispers of gossip.

But a change has come about of late. The wedding is no longer simply, in contemporary Lebanon, a means of underscoring a union or restating the importance of a conjunction of feeling and kin and interest, but an end in itself—something that matters in its own right, in and for itself, as a social performance, a way of signalling status and discernment. The wedding—rather than the marriage itself—has seen its importance grow as a short-term investment of social capital, a high-stakes bet which, if well executed, can lead to generous returns for the bride and groom and their families. They will be seen as people of taste and means, fun people who put on a good party for those around them. And this suggests, too, that for some the wedding is also a masque—an occasion to slip for a short while out of the bounds of everyday existence, with its constraints and drudgery, and to become the central actors of a familiar play. In this sense, these products of the aspirational imagination have increasingly short-term effects: they are there to impress, to be remarked upon, to be recorded on social media, to be ranked against the dozens of other weddings that litter the night skies with fireworks and dance music all through the summer months, as much as to serve longer-term purposes. It is not for nothing that so many weddings nowadays have their own Instagram feeds and hashtags and invitation websites and Facebook pages—archives of ersatz joy, short-term stimuli there to garner as many likes and hits as possible before slipping into quiet oblivion, forgotten by all until, perhaps, an algorithm throws them back into view with the coming of an anniversary.

For, like the scenes played out in the clubs and bars of Beirut, Batroun, and Jbeil, there is something hyperreal about these weddings. They accentuate conventional features of the ordinary world—over-emphasising gender roles in particular, as though bride and groom were characters in a crude comedy of manners. The groom must be sleek, suave, the very picture of an outmoded cinematic kind of sophistication in his glossy dinner suit, with his resplendently slicked back hair reflecting the strobe lights. The suit may be a little bit too tight, stretched beyond comfort by excess fat or surplus muscle, the sure signifiers of time to oneself and money to spare. The bride, for her part, must resemble the kind of sugar confection that sits atop a wedding cake. Encased in a shining assemblage of sequin and lace, a rigid frame that moulds her body into an hourglass frame, she is weighted down with an array of jewels, her hair solid with spray, her face frozen and concealed beneath a mask of powder and eye-shadow. But there is often one disquieting detail in this picture of connubial perfection—a disjuncture between the curves the dress suggests, and the breastbones that jut through above the décolleté. For the bride is often so thin, these days, as to resemble a child playing at dress-up in her mother's clothes. I remember attending one ceremony in which the bride had lost so much weight because of her crash diet that her dress—already taken in once—no longer fit her on the day; slipping off her bony frame, it had to be held up with safety pins. She spent much of the day clutching at it with one hand while she went about absent-mindedly greeting well-wishers and swirling to the music. This unresolved aesthetic contradiction between the Botticelli-like, desirable figure suggested by this fabric frame and the bride's own diminished, unwell, waif-like body is not the only jarring note. It is often heightened by the age difference between bride and groom—an inevitable consequence of Lebanon's particular demographic make-up and political economy. For both a gender ratio unusually favourable to men and economic conditions unusually unfavourable to social mobility mean that men often delay marriage until their late thirties or forties, when they have built up—or come into—the necessary capital. I can think of several such marriages. In at least one case, the bride had only recently broken up with someone her own age, a man ultimately deemed unsuitable for marriage because, though he had a nice car and an expensive watch and his own apartment, his position retained the insecurity of youth. In all these ways, aesthetic as well as material, contemporary Lebanese weddings seem to accentuate features of the ordinary—the expectations, the craving for status and acceptance and comfort, and the sense of life as a fragile thing, always one slip away from social discomfiture and economic crisis.

In other ways, however, the wedding marks an escape from the ordinary, a realm of absurd play that follows its own conventions. It is, for instance, de rigueur for some to have a *zaffe*, or sword-dancing display, or fireworks, strobes and a DJ, turning their wedding into a fantasia of village life or an attempt to have their very own private nightclub for an evening. Every night for a month, I would stand on my aunt's balcony, which overlooks the coastal highway from Beirut to the north and, beyond it, a thick glut of shops and restaurants and gyms and beach resorts leading all the way down to the shoreline, and watch the fluorescent strobes tear into the sky like cannons of light. After a while, the choreography became entirely predictable and I came to know when the fireworks would be launched, or when the DJ would drop one of the three tracks he came back to every night, the big tunes of the summer, songs whose breakdowns and choruses would be met with the same whoops and out-of-tune singing each night.

This is something that few who get married in Lebanon nowadays will acknowledge about their own ceremonies, though they are all too happy to say it about those of others: all these supposedly singular moments of joy, these special, exceptional confections, in many ways repeat each other, slight variations on an anodyne theme. Ultimately, they are the iterative products of late capitalist consumption, wares picked out from catalogues or calqued from social media and magazines.

Indeed, there are many who consciously attempt to emulate the opulent parties of the rich and famous, like the party thrown by PSP MP Ghazi Aridi—one of Walid Jumblatt's most trusted and longstanding right-hand-men—for the wedding of his son Omar to Rhea Hindi, herself, appropriately enough, an event planner. Many in the press and on social media derided the ceremony's fantastical cost, which they condemned as particularly unseemly in times of economic strife and suffering. (The bride's three dresses, all the work of the designer Rami Kadi, were rumoured to have cost $120,000.) Others, however, looked longingly at this display of expense, attempting to find things they could copy on a budget—perhaps the miniature recreation of Beiteddine palace from which the bride and groom appeared to greet their guests, like faded pop singers on a reunion tour, or the way the strobes fell across the dancefloor. They could turn for inspiration not just to websites like arabiaweddings.com, which provides pages after pages of 'real luxury weddings' and 'luxury wedding inspirations', but also to the site of Rhea Hindi's own company, FIFT15N, with its snapshots of 'mega production weddings' held in venues like BIEL or the ruins of the Sursock family's old palace, in the mountain town of Sofar—once a favourite summer spot for the moneyed classes of

Egypt, Iraq or Saudi Arabia, who flocked to its casinos, hotels, and cool night air.[80] Among these one finds, of course, Hindi's own wedding to Omar Aridi. Here again commerce and celebration are muddled together, and hedonistic excess and ostentation come to stand—or stand in—for joy and pleasure.

It is telling that while some choose to hold their festivities in a mountain monastery or church, or in the old family home up in their village, the better to underscore their humility, their attachment to their origins and fondness for family and home, many others prefer the apparent sophistication offered by beach complexes, hotels, or country clubs. And, for those who can afford them, weddings abroad in Mykonos or Santorini, Paris, St Tropez or Forte dei Marmi have become increasingly desirable. For these are destinations that signal distinction and 'prestige' while remaining familiar enough. This fashion for the foreign is in part a product of the 'security situation'—as so many call the sense of anxiety that stalks the Lebanese, ever fearful of another car bomb, another pitched gun battle in the streets, another assassination. As Nabil Baz, the founder of Promofair, an industry exhibition for events organisers, explained to a journalist: 'in this unstable context, it is difficult to plan in advance', and many venues that were fully booked in 2012 lay empty three years later.[81] Not only this, but there is the precedent set by celebrities like the pop singer Myriam Fares, who incorporated into one of her music videos images of her own 2014 wedding, in which she tied the knot with the Lebanese-American Danny Mitri on a glass pontoon launched across an infinity pool, so that the guests could watch them walk down the aisle towards the blue-tinted horizon.[82] The couple's second anniversary provided further opportunity for leveraging life moments into little nuggets of self-promotion. Returning to Santorini, Fares—chin up, head turned in a coquettish pose, lips pursed into a pout—posed in a variety of swimsuits and sun-hats against a background of cloudless blue skies, small basalt islands, and still seas, their immaculate cover broken only by the foam trail of a jet ski.[83] Life and commerce become entangled here. There is no privacy, no companionate intimacy. Rather, everything is to be shared. Each moment is an artefact, a tempting projection of pleasure and beauty and youth and abandon, carefully designed to draw in the viewer. Nothing is spontaneous or unconsidered; every gesture, every move is deliberate. The troubling thing, of course, is that such tactics for turning life into a performance of constant enjoyment and unfettered consumption are no longer the preserve of the famous. I recall one wedding held in an orchard, in which the branches of the apple trees were garlanded with small cut-out flowers and love hearts, each one inscribed with the wedding's hashtag, a small invitation to chronicle its unfolding on Instagram. It is not the moment that matters, but rather its digital alter ego, a hyperreal representation of frozen smiles, of catered dishes captured in soft focus and beautiful, unwilted flowers. It is in this other world that the event now exists, a scrolling slideshow of smartphone images out of which memories are made. The evanescent, addictive gratification of digital appreciation— of carefully tallied likes, of emoji hearts and laughing faces and unicorns—matters more than the moment itself.

Such extravagance does not come cheap. As one well-known wedding planner, Alain Hadifé, explained in 2014, 'the majority of weddings cost between 20,000 and 40,000 dollars ... but there are also many whose budget is as high as 100,000 dollars'. While Hadifé sought to insist on the rarity of weddings on which 'colossal sums, running into the millions, were spent', it is clear that what he might consider piddling sums remain substantial investments for the bulk of those seeking to tie the knot.[84] It is not surprising, then, that for many, weddings—like cars or new-build apartments, those other essential accoutrements of bourgeois comfort—lead to dependence on others: on gifts or loans from relatives or even from employers and political patrons, who are duly invited as guests of honour to the festivities and thanked in the speeches given by the parents of the bride and groom. Others have come to rely—at least in part—on the wedding loans that several Lebanese banks have introduced in recent years, like that offered by Banque Libano-Française, which offers a 'Wedding Package ... to finance all your wedding expenses with no concerns at all'. Customers can borrow up to $30,000 over a period of four years, repayable in forty-five monthly instalments at an APR of 12.76 per cent.[85] In similar fashion, Byblos Bank vaunts its own wedding loan as a means of providing 'the financing you need to make sure your big day will always be one to remember'. To enjoy the benefits of its loans—up to $20,000, at an APR of 13.996 per cent— applicants must demonstrate that they are Lebanese citizens, that they are under forty years old and in good health, that they have worked in the same field for at least two years, and that they have a monthly income of at least 900,000LL—or $600.[86] There is no point indulging in easy moralism, castigating those who depend on these loans for their discreditable profligacy. Such is the burden of expectations—familial and personal and social—that many feel obligated, regardless of their own circumstances, to replicate something of the ostentation they have seen elsewhere.

This conspicuous, ephemeral consumption—$50,000 or $100,000 burned away in a few hours of half-eaten bowls of hummus, discarded slices of wedding cake, first dances and perfunctory fireworks—draws some further into the webs of credit on which the Lebanese economy rests. For those who are canny or cynical enough, however, these inflationary tendencies present opportunities as well as risks. It has become increasingly common in recent years for the bride and groom to request cash gifts, instead of or alongside the white goods and crockery of the wedding list. The conventional justifications for this are not unsound. When real estate prices are so high, and salaries so stubbornly low, the newly married surely deserve a little helping hand. But some careful calculations and budgeting can allow the bride and groom to turn a profit, transforming the wedding into an occasion for speculation. Transactional, atomised, interested, these are the ways of contemporary Lebanon, that consumptive society dreaming feverish dreams of money and things.

The mall

It is Wednesday morning, on an intensely hot day in late September. Summer, it seems, shows no sign of fading. I am early for a family lunch and so, with an hour or so to kill, I deviate from my usual path through central Beirut into the renovated—or reinvented—souks opened in 2009. Perhaps it is because of the heat, or the fact that we are in the lull before lunch, that fallow hour in which restaurant parking valets and waiters loll about, chatting or scrolling through social media, but there is scarcely anyone about. A few men sit out at the terraces of the expensive cafés, drinking espresso while they read the paper or do the crossword, or conducting business meetings over an *arghileh*. In Souk al-Tawileh, the 'long market' that stretches out like a pointed arm from the centre of the city towards the sea, forming the nave of this new complex of consumption, there are only one or two young couples ambling with arms interlaced, whispering to each other and only occasionally looking in to this or that shop window. The shop hands sit idle. The odd tourist passes by, wearing that slightly dazed look peculiar to those who visit Beirut, like restaurant customers served the wrong main course. The jewellery souk, nestled behind the medieval Islamic scholar al-Uza'i's mausoleum, is even emptier. I find a bench to jot down a note or two. It is only after a few minutes that I realise the young woman sitting close by, in her smart white shirt and navy trousers and high heels, works in one these shops. She has given up hope of a customer passing through and abandoned her station, refocusing her energies on the mobile phone screen she is so intently examining.

Though I hate to admit it, there is something vaguely appealing about the architecture of the souks—and in particular the 'south souks', designed by the Spanish architect Rafael Moneo with his Lebanese counterpart Samir Khairallah. They are all openness and shade and light, the sun dappling the ground and creating a gentle chiaroscuro effect. And yet there is also a sense of disappointment about the place. Part of it is to do with the architecture itself, which seems to treat consumption as an act of veneration to be carried out in quiet, reflective stillness. But it is also to do with the fact that so many of the shops have been let to Western high street brands like Zara or Geox, giving the impression that beneath these high vaults, there is the most anodyne of shopping thoroughfares. And it is also that all of it is so empty, so motionless and stuck in a rut. By any standard, then, the place seems a failure. It is a desperate offence to those who oppose Solidere's vision for the central parts of Beirut and who long for the times when these alleyways and passages overflowed with people of all classes, here to buy vegetables or shirts, slippers, chocolate, coffee beans and Arabic sweets dripping with syrup, when the markets were spaces of encounter and surprise and collective enjoyment, owned and used by the multitudes. But it also cannot but be a disappointment to those who believed Solidere's broken promises of affluence, and who still continue to hope, perhaps, that the good years will return if only the demonstrators could be kept at bay, foreign meddling cease, and foreign investment return, men like Nicolas

Shammas, the president of the Beirut Traders' Association, who has transformed himself in recent years into a spokesman for the city's commercial enterprises, complaining of the deleterious effects of public sector pay rises, tax reforms, and ongoing political protests on the capital's central business district.

It was Shammas who, in late September 2015, when the demonstrations and sit-ins of the 'rubbish crisis' were still at their height, coined the awkward term Abu Rukhusa—roughly, 'Father Cheapness' or 'Mr Economy'—to describe the attempts of some to degrade and diminish the centre of city, destroying his dreams of an exclusive realm of affluence and expensive good taste. This was, he insisted, a 'commercial centre', which hosted 'the most important Lebanese banks, of which we are proud, the most prestigious restaurants and hotels, and the most excellent shops'. It was a 'point of pride' for Lebanon, and it was 'unacceptable' that it should be transformed into anything but a site of 'progress' and a 'meeting point for the entire Arab world'.[87] For all Shammas' attempts to insist he did not seek to single out any one social group, that he 'despised class warfare' and wished for the centre of Beirut to be truly open to all, a thriving commercial district in which Lebanese from all walks of life felt welcome, many remained unconvinced.[88]

The riposte was as sharp as it was rapid. Only three days after his press conference, Badna Nhasib—'we want accounts'—one of the two main groups spearheading the protests of those weeks, organised a Suq Abu Rukhusa, or Abu Rukhusa market, in Riyad al-Sulh Square, long a meeting-ground for demonstrators. This displayed all the plebeian qualities that Shammas appeared to despise. Some set their goods out on the bare ground; others transformed tables and planks of wood into makeshift stalls, selling freshly pressed fruit juices, plastic beakers of *hummus balila*, or whole chickpeas, and hot popcorn. Among the streetsellers were young designers and artists selling prints and CDs of their work. Nothing sold for more than a couple of thousand Lebanese lira—less than a dollar and a half—and many simply gave away free bags of crisps and unwanted clothes. This was a deliberate show of demotic defiance, harking back to the days when, as one passer-by put it, the neighbourhood was open 'to those of all classes [*mustawayyet*]'. Nowadays, this middle-aged man complained, one needed a *wasta*—or the intercession of a patron—to even gain access to the area.[89]

Demotic pleasures

And yet, amidst all these exclusive enclaves, there continue to exist other, fugitive, spaces. Though they almost seem defined by their fragility, their apparent ephemerality, these are places where Lebanese of different classes, but also Syrian or Palestinian refugees and Sri Lankan, Filipino or Nepalese migrant workers, can escape for a while to enjoy straightforward, relatively inexpensive forms of leisure, snatching a few moments of pleasure from the day. One evening in mid-September I went for a run on the Corniche, the long walkway that snakes along Beirut's seafront. It had been a few weeks since I had done any exercise, and I was starting to feel the toll of heavy food—hummus loaded with tahini, sweet, sugary white bread, meat doused in the sweet thick tang of pomegranate molasses. It was still hot, even after five o'clock. But I was determined to go just a little further, just a few hundred metres more—in part because I felt so slothful, the laziness and heat enrobing me like an added weight on my shoulders, but also because I was captivated by the motley crowd that had come down to the shoreline. There were a few Nike-suited denizens of the middle classes taking, like me, their evening constitutional—men stripped down to the waist, the better to reveal the small patches of hair in the small of their back, wearing nothing but Dayglo orange shorts and expensive shoes, and women in tight leggings whose elaborate patterns ran up their calves like fluorescent tattoos. One or two in the crowd ran determinedly, cussedly, as though to prove someone wrong. But many more walked, some barely strolling, others marching at a fast, nervous pace, a Bluetooth headset at the ready so that they could chat away or attend to their business while working out.

On the rocks below, fishermen cast their long rods into the dirty Mediterranean—old men who have been here for decades and have watched this sea blacken and grow more toxic, but who still come out, their muscles now withered, sagging slightly beneath their short-sleeved shirts, others in their twenties or thirties still full of the assuredness of youth, with their deep tans and garish swimming trunks. Groups of swimmers bobbed up and down in the waves. Others lolled, sunbathing and smoking their *arghileh* on the rocks, seemingly impervious to the thin film of scum that covered their surface. Loud, percussive Arabic pop music rang out, drifting up to the Corniche and intermingling with the shouts of the divers who plunged swallow-like from its metal barriers.

And then there were those who had come simply to be here—to stretch their legs for a little while or to lounge on one of the benches scattered along the seafront in a rare concession to publicness. Young men, their legs spread wide apart, who smoke cigarette after cigarette and drink Pepsi and ogle passing women with as much subtlety as they can muster. Syrian families—husbands and wives growing old together, who shyly take selfies against the sea and the sky, laughing at the audaciousness, the silliness of this brazen act, and young couples, whose toddlers run about as the parents, lean, delicate boys and girls who look barely out of their teens, look on indulgently. Domestic workers, Filipino and Nepalese and Ethiopian women dressed up in jeans skirts and boots, and walking along in laughing clusters of excitement, and one West African couple, her arm laced around him as he gazes absently at his mobile phone. As the political anthropologist Laleh Khalili has written, 'the distinguishing feature of promenading on the Corniche is that it is a form of leisure that requires no exchange of money'.[90] One can just be there, for free. There is no admission fee to enjoy its passing pleasures.

But even the forms of consumption that are on offer here are affordable. A strong Arabic coffee poured out of his copper pot by one of the *'ahwaji*-s, or coffee-sellers, who walk up and down, clinking their cups together to call for custom as they always have done; a cup of yellow lupin beans sitting in their brine, all texture and saline hit; a *ka'k*, or sweet sesame bread lathered in Picon cream cheese—all can be bought here for a dollar or less, a fraction of the prices in the Starbucks just up the street. There are not many of these spaces of demotic encounter, of democratic consumption, left in Beirut, but a few of them survive here and there, like flowers growing through the rubble. I can think, for instance, of the coffee shop I walked by daily during my last spell in Beirut, a small place with one or two flimsy plastic tables jammed up against the outside wall, at which pairs of men sit, playing *tawleh*, backgammon. One day I watched on as an argument broke out between two players over the count. While one insisted calmly that he was ahead, the other loudly protested, hitting the table, running his hands through his thin, swept-back hair in mock disbelief, swivelling round to elicit the sympathies of onlookers. The small audience that gathered round understood this to be the performance that it was, nudging each other and laughing and lighting cigarettes to enjoy the show as the two men dug their heels in. Before long, though, the sore loser realised that all his showmanship was unlikely to secure him the turn-around he sought. The storm blew over, and both men returned to their calm play, the silence only occasionally broken by the odd exhalation of delight at a winning move. There is something distinctly masculine about this form of play, with its deliberate gestures, its loud, virile assertions and force, its raucous laughter, its subterfuges and boasts, claims and counter-claims.

But other such places are more open, less clearly confined to one gender. This is the case of the *man'ushe* oven just next door, where I would regularly stop to pick up some lunch. The place is just a small corner shop occupying one side of an intersection. Behind a high counter piled with the bakery's goods—folded over *mana'ish* covered in *za'tar*, gooey melted cheese or *kishk*, the fermented bulgur wheat that is such a sturdy winter staple; spinach triangles and *lahm bi-'ajin*—one or two youngish Syrian men take orders. As the orders arrive, they shovel the doughy confections into the oven, pulling them out after a minute or two, before stuffing them to the customer's requirements with mint leaves, cucumber, black olives and large, soft mountain tomatoes, and wrapping them tightly in greaseproof paper. On a plastic chair a couple of metres away, the shop's octogenarian owner silently sits watching proceedings, occasionally exchanging a burned away cigarette for a new one or tapping away one of the flies bothering his rheumy, red-lined eyes. There is always a clump of customers coagulating around the counter—gendarmes in uniform picking up bags of *mana'ish* for their colleagues, young men in smart business suits and polished shoes, headscarf-wearing middle-aged women returning from a visit to the American hospital, nearby, with their teenage daughters. Some sit, as I do, besides an old tree that throws shade into the burning street, sharing wry smiles as we watch the gridlocked traffic, a few feet away, and the faces of the drivers as they grow more frustrated with each passing minute. Others stand, eating busily. All, though, are enclosed in a bubble of conversation, as loud voices peal over the hum and throb of the traffic, exchanging greetings and news and jokes.

These are older, more demotic, forms of sociability. But even as they are increasingly pushed out of the city, they have been re-appropriated by entrepreneurs eager to distil their *sha'bi*, or popular, appeal into commodity form. Out of this desire have been born restaurants like Al-Falamanki, the 500-seat emporium of mezze that opened in Achrafieh in 2008. Amidst a garden planted with lemon and orange trees and lush bougainvillea are strewn old sofas. Their 1940s or 1950s wood-frames painted with fresh varnish, they are upholstered in 'traditional' fabrics, all colourful geometrical patterns. Inside, the décor is that of an 'old' Lebanese home: tiles of many hues, tinted glass *arghileh*-s, and family photos, many of them honouring Khalil al-Falamanki, the father of one of the restaurant's founders, Anis. A quasi-mythical figure, Khalil was first a *bahlawan* or wrestler who became, like others of his peers, a *qabaday* or strongman, working as a bodyguard for the Egyptian businessman Tarek al-Fakhry in the 1950s and 1960s. In these images, Falamanki appears a figure of bonhomie, the very embodiment, with his belly, his lustrous moustache, his white summer suit, a *tarbush* atop his head, of Lebanon's pre-civil war 'golden age'. But if at one level the restaurant is a fond tribute to a time that many regard as more carefree, a glamorous era of Hollywood stars, Egyptian *tarab* singers, and gambling trips to Las Vegas and Monte Carlo, at another level it is a knowing and canny attempt to capture and capitalise upon this nostalgia, this aching desire to return to a better, more innocent past, so palpable in the many Facebook pages, Tumblr feeds and coffee-table tomes that eulogise this lost age of innocence. This is a place 'designed to take you back to the village you grew up in … the perfect venue for one to sit and play a game of cards or backgammon, while listening to artists such as Fairuz playing in the background'.[91] As Mario Haddad, the restaurateur who developed this concept, explained, even the tableware is 'intended' to evoke 'the typical Lebanese village setting, complete with vinyl, plastic table covers, randomly chosen crockery and cutlery, common synthetic napkins, [and] plastic cups'.[92] But, as Haddad is all too aware, the prices are far higher than those you would find in a small *furn*, or in a roadside restaurant selling grilled chicken and French fries lathered in garlic sauce. A thyme *man'ushe* will set the customer back 4,750LL, or just over three dollars, a bowl of *tabbouleh* or *fattoush* 9,000LL, or six dollars, a bowl of *hummus* with meat and

357

pine nuts 14,000LL, or almost ten dollars.[93] And yet none of this makes Al-Falamanki any less successful. On summer nights or during Ramadan, queues snake out of its doors and security guards monitor its entrances like nightclub bouncers. The food, and the music, play their part. But they are, of course, impossible to detach from the wider effect of the place, the particular atmosphere of this restaurant with its *qahwaji*-s and its stick-thin *narji*-s, or 'firemen', replenishing the coals on smokers' *arghileh*-s, whose uniforms appear drawn out of an old photo album. All of this comes together to invoke an invented 'Lebanese' past, detached from any particular place or region, and riddled with canny inter-sectarian cues and clues, a site of memory in which all can feel at home regardless of confession. For this is a place that conjures up at once the mythical mountain home of Christian lore and the old popular cafés of Sunni Beirut, with their *arghileh*-smoking, their story-telling and agitated board games, and their clientele, those charismatic, jovial, *tarbush*-wearing strongmen like Khalil al-Falamanki. These places, which exist now only in dog-eared anecdotes and folk-loric histories that eulogise the Beirut of old, are almost always envisioned as venues of male camaraderie.

And yet, even as entrepreneurs like Haddad have attempted to make them accessible to a mixed public of young middle-class men and women willing to pay for this ersatz experience, newer forms of homosocial leisure have appeared in Lebanon. One is the women's-only beach, of the kind frequented by Hala, Sara and Sirene, the three young Palestinian women whose leisure habits Laleh Khalili followed. The beach that they favoured, Bellevue, is in many ways typical. A private enterprise, it charges a fee of around $10 on weekdays, and a little more on weekends. For this, one gains access to a complex containing two swimming pools with slides for children, two paddling pools for toddlers, and two adult-only pools, as well as a sand beach and seating areas with plastic tables and chairs, sun loungers and parasols. Customers can also purchase food, drinks and shisha from several kiosks distributed about the premises. There is also a dancefloor in a 'thatched gazebo', where a DJ will play Lebanese and Arabic pop music.[94] But what distinguishes Bellevue, and other venues like it, is that only women and their children are allowed entry. For some, these places are attractive because they allow for an escape from the unwelcome attentions of men—from stray gazes to insistent conversation and worse—offering an opportunity to socialise among women, to chat and laugh and be without these niggles, anxieties and constraints. For others, however, there is a moral imperative here. Like wearing the headscarf or engaging in charitable acts—forms of behaviour so brilliantly chronicled by the anthropologist Lara Deeb in her work on the pious Shia women of southern Beirut—keeping strict gender segregation is a means of manifesting one's commitment to certain norms of ethical conduct.[95]

Indeed, the women's-only beach is just one of the forms of leisure that have attempted to cleave to the desires of Lebanon's Muslims, in particular, to enjoy themselves while adhering to the moral imperatives of public piety. Deeb, together with Mona Harb, has tracked the emergence of what the two scholars call 'leisurely Islam', examining the workings of restaurants, cafés, malls, and amusement parks that have appeared in recent years in the southern Beirut neighbourhoods of Ghobeiri and Chiyah. These have rapidly filled the vacuum in leisure production in the *dahiyeh*, catering to its relatively affluent middle-class denizens, who wanted to go out for a meal, buy some clothes, go to the gym, or sip a glass of mango juice or a coffee without having to go 'outside' the neighbourhood and drive along gridlocked roads into Beirut proper. As Ali, one young respondent, told Deeb and Harb, 'we used to go to Beirut and spend the whole evening looking for a place to sit where we could feel comfortable. ... Now we have many places and cafés here and they are the same as Beirut and near our homes. I am living here, and I am happy here'. As this suggests, there is a complex admixture of motives here: convenience and the comforting sense of being at home, on familiar ground, but also for some, moral and political considerations. As another of their interlocutors, Abdallah, put it in an interview with Deeb and Harb, in downtown—the common shorthand for Beirut's central district—'there's alcohol, there is loud music, songs, behaviour that doesn't relate to my piety in any way'. *Dahiyeh*, by contrast, was as another respondent put it, 'home, as if I opened the door of my living room and went in!' People behaved in ways that were socially acceptable and, just as importantly, predictable, conforming as they did to the reigning moral injunctions. As one of Deeb and Harb's female respondents, Danya, put it, 'in Dahiya, the environment imposes itself'. Just as one couldn't expect to go to Verdun or Manara in west Beirut and find places that didn't serve alcohol or play music, so too did all who lived and went out in Ghobeiri and Haret el-Hreik have to accept its social expectations and resident norms, regardless of their sect or political persuasion. Equally important for some were political considerations—an ineffable sense of tension, of being made to 'feel uncomfortable' or 'different' in other parts of Beirut, which made one have to 'think about where to go' in order not to 'get into trouble' and avoid unpleasant experiences, from insistent stares and whispered comments to hostile confrontations.[96] In short, going out in their own neighbourhoods has come to seem, for many inhabitants of the *dahiyeh*, at once more convenient and more morally correct, but also more secure in the years since 2005.

Accordingly, a host of businesses have sprung up to cater to local residents' tastes and needs. Despite the 2006 war, 63.8 per cent of the venues that Harb and Deeb surveyed opened their doors between 2006 and 2008. The first burst of commercial activity had begun earlier in the decade under rather different circumstances. As the Hizballah mayor of Ghobeiri, Hajj Abu Sa'id explained, after the *tahrir*, or liberation—the Israeli withdrawal from southern Lebanon in 2000—many 'started to think more about investment ... Many tourist places opened, amusement parks, different types of restaurants, entertainment places, different types of cafés, and lots of gyms'. Ironically, though, the *dahiyeh*'s burgeoning leisure industry was given a spur by the political polarisation of the years after 2005, when people developed—as one respondent put it—*ta'assub la manta'itun*, a 'territorial bias' or sense of allegiance 'towards their area'. As one respondent put it, after the street clashes of 2008 'I don't buy a thing from outside Dahiya! I won't go to cafés outside Dahiya! Never!'[97]

Many of the venues that have opened in these years do not serve alcohol—or do so only in highly circumscribed circumstances—and will use only halal meat, in a deliberate effort to foster a *hala islamiyya*, or Islamic atmosphere. In other ways, however, these venues are manifestations of the way in which Islamic *qiyam*, or values, have shifted in recent years with what many call the *infitah*, or opening up, of both Hizballah and its public. As one young woman explained to Deeb and Harb, it once would have been '*ayb*, or shameful, even for pious married couples to go out for a meal together in a restaurant, an overt show of public intimacy that would have called their moral rigour into question. And yet, as new restaurants like Al-Saha opened in the early 2000s and grew in reputation, 'the idea of going out to eat and socialise became first acceptable, and then normalized in the community'. *Infitah*, then, was both cause and effect of the opening of these new locales of leisure, as the inhabitants of Chiyah or Jnah came to think of it as acceptable for a couple to share a meal in public or a young woman to sit alone, smoking the *arghileh*—a sight that many Lebanese, of all confessions, would have deemed unseemly only a few years earlier.[98]

There were limits to such freedoms. Many, for instance, criticised young couples who kissed in public, or even held hands. In coded terms, they would tell Harb and Deeb that they did not 'respect themselves in front of others', failing to uphold expected norms of moral conduct. More generally, some expressed disdain for those who made a show of themselves, like the preening young men criticised by some for attempting to draw attention to themselves. And yet, these prescriptions are far from hegemonic. Some insisted in their discussions with Deeb and Harb that no-one had the authority to dictate and regulate their behaviour. As one young man put it: 'It is my car! ... And my area! No-one can say anything to me about what I do here! Whoever he is!' What he wanted to listen to, whether it was the Dutch DJ Tiesto's trance mixes or the Qur'an, was entirely his business, and his alone. Not even Hizballah, he insisted, could exercise its disciplining powers over him. Such loose talk, with its insistence on individual freedom, is in some ways the mirror of the ostentatious piety that Lara Deeb has examined elsewhere. Like this form of religiosity, it privileges the capacity of the individual subject to reason for him or herself. And yet such similarities should not be exaggerated, for it also positions itself explicitly against this way of being in the world, stressing with relish the right to private pleasures and enjoyments and rejecting the ethical oversight of religious and political authorities. Others, conscious of the need for a partner, find ways of marrying piety and bodily display. Young men wear rings containing a *hijab*, or 'protective ... Qur'anic verse' on a 'small slip of paper'; they carry about Hizballah or Amal paraphernalia in an attempt to convey their convictions and 'proximity' to the resistance, and choose political anthems or snippets of

Nasrallah's speeches for their ringtones. Young women, even when they wear the headscarf, do not shy away from 'form-fitting' smocks, 'heels and make-up'.[99]

But these forms of public and private piety are not exclusive to Lebanon's Muslim communities. If Shia taxi drivers adorn their vehicles with images of treasured figures such as Ali and Husain, keep photos of Sayyid Hassan Nasrallah in their wallets, and play songs of grief and devotion during 'Ashura, the yearly commemoration of Husain's martyrdom at Karbala, then Christian drivers will attempt to keep out of harm's way with crosses and rosaries draped around their rear-view mirrors, or with stickers and hanging trinkets depicting the Virgin Mary, Mar Charbel, Mar Marun or Mar Elias—St Elijah—who, armed with a sword, acts as protector and intercessor. Many a time have I seen drivers fervently cross themselves on passing a church—quiet, private gestures, but ones they have no qualm about making in public. Supermarkets in Kisrwan or Jbeil will devote an aisle or half an aisle entirely to religious products, from keyrings to candles adorned with the faces of Jesus Christ and the Virgin, and St Rita and St Anthony, those beloved patrons of lost causes, or more contemporary but no less revered figures like Padre Pio, the Italian saint for whom some Lebanese Christians have a particular devotion. On roadsides and at the entrances of apartment buildings are set small ex-votos, full of small bouquets of plastic flowers and candles and rosaries and prayer sheets.

All these markers of devotion, these signs of piety remind us of the porousness between private piety and public religion. This is in part a function of the ways in which belief and belonging are so intimately bound together. For all the statues of Mar Elias, crucifix around his neck, sword raised high above his head, that stand tall at the entrances to Christian neighbourhoods do not just perform a devotional, protective function. They also serve as ostentatious markers of confessional community, defining these places as Christian preserves. And these two functions meld into one another, for what are the harms that Mar Elias is there to ward off if not those of intrusion by 'foreign' religious foes, outsiders to the region and its confession? In many ways, then, Elias— 'noble, heroic, and faithful to [his] religion'—stands for the way some Maronites would like to their community to be.[100] This is a reminder, then, that sectarianism is not just a political or a socio-economic category. Religious figures and tropes and symbols are always involved in the production of confessional community and sectarian space.

Some, indeed, are all too aware of what is at stake here. This is apparent from the story H.H., a 30-year-old Shia taxi driver from Beirut's southern suburbs, recounted of his navigations and negotiations of the city's neighbourhoods. After the fights that broke out at the Arab University in January 2007 between supporters of the Future Movement, on the one hand, and Amal and Hizballah, on the other, he did not return to the staunchly Sunni area of Tariq el-Jdideh for seven months. But, after a while, he resigned himself to the need to pass through the neighbourhood again. And so he stripped his car of all confessional markers and signs of political allegiance, removing the 'sectarian' stickers that used to adorn his dashboard and the cassettes of patriotic songs he listened to, like the Wilaya Group's 'Get up and free yourself, my people', an ode to resistance against Israel. Where there once was an image of Sayyid Hassan Nasrallah, there is now his daughter's name. But he has not let go of the Sayyid's photo entirely; it now sits safely hidden in his wallet.[101] But just as drivers must take precautions to conceal their confession when passing through seemingly foreign areas, so too do some deem unfamiliar signs in familiar places as deliberate slights. Driving through the mixed Beirut neighbourhood of Sanayyeh one day in the lead-up to 'Ashura—a commemoration invested in recent years with a sharp political meaning, the death of Husain coming to symbolise not just the Shia community's long history of persecution and exclusion, but also its resistance in the face of oppression—my driver burst out in rage, gesturing in exasperation at the black flags placed every few metres along the pavement. *Hayda istifzaz*—'this is provocation'—he practically shouted, safe in the knowledge of his passenger's confession, 'and you know why they put these here, it's only because Al-Mustaqbal'—the Hariri family's television channel, whose offices were nearby—'is here'.

But if some view these out-of-place religious signs as overtly political insults, transgressive acts which confound the distinction between pious observance and partisan enmity, it is precisely because all groups will sometimes insist on the need to separate out the religious and the political. As 'Ashura approached again in September 2017, the Sunni women's mosque of Ain al-Mreisse was encircled by a forest of signs:

363

banners evoking the martyrdom of Husain, but also posters showing Nabih Berri, Amal's current leader, alongside its founder, Musa al-Sadr, whose disappearance on a visit to Libya in 1978 echoes, for many of his supporters, the occultation of past Shia imams. On the small verge by the mosque, someone had pinned up a lapidary response on a small, black poster: 'the mosque belongs to God, and he who attacks it is an enemy of the faith'. When I returned the next day, all the signs, banners, and posters had been taken down. How much this had to do with the response pinned to an electricity pylon in the street, and how much with the provocations and backroom deals of the political elite, is open to question. (It was perhaps no coincidence that, at that very moment, Berri was caught up in a dispute with the prime minister, Saad Hariri, over the latter's proposal to introduce biometric identity cards ahead of the 2018 parliamentary elections.) Nevertheless, this remains a revealing message. Those who responded to what they saw as a symbolic offensive by Amal supporters drew a clear and emphatic distinction between religion and the practice of politics. There was no place in the latter for attacks upon another's faith or places of worship. This was an unwarranted transgression, an impermissible act that put their political antagonists beyond the pale, proving once more that they were not moral actors but crude opportunists.

It is true, of course, that this was itself a form of political rhetoric that drew upon the force of religious conviction to buttress its point, a means of undermining one's opponents by questioning their rectitude and challenging their right to act as they did. But it remains, all the same, a reminder of the ways in which religion performs different, and sometimes jarring, roles in Lebanon, and of the need to distinguish between devotion and confession, piety and sectarianism. This is a distinction the Lebanese themselves tend to disregard, instead setting 'secularism', understood both as a separation of the religious and the political and as a lack of religious conviction, against religion and confessionalism, bundled together as a natural pairing. And yet, faith and confession are not inseparable and interchangeable categories. In August 2017, a young couple, Marwa and Boutros—he a Greek Catholic, she a Shia, both equally devout—married without changing their faith. As Lara Deeb has pointed out recently, there was nothing unusual in this. 'Mixed couples are more common than people imagine, and exist to varying degrees across generations, classes, and communities.' What was distinctive, however, was the couple's very open religiosity and their insistence on holding both Christian and Muslim ceremonies to sanctify their union—a Shia *katb kitab*, or signing of the book, and a Melkite or Greek Catholic church wedding, both 'sanctioned by their respective clerics'. While the Melkite Bishop of Tyre gave his blessing to the church wedding, a Shia *sayyid* issued a fatwa making it clear 'there was no reason a Muslim woman could not marry a non-Muslim man if she entered the marriage of her free will'. If Christian women could marry Muslim men without either party converting, as both Shia and Sunni jurisprudents accept, then why could Muslim women not to do the same? In short, it was, as Deeb put it, the 'unapologetically and insistently inter*religious*' nature of this union that so many of those who commented on it on social media found disquieting, and not its inter-confessionalism.[102]

This underlies the way in which sect and faith are not coterminous. It is possible in contemporary Lebanon to consider one's faith of great personal importance, as Marwa and Boutros do, and yet not regard it as an impediment to marrying a partner of another confession. Conversely, it is just as possible to belong to the same confession—the same 'religious group'—as one's spouse and yet insist upon a civil marriage because of one's lack of religious belief or dislike for sectarian strictures. And it is possible to have little time for religious observance, and yet still refuse to countenance even the thought of marrying—or seeing one's children marry—a member of another community, because this act would constitute a form of grave social transgression, a wrenching break with one's structures of belonging that would leave one out in the cold, stripped of the blanket of community. Deeb is surely right to argue that this underlines the need to see sectarianism as a category of practice, one which the Lebanese invest with a deep and varied social meaning. But it is also a reminder of the distinction, so often elided, between religion and confession. The two are used as interchangeable in law and political rhetoric and everyday situations. But there is still a difference to be drawn between belief as such and sectarianism as a web of institutional bodies and legal mechanisms, political expectations and social tropes that entrap the Lebanese, shaping their everyday lives. This distinction is never watertight. Religious tropes and symbols inevitably bleed into political discourse, just as the social and political structures and strictures of community shape religious practice. But it does matter.

Conclusion

Lebanon seems at times a country infatuated with the fatuous, the superficial and the inane. Its high society is focused on vapid appearances, as though the shape of one's nose or the sharpness of one's cheekbones, the swell of one's biceps or breasts, the watch one wears and the cigar one smokes were the makings of the person, rather than mere outward trappings. Everyone must be seen in the same nightclubs, the same beach resorts, the same exclusive hotels and restaurants; they must have the same lavish weddings, if they are to matter, if they are to be assigned any social worth and standing. It is perhaps this, more than anything else, that accounts for the particular pull of nocturnal forms of pleasure, with all the opportunities they offer for self-assertion and show. The measure of the man is taken in material terms.

So prevalent are these forms of conspicuous consumption and ostentatious self-fashioning, so predictable and reiterative the forms that they take, so tangled the webs of expectation in which so many Lebanese are caught, that it almost verges on the banal to point this out. And yet there remains something striking about the sheer power of dominant modes of consumption here. They reverberate through the melodramatic *musalsalat*, or TV series, produced for Ramadan, whose stories of family rows and heartbroken couples play out in opulent settings—showrooms for the bourgeois dream—and are picked up in the talk shows and reality programmes that run alongside them. But if they saturate the airwaves, then they also shape social structures, reinforcing particular understandings of gender—and, in particular, of womanhood—which pervade society, contributing to a sense that the female subject remains reliant on the male, that she must remain pliant and passive, an aestheticized receptacle for the ambitions of the men about her.

Of course, we should never think of this economy of display as a monopolistic one, in which one set of discursive and aesthetic and material conventions is able to impose its hegemony over others. I have pointed, in the latter stages of this chapter, to the growing prominence of pious forms of leisure that seek to combine ethical uprightness with public consumption, but also to various modes of fugitive, demotic leisure—forms of relish that find themselves increasingly pushed to the margins of the city by rampant development, and yet which continue to provide enjoyment, delight, and relief for many, a small escape from the overbearing tedium of the days. But there are other alternatives, too, from the mountain restaurants at which entire families will commandeer a table for a long Sunday lunch of mezze, grilled meat and arak, to the 'intellectual' bars of Mar Mikhael and Hamra, full of laughing young women with their Marlboros and young men with furrowed brows and glasses of whisky. In short, the view of public space as a territory to be colonised by private interests and private ambitions, an arena in which individuals can parade and compete for status and distinction and in which religious and political communities can state their differences, though so very nearly hegemonic, has not yet won out. Other, alternative conceptions of what it means to live in public still perdure, gaining new ground in moments of crisis. It is to these that the next chapter turns.

8

TAL 'IT RIHATKUM, OR 'YOU STINK'

ON WASTE AND THE LEBANESE BODY POLITIC

On Monday 20 July 2015, they stopped collecting the rubbish in Beirut. Within days, the familiar green bins that line the streets of the Lebanese capital were overflowing with mounds of rubbish that emerged from within like ragtag zombies pulling themselves from out the grave. Long trails of bursting, leaking bin bags lined the streets, the smell of their decomposing contents only made worse by the overbearing July heat. Soon, the entire city was covered in the thick, sickly sweet stench of rot, hovering in the still summer air. For many, it seemed as though the country had been invaded by trash, the everyday matter that the Lebanese, like others, throw away with nary a thought for its journey into the half-world of the landfill, suddenly manifesting its presence like a repressed thought returning in nightmarish form. As John Scanlan has written, we rarely think of the 'shadow city' of waste that runs beneath all the 'familiar' markers of urban space, 'the streets and houses, public spaces and commercial zones', living in blissful 'ignorance of [the] ruin [and] decay' around us. If the 'city is life', 'garbage is death', always there, 'an unwelcome shadow that ... resists any of our attempts to disconnect from it'.[1]

Now, though, there seemed to be no getting away from its abject, unsettling, repulsive presence. This was nothing less than the 'abrupt' appearance of a strange if 'distantly familiar' force that 'harassed' the Lebanese incessantly as they attempted to go about their everyday lives, provoking a 'violent and obscure revolt' against this unexpected and incomprehensible threat.[2] No matter where one went, whether in Beirut or in its suburbs or other parts of Mount Lebanon (wherever, in fact, that the waste management contractor Sukleen and its sister company Sukomi had operated) one found the same thing: hundreds and thousands of plastic bags and bin bags and cardboard boxes and pallets, all filled with vegetable peel and plastic water bottles, discarded takeaway wrappers and dirty toilet paper. By the end of the week, angry young men had taken matters into their own hands, tipping bins over into the street and setting their contents alight. That Friday night was stained with the acrid smell of waste going up in flames.

A few months later, a friend recalled how he had stopped at a red light at an intersection in the working-class quarter of Bashoura the morning after these first, improvised protests, and watched a burning bin roll down the street in front of him. I found in the story no contempt for those who set the blaze, none of that uneasy fear of the people that sometimes marks the speech of middle-class Lebanese, but only a sense of the absurdity of the situation. There he was wearing his seatbelt, stopped at the lights, still believing that he lived in a country where laws might mean something, might have a shared value for both the citizens and the politicians in power. At that moment, he realised this was just a delusion. He was not alone in speaking to me of the trash crisis in such terms, as a moment when the mask of power fell away, revealing the growing disjuncture between the desires and frustrations of a citizenry pining for a less uncertain, difficult life, and the indolence and incompetence of the political class, whose slovenly response showed its utter disregard for the concerns of the people. In short, the rubbish crisis was the 'trauma which destabilises the symbolic order' in which the Lebanese lived, a 'radical political rupture' which stripped them once and for all of their delusions, making apparent the fragile underpinnings of their life.[3] It was precisely this disjuncture between the unanswered requests and disregarded rights of the people, and the working of what many came to call al-tabaqa al-siyasiyya, or 'the political class', with its cronyism, its prevarication, and its endless self-interest that lay at the heart of the protests that began in the dog days of July. In short, people pined for the rule of law—for justice and equity and efficiency—and not for the lawless rulers they had at present.

Within weeks, images had gone viral of lorries and rubbish trucks pouring their fetid contents out on isolated mountain roads, the rubbish collapsing down into the valley beneath like a waterfall, and of the concrete channel through which Nahr Beirut, the capital's river, now just a shrivelled-up dirty stream, runs, filled to the brim with waste. By this point, the small protests of the first few days and weeks had grown into the largest non-partisan public gatherings that Lebanon had witnessed since the first demonstrations of February 2005. The demonstrations of the summer and autumn of 2015 brought together an array of different constituencies with diverse expectations and approaches, from the rowdy irreverence of working-class boys and men who delighted in mocking the politicians who had long regarded them as loyal, unquestioning underlings, to the self-conscious dignity of middle-class students and activists, with their sit-ins and hunger strikes, and the longing of some for a technocratic government of experts equipped with the knowledge and zeal to remedy Lebanon's manifold infrastructural problems. Before long, the uneasy, temporary coalition of these weeks had splintered again, as smaller groups undertook their own micro-actions organised through word of mouth or social media, performances of the possible in which they took the status quo to task and sketched out utopian visions of another future.

As activists and campaigners pondered how to build on the disaffection of these months and considered what was to be done, this longing for alternative futures—indeed, for any future at all, rather than the permanent present into which Lebanon had seemingly sunk—gave rise to Beirut Madinati—'Beirut is my city'—an electoral coalition of architects, engineers and urban planners, lawyers, pharmacists and academics. These professionals sought local office in the municipal elections of May 2016 on the basis of their dual qualification, as experts who possessed the training and experience to resolve Beirut's infrastructural woes, and as proud inhabitants of the city, committed to its renewal. For all the enormous enthusiasm that this new force generated, though, Lebanon's politicians found a way to rally, closing ranks in the face of the unprecedented challenges of these years. If the rubbish crisis of July 2015 appeared to undermine the very basis of the

Lebanese political system, then the appearance of Beirut Madinati seemed inadvertently to pave the way towards political reconciliation and reconsolidation. It is this arc from street protests to electoral politics, and from crisis to consolidation, that this chapter surveys. But, before doing so, we must attend to the matter at hand—the rubbish that took over Lebanon's streets and roads.

Waste mismanagement

The *azmat al-nufayyat*, or 'trash crisis' had been a long time coming, the product of years of mistakes, decisions left for another day and solutions pushed down the river. For this was not Lebanon's first waste crisis. By the time I arrived in Lebanon for a research trip in early September, some of the rubbish had been cleared from Beirut's streets, but the stench of rotting matter still hung heavy over the city. On high-up mountain roads, one would turn a corner to find a trail of half-burned waste bags along the road, their entrails spilling out, small billows of smoke rising out here and there, the failing breath of a dying fire. It was after driving along one of these roads with my aunt and cousin that she turned to me and said, 'well of course, they never collected the rubbish during the war. Everyone just dumped their waste on the street'. And, of course, it was true. I remember the rivers of waste that formed in the valleys I used to play in as a child, up in the mountains above Beirut, as bin-liners thrown from passing cars would tumble down the hillside. In some ways, indeed, the crisis of 2015 was also a product of the civil war and the particular mode of political thinking it had bred, one focused entirely on the short-term, the exceptional and the temporary—on the next six months, the next year—but utterly uninterested in, or incapable of, devising dispensations for the long run. During the war, much of the waste of Beirut and Mount Lebanon, when it was collected at all, was dumped untreated into two sites: the great seething mass of the Normandy landfill and the Burj Hammoud landfill, which abutted the working-class Armenian neighbourhood of the same name. These two sites remained in use for much of the 1990s: while the Normandy landfill took in the bulldozed remains of central Beirut, the brick and mortar and concrete and steel of its markets, its cafés and banks as they were pulled down by

Solidere's bulldozers, the Burj Hammoud landfill finally closed down only in 1997.

In the wake of this closure, the then-minister of the environment, the Druze politician Akram Chehayeb—a close ally of Walid Jumblatt and a member of his Progressive Socialist Party—cast about for a means to reform and rationalise Lebanon's waste management system. Chehayeb had initially favoured transforming the old incinerators at Karantina, a working-class district near the port of Beirut, and the southern suburb of 'Amrusiyyeh, into modern waste treatment facilities. His proposals, however, faced obdurate opposition from local residents. When the government dismissed their concerns, the inhabitants of 'Amrusiyyeh took matters into their own hands, setting fire to the plant in their town. In the face of this discomfiture, Chehayeb was forced to abandon his plans for comprehensive reform.[4] Instead, he devised what he called the Emergency Plan for the Greater Beirut Area. A sanitary landfill would be created in the village of Naameh, about 20 kilometres to the south of Beirut, to treat the waste of the capital and the Governorate of Mount Lebanon, an area covering about a fifth of Lebanon, but in which perhaps three quarters of the country's population is concentrated. This was only a temporary measure. The landfill would be in operation for only ten years, taking no more than two million tonnes of waste.[5] What's more, this was far from a comprehensive, national plan—a point on which Chehayeb was clear. Local authorities and ordinary inhabitants in Lebanon's six other governorates had to find alternative means of ridding themselves of the unwanted by-products of everyday life. And, though many Lebanese municipalities have had to put in place collection and sorting facilities, only the eastern town of Zahle had a sanitary landfill before 2014.[6] It is no surprise, then, that other 'wild' or unregulated dumping grounds survived and proliferated across the country. The most infamous of these, the 50-metre-high mountain of detritus that had accumulated over forty years of fly-tipping in the harbour of the southern port-town of Saida, finally closed in 2014. (I remember being haunted by its almost phantasmagorical appearance, as though all the flotsam and jetsam the waves carried had been pulled together by an awesome magnetic force-field.) This mountain of waste was replaced by a new landfill, a triage and recycling factory, and a composting unit, built with the assistance of the EU and the UNDP. But though this 'nightmarish' mound had now been pulled down and the 'pestilential' scent that had washed across the city almost disappeared, there still remained, even before the rubbish crisis of the summer of 2015, over 700 'wild', or unregulated, dumping sites across Lebanon.[7] In 2013, it was estimated that while 48% of Lebanon's municipal solid waste was disposed of in sanitary landfills, 29% was simply dumped without any treatment or triage in unregulated sites. Only 8% was recycled, and 15% composted.[8] The cost to the environment of all of this is incalculable. One day, while out on a boat on the Mediterranean, I sat and looked out over the waves. Amidst the churning water there bobbed used tampons and nappies, but also a shopping caddy and, most incongruous of all, a skateboard—still with its wheels on.

All the while, the landfill at Naameh remained open, serving as the burial ground for almost half of Lebanon's waste. An unending caravan of rubbish trucks trailed through the surrounding villages day and night, bringing another 2,800 tonnes of rubbish each day. In 2015, it was estimated that some fifteen million tonnes of waste had been buried over an area of 200,000 square metres.[9] Aerial photos show a vast site barren of vegetation, what was once a 'deep valley' that used to serve—in the words of the engineer Ajwad Ayache—as a 'playground for many, many kids from the neighbouring villages' now a 'mountain', layer upon layer of waste piled high beneath the churned-up earth.[10] By the 2010s, Naameh's inhabitants had long since come to look upon the landfill as a noxious blight upon their lives. Visiting journalists found only anxiety and concern for the future. Some worried that Sukleen, the waste disposal company that manages Naameh, had ignored the most elementary guidelines. The environmental activist Paul Abi Rached, who worked alongside local residents, complained that, despite Sukleen's contractual obligation to sort the waste arriving at the site, 'nothing was sorted'.[11] Ayache spoke of 'remains, animal remains, human remains, hospital garbage, any kind of garbage' being buried.[12] Others expressed their fears that Sukleen had failed to install an adequate number of release pipes to cope with the 1,200 cubic metres of methane that the landfill apparently produced every hour, and that it burned some of the rubbish rather than treating and burying it. Their land, the inhabitants complained, was polluted by the outflow that leached into the earth and the organic gases that built up, trapped beneath the surface, and their air by the foul-smelling smoke that rose up from the mounds of waste, particularly at night. From 9:00 p.m. to 6:00 a.m., the east wind would bring an 'unbearable, fetid odour' in from the landfill, particularly in summer. The village was infested with 'more and more rats and flies'. Residents reported 'an abnormally high incidence' of 'diarrhoea, pulmonary infections', 'skin allergies' and 'asthma'.[13] Some even spoke of an increase in the number of local cancer patients, telling sad stories of middle-aged men and young girls dying before their time.[14]

It is hardly surprising that the inhabitants of the surrounding villages of Naameh, Ain Drafil, and Haret Naameh had been demanding the landfill's closure almost since the day it began its operations. The first protests took place in 1998, a year after it opened its doors. Local residents' anger only grew when they learned that the landfill, which was scheduled to cease operations in 2008, would remain open for another three years. In 2011, another three-year extension was granted.[15] In 2013, a group of local residents formed the Campaign to Close the Naameh Dumpsite, working with Lebanese environmental activists like Abi Rached to raise awareness of their plight.[16] When they learned in January 2014 that the government was contemplating yet another extension, they resorted to direct action to manifest their anger at years of broken commitments and neglect. On 17 January, they began a sit-in, blocking the entrance to the landfill to Sukleen's trucks. For a week, the rubbish went uncollected in Beirut and Mount Lebanon, the streets piled high with wasting bags. Their demands were simple: no more extensions and a guarantee that the landfill would close for good a year hence, in January 2015, and no more organic waste. The response from politicians and officials was telling. For at the same time as the protesters received reassurances from Walid Jumblatt and Talal Arslan that they would work towards the landfill's closure in 2015, their camp was raided by security forces who tore down their demonstrators' tents and banners, arresting several demonstrators, including the engineer and activist Ajwad Ayache. The sit-in had lasted a week, effectively paralysing waste collection in the capital and the surrounding regions.[17] The incoherent, garbled mix of emollient words and forceful action, of commitments and coercion, which brought it to an end was a telling portent of what lay ahead.

So, too, was the way in which hastily made promises just as quickly fell by the wayside. For the inhabitants of Naameh and the surrounding villages learned to their dismay in January 2015 that the new minister of the environment, Mohammad Machnouq, had extended the landfill's life and Sukleen's contract for another renewable three-month term—a stay of execution of six months, which he justified by the need to implement a new national plan for waste management. Once again, the inhabitants fell into action, organising a demonstration on the landfill on the Saturday on which it was supposed to cease operations. Photos of the day show a solemn, resolute crowd of men—and a few women—grouped in a circle, heads bowed as they listen to one of their lot. Around them stands a phalanx of agents of the Internal Security Forces, perhaps as numerous as the demonstrators. The words of one of those who went to the landfill that day showed their disappointment and anger:

> We have gone back to the starting point. Yes to life, no to death. The politicians have said their plans [for a national waste management policy] have the support of civil society. We tell them: we are civil society. You are poisoning us. We deserve life. This landfill is killing us in our bedrooms. Shame on you for making your agreements at our expense.[18]

As the deadline set for mid-July approached, the inhabitants of the region and their supporters were no longer willing to take the politicians at their word. On 17 July, the date on which Sukleen's contract was set to expire, they once again occupied the entrance to the landfill. If the government was not prepared to close the site, then they would force its hand. Just as in January 2014, their actions paralysed waste collection in Beirut and Mount Lebanon. Not for the first time, Lebanon's rulers had failed to heed the lessons of the recent past. Thus began the 'trash crisis' of 2015.

This is, at one level, a story of environmental degradation and local mobilisation, of a community protesting the blight forced into its midst. But it is also, of course, one of political extemporisation and prevarication, as successive cabinets' reluctance to tackle the matter of waste turned a site intended only as a stop-gap measure into a permanent sore. In this sense, it is impossible to disentangle from the economic policies of the 1990s and the 2000s—and, in particular, from the botched attempts to privatise waste management as part of a neoliberal restructuring of service provision. Before the civil war, waste collection had been, by law, carried out by local authorities, and bin men and street cleaners were public workers, employed by Lebanon's municipalities.[19] Post-war cabinets, however, had little faith in a public sector decimated by a decade and a half of civil strife. In 1994, Rafiq Hariri's government granted the contract for street-cleaning and rubbish collection in Beirut and Mount Lebanon to Sukleen, a subsidiary of Averda, the waste management company that the Lebanese engineer Maysarah Khalil Sukkar—a former business partner of Hariri—had established in Saudi Arabia in 1970.[20] In 1998, Sukleen's sister company, Sukomi, won the contract to treat and landfill that waste, taking over the administration of Naameh.[21] (Small wonder, then, that local inhabitants should simply call the landfill outside their village Sukleen.)

These deals, however, have not resulted in the cost efficiency that advocates of privatisation proclaim as one of its chief benefits. On the contrary. The initial contract signed with Averda was worth $3.6 million per year.[22] By 2015, the Lebanese state was spending somewhere between $142 million and $153 million dollars per year on waste management. This, it is clear, has not simply been a consequence of the expansion of Averda's remit—though it does account for some of this—but also of ever-rising costs. By some estimates, the cost of solid waste collection grew in real terms at an annual rate of 5 per cent between 2002 and 2015. In 2012, Bassam Sabbagh, an official at the Ministry of the Environment, put the cost of Averda's contract at $140 dollars per tonne.[23] According to the environmental activist Paul Abi Rached, thirty dollars of this supposedly went on sorting—a contractual obligation but one that, he alleges, Averda has systematically neglected.[24] Forty-five dollars, meanwhile, went on 'dumping alone'; the global average is $11.[25] According to *Le Monde*'s Beirut correspondent, Laure Stephan, the waste treatment facilities at Naameh were considered 'among the most expensive in the world'.[26]

What makes these figures even more remarkable, of course, is that Averda was responsible for waste collection and treatment only in two of the country's eight governorates. Though the detritus produced in Beirut and Mount Lebanon did amount, by some estimates, to 70 per cent of Lebanon's total waste, the arrangements put in place in the 1990s were never intended to provide nation-wide coverage.

Municipalities in other regions were left in charge of their own waste, devising whatever mechanisms they saw fit for its disposal and paying for it out of their own budgets. This, then, had only ever amounted to a partial privatisation of waste management. But to cope with the rising costs of outsourcing, the Lebanese state resorted to measures which placed the burden of its obligations towards Averda on Lebanon's municipalities. In 2000, a decree was passed authorising the Council of Ministers—the cabinet—to draw funds from the Independent Municipalities Fund to pay for private waste management contracts benefiting only some municipalities. Though the Court of Accounts ruled this arrangement unconstitutional, the 2001 budget allowed the government to charge those municipalities in which waste collection was outsourced to private providers 40 per cent of their share of the Independent Municipal Fund. As Sami Atallah, the executive director of the Centre for Lebanese Policy Studies, has pointed out, this was rather odd, for the sums the government charged to municipalities had no definite relation to the cost that Averda charged the state. In other words, particular municipalities had no way of knowing for certain whether they were being under-charged or over-charged for waste collection, and whether this flat rate represented a subsidy or a levy. What made the matter stranger still was that the sums collected from local authorities covered only 22 per cent of the total cost of waste collection in 2009. When Atallah asked how the remaining expenditure was being met, he was told that the Council for Development and Reconstruction—the powerful quasi-autonomous overseen by Hariri loyalists—was covering these costs, but 'registering [them] as debt to municipalities'.[27] One way or another, then, local authorities that had no say in how waste should be collected had ended up subsidising the central state's deficit financing and its piecemeal and dysfunctional arrangements with the private sector.

In March 2014, the then-prime minister, Tammam Salam, attempted to address this situation, creating a ministerial commission to devise a national masterplan for waste management. On 12 January 2015, just three days before the Naameh landfill was due to close, the cabinet approved the subcommittee's recommendations. Under this plan, Lebanon was to be divided into six operating regions: Beirut and its immediate suburbs; the Matn, Kisrwan, and Jbeil; Baabda, Aley, and the

Chouf; the Beqaa; the north, including Tripoli and Akkar; and the south, including Nabatiyyeh. The first three of these regions were put out to tender immediately, with the other three following at a later date. The winners of the three bids would be announced in April 2015. Contracts were to be awarded, either to individual companies or consortiums, for an initial period of seven years, renewable for a further three. Bidders had to fulfil a number of technical and financial conditions to be deemed eligible: local companies 'bidding alone' had to possess 'experience in both collection and disposal'. Any partnerships had to include three partners: one international, one local, and one either local or international; any one of these could meet the 'experience requirements'. In addition, bidders had to have a minimum annual turnover of $80 million to be considered in Beirut, $65 million in the Matn, Kisrwan and Jbeil, and $50 million for Baabda, Aley, and the Chouf. What's more, the successful bidders had to commit to landfilling no more than 40 per cent of solid waste in the first three years of the contract, and 25 per cent in subsequent years. While the state had drawn up a list of potential sites for waste management facilities—most of them, according to one source, old quarries or dumping grounds—it remained up to the company to secure the land rights, to choose how to process the waste, and to build and maintain at its own cost 'sanitary landfills, sorting and composting facilities', incinerators, and recycling and 'waste-to-energy plants'.[28]

This financial burden was alleviated somewhat by the €35 million the Lebanese government had obtained from the European Commission in 2013–14 to fund the construction of 'six sanitary landfills and seven sorting, composting [and] refuse-derived fuel … facilities' and the rehabilitation of two existing facilities.[29] All the same, the conditions of tender represented a significant undertaking for any interested party, and the Council for Development and Reconstruction struggled to attract bids. When the deadline passed in April 2015, three bids had been made for the zone encompassing the Matn, Kisrwan, and Jbeil, but only one for that grouping together Baabda, Aley, and the Chouf. Beirut had received no offers. In the face of this fiasco, the deadline was extended once again until 15 July, just two days before Averda's contract was due to expire. Even had a bidder come forward, and even had the government deemed it a fit operator, this was an impossible deadline. In the event, though, no bidder could be found.[30] With Averda's contract having finally lapsed and the inhabitants of Naameh blockading the landfill, the rubbish began to pile up.

If the decision to set a deadline for prospective new operators to submit bids just two days before the old operator's contract expired seemed at best incompetent, then many informed observers saw more nefarious forces at work. Bassam Farhat, the CDR official who handled waste management, described the new plan adopted by the Salam cabinet as the product of a 'political decision'. When a journalist from *Executive Magazine* asked him whether this meant that the plan was 'flawed or ignored advice from agencies like the CDR and the Ministry of [the] Environment ... he said the cabinet had all the relevant information needed to make the best decision but "in the end, it was their decision"'.[31] Farhat was not alone in suggesting that the plan was a politicised product of grand compromise between Lebanon's factional leaders. In the wake of a stormy cabinet session on 9 January 2015, the ministers of the Kata'ib party—which, under the leadership of Samy Gemayel, has attempted to portray itself as an advocate of decentralisation to local authorities and an opponent of political corruption—expressed their concerns that the proposals left it up to private companies to secure the sites for their installations. This, they explained, would leave these companies 'at the mercy of influential local leaders, favouring those who were willing to bend to the latter's demands'. Far better, they suggested, would be to allow the central state and local municipalities to work together to choose suitable landfill sites ahead of the tender adjudications. This would 'protect the companies' from undue influence, rather than 'leaving them prey to local forces'.[32]

Such dark mutterings appeared to be fuelled by the suspicion that powerful politicians with extensive business interests and networks of influence had been busy preparing for the day when Averda's contract would finally expire, readying their own bids or lending their support to those of friends and clients. Indeed, several sources testified that Walid Jumblatt, for one, had shown an interest in moving into waste management. The businessman Riad al-Assaad, whose company, South for Construction, was one of the few to submit a bid to the CDR in 2015, insisted that he had only become interested in waste because of Jumblatt. Assaad, himself the scion of a fallen Shia political dynasty from southern Lebanon, told *Executive Magazine* that he and Jumblatt's sons, Taymour and Aslan, had incorporated EcoPark Holdings in mid-2014 to serve as a parent company for several 'special purpose vehicles' which would each handle a separate part of the waste stream. Though Jumblatt had apparently lost interest, his sons were still listed as members of the company's board on the Beirut commercial registry.[33] In a striking coincidence, Jumblatt warned in November 2014 in his weekly column for the PSP newspaper *al-Anba* that the party would respond to any further 'unjustified prevarication' over the Naameh landfill by calling for 'a vast popular movement' to 'pressure' the government to find a 'radical solution' to the problem of waste.[34] (It should be pointed out that Naameh falls within Jumblatt's own parliamentary district of the Chouf, and he was doing no more, in a sense, than representing his constituents.) In January 2015, Wael Abou Faour and Akram Chehayeb, the ministers representing the PSP in cabinet, again insisted that Naameh had to close, and warned of a 'great waste crisis' should no contingency plan be put in place.[35] They were not wrong, of course. But if some saw these tractations as attempts to break Averda's quasi-monopoly over private waste collection and enter a potentially lucrative market, redistributing the spoils of privatisation once again amongst Lebanon's political and financial elite, others alleged that the government showed no desire to break with the status quo. In July 2015, Riad al-Assaad complained that 'the tenders were rigged to keep the incumbent in place'. (In August, Averda issued a statement denying that it had ever intended to present a bid, slamming the conditions imposed on prospective contractors.)[36] As politicians, high functionaries, and businessmen threw the blame around, there was one thing that all could agree on: the entire process had been a flawed one, plagued by sectional interests and inscrutable calculations.

This was scant consolation to the inhabitants of Beirut and Mount Lebanon as they watched—and smelled—the refuse accumulate outside their homes. In Beirut alone, around 450 tonnes of waste were being left on the streets each day.[37] Despite the catastrophic scale of the problem, the government proved slow to act. A week into the crisis, it had still not found a way out of the impasse. In part, its path was blocked by the firm refusal of local authorities across Lebanon to take in Beirut's waste. In the southern village of Kfour, whose landfill was used to bury the refuse of the region, the inhabitants held a sit-in to call for the site's closure; echoing the rhetoric heard at Naameh, they accused it of 'poisoning the lives of residents for kilometres around' and 'ruining fields and orchards of fruit trees'. The mayor of Hebline, a Christian village near Jbeil which was also the location of a landfill serving local needs, was so panicked by the notion that dumpsters might begin to overwhelm his tiny hamlet, perched on a hill overlooking the Mediterranean, that he secured a meeting with the former president Michel Sleiman. The federation of mayors of Akkar, the remote, poor northern region that the cabinet looked to as a possible dumping ground for Beirut's rubbish, announced their 'complete refusal of the despatch of refuse to the district'. The local MPs Mouin Merhebi and Khaled Zahramane were quick, too, to denounce what they saw as an iniquitous plan, breaking ranks with their colleagues in the Lebanon First parliamentary bloc, many of whom represented districts in Beirut and were eager to find a rapid solution at any cost. Merhebi even went so far as to threaten direct action to close the road to the landfill at Srar to any dumpsters coming from Beirut. 'They forget us', he complained bitterly, 'when it comes to budgets for equitable development, but remember us when they have to get rid of the rubbish.'[38] While some complained of neglect and opportunism, others saw proposals to send rubbish to given regions as evidence of disregard for particular communities. Plans in late July to use mountainous sites and deserted quarries in the Kisrwan were scuppered when the Free Patriotic Movement refused to support this initiative, fearing that these Christian regions would be forced to take in—as one journalist put it—'the waste of others'.[39]

By late July, it had become apparent that no Lebanese region was prepared to take Beirut's waste. On 29 July, the city's governor, Ziad Chbib, announced that Sukleen would be called upon once again. Under this hastily cobbled-together 'emergency plan', the company would collect the 5,000 tonnes of rubbish that had lingered, rotting, in the streets of the capital over the previous two weeks, taking them to a site in the working-class district of Karantina. It was not long, however, before it was found that the chosen site, a vacant lot near the port, also happened to be adjacent to the Bakalian mills, which produced around 40 per cent of Lebanon's flour. Would the rubbish crisis, journalists asked anxiously, now be followed by a 'bread crisis'? A site in the capital's southern suburbs that had been used to store the rubbish of the *dahiyeh*, meanwhile, was closed when aviation experts expressed their fears that the large number of birds attracted by these rich pickings posed a threat to the planes landing at the nearby international airport.[40] Things, in short, appeared to be falling apart, as one cataclysm piled atop another and as anxious politicians floundered haplessly, trading accusations of incompetence and malfeasance.

Of dirt and disorder

In recent decades, scholars have shown how the imperial language of dirt was passed down to the new postcolonial elites that inherited the mantle of rule in the mid-twentieth century. But if, for colonial administrators, the colony as a whole was defined by what the anthropologist Mary Douglas called 'matter out of place'—streets littered with waste and strewn with shit and puddles of filthy water, which seemed to stand for this 'teeming, threatening environment'—these anxieties about dirt have been displaced in more recent decades onto the lower orders.[41] It is they who present a threat to the craving for cleanliness, order, and hygiene of the new rulers—with their dreams of uncluttered streets free of stinking detritus and jostling, chaotic crowds. In this vision, tidiness and cleanliness represent 'modernity [and] ... civic consciousness', the 'popular practices' of the city an atavistic attachment to tradition, holding the nation back and preventing it from moving into the promised future.[42] As Nicholas Hopkins and Sohair Mehanna have suggested in their examination of local environmental concerns in Egypt, the trope of the 'ignorant citizen', whose lack of learning renders him 'careless or malicious', remains a powerful way of understanding the blight of waste and pollution.[43]

In the Middle East as in South Asia, then, postcolonial elites have grown used to painting 'the people' as an amorphous, uncouth mass, whose inability to police themselves and to distinguish between the private and the public render them refractory to modernity. Lacking any sense of civic pride or political understanding, the people can never make up a public. How could they, incapable as they are of living by the ethics of public life? As the positive aspirations of self-determination have given way in many places to the strictures of authoritarian power—or, at the very least, to the dominance of an ossified political class—this discourse has increasingly been used to justify the suspension of democratic norms and the institution of a state of exception. For how can the people be entrusted to make correct use of their rights when they can barely comport themselves in a civilised fashion, let alone understand the workings of democracy? This is the discourse on which Hosni Mubarak drew when, in the dying days of his presidency, he cast those demonstrating in Tahrir Square as *juhhala'*— 'ignorant people'. Invective like this reminds us, too, that as the self-conscious bourgeois politeness of the early post-colony has given way to cruder, more brutal discourses of sovereign power, so have knowledge and informed insight come to be equated in new and more flagrant ways with wealth, and ignorance and uncomprehending rashness with impotent poverty. Capital has come to take the place of inherited status and racial difference as the essential trapping of power. For it is wealth that imbues the elite with the self-assurance and poise that birth once provided, and that allows its members to hold on to security, cleanliness, and order, freeing them from the noisome inconveniences of the post-colony. To those in favour belong crisp, immaculately laundered white shirts, polished cars and carefully tended lawns. Those who live outside, beyond the confines of the gated communities and guarded compounds, must make do with a world of dust and refuse.

This is a way of thinking that some have adhered to in post-war Lebanon, attempting to enforce strict demarcations between those who belong to this world of cleanness and quiet, of expensive trinkets and polished surfaces, and those who do not, because they are too loud, too dirty, too poor, because they lack the wherewithal and knowledge to gain access. This discursive distinction, this cleavage of the city in two, can take at times a sectarian turn, as Christians or Sunnis will dismiss the Shia in caustic terms as *bajam*, dirt, or *za'ran*, street thugs. But it has also increasingly shaped the way in which Lebanon's 'luxury' homes are designed and marketed, as 'exclusive' preserves enclosed from the world without, undergirding attempts to change the character of particular neighbourhoods and to enclose hitherto public space. It is there, for instance, in the comments of Nicolas Shammas, the president of the Beirut Traders' Association, when, in a fit of anger, he blurted out that 'it was forbidden' to cheapen and diminish the commercial centre, that place of refined hotels and expensive shops and exclusive banks; addressing the 'infernal' protesters, he told them 'it is not yours'.[44] And it is there, too, in the signs that used to guard the entrance to Zaitunay Bay, with their proprietorial prohibitions on smoking the shisha, roller-skating, loud talking and the like. But this discourse is not the preserve of private entrepreneurs. Public officials, too, make use of these terms. To the fury of civil society activists, the mayor of Beirut, Bilal Hamad, has long insisted on keeping the city's largest green space, Horsh Beirut—literally, 'the forest of Beirut'—closed to the public. As the architect and activist Abir Saksouk-Sasso has argued, Hamad adheres to the same logic as Shammas or the managers of Zaitunay Bay, fearing that 'various social groups using public space in unpredictable ways—unfit within this narrow perceived appropriate lifestyle—act as a threat to the constructed image of the city; the public is hence seen as "ugly"'. In justifying the continued closure of Horsh Beirut, Hamad had, according to Saksouk-Sasso, listed 'various informal activities that he considers a threat … including picnics, eating, walking on the grass, smoking shisha or engaging in political debates'. In other words, 'the "public" is only seen as worthy of this space if it behaves according to a classed understanding of what a public might be'.[45] Public space, for its part, had to be 'sterile', policed, and kept free of the people that Hamad described, according to another source, as *jahilin*—'the ignorant'.[46]

This, however, is a discourse that has never acquired hegemonic status in Lebanon, that has never been able to force itself upon all as the only way of thinking about the city. For just as Zaitunay Bay has now been transformed into a promenading site for young working-class men and women, a curious extension of the Corniche into which they can stroll to gawp, in an amused, incredulous way, at the menus and take a few selfies in front of the yachts before walking away again, so too was Shammas forced to apologise for his comments in the face of a social media storm, fulminating as parts of the downtown area were used for the Suq Abu Rukhusa, with its cheap food stalls and discounted artisan pieces. Indeed, this was a direct consequence of the upswell of popular sentiment that began to gather force in July and August 2015, and which turned this rhetoric on its head. For those who participated in the demonstrations of these weeks, and who feverishly chronicled their thoughts and actions on social media, were in no doubt that the members of *al-tabaqa al-siyasiyya*, 'the political class', had lost the power to berate the citizenry down below from the commanding heights of the state, to demean and denounce and shower contempt on their constituents from their well-guarded enclaves. In these weeks, the language of dirt, filth, and refuse, was transformed from a language of order, used to instil compliance and to dismiss the demands of the people, into an insurgent language, full of contempt for the politicians and their incompetence and corruption.

The first protests began just days after the rubbish had begun to pile up in the streets of Beirut. On Friday 24 July, a week to the day after the closure of the Naameh landfill, young men from the working-class districts of Bashoura and Khandaq al-Ghamiq—just a few short minutes' walk from the downtown, with its opulent, empty cafes and unlet corporate offices—pulled and dragged overflowing rubbish skips into the road before setting them alight. The acrid smell of burning waste fell over the city. Images from that evening show a landscape invested with waste, streets taken over by matter out of place: rubbish bags lying burst on the tarmac, their decomposing contents strewn about; cars delicately edging their way through these fields of rot, moving in single file past the overturned bins lying there like sleeping cattle; white smoke rising up into the fading sun, its pristine colour belying its foul odour; confused security agents standing by the roadside, attempting as best they could to put out the wild fires.[47] Some were quick to draw parallels with the protests of 2006 and 2008, regarding them as manifestations of a desire to sow sectarian disorder. The French-language daily *L'Orient-Le Jour* would thus insist that the young scooter-riding men who had thrown filled rubbish bags at the residences of the current and former prime ministers, Tammam Salam and Fouad Siniora, had shouted, *Allah, Nasrallah w bas*—'God, Nasrallah, and nothing else'—as they did so. Others dismissed them as acts of pre-political anger, the uncouth manifestation of an incoherent popular will. The Amal minister Ali Hassan Khalil, seeking to defuse allegations that his own party and Hizballah had tried to infuse the protests with sectarian overtones, using them to exert pressure on their opponents, described the young men who had defiled the homes of Salam and

Siniora as *za'ran*, or thugs. This was a reading shared by the Future Movement, which warned of the actions of 'undisciplined partisans' whose behaviour did not reflect their leaders' directives.[48] But when the journalist Moe Ali Nayel spoke to some of the young men involved in these protests, he found only frustration at the seething economic inequality that they faced. 'We are on the street, jobless, and with no place to go', they told him, recounting tales of how the state punished them, confiscating their scooters, rounding them up and inflicting beatings on them, while a 'small ruling class' enjoyed 'state security protection and legal immunity'.[49] These two elements—an insurgent working-class sense of 'disenfranchisement' and the efforts of Lebanon's politicians to close ranks and to portray the protests as beyond the law—would be a constant motif through the demonstrations of the coming weeks.

So too would the efforts of activists—many of them middle-class university students and civil society campaigners—to coordinate and canalise the protests. Early evidence of this came on Saturday 25 July, when a sit-in was staged in *shari' al-bnuk*, the 'street of banks' in central Beirut. The timing—the demonstration was called for 5:00 p.m. on a weekend evening, when people would be free of work and social obligations—was telling evidence of the organisers' desire to appeal to a middle-class public. For the first time, the hashtag slogan #YouStink—*tal'it rihatkum*, in Arabic—was used to denounce the stench of political malfeasance.[50] Over the next few weeks, it would gain wide currency, a viral rallying cry and a digital token of disgust and disaffection. At the same time, Tal'it Rihatkum would become a movement, or rather a nucleus of committed activists who coordinated activities online and in the streets, seeking to maintain the momentum of popular discontent and to channel the sense of public frustration and anger and anxiety into a broader challenge to the authority of a corrupt and kleptocratic political class. These aims it shared with the other movement that emerged in these weeks, Badna Nhasib, or 'we want accounts'. Their names—direct, slogan-like and, in the case of Badna Nhasib, programmatic in a way quite different to the empty, pious phrases with which Lebanese parties and parliamentary blocs garland themselves—hinted at the concerns of the hard core of activists who established them. Many of them long committed to causes as varied as anti-sectarianism and anti-corruption, labour militancy and migrant workers' rights, urban conservation, women's rights and LGBTQ+ advocacy, they shared a common abhorrence for Lebanon's politicians and their self-interested pursuit of neoliberal policies.

And yet the two movements, though often bundled together, had rather different objectives. Tal'it Rihatkum focused predominantly on clearly defined short-term objectives that its leading lights regarded as within reach: the devolution of responsibility for waste management to Lebanon's municipalities; the resignation of the minister of the environment, Mohammad Machnouq; immediate parliamentary elections; and accountability for the security services that had used excessive force against demonstrators. Badna Nhasib, meanwhile, had rather more ambitious aims. As one of its leading figures, Georges Azar, explained to *The Daily Star*, 'we think that replacing someone like the environment minister is not the solution to our problems. The real problem is the sectarian regime that is dividing us.' In short, resignations and elections were no more than efforts to tinker with a broken machine. The Lebanese state, Badna Nhasib argued, was a *nizam al-ta'ifi* and a *dawlet al-muhasasat*—a 'sectarian regime' and a 'state of allotments', whose sole purpose was to distribute the spoils of the country's economy among its sectarian leaders and their privileged clients and friends. It was time, in Azar's words, for a 'popular movement that pulls people away from sectarian identity and towards a national one'. 'What we want to do is to change society, not only the positions in our government.'[51]

These calls for action struck a chord with many who, without necessarily sharing all of these movements' objectives, shared their disgust at the state of the streets and the conduct of the government and were increasingly willing to vent their frustration in the capital's streets and public squares. Particularly significant were the events on 19 August, when demonstrators who had gathered near Riyad al-Sulh Square, in the very centre of Beirut, were brutally beaten back by riot police. Footage filmed earlier that day shows a peaceful protest: young men and women dressed for summer marching through the street, chanting their slogans, or sitting cross-legged in small circles listening to the movement's most prominent figures discuss the country's predicament. Despite the frustration evident in the words of these speeches—

al-zbeleh ma bta'rif ta'ifeh, al-mard ma bya'rif ta'ifeh, al-fu'r ma bya'rif ta'ifeh, al-ju' ma bya'rif ta'ifeh, 'rubbish and illness and poverty and hunger know no confession', Assaad Thebian is shown saying, sitting on another demonstrator's shoulders—the crowd seems well-natured and in good spirits. By mid-afternoon, however, the situation had turned. First the security services used water-cannon in their attempts to repel the demonstrators and to keep them away from the streets around parliament, the prime minister's office and the Ministry of the Environment. Then, when this failed to disperse the crowds, security agents advanced on the protesters. Unsteady mobile phone footage shows them, in their helmets and padded uniforms, sheltering behind their shields as they rain hard blows down on the young men and women before them.[52]

One of the clips that went viral makes for excruciating viewing: a tense stand-off, as demonstrators attempt to reason with the agents whose faces are a few centimetres from their own, then a sudden release of violence; one of the agents pushes a woman back, she pushes back, her open palm on his shield, and then the blows start coming down. Panicked screams. Officers attempt to calm their men, to separate them from the crowd. But both sides are now anxious, angry. Insults are exchanged, and agents suddenly surge forward, appearing to single out particular demonstrators whose words have slighted them. One agent lunges for a woman filming the events on her mobile phone. 'You are attacking a woman, shame on you,' someone in the crowd screams. Then the policemen again throw themselves forward, this time faster, sending the crowd running back. All around the person filming you can hear shouts of *baltajiyyeh, baltajiyyeh*—'thugs, thugs'. The whole thing lasts only three and a half minutes. But it is unbearably visceral, claustrophobic, tense.[53] Four of Tal'it Rihatkum's main figures—Thebian, Lucien Bourjeily, Hassan Chammas and Waref Sleiman—were detained that day, before being released. One demonstrator, Bilal Allaw, was so badly beaten that he had to be rushed to hospital with a broken jaw. By nightfall, the violence had finally achieved its effect. Many had fled, and the protest was called off. As the blogger Elie Fares put it in a laconic tweet, just before 7:00 p.m.: 'Protesters have been called to go home and not to leave any trash behind. There's enough of those in government'.[54]

If the government's intention was to defuse the protests, discouraging others from descending into the streets, then its actions backfired. For the sight of this seemingly unwarranted aggression only served to galvanise many. To the protest movement's demands for a sound resolution to the rubbish crisis and for an end to the political atrophy that had left Lebanon's parliament a withered branch were now added calls for justice for the demonstrators hurt and arrested on 19 August and for an end to police aggression. The following weekend, large crowds descended on central Beirut. On Saturday 22 August, there were perhaps as many as 10,000 people gathered in Martyrs' Square; on Sunday 23 August, as many as 15,000. But, once again, the demonstrations turned violent, as security agents and soldiers attempted to keep the crowds out of the streets around parliament. One young woman caught the scene on film as soldiers responded to demonstrators throwing projectiles—stones, sticks, plastic chairs—by firing into the air and cocking their guns at the crowd. As panicked protesters ran backwards, shouts of *shabbiha, shabbiha*—'thugs, thugs'—and *'ayb al-shum*—'shame on you'—rang out.[55]

And yet, the violence was still not enough to quell popular anger. On 29 August came the largest demonstration of all. Aerial photos and drone footage showed Martyrs' Square, that vast, empty space in the heart of the city, filled with demonstrators, waving Lebanese flags and chanting *thawra, thawra*—'revolution, revolution'. As one demonstrator told a journalist, 'we need a revolution to free ourselves from these politicians. We want power, we want water, we don't want rubbish in the streets. We want these politicians to get lost.'[56] This time, there was to be little violence. For rather than relying upon policemen and soldiers to keep the demonstrators back, the security forces had effectively turned the area around parliament into a fortified enclave guarded by concrete breezeblocks and layers of barbed wire. Safe behind their barriers, the security forces watched as young men desperately pulled at the barbed wire. This was a security zone that some compared, with bitter derision, to Baghdad's Green Zone—a comparison that spoke not just of the lengths to which Lebanese politicians had gone to protect their sanctum, but also to the extent that many viewed them as illegitimate, alien occupiers who had usurped the sovereignty of the Lebanese people and were bleeding the land dry.[57]

But by this point, Tal'it Rihatkum had lost control of the demonstrations, after denouncing the violence of 22 August as the work of 'agent provocateurs, hooligans and thugs' in the pay of politicians who had infiltrated the protests to sow unrest and to undermine their peaceful intentions. These comments provoked bitter controversy and recrimination, particularly for those for whom they revealed the class cleavage between Tal'it Rihatkum's largely middle-class members and the young working-class men and boys who had joined the demonstrations in large numbers over the course of August. If some feared the latter, wary of their supposed potential for violence or anxious that they might be doing the bidding of this or that sectarian leader, others insisted that these claims were baseless, the mere products of pusillanimous bourgeois minds. Despite the movement's subsequent attempts at reconciliation, the damage had been done: it could no longer claim to be the sole voice and coordinating force of the contestation movement.[58] Over the following weeks, events would slip out of its grasp.

I arrived in Beirut too late to witness these initial protests, but was there for the events on 9 September, called to coincide with yet another round of the national dialogue sessions called by the speaker of parliament, Nabih Berri. For almost two days the city had been in the midst of a sandstorm that had come in from the Syrian desert to the east. Shops, schools, and universities in the capital closed down, and the news carried reports of respiratory problems and low visibility. On the day of the protest, anticipation mingled on social media with fears that violence and dust would put off many from attending, like further portents of the apocalypse soon to engulf Lebanon. I remember sitting in my hotel room for much of the afternoon, relying on a vacillating internet connection to watch a live stream of protesters—mere kids, eighteen or nineteen years old, their limbs thin, not yet thickened by age, their faces covered up with black scarves and Palestinian *keffiyeh*-s—pelt eggs at the blacked-out armoured Mercedes that swept towards parliament, carrying the leaders of Lebanon's political parties to yet another round of extemporisation and prevarication. Over and over I watched the same short clip, trying to gain a sense of what was happening. Shouts of *haramiyyeh, haramiyyeh*—'thieves, thieves'—then a quick flick of the arm sending another projectile towards a car speeding past, a leg stretched out in an angry kick at the politicians entering the private securitised precinct of parliament square. Twenty-one seconds, and again it starts, decades of seething frustration distilled into a third of a minute.

At about half past five, I decided to head down to the demonstration. After about half an hour's walk along the seafront, I reached the bottom of Martyrs' Square, past the spot where I had watched that scene unfold digitally, still strewn with broken eggshells and yolks spattered like mucus over the asphalt. Following the sound of speeches, I trailed a small trickle of people climbing up the hill, and through the gaps in a car park fence, to the square. The crowd was smaller than that many had reported on 29 August, but it was still big—bigger, at least, than I had expected from the live feeds on social media. More people had come out now that work had ended and the storm, which had exacerbated Beirut's pollution problems, had abated a little. All in all, there were probably a few thousand in attendance, though some organisers would later put the figure higher. The crowd was a motley one: youngish middle-class parents with their designer eyeglasses and slogan-bearing t-shirts, carrying their babies in slings hung about their chests, or letting their toddlers stumble alongside them; older, well-to-do couples wandering about like dazed tourists in their sunglasses and designer shirts; students with their facemasks—as much a badge of protest against the ambient stench and permanent pollution as a measure against the sand particles—but also wizened trade unionists holding up their banners and groups of boys from the working-class neighbourhood of Khandaq al-Ghamiq, providing a pulse to this uncoordinated mass with their *darbakeh* drums and their mocking, irreverent chants.

On the edge of the square sat a large stage hastily erected for the occasion, with a video screen and impressive speakers, of the kind one sees more often at music festivals, suspended precariously either side. Tal'it Rihatkum, in its attempts to regain some legitimacy, had done its best to turn this latest demonstration into a multimedia extravaganza, showcasing the different strands of the movement it hoped were coalescing in opposition to the government and its deleterious policies. At times, these efforts to demonstrate the protests' wide appeal seemed ill-thought out. This was particularly the case when two soap stars were wheeled out to show their support for the cause. While one attempted to make a melodramatic political speech full of allusions to the politicians in their palaces, the other confined herself to shouting *intu helwin*, 'you're beautiful', over and over again at the crowd, her words wheeling into feedback as people stood about with a sense of discomfort on their faces. At such moments, the organisers' attempts to be all things to all people, to show that theirs was not just a fringe movement of a few disaffected radicals but one that could appeal to those who prefer their *musalsalat*, or telenovelas, to political talk shows, provoked only a sense of disjoint and drift. No-one seemed sure what was really happening here, or what the point of it all was.

At other moments, however, the event did appear to cohere into something more cogent, the manifestation of a movement with clear desiderata. As the evening gained on the day, speakers from across the regions affected by the various 'rubbish plans' proposed by this minister or that took to the rostrum in turn. The representative of the local committee of Akkar, where a new landfill was being mooted, gained loud cheers from the audience when she repeated the slogans that had rapidly gained currency in recent weeks: *'Akkar mish mikab, 'Akkar mish zbeleh, 'Akkar mish lil-bi'*—'Akkar is not a dumping site', 'Akkar is not rubbish', 'Akkar is not for sale'. Tripoli's representative spoke of this latest crisis as the culmination of years of neglect, when the city had been left to its own internecine squabbles by governments unable or unwilling to address its problems. Its inhabitants, he reminded the crowd, had lived through six years of fighting. Three quarters of them were now unemployed. Only their innate resilience—*sumud*—and dignity—*karama*—had allowed them to remain. The speaker from Naameh was the oldest by some way, a wiry dark-haired man well into middle age, who had gained experience of protest and negotiation over years of opposition to the landfill that had blighted his small town. He gave one of the most impassioned speeches of all as night fell, weaving many of the phrases that had become leitmotifs of the protests into his defence of local rights. He recounted his efforts to alleviate the problems created by rubbish, telling the crowd that the politicians met with us only to say that they had met with us ... This was nothing short of a *mu'amara*, a 'conspiracy' against us, the people. 'That is their dialogue, that is their aim', he said, 'they don't know anything else' but the politics of 'sectarian division'. But we do not want the protection or pity of anyone, he continued. *Badna al-haqq*, 'we want the truth', we want justice and what is rightfully ours. We rose up to reclaim our independence, and to create a democratic state. 'Yes to the state', he insisted, but 'no to the state of corruption and *muhasasat*', or the division of the spoils. It is they, the political class, who stink with the rot of corruption. It is not just the rubbish that suffocates and chokes us— *byikhni'na*—but also the electricity and the water that don't come, the education system's failings, the lack of employment and low wages.

These were speeches that harped on the tropes of patria, of homeland, of popular accord and popular rights. Many presented the political as a contest for control of the state, pitting the citizen, *al-muwatin*, against *al-tabaqa al-siyasiyya*. In this starkly binary vision, the citizenry, the people, were cast as long suffering, oppressed and blighted by incompetence and self-interested neglect, those who hold power as unworthy of it, corrupted, indolent, and incapable of achieving anything but their own survival. In this sense, these speeches seem to encapsulate the discontent and sense of possibility of those days—in their attempts to weave a series of local narratives into a national cause, in their frustration, in their desire for doing away with the post-war consensus, their vague, utopian striving for a new commonwealth. This was echoed by the crowd, as cries of *al-sha'b*, 'the people', gained in amplitude, repeated again and again in triplets, or as all chanted *la arb'ata'sh w la tmene, ana muwatin lubnani*—'Not 14 [March] and not 8 [March], I am a Lebanese citizen'—or sang along to the national anthem boomed out from the speakers above the stage. But there was also an angrier, more irreverent streak running through many of the chants and songs I heard that evening. Shouts broke out of *yasqut yasqut hukm al-az'ar*—echoing the chant of *al-sha'b yurid isqat al-nizam*, 'the people want the downfall of the regime', that had become the rallying cry of Arab capitals in early 2011, but turning it into an even angrier condemnation of the 'rule of crooks'. Many of the chants had something humorous about them, mocking rhymes putting the playful metre of children's songs to satirical ends. One of these was *arb'ata'sh w tmene 'amlu al-balad dekene*, or '14 [March] and 8 [March] have turned the country into a corner shop' where everything is for sale at knockdown prices. Another took the tune and opening words of 'Jingle Bells'— 'Leilet Eid' in Arabic. *Leilet 'eid, leilet 'eid, haida majlis al-zbeleh, majlis al-tamdid*, the demonstrators sang, mocking 'the assembly of rubbish, the parliament of prolongation', contrasting their representatives' inability to provide solutions to the trash crisis with their readiness to extend their own terms in office—one of the few measures that had reached any kind of consensus across the political class in recent years.

Later, on social media, some complained that the demonstration was too much like a *mahrajan*—a festival or show. By this they seem to have meant that its organisers were too eager to turn the evening into a carefully choreographed display of dissent. Too controlling and too bumbling in their efforts to plan proceedings, too anxious to persuade the media that their movement had traction and support, they had succeeded only in arresting its momentum and diluting its revolutionary potential. But this desire to manage tightly the ungovernable force of protest, turning discontent into slick, insipid political entertainment, competed with another more carnivalesque sense of the political, more wilfully chaotic, more improvised and unpredictable, more biting in its scorn, a Lebanese 'rough music' designed to humiliate the country's politicians and push them into retreat.

As night fell and most of the crowd drifted away, a small group of perhaps a few hundred moved south through Martyrs' Square, away from the main site of the demonstration and towards the barricades that closed off access to parliament and the Ministry of the Environment. From the margins, I watched as a small group of teenagers—perhaps from Khandaq al-Ghamiq or Siray or Bashoura—provided a pulse to the protest. Their limbs shiny with sweat under the streetlights, they beat out a propulsive rhythm on their drums, while one of them—hardly a teenager at all, but still a young boy, his hair shaped into a brush cut above a podgy face rimmed with heavy glasses—called out mocking, funny slogans through a megaphone. Later, as I walked home, I saw young men and women in green t-shirts emblazoned with the #YouStink hashtag slogan, their mouths covered with sanitary facemasks, cleaning up the rubbish the demonstrators had left behind, a pick-up operation designed to keep the movement true to its aspirations. On the one hand, the 'disenfranchised young men' from 'marginalised and poverty-stricken areas' that the journalist Moe Ali Nayel described; on the other, diligent, well-meaning, middle-class university students. For all the intense focus on You Stink, the ones were as much a part of these events as the others. But though they occupied the same space and shared the same broad aspiration towards *'adala ijtima'iyya*, or 'social justice'—one of the leitmotifs of these days and weeks—they had different horizons of expectation and resorted to quite different tactics.

Indeed, it is one of the paradoxes of these weeks of contestation that the different actors who took part in these events often chose tactics that seemed out of keeping with their aspirations and ambitions. While Tal'it Rihatkum remained committed to immediate objectives—and, in particular, the resignation of the embattled Mohammad Machnouq—it drew increasingly upon the solemn, dignified repertoire of non-violence. On 1 September, activists from the group occupied the Ministry of the Environment, in downtown Beirut. After nine hours, they were brutally ejected. According to the film director and environmental activist Lucien Bou Rjaily, who had helped to organise the protest, the security services had first prohibited the demonstrators from using the building's bathrooms. Then they barred them from getting food and water into the building. Finally, they closed all the windows and turned off the air conditioning, leaving the demonstrators sweltering. Once they had thrown out the cameramen and journalists who crowded the corridors, they dragged the demonstrators from their positions on the floor, beating them and pulling them along the ground. Throughout, Abou Rjaily was at pains to stress, the demonstrators had remained 'peaceful'.[59] On 4 September, a group of students and activists began a hunger strike in Martyrs' Square, determined to fast until Machnouq left office.[60] There was undoubtedly something deeply brave and affecting about these gestures. They seemed to be acts of grave, considered commitment and of genuine courage. And yet, they did not succeed in securing even the smallest of concessions from the government. Several of the hunger strikers were hospitalised, their bodies pushed to their very limits. Machnouq, however, stayed where he was, resolutely refusing to resign.

On the other hand, Badna Nhasib and their allies seemed to combine a utopian longing for a reformed state with a propensity for tactics that seemed to draw on the capacity for irreverent insurrection of the *shabab*, the 'young men' who had come down into Martyrs' Square from Beirut's working-class neighbourhoods. Over the course of September, they staged a series of fast-moving, subversive occupations and operations, designed to take up public space, to make it their own, erasing the marks of the present and transforming it into a theatre in which to act out visions of the future.

Some of these events, like the actions of the small group who had pelted the SUVs and armoured Mercedes of the politicians entering parliament with eggs and rotting vegetables, were strikingly simple in their methods. Others, though they shared the same subversive impulse, showed a rather more performative bent, coming to seem almost like happenings or pieces of live art. This understanding of the importance of 'symbolic' performances to capture the attention of the public and to impel it towards revolutionary change was apparent even in the earliest days of the contestation movement. On 24 July, a group of members of the Lebanese Communist Party had taken bags of rubbish down to Zaitunay Bay. 'As you know', one of them explained to a television reporter, 'this place has a particular significance, as it used to be the entrance to the Normandy landfill. We are calling on the people [al-'alam] ... if the government does not find another dumping ground or landfill, to throw their rubbish here as, in any case, these are public properties stolen by ... a corrupt political class'. As another of the protesters that day put it, this was a 'symbolic' action. It could not stand in for 'real action'—al-shi al-fii 'li—for popular movements calling for wholesale change. But it could draw attention, not just to the symptoms of the crisis, but also to its underlying causes.[61]

Many of the demonstrations of September showed a similar desire to speak truth to power and to take back the commonweal. On 4 September, activists from Badna Nhasib launched what Al-Nahar called a 'surprise raid' on the Corniche, sabotaging the parking meters that had been installed along Beirut's seafront by placing stickers over their coin-slots. Their reasoning was simple. This was public land, and the people should not have to pay to use it.[62] On 12 September activists staged a gathering at Zaitunay Bay. Singing, playing music, dancing the dabkeh, sitting on the marina's boards to eat the picnics they had brought with them, they flaunted its rules and regulations in a playful, joy-filled manner. To underpin their irreverence, to insist that one enjoy oneself even while manifesting one's discontent, some even wore red clown noses. After a couple of hours, the journalist Habib Battah recounted, the crowd decided to walk down the Corniche and towards Daliet al-Raouche. Some had brought pliers in their bags, and began to cut through the wire fence that closed off the Dalieh. The policemen who were there simply watched on, doing nothing, as the joyful crowd tore away the barrier that had kept them from the sea and walked down to the shore, chanting hoarse celebrations.[63]

Perhaps we should not overstate the differences between these two strands of contestation, the one solemn and still in its efforts to invite the shameful violence of the state, the other full of jubilation and the exhilarating potential of subversion, for there could be, at times, significant overlaps in their language. From his hospital bed, Lucien Bou Rjaily, one of the organisers of the sit-in held in the Ministry of the Environment, wrote a stinging message to the minister of the interior, Nouhad Machnouq, and the entire political class of which he was a part:

> Why did you throw out the media ... before breaking us with your barbaric, your beastly and dictatorial boots and batons? You are a dictatorship of shame, you are without honour and without morals. Because we were 100 per cent peaceful, you cut the cameras covering the crime. You are a mafia and you have taken over the entire state with your corruption. But the people will bring you to account, and soon.[64]

Such discursive overlaps notwithstanding, it does seem the case that these two strands were using increasingly divergent means to pursue different ends.

Despite these growing cleavages, the demonstrations of these weeks remained, for some, portents of a coming revolution. The scholar Nadia Bou Ali, for instance, called upon the 'uprising ... to be affirmed, supported and pushed to reach its radical potentials'. To insist on the unpolitical or depoliticised nature of the demonstrations was a mistake, she declared. What was needed was a new definition of the political, one that replaced the language of *nashitin*, or activists, with that of *thuwwar*, or revolutionaries, and that of violence and non-violence by 'state violence versus revolutionary violence'. Only once truly radical could 'the revolt' hope to 'establish a coherent program against the capitalist neo-liberal state without resorting to its own slogans of "democracy", "technocratic government", and "reform"'.[65] Others drew upon the visual and discursive resources of revolutions past to mount mordant attacks on Lebanon's politicians. In a series of striking posters, the graphic designer Jana Traboulsi mocked these men and their theft of public wealth and public space. *Taht rasif Solidere arduna*, one read—'under Solidere's pavements is our earth'. Playfully appropriating the company's logo, this was an image that echoed the Situationist slogan of May 1968—*sous les pavés, la plage*—redeploying it to make a claim for repossessing wrongly acquired public goods. A similar visual pun underpinned another of Traboulsi's images, which used the distinctive design used by the municipality of Beirut to write the city's name to claim 'this is not Beirut, this is the logo of a private company that owns the centre of Beirut'. In her accompanying notes, Traboulsi made clear her aims. 'City-centers are named as such because they gather people. They should not belong [to], be managed, or controlled by a few. ... They are where all inhabitants walk, meet, stroll, buy, stop, rejoin ... They are where we contest and subvert. They will always be as such.'⁶⁶ 'Now, at this historical moment of the country's movements and struggles, I am now part of an "us". ... We have legitimacy and people power.'⁶⁷ There were many who shared this novel sense of shared desires and objectives, a common sense of working together in collective action to build a different future.

Others, however, dismissed the protests out of hand. As one well-to-do woman told me, they were nothing but *enfantillages qui ne mèneront à rien*—mere 'kid's play, which would come to naught'. There was a sense of weariness and disillusion here—a sense that nothing could ever change for the better, no matter what—but also a contempt for the young men and women who had streamed out into the streets. Others saw the protests through the prism of conspiracy. One acquaintance in his early thirties told me a long and elaborate story of how the demonstrations had been orchestrated by an old schoolmate of his, who had worked in Washington, D.C. for an NGO before being sent out to Tunisia to train protesters in social media tactics and then to Syria, where he had trained members of the Syrian opposition. Now he was back in Lebanon. He was, as my acquaintance told me, 'a clever guy, too clever to be played'. But his presence at the heart of the protests showed that they were being spurred on by the United States. Once again, geopolitical grand strategies were being plotted out in distant capitals whose implementation would cost the Lebanese dear, and once again Washington had played its hand badly. The US–Iran nuclear deal had led to a détente, and allowed Russia a free hand in Syria. Saudi Arabia was weak and distracted by Yemen. The Christians in Lebanon were at their lowest ebb, disillusioned and broken by years of infighting and vain hopes. Hizballah saw this as a moment of opportunity; it would use Aoun's vanity and appetite for the presidency to stall any attempts to resolve the rubbish crisis, pushing the people to breaking point and undermining yet further any lingering trust in government. When all hope seemed lost, the party would seize the moment to call for a constitutional assembly, which would enable it to introduce the reforms it had long sought to bolster its own position. 'The cards', he insisted, 'all lined up'. The arc of history had tended towards this final, awful point since 2002. Such is the impervious logic of conspiracy, with its reworking of facts into a teleological narrative of fear.

There is no doubt, however, that these days and weeks marked a moment of remarkable democratic opening, defined by a desire to speak and discuss, to unburden oneself of frustrations and to share concerns, but also to pool knowledge and experience and views, to construct new alliances that paid little heed to partisan or sectarian differences, in the hope that something might give and that paths might be found out of the obscurity. In mid-September, I attended an open meeting at Masrah al-Madina, the Hamra theatre owned by the actor Nidal Achkar. All those who spoke that evening, from well-known activists like the lawyer Nizar Saghieh and the economist and ex-minister Charbel Nahhas, to ordinary members of the audience who had been galvanised into action by the effects of waste on their communities, shared a common sense of outrage at decades of institutional failure, resignation, and inaction. As one panel member put it, the problem was not an environmental one, but a problem of the state. This was, he went on, picking up a phrase used over and again in these weeks, a state of *muhasasat*—'the division of the spoils'. 'We are', he concluded, 'in a political crisis'. Another put it in even sharper terms: 'the past was all corruption … the future is all rose-tinted dreams, but in the present, we have a duty not to waste time in empty talk. Cholera is on its way and we need an alternative to the plan' the government had put forward. Others echoed this call for urgent action, born of a deep fear of what the first rains would bring, flooding the streets with rotting waste and spreading disease through the city. There was a need to 'confront the plan with force', to call out the names of those who were corrupt and who had dragged Lebanon to this point and to bring them to justice. What was at stake here was the 'dignity of the Lebanese people'.

But amidst the anger and despair, there was also a desire to know what could be done—a desire for collective action and concerted change. Some spoke in crude terms of the constraints that Lebanon faced. 'Kuwait', one audience member opined, 'is a desert country, there is room there for landfills. In Lebanon there isn't more than a kilometre between one village and the next'. Others recalled the mistakes of the past. There could be no return, another audience member insisted, to the days of the Normandy landfill, when waste was simply thrown into the sea, creating mounds of rubbish. To do this, however, required a sea change in attitudes across society and government. Several speakers insisted on the need to see waste not as a 'problem, but as a source of revenues'. As one panel member put it 'rubbish is a public property, the whole world is extracting money from rubbish ... nothing is to be thrown away'. Why was it, for instance, that Lebanon imported recycled glass from Jordan, when it didn't know what to do with its own glass, or that a country in which more than half the population relied on bottled water imported recycled plastics from Saudi Arabia or the United Arab Emirates? Why not seize on the opportunities that waste presented, turning refuse, say, into compost that could be sold for $15 a bag? There was a need, then, not just for recrimination and accountability, for parsing the mistakes of the past and assigning blame, but also for building a new future by devising a comprehensive waste management policy in line with regional and global trends.[68]

Beirut Madinati

Already, in the heady, frantic days of September 2015, some were beginning to think of ways to build on the angry energy unleashed by the rubbish crisis. Many older civil society activists who had helped to coordinate campaigns against the gentrification of Beirut, the razing of old neighbourhoods to build new, ineffective highways, the demolition of old buildings to erect empty, luxury high-rises, and the enclosure or destruction of public spaces greeted the protests of these weeks with ambivalence. On the one hand, they saw these—as an architect and activist told me in September 2015—as a manifestation of growing 'unity' and 'solidarity' between different constituencies, revealing the 'common ground' that bound together previously disparate campaigns and causes, from heritage and environmental protection to anti-sectarianism and anti-corruption.[69] As an urban planner who would go on to be involved in Beirut Madinati told me in September 2015, these questions were intimately tied up, for the collapse of waste management suddenly threw into sharp relief all the other systemic failures of infrastructure—and all, ultimately, could be traced back to the way in which the zu'ama had 'distributed out [Beirut's] neighbourhoods among themselves' in the wake of the civil war, leading to the piecemeal, uneven provision that had characterised the subsequent decades.[70]

On the other hand, they were sharply aware of the generational divide that separated them from the shabab al-sghar, the 'young kids'. 'The movement', in the words of the architect I spoke to, 'is not us'. It was deeply 'useful' for 'building awareness' of the underlying issues. But there was, at the same time, the need for a civil society of experts, professional men and women—architects, urbanists, lawyers, people with connections, who had worked with the Ministry of Culture, say, and knew the correct procedures. The architect was clear that there was space for both tactics, that there shouldn't be any difference, as she put it, between the 'professional activists' and the 'ground activists', but constant dialogue.[71]

Others, however, were not so sure. For the urban planner I spoke with, the acephalous, fragmented nature of these movements was not a strength, but a profound failing, stymying their capacity for effective action. Many of the people involved, she told me, mistrust each other's positions, each other's views. Like the architect, she felt that many of those at the forefront were just 'kids' who lacked political experience. There could be no clearer evidence of this than the hunger strikers' demand for Mohammed Machnouq's resignation. As she put it, he was but an insignificant pawn, a useful placeman. The cards were not in his hands; he lacked the power to resign, for the decision did not ultimately rest with him, but with his superiors. Failing to realise this, the protesters had naively set themselves an unrealisable goal. Equally frustrating was their tendency to think only in the short term, caught up in the fervent rush of the moment. 'At the minute', she explained, 'the horizon is the next event, the next day'. The questions that were being asked were purely tactical ones, of numbers, of momentum: 'will they bring people down against the *tawlat al-hiwar*'—the national dialogue sessions held in parliament—'or not?'[72] Implicit in these comments was a desire for a longer-term strategy.

This pessimism was echoed by another older academic in his late thirties, who had gained experience of political activism in the late 1990s and early 2000s. The 'hashtag movements', as he called them, were in clear danger of running out of steam and being outmanoeuvred. They could muster, at most, a couple of hundred dedicated activists willing to come down into the streets. The political parties could bring twice that many into the streets at the drop of a hat. Operating in the space between 14 March and 8 March, the protesters depended on the equilibrium between these two forces—the stable existence of a chasm in which they could stand. But should the two blocs forge a tactical alliance to ward off this challenge to their authority, as they appeared to be doing, then the movements would be trapped and asphyxiated. What's more, he too thought that in their naïve eagerness they had committed grave tactical errors, such as singling out Nabih Berri for criticism—a perceived slight that his followers in the street and the security services would not easily forget. In the short term, then, they were destined to peter out, like the brief efflorescence of civil society activism in 1998 shut down by Hariri and Lahoud, or like the activism of 2003 to 2005, which ended with the *intifadat al-arz*, the cedar uprising, and the consolidation of the main political blocs. And yet this was no tragic failure, for the movements had brought something new into the country—new, younger, faces had infused civil society with a sense of possibility it was in danger of losing, as its stalwarts slipped into a jaded and weary middle age.[73] As the urban planner insisted, there was a need to build on the energy of the protests, but also for 'careful, effective planning' if those galvanised by the rubbish crisis were ever to look towards a more distant horizon of possibility. Now was the time to channel the palpable desire for change into a more structured political movement capable of 'capturing' the municipality of Beirut and bringing reform from within its institutions.

Of this equivocal sense of possibility was born the movement that would come to be known as Beirut Madinati. Its members shared a sense that administrative decentralisation and technocratic oversight could go hand-in-hand. For, as the urban planner explained to me, Lebanese law gave municipalities extensive powers which they did not exercise at present. There was therefore the need for a 'more efficient, responsive model of municipal government', which might use its extensive prerogatives to improve the lives of the citizenry.[74]

It would be tempting to see those who pushed for such change from within as following a global trend to see the city as the prime site of governance, a municipal island unto itself that could provide its inhabitants with the life that they desired. It may well be that, for some, such global arguments about urban planning were at the forefront of their minds. But when asked, several rejected these transregional comparisons in favour of more immediate precedents and influences. For the academic, the institutional memory of earlier civil society campaigns in Lebanon, with their desire to preserve the urban fabric and their insistence on anti-corruption, anti-sectarianism, and the importance of local decision-making, was crucial. Movements such as Indignados, Podemos, or Syriza were not their foremost inspiration.[75] The architect articulated this in even more forceful fashion. The significant precedent for the actions of 2015, she stressed, was that presented by the Arab revolutions of 2011. Despite all that happened since, they remained a positive development, which had set down a model of organisation, creating a sense that grassroots activism, loosely coordinated through the viral networks of social media, could be effective and could, perhaps, given the right conditions, translate into electoral gains and meaningful, substantive political transformations. The anti-austerity campaigns, movements, and parties of France, Spain, Greece or the United States—Occupy Wall Street, Nuit Debout, Indignados, Podemos, Syriza, and their like—did not occupy a central place in the minds of those pushing for change in Beirut. They were a 'beautiful parallel', to be sure, but nothing more than that.[76]

There were some, though, who did draw upon the rhetoric of these other movements to articulate their grievances and their vision of reform. In a widely circulated open letter, the academics Mona Harb and Mona Fawaz asked Beirut's mayor, Bilal Hamad, 'are you the mayor of the 1 per cent or the mayor of the 99 per cent?' Beneath this deliberate echo of the slogan that Occupy had made famous four years earlier, they delivered a stinging rebuke to Hamad's pleas of municipal impotence. Was it really the governor of Greater Beirut, Harb and Fawaz asked, who had 'stopped the project to improve the built fabric of the city, the creation of pedestrian paths, and the planting of trees' and who had failed to 'implement municipal policies that had succeeded in numerous cities across the world'? Would the governor have 'delayed the opening of Horsh Beirut, the only walking place in the area, had the mayor supported the organisations that had called for its opening for more than a decade'? Would the Council for Development and Reconstruction have attempted to 'destroy entire neighbourhoods in Achrafieh to build the Fouad Boutros highway', on the basis of an old and outmoded design plan, 'had the mayor stood with the inhabitants of the neighbourhoods and the activists who had worked to prevent the project'? And how 'could your office still see private cars as an acceptable solution' to Beirut's traffic problems, making no attempt to coordinate 'public transport'? Hamad had failed, Fawaz and Harb concluded, not just to use his considerable powers to provide better lives of Beirut's citizens. He had also missed a historic opportunity to work with the 'civil organisations that had worked to improve … conditions' in the city, and whose frustration had resulted in their taking their 'demands into the streets'. In short, they told Hamad, 'you have failed to serve your constituents, who brought you to office, because of your constant attempts to maintain the support and satisfaction of the 1 per cent'. The time had come to 'abandon the traditional political and confessional elite and to elect true defenders of the city and its way of life'.[77] This letter would effectively come to serve over the coming months as Beirut Madinati's founding charter and manifesto, an incandescent appeal to the public which conveyed the movement's aspirations.

But this was only one part of the sophisticated communication strategy that the movement developed in the lead-up to the municipal elections of June 2016. Central to this were the campaign videos that it produced showcasing its candidates, short, straight-to-camera monologues, plainly designed for viral dissemination through social media and rapid viewing. None lasted more than a minute or two, and even the casual, distracted viewer scrolling through their newsfeed or clicking between tabs could find something memorable in them. All proceeded in much the same fashion, with the candidate introducing and giving a brief account of themselves, their professional life and upbringing before focusing on their dedication to a particular cause or campaign and on what they hoped to achieve through standing as a candidate, and all ended with the same message: *sawwit Bayrut madinati, la'iha lil-intikhabat al-baladiyya 2016*, 'vote for the Beirut Madinati list in the 2016 municipal elections'. These videos were not just structured in the same fashion, but also conveyed the same substantive message.

In one, 'Abd al-Halim Jabr introduces himself as 'an architect, a consultant in urban planning, and a university professor'. But, just as importantly, he 'was born in Zuqaq al-Blat, and grew up in Hamad Street in Tariq al-Jdideh and Mar Elias street in Musaytbeh'. Jabr goes on: 'I am an activist involved in efforts to protect the old buildings of Beirut's shoreline, but for the last few years I have concentrated more on the traffic crisis in Beirut. Congestion and the near-total reliance on the car are a disease, and for the last eighteen years Beirut municipality have been out of the picture ... I am part of an organisation that opposed the construction of the Fouad Boutros highway in Achrafieh, and that succeeded in stopping [the project], as it would only lower congestion by 3 per cent', while leading to the flattening of old, working-class neighbourhoods and the asphalting over of some of Beirut's few remaining green spaces. 'Among our priorities', Jabr concludes, 'is to find an alternative plan for transport in Beirut, for all of its citizens and their needs. It is our right to get [somewhere] without getting stuck in a traffic jam. It is our right to walk on safe, comfortable pavements', rather than the narrow gangways colonised by bins and parked scooters and bollards that are typical of the city's streets. 'It is our right to go about Beirut without stress. Beirut is my city, and I want to work towards giving it a better life.'[78]

This video was typical of the three-pronged approach that Beirut Madinati adopted to persuade voters. Its candidates were professionals, deeply qualified to address the city's infrastructural problems and to provide its citizens with a better quality of life. They were themselves inhabitants of Beirut, who possessed longstanding and affectionate ties to the city and its neighbourhoods. And they had built up insight, gathering up ideas and plans and policies to keep in the storehouse of their minds, over years of involvement in civil society campaigns against gentrification, road building, and coastal constructions. More than that, they also possessed one final, unstated, qualification: they were not politicians. What some would have viewed as a flaw—their lack of active experience of government—these videos portrayed as a strength. This was a strategy that relied upon certain normative assumptions—about the neutrality and moral cleanliness of civil society, with its detachment from government and its malfeasance and misplaced ambitions, and about the self-evident worth of technocratic expertise. But it also rested upon the understanding that those who knew the city and its neighbourhoods, who had been born and grown up there, who loved it and cared for it, were best placed to remedy its problems. Emotional attachment and affective concern mattered as much here as technocratic competence.

As this suggests, the movement portrayed itself as deeply democratic. It was, to be sure, an alternative to the political status quo. But it was not an alternative to politics. Rather, as a coalition of ordinary citizens presenting themselves as candidates to represent those who, like them, were affected by the quotidian stresses of the city and wished to find remedies to these chronic aches, it offered a singular opportunity to renew and reconceive of the political. This movement alone could transform it from an instrument of interest, a display of constant enmity and incompetence, into a utilitarian pursuit, providing the greatest happiness for the greatest number. It was, in short, a movement of the people and for the people.

These videos, introducing the list's candidates to its public, were accompanied by a host of others designed to underpin its message of change, of togetherness and concern and competence. Some adopted a more pedagogical stance, seeking to educate prospective voters in what the municipality could achieve and reinforcing Beirut Madinati's message that the town hall could be an effective locus for change. Many were playful, semi-animated, short clips like those entitled simply *Bayrut shu na'sa?*—or Beirut, what is she missing? One, just thirty-eight seconds long, focused on the pavement. It began by showing a still of Tariq al-Jdideh, the narrow road shrunken still further by cars parked either side and devoid of pedestrian crossings, the pavement, bereft of passers-by, barely a couple of metres across, the only sign of municipal investment a few sorry-looking trees. Beneath it was a simple caption: *Tariq al-jdideh, aj'et siyyarat*—or 'Tariq al-Jdideh, crowded with cars'. As a jaunty tune played, an invisible hand redrew this streetscape into a more comforting, liveable shape. The pavement was widened. Along the concrete wall on one side, simple corrugated iron stalls went up for local street vendors. New, fully grown, healthy trees were planted, providing a thick cover. A zebra crossing appeared. A new caption appeared: *Tariq al-jdideh, mush bas lil-siyyarat*, 'Tariq al-Jdideh, not just for cars'. Finally, cartoon characters popped up: an intellectual-looking man in middle age, with grey hair and glasses, holding papers under his arm, as he smiled in delight at this new vision. Cyclists crossing the road. A smiling couple walking their baby in a stroller. Men in sports gear chatting happily with the local vendors. A picture, in other words, of possibility, of what could be done with the seemingly unprepossessing raw material of the city, remaking the unliveable and the austere into a space of civic life and togetherness, of conversation and conviviality.[79]

Another video produced about the same time sought to familiarise voters with the municipality's extensive prerogatives, giving them a sense of just how much was at stake in the upcoming elections. Drawn in a stylised black-and-white hand reminiscent of graphic novels, the clip shows a bus caught in Beirut gridlock. An exasperated driver—all caricature, with his white vest, his hairy arms, thick eyebrows, balding pate and black moustache—shouts out to everyone to get off. 'The road ahead is closed', he groans, as a pile of cars, all at awkward angles to each other, stretches out before him. 'When will they solve the problem with traffic?' a serious-looking young woman asks. 'It's up to the state', an older man exclaims. The presidential seat is shown, empty under a Lebanese flag. 'What has the president got to do with it?' the woman retorts, 'the municipality can also find solutions'. At this point, a voiceover takes over, the basso male voice deliberately evocative of that used in Lebanese commercials. 'The municipality', it calmly explains, 'cannot just resolve the traffic problem, it has extensive and particular prerogatives and it possesses a form of authority, as the governor holds executive powers and has oversight over the decisions taken by the municipal council'. 'And now what should I do?' an elderly woman asks. 'And now you can vote', answers the voice, calm, assured and reassuring.[80]

This clip is distinctive in a number of ways—for its playful parody of the norms of television advertising, but also for its willingness to take its audience's capacity for reasoned decision-making seriously, urging voters to go to the ballots, while explaining to them what their vote can achieve, rather than providing them with vacuous slogans portraying politics as a militaristic, masculine matter of honour and pride, of enmity, amity and existential survival. While taking a pedagogical tone, it sought to include a variety of voices, presenting the political sphere as one of dialogue rather than of acquiescence, of obedience. And, again, it was short. At barely forty-five seconds, it was designed for the accelerated, scattershot rhythm of social media. Almost like a tweet, it sought to compress information into a capsule, like a message squeezed into a bottle.

Other videos sought to draw the young in by other means. One clip, for instance, showed Hamed Sinno, the singer of the band Mashrou3 Leila, in conversation with the political talk show host Marcel Ghanem. When asked whether he still attends demonstrations, Sinno answers squarely that he would rather support a movement like Beirut Madinati than go down into the streets, for its candidates were all *muthaqqafin*— literally, 'cultured' people. Often used nowadays simply to connote intellectuals, this is a term that still retains something of its first meaning, with its evocation of civility and sophistication and learning. And 'as intellectuals, as activists, as lawyers and writers', Beirut Madinati's members were 'trying to change things in the country'. They had 'found a way', Sinno continued, of 'working within the system to change the things that we go down to demonstrate about'. This was, in short, effective, meaningful political action, and not just the ephemeral upsurge of interest that comes with each passing moment of mobilisation.

But if part of Beirut Madinati's strategy was to get out the young who had never voted before, it also sought in other videos to deflect the criticism that it was not representative of Beirut's complex demographic make-up—that it was only an expression of young, middle-class, professional technocratic ambition, with little access to older generations. One showed Amin Daouk, a member of one of Beirut's best-known Sunni families and the head of the Maqasid—the oldest Sunni charitable organisation in the city, established in 1878. In his avuncular fashion, he explained that he was with the *shabab*—the young men and women who made up Beirut Madinati. They were a 'breath of fresh air' who had redefined what politics could be, and stripping the term of the negative connotations it had become encrusted with over 'thirty or forty years'. Free of 'political'—or, in other words, partisan—associations, they had a 'proper vision' and were ready to do 'proper work'. In a similar vein, another video was of Kamal Bekhazi, the director of the Bekhazi Hospital in Hamra—and a member of a well-known and long-established Greek Orthodox family of Ras Beirut—explaining why he had stood for the municipal council in the past, and why he would be supporting Beirut Madinati this time around. In canny fashion, the movement sought to show how it had caught the attentions of an older generation. It could speak, these videos suggested, not just for the young and the fashionable, but also for men like Daouk and Bekhazi—stolidly respectable professionals of a certain age, deeply rooted in the city and its history, who had perhaps been side-lined by the political and economic developments of the 1990s and early 2000s and the ascent of new post-war elites, but who had not given up their hopes for Beirut.

And while these two videos elicited the views of members of the old notability, others showcased a rather more demotic sensibility. In one, the owner of a popular men's hair salon explained that he had been offered many opportunities to move abroad, to Canada or Australia, but 'he had refused, because he loves Beirut'. The city, he went on, was in 'his heart, it was his home'. Everything about it suited him and meant something to him. There was, he concluded with a warm, rueful smile, just no 'alternative to Beirut'. In another, the owner of Al Soussi—one of the city's popular culinary institutions, fêted by CNN as 'one of the best breakfasts in the world'—exclaimed that he could as much leave Beirut as a fish could leave the water, slamming his open hand on his kitchen counter in an emphatic gesture. This was an astute political strategy, a way of suggesting that this was truly a civic movement of the people and for the people—one that was once firmly rooted in a place and supported by the people that gave the city its distinctive timbre and rhythm and sense of life, and that understood the city as a political community and space of possibility.

And yet, for all its elegant graphic design and carefully calibrated political communications, and for all the enthusiasm it unleashed across social media, Beirut Madinati did not achieve the victory that some had hoped for in the municipal elections. Obtaining 32 per cent of the vote, it failed to secure a single seat on the municipal council. But, despite this, many of those who participated were understandably proud of what they had achieved in the face of concerted opposition from Lebanon's political establishment. Fearful of a discomfiture born of popular discontent, 14 March and 8 March had banded together into a single electoral coalition, the Bayarita—or Beirutis—list. As the activist and blogger Gino Raidy pointed out, securing almost a third 'of the vote in the face of a coalition that includes ALL of Lebanon's ruling parties and groups' remained a sizeable achievement, especially when one reckoned with the 'harassment, fraud, bribes, ... outright vote destruction' and 'sectarian rhetoric' to which their opponents had resorted to avoid 'an embarrassing loss'. There was much hope and consolation to be found in the fact that Beirut Madinati had secured a greater share of the vote than any single one of Lebanon's established political parties, 'with a campaign that spent less than what the political parties spend on a neighbourhood, with secular values, a gender-balanced list of candidates and volunteers who work without pay and, most important of all, candidates unburdened by sectarian, political or familial/feudal considerations'.[81]

But there was no getting away from the fact that Beirut Madinati had been locked out of office. Unable to secure a seat at the table, it has been forced to fall back on its skilled use of social media to continue its work. It has created an alternative municipal council, which serves to call the municipality's current tenants to account. And it has produced another series of videos—all eye-catching infographics and clear voiceovers—showing what might have already been achieved in a year. Disseminated through Facebook and Instagram, these clips seek to show their followers that an alternative course is possible, one in which renovation of Beirut's infrastructure and urban fabric can go hand in hand with regulatory reform. One video, for instance, begins with familiar images of gridlocked roads, before slipping into an alternate universe of unexplored possibility. Now was the time, the female voice explains with the aid of illustrated graphics, in which work might have begun on tackling the Lebanese capital's 'veritable transport crisis', caused by an excessive reliance on the car, 'at the expense of alternative modes of getting about and public transport'. Renovation might have begun on portions of the road network, such as that which connects

411

Horsh Beirut—the city's most extensive public green space—to the city centre, work that would have not just lightened the congestion on the roads, but also led to the improvement and embellishment of their environs. And, in a year, efforts could also have been made to coordinate with adjoining municipalities' transport providers—in the main, the private mini-bus companies that ferry customers to and fro across Beirut and its surroundings—to create a 'public, shared' transport network that would enable users to get into the capital without having to rely on their cars.

Another video sketched out all the new regulatory schemes that would have been introduced by a municipality led by Beirut Madinati for urban planning—suspending all construction work along a portion of the city's seafront for a period of three years, abrogating all the 'exceptions' that had enabled the 'privatisation' of the coast, and devising new schemes that might bring Beirut's inhabitants closer to their shoreline by removing barriers, building steps down to the beach, laying down cycle paths and planting palm trees. Here, too, the movement harnessed its members' training in graphic design and architectural draughtsmanship to distil complex matters of regulation and planning into short, easily digestible visions of what might have been. A third stuck a more discordant note. A year on from the municipal elections, it noted, the garbage crisis still had not been resolved. In that year, the municipality could have coordinated with civil society to create programmes for recycling at the source, which would have explained to the city's inhabitants the importance of sorting their rubbish. This could have in turn set the foundations for a new industrial sector, working in coordination with private companies that had already begun to explore the commercial potential of recycling, creating hundreds of job opportunities, and reducing the volume of waste by a third. But, as plangent notes played in the background, the screen faded to black and a simple slogan appeared in white—*sini w ma tghayyar shi*, 'a year, and nothing has changed'.[82] And there is no denying that nothing has changed, and there still remains a stark contrast between these products of the counterfactual imagination, with their optimistic vision of a better Beirut, a better Lebanon, and the dull melodrama of political life, with its tantrums and fallings-out, its demands and ultimatums and threats and counter-threats, its reconciliations and resignations and its improvised agendas and inscrutable, ineffective laws.

31 October 2016—the apotheosis

Mobile phones lain out before them, silvery ties hanging loose at the collar, making them look like badly wrapped Christmas presents, 127 men—and two women—sat joking and gossiping in the hemicycle. Above them were crowded journalists, diplomats and sundry grandees, who had filled the public gallery for the happy occasion. For the forty-sixth time in twenty-nine months, a session of parliament had been called to elect a new president. This time, though, things were different. What was once thought impossible was now impending: Michel Aoun was about to realise his life's ambition, becoming Lebanon's president. For the session's outcome was a foregone conclusion, the result of months of careful negotiations to open Aoun's path to the presidency.

First had come Samir Geagea's dramatic decision to declare his support for Aoun's presidential bid. After more than a year of meetings between representatives of the Lebanese Forces and the Free Patriotic Movement, Geagea's formal endorsement finally came on 18 January 2016, when Geagea received Aoun at his residence at Me'rab. After a brief, if far from private, tête-a-tête in front of the cameras, the two men gave a joint press conference. Laid out before them on the desk were garish fake white roses, behind them an immense Lebanese flag. Addressing an audience made up of journalists and representatives of both parties—including Geagea's wife Sethrida, her fellow Lebanese Forces MPs Antoine Zahra and Georges Adwan, and Aoun's son-in-law, Gebran Bassil—Geagea read out a prepared statement. The presidential vacuum, he said, had gone on too long. It was time for an act 'out of the ordinary'—a 'rescue operation that might offer succour to others'. For all the ostentatious display of hospitality that came with this occasion, Geagea could not resist presenting himself as Aoun's saviour, whose magnanimous intercession had opened the way towards the presidency. His words were appreciated by the faithful. While Bassil and Adwan, rivals now united in newfound camaraderie, laughed in the front row, Geagea's supporters at the back of the hall broke out into wolf whistles and chants of *ha-kim*, *ha-kim*—repeating over and over

Geagea's nickname. There were other moments of levity amidst the pious proclamations of enduring 'belief in Lebanon', respect for the principle of coexistence, and 'support for the army' as the 'sole representative of the state's power'. As Geagea reached the sixth of his ten terms of engagement, stressing the need for Lebanon to respect its international obligations, Aoun couldn't resist pointing at Bassil—then the foreign minister—with a little smile. Raising his hooded eyes from the page, Geagea broke away from the formal Arabic of his text to join in the teasing—*baddak ya'mila*, he said, 'it's your job to do it', and then, as guffaws rippled through the room and Bassil kept laughing to himself, *shu, 'ajbetak hayde*—'you liked that one, didn't you'.[83]

Many found the sight of these two men of another generation, once resolute enemies who had fought a bitter and costly war for supremacy over Lebanon's Christians, now joshing together with the complacency of those in power as disconcerting as it was distasteful. Indeed, there was something surreal about these old foes sharing the stage, declaring their faith in the Ta'if accord they had each resisted, denouncing Israel as an enemy of the Lebanese people, and insisting that the dark memories of the past should be wiped way, while their acolytes laughed and shared whispered asides like old friends. Amidst the forced bonhomie, the faces of some could not help belie the cost of this move to the Lebanese Forces. Geagea's wife, Sethrida, kept her eyes firmly on her husband throughout his speech, intently ignoring her neighbour, the Aounist MP Ibrahim Kanaan; only occasionally did a tender smile pass her lips as her husband made one declaration or another. Geagea's close aide Antoine Zahra, meanwhile, sat impassively as others laughed and applauded around him, his heavy-lidded eyes betraying a hint of dubiousness about the enterprise. But though some perhaps remained doubtful, Geagea's support went some considerable way towards firming up Aoun's bid.

One by one, others heeded Geagea's call to rally to Aoun in the 'national interest'. The Kata'ib abandoned their attempts to see Amin Gemayel elected president for a second time, more than thirty years after his first term. Walid Jumblatt announced the withdrawal of his party's candidate for the presidency, Henri Helou, while insisting that he would remain neutral. And, perhaps most importantly, Saad Hariri abandoned his ill-fated support for Sleiman Frangieh, the heir to a long line of haughty, brutal Maronite notables from the northern reaches of Mount Lebanon who had remained close to the Syrian regime throughout the 1990s and 2000s. Hariri's support for Frangieh, announced in November 2015, had never been overly effusive—at one point he had described him simply as 'the only [candidate] left'—and he rapidly understood the damage it could do to his own political standing and alliance with Christian parties like the Lebanese Forces and the Kata'ib, on whose continued participation in 14 March he counted.[84] Distanced from Lebanese politics after his humiliating ousting from the premiership, Hariri had spent the ensuing years licking his wounds in exile, forever deferring his return to Lebanon because of assassination fears. Now he sensed his opportunity for a comeback, understanding that his support for Aoun could be rewarded with the premiership. Finally, on 20 October 2016, Hariri gave Aoun his endorsement in a press conference that it is hard not to see as a deliberate pitch for the prime minister's office. His once hesitant Arabic now more confident and practised, Hariri repeatedly invoked his father, speaking of his capacity for putting Lebanon and its people above his own inclinations and interests.[85]

The pieces had all fallen into place. Now all that remained was for Aoun to be elected—a mere formality on the face of it, were it not for the incompetence and deliberate sabotage of his colleagues. On the appointed day, the members of Aoun's parliamentary bloc had been the first to arrive, like eager fans waiting for their idol. As they sat impatiently, their colleagues trickled in as the public galleries above filled with spectators, before Aoun, Hariri and Frangieh, and, finally, the parliamentary speaker, Nabih Berri, made their entrances to loud applause. Never one to shrink away from acknowledging the absurd, surreal quality of Lebanese parliamentary life—in which he plays, of course, such a large part—Berri quipped to his captive audience, *jdideh hay*—'that's a new one for me'. Then came the rollcall, and the announcement that no MPs had sent their apologies—prompting a look of theatrical surprise from Berri and applause from the chamber. The Future MP Nouhad Machnouq shouted out, 'democratic life has returned', Berri responded, 'we waited for it for two and a half years'.

Finally, the ballot papers were distributed and it was time to vote. But Aoun's hopes of being elected in the first round were to be disappointed. Aoun gained eighty-four votes—just short of the two-thirds he needed. Thirty-six MPs cast blank ballots, five wrote the words 'the cedar revolution continues in the service of Lebanon' on their ballots, and one voted for Gilberte Zwayn. In a turn few could have foreseen, one MP had voted for the Lebanese pop singer and provocatrice Myriam Klink, whose Facebook page describes her as a 'Mega star, supermodel, Singer, queen'. A platinum blonde best known for her revealing stage outfits, Klink had recently launched an idiosyncratic political career by declaring herself ruler of the 'Kingdom of Klinkistan' and announcing her ambitions to be Lebanese president, undeterred by the fact that, as a Greek Orthodox, she did not qualify—though this was, perhaps, in the circumstances, not the most important of considerations. Suspicions that this was Walid Jumblatt's way of spoiling his ballot were hardly abated by the way he spent the session slumped back in his chair with a gnomic smile on his face, now and then picking up his phone to toy with his emoji-strewn Twitter feed. The vote moved to a second round, in which Aoun needed only sixty-five votes—half the MPs plus one. But this time, too, things went wrong. Three counts of the vote revealed that one MP appeared to have cast two ballots. Berri called a third round, and again the same result came back. Throughout, Aoun had to sit like a groom waiting for his bride—the thin smile stretched across his lips barely suppressing his nerves.

Putting on his best schoolmaster airs, Berri instructed his colleagues: 'we are not alone in this chamber. All of Lebanon is watching us, as are … supporters of Lebanon. This is no joke so please, if you will…' His sermon having received a dutiful round of applause, a fourth round of voting was called. This time, the MPs would have to file to the front of the chamber to cast their ballots under the watchful gaze of Marwan Hamadeh and Antoine Zahra. As Aoun and his nephew and colleague Alain Aoun anxiously totted up the votes, it became apparent that his time had finally come. The sixty-fifth vote for Aoun was greeted by loud applause and whoops, as his MPs punched the air like substitutes celebrating their team's victory in a cup final, their suit jackets flapping about their soft middles. The final count would give Aoun a solid majority—eighty-three votes, against thirty-six blank ballots, a vote for Sethrida Geagea, and seven spoilt ballots. In a final surreal touch, these included a stray vote for Zorba the Greek—discounted by Berri on the grounds that, as both a Greek national and, therefore, a Greek Orthodox, Zorba could not be a legitimate candidate.[86]

The comedy was not over yet. After the necessary procedural business, Berri addressed his fellow MPs. Insisting that Aoun's election was 'not an ending but a beginning', he used the occasion to call for a new foreign and defence policy capable of confronting Israel's attempts to weaken its Arab neighbours, a new electoral law, and a renewal of democratic politics—words that might have seemed incongruous to some coming from the lips of a 79-year-old man who had been speaker of parliament since 1992. And then he called forth Aoun—only a few months shy of his eighty-second birthday—to take the oath. While a hesitant Aoun was guided through his steps by Berri—one old man helping an older man along—Zahra, Hamadeh and others gestured to their fellow MPs to rise to their feet. As some ignored their urgent arm waving, Berri looked up for a moment, issuing a sharp order, before returning to Aoun. Picking up the wrong piece of paper, then the right one, Aoun began reading—only to be corrected by Berri for fluffing his first line. As he continued, gaining a little assurance, Berri peered over his shoulder, mouthing the words like a teacher watching over a nervous student, before enjoining the MPs to applaud. That was it—after more than two and a half years, Lebanon had a president.[87] For all the jokes and political theatre and posturing, nothing much seemed to have changed.

All that remained now was for a government to be formed. As expected, Saad Hariri was entrusted with this task. After a mercifully short period of concertation, the new cabinet was announced on Sunday 18 December 2016. Thirty strong, it was billed as a national unity government bringing together all of Lebanon's many parties and factions. Only the Kata'ib refused to take part—their leader, Sami Gemayel, rejecting the offer of a secretary of state without portfolio as a derisory attempt to exclude his party from the government. Though the cabinet included some innovations—a minister for combating corruption, and a minister for women's affairs who, much to the appalled amusement of social media users, was a man—many of those nominated had previously served. Old hands like Gebran Bassil, Nouhad Machnouq, and the Hizballah ministers Mohammed Fneish and Hussein al-Hajj Hassan kept the positions they had held in Tammam

Salam's government. Others returned to cabinet after an absence of some years. This was the case, for instance, of Marwan Hamadeh, appointed education minister, or Rafiq Hariri's old ally, Ghattas Khoury, appointed minister of culture, but also of old Damascus loyalists like the Syrian Social Nationalist Party leader Ali Qanso and the Druze politician Talal Arslan, who had occupied a succession of ministerial posts in the 1990s and early 2000s, but had been left out in the cold since 2009. Many of these men were well into middle age, wizened members of the old guard who had found their way during the civil war and the long years of Syrian overrule. This hardly felt like the new beginning that Berri heralded in his speech on Aoun's inauguration. If anything, the younger Hariri's second cabinet called to mind Marx's quip that history has a way of repeating itself, 'the first time as tragedy, the second time as farce'.

Conclusion

At a most elemental level, the waste crisis that broke out in the summer of 2015 was an environmental disaster, a trauma that revealed just how fragile and tenuous was the order that humans impose on the world about them, how rapidly waste could assert itself, invading the city. But it was also a distinctly Lebanese affair, a symptom of the ills that have plagued this body politic since 2005. For it was at once the product of the politics of extemporisation, a way of thinking about policy strictly in terms of ad hoc measures and temporary plans, exceptional contingencies and emergency measures, and of the neoliberal redistribution of public goods and public services into private hands—a redistribution that necessitated, as we have seen, the intensive intervention of the state. If these are familiar features of our twenty-first-century world, then so too are the allegations of malpractice, corporate corner-cutting and corruption that swirled about the trash crisis from its very beginning, rumours given a particular inflection by the charged language of sectarianism.

Indeed, if there was one feature that united the various constituencies that came together in protest at the government's lack of initiative that summer, it was a growing disgust with confessionalism. Many of the activists who rallied in July and August 2015 had been active in the past in campaigns for labour reform or gender equality, for the preservation of the built heritage and social fabric of the city, for the protection of public space from rampant privatisation and redevelopment. But now they argued, with growing force, that all these various symptoms had a single aetiology. All were rooted, in short, in what many called *al-ta'ifiyya al-siyasiyya*, or political sectarianism, a system devised to keep Lebanon's citizenry divided and devoid of a sense of common feeling, while the 'political class' profited from the *muhasasat*, or division of the spoils of state. If a few initially saw revolution as the only means of upsetting this system and creating a new, more democratic dispensation founded on a shared sense of popular sovereignty, many more came to favour a more gradualist approach, and the construction of a new state defined at once by popular commitment and competent, expert governance. This was, in a sense, the political vision of Beirut Madinati, with its technocratic populism and its dissatisfaction with the inequalities and iniquities of the established order. For a brief time in 2015 and 2016, fissures seemed to appear in the remarkably sturdy edifice of Lebanese politics, and another way of thinking about society, about community, about sovereignty, appeared possible. But if the municipal elections of 2016 demonstrated anything, it was the remarkable capacity of Lebanon's political parties to close ranks. Even as they remained deeply dismissive of each other and incapable of devising an effective solution to the country's infrastructural woes, they proved prepared, nevertheless, to put their collective survival above all else— a rare manifestation of common purpose which snuffed out the flickering light of change, leaving Lebanon lingering still in obscurity.

CONCLUSION

Little has changed since those angry, heady days of 2015. When I was last in Beirut, in September 2017, the Lebanese army and Hizballah had recently fought, and won, a series of battles against Jabhat Fatah al-Sham and IS in the barren hills of the Lebanese borderlands. While some expressed disquiet at Hizballah's ever-growing autonomy and juggernaut-like strength, others celebrated this as a decisive victory over the dark forces of *takfiri* Islam. In truth, though, the ragtag band of straggly-bearded, dishevelled fighters that emerged from their hiding spots in the high ground to board their coaches to Idlib did not look much like formidable foes. The Lebanese press, if it was not anatomising this success, was dissecting the latest political row—an unseemly spat between Saad Hariri and his Future Movement colleagues, who were eager to introduce new biometric identity cards ahead of the 2018 parliamentary elections, and Amal, whose leader, Nabih Berri, adamantly opposed this innovation. As so often is the case in Lebanon, high politics appeared driven by low pecuniary considerations: how much was this scheme going to cost? Would it leave the supporters of this or that party out of pocket and discourage them from heading to the polls? And who, exactly, would it favour? Whose pockets would it line? For this was to be, of course, a public–private initiative, undertaken with a corporate partner.

But if the last heat of September brought with it reminders of the pettiness and venality of Lebanese politics and the troubling militarisation of Lebanese society—of the unquestioning veneration of some for the army, that apparent bastion of national unity and sovereignty, and

421

of the increasingly bitter rows over Hizballah's arsenal and foreign adventures—with the onset of winter came yet another crisis. On 4 November 2017, Saad Hariri, announced his resignation as prime minister over the airwaves from Riyadh. His life was under threat, he explained, and he could no longer continue as Lebanon's prime minister in the present circumstances, when Hizballah and Iran continued to interfere with impunity in the sovereign affairs of Arab states. Lebanon's politicians reacted with shock and panic to this unexpected news. President Michel Aoun said that he had only been informed of the resignation by phone from Saudi Arabia, and that he could not and would not accept it until Hariri returned to Beirut and explained in person his reasons for so suddenly quitting office. Hariri's relations with Hizballah had seemed cordial enough in recent months and, despite their profound difference of opinions over Syria, they appeared to be putting inner stability ahead of foreign questions. What's more, only the day before leaving for Riyadh, Hariri had met with the Iranian official Ali Akbar Velayati, a former foreign minister who now served as a senior adviser on foreign affairs to Ali Khamenei. Bereft of information, many soon turned towards conspiracy: Hariri, a Saudi citizen with close friends among the kingdom's tentacular royal family, had been privy to a palace coup against King Salman and his son, Crown Prince Muhammad bin Salman (known by his initials MBS), and had been arrested for failing to disclose its details; Hariri was being punished over the failure of Saudi Oger, the family construction firm, which had recently gone belly-up; Hariri had been caught up in the anti-corruption campaign that Muhammad had recently launched, and which had caught such eminent figures as Walid bin Talal in its snares, as Muhammad ruthlessly consolidated his own political and financial position and confiscated his rivals' assets.

Rapidly, though, another narrative, just as strange and disturbing, began to emerge. Determined to prevail over Iran and its proxies—the Houthis in Yemen, who had launched a missile on Riyadh only a few days earlier and, of course, Hizballah in Lebanon and Syria—and to buttress Saudi Arabia's position as the dominant Sunni power in the region, recently threatened by Qatar and Turkey, MBS had decided that Hariri was at once too weak, too willing to compromise with Hizballah, and too intent upon going his own way and ignoring the diktats from Riyadh. He was, in effect, too Lebanese and not Saudi enough, privileging the former's domestic stability over the latter's foreign ambitions. He had to be replaced by a more pliant figure, willing to do Riyadh's bidding and confront Hizballah head-on.[1]

But if this was the plan, it soon backfired. While Aoun and others deplored Saudi Arabia's actions as an unprecedented intervention in Lebanon's internal affairs, Hariri's supporters rallied behind him. The same message was everywhere—on stickers and posters hastily put up on Beirut's streets, but also on social media and television broadcasts: *kilna Sa'd*, 'we are all Saad'. Saudi Arabia's Western allies, too, felt that this was a step too far, and Emmanuel Macron, in particular, soon began to exert pressure on Riyadh to release Hariri and allow him to return to Beirut. On 18 November, Hariri left Riyadh for Paris, where he was reunited with his wife and children, and invited for a friendly family lunch at the Elysée Palace with the Macrons.[2] Hariri was back in Beirut by 22 November, Lebanon's Independence Day. Before the jubilant crowds that had gathered in central Beirut to greet him, with their banners and sky-blue Future Movement flags, Hariri announced—his voice hoarse, his eyes tired—that he would be staying in Lebanon, and that he remained resolute in his defence of all the principles he held dear: stability, independence, moderation, the nation above all else.[3] On 5 December, Hariri officially rescinded his resignation before the cabinet. Lebanon, he insisted, had been 'sheltered from the fires raging in other parts of the region, thanks to the unity of its people and its attachment to civil order'. But for this to remain true, the country had 'to keep its distance from exterior conflicts', while continuing to 'consolidate its relations with friendly and brotherly states'.[4] Bland words, perhaps, but ones by which a harried prime minister attempted to steer a path between the Scylla of Hizballah and the Charybdis of Saudi Arabia.

Still, though, the ugly political rows continue. In January 2018, Berri and Aoun fell out over the question of military promotions—at once a matter of clientelism and one of confessional rights and consideration, with Berri incensed that Aoun had bypassed the minister of defence, a representative of Amal. As both men dug their heels in, accusing each other of exceeding their constitutional prerogatives, the dispute dragged on. It soon became more acrimonious still, when someone leaked a video of Gebran Bassil, the foreign minister, Aoun's son-in-law and president of the FPM, calling Berri a *baltaji*, a thug. Within hours, Berri's supporters had taken to the streets to demand an immediate apology for this slight. In the Hermel, they surrounded FPM offices, chanting slogans and throwing projectiles at their windows. In the mixed suburb of Hadath, they were met with FPM supporters, determined to defend what they saw as their own territory. The army had to be called in to keep both sides apart. As the sour smell of sectarian rancour spread through the streets, both sides reeled back from the void, staging a very public reconciliation in early February.

It is clear, however, that all is not well in Lebanon. The prestidigitation tricks of the Central Bank have now been forgotten, and yet Lebanon's currency still appears volatile and its foreign debt levels unsustainable, its economy balanced on the thin threads of trust like a high-wire walker above the abyss. Efforts to resolve the longstanding row over public sector pay, which had mired Lebanon in bitter disputes and strikes since 2011, finally came to fruition in September 2017, when the cabinet approved a new pay-scale. Even this victory, though, was marred by clumsiness, when the courts ruled that the tax hikes the government had initially hoped would finance the rise in salaries were unconstitutional. What's more, it has done little to dissipate disagreement between Lebanon's private schools, many of which claim they cannot afford to pay their teachers according to the new scale, and their employees, who insist that they cannot afford to live on their old salaries. Teachers across the private sector walked out for a three-day strike in November 2017, but still the issue is unresolved, these industrial disputes an indication of the economic strains and pinches that many in Lebanon have to live with.[5] The electricity still stutters and cuts out, and the energy minister's attempts to make up for shortfalls in supply by leasing three Turkish floating power stations have been referred to the courts because of concerns over the financial propriety of the tender process. The rubbish crisis still has not been resolved. As the temporary dumping grounds created on the Costa Brava beach and in Burj Hammoud reach saturation point, civil society activists continue to warn of impending infrastructural collapse and environmental disaster. In September 2017, the minister of the environment was forced to apologise after he was caught on camera telling local residents in Costa Brava that the rubbish should not have been piled up on their beach; the idea, he explained, was always to throw it into the sea. In October, the cabinet approved a new long-term plan, based on the idea of 'waste to energy': an attractively simple idea for the politicians—who would be able to kill two birds with one stone by building a series of incinerators that would burn Lebanon's rubbish and provide its national grid with supplementary power—but one decried by civil society activists and academics, who warn of spiralling costs, malpractice, and potential environmental risks.[6] In the meantime, the rubbish continues to pile up. On 15 January 2018, a Hamas cadre was injured in a car bomb in Saida, an indication for some of the internecine splits that threaten to splinter Palestinian society in Lebanon, and for others of Israel's determination to chase down its enemies, bringing violence to Lebanon yet again.[7] On 8 March, a Syrian toddler died when her family's tent, in one of the camps of the Beqaa, caught fire.[8] We do not know yet whether this was another in the series of arson attacks on informal encampments that began in the summer of 2017, or whether her parents were simply attempting to keep warm or cook some food, but the fire is a further reminder of the precarity that Syrian refugees in Lebanon live with, and of the xenophobia that leads the government to refuse them adequate shelter—sending some of their flimsy homes up in flames.

And yet, the country's politicians seem to be turning their attention away from the present and its problems, and towards the promises of the future. The newspapers have begun to fixate on the upcoming elections, still scheduled for May 2018, examining the chances of this or that candidate to hold on to a majority or to cause an upset, and anatomising the unexpected alliances and strategic understandings drawn up by various parties. Talk is now focusing, for instance, on the end of the alliance between Hizballah and the FPM, and the birth of a new 'blue–orange' coalition uniting Aoun's movement and Hariri's Future Movement.[9] A brutal campaign is being waged by the Syrian regime and Russian forces on the eastern Ghouta, outside Damascus, and yet many in Lebanon continue to talk, with blithe inhumanity and seemingly endless resources of Panglossian optimism, of the windfalls of Syrian reconstruction—of how the ports of Beirut and Tripoli could be turned into conduit points for all the building material, of how

Lebanon could serve as an attractive rear-base for all the international agencies and corporations that would flood into Syria to help remake the country, and of the potential profits for Lebanese contractors, engineers, and banks. More and more, commentators in Beirut, Washington, and Tel Aviv talk of a new Israeli war on Lebanon, spurred on by the IDF's desire to cut Hizballah down to size, but also by the growing rapprochement between Israel and Saudi Arabia, a new marriage of convenience born of the two countries' shared fear of Iran and its growing influence through the Middle East. Despite the spectre of war, many in Lebanon seem entranced by the windfalls of offshore gas. The bid put forward by a consortium led by Total has been accepted, and the Lebanese government is readying itself to sign the exploitation contracts. Buoyed by this news, many foresee a bright new future as a carbon economy now that the work of boring down into the seafloor in Lebanon's exclusive economic zone is finally set to begin, after so many delays and false dawns.[10] But what are we to make of these radiant projections, when so much still appears broken in the present, when the lives of the Lebanese still seem so wearyingly, disconcertingly hard, when such simple things as getting to work through the morning traffic or Skyping a friend abroad require bottomless reserves of patience, and when so many worry aloud at the state's growing intolerance of dissent? These dreams and delusions of the future seem both too much for the Lebanese, and not quite enough.

AFTERWORD

When I finished writing this book in late winter 2018, weary and jaded, I could not have foreseen what would come to pass. Even a few short weeks ago, the events that have held Lebanon in their sway since 17 October 2019 seemed inconceivable. I was last in Lebanon in May and June 2019. The country seemed then in the grip of a malaise as deep as I could remember. When we went to buy a friend's daughter a present, the malls were ghostly in their emptiness, the shop attendants idling with phones in hand, their eyes glazed over with tedium. More striking still was how young they all were, just kids in their late teens or early twenties, as though an entire generation had gone missing—as it has, in a sense, with so many taking flight as soon as they can finish their studies or can afford to go abroad, uncertain whether they will return. When we went to have dinner in an old haunt on our last night in Beirut, our meal broken by the loud yaps of a drunk young American expounding on his aggressive dating strategies and bold plans for restructuring the Jordanian economy, the waiter walked through the half-empty space, wishing each table in turn a safe flight. No-one here, it suddenly occurred to me, as I looked around, half-drunk, lives in Lebanon.

Deep economic morass was only compounded by the staleness and stasis of the country's politics. After the evanescent anger and hope of 2015 and 2016, the parliamentary elections of May 2018 seemed an anti-climax. Some had hoped the new electoral law, various iterations of which had been debated by Lebanon's politicians for more than a decade, might create a space for lists of independent candidates, not aligned to one or another of the dominant political blocs, and for a political life less beholden to the logic of confessionalism. In the event, the law's labyrinthine complexities created only befuddlement, adding to the general sense of listless disinterest. Tellingly, though these were the first national polls since 2009, many voters simply stayed away, and the turn-out fell below 50 per cent. Significant losses for the Future Movement coupled with the Free Patriotic Movement's strong performance were widely seen, both at home and abroad, as confirmation of Hizballah's growing dominance over Lebanon. There was some truth to this reading. Michel Aoun, the party's longstanding ally, was ensconced in the presidential palace, and the FPM, headed by his son-in-law Gebran Bassil, was now the single largest parliamentary grouping, with twenty-nine seats. For his part, Hariri seemed not to have recovered from his debasing trip to Saudi Arabia, while trust in his party's capacity to provide for its supporters and speak for Lebanon's Sunnis had been steadily eroded both by years of growing precarity and perceived neglect—particularly evident in places like Tripoli and Saida—and the painful open sore of the Syrian war.

Beneath the headline figures, however, the depressing truth was that little had changed with the elections, which brought only disappointment to those who had hoped for a breakthrough for civil society candidates. In the end, only one such candidate—the journalist Paula Yacoubian—won a seat. And what was new did not bode well. The election of former army or intelligence officers like Chamel Roukoz, Ashraf Rifi and Jamil Sayyid spoke of the growing militarisation of Lebanese politics—with another former military man, of course, in the presidential palace. And the reappearance on the scene of men like Sayyed or Elie Ferzli, loyal allies of Damascus banished from the political scene, seemingly for good, in 2005, suggested that many in Lebanon regarded the Syrian war's outcome as a foregone conclusion. More than this, the return of these despised Lazaruses seemed the clearest indication that the country's politicians were a closed case. As in an outlandish soap opera, some disappeared for a while, and others returned miraculously from the dead. But all were ultimately interchangeable. Unrepentant and unaccountable, their old offences held, in the eyes of their peers, about as much significance as their old promises.

Just as wearisome as the election results were the negotiations to form a new government, headed up by Saad Hariri. These dragged on for nine months, as the FPM insisted on seeing its self-proclaimed status as the representative of Lebanon's Christians confirmed by a respectable share of cabinet seats, and as Hizballah sought to keep Hariri in check by imposing on him its Sunni allies. Finally, another national unity cabinet—in truth, a fudge dominated by the overbearing Aoun and Bassil, who together claimed eleven ministers—was formed in January 2019. Its mission was to implement the structural reforms international donors had called for at the CEDRE conference, held in Paris in April 2018. There, France, the United States, the IMF and others had pledged over $10 billion in loans and aid, whose release was conditional on what the French government blandly described as 'challenging fiscal consolidation'—in other words, on raising taxes and cutting state expenditure, hardly the most popular tandem of measures at the best of times.[1]

Indeed, one did not have to look far to find manifestations of growing discontent. The spring and early summer of 2019 were marked by a series of strikes, as public sector workers, teachers, university lecturers and retired soldiers protested against proposed cuts to their salaries and pensions. While teachers had grown accustomed to industrial action, having only recently secured wage increases after drawn-out negotiations with the Ministry of Education, the veterans' protests were a sign of just how dire things had become for many: holding a sit-in beneath the prime minister's offices in central Beirut, they spoke of their fury and desperation, of their desire for dignity and respect from the state they had served, but also of their very real struggles to make ends meet. In the face of this anger, politicians fell back on nativist rhetoric—with the minister of labour imposing harsh new registration measures on foreign residents, provoking widespread protests among Lebanon's Palestinians. But if they hoped that such populist tactics would be enough to diffuse the situation, they were wrong.

For the onset of autumn brought no let-up from the sense of crisis. In September 2019, rumours began to circulate of ATMs running dry and of money-changers hiking up the price of dollars, feeding anxiety about a possible currency crisis and devaluation of the Lebanese lira, pegged to the dollar since 1997. In an economy so heavily reliant on imports of everything from wheat and other staples to energy supplies, and in which so many who kept current and savings accounts in the local currency counted on its easy convertibility into dollars, devaluation would have spelled disaster. Despite reassurances from the longstanding central bank governor, Riad Salame, that all was well, fear of economic catastrophe was rapidly morphing into anger at the government.

This only increased when over a hundred wildfires broke out across the country on 14 October, devastating swathes of what is left of Lebanon's forests and endangering homes and powerlines. As Laure Stephan, *Le Monde*'s Beirut correspondent, noted, sadness rapidly yielded to anger, particularly when it was discovered that the country lacked forest-guards because the cabinet still could not agree, after years of unedifying squabbles, on the confessional distribution of public appointments, and that three Canadair fire-fighting helicopters, purchased at considerable expense in 2009, had been grounded. The helicopters had not been properly maintained, and had simply fallen into disrepair. In the absence of state intervention, the Lebanese were forced to fall back on the volunteers of the Civil Guard and the help of Cyprus, Jordan and Greece.[2] There could perhaps be no sadder, and truer, encapsulation of the governing class's profligacy, neglect and casual reliance on foreign assistance. To many, they simply looked like spoilt brats who could always count on others to get them out of dire straits.

Then, on 17 October 2019, came the announcement, as part of the raft of fiscal measures intended to appease foreign lenders, of a charge on WhatsApp calls. Given Lebanon's patchy, sluggish network, these are perhaps not much better than crackly mobile calls. But they do have the advantage, at least, of being cheap, serving as a convenient work-around for those who cannot, or will not, pay the high charges imposed by operators. It is one of austerity's ironies that, for all its proponents' insistence that we are all in it together, pinching our pennies and tightening our belts in a common show of discipline and prudence, it often serves only to underline the stark economic—and cultural—inequalities running through society. For so often it is the small charges and impositions, those that seem most innocuous or insignificant to those in power, that prove the most provocative and intolerable to others. So it has proved in Lebanon, just as it has in Brazil in 2013 and 2015, or in autumn 2019 in Chile, where transport fare hikes caused public anger to boil over.

Rapidly, though, the demonstrations morphed into something more than simple tax protests, with protesters' demands expanding to call for the cabinet's resignation and the appointment of a new government of experts; early parliamentary elections; a concerted effort to end corruption and to bring to heel those who had asset-stripped the Lebanese state since the end of the civil war, appropriating public funds or funnelling them to their allies and clients; and the abolition of political sectarianism. In short, this is nothing less, in many participants' eyes, than a revolution. This is reflected in the slogans they use, both in the streets and on social media, where images and clips circulate under the hashtags *#lubnan_yathur*—'Lebanon revolts'—and *#lubnan_yantafid*, or 'Lebanon rises up'. The emblematic cry of the Arab spring, *al-sha'b yurid isqat al-nizam*, 'the people want the downfall of the regime', had been heard during the trash protests in 2015. Then, many had still been wary of uttering such transformative, subversive words. Now, however, few in downtown Beirut, Tripoli, Sur, Zouk and other epicentres of the uprising seem to have any qualms about calling for the entire system to be overturned, the political class a rotten tree that must be pulled out of the ground. For all that some protesters have singled out particular politicians whom they regard as especially corrupt—none more so, perhaps, than Aoun's son-in-law and heir apparent, Gebran Bassil, whose naked pursuit of power, ostentatiousness and use of crude nativist and confessional rhetoric to strengthen his shaky hold over the FPM have alienated many, even within his movement—many have been at pains to stress that all politicians were at fault here. None could be excused or redeemed. It was time to remake the system, rather than tinker with its parts. As another of the chants that have echoed through the streets and public squares of Lebanon in recent weeks has it: *killun ya'ni killun*, 'all of them means all of them'.

Clearly, the 'uprising of 17 October', as many Lebanese have taken to calling their revolution, has not emerged from the ether, with growing numbers expressing disgust in recent years at the disjuncture between the opulent comfort of their politicians' world, and the pollution, environmental degradation, infrastructural failure, anxiety and straitened circumstances of their own lives. What's more, the protests do share certain features with earlier moments of mobilisation in 2005 and 2015, not least a marked penchant for mutinous political humour and carnivalesque merriment. The Lebanese continue to show a remarkable capacity for harnessing their disaffection, transforming it into memorable slogans and mocking memes, and refusing to regard politics as an austere, cerebral pursuit. To protest, they understand, is an inherently physical act, a statement of one's presence in the world, of one's capacity to move, to cry, to sing and shout and make common voice with others. In Beirut, where bands, balloon sellers and snack vendors mingle with the crowds, or in the northern city of Tripoli, where the local DJ Mehdi Karimeh turned the central square of Sahat al-Nour into a massive dance party, the crowds have insisted on having fun. This is a world away from the heedless, nihilistic hedonism of Beirut's chichi clubs, with their stiff social conventions and conspicuous flaunting of wealth. Instead, it is joy as a kind of resistance, as emancipation from the ordinary. What better way for the Lebanese to turn their noses up at their politicians than by refusing to be defeated by despair, channelling their anger and frustration into joyous communion?

In other ways, too, the protests of recent weeks have built on those of 2015. One can see this in their commitment to horizontal organisation and open debate, in their insistence on civility—on peaceful protest, on cleaning up after themselves, on avoiding misogynistic or homophobic slurs, and on treating soldiers and policemen as simple citizens rather than agents of a repressive state—and in their commitment to reclaiming the country's urban spaces, from roads and squares to controversial private developments, like Zaitunay Bay or Eden Rock in Beirut. These are more than theoretical stances: women have played a prominent part in organising, as have young, working-class men, whom some had once dismissed warily as agents of unruliness.

But the sheer scale of these protests is unprecedented. For the first time, demands that had long been the preserve of a small core of hardened activists—not least the abolition of the confessional system—have been taken up by a wide swathe of the Lebanese. Indeed, calls for systemic change have resonated across the country. This, in itself, is new too. Where previous protests could be overly focused on Beirut and rely on a relatively small set of middle-class activists drawn from student politics and civil society, Nabatiyyeh and Sur, Tripoli and Zouk, and down-at-heel Beirut suburbs like Ayn al-Rummaneh have all emerged in recent weeks as significant centres of mobilisation. In short, the movement that began in mid-October has rapidly become a nation-wide one, cutting across regional, confessional and class lines. Opposition to austerity, then, has succeeded in crystallising the dispersed, diffuse discontent that seeped through Lebanese society in recent years, turning hopelessness into hope. Out of disillusion has been born a bold new vision of the future.

In response, Lebanon's politicians have offered little. Saad Hariri, it is true, resigned on 29 October, after the measures he proposed failed to satisfy the demonstrators. Others, though, have remained obdurate in resisting the protesters' calls for reform. While the president, Michel Aoun, has appeared uncertain—a weary, ailing figure—his son-in-law, the target of so much concentrated ire, has shown no inclination to give away his power, suggesting in a speech that politicians should retain a stake in the selection of a new cabinet of neutral technocrats. For his part, Sayyid Hassan Nasrallah has dismissed the protests as the work of foreign plotters intent on undermining Lebanon's sovereignty—a familiar refrain that has provided grist to the mill of sundry online conspiracy theorists.[3] Like sitting tenants refusing to be evicted, Lebanon's politicians appear intent on simply waiting it out, in the hope that the protesters will soon tire themselves out and return home, leaving the status quo untouched. No-one knows where we go from here. But we have already gone much further than anyone might have hoped, or dreamed, a mere month ago. To turn back now must surely be impossible.

7 November 2019

NOTES

INTRODUCTION: LEBANON AND THE TWENTY-FIRST CENTURY

1. https://web.archive.org/web/20120206055402/http://news.usti.net/home/news/cn/?/world.mideast.misc/1/wed/bq/Alebanon-war-deaths.RYBR_GDS.html; http://www.pcm.gov.lb/Admin/Dynamic File.aspx?PHName=Document&PageID=3915&published=1
2. http://data.unhcr.org/syrianrefugees/country.php?id=122
3. John and Jean Comaroff, *Law and Disorder in the Postcolony* (Chicago, IL: University of Chicago Press, 2006), ix.
4. Fredric Jameson, 'The Aesthetics of Singularity', *New Left Review* 92 (March/April 2015), 120.
5. Achille Mbembe, *On the Postcolony* (Berkeley, CA: University of California Press, 2001), 16–17.
6. Jameson, 'Aesthetics', 120.
7. Mbembe, *Postcolony*, 16–17.
8. Jameson, 'Aesthetics', 120.
9. Craig Larkin, *Memory and Conflict in Lebanon: Remembering and Forgetting the Past* (London: Routledge, 2012); Sune Haugbolle, *War and Memory in Lebanon* (Cambridge: Cambridge University Press, 2010).
10. https://data.worldbank.org/country/Lebanon
11. http://www.finance.gov.lb/enUS/finance/PublicDebt/Documents/Quarterly%20Debt%20Report/2014/Debt%20and%20Debt%20Markets%20QIV%202014.pdf
12. http://www.tradingeconomics.com/lebanon/unemployment-rate
13. https://www.lorientlejour.com/article/1090855/le-nombre-de-palestiniens-au-liban-nexcede-pas-les-174-422-personnes.html
14. http://syrianrefugees.eu/timeline/
15. http://data.unhcr.org/syrianrefugees/country.php?id=122
16. https://data.unhcr.org/syrianrefugees/download.php?id=8649

17. https://data.unhcr.org/syrianrefugees/download.php?id=10006
18. Tom Najem, *Lebanon: The Politics of a Penetrated Society* (London: Routledge, 2012), 1.
19. Michael Kerr, 'Before the Revolution', in Are Knudsen and Michael Kerr, eds, *Lebanon after the Cedar Revolution* (London: Hurst, 2012), 24.
20. Are Knudsen and Michael Kerr, 'Introduction: The Cedar Revolution and Beyond', in Are Knudsen and Michael Kerr, eds, *Lebanon after the Cedar Revolution* (London: Hurst, 2012), 5.
21. Imad Salamey, *The Government and Politics of Lebanon* (London: Routledge, 2013), xii; Najem, *A Penetrated Society*, 1.
22. Kerr, 'Before the Revolution', 26.
23. Ibid., 32.
24. Najem, *A Penetrated Society*, 3; Hanna Ziadeh, *Sectarianism and Intercommunal Nation-Building in Lebanon* (London: Hurst, 2006), 6.
25. Ziadeh, *Intercommunal Nation-Building*, 8; Amal Hamdan, 'The Limits of Corporate Consociation: Taif and the Crisis of Power-Sharing in Lebanon since 2005', in Are Knudsen and Michael Kerr, eds, *Lebanon after the Cedar Revolution* (London: Hurst, 2012), 59.
26. Najem, *A Penetrated Society*.
27. Marie-Joëlle Zahar, 'Foreign Interventions, Power Sharing and the Dynamics of Conflict and Coexistence in Lebanon', in Are Knudsen and Michael Kerr, eds, *Lebanon after the Cedar Revolution* (London: Hurst, 2012), 64, 80.
28. Thomas Carlyle, *On Heroes, Hero-Worship and the Heroic in History*, in F. Randolph Ludovico, ed., *The Selected Works of Thomas Carlyle* (n.p.: The Bibliotheca Cakravarti Foundation), 91.
29. Ibid.
30. Mbembe, *On the Postcolony*, 16.
31. Ibid.
32. Kathleen Stewart, *Ordinary Affects* (Durham, NC: Duke University Press, 2007), 1.
33. Mbembe, *On the Postcolony*, 15.
34. Michel Foucault, cited in Joan Wallach Scott, Andrew Aisenberg, Brian Connolly, Ben Kafka, Sylvia Schafer, and Mrinalini Sinha, 'Introducing History of the Present', *History of the Present* 1 (2011), available at http://historyofthepresent.org/1.1/introduction.html
35. Ibid.
36. Mbembe, *On the Postcolony*, 6.
37. Patrick Chabal and Jean-Pascal Deloz, *Africa Works: Disorder as Political Instrument* (Oxford: James Currey, 1999), xv, xvii.
38. Naveeda Khan, 'Introduction', in Naveeda Khan, ed., *Beyond Crisis: Re-evaluating Pakistan* (London: Routledge, 2010), 1.

39. Michel Foucault, *Le Gouvernement de soi et des autres: Cours au Collège de France (1982–1983)* (Paris: Gallimard, 2003), 13, 22.

1. *INTIFADAT AL-ISTIQLAL*, OR THE INDEPENDENCE UPRISING—THE MOMENT THAT PASSED

1. Nicholas Blanford, *Killing Mr Lebanon: The Assassination of Rafik Hariri and its Impact on the Middle East* (London: IB Tauris, 2006), 1–12.
2. Special Tribunal for Lebanon, 'The Prosecutor v. Mustafa Amine Badreddine, Salim Jamil Ayyash, Hussein Hassan Oneissi & Assad Hassan Sabra—Indictment' (The Hague, Special Tribunal for Lebanon, 2011), 20.
3. Ibid.; Joshua Hammer, 'Getting Away With Murder?', The Atlantic (December 2008), http://www.theatlantic.com/magazine/archive/2008/12/getting-away-with-murder/307149/
4. Blanford, *Killing Mr Lebanon*, 85.
5. Ibid., 89.
6. Ibid., 87.
7. Ibid., 91.
8. https://www.congress.gov/108/plaws/publ175/PLAW-108publ175.pdf
9. Blanford, *Killing Mr Lebanon*, 100–1.
10. Ibid., 92.
11. http://www.unsco.org/Documents/Resolutions/S_RES_1559(2004).pdf; http://www.un.org/press/en/2004/sc8181.doc.htm
12. Blanford, *Killing Mr Lebanon*, 141.
13. Michael Young, *The Ghosts of Martyrs Square: An Eyewitness Account of Lebanon's Life Struggle* (New York: Simon & Schuster, 2010), 24. See also Blanford, *Killing Mr Lebanon*, 140.
14. Blanford, *Killing Mr Lebanon*, 142–3.
15. https://www.youtube.com/watch?v=iZ7b773WM94; https://www.youtube.com/watch?v=YITd5SXiRvs
16. Young, *Ghosts of Martyrs Square*, 28.
17. https://www.youtube.com/watch?v=LpCv2qbhsKs
18. Anonymous interview, Beirut, August 2012.
19. Young, *Ghosts of Martyrs Square*, 34–5.
20. Ibid., 39.
21. http://commdocs.house.gov/committees/intlrel/hfa24515.000/hfa24515_0.HTM
22. http://news.bbc.co.uk/1/hi/in_pictures/4304639.stm
23. http://news.bbc.co.uk/1/hi/in_pictures/4304639.stm
24. Young, *Ghosts of Martyrs Square*, 50.

25. http://news.bbc.co.uk/1/hi/world/middle_east/4305927.stm#

26. https://www.youtube.com/watch?v=LpCv2qbhsKs

27. Young, *Ghosts of Martyrs Square*, 50.

28. https://www.youtube.com/watch?v=YMf-bvXZQzY&t=613s

29. https://www.youtube.com/watch?v=YMf-bvXZQzY&t=613s

30. https://www.youtube.com/watch?v=AMmBuP-tK_s

31. https://www.youtube.com/watch?v=AMmBuP-tK_s

32. Blanford, 158–9, 162.

33. https://documents-dds-ny.un.org/doc/UNDOC/GEN/N05/299/98/PDF/N0529998.pdf?OpenElement

34. Blanford, *Killing Mr Lebanon*, 167.

35. Ibid.

36. https://now.mmedia.me/Library/Files/EnglishDocumentation/Political%20agreements%20and%20manifestos/hezbollah-FPM.pdf

37. https://www.youtube.com/watch?v=Syx2bp91WSI

38. http://www.washingtonpost.com/wp-dyn/articles/A19372–2005Apr1.html

39. https://www.lorientlejour.com/article/503733/Une_foule_indignee_s%27en_prend_au_Premier_ministre_et_aux_officiels_accourus_sur_les_lieux_du_drameSamir_Kassir_tue_dans_un_attentat_a_la_voiture_pie.html

40. https://www.lorientlejour.com/article/503736/Tueni_a_%3C%3C_L%27Orient-Le_Jour_%3E%3E_%3A_Le_Liban_n%27a_pas_encore_ete_libere_du_regime_securitaire_libano-syrien.html

41. https://www.lorientlejour.com/article/503739/Hamade_%3A_%3C%3C_Les_residus_du_regimesecuritaire_syro-libanais_sont_encore_la_%3E%3E.html

42. https://www.lorientlejour.com/article/503735/Les_collegues_de_Kassir_%3C%3C_choques_%3E%3E_par_l%27elimination_d%27un_editorialiste_libreA_son_bureau_d%27%3C%3C_an-Nahar_%3E%3E%2C_une_rose%2Cun_d.html

43. https://www.lorientlejour.com/article/503728/Samir_Kassir_tue_dans_un_attentat_a_la_voiture_piegee_a_Achrafieh_La_pensee_libre_assassineeL%27opposition_reclame_la_demission_de_Lahoud_et_appelle_a.html

44. Blanford, *Killing Mr Lebanon*, 181–2. https://www.lorientlejour.com/article/519601/La_route_des_usines_de_Mkalles%2C_un_veritable_champ_de_batailleLe_rendez-vous_avec_la_mort_de_Gebran_Tueni.html

2. *AL-HAWADITH*, OR THE EVENTS—LEBANON'S TUMULTUOUS YEARS

1. http://usatoday30.usatoday.com/news/world/2006-08-01-mideast-fighting_x.htm; https://web.archive.org/web/20080215135534/http://asia.news.yahoo.com/060813/3/2of6v.html

2. https://www.flickr.com/photos/koldo/209516561/in/set-72157594209999922/

3. http://articles.latimes.com/2006/aug/10/world/fg-litani10

4. https://web.archive.org/web/20140115164420/http://www.pbs.org/newshour/bb/middle_east/july-dec06/israel_07–12.html

5. Human Rights Watch, *Why They Died: Civilian Casualties in Lebanon during the 2006 War* (September 2007), 38.

6. Ibid., 39.

7. Ibid., 43.

8. Ibid., 47.

9. Ibid., 46.

10. Ibid., 6.

11. Ibid., 7.

12. Ibid., 8.

13. Ibid., 65.

14. Ibid., 9–11.

15. Human Rights Watch, *Flooding South Lebanon: Israel's Use of Cluster Munitions in Lebanon in July and August 2006* (February 2008), 3, 6–7.

16. Ibid., 43.

17. Ibid., 50.

18. Ibid., 36, 40–43.

19. Ibid., 63.

20. Ibid., 49.

21. http://time.com/4398489/lebanon-war-10-years-later-photos/

22. http://news.bbc.co.uk/1/hi/world/middle_east/6385969.stm

23. http://news.bbc.co.uk/1/hi/world/middle_east/6385969.stm

24. Fuad I. Khuri, *From Village to Suburb: Order and Change in Greater Beirut* (Chicago, IL: University of Chicago Press, 1975).

25. http://news.bbc.co.uk/1/hi/world/middle_east/6385969.stm

26. https://www.youtube.com/watch?v=LIo4dh884hE

27. These images can be seen on http://warkerblog.blogspot.co.uk

28. http://warkerblog.blogspot.co.uk

29. https://paddle8.com/work/ali-cherri/33622-untitled-to-the-lebanese-citizens

30. http://www.beirutreport.com/2014/06/lebanese-war-art.html

31. https://www.youtube.com/watch?v=KRVvPEEAmck

32. http://news.bbc.co.uk/1/hi/world/americas/6107224.stm

33. https://www.lorientlejour.com/article/542998/Le_Hezbollah_relance_sa_campagne_pour_la_formationd'un_gouvernement_d'union%3C%3C_Pas_de_rencontre_entre_Nasrallah_et_Hariri_si_elle_ne_vise_pas_d.html

34. https://www.lorientlejour.com/article/543620/%3C%3C_Les_negociations_sur_les_prisonniers_sont_en_bonne_voie_%3E%3E%2Caffirme_le_chef_du_HezbollahNasrallah_accuse_la_majorite_de_vouloir_faire_du_L.html

35. https://www.lorientlejour.com/article/544039/Saad_Hariri_%3A_%3C%3C_Pas_question_d%27un_tiers_de_blocageen_presence_d%27un_president_de_blocage_%3E%3E.html

36. https://www.lorientlejour.com/article/544635/Le_dialogue_avorte_samedi%2C_les_ministres_Amal_et_Hezbollah_demissionnent%2C_Lahoud_et_Siniora_font_la_guerre_des_communiques_et_le_Conseil_des_minis.html.

37. http://www.independent.co.uk/voices/commentators/fisk/robert-fisk-gemayels-mourners-know-that-in-lebanon-nothing-is-what-it-seems-425427.html

38. https://www.lorientlejour.com/article/545442/Le_ministre_de_l%27Industrie_conduisait_depuis_quelques_heures_la_Kia_qu%27il_avait_louee_a_une_agence_Pierre_Gemayel_assassine_hier%2C_a_Jdeide%2Cd%2.html

39. https://www.lorientlejour.com/article/545630/%253C%253C_A_bas_la_Syrie%252C_a_bas_Lahoud_%253E%253E_ou_%253C%253C_General%252C_tu_es_des_notres_ou_des_leurs_%253E%253EDes_centaines_de_milliers_de_manifestants_crien.html

40. https://www.lorientlejour.com/article/546373/Pour_les_centaines_de_milliers_de_manifestants%2C_un_seul_leitmotiv_%3A_%3C%3C_Siniora_va-t-en_%21_%3E%3EDemonstration_de_force_de_l%27oppositiondans_.html

41. https://www.lorientlejour.com/article/546559/Qui_a_tue_le_partisan_d%27Amal_Ahmad_Mahmoud_Entre_Tarik_Jdide_et_la_banlieue_sud%2C_la_tension_est_a_son_paroxysme.html

42. https://www.lorientlejour.com/article/550610/Les_ecoles_catholiques_ouvriront_leurs_portes_aujourd%27huiLa_vie_a_repris_dans_toutes_les_regions_du_Liban_.html

43. https://www.lorientlejour.com/article/550706/Une_dispute_entre_etudiants_a_l%27Universite_arabe_degenere_en_affrontements_entre_partisans_de_la_majorite_et_ceux_de_l%27oppositionScenes_de_guerre_.html

44. https://www.lorientlejour.com/article/546550/ECLAIRAGE_-_Le_sit-in_semble_s%27installer_dans_la_duree_et_5_000_jeunes_

assurent_des_permanences_la_nuitLa_presence_aouniste%2C_un_des_ principauxmote.html

45. https://www.lorientlejour.com/article/546472/Frangie_affirme_etre_ pret_a_%3C%3C_feter_Noel%2C_al-Adha%2C_le_Nouvel_An_et_ Paques_%3E%3E_sur_le_lieu_du_sit-in_.html

46. http://www.scoop.co.nz/stories/WL0612/S00323/cablegate-lebanon-siniora-hits-back-at-nasrallahs.htm

47. http://www.washingtonpost.com/wp-dyn/content/article/2007/ 12/01/AR2007120100357_pf.html

48. https://now.mmedia.me/lb/en/commentary/chronology_of_a_crisis; http://www.lorientlejour.com/article/560369/Quarante_tues%2C_ dont_23_soldats_libanais%2C_au_cours_d%27affrontements_a_l% 27arme_lourde_Des_combats_de_rue_acharnes_dans_les_dedales_de_ Tripoli_oppo.html

49. http://www.lorientlejour.com/article/554738/Attentat_de_Ain_ Alak_-_Fateh_al-Islam_nie_toute_implication%2C_mais_se_fait_men-acantUn_reseau_terroriste_demantele%2Cles_SR_syriens_pointes_du_ doigt.html

50. http://www.lorientlejour.com/article/560369/Quarante_tues%2C_ dont_23_soldats_libanais%2C_au_cours_d%27affrontements_a_l% 27arme_lourde_Des_combats_de_rue_acharnes_dans_les_dedales_de_ Tripoli_oppo.html

51. https://now.mmedia.me/lb/en/commentary/chronology_of_ a_crisis

52. https://now.mmedia.me/lb/en/commentary/the_story_of_nahr_ al-bared

53. https://now.mmedia.me/lb/en/archive/intensified_shelling_at_nahr_ al-bared

54. https://now.mmedia.me/lb/en/commentary/chronology_of_a_ crisis

55. https://now.mmedia.me/lb/en/archive/army_cleansing_fatah_ al-islam_position_in_nahr_al-bared

56. https://now.mmedia.me/lb/en/archive/final_assault_on_nahr_ al-bared_is_imminent

57. https://now.mmedia.me/lb/en/archive/final_assault_on_nahr_ al-bared_is_imminent

58. http://news.bbc.co.uk/1/hi/world/middle_east/7775239.stm

59. https://now.mmedia.me/lb/en/archive/palestinians_say_nahr_ al-bared_camp_is_not_livable_

60. https://now.mmedia.me/lb/en/archive/nahr_al-bared_reconstruc-tion_donors_conference_begins_in_vienna; http://www.irinnews.org/ report/80666/lebanon-despair-trauma-discontent-among-nahr-al-bared's-impoverished-palestinians

61. https://now.mmedia.me/lb/en/archive/nahr_al-bared_reconstruction_donors_conference_begins_in_vienna

62. http://www.lorientlejour.com/article/560891/Une_branche_d%27el-Qaeda_promet_des_%3C%3C+mers_de_sang+%3E%3E_aux_chretiens_du_Liban.html

63. See Bernard Rougier, *Everyday Jihad: The Rise of Militant Islam among Palestinians in Northern Lebanon* (Cambridge, MA: Harvard University Press, 2007); and Bernard Rougier, *The Sunni Tragedy in the Middle East: Northern Lebanon from al-Qaeda to ISIS* (Princeton, NJ: Princeton University Press, 2015); Thomas Pierret, 'Al-Ahbash', *The Encyclopaedia of Islam*, 3rd ed. (Leiden: Brill: 2010), vol. 2, 35–7; Jacob Skovgaard-Petersen, 'The Sunni Religious Scene in Beirut', *Mediterranean Politics* 3 (1998), 69–80.

64. See Faisal Devji, 'A Life on the Surface', http://www.hurstpublishers.com/a-life-on-the-surface/

65. http://www.lorientlejour.com/article/554822/Pour_le_PSP%2C_Ain_Alak_est_la_preuve_de_l%27implication_du_regime_de_Damas_dans_la_serie_des_attentats_terroristesMoallem_nie_tout_lien_de_la_Syrie_a.html

66. http://news.bbc.co.uk/1/hi/world/middle_east/7775239.stm; see also Rougier, *The Sunni Tragedy in the Middle East*, chapters 4–5.

67. http://www.lorientlejour.com/article/560887/Pronant_une_solution_%3C%3C+politique+%3E%3E_au_probleme_de_Fateh_el-Islam%2C_le_chef_du_Hezbollah_refuse_de_%3C%3C+couvrir+%3E%3E_une_nouvelle_%3C%3C.html

68. http://www.lorientlejour.com/article/560889/Siniora+%3A_En_ne_condamnant_pas_de_maniere_claire_Fateh_el-Islam%2C_c%27est_comme_si_Nasrallah_le_cautionnait.html

69. http://www.lorientlejour.com/article/560882/Les_forces_politiques_expriment_un_appui_inconditionnel_a_l%27armee_Kanaan_%3A_L%27entente_avec_le_Hezbollah_ne_nous_empeche_pas_d%27avoir_des_points_.html

70. http://www.lorientlejour.com/article/589074/Le_chef_du_PSP_revele_l%27existence_d%27un_reseau_de_telecommunications_du_Hezbollah_reliant_le_Sud_au_HermelJoumblatt_met_en_garde_contre_une_operati.html

71. http://www.lorientlejour.com/article/589075/Hamade_demande_au_Conseil_des_ministres_d%27examiner_le_dossier_du_reseau_telephonique_illegal_du_Hezbollah.html

72. http://www.lorientlejour.com/article/589276/Le_gouvernement_determine_a_eradiquer_les+abus_du_parti_chiite%2C_le_chef_de_la_securite_de_l%27aeroport_mute%2C_le_salaire_minimum_releve_de_200+000_.html

73. http://www.lorientlejour.com/article/589353/Scenes_de_guerre_a_
Mazraa%2C_Cola%2C_Noueyri_et_Basta%2C_hier_dans_la_capital-
eLa_longue_journee_d%27affrontements_a_Beyrouthse_termine_par_
le_blocus_d.html

74. https://www.youtube.com/watch?v=6hRwn3kJ_xE&t=255s

75. https://www.youtube.com/watch?v=6hRwn3kJ_xE&t=255s

76. http://www.lorientlejour.com/article/589353/Scenes_de_guerre_a_
Mazraa%2C_Cola%2C_Noueyri_et_Basta%2C_hier_dans_la_capital-
eLa_longue_journee_d%27affrontements_a_Beyrouthse_termine_par_
le_blocus_d.html

77. https://www.youtube.com/watch?v=KlnNND5sGHg

78. http://peacemaker.un.org/sites/peacemaker.un.org/files/Lebanon_
DohaAgreement2008_Engl.pdf

79. http://www.nytimes.com/2008/05/10/world/middleeast/10lebanon.

3. *AL-FARAGH*, OR THE VACUUM—LEBANON BETWEEN TWO PRESIDENTS

1. http://l7.alamy.com/zooms/d0adf1b7b29a4e6f8e4b88dea909ae87/
lebanons-christian-leaders-michel-al-murr-l-and-ghassan-toweiny-arrive-
gmnm03.jpg; https://www.khazen.org/images/stories/7may2008/
221.jpg

2. http://www.meforum.org/meib/articles/0007_l1.htm

3. http://news.bbc.co.uk/1/hi/world/middle_east/7412170.stm

4. http://www.independent.co.uk/news/world/middle-east/lebanon-
elects-head-of-state-834384.html; https://www.lorientlejour.com/arti-
cle/590726/Le_commandant_de_l%27armee_obtient_118_voix_con-
tre_6_bulletins_blancs_et_3_divers%2C_en_presence_d%27une_
impressionnante_representation_arabe_et_inter.html

5. http://www.dailystar.com.lb/News/Lebanon-News/2008/Jun-
02/49931-suleiman-calls-for-removal-of-posters-bearing-his-likeness.
ashx

6. https://www.theguardian.com/world/2008/may/26/lebanon

7. https://www.lorientlejour.com/article/590726/Le_commandant_
de_l%27armee_obtient_118_voix_contre_6_bulletins_blancs_et_3_
divers%2C_en_presence_d%27une_impressionnante_representation_
arabe_et_inter.html

8. http://peacemaker.un.org/sites/peacemaker.un.org/files/Lebanon_
DohaAgreement2008_Engl.pdf

9. http://www.ifes.org/sites/default/files/ifes_lebanon_esb_paper
030209_0.pdf

10. This account of the electioneering draws in part on Daniel Corstange's

useful summary 'The parliamentary election in Lebanon, June 2009', *Electoral Studies* 29 (2010), 287.

11. http://www.elections.gov.lb/Parliamentary/Elections-Results/2009-Real-time-Results/The-2009-MPs.aspx

12. http://www.elections.gov.lb/Parliamentary/Elections-Results/2009-Real-time-Results/The-2009-MPs.aspx

13. http://www.nytimes.com/2009/04/23/world/middleeast/23lebanon.html

14. Daniel Corstange, 'Vote trafficking in Lebanon', *International Journal of Middle East Studies* 44 (2012), 492.

15. https://qifanabki.com/2009/07/25/how-many-lebanese-were-flown-in-to-vote/

16. http://www.reuters.com/article/idININdia-40016820090601

17. Corstange, 'Vote-buying', 495–6, 497.

18. https://www.theatlantic.com/magazine/archive/2008/12/getting-away-with-murder/307149/; http://www.nytimes.com/1983/08/26/world/french-consulate-bombed-in-berlin.html

19. https://documents-dds-ny.un.org/doc/UNDOC/GEN/N05/563/67/PDF/N0556367.pdf?OpenElement

20. https://documents-dds-ny.un.org/doc/UNDOC/GEN/N05/563/67/PDF/N0556367.pdf?OpenElement

21. Joshua Hammer, 'Getting Away With Murder?', The Atlantic (December 2008), https://www.theatlantic.com/magazine/archive/2008/12/getting-away-with-murder/307149/

22. Ibid.

23. Ibid.

24. Ibid.

25. Ibid.

26. https://www.alarabiya.net/articles/2009/04/29/71647.html

27. https://www.lorientlejour.com/article/618460/Sayyed+%3A_J%27ai_ete_victime_d%27une_manoeuvre__de_la_commission_d%27enquete_internationale.html

28. https://www.lorientlejour.com/article/618626/Mehlis_et_Abdo_seront_entendus_par_une_juge_d%27instruction_a_Paris%2C_suite_a_la_plainte_de_Sayyed.html

29. http://www.spiegel.de/international/world/breakthrough-in-tribunal-investigation-new-evidence-points-to-hezbollah-in-hariri-murder-a-626412.html

30. https://now.mmedia.me/lb/en/archive/jumblatt_i_intend_to_fix_my_relationship_with_syria_i_do_not_know_who_killed_rafik_harir

31. http://www.nytimes.com/2009/06/04/us/politics/04obama.text.html

32. https://www.youtube.com/watch?v=cm5fgaFTAuQ

33. https://www.lorientlejour.com/article/629698/Jamil_el-Sayyed_
tire_a_boulets__rouges_dans_toutes_les_directions.html

34. https://www.lorientlejour.com/article/629949/Machnouk+%3A_
C%27est_un_paon_a_la_solde_de_la_Syrie.html

35. http://www.lepoint.fr/actualites-monde/2009–09–17/assassinat-
d-hariri-la-syrie-accuse-les-premiers-enqueteurs-de/924/0/378283

36. https://www.lorientlejour.com/article/629812/Le_dossier_du_tribu-
nal_prend_progressivement_le_dessus_sur_celui_du_gouvernement.
html

37. https://www.lorientlejour.com/article/665606/Assassinat_
Hariri%253A_Nasrallah_propose_une_commission_libanaise_ad_hoc_
pour_elucider_laffaire_des_4_faux_temoins.html

38. https://www.lorientlejour.com/article/665518/Aoun%2B%253A_
Le_TSL_est_tombe_car_il_s%2527est_base_sur_de_faux_temoins_
pour_accuser_la_Syrie.html

39. https://www.lorientlejour.com/article/667387/Le_Hezbollah_dif-
fuse_des_%2522images_israeliennes%2522_du_site_du_meurtre_de_
Hariri.html

40. https://www.lorientlejour.com/article/668438/Le_gouvernement_
charge_le_ministre_de_la_Justice_d%2527une_%253C%253C%
2Bmission_d%2527information%2B%253E%253E_dans_l%2527
affaire_des_%253C%253C%2Bfaux_temoins%2B%253E%253E_.html;
https://www.lorientlejour.com/article/665606/Assassinat_
Hariri%253A_Nasrallah_propose_une_commission_libanaise_ad_hoc_
pour_elucider_laffaire_des_4_faux_temoins.html

41. https://now.mmedia.me/lb/en/archive/hariri_says_false_witnesses_
misled_stl_

42. https://www.lorientlejour.com/article/674722/L%2527affaire_
des_%253C%253C%2Bfaux_temoins%2B%253E%253E_
creuse_l%2527abime_entre_le_14_et_le_8_Mars%252C_Sleiman_
reporte_la_suite_du_debat_au_20_octobre.html

43. https://www.lorientlejour.com/article/671188/Faux_
temoins%2B%253A_le_Hezbollah_hausse_a_nouveau_le_ton.html

44. https://www.lorientlejour.com/article/678306/Le_14_Mars_reste_
ferme%2B%253A_oui_au_TSL%252C_non_au_vote_sur_le_dossier_
des_faux_temoins.html

45. http://www.bbc.co.uk/news/world-middle-east-10813301

46. http://edition.cnn.com/arabic/2011/middle_east/1/12/lebanon.
hariri/index.html

47. http://carnegie-mec.org/2011/01/17/lebanon-descends-into-long-
crisis-pub-42308

48. Ibid.
49. Special Tribunal for Lebanon, 'The Prosecutor v. Mustafa Amine Badreddine, Salim Jamil Ayyash, Hussein Hassan Oneissi & Assad Hassan Sabra—Indictment' (The Hague, Special Tribunal for Lebanon, 2011).
50. http://www.bbc.co.uk/news/world-middle-east-36284621
51. http://www.reuters.com/article/us-lebanon-idUSTRE75T2LG 20110630
52. https://www.lorientlejour.com/article/710836/Nasrallah+%3A_Les_quatre_personnes_recherchees_ne__seront_remises_au_TSL_ni_aujourd%27hui_ni_dans_300_ans....html
53. https://www.lorientlejour.com/article/734251/%3C%3C+Mon_insistance_a_verser_notre_contribution_tient_a_mon_souci_de_pre-server_le_Liban+%3E%3E.html
54. Much of this paragraph relies on Joseph Daher, 'Hezbollah and the Workers', https://jacobinmag.com/2016/12/hezbollah-lebanon-iran-islamic-revolution-labor/
55. https://www.wsj.com/articles/SB10001424052970203833310457707 1960384240668
56. http://www.dailystar.com.lb//News/Lebanon-News/2011/Apr-18/136762-syria-lebanon-stability-interdependent-conference.ashx
57. http://www.dailystar.com.lb//News/Lebanon-News/2011/Apr-18/136762-syria-lebanon-stability-interdependent-conference.ashx
58. http://www.naharnet.com/stories/ar/17575-ما-أقوى-اليوم-سوريا-فرنجيه-باق-والنظام-بالأمس-كانت#new-comment
59. http://www.dailystar.com.lb//News/Lebanon-News/2011/Apr-18/136762-syria-lebanon-stability-interdependent-conference.ashx
60. http://www.naharnet.com/stories/ar/30059
61. http://www.naharnet.com/stories/ar/30061
62. http://www.naharnet.com/stories/ar/21548
63. https://www.youtube.com/watch?v=Mmdp13CQHAs
64. http://www.naharnet.com/stories/ar/12117
65. http://www.naharnet.com/stories/ar/29194
66. https://now.mmedia.me/lb/en/nownews/ghosn_stresses_al-qaeda_presence_in_lebanon
67. http://www.naharnet.com/stories/ar/29701
68. https://now.mmedia.me/lb/en/archive/syrian_gunfire_wounds_10_at_lebanese_border1
69. http://www.naharnet.com/stories/ar/29697-معلومات-ينفي-الله-حزب-الجمعة-صور-الى-سوريا-من-وصلتا-جثتين-سحبه#new-comment
70. http://www.dailystar.com.lb/News/Politics/2012/Feb-11/162878-syrian-massacres-jolt-north-lebanon.ashx

71. http://www.naharnet.com/stories/ar/28871

72. https://www.lorientlejour.com/article/765693/Le_%3C%3C+port_phenicien_de_Beyrouth+%3E%3E_detruit_a_coups_de_pelleteuse.html

73. https://www.theguardian.com/world/2012/jun/01/houla-massacre-reconstructing-25-may

74. http://www.unhcr.org/uk/news/latest/2014/4/533c1d5b9/number-syrian-refugees-lebanon-passes-1-million-mark.html

75. https://www.annahar.com/article/32456-ميقاتي-:-سياسة-ناي-بالنفس-طوقت-فتنة

76. http://english.alarabiya.net/articles/2013/02/17/266843.html

77. https://www.yahoo.com/news/hezbollah-chief-says-group-fighting-syria-162721809.html

78. http://www.reuters.com/article/uk-lebanon-mikati-idUKBRE92M0E120130323

79. http://www.unhcr.org/uk/news/latest/2014/4/533c1d5b9/number-syrian-refugees-lebanon-passes-1-million-mark.html

4. *AL-ZA'AMA*—ON POLITICAL LEADERSHIP AND PARTISANSHIP IN LEBANON

1. Sami Hermez, *War is Coming: Between Past and Future Violence in Lebanon* (Philadelphia, PA: University of Pennsylvania Press, 2017), 2–4.

2. Michael Gilsenan, *Lords of the Lebanese Marches: Violence and Narrative in an Arab Society* (London: IB Tauris, 1996), 22.

3. Leonard Hottinger, 'Zu'ama in Historical Perspective', in Leonard Binder, ed., *Politics in Lebanon* (New York: Wiley, 1966), 85–6, 97–9.

4. Michael Johnson, *Class and Client in Beirut: The Sunni Muslim Community and the Lebanese State 1840–1985* (London: Ithaca Press, 1986), 3, 5.

5. Rola El-Husseini, *Pax Syriana: Elite Politics in Post-War Lebanon* (Syracuse, NY: Syracuse University Press, 2012), xvii.

6. See Hannes Baumann, *Citizen Hariri: Lebanon's Neoliberal Reconstruction* (London: Hurst, 2016).

7. See Lina Khatib, Dina Matar and Atef Alshaer, *The Hizbullah Phenomenon: Politics and Communication* (London: Hurst, 2014).

8. Franck Mermier and Sabrina Mervin, 'Introduction: Une approche anthropologique du leadership au Liban', in Franck Mermier and Sabrina Mervin, eds, *Leaders et Partisans au Liban* (Paris: Karthala, 2012), 10.

9. Gilsenan, *Lords of the Lebanese Marches*, xi–xii.

10. Hannes Baumann, 'The New "Contractor Bourgeoisie" in Lebanese Politics: Hariri, Mikati, and Fares', in Are Knudsen and Michael Kerr, eds, *Lebanon after the Cedar Revolution* (London: Hurst, 2012), 125–44.

11. Majed Halawi, *A Lebanon Defied: Musa al-Sadr and the Shi'a Community* (Boulder, CO: Westview, 1992); Augustus Norton, *Amal and the Shi'a: Struggle for the Soul of Lebanon* (Austin, TX: University of Texas Press, 1987); Augustus Norton, *Hezbollah: A Short History* (Princeton, NJ: Princeton University Press, 2009).

12. See Elizabeth Picard, 'Une sociologie historique du *za'îm* libanais', in Charles Chartouni, ed., *Histoire, société et pouvoir aux Proche Orients (travaux dédiés à Toufic Touma)*, vol. 1 (Paris: Geuthner), 157–72.

13. El-Husseini, *Pax Syriana*.

14. Baumann, 'The New "Contractor Bourgeoisie"'.

15. Michael Johnson, *All Honourable Men: The Social Origins of War in Lebanon* (London: IB Tauris, 2002).

16. Mona Harb, *Le Hezbollah à Beyrouth (1985–2005): De la banlieue à la ville* (Paris: IFPO-Karthala, 2006), 189.

17. Myriam Catusse and Joseph Alagha, 'Les Services sociaux du Hezbollah: effort de guerre, *ethos* religieux et ressources politiques', in Sabrina Mervin, ed., *Le Hezbollah: Etat des lieux* (Arles: Actes Sud-IFPO, 2008), 117–40, 122–26. For a detailed treatment, see Mona Harb, *Le Hezbollah à Beyrouth (1985–2005): De la banlieue à la ville* (Paris: IFPO-Karthala, 2006).

18. Catusse and Alagha, 'Les Services sociaux du Hezbollah', 127; Sabrina Mervin, 'Le Lien iranien', in Mervin, ed., *Le Hezbollah*, 82–5; Amal Saad-Ghorayeb, *Hizbu'llah: Politics and Religion* (London: Pluto Press, 2002).

19. Mona Harb, *Le Hezbollah à Beyrouth*, 111–14.

20. Mona Fawaz, 'La Reconstruction de Haret Hreik (Beyrouth)', in Mervin, ed., 143; Fawaz, 'The Politics of Property in Planning: Hezbollah's Reconstruction of Haret Hreik (Beirut, Lebanon) as a Case Study', *International Journal of Urban and Regional Research* 38 (2014), 931.

21. Harb, *Le Hezbollah à Beyrouth*, 96, 104, 112.

22. Ibid., 113–14; Catusse and Alagha, 'Les Services sociaux du Hezbollah', 125–6.

23. Eric Lob, 'Development, Mobilization and War: The Iranian Construction Jehad, Construction Mobilization and Trench Builders Association (1979–2013)', *Middle East Critique* (2017), 2–9.

24. For more on this, see Lara Deeb, *An Enchanted Modern: Gender and Public Piety in Shi'i Lebanon* (Princeton, NJ: Princeton University Press, 2006).

25. http://www.almahdischools.edu.lb/الخريطة-على-مواقعنا?view=contactmap

26. Mona Fawaz, *Le Hezbollah à Beyrouth*, 96; http://www.almahdischools.edu.lb/2013-02-12-12-47-46/من-نحن.html

27. Catherine Le Thomas, 'Formation et Socialisation: un projet de (con-tre-)société', in Mervin, ed., *Le Hezbollah*, 154.

28. http://www.almahdischools.edu.lb/28–2013-01-20-19-46نحن-من.html

29. http://www.almahdischools.org/component/k2/item/5969--حفل صور ع-المهدي-ثانوية-في-السنوي-التفوق.html

30. https://www.facebook.com/-614602818555المهدي-مدارس-خريجي-رابطة 782/

31. Catherine Le Thomas, 'Le Paysage scout chiite', in Franck Mermier and Sabrina Mervin, eds, *Leaders et Partisans au Liban* (Paris: Karthala, 2012), 288.

32. Catherine Le Thomas, 'Les Scouts al-Mahdî: une génération résistante', in Mervin, ed., 175; Le Thomas, 'Le Paysage', 297–8.

33. Le Thomas, 'Les Scouts', 175; Le Thomas, 'Le Paysage', 290, 296.

34. https://www.alrassoul.org/ar/المقاومة-جرحى-يزور-قرداحي-جورج-الإعلامي

35. https://www.alrassoul.org/ar/العالمي-اليوم-بمناسبة-طبي-مؤتمر- القانونية-للقبالة

36. http://www.hayaa.org/essaydetails.php?eid=31749&cid=560

37. Melani Cammett, *Compassionate Communalism: Welfare and Sectarianism in Lebanon* (Ithaca: Cornell University Press, 2014), 155.

38. Cammett, *Compassionate Communalism*, 157–60.

39. Baumann, *Citizen Hariri*, 47; Cammett, *Compassionate Communalism*, 139.

40. Baumann, *Citizen Hariri*, 49.

41. Ibid., 48–51.

42. Ibid., fn. 99, 111.

43. Melani Cammett and Sukriti Issar, 'Bricks and Mortars Clientelism: Sectarianism and the Logics of Welfare Allocation in Lebanon', *World Politics* 62 (2010), 381–421.

44. http://rhf.org.lb/?q=node/89#overlay-context=content/rafik-hariri-un-habitat-memorial-award; http://rhf.org.lb/?q=node/82#overlay-context=content/rafik-hariri-un-habitat-memorial-award

45. http://rhf.org.lb/?q=node/91#overlay-context=content/rafik-hariri-un-habitat-memorial-award

46. Baumann, *Citizen Hariri*, 110–111.

47. Cammett, *Compassionate Commualism*, 149; http://www.yellowpages.com.lb/en/business/medical-centers/hariri-foundation-dhss1

48. Cammett, *Compassionate Communalism*, 149.

49. Ibid., 146.

50. Ibid., 150–51.

51. http://rhf.org.lb/?q=content/social-health-care-services-0#overlay-context=content/social-health-care-services-0; http://www.haririmed.org/pages/frmDepartmentsdoctors.aspx.

52. http://www.yellowpages.com.lb/en/business/medical-centers/hariri-foundation-dhss1.

53. Cammett, *Compassionate Communalism*, 141.
54. http://rhf.org.lb/?q=content/office-hariri-relief-services-0.
55. Cammett, *Compassionate Communalism*, 142. See also Daniel Corstange, 'Vote trafficking in Lebanon', *International Journal of Middle East Studies* 44 (2012), 485.
56. Cammett, *Compassionate Communalism*, 141–2.
57. http://www.higher-edu.gov.lb/english/privuniv/hariri.htm
58. https://www.rhu.edu.lb/about-rhu/history
59. https://www.rhu.edu.lb/Library/Assets/Gallery/Files/tuitionandfees.pdf
60. https://www.aub.edu.lb/comptroller/Documents/docs/Tuition%20Sch%202016–17.pdf
61. https://www.rhu.edu.lb/admission/scholarship-and-financial-support; https://www.rhu.edu.lb/student-affair/financial-aid-program
62. https://www.rhu.edu.lb/about-rhu/history
63. https://www.rhu.edu.lb/about-rhu/mission-statement
64. https://www.facebook.com/rhualumnia/?ref=bookmarks
65. https://www.rhu.edu.lb/about-rhu/leadership/board-of-deans; https://www.linkedin.com/in/prof-ahmad-smaili-09ba1527/?ppe=1
66. Roschanack Shaery-Eisenlohr, *Shi'ite Lebanon: Transnational Religion and the Making of National Identities* (New York: Columbia University Press, 2011).
67. Baumann, *Citizen Hariri*, 53.
68. Cammett, *Compassionate Communalism*, 161–3; http://www.amaleducation.com/ar-about-us
69. Harb, *Le Hezbollah à Beyrouth*, 69–74.
70. Cammett, *Compassionate Communalism*, 173, 175–6; Chantal Mazaeff, 'L'action des Forces libanaises à Aïn al-Remmané: un intense travail de réhabilitation et de socialisation politique', in Franck Mermier and Sabrina Mervin, eds, *Leaders et Partisans au Liban* (Paris: Karthala, 2012), 269.
71. https://www.oroom.org/forum/threads/8-oranges.9542/page-2
72. http://www.dailystar.com.lb/News/Lebanon-News/2006/Feb-27/7559-turning-the-world-orange-fpm-members-set-up-private-company.ashx
73. This paragraph relies heavily on Isabelle Rivoal's wonderful description of these scenes. Isabelle Rivoal, 'Intimité, mise en scène et distance dans la relation politique au Liban', in Franck Mermier and Sabrina Mervin, eds, *Leaders et Partisans au Liban* (Paris: Karthala, 2012), 152–3.
74. Michael Gilsenan, *Recognizing Islam: An Anthropologist's Introduction* (London: Croom Helm, 1982), 102.

75. On Hizballah's media, see Lina Khatib and Dina Matar with Atef Alshaer, *The Hizbullah Phenomenon: Politics and Communication* (London: Hurst & Company, 2014); and Olfa Lamloum, 'Le Hezbollah au miroir de ses médias', in Mervin, ed., *Le Hezbollah*, 21–45.

76. Chawkat Ichti, 'La place du leadership traditionnel dans les partis politiques modernes: le cas de la *za'âma* des Arslan', in Franck Mermier and Sabrina Mervin, eds, *Leaders et Partisans au Liban* (Paris: Karthala, 2012), 461–79 and especially 471–5.

77. Chawki Douayhi, 'Réflexions autour de la *za'âma* aronite au Liban-Nord', in Franck Mermier and Sabrina Mervin, eds, *Leaders et Partisans au Liban* (Paris: Karthala, 2012), 491.

78. https://elmarada.org/المردة

79. Douayhi, 'Réflexions', 491–2.

80. Douayhi, 'Réflexions', 485.

81. https://www.youtube.com/watch?v=Ae2TbQ04pOA

82. Johnson, *Class and Client*; Philip S. Khoury, ''Abu 'Ali al-Kilawi: A Damascus Qabaday', in Edmund Burke III, ed., *Struggle and Survival in the Modern Middle East* (London: IB Tauris, 1993), 179–90.

83. Harb, *Le Hezbollah à Beyrouth*, 79.

84. http://sawte.com/showthread.php?t=14265

85. Ward Vloeberghs, 'Worshipping the Martyr President: The *Darih* of Rafiq Hariri in Beirut', in Pedro Pinto, Baudouin Dupret, Thomas Pierret, and Kathryn Spellman-Poots, eds, *Ethnographies of Islam: Ritual Performances and Everyday Practices* (Edinburgh: Edinburgh University Press, 2012), 87.

86. Schaery-Eisenlohr, *Shi'ite Lebanon*.

87. Philippe Abirached, 'Charisme, pouvoir et communauté politique: la figure de Michel Aoun', in Franck Mermier and Sabrina Mervin, eds, *Leaders et Partisans au Liban* (Paris: Karthala, 2012), 36, 37.

88. Bruno Lefort, 'Représentations du leadership et mémoires vives chez les militants aounistes', in Franck Mermier and Sabrina Mervin, eds, *Leaders et Partisans au Liban* (Paris: Karthala, 2012), 228–9.

89. Emma Aubin-Boltanski, 'Samir Geagea: le guerrier, le martyr, et le *za'îm*', in Franck Mermier and Sabrina Mervin, eds, *Leaders et Partisans au Liban* (Paris: Karthala, 2012), 63–4, 68, 69, 72.

90. Abirached, 'Charisme', 42.

91. Michel Aoun and Frédéric Domont, *Une certaine vision du Liban: entretiens avec Frédéric Domont* (Paris: Fayard, 2007), 49.

92. Aubin-Boltanski, 'Samir Geagea', 68–9.

93. Abirached, 'Charisme', 53.

94. Lefort, 'Représentations', 241, 240.

95. https://www.youtube.com/watch?v=DLpZOfQEbqs

96. https://www.youtube.com/watch?v=YUZxu1jcPM8

97. https://www.youtube.com/watch?v=Z1EmlHQmpJA

98. Aubin-Boltanski, 'Samir Geagea', 59.

99. Harb, *Le Hezbollah à Beyrouth*, 79.

100. Mazaeff, 'L'action des Forces libanaises', 279.

101. https://www.youtube.com/watch?time_continue=85&v=JF1sEv-E2mo

102. https://www.oroom.org/forum/threads/ex-fpmers-forming-lists-against-fpm.52567/page-1 and following.

5. *AL-MISHWAR*, OR THE WALK—ON SPACE AND CAPITAL IN CONTEMPORARY LEBANON

1. Hannes Baumann, 'The New "Contractor Bourgeoisie" in Lebanese Politics: Hariri, Miqati and Fares', in Are Knudsen and Michael Kerr, eds, *Lebanon After the Cedar Revolution* (London: Hurst, 2012), 125–44.

2. See in particular Hannes Baumman, *Citizen Hariri: Lebanon's Neoliberal Reconstruction* (London: Hurst, 2016); and Hadi Makarem, 'Actually Existing Neoliberalism: The Reconstruction of Downtown Beirut in Post-Civil war Lebanon', unpublished Ph.D. dissertation (University of London, 2014).

3. http://www.undp.org.lb/programme/governance/advocacy/nhdr/nhdr97/chpt2.pdf

4. Much ink has been spilled in discussing the reconstruction of central Beirut. See, in particular, Makarem, 'Actually Existing Neoliberalism'; Saree Makdisi, 'Laying Claim to Beirut: Urban Narrative and Spatial Identity in the Age of Solidere', *Critical Inquiry* 23, 2 (1997), 660–7; Peter Rowe and Hashim Sarkis, eds, *Projecting Beirut: Episodes in the Construction and Reconstruction of a Modern City* (Munich: Prestel, 1998); Aseel Sawalha, *Reconstructing Beirut: Memory and Space in a Postwar Arab City* (Austin, TX: University of Texas Press, 2011); Heiko Schmid, 'Privatized Urbanity or a Politicized Society? Reconstruction in Beirut after the Civil War', *European Planning Studies* 14, 3 (2006), 365–81.

5. This paragraph is largely based on Baumann, *Citizen Hariri*, 59–67.

6. Baumann, *Citizen Hariri*, 70–81, 96.

7. Ibid.

8. This and the following paragraphs depend in large part on Rosalie Berthier, 'Abracada... broke: Lebanon's Banking on Magic', http://www.synaps.network/abracada-broke. I am immensely grateful to Nasri Atallah for drawing this piece to my attention, and to Berthier for her investigative work and incisive analysis.

9. Interview with Nassib Ghobril, Beirut, 8 August 2012.
10. Berthier, 'Abracada... broke', http://www.synaps.network/abracada-broke
11. 'Al-Hariri: al-hukuma musamama 'ala tanfidh qanun al-salsala', *Al-Balad* (25/09/2017), 4.
12. Berthier, 'Abracada... broke', http://www.synaps.network/abracada-broke
13. Interview with Nassib Ghobril, Beirut, 8 August 2012.
14. Berthier, 'Abracada... broke', http://www.synaps.network/abracada-broke
15. Interview with Nassib Ghobril, Beirut, 8 August 2012.
16. Ibid.
17. See Byblos Bank, Economic Research and Analysis Department, 'The Global Crisis and Expatriates' Remittances to Lebanon: Trends and Elements of Resilience' (Beirut: Byblos Bank, 2011).
18. http://www.economy.gov.lb/public/uploads/files/1713_2575_2974.pdf
19. Interview with Nassib Ghobril, Beirut, 08/08/2012.
20. https://www.youtube.com/watch?v=Fh_EyLpsL80
21. http://www.plusproperties.com.lb/6/apartments-lebanon-tilal-bhersaf/project_details
22. Anonymous interview, Beirut, 19/09/2017.
23. Dilip Ratha, Sanket Mohapatra, and Ani Silwal, *The Migration Remittances Factbook 2011* (Washington, DC: World Bank, 2011).
24. Marwan Abi Samra, *L'Emigration libanaise et son impact sur l'économie et le développement* (Geneva: ILO, 2010), 79. See also Boutros Labaki, *The Role of Transnational Communities in Fostering Development in Countries of Origin: The Case of Lebanon* (Beirut: ESCWA, 2006).
25. http://cadmus.eui.eu/bitstream/handle/1814/46504/RSCAS_PB_2017_12_MPC.pdf?sequence=1
26. Abi Samra, *L'émigration libanaise*, 27.
27. http://www.cas.gov.lb/images/Mics3/MISC3_new/International%20migration%20in%202009.pdf
28. http://www.investinlebanon.gov.lb/Content/uploads/Salary_Scales_in_Lebanon_2013.pdf. https://www.alfa.com.lb/post/plans.aspx?language=1.http://blogbaladi.com/alfa-and-touch-new-reduced-mobile-internet-prices/
29. http://www.cas.gov.lb/images/Mics3/MISC3_new/International%20migration%20in%202009.pdf
30. https://openknowledge.worldbank.org/bitstream/handle/10986/23743/9781464803192.pdf?sequence=3
31. Al Jumhuriyya al-Lubnaniyya, Wizarat al-Kharijiyya wa al-Mughtaribin, al-Mudiriyya al-'Amma li-l-Mughatiribin, 'Kalimat mudir 'amm al-

mughtaribin al-ustadh Haytham Jum'ah fi al-yawm al-'alami li-l-mugh-
tarib al-lubnani fi 09/03/2008'.

32. http://www.tayyar.org/News/Lebanon/46537
33. 'Basil aftataha mu'tamar al-taqa al-ightirabiyya fi Las Vegas', *Sada al-Balad* (25/09/2017).
34. Berthier, 'Abracada... broke', http://www.synaps.network/abracada-broke
35. http://zaitunaybay.com
36. http://stowcapitalpartners.com/property/beirut-waterfront/
37. http://www.solidere.com/city-center/solidere-developments/real-estate/zaitunay-bay
38. Ibid.
39. http://zaitunaybay.com/where-to-eat
40. http://www.nytimes.com/2012/02/19/travel/in-beirut-the-zaitunay-bay-promenade-opens.html?mcubz=1
41. http://stowcapitalpartners.com/property/beirut-waterfront/
42. http://www.nytimes.com/2012/02/19/travel/in-beirut-the-zaitunay-bay-promenade-opens.html?mcubz=1
43. http://www.executive-magazine.com/business-finance/business/stowing-the-rich
44. http://www.solidere.com/city-center/solidere-developments/real-estate/zaitunay-bay
45. http://stowcapitalpartners.com/property/beirut-waterfront/; http://leyachtclubbeirut.com
46. http://www.executive-magazine.com/business-finance/business/stowing-the-rich
47. http://leyachtclubbeirut.com/the-club.php?section=5
48. http://leyachtclubbeirut.com/the-club-suites.php
49. http://www.executive-magazine.com/business-finance/business/stowing-the-rich
50. http://leyachtclubbeirut.com/explore.php
51. http://leyachtclubbeirut.com/the-club-residences.php
52. https://www.theverge.com/2016/8/3/12325104/airbnb-aesthetic-global-minimalism-startup-gentrification
53. S. Sadek and M. El-Fadel, 'The Normandy Landfill: A Case Study in Solid Waste Management', *Journal of Natural Resources and Life Sciences Education* 29 (2000), 155–61.
54. http://www.hydromar-sal.com/normandy.html; http://english.al-akhbar.com/content/solidere's-final-frontier
55. For detailed consideration of this, see Hadi Makarem, 'Actually Existing Neoliberalism'.
56. http://english.al-akhbar.com/content/beirut's-zaitunay-bay-corruption-boardwalk

57. http://www.solidere.com/sites/default/files/attached/ar2004.pdf

58. http://stowcapitalpartners.com/united-kingdom/investment/; http://stowcapitalpartners.com/property/33-davies-street/

59. http://investinlebanon.gov.lb/Content/uploads/SideBlock/130308125455184~IDAL-INVESTMENT%20LAW%20360.pdf

60. http://investinlebanon.gov.lb/en/about_us/who_we_are

61. http://investinlebanon.gov.lb/Content/uploads/SideBlock/130308125455184~IDAL-INVESTMENT%20LAW%20360.pdf

62. https://www.theguardian.com/world/2007/jun/07/bae6

63. Ibid.; http://english.al-akhbar.com/content/beirut's-zaitunay-bay-corruption-boardwalk

64. http://www.executive-magazine.com/business-finance/business/stowing-the-rich

65. http://jo.pcm.gov.lb/j2006/j14/default.htm

66. http://english.al-akhbar.com/content/lebanese-ministers-open-floodgates-corruption

67. http://www.beirutreport.com/2015/07/private-security-confront-police-at-zaitunay-bay.html

68. See Neil Brenner and Nik Theodore, eds, *Spaces of Neoliberalism: Urban Restructuring in North America and Western Europe* (Oxford: Blackwell, 2002); Anna Minton, *Ground Control: Fear and Happiness in the Twenty-First Century* (London: Penguin, 2009).

69. http://samabeirut.com/explore

70. Hicham El-Achkar, 'The Role of the State in Initiating Gentrification: The Case of the Neighbourhood of Achrafieh in Beirut', unpublished MA thesis (Lebanese University, 2011), 81.

71. Marieke Krijnen and Mona Fawaz, 'Exception as the Rule: High-End Developments in Neoliberal Beirut', *Built Environment* 36, 2 (2010), 246. See, for an important rejoinder to this discourse of statelessness, Jamil Mouawad, 'The Negotiated State: State-Society Relations in Lebanon', unpublished Ph.D. dissertation (University of London, 2015).

72. Krijnen and Fawaz, 'Exception as the Rule', 246.

73. El-Achkar, 'The Role of the State', 52.

74. Krijnen and Fawaz, 'Exception as the Rule', 248–51.

75. Krijnen and Fawaz, 'Exception as the Rule', 252–4, 256. Italics in the original.

76. https://www.lecommercedulevant.com/article/27621-les-prix-moyens-quartier-par-quartier#

77. Nadia Alaily-Mattar, 'Beyond Gated Communities? Detachment and Concentration in Networked Nodes of Affluence in the City of Beirut', *Urban Design International* 13 (2008).

78. http://www.jadaliyya.com/Details/23615/Lebanese-Ideology-and-Boutros-Harb-Separate,-But-%5B-Kind-of%5D-Equal

79. https://www.youtube.com/watch?v=9wYq68tFbac

80. http://www.lorientlejour.com/article/683826/Harb_fait_etat_de_plans_visant_a_acheter_les_biens-fonds_des_chretiens_dans_certaines_regions.html

81. El-Achkar, 'The Role of the State'; Marieke Krijnen, 'Filling Every Gap: Real Estate Development in Beirut', http://www.jadaliyya.com/Details/29724/Filling-Every-Gap-Real-Estate-Development-in-Beirut

82. El-Achkar, 'The Role of the State', 56.

83. Krijnen, 'Filling Every Gap'; El-Achkar, 'The Role of the State'.

84. El-Achkar, 'The Role of the State', 53.

85. Krijnen, 'Filling Every Gap'.

86. El-Achkar, 'The Role of the State', 51.

87. Alaily-Mattar, 'Beyond Gated Communities?', 264, 266.

88. Alaily-Mattar, 'Beyond Gated Communities', 265, 268.

89. El-Achkar, 'The Role of the State', 128–9.

90. Hicham El-Achkar, 'The Lebanese State as Initiator of Gentrification in Achrafieh', http://ifpo.hypotheses.org/3834

91. http://www.archdaily.com/872480/spurred-by-privatization-beiruts-working-class-is-colonizing-the-citys-periphery

92. https://www.lorientlejour.com/article/742217/Le_double_drame_des_Soudanais_de_limmeuble_Fassouh.html

93. http://www.aljazeera.com/news/middleeast/2012/01/201211618 2913687213.html

94. https://www.lorientlejour.com/article/745292/Fassouh+%3A_les_conclusions_des_experts_remises_a_Charbel.html; https://www.lorientlejour.com/article/743568/Tragedie_de_Fassouh+%3A_trois_scenarios_envisageables....html

95. http://www.aljazeera.com/news/middleeast/2012/01/2012116 182913687213.html

96. https://www.lorientlejour.com/article/742217/Le_double_drame_des_Soudanais_de_limmeuble_Fassouh.html

97. https://www.lorientlejour.com/article/754865/Fassouh%2C_trois_mois_apres_la_catastrophe.html

98. https://www.lorientlejour.com/article/757477/Albert_Yazbeck%2C_28e_victime_de_l%27effondrement_de_Fassouh.html; https://www.lorientlejour.com/article/741649/Mandats_d%27arret_contre_les_deux__coproprietaires_de_l%27immeuble_en_ruines.html

99. https://www.lorientlejour.com/article/790620/Les_proprietaires_des_anciens_logements_appellent_a_une_nouvelle_loi_sur_les_loyers_pour_eviter_un_nouveau_Fassouh.html; https://www.lorientle-

jour.com/article/748402/Proprietaires_vs_locataires+%3A_le_
debat_dont_tout_le_monde_se_lave_les_mains.html

100. https://sakanbeirut.files.wordpress.com/2012/12/1396354598-
d985d8b4d8b1d988d8b9-d982d8a7d986d988d986-d8a7d984d8a-
7d98ad8acd8a7d8b1d8a7d8aa.pdf

101. https://www.lorientlejour.com/article/753165/Le_nouveau_projet_
de_loi_sur_les_loyers%2C_detonateur_de_la_crise_sociale_.html

102. https://sakanbeirut.files.wordpress.com/2012/12/1396354598-
d985d8b4d8b1d988d8b9-d982d8a7d986d988d986-d8a7d984d8a-
7d98ad8acd8a7d8b1d8a7d8aa.pdf

103. https://www.lorientlejour.com/article/753165/Le_nouveau_projet_
de_loi_sur_les_loyers%2C_detonateur_de_la_crise_sociale_.html

104. Ibid.

105. http://www.jadaliyya.com/Details/31561/Lebanon-Rejecting-the-
New-Rent-Law-An-Open-Letter-to-the-ParliamentError! Hyperlink
reference not valid.

106. http://www.jadaliyya.com/Details/33070/New-Texts-Out-Now-
Nadine-Bekdache,-Evicting-Sovereignty-Lebanon%60s-Housing-
Tenants-from-Citizens-to-Obstacles

107. http://www.jadaliyya.com/Details/31561/Lebanon-Rejecting-the-New-
Rent-Law-An-Open-Letter-to-the-Parliament

108. El-Achkar, 'The Role of the State', 130.

109. https://www.youtube.com/watch?time_continue=122&v=
bRGgM4M9L2g

110. http://www.cas.gov.lb/images/Mics3/MISC3_new/International%20
migration%20in%202009.pdf

111. https://www.reuters.com/article/us-lebanon-electricity/no-light-at-
end-of-tunnel-for-lebanons-power-crisis-idUSKCN0SK1LH20151026

112. https://www.lorientlejour.com/article/1051966/tensions-entre-les-
proprietaires-de-generateurs-et-le-ministere-de-lenergie.html

113. https://www.reuters.com/article/us-lebanon-electricity/no-light-at-
end-of-tunnel-for-lebanons-power-crisis-idUSKCN0SK1
LH20151026

114. https://www.lorientlejour.com/article/1052762/generateurs-le-gou-
vernement-veut-mieux-controler-les-prix.html

115. https://www.lorientlejour.com/article/1051966/tensions-entre-les-
proprietaires-de-generateurs-et-le-ministere-de-lenergie.html

116. https://www.lorientlejour.com/article/1052762/generateurs-le-gou-
vernement-veut-mieux-controler-les-prix.html

117. S.R., 'Le plan de Gebran Bassil pour l'électricité', *Le Commerce du
Levant* (July 2010), 46–50.

118. Ibid.

119. Salwa Ismail, *Political Life in Cairo's New Quarters: Encountering the*

Everyday State (Minneapolis, MN: University of Minnesota Press, 2006), xx. See also Nikolas Rose, *Powers of Freedom: Reframing Political Thought* (Cambridge: Cambridge University Press, 1999); and Nikolas Rose, 'Governing Advanced Liberal Democracies', in Andrew Barry, Thomas Osborne, and Nikolas Rose, eds, *Foucault and Political Reason: Liberalism, Neo-Liberalism, and Rationalities of Rule* (Chicago: University of Chicago Press, 1996), 37–64.

120. S.R., 'Le plan de Gebran Bassil'.

121. http://www.dailystar.com.lb//News/Lebanon-News/2017/Mar-31/399979-lebanon-energy-minister-says-new-power-plan-to-provide-7-additional-hours-of-feed.ashx

122. https://www.lorientlejour.com/article/1062808/electricite-lete-sera-t-il-plus-clement-pour-les-libanais-.html

123. https://www.lorientlejour.com/article/1064600/appel-doffres-pour-les-navires-centrales-abi-khalil-se-justifie.html; https://www.lorientlejour.com/article/1064191/lappel-doffres-pour-les-navires-centrales-a-du-plomb-dans-laile.html

124. https://www.lorientlejour.com/article/1066342/edl-augmente-ses-importations-delectricite-de-syrie.html

125. http://www.dailystar.com.lb//News/Lebanon-News/2017/Mar-31/399979-lebanon-energy-minister-says-new-power-plan-to-provide-7-additional-hours-of-feed.ashx

126. https://www.reuters.com/article/us-lebanon-electricity/no-light-at-end-of-tunnel-for-lebanons-power-crisis-idUSKCN0SK1LH20151026

127. Interview with Guita Hourani, 20/08/2012.

128. Ismail, *Political Life*, xx–xxi.

129. Mona Fawaz, 'The Politics of Property in Planning: Hezbollah's Reconstruction of Haret Hreik (Beirut, Lebanon) as a Case Study', *International Journal of Urban and Regional Research* 38 (2014), 922–34.

130. https://lb.usembassy.gov/our-relationship/policy-history/embassy-fact-sheets/; https://www.reuters.com/article/us-lebanon-military-usa/lebanese-army-to-get-120-million-in-u-s-aid-idUSKBN1E72J6

131. I draw here on Baumann, *Citizen Hariri*.

132. https://tradingeconomics.com/lebanon/external-debt

133. Baumann, *Citizen Hariri*.

134. Ismail, *Political Life*.

6. *AL-AKHARIN*, OR THE OTHERS—ON LEBANON'S REFUGEES AND MIGRANT WORKERS

1. https://stateofmind13.com/2015/02/18/0-3-of-lebanese-own-50-of-lebanon/

2. Wolfgang Sachs, *For Love of the Automobile: Looking Back into the History of our Desires* (Berkeley, CA: University of California Press, 1992), 8.

3. Sudhir Chella Rajan, *The Enigma of Automobility: Democratic Politics and Pollution Control* (Pittsburgh, PA: University of Pittsburgh Press, 1996), 81.

4. https://www.lorientlejour.com/article/1090855/le-nombre-de-palestiniens-au-liban-nexcede-pas-les-174-422-personnes.html

5. https://www.unrwa.org/where-we-work/lebanon

6. See, for instance, Jad Chaaban, Hala Ghattas, Rima Habib, Sari Hanafi, Nadine Sahyoun, Nisreen Salti, Karin Seyfert, Nadia Naamani, 'Socio-Economic Survey of Palestinian Refugees in Lebanon', (Beirut: American University of Beirut and UNRWA, 2010), available at https://www.unrwa.org/userfiles/2011012074253.pdf. This report put the number of Palestinians living in Lebanon at 260–280,000.

7. https://www.lorientlejour.com/article/1090855/le-nombre-de-palestiniens-au-liban-nexcede-pas-les-174-422-personnes.html

8. http://www.wipo.int/edocs/lexdocs/laws/en/lb/lb018en.pdf

9. http://prrn.mcgill.ca/research/papers/brynen2_09.htm

10. Julie Peteet, *Landscape of Hope and Despair: Palestinian Refugee Camps* (Philadelphia, PA: University of Pennsylvania Press, 2005), 172, 224.

11. Bernard Rougier, *Everyday Jihad: The Rise of Militant Islam among Palestinians in Northern Lebanon* (Cambridge, MA: Harvard University Press, 2007), 18.

12. Chaaban et al., 'Socio-Economic Survey'.

13. Sari Hanafi, 'Governing the Palestinian Refugee Camps in Lebanon and Syria: The Cases of Nahr al-Bared and Yarmouk Camps', in Sari Hanafi and Are Knudsen, eds, *Palestinian Refugees: Identity, Space and Place in the Levant* (Abingdon: Routledge, 2011), 29–49.

14. Hanafi, 'Governing the Palestinian Refugee Camps', 44–5; Rougier, *Everyday Jihad*.

15. https://www.lorientlejour.com/article/1068902/cessez-le-feu-a-ain-el-heloue-apres-une-victoire-du-fateh-dans-le-quartier-de-tireh.html

16. Hanafi, 'Governing the Palestinian Refugee Camps', 34–5.

17. Anonymous interview, Jal al-Dib, 7 August 2012.

18. Anonymous interview, Jal al-Dib, 7 August 2012.

19. http://www.refworld.org/publisher,NATLEGBOD,,LBN,4c3c630f2,0.html

20. Sergio Bianchi, 'Community Participation and Human Rights Advocacy: Questions Arising from the Campaign About the Right to Work of Palestinian Refugees in Lebanon', in Sari Hanafi and Are Knudsen, eds, *Palestinian Refugees: Identity, Space and Place in the Levant* (Abingdon: Routledge, 2011), 165.

21. http://www.refworld.org/publisher,NATLEGBOD,,LBN,4c3c5fc 57d,0.html

22. http://www.refworld.org/docid/460a2b252.html

23. International Labour Organization, 'Palestinian Employment in Lebanon: Facts and Challenges', http://www.ilo.org/wcmsp5/groups/ public/—arabstates/—ro-beirut/documents/publication/ wcms_236502.pdf

24. Bianchi, 'Community Participation', 165.

25. Are Knudsen, 'The Law, the Loss, and the Lives of Palestinian Refugees in Lebanon', CMI Working Paper (Bergen: Chr. Michelsen Institute, 2007),   https://www.cmi.no/publications/ file/2607-the-law-the-loss-and-the-lives-of-palestinian.pdf.

26. http://www.lpdc.gov.lb/property-ownership/the-palestinian-refugee-and-the-property-ownership/56/en

27. Peeteet, *Landscape of Hope and Despair*, 174, 225–26.

28. Anonymous interview, Jal al-Dib, 7 August 2012.

29. Are Knudsen, 'Nahr al-Bared: The Political Fall-Out of a Refugee Disaster', in Sari Hanafi and Are Knudsen, eds, *Palestinian Refugees: Identity, Space and Place in the Levant* (Abingdon: Routledge, 2011), 100–6.

30. Anonymous interview, Jal al-Dib, 7 August 2012.

31. http://www.lpdc.gov.lb/DocumentFiles/%20قرار%20وزير%20العمل%I%20سجعان%20قزي%I%20المتعلق%20بالمهن%20I%20الواجب%20حصرها%20% باللبنانيين866-635996807061756866.pdf

32. International Labour Organization, 'Palestinian Employment in Lebanon: Facts and Challenges', http://www.ilo.org/wcmsp5/groups/ public/—arabstates/—ro-beirut/documents/publication/wcms_ 236502.pdf

33. International Labour Organization, 'Palestinian Employment in Lebanon: Facts and Challenges', http://www.ilo.org/wcmsp5/groups/ public/—arabstates/—ro-beirut/documents/publication/ wcms_236502.pdf

34. Anonymous interview, Jal al-Dib, 7 August 2012.

35. International Labour Organization, 'Palestinian Employment in Lebanon: Facts and Challenges', http://www.ilo.org/wcmsp5/groups/ public/—arabstates/—ro-beirut/documents/publication/wcms_ 236502.pdf

36. https://www.lorientlejour.com/article/1090855/le-nombre-de-pales-tiniens-au-liban-nexcede-pas-les-174-422-personnes.html; https:// tradingeconomics.com/lebanon/unemployment-rate

37. https://www.lorientlejour.com/article/1090855/le-nombre-de-pales-tiniens-au-liban-nexcede-pas-les-174-422-personnes.html

38. Mohamed Kamel Doraï, 'Palestinian Refugee Camps in Lebanon: Migration, Mobility and the Urbanization Process', in Sari Hanafi and Are Knudsen, eds., *Palestinian Refugees: Identity, Space and Place in the Levant* (Abingdon: Routledge, 2011), 67–80.

39. International Labour Organization, 'Palestinian Employment in Lebanon: Facts and Challenges', http://www.ilo.org/wcmsp5/groups/public/—arabstates/—ro-beirut/documents/publication/wcms_236502.pdf.

40. Chaaban et al., 'Socio-Economic Survey', https://www.unrwa.org/userfiles/2011012074253.pdf

41. International Labour Organization, 'Palestinian Employment in Lebanon: Facts and Challenges', http://www.ilo.org/wcmsp5/groups/public/—arabstates/—ro-beirut/documents/publication/wcms_236502.pdf

42. https://www.unrwa.org/where-we-work/lebanon/wavel-camp

43. https://www.unrwa.org/where-we-work/lebanon/ein-el-hilweh-camp

44. https://www.unrwa.org/where-we-work/lebanon/shatila-camp

45. Doraï, 'Palestinian Refugee Camps in Lebanon', in Hanafi and Knudsen, eds., *Palestinian Refugees*, 77.

46. https://www.unrwa.org/where-we-work/lebanon/burj-shemali-camp

47. Chaaban et al., 'Socio-Economic Survey', https://www.unrwa.org/userfiles/2011012074253.pdf

48. Ibid.

49. Peteet of Hope and Despair, *Landscape*, 198, 210.

50. Hannah Arendt, 'The Perplexities of the Rights of Man', in Peter Baehr, ed., *The Portable Hannah Arendt* (London: Penguin Books, 2000), 36.

51. Sylvain Perdigon, 'For Us It is Otherwise: Three Sketches on Making Poverty Sensible in the Palestinian Refugee Camps of Lebanon', *Current Anthropology* 56 (2015), 88–96.

52. Isabell Lorey, *State of Insecurity: Government of the Precarious* (London: Verso, 2015), 1, 10.

53. Sylvain Perdigon, 'The One Still Surviving and Viable Institution', in Sari Hanafi and Are Knudsen, eds, *Palestinian Refugees: Identity, Space and Place in the Levant* (Abingdon: Routledge, 2011), 178.

54. http://data.unhcr.org/syrianrefugees/country.php?id=122

55. UNHCR, 'Vulnerability Assessment of Syrian Refugees in Lebanon 2017' (Geneva: UNHCR, 2017).

56. Ibid.

57. https://www.thenation.com/article/will-lebanon-force-a-million-syrian-refugees-to-return-to-a-war-zone/

58. https://www.lorientlejour.com/article/957670/militaires-libanais-enleves-un-echange-avec-les-jihadistes-se-heurte-a-des-obstacles-securite.html
59. https://www.aljazeera.com/news/2017/08/lebanese-army-begins-offensive-isil-border-170819035851822.html
60. https://www.aljazeera.com/news/2017/08/lebanon-finds-suspected-remains-isil-held-soldiers-170827161154135.html
61. https://www.thenation.com/article/will-lebanon-force-a-million-syrian-refugees-to-return-to-a-war-zone/
62. UNHCR, 'Vulnerability Assessment'.
63. https://www.lorientlejour.com/article/1076404/sit-in-a-zghorta-pour-reclamer-le-depart-des-refugies-syriens.html
64. UNHCR, 'Vulnerability Assessment'.
65. Elizabeth Saleh, 'The Master Cockroach: Scrap Metal and Syrian Labour in Beirut's Informal Economy, *Contemporary Levant* 1 (2016), 94–5.
66. John Chalcraft, *The Invisible Cage: Syrian Migrant Workers in Lebanon* (Palo Alto, CA: Stanford University Press, 2009).
67. Barbara Ehrenreich and Arlie Russell Hochschild, 'Introduction', in Barbara Ehrenreich and Arlie Russell Hochschild, eds, *Global Women: Nannies, Maids, and Sex Workers in the New Economy* (London: Granta, 2001), 4.
68. See Ray Jureidini and Nayla Moukarbel, 'Female Sri Lankan Domestic Workers in Lebanon: A Case of 'Contract Slavery'?', *Journal of Ethnic and Migration Studies* 30, 4 (2004), 581–607; and Michael Young, 'Migrant Workers in Lebanon', http://www.lnf.org.lb/migrationnetwork/mig1.html. See also Nayla Moukarbel, *Sri Lankan Maids in Lebanon: A Case of 'Symbolic Violence' and 'Everyday Forms of Resistance'* (Amsterdam: Amsterdam University Press, 2009).
69. http://www.lnf.org.lb/migrationnetwork/mig1.html
70. Kathleen Hamill, *Trafficking of Migrant Domestic Workers in Lebanon: A Legal Analysis* (Beirut: Kafa, 2011), 24.
71. https://www.youtube.com/watch?v=QNwm57e19FI
72. Hamill, *Trafficking of Migrant Domestic Workers*, 24.
73. https://www.youtube.com/watch?v=iWn7ykF6qHs; https://www.youtube.com/watch?v=-z_Tou3CSOg
74. Hamill, *Trafficking of Migrant Domestic Workers*, 25.
75. Barbara Ehrenreich, 'Maid to order', in Ehrenreich and Hochschild, eds., *Global Women*, 85–103.
76. Ehrenreich, 'Maid to order', 102. Melanie Cooper, *Family Values: Between Neoliberalism and the New Social Conservatism* (Cambridge, MA: MIT Press, 2017).

77. See Akram Khater, *Inventing Home: Emigration, Gender, and the Middle Class in Lebanon, 1870–1920* (Berkeley, CA: University of California Press, 2001).

78. Nicole Constable, 'Filipino Workers in Hong Kong Homes: Household Rules and Relations', in Ehrenreich and Hochschild, eds, *Global Women*, 116.

79. https://www.khaleejtimes.com/editorials-columns/collateral-damage-sri-lanka-caught-in-israel-lebanon-war

80. https://www.hrw.org/reports/2007/lebanon0907/10.htm

81. Lina Abu Habib, 'The use and abuse of female domestic workers from Sri Lanka in Lebanon', *Gender & Development* 6, 1 (1998), 56.

82. https://www.youtube.com/watch?v=ZNMJeEa5jVQ&t=63s

83. https://www.youtube.com/watch?v=-z_Tou3CSOg

84. https://www.youtube.com/watch?v=-z_Tou3CSOg

85. Ann Laura Stoler, *Carnal Knowledge and Imperial Power: Race and the Intimate in Colonial Rule* (Berkeley, CA: University of California Press, 2002).

86. Hamill, *Trafficking of Migrant Domestic Workers*, 30.

87. https://www.youtube.com/watch?v=svhP1Kw62sg

88. Jureidini and Moukarbel, 'Female Sri Lankan Domestic Workers', 587.

89. https://www.youtube.com/watch?v=nCpCmY71O5A

90. https://www.youtube.com/watch?v=svhP1Kw62sg

91. https://www.youtube.com/watch?v=u0LWs29xe2E

92. https://www.youtube.com/watch?v=Na0_8qU2kZw

93. https://www.youtube.com/watch?v=wrtL9ZvYVKk

94. http://www.menassat.com/?q=en/news-articles/6543-breaking-prevalent-equation-sri-lankan-maid

95. https://armlebanon.org

96. https://armlebanon.org/about

97. https://www.facebook.com/Domestic-Workers-Union-In-Lebanon-founding-Committee-553197294739276/

98. https://www.youtube.com/watch?v=J90NGBCzqEA

99. https://www.hrw.org/news/2008/08/26/lebanon-migrant-domestic-workers-dying-every-week

100. https://www.hrw.org/news/2009/11/09/lebanon-deadly-month-domestic-workers

101. https://www.hrw.org/news/2008/08/26/lebanon-migrant-domestic-workers-dying-every-week

102. Hamill, *Trafficking of Migrant Domestic Workers*, 21–2.

103. https://www.hrw.org/news/2012/03/23/lebanon-stop-abuse-domestic-workers

104. http://us7.campaign-archive1.com/?u=9603efee89352bfcc5de5fc67&id=ed284f9da3

105. https://www.hrw.org/news/2016/12/13/lebanon-deports-domestic-worker-rights-organizer

106. http://www.al-monitor.com/pulse/originals/2014/11/lebanon-migrant-domestic-workers-situation.html

7. *AL-SAHRA*, OR THE NIGHT OUT—ON LEISURE AND PLEASURE IN CONTEMPORARY LEBANON

1. https://www.youtube.com/watch?time_continue=132&v=-CQ5vrzc-8E

2. http://www.ourmaninbeirut.com/2011/09/nation-blanding-hedonism-and-the-underselling-of-beirut/

3. https://www.youtube.com/watch?time_continue=132&v=-CQ5vrzc-8E

4. https://www.pinterest.co.uk/4aj9/lebanon/

5. https://www.jadaoun.com/category/lebanon-news-under-rug-swept/looks-like-beirut-award/

6. Thorstein Veblen, *The Theory of the Leisure Class* (n.p.), 19.

7. http://desktop.beiruting.com/lemag/Top_10_Lebanese_stores_to_visit_this_Black_ Friday/8925

8. http://desktop.beiruting.com/lemag/Lebanon_Among_The_World's_Sexiest_People/6501

9. http://desktop.beiruting.com/lemag/Beirut_Tops_The_Best_nternational_Cities_for_Food/7177

10. Jared McCormick, 'Hairy Chest, Will Travel: Tourism, Identity and Sexuality in the Levant', *Journal of Middle East Women's Studies* 7, 3 (2011), 87. I am grateful to Adriana Qubaia for pointing me to this article.

11. https://www.lorientlejour.com/article/771255/Nouveau_scandale_des_tests_de_la_honte+%3A_apres_une_arrestation_en_masse%2C_trois_homosexuels_deferes_devant_le_parquet.html

12. https://www.youtube.com/watch?v=lgJdeFvMH5A

13. https://www.ft.com/content/de552c4c-fcb5-11db-9971-000b5df10621

14. Ibid.

15. http://news.bbc.co.uk/1/hi/world/middle_east/6577497.stm

16. http://www.aurora-clinics.co.uk/general-news/beirut-now-the-cosmetic-surgery-capital-of-the-world/

17. https://www.al-monitor.com/pulse/originals/2015/02/lebanon-beauty-standards-women-plastic-surgery.html

18. https://www.ft.com/content/de552c4c-fcb5–11db-9971–000b5df10621; https://www.al-monitor.com/pulse/originals/2015/02/lebanon-beauty-standards-women-plastic-surgery.html

19. http://www.latimes.com/world/la-fg-skinloans29jan29-story.html

20. https://www.al-monitor.com/pulse/originals/2015/02/lebanon-beauty-standards-women-plastic-surgery.html

21. Ibid.

22. https://www.al-monitor.com/pulse/originals/2015/02/lebanon-beauty-standards-women-plastic-surgery.html

23. https://www.youtube.com/watch?v=hKZzSO5Um8E

24. https://www.silkor.com/lebanon/en/service/coolsculpting; http://cosmeticsurgery.silkor.com

25. https://www.silkor.com/lebanon/en/locations

26. http://www.latimes.com/world/la-fg-skinloans29jan29-story.html

27. http://news.bbc.co.uk/1/hi/world/middle_east/6577497.stm; http://www.latimes.com/world/la-fg-skinloans29jan29-story.html

28. http://www.signsofconflict.com/Publications/essay_details?id=11#_edn16

29. http://feminist-collective.blogspot.co.uk/2009/04/top-12-reasons-why-billboard-campaign.html

30. Suad Joseph, ed., *Arab Families: Gender, Self, and Family* (Syracuse, NY: Syracuse University Press, 1999); Suad Joseph, ed., *Gender and Citizenship in the Middle East* (Syracuse, NY: Syracuse University Press, 2000).

31. https://www.thenational.ae/world/mena/law-that-deprives-lebanon-s-children-of-their-nationality-1.473073

32. http://www.al-akhbar.com/node/245663

33. http://www.naharnet.com/stories/ar/68663--نساء-لبنان-يعتصمن-على-الطريق-المؤدي-لقصر-بعبدا   مطالبين-بحق-منح-جنسيتهن-لأولادهن-حقوقنا-ليست-مادة-إنتخابية

34. http://www.al-akhbar.com/node/245663

35. https://www.thenational.ae/world/mena/law-that-deprives-lebanon-s-children-of-their-nationality-1.473073

36. http://www.naharnet.com/stories/ar/68663--نساء-لبنان-يعتصمن-على-الطريق-المؤدي-لقصر-بعبدا   مطالبين-بحق-منح-جنسيتهن-لأولادهن-حقوقنا-ليست-مادة-إنتخابية

37. http://www.al-akhbar.com/node/245663

38. https://www.thenational.ae/world/mena/law-that-deprives-lebanon-s-children-of-their-nationality-1.473073

39. Maya Mikdashi, 'Religious Conversion and Da'wa Secularism: Two Practices of Citizenship in Lebanon', unpublished Ph.D. dissertation, Columbia University (2014).

40. https://www.lorientlejour.com/article/921195/le-mariage-civil-un-droit-fondamental-.html

41. https://www.lorientlejour.com/article/909366/impossible-denregistrer-les-mariages-civils-contractes-au-liban-reconnait-machnouk.html

42. https://www.lorientlejour.com/article/921195/le-mariage-civil-un-droit-fondamental-.html

43. https://www.lorientlejour.com/article/909366/impossible-denregistrer-les-mariages-civils-contractes-au-liban-reconnait-machnouk.html

44. https://www.lorientlejour.com/article/811863/historique-le-premier-mariage-civil-consacre-par-letat-libanais.html

45. https://www.lorientlejour.com/article/909366/impossible-denregistrer-les-mariages-civils-contractes-au-liban-reconnait-machnouk.html

46. http://ritakml.info/2014/02/06/civil-marriage-for-lebanese-citizens-diy-or-via-travel-agency/

47. Ibid.

48. https://www.lorientlejour.com/article/709565/Dar_el-Fatwa_rejette_le_projet_de_loi_sur_la_protection_des_femmes_de_la_violence_familiale.html

49. https://now.mmedia.me/lb/en/reportsfeatures/the_marriage_exception

50. https://www.lorientlejour.com/article/715834/Le_Conseil_de_la_femme_libanaise_repond_a_Dar_el-Fatwa.html

51. https://www.lorientlejour.com/article/861261/les-remarques-de-kafa.html; http://www.kafa.org.lb/ZalfaFAQ/1/قانون-حول-زلفا-تساؤلات-العنف-الأسري

52. https://www.lorientlejour.com/article/861423/la-seance-pleniere-trahit-la-supercherie-de-la-gestion-parlementaire.html; https://www.lorientlejour.com/article/861424/loi-sur-la-violence-domestique-la-societe-civile-trahie-par-ses-deputes.html

53. https://www.lorientlejour.com/article/882954/loi-sur-la-violence-domestique-quid-de-lapplication-et-de-lefficacite-.html; see also http://www.kafa.org.lb/ZalfaFAQ/1/الأسري-العنف-قانون-حول-زلفا-تساؤلات

54. https://www.lorientlejour.com/article/1022331/des-mariees-ensanglantees-devant-le-parlement-pour-labrogation-de-larticle-522-du-code-penal.html

55. http://www.kafa.org.lb/kafa-news/127/بالكامل-تلغ-لم-522-المادة-the-remaining-effects-of

56. https://www.lorientlejour.com/article/1067513/le-parlement-abroge-larticle-522-du-code-penal.html

57. https://www.lorientlejour.com/article/822903/il-bat-sa-femme-jusqua-la-mort.html

58. https://www.lorientlejour.com/article/853653/manal-assi-un-crime-conjugal-de-trop-.html

59. https://www.lorientlejour.com/article/855064/deces-de-christelle-abou-chacra-lhypothese-du-meurtre-soulevee-par-la-famille.html

60. https://www.lorientlejour.com/article/860383/rakya-24-ans-enceinte-nouvelle-victime-de-la-violence-domestique-au-liban.html

61. https://www.lorientlejour.com/article/898083/nisrine-rouhana-nouvelle-victime-de-la-violence-domestique-au-liban.html

62. https://www.lorientlejour.com/article/1074649/une-jeune-femme-tuee-par-son-concierge-syrien-a-miziara.html

63. https://www.lorientlejour.com/article/1075556/les-syriens-doivent-partir-on-ne-peut-pas-leur-faire-confiance-.html

64. https://twitter.com/chehayebk/status/944585788641234945

65. https://twitter.com/leloveluck/status/944586555888427008

66. https://twitter.com/chehayebk/status/944585788641234945

67. https://www.lorientlejour.com/article/1091143/ca-aurait-pu-etre-moi-rassemblement-a-beyrouth-apres-le-meurtre-de-plusieurs-femmes.html

68. https://www.lorientlejour.com/article/1091191/malak-23-ans-nouvelle-victime-de-la-violence-conjugale-au-liban.html

69. http://english.al-akhbar.com/content/where-find-lebanon's-worst-seafront-violations

70. http://www.beirutreport.com/2017/06/the-violent-face-of-real-estate-development-in-lebanon.html

71. http://executive-bulletin.com/business/real-estate/eden-rock-resort-launching-event

72. https://www.theguardian.com/cities/2017/feb/02/beiruts-public-space-last-beach-residents-fear-privatisation-ramlet-al-baida

73. http://www.executive-magazine.com/business-finance/real-estate/seashore-inc

74. https://www.lorientlejour.com/article/1064991/un-rapport-accablant-pour-le-chantier-controverse-sur-la-plage.html

75. https://www.facebook.com/nahnoo.org/photos/a.730483513644488.1073741834.417957431563766/2250102731682551/?type=3&theater; https://www.lorientlejour.com/article/930858/la-juge-el-hassan-revient-sur-sa-decision-de-fermer-lacces-a-ramlet-el-baida.html

76. http://www.beirutreport.com/2014/06/the-fencing-of-dalieh.html

77. https://dalieh.org/assets/booklet-en.pdf

78. https://dalieh.org/assets/booklet-en.pdf

79. Dictaphone Group, *Hadha al-Bahr li.*

80. http://www.fifteenco.com

81. https://www.lorientlejour.com/article/934748/les-wedding-planners-misent-sur-le-creneau-des-mariages-a-letranger.html

82. https://www.arabiaweddings.com/luxury/real-weddings/myriam-fares-and-dany-mitris-wedding

83. http://www.mondanite.net/article/3281/myriam-fares-and-dany-mitri-celebrate-2nd-annivers

84. https://www.lorientlejour.com/article/887210/mariages-au-liban-fastes-de-cour-et-somptueuses-ceremonies.html

85. https://www.eblf.com/en/Wedding-Loan-263

86. https://www.byblosbank.com/personal/loans/wedding-loan

87. https://www.youtube.com/watch?v=Bog_aECcziA

88. https://www.youtube.com/watch?v=WZ2sCbXiEHI

89. https://www.youtube.com/watch?v=Jc3ctYpidQA

90. Laleh Khalili, 'The Politics of Pleasure: Promenading on the Corniche and Beachgoing', *Environment and Planning D: Society and Space* (2015), 8.

91. http://alfalamanki.com

92. http://shouraeyak.com/a-conversation-with-mario-haddad-jr-part-ii/

93. http://alfalamanki.com/uploads/607944589Falamanki_Final.pdf

94. Khalili, 'The Politics of Pleasure', 4–5.

95. Lara Deeb, *An Enchanted Modern: Gender and Public Piety in Shi'i Lebanon* (Princeton, NJ: Princeton University Press, 2006).

96. Lara Deeb and Mona Harb, *Leisurely Islam: Negotiating Geography and Morality in Shi'ite South Beirut* (Princeton, NJ: Princeton University Press, 2013), 183.

97. Ibid., 53, 103, 188.

98. Ibid., 63–5.

99. Ibid., 100–1, 165,170.

100. http://www.discoverlebanon.com/en/panoramic_views/mount_lebanon/el_maten/mar_elias.php

101. Hiba Bou Akar and Mohamad Hafeda, *Narrating Beirut from its Borderlines* (Beirut: Heinrich Böll Foundation, 2011), 22–3. The translation from the Arabic is my own.

102. http://www.jadaliyya.com/Details/34552/"Til-Sect-Do-You-Part"-On-Sectarianism-and-Intermarriage-in-Lebanon

8. *TAL 'IT RIHATKUM*, OR 'YOU STINK'—ON WASTE AND THE LEBANESE BODY POLITIC

1. John Scanlan, *On Garbage* (London: Reaktion Books, 2005), 36, 154, 157.

2. Julia Kristeva, *Pouvoirs de l'horreur: essai sur l'abjection* (Paris: Editions du Seuil, 1980), 9, 12.

3. Slavoj Žižek, *Event: Philosophy in Transit* (Harmondsworth: Penguin, 2014).

4. Ziad Abu-Rish, 'Garbage Politics', http://www.jadaliyya.com/Details/33377/Garbage-Politics

5. https://www.lorientlejour.com/article/934360/la-dechetterie-de-naame-une-fabrique-a-cancers-pour-ses-habitants.html

6. http://www.executive-magazine.com/economics-policy/waste-management-cleaning-up

7. https://www.lorientlejour.com/article/896607/celebration-en-grande-pompe-de-la-premiere-phase-de-traitement-du-depotoir-de-saida.html

8. http://www.executive-magazine.com/economics-policy/waste-management-cleaning-up

9. https://www.lorientlejour.com/article/934360/la-dechetterie-de-naame-une-fabrique-a-cancers-pour-ses-habitants.html; http://www.lesclesdumoyenorient.com/Le-gouvernement-libanais-devant-la-crise-des-dechets-et-le-mecontentement-de-la.html

10. https://www.youtube.com/watch?time_continue=41&v=o_vcFpW7Aqs

11. https://www.lorientlejour.com/article/851907/decharge-de-naame-les-manifestants-suspendent-leur-sit-in.html

12. https://www.youtube.com/watch?time_continue=41&v=o_vcFpW7Aqs

13. https://www.lorientlejour.com/article/934360/la-dechetterie-de-naame-une-fabrique-a-cancers-pour-ses-habitants.html

14. https://www.youtube.com/watch?time_continue=41&v=o_vcFpW7Aqs

15. http://www.executive-magazine.com/economics-policy/waste-management-cleaning-up

16. Ziad Abu-Rish, 'Garbage Politics', http://www.jadaliyya.com/Details/33377/Garbage-Politics

17. https://www.lorientlejour.com/article/851907/decharge-de-naame-les-manifestants-suspendent-leur-sit-in.html

18. https://www.lorientlejour.com/article/906606/manifestation-contre-le-maintien-de-la-decharge-de-naame.html

19. Ziad Abu-Rish, 'Garbage Politics', http://www.jadaliyya.com/Details/33377/Garbage-Politics

20. https://www.averda.com/about-us/history; http://www.sukleen.com/who_we_are.html

21. http://www.executive-magazine.com/economics-policy/waste-management-cleaning-up

22. http://www.lcps-lebanon.org/featuredArticle.php?id=48

23. http://www.executive-magazine.com/economics-policy/waste-management-cleaning-up

24. https://www.lorientlejour.com/article/851907/decharge-de-naame-les-manifestants-suspendent-leur-sit-in.html

25. Ziad Abu-Rish, 'Garbage Politics', http://www.jadaliyya.com/Details/33377/Garbage-Politics

26. http://www.lesclesdumoyenorient.com/Le-gouvernement-libanais-devant-la-crise-des-dechets-et-le-mecontentement-de-la.html

27. http://www.lcps-lebanon.org/featuredArticle.php?id=48

28. http://www.executive-magazine.com/economics-policy/waste-management-cleaning-up

29. Ibid.

30. https://www.lorientlejour.com/article/938102/crise-des-dechets-bey-routh-a-enfin-trois-offres.html

31. http://www.executive-magazine.com/economics-policy/waste-management-cleaning-up

32. https://www.lorientlejour.com/article/904756/le-plan-pour-les-dechets-gele-lactivite-du-gouvernement.html

33. http://www.executive-magazine.com/special-report/wastemis management

34. https://www.lorientlejour.com/article/897783/decharge-de-naame-en-cas-datermoiements-le-psp-appellera-a-un-mouvement-populaire-affirme-joumblatt.html

35. https://www.lorientlejour.com/article/904756/le-plan-pour-les-dechets-gele-lactivite-du-gouvernement.html

36. http://www.executive-magazine.com/special-report/wastemis management

37. http://www.lesclesdumoyenorient.com/Le-gouvernement-libanais-devant-la-crise-des-dechets-et-le-mecontentement-de-la.html

38. https://www.lorientlejour.com/article/935718/beyrouth-dans-limpasse-a-la-recherche-dune-decharge.html

39. https://www.lorientlejour.com/article/936839/le-gouvernement-tient-bon-face-a-une-crise-des-dechets-partie-pour-durer.html

40. https://www.lorientlejour.com/article/936821/un-nouveau-plan-durgence-pour-beyrouth-a-la-quarantaine.html

41. Mary Douglas, *Purity and Danger: An Analysis of the Concepts of Pollution and Taboo* (London: Routledge, 2005 [1966]); Warwick Anderson, 'Excremental colonialism: public health and the poetics of pollution', *Critical Inquiry* 21 (1995), 643.

42. Dipesh Chakrabarty, 'Open space/public space: garbage, modernity and India', *South Asia: Journal of South Asian Studies* 14 (1991), 15–31, 16, 18.

43. Nicholas Hopkins and Sohair R. Mehanna, 'Social action against everyday pollution in Egypt', *Human Organization* 59 (2000), 251.

44. https://www.youtube.com/watch?v=Bog_aECcziA

45. https://skift.com/2012/07/29/amidst-growing-visitor-numbers-beirut-struggles-to-make-sense-of-its-public-spaces/

46. https://skift.com/2012/07/29/amidst-growing-visitor-numbers-beirut-struggles-to-make-sense-of-its-public-spaces/; Anonymous interview, Hamra, Beirut, 16 September 2015.

47. https://www.lorientlejour.com/article/935993/a-beyrouth-des-routes-coupees-par-des-bennes-en-feu-et-des-ordures.html

48. https://www.lorientlejour.com/article/936839/le-gouvernement-tient-bon-face-a-une-crise-des-dechets-partie-pour-durer.html

49. http://www.jadaliyya.com/Details/32406/Quick-Thoughts-Moe-Ali-Nayel-on-Lebanon's-Garbage-Crisis-and-Protest-Movement

50. https://www.lorientlejour.com/article/936143/crise-des-dechets-des-activistes-bloquent-la-rue-des-banques-a-beyrouth.html

51. http://www.dailystar.com.lb//News/Lebanon-News/2015/Sep-07/314217-groups-making-up-the-protest-movements.ashx

52. https://www.nytimes.com/2015/08/20/world/middleeast/lebanese-police-beat-you-stink-activists-in-beirut.html

53. https://www.facebook.com/tol3etre7etkom/videos/1628085397453575/?pnref=story

54. https://www.nytimes.com/2015/08/20/world/middleeast/lebanese-police-beat-you-stink-activists-in-beirut.html

55. https://www.facebook.com/Zaynoun/videos/10153548422469841/

56. https://www.reuters.com/article/us-lebanon-crisis-politics/thousands-rally-in-beirut-against-political-leaders-rot-idUSKCN0QY08S20150830

57. http://www.jadaliyya.com/Details/32406/Quick-Thoughts-Moe-Ali-Nayel-on-Lebanon's-Garbage-Crisis-and-Protest-Movement

58. Ibid.

59. https://www.lorientlejour.com/article/942312/lucien-bou-rjeily-a-lolj-mardi-on-a-clairement-voulu-amputer-le-mouvement-vous-puez-.html

60. https://newspaper.annahar.com/article/264790--من-التحرك-حمى-id?=الباركميتر-إلى-الرئاسة-عون -عشية-تظاهرته -إزالة-الجمهورية-الباطلة 264790

61. http://www.beirutreport.com/2015/07/private-security-confront-police-at-zaitunay-bay.html

62. https://newspaper.annahar.com/article/264790-حمى-التحرك-من-الباركميتر-إلى-الرئاسة-عون-عشية-تظاهرته-إزالة-الجمهورية-الباطلة؟id=264790

63. http://www.beirutreport.com/2015/09/how-activists-reclaimed-beiruts-coast-and-why-it-matters.html

64. https://www.annahar.com/article/264255-ماذا-قال-لوسيان-ابو-رجيلة-من-المستشفى-لنهاد-المشنوق-id=264255?

65. http://www.jadaliyya.com/Details/32408/Beirut-Revolt-What-Is-to-be-Done

66. http://www.jadaliyya.com/Details/32443/We-Are,-You-Are

67. http://www.jadaliyya.com/Details/32491

68. Field notes, meeting at Metro Madina, Beirut, 15 September 2015.

69. Anonymous interview, Mar Mikhail, Beirut, 16 September 2015.

70. Anonymous interview, Hamra, Beirut, 16 September 2015.

71. Anon., interview 16/09/2015, Mar Mikhail, Beirut.

72. Anon., interview 16/09/2015, Hamra, Beirut.

73. Anon., interview 17/09/2015, Hamra, Beirut.

74. Anon., interview 16/09/2015, Hamra, Beirut.

75. Anon., interview 17/09/2015, Hamra, Beirut.

76. Anon., interview 16/09/2015, Mar Mikhail, Beirut.

77. https://newspaper.annahar.com/article/267021-هل-أنت-رئيس-عن-ال-أم-عن-ال-99--1

78. https://www.facebook.com/BeirutMadinati/videos/1028680993878321/

79. https://www.facebook.com/BeirutMadinati/videos/1027813993965021/

80. https://www.facebook.com/BeirutMadinati/videos/1029935923752828/

81. https://ginosblog.com/beirut-madinati-post-election-fever-e63717738f68

82. https://www.facebook.com/BeirutMadinati/app/151858328287166/

83. https://www.youtube.com/watch?v=scJAbrJ16M4

84. http://www.lorientlejour.com/article/970277/hariri-explique-les-motivations-de-son-soutien-a-frangie.html; http://www.al-monitor.com/pulse/originals/2015/12/lebanon-president-franjieh-bid-hariri.html

85. https://www.youtube.com/watch?v=aEYiMI073Ew

86. https://www.youtube.com/watch?v=ZLatbdz-Ruw

87. https://www.youtube.com/watch?v=-1K6RNi9fmQ&t=190s

EPILOGUE

1. https://www.nytimes.com/2017/12/24/world/middleeast/saudi-arabia-saad-hariri-mohammed-bin-salman-lebanon.html

2. https://www.lorientlejour.com/article/1093075/la-demission-enigmatique-de-hariri-annoncee-a-riyad.html

3. https://www.youtube.com/watch?v=4YI_z5ZebmQ
4. https://www.lorientlejour.com/article/1087897/a-baabda-unanimite-autour-dune-politique-de-distanciation-qui-a-tout-dune-declaration-din-tention.html
5. https://www.lorientlejour.com/article/1092718/au-liban-lecole-pri-vee-en-crise-aigue-depuis-ladoption-de-lechelle-des-salaires.html
6. https://www.lorientlejour.com/article/1092745/dechets-une-annee-pour-quasiment-rien.html
7. https://www.lorientlejour.com/article/1094318/un-responsable-du-hamas-blesse-dans-un-attentat-a-la-voiture-piegee-a-saida.html
8. https://twitter.com/UNHCRGirard/status/971828070939332609
9. https://www.lorientlejour.com/article/1099718/le-bloc-courant-du-futur-cpl-ne-permettra-pas-au-hezbollah-de-dominer-la-chambre.html
10. https://www.lorientlejour.com/article/1092719/une-annee-decisive-pour-le-dossier-du-gaz-libanais.html

AFTERWORD

1. https://www.diplomatie.gouv.fr/IMG/pdf/cedre_statement-en-_final_ang_cle8179fb.pdf
2. https://www.lemonde.fr/planete/article/2019/10/16/le-liban-sous-le-choc-apres-une-vague-d-incendies_6015763_3244.html
3. https://www.lorientlejour.com/article/1193799/ceux-qui-voient-un-complot-derriere-la-revolte-libanaise.html

BIBLIOGRAPHY

Interviews

Anonymous, Jal al-Dib, 7 August 2012.
Anonymous, Mar Mikhail, Beirut, 16 September 2015.
Anonymous, Hamra, Beirut, 16 September 2015.
Anonymous, Hamra, Beirut, 17 September 2015.
Anonymous, Beirut, 19 September 2017.
Guita Hourani, Louaize, 20 August 2012.
Nassib Ghobril, Beirut, 8 August 2012.

Digital material

Al-Akhbar
Al-Arabiya
Al-Jazeera
Al-Nahar
Al-Safir
BBC
Beirut Report
Der Spiegel
Jadaliyya
L'Orient-Le Jour
Qifa Nabki

Published material

Abi Samra, Marwan, *L'Emigration libanaise et son impact sur l'économie et le dével-oppement* (Geneva: ILO, 2010).
Abirached, Philippe, 'Charisme, pouvoir et communauté politique: la figure de Michel Aoun', in Franck Mermier and Sabrina Mervin, eds, *Leaders et Partisans au Liban* (Paris: Karthala, 2012).

BIBLIOGRAPHY

Abu-Rish, Ziad, 'Garbage Politics', http://www.jadaliyya.com/Details/33377/Garbage-Politics

El-Achkar, Hicham, 'The Role of the State in Initiating Gentrification: The Case of the Neighbourhood of Achrafieh in Beirut', unpublished MA thesis (Lebanese University, 2011).

———— 'The Lebanese State as Initiator of Gentrification in Achrafieh', http://ifpo.hypotheses.org/3834

Alaily-Mattar, Nadia, 'Beyond Gated Communities? Detachment and Concentration in Networked Nodes of Affluence in the City of Beirut', *Urban Design International* 13 (2008), 263–71.

Anderson, Warwick, 'Excremental colonialism: public health and the poetics of pollution', *Critical Inquiry* 21 (1995), 640–69.

Aoun, Michel and Frédéric Domont, *Une certaine vision du Liban: entretiens avec Frédéric Domont* (Paris: Fayard, 2007).

Arendt, Hannah, 'The Perplexities of the Rights of Man', in Peter Baehr, ed., *The Portable Hannah Arendt* (London: Penguin Books, 2000), 31–45.

Aubin-Boltanski, Emma, 'Samir Geagea: le guerrier, le martyr, et le *za'îm*', in Franck Mermier and Sabrina Mervin, eds, *Leaders et Partisans au Liban* (Paris: Karthala, 2012).

Baumann, Hannes, 'The New "Contractor Bourgeoisie" in Lebanese Politics: Hariri, Mikati, and Fares', in Are Knudsen and Michael Kerr, eds, *Lebanon after the Cedar Revolution* (London: Hurst, 2012), 125–144.

———— *Citizen Hariri: Lebanon's Neoliberal Reconstruction* (London: Hurst, 2016).

Berthier, Rosalie, 'Abracada... broke: Lebanon's Banking on Magic', http://www.synaps.network/abracada-broke

Bianchi, Sergio, 'Community Participation and Human Rights Advocacy: Questions Arising from the Campaign About the Right to Work of Palestinian Refugees in Lebanon', in Sari Hanafi and Are Knudsen, eds, *Palestinian Refugees: Identity, Space and Place in the Levant* (Abingdon: Routledge, 2011), 163–86.

Blanford, Nicholas, *Killing Mr Lebanon: The Assassination of Rafik Hariri and its Impact on the Middle East* (London: IB Tauris, 2006).

Bou Akar, Hiba and Mohamad Hafeda, *Narrating Beirut from its Borderlines* (Beirut: Heinrich Böll Foundation, 2011).

Brenner, Neil and Nik Theodore, eds, *Spaces of Neoliberalism: Urban Restructuring in North America and Western Europe* (Oxford: Blackwell, 2002).

Byblos Bank, Economic Research and Analysis Department, 'The Global Crisis and Expatriates' Remittances to Lebanon: Trends and Elements of Resilience' (Beirut: Byblos Bank, 2011).

Cammett, Melani, *Compassionate Communalism: Welfare and Sectarianism in Lebanon* (Ithaca: Cornell University Press, 2014).

Cammett, Melani and Sukriti Issar, 'Bricks and Mortars Clientelism: Sectarianism and the Logics of Welfare Allocation in Lebanon', *World Politics* 62 (2010), 381–421.

Carlyle, Thomas, *On Heroes, Hero-Worship and the Heroic in History*, in F. Randolph Ludovico, ed., *The Selected Works of Thomas Carlyle* (n.p.: The Bibliotheca Cakravarti Foundation).

Catusse, Myriam and Joseph Alagha, 'Les services sociaux du Hezbollah: effort de guerre, *ethos* religieux et ressources politiques', in Sabrina Mervin, ed., *Le Hezbollah: Etat des lieux* (Arles: Actes Sud-IFPO, 2008), 117–40.

Chabal, Patrick and Jean-Pascal Deloz, *Africa Works: Disorder as Political Instrument* (Oxford: James Currey, 1999).

Chalcraft, John, *The Invisible Cage: Syrian Migrant Workers in Lebanon* (Palo Alto, CA: Stanford University Press, 2009).

Chakrabarty, Dipesh, 'Open space/public space: garbage, modernity and India', *South Asia: Journal of South Asian Studies* 14 (1991), 15–31.

Comaroff, John and Jean, *Law and Disorder in the Postcolony* (Chicago, IL: University of Chicago Press, 2006).

Constable, Nicole, 'Filipino Workers in Hong Kong Homes: Household Rules and Relations', in Barbara Ehrenreich and Arlie Russell Hochschild, eds, *Global Women: Nannies, Maids, and Sex Workers in the New Economy* (London: Granta, 2001), 115–41.

Cooper, Melanie, *Family Values: Between Neoliberalism and the New Social Conservatism* (Cambridge, MA: MIT Press, 2017).

Corstange, Daniel, 'The parliamentary election in Lebanon, June 2009', *Electoral Studies* 29 (2010), 285–9.

———— 'Vote trafficking in Lebanon', *International Journal of Middle East Studies* 44 (2012), 483–505.

Daher, Joseph, 'Hezbollah and the Workers', https://jacobinmag.com/2016/12/hezbollah-lebanon-iran-islamic-revolution-labor/

Deeb, Lara, *An Enchanted Modern: Gender and Public Piety in Shi'i Lebanon* (Princeton, NJ: Princeton University Press, 2006).

Deeb, Lara and Mona Harb, *Leisurely Islam: Negotiating Geography and Morality in Shi'ite South Beirut* (Princeton, NJ: Princeton University Press, 2013).

Devji, Faisal, 'A Life on the Surface', http://www.hurstpublishers.com/a-life-on-the-surface/

Doraï, Mohamed Kamel, 'Palestinian Refugee Camps in Lebanon: Migration, Mobility and the Urbanization Process', in Sari Hanafi and Are Knudsen, eds, *Palestinian Refugees: Identity, Space and Place in the Levant* (Abingdon: Routledge, 2011), 67–80.

Douayhi, Chawki, 'Réflexions autour de la *za'âma* maronite au Liban-Nord', in Franck Mermier and Sabrina Mervin, eds, *Leaders et Partisans au Liban* (Paris: Karthala, 2012).

BIBLIOGRAPHY

Douglas, Mary, *Purity and Danger: An Analysis of the Concepts of Pollution and Taboo* (London: Routledge, 2005 [1966]).

Ehrenreich, Barbara, 'Maid to order', in Barbara Ehrenreich and Arlie Russell Hochschild, eds, *Global Women: Nannies, Maids, and Sex Workers in the New Economy* (London: Granta, 2001), 85–103.

Ehrenreich, Barbara and Arlie Russell Hochschild, eds, *Global Women: Nannies, Maids, and Sex Workers in the New Economy* (London: Granta, 2001).

Ehrenreich, Barbara and Arlie Russell Hochschild, 'Introduction', in Barbara Ehrenreich and Arlie Russell Hochschild, eds, *Global Women: Nannies, Maids, and Sex Workers in the New Economy* (London: Granta, 2001), 1–13.

Fawaz, Mona, 'La Reconstruction de Haret Hreik (Beyrouth)', in Sabrina Mervin, ed., *Le Hezbollah: Etat des lieux* (Arles: Actes Sud-IFPO, 2008), 141–5.

————— 'The Politics of Property in Planning: Hezbollah's Reconstruction of Haret Hreik (Beirut, Lebanon) as a Case Study', *International Journal of Urban and Regional Research* 38 (2014), 922–34.

Foucault, Michel, *Le Gouvernement de soi et des autres: Cours au Collège de France (1982–1983)* (Paris: Gallimard, 2003).

Gilsenan, Michael, *Lords of the Lebanese Marches: Violence and Narrative in an Arab Society* (London: IB Tauris, 1996).

Halawi, Majed, *A Lebanon Defied: Musa al-Sadr and the Shi'a Community* (Boulder, CO: Westview, 1992).

Hamdan, Amal, 'The Limits of Corporate Consociation: Taif and the Crisis of Power-Sharing in Lebanon since 2005', in Are Knudsen and Michael Kerr, eds, *Lebanon after the Cedar Revolution* (London: Hurst, 2012), 39–61.

Hammer, Joshua, 'Getting Away with Murder?', https://www.theatlantic.com/magazine/archive/2008/12/getting-away-with-murder/307149/

Hamill, Kathleen, *Trafficking of Migrant Domestic Workers in Lebanon: A Legal Analysis* (Beirut: Kafa, 2011).

Hanafi, Sari, 'Governing the Palestinian Refugee Camps in Lebanon and Syria: The Cases of Nahr al-Bared and Yarmouk Camps', in Sari Hanafi and Are Knudsen, eds, *Palestinian Refugees: Identity, Space and Place in the Levant* (Abingdon: Routledge, 2011), 29–49.

Harb, Mona, *Le Hezbollah à Beyrouth (1985–2005): De la banlieue à la ville* (Paris: IFPO-Karthala, 2006).

Haugbolle, Sune, *War and Memory in Lebanon* (Cambridge: Cambridge University Press, 2010).

Hermez, Sami, *War is Coming: Between Past and Future Violence in Lebanon* (Philadelphia, PA: University of Pennsylvania Press, 2017).

Hopkins, Nicholas and Sohair R. Mehanna, 'Social action against everyday pollution in Egypt', *Human Organization* 59 (2000), 245–54.

Hottinger, Leonard, 'Zu'ama in Historical Perspective', in Leonard Binder, ed., *Politics in Lebanon* (New York: Wiley, 1966), 85–105.

BIBLIOGRAPHY

Human Rights Watch, *Why They Died: Civilian Casualties in Lebanon during the 2006 War* (September 2007).

———— *Flooding South Lebanon: Israel's Use of Cluster Munitions in Lebanon in July and August 2006* (February 2008).

El-Husseini, Rola, *Pax Syriana: Elite Politics in Post-War Lebanon* (Syracuse, NY: Syracuse University Press, 2012).

Ichti, Chawkat, 'La place du leadership traditionnel dans les partis politiques modernes: le cas de la *za'âma* des Arslan', in Franck Mermier and Sabrina Mervin, eds, *Leaders et Partisans au Liban* (Paris: Karthala, 2012), 461–79.

International Labour Organisation, 'Palestinian Employment in Lebanon: Facts and Challenges', http://www.ilo.org/wcmsp5/groups/public/—arabstates/—ro-beirut/documents/publication/wcms_236502.pdf

Ismail, Salwa, *Political Life in Cairo's New Quarters: Encountering the Everyday State* (Minneapolis, MN: University of Minnesota Press, 2006).

Jameson, Fredric, 'The Aesthetics of Singularity', *New Left Review* 92 (March/April 2015), 101–32.

Johnson, Michael, *Class and Client in Beirut: The Sunni Muslim Community and the Lebanese State 1840–1985* (London: Ithaca Press, 1986).

———— *All Honourable Men: The Social Origins of War in Lebanon* (London: IB Tauris, 2002).

Joseph, Suad, ed., *Arab Families: Gender, Self, and Family* (Syracuse, NY: Syracuse University Press, 1999).

———— *Gender and Citizenship in the Middle East* (Syracuse, NY: Syracuse University Press, 2000).

Jureidini, Ray and Nayla Moukarbel, 'Female Sri Lankan Domestic Workers in Lebanon: A Case of "Contract Slavery"?', *Journal of Ethnic and Migration Studies* 30, 4 (2004), 581–607.

Kerr, Michael, 'Before the Revolution', in Are Knudsen and Michael Kerr, eds, *Lebanon after the Cedar Revolution* (London: Hurst, 2012), 23–38.

Khalili, Laleh, 'The Politics of Pleasure: Promenading on the Corniche and Beachgoing', *Environment and Planning D: Society and Space* (2015), 583–600.

Khan, Naveeda, 'Introduction', in Naveeda Khan, ed., *Beyond Crisis: Re-evaluating Pakistan* (London: Routledge, 2010), 1–28.

Khater, Akram, *Inventing Home: Emigration, Gender, and the Middle Class in Lebanon, 1870–1920* (Berkeley, CA: University of California Press, 2001).

Khatib, Lina, Dina Matar and Atef Alshaer, *The Hizbullah Phenomenon: Politics and Communication* (London: Hurst, 2014).

Khoury, Philip S., 'Abu 'Ali al-Kilawi: A Damascus Qabaday', in Edmund Burke III, ed., *Struggle and Survival in the Modern Middle East* (London: IB Tauris, 1993), 179–90.

Knudsen, Are, 'The Law, the Loss, and the Lives of Palestinian Refugees in

Lebanon', CMI Working Paper (Bergen: Chr. Michelsen Institute, 2007), https://www.cmi.no/publications/file/2607-the-law-the-loss-and-the-lives-of-palestinian.pdf

———— 'Nahr al-Bared: The Political Fall-Out of a Refugee Disaster', in Sari Hanafi and Are Knudsen, eds, *Palestinian Refugees: Identity, Space and Place in the Levant* (Abingdon: Routledge, 2011), 97–110.

Knudsen, Are and Michael Kerr, eds, *Lebanon after the Cedar Revolution* (London: Hurst, 2012).

Knudsen, Are and Michael Kerr, 'Introduction: The Cedar Revolution and Beyond', in Are Knudsen and Michael Kerr, eds, *Lebanon after the Cedar Revolution* (London: Hurst, 2012), 3–22.

Krijnen, Marieke, 'Filling Every Gap: Real Estate Development in Beirut', http://www.jadaliyya.com/Details/29724/Filling-Every-Gap-Real-Estate-Development-in-Beirut

Krijnen, Marieke and Mona Fawaz, 'Exception as the Rule: High-End Developments in Neoliberal Beirut', *Built Environment* 36, 2 (2010), 245–59.

Kristeva, Julia, *Pouvoirs de l'horreur: essai sur l'abjection* (Paris: Editions du Seuil, 1980).

Labaki, Boutros, *The Role of Transnational Communities in Fostering Development in Countries of Origin: The Case of Lebanon* (Beirut: ESCWA, 2006).

Lamloum, Olfa, 'Le Hezbollah au miroir de ses médias', in Sabrina Mervin, ed., *Le Hezbollah: Etat des lieux* (Arles: Actes Sud-IFPO, 2008), 21–45.

Larkin, Craig, *Memory and Conflict in Lebanon: Remembering and Forgetting the Past* (London: Routledge, 2012).

Lefort, Bruno, 'Représentations du leadership et mémoires vives chez les militants aounistes', in Franck Mermier and Sabrina Mervin, eds, *Leaders et Partisans au Liban* (Paris: Karthala, 2012), 221–62.

Le Thomas, Catherine, 'Formation et Socialisation: un projet de (contre-) société', in Sabrina Mervin, ed., *Le Hezbollah: Etat des lieux* (Arles: Actes Sud-IFPO, 2008), 147–72.

———— 'Les Scouts al-Mahdî: une génération résistante', in Sabrina Mervin, ed., *Le Hezbollah: Etat des lieux* (Arles: Actes Sud-IFPO, 2008), 173–9.

———— 'Le Paysage Scout Chiite', in Franck Mermier and Sabrina Mervin, eds, *Leaders et Partisans au Liban* (Paris: Karthala, 2012), 285–304.

Lob, Eric, 'Development, Mobilization and War: The Iranian Construction Jehad, Construction Mobilization and Trench Builders Association (1979–2013)', *Middle East Critique* (2017), 1–20.

Lorey, Isabell, *State of Insecurity: Government of the Precarious* (London: Verso, 2015).

Makarem, Hadi, 'Actually Existing Neoliberalism: The Reconstruction of Downtown Beirut in Post-Civil War Lebanon', unpublished Ph.D. dissertation (University of London, 2014).

BIBLIOGRAPHY

Makdisi, Saree, 'Laying Claim to Beirut: Urban Narrative and Spatial Identity in the Age of Solidere', *Critical Inquiry* 23, 2 (1997), 660–705.

Mazaeff, Chantal, 'L'action des Forces libanaises à Aïn ʿal-Remmané: un intense travail de réhabilitation et de socialisation politique', in Franck Mermier and Sabrina Mervin, eds, *Leaders et Partisans au Liban* (Paris: Karthala, 2012).

Mbembe, Achille, *On the Postcolony* (Berkeley, CA: University of California Press, 2001).

McCormick, Jared, 'Hairy Chest, Will Travel: Tourism, Identity and Sexuality in the Levant', *Journal of Middle East Women's Studies* 7, 3 (2011), 71–97.

Mermier, Franck and Sabrina Mervin, eds, *Leaders et Partisans au Liban* (Paris: Karthala, 2012).

Mermier, Franck and Sabrina Mervin, 'Introduction: Une approche anthropologique du leadership au Liban', in Franck Mermier and Sabrina Mervin, eds, *Leaders et Partisans au Liban* (Paris: Karthala, 2012), 7–32.

Mervin, Sabrina, ed., *Le Hezbollah: Etat des lieux* (Arles: Actes Sud-IFPO, 2008).

Mervin, Sabrina, 'Le Lien iranien', in Sabrina Mervin, ed., *Le Hezbollah: Etat des lieux* (Arles: Actes Sud-IFPO, 2008), 75–87.

Mikdashi, Maya, 'Religious Conversion and Da'wa Secularism: Two Practices of Citizenship in Lebanon', unpublished Ph.D. dissertation, Columbia University (2014).

Minton, Anna, *Ground Control: Fear and Happiness in the Twenty-First Century* (London: Penguin, 2009).

Mouawad, Jamil, 'The Negotiated State: State-Society Relations in Lebanon', unpublished Ph.D. dissertation (University of London, 2015).

Moukarbel, Nayla, *Sri Lankan Maids in Lebanon: A Case of 'Symbolic Violence' and 'Everyday Forms of Resistance'* (Amsterdam: Amsterdam University Press, 2009).

Najem, Tom, *Lebanon: The Politics of a Penetrated Society* (London: Routledge, 2012).

Norton, Augustus, *Amal and the Shi'a: Struggle for the Soul of Lebanon* (Austin, TX: University of Texas Press, 1987).

——— *Hezbollah: A Short History* (Princeton, NJ: Princeton University Press, 2009).

Perdigon, Sylvain, 'The One Still Surviving and Viable Institution', in Sari Hanafi and Are Knudsen, eds, *Palestinian Refugees: Identity, Space and Place in the Levant* (Abingdon: Routledge, 2011), 165–79.

——— 'For Us It is Otherwise: Three Sketches on Making Poverty Sensible in the Palestinian Refugee Camps of Lebanon', *Current Anthropology* 56 (2015), 88–96.

Peteet, Julie, *Landscape of Hope and Despair: Palestinian Refugee Camps* (Philadelphia, PA: University of Pennsylvania Press, 2005).

BIBLIOGRAPHY

Picard, Elizabeth, 'Une sociologie historique du *za'îm* libanais', in Charles Chartouni, ed., *Histoire, société et pouvoir aux Proche Orients (travaux dédiés à Toufic Touma)*, vol. 1 (Paris: Geuthner), 157–72.

Pierret, Thomas, 'Al-Ahbash', *The Encyclopaedia of Islam*, 3rd ed. (Leiden: Brill: 2010), vol. 2, 35–7.

S.R., 'Le plan de Gebran Bassil pour l'électricité', *Le Commerce du Levant* (July 2010), 46–50.

Rajan, Sudhir Chella, *The Enigma of Automobility: Democratic Politics and Pollution Control* (Pittsburgh, PA: University of Pittsburgh Press, 1996).

Ratha, Dilip, Sanket Mohapatra, and Ani Silwal, *The Migration Remittances Factbook 2011* (Washington, DC: World Bank, 2011).

Rivoal, Isabelle, 'Intimité, mise en scène et distance dans la relation politique au Liban', in Franck Mermier and Sabrina Mervin, eds, *Leaders et Partisans au Liban* (Paris: Karthala, 2012).

Rose, Nikolas, *Powers of Freedom: Reframing Political Thought* (Cambridge: Cambridge University Press, 1999).

———— 'Governing Advanced Liberal Democracies', in Andrew Barry, Thomas Osborne, and Nikolas Rose, eds, *Foucault and Political Reason: Liberalism, Neo-Liberalism, and Rationalities of Rule* (Chicago: University of Chicago Press, 1996), 37–64.

Rougier, Bernard, *Everyday Jihad: The Rise of Militant Islam among Palestinians in Northern Lebanon* (Cambridge, MA: Harvard University Press, 2007).

———— *The Sunni Tragedy in the Middle East: Northern Lebanon from al-Qaeda to ISIS* (Princeton, NJ: Princeton University Press, 2015).

Rowe, Peter and Hashim Sarkis, eds, *Projecting Beirut: Episodes in the Construction and Reconstruction of a Modern City* (Munich: Prestel, 1998).

Saad-Ghorayeb, Amal, *Hizbu'llah: Politics and Religion* (London: Pluto Press, 2002).

Sachs, Wolfgang, *For Love of the Automobile: Looking Back into the History of our Desires* (Berkeley, CA: University of California Press, 1992).

Sadek, S. and M. El-Fadel, 'The Normandy Landfill: A Case Study in Solid Waste Management', *Journal of Natural Resources and Life Sciences Education* 29 (2000), 155–61.

Salamey, Imad, *The Government and Politics of Lebanon* (London: Routledge, 2013).

Saleh, Elizabeth, 'The Master Cockroach: Scrap Metal and Syrian Labour in Beirut's Informal Economy, *Contemporary Levant* 1 (2016).

Sawalha, Aseel, *Reconstructing Beirut: Memory and Space in a Postwar Arab City* (Austin, TX: University of Texas Press, 2011).

Shaery-Eisenlohr, Roschanack, *Shi'ite Lebanon: Transnational Religion and the Making of National Identities* (New York: Columbia University Press, 2011).

Scanlan, John, *On Garbage* (London: Reaktion Books, 2005).

BIBLIOGRAPHY

Schmid, Heiko, 'Privatized Urbanity or a Politicized Society? Reconstruction in Beirut after the Civil War', *European Planning Studies* 14, 3 (2006), 365–81.

Scott, Joan Wallach, Andrew Aisenberg, Brian Connolly, Ben Kafka, Sylvia Schafer, and Mrinalini Sinha, 'Introducing History of the Present', *History of the Present* 1 (2011), available at http://historyofthepresent.org/1.1/introduction.html

Skovgaard-Petersen, Jacob, 'The Sunni Religious Scene in Beirut', *Mediterranean Politics* 3 (1998), 69–80.

Special Tribunal for Lebanon, 'The Prosecutor v. Mustafa Amine Badreddine, Salim Jamil Ayyash, Hussein Hassan Oneissi & Assad Hassan Sabra—Indictment' (The Hague, Special Tribunal for Lebanon, 2011).

Stewart, Kathleen, *Ordinary Affects* (Durham, NC: Duke University Press, 2007).

Stoler, Ann Laura, *Carnal Knowledge and Imperial Power: Race and the Intimate in Colonial Rule* (Berkeley, CA: University of California Press, 2002).

UNHCR, 'Vulnerability Assessment of Syrian Refugees in Lebanon 2017' (Geneva: UNHCR, 2017).

Veblen, Thorstein, *The Theory of the Leisure Class* (n.p.).

Vloeberghs, Ward, 'Worshipping the Martyr President: The *Darih* of Rafiq Hariri in Beirut', in Pedro Pinto, Baudouin Dupret, Thomas Pierret, and Kathryn Spellman-Poots, eds, *Ethnographies of Islam: Ritual Performances and Everyday Practices* (Edinburgh: Edinburgh University Press, 2012), 80–93.

Young, Michael, 'Migrant Workers in Lebanon', http://www.lnf.org.lb/migrationnetwork/mig1.html

Young, Michael, *The Ghosts of Martyrs Square: An Eyewitness Account of Lebanon's Life Struggle* (New York: Simon & Schuster, 2010).

Zahar, Marie-Joëlle, 'Foreign Interventions, Power Sharing and the Dynamics of Conflict and Coexistence in Lebanon', in Are Knudsen and Michael Kerr, eds, *Lebanon after the Cedar Revolution* (London: Hurst, 2012), 63–82.

Ziadeh, Hanna, *Sectarianism and Intercommunal Nation-Building in Lebanon* (London: Hurst, 2006).

Žižek, Slavoj, *Event: Philosophy in Transit* (Harmondsworth: Penguin, 2014).

INDEX

INDEX

INDEX

'Aysha Bakkar, 175
Ayyash, Salim, 131
Azar, Georges, 388
Azar, Raymond, 113, 115, 119
al-Azhar University, 121
Azour, Jihad, 49, 213
Azzi, John, 327

Ba'arshit, 66
Baabda, 47, 54, 80, 106, 107, 174, 179, 199, 259, 378, 379
Baalbek, 92, 105, 165, 175, 192
Baath Party
  of Lebanon, 115, 143, 265
  of Syria, 6, 30, 36, 54, 64, 88, 113, 136, 137, 266, 285
Bab al-Tebbaneh, Tripoli, 1, 141, 144–5
Bab Idriss, 209
baba ghanuj, 243
Babel Bay, 227
Bachir Gemayel Foundation, 246
backgammon, 84, 153, 242, 344, 355, 357
Baddawi refugee camp, 88, 263, 267, 268, 273
Badna Nhasib, 387–8, 396, 397
Badreddin, Mustafa, 9, 131–2, 191
Baer, Robert, 133
Baghdad, Iraq, 390
Bahamas, 3
bahlawan, 357
Bahrain, 11, 136
Baitamouni, Samir, 340
Bakalian mills, 382
balconies, 237
Baltika beer, 262
banat, 289
Bangladesh, 288
Banias, 143
Bank Audi, 216
banking, 5, 10, 216, 219, 220, 222, 257

BankMed, 85
Banque du Liban, 218–19, 220, 221, 222, 424
Banque Libano-Française, 216, 350
Banque Méditerranée, 216
Baraili, Menuka, 292, 294, 295, 297, 305
Barbir, Beirut, 93, 95
Baroud, Ziad, 104, 130, 335
barrel bombs, 10, 136
Bashoura, Beirut, 210, 370, 386, 395
Basic Instinct, 313
Bassil, Gebran
  and cabinet resignations (2011), 128
  and diaspora, 225–6
  Hizballah, MoU with (2006), 51
  military promotions dispute (2018), 424
  Ministry of Energy, 111, 145–6, 252, 253
  Ministry of Telecommunications, 103, 110
  parliamentary election (2009), 107, 110
  parliamentary election (2018), 428–9
  presidency of FPM, candidacy for (2015), 203–5
  presidential election (2016), 413, 414, 417
  protests (2019), 431
Basta al-Fawqa, 141
Basta, Beirut, 169, 210
Batroun, 106, 107, 109, 175, 346
Battah, Habib, 234, 342, 397–8
Baumann, Hannes, 159, 213, 214, 217, 258
Baz, Nabil, 349
al-Bazzi, Karam, 338
Bcharreh, 105, 107, 175, 186, 197

INDEX

INDEX

INDEX

INDEX

INDEX

INDEX